ISBN 978-1-5279-7448-7
PIBN 10928466

1 MONTH OF
FREE
READING

at
www.ForgottenBooks.com

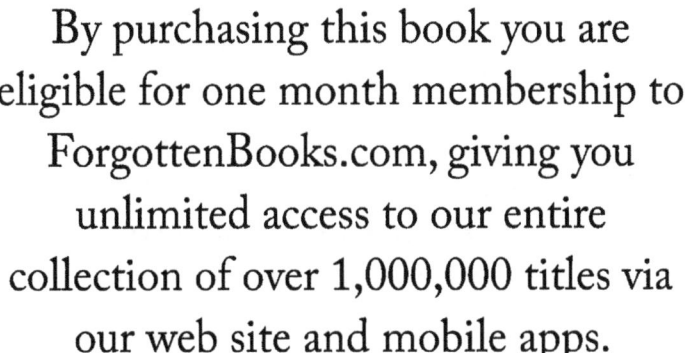

By purchasing this book you are eligible for one month membership to ForgottenBooks.com, giving you unlimited access to our entire collection of over 1,000,000 titles via our web site and mobile apps.

To claim your free month visit: www.forgottenbooks.com/free928466

English
Français
Deutsche
Italiano
Español
Português

www.forgottenbooks.com

Mythology Photography **Fiction**
Fishing Christianity **Art** Cooking
Essays Buddhism Freemasonry
Medicine **Biology** Music **Ancient
Egypt** Evolution Carpentry Physics
Dance Geology **Mathematics** Fitness
Shakespeare **Folklore** Yoga Marketing
Confidence Immortality Biographies
Poetry **Psychology** Witchcraft
Electronics Chemistry History **Law**
Accounting **Philosophy** Anthropology
Alchemy Drama Quantum Mechanics
Atheism Sexual Health **Ancient History**
Entrepreneurship Languages Sport
Paleontology Needlework Islam
Metaphysics Investment Archaeology
Parenting Statistics Criminology
Motivational

REPORTS

OF

CASES ARGUED AND ADJUDGED

IN

HE SUPREME COURT

OF

THE UNITED STATES.

DECEMBER TERM, 1852.

———

By BENJAMIN C. HOWARD,

UNSELLOR AT LAW AND REPORTER OF THE DECISIONS OF THE SUPREME
COURT OF THE UNITED STATES.

———

VOL. XIV.

———

BOSTON:
LITTLE, BROWN AND COMPANY,
Law Publishers and Booksellers.
1853.

Entered according to Act of Congress, in the year 1853, by
LITTLE, BROWN AND COMPANY,
in the Clerk's Office of the District Court of the District of Massachusetts.

RIVERSIDE, CAMBRIDGE:
PRINTED BY H. O. HOUGHTON AND COMPANY.

STEREOTYPED BY STONE AND SMART.

PROCEEDINGS

IN RELATION TO THE

DEATH OF THE LATE JUDGE McKINLEY.

————

AT the opening of the Court, this morning, Mr. Crittenden, the Attorney-General of the United States, addressed the Court as follows:—

That since its adjournment yesterday, the members of the Bar and officers of the Court held a meeting and had adopted resolutions expressive of their high sense of the public and private worth of the Hon. John McKinley, lately one of the Justices of this Court, and their deep regret at his death. By the same meeting I was requested to present those resolutions to the Court, and to ask that they might be entered on their records, and I rise now to perform that honored task.

Besides the private grief which naturally attend it, the death of a member of this Court, which is the head of a great, essential, and vital department of the Government, must always be an event of public interest and importance.

I had the good fortune to be acquainted with Judge McKinley from my earliest manhood. In the relations of private life he was frank, hospitable, affectionate. In his manners he was simple and unaffected, and his character was uniformly marked with manliness, integrity and honor. Elevation to the Bench of the Supreme Court made no change in him. His honors were borne meekly, without ostentation or presumption.

He was a candid, impartial, and righteous Judge. Shrinking from no responsibility, he was fearless in the performance of his duty, seeking only to do right, and fearing nothing but to do wrong.

For many of the last years of his life he was enfeebled and afflicted by disease, and his active usefulness interrupted and impaired; but his devotion to his official duties remained unabated, and his death was probably hastened by his last ineffectual attempt at their performance by attending the last term of this Court.

Death has now set her seal to his character, making it unchangeable forever; and, I think, it may be truly inscribed upon his monument that as a private gentleman, and as a public magistrate, he was without fear and without reproach.

This occasion cannot but remind us of other afflicting losses which have recently befallen us. The present, indeed, has been a sad year for the profession of the law. In a few short months it has been bereaved of its brightest and greatest ornaments. Clay, Webster and Sergeant, have gone to their immortal rest in quick succession. We had scarcely returned from the grave of one of them, till we were summoned to the funeral of another. Like bright stars they have sunk below the horizon, and have left the land in wide-spread gloom. This hall, that knew them so well, shall know them no more. Their wisdom has no utterance now, and the voice of their eloquence shall be heard here no more forever.

This hall itself seems as though it was sensible of its loss, and even these marble pillars seem to sympathize as they stand around us like so many majestic mourners.

But we will have consolation in the remembrance of these illustrious men. Their *names* will remain to us, and be like a light kindled in the sky to shine upon us, and to guide our course. We may hope, too, that the memory of them, and their great examples, will create a virtuous emulation which may raise up men worthy to be their successors in the service of their country, its constitution and its laws.

For this digression and these allusions to Clay, Webster, and Sergeant, I hope the occasion may be considered as a sufficient excuse; and I will not trespass by another word, except only to move that these resolutions, in relation to Judge McKinley, when they shall have been read by the Clerk, may be entered on the records of this Court.

At a meeting of the members of the Bar and officers of the Court, held in the Supreme Court Room on Tuesday, the 7th day of December, 1852, the Honorable Solomon W. Downs, of Louisiana, was called to the Chair, and John A. Campbell, Esquire, of Alabama, appointed Secretary.

On motion of Richard S. Coxe, Esquire, it was resolved that a committee of three gentlemen be appointed by the Chair to prepare and report to the meeting resolutions on the occasion of the lamented death of the Honorable John McKinley, one of the Associate Justices of the Supreme Court of the United States.

Whereupon the Chair appointed Richard S. Coxe, Esquire, of the District of Columbia, Reverdy Johnson, Esquire, of Maryland, and William Rawle, Esquire, of Pennsylvania, to constitute the committee.

Mr. Coxe, on behalf of the committee, reported to the meeting the following resolutions, which were unanimously adopted : —

Resolved, That among the afflictive dispensations with which it has pleased Almighty God to visit us, in common with the entire nation, during the last few months, we are especially called upon to deplore the death of the Honorable John McKinley, who, for the period of fifteen years, had filled an honorable position on the Bench of the Supreme Court, which he adorned by his simple purity of character, his learning, industry, and courtesy of manner.

Resolved, That this meeting deeply lament the death of Judge McKinley, and will cherish an affectionate remembrance of his many virtues and eminent worth as a judge, a patriot, and a man, and that we will wear the usual badge of mourning during the residue of the term.

Resolved, That the Chairman and Secretary of this meeting transmit a copy of these proceedings to the family of the deceased, and to assure them of our sincere condolence on account of the bereavement which they have sustained.

Resolved, That the Attorney-General be requested to present these proceedings to the Court, with a request that they be entered on its minutes.   S. W. DOWNS, *Chairman.*

J. A. CAMPBELL, *Secretary.*

To which Mr. Chief Justice Taney replied:—

When the Court assembled at the last term, one of its first acts was to express its sorrow for the loss of a highly respected member of the Court, who died in the preceding vacation. And now, when we meet again, we have to lament the death of another who has fallen since the last adjournment.

We cordially unite with the Bar in all that they have said of the character and worth of Judge McKinley. He was a member of this Court for fifteen years, and we knew him well. He was a sound lawyer, faithful and assiduous in the discharge of his duties while his health was sufficient to undergo the labor. And his life was most probably shortened by the effort he made to attend this Court at the last adjourned term, when his health had become too infirm to encounter the fatigue of a journey to Washington. He was frank and firm in his social intercourse, as well as in the discharge of his judicial duties. And no man could be more free from guile, or more honestly endeavor to fulfil the obligations which his office imposed upon him. We truly deplore his death.

We have indeed met together at the present term under circumstances peculiarly painful. And when we are speaking of the loss sustained by the death of a Brother of the Bench, we unavoidably call to mind the three distinguished members of the Bar who have also died since the last session of the Court. Very soon after the adjournment the death of Henr Clay was announced. In a few months afterwards Daniel Webster followed him; and before this term commenced the name of John Sergeant was added to the melancholy list. These gentlemen have all for the last thirty years been identified with the proceedings of this Court, standing always in the foremost ranks of the profession, and ornamenting it by their genius, their learning, and their eloquence. And while they were maintaining this distinguished position before the judicial tribunals, they were able at the same time to place their names among the leading and eminent statesmen of the day, exercising a strong and wide influence upon the great political questions which were agitated during the period in which they lived.

The interval between the last and present session of the Court has been a brief one. But sad events have been crowded in it. And we shall direct the proceedings of the Bar and this response to be entered on the records of the Court, as the evidence of the deep sense which the Court entertain of the loss sustained at the Bar as well as on the Bench.

LIST OF ATTORNEYS AND COUNSELLORS,

JOHN H. CLIFFORD,	*Massachusetts.*
LUCIUS C. DUNCAN,	*Louisiana.*
S. S. BAXTER,	*Virginia.*
EBENEZER ALLEN,	*Texas.*
J. GLANCEY JONES,	*Pennsylvania.*
CHARLES EDWARDS,	*New York.*
JAMES T. BRADY,	*Do.*
GEORGE F. COMSTOCK,	*Do.*
LEVI S. CHATFIELD,	*Do.*
ROBERT M. CHARLTON,	*Georgia.*
JOHN M. MARTIN,	*New York.*
S. G. HAVEN,	*Do.*
P. D. VROOM,	*New Jersey.*
JAMES W. GERARD, JR.,	*New York.*
RICHARD J. BOWIE,	*Maryland.*
PLATT SMITH,	*Iowa.*
GEORGE D. DOWLING,	*New York.*
C. O. LOOMIS,	*Pennsylvania.*
WILLIAM CULLOM,	*Tennessee.*
BENJAMIN F. THOMAS,	*Massachusetts.*
BYRON GORDON DANIELS,	*New York.*
JOSHUA D. BALL,	*Massachusetts*
CHARLES S. LESTER,	*New York.*
CALVIN K. AVERILL,	*Do.*
CHEYNEY H. HOUSEKEEPER,	*Pennsylvania*
W. ARTHUR JACKSON,	*Do.*
WILLIAM PRESTON,	*Kentucky.*
SIDNEY WEBSTER,	*New Hampshire.*
JOHN L. PENDERY,	*Ohio.*
DANIEL MACE,	*Indiana.*
HENRY B. NORTHUP,	*New York.*
HENRY S. MAGRAW,	*Pennsylvania*
ALEXANDER HAMILTON, JR.,	*New York*

JOSEPH HOWARD,	*Ohio.*
CHARLES J. HULL,	*Illinois.*
THOMAS SHANKLAND,	*New York.*
THOMAS S. ALEXANDER,	*Maryland.*
DAVID QUINN,	*Ohio.*
JOSEPH J. MERRICK,	*Maryland.*
SIDNEY G. FISHER,	*Pennsylvania.*
WILLIAM H. BELL,	*New York.*
ISRAEL GARRARD,	*Ohio.*
GEORGE W. THOMPSON,	*Do.*
NIMROD H. JOHNSON,	*Indiana.*
HORACE BINNEY, JR.,	*Pennsylvania.*
EDWARD F. HODGES,	*Massachusetts.*
ISAIAH T. WILLIAMS,	*New York.*
SAMUEL BLATCHFORD,	*Do.*
HENRY DAMPIER LAPAUGH,	*Do.*
M. HALE SMITH,	*Massachusetts.*
WEBSTER KELLEY,	*Do.*
J. KERSHNER,	*New York.*
W. A. BEACH,	*Do.*
ALBERT W. PAINE,	*Maine.*
HIRAM O. ALDEN,	*Do.*
CALVIN C. PARKS,	*Illinois.*
THOMAS C. WELCH,	*New York.*
JOSEPH CENTER,	*Do.*
JAMES M. SPENCER,	*Indiana.*
FRANCIS TUKEY,	*Massachusetts.*
ROBERT TOOMBS,	*Georgia.*
J. M. ELAM,	*Louisiana.*
CHARLES D. MEAD	*New York.*
NELSON DEWEY,	*Wisconsin.*
ELIJAH P. BROOKS,	*New York.*
H. J. JEWETT,	*Ohio.*
ELIAS S. TERRY,	*Indiana.*
JAMES W. BORDEN,	*Do.*
JOHN W. HOWE,	*Pennsylvania.*
THOMAS A. OSBORNE,	*New York.*
BENJAMIN T. DU VAL,	*Arkansas.*
N. H. PURPLE,	*Illinois.*
JACOB J. NOAH,	*Minnesota Territory.*
ALEXANDER DAVIDSON,	*Michigan.*
GEORGE G. BLODGET,	*Illinois.*
E. A. GRAVES,	*Kentucky.*

LINCOLN CLARK,	*Iowa*
DON. A. J. UPHAM,	*Wisconsin*
E. PEYRE FERRY,	*Illinois.*
VOLNEY FRENCH,	*Wisconsin.*
JOHN DELANY,	*Do.*
OSMAN A. LYMAN,	*Ohio.*
CHARLES R. BREWSTER,	*South Carolina.*
ELLIS D. TREVILLE,	*Do.*
LEWIS C. GROVER,	*New Jersey.*
HENRY K. VIELE,	*New York.*
EDMOND L. GOOLD,	*Louisiana.*
H. S. WALBRIDGE,	*New York.*
B. RUSH BAGG,	*Michigan.*
WILLIAM ASHLEY HILLYER,	*New York.*
THOMAS J. GALLAGHER,	*Ohio.*
T. PASSMORE HANBEST,	*Pennsylvania.*
JAMES ROSS SNOWDON,	*Do.*
FLAMEN BALL,	*Ohio.*
J. S. CARPENTIER,	*New York.*
JOHN MILTON ADAMS,	*Maine.*
N. TITUS WAKEMAN,	*Missouri.*
GEO. VAN SANTVOORD,	*New York.*
J. E. CALHOUN,	*South Carolina.*
LOUIS BLANDING,	*Do.*
JOSIAH SUTHERLAND,	*New York.*
J. HOPKINS STEWART,	*Do.*

LIST OF CASES REPORTED.

OMISSION.

At page 11 in this volume, before the words, " It appears in this case, that a suit was brought," &c., the following words are omitted, viz. :

" Mr. Chief Justice Taney delivered the opinion of the court."

ERRATUM.

In 13th Howard, page 381, in the syllabus of the case of Howard et al. *v.* Ingersoll, it is said,

" The boundary line runs along the top of this high western bank, leaving the bed of the river and the western shelving shore within the jurisdiction of Georgia."

This is an error. It should read,

" The boundary line runs up the river, on and along its western bank, and the jurisdiction of Georgia in the soil extends over to the line which is washed by the water, wherever it covers the bed of the river within its banks."

THE DECISIONS

SUPREME COURT OF THE UNITEL STATES,

AT

DECEMBER TERM, 1852.

ANDREW WYLIE, JR., ADMINISTRATOR OF SAMUEL BALDWIN, APPELLANT, *v.* RICHARD S. COXE.

An appeal will not lie to this court from a refusal of the court below to open a prior decree, and grant a rehearing. The decision of this point rests entirely in the sound discretion of the court below.

The case of Brockett *v.* Brockett, (2 How. 240,) explained.

Two appeals having been taken, one from the original decree, and the other from the refusal to open it, the latter must be dismissed, and the case stand for hearing upon the first appeal.

A motion for a mandate upon the court below, to carry the decree into execution, overruled.

THIS was an appeal from the Circuit Court of the United States, for the District of Columbia.

It was brought before the court upon the following motion: —

The appellee in this case moves the court to dismiss the second appeal in this record from the order of the Circuit Court, overruling a motion to open the decree and grant a rehearing. And, also, to award a writ of *procedendo*, commanding the said Circuit Court to proceed and execute the first decree.

RICHARD S. COXE,
Dec. 22d, 1852.   *In pro. per.*

Mr. Chief Justice TANEY delivered the opinion oi the court

This is an appeal from the decree of the Circuit Court, for the District of Columbia.

The bill was filed by the appellee, to recover a sum of money which he alleged was due to him for services rendered to the appellant, as administrator, and to Baldwin, the intestate, in his lifetime, in recovering a large sum of money, which was due to the said Baldwin from the Mexican government. The case proceeded to final hearing; and, on the 28th of April, 1852, the court passed its decree, directing the appellant, as administrator, to pay to the appellee $3,750, with interest from the 16th of May, 1851, until paid.

From this decree the appellant prayed an appeal to this court, and executed an appeal-bond in the usual form, in the penalty of $200. The bond is dated on the 6th of May, 1852, and on the same day was left for approval in the clerk's office, and, as appears by an indorsement upon it, was approved and filed on the 13th of the same month.

On the 13th of May, 1852, the appellant filed a petition for a rehearing, and on the same day moved to open the decree. The appellee answered the petition on the 19th. And, on the 22d, the motion to open the decree and for a rehearing, was overruled by the court. And, thereupon, the appellant prayed an appeal, as well from this order as from the decree of April 28th; and on the same day executed an appeal-bond in the penalty of $7,500, which was approved by the court.

The case is therefore here upon two appeals: 1st, from the final decree, directing the payment of the money; and, 2d, from the order overruling the motion to open this decree and grant a rehearing.

In relation to the order, it is plain that no appeal will lie from the refusal of a motion to open the decree and grant a rehearing. The decision of such a motion rests in the sound discretion of the court below, and no appeal will lie from it.

The case of Brockett v. Brockett, (2 How. 240,) which was relied on in the argument, was decided on different ground. In that case, before any appeal was taken, a petition was filed to open the decree for certain purposes, and the court referred it to a commissioner to examine and report on the matters stated in the petition. Upon his report, the court refused to open the decree, and the party thereupon appealed from this refusal, as well as the original decree, and gave bond, with sufficient security, to prosecute the appeal. This bond was given within ten days of the refusal of the motion, but was more than a month after the original decree. And the court held that this appeal was well taken; not because an appeal will lie from the refusal of a motion to open the decree and grant a rehearing, but because the court regarded the original decree as suspended by the action of the court on the motion, and that it was not effectual and final until the motion was overruled.

sufficient special bail, in the sum of one hundred and thirty-three dollars and thirty-three and one third cents, because of the omission to serve your petitioner with a copy of the declaration, according to the terms of the aforesaid act of 1715, c. 40, § 3; and your petitioner then and there tendered in open court good and sufficient bail, in the last-mentioned sum of money. The sufficiency of said bail for said amount was fully admitted by said court, as will appear by reference to said transcript of the record; but the court overruled said application upon the express ground that your petitioner was bound to enter special bail to said action, in the amount of the sum sworn to in the affidavit of said Ewing, which sum is shown in said affidavit to be four thousand nine hundred and seventy dollars. Your petitioner is advised that the aforesaid recited act of the legislature of Maryland is in full force in Washington county aforesaid; and that, under and by virtue of said law, it was the duty of the marshal to require no greater appearance-bail, and of the court to require no greater special bail than the amount specified in said act, where no copy of the declaration is sent to be served with the writ; and your petitioner is also advised, that there is in said affidavit no legal cause of bail whatever. Wherefore, inasmuch as the said Circuit Court has refused both of said applications for an appearance on the part of your petitioner to said suit, and as the law provides no other adequate remedy in the premises, whereby your petitioner can, before the final determination of said suit, regain his personal liberty, whereof he is now illegally and unjustifiably deprived, your petitioner prays that the writ of mandamus may be issued and directed to the Judges of said Circuit Court, commanding and enjoining them to receive the appearance of your petitioner to said action, either without requiring special bail, or upon your petitioner causing good and sufficient special bail to be entered to said action, in the sum of one hundred and thirty-three dollars and thirty-three cents and one third of a cent.

And, as in duty bound, your petitioner will ever pray, &c.

ROBERT J. BRENT, *for Petitioner.*

District of Columbia, Washington County, to wit:

Before the subscriber, a justice of the peace of the District of Columbia, in and for Washington county, personally appears David Taylor, the within petitioner, and made oath on the Holy Evangely of Almighty God, that the facts, as stated in the said petition, are true, to the best of his knowledge and belief.   J. W. BECK, *J. P.*

Dec. 10, 1852.

i *

District of Columbia, ss.

At a Circuit Court of the District of Columbia, begun and held in and for the county of Washington, at the city of Washington, on the third Monday of October, being the eighteenth day of the same month, in the year of our Lord one thousand eight hundred and fifty-two, and of the independence of the United States the seventy-seventh.

Present, WILLIAM CRANCH, *Chief Judge.*
THE HON. JAMES S. MORSELL, and } *Assistant*
JAMES DUNLOP, } *Judges.*
RICHARD WALLACH, Esquire, *Marshal.*
JOHN A. SMITH, *Clerk.*

In the records of proceedings of the said court, amongst others, are the following, to wit : —

THOMAS EWING, JR. }
v. }
DAVID TAYLOR. }

Be it remembered, to wit, on the 4th day of October, 1852, the said plaintiff, by Charles S. Wallach, Esquire, his attorney, prosecuted and sued forth out of the Circuit Court here, the United States writ of *capias ad respondendum,* directed to the marshal of the District of Columbia, in form following, to wit : —

District of Columbia, to wit :

The United States of America, to the Marshal of the District of Columbia, Greeting :

We command you, that you take David Taylor, late of Washington county, if he shall be found within the county of Washington, in your said district, and him safely keep, so that you have his body before the Circuit Court of the District of Columbia, to be held for the county aforesaid, at the city of Washington, on the 3d Monday of October instant, to answer unto Thomas Ewing, Jr., in a plea of trespass on the case, and so forth.

Hereof fail not at your peril, and have you then and there this writ.

Witness WILLIAM CRANCH, Esq., Chief Judge of our said court, at the city of Washington, the 22d day of May, Anno Domini one thousand eight hundred and fifty-two.

Issued this 4th day of October, 1852.
Wallach.
JNO. A. SMITH, *Clerk.*

District of Columbia, Washington County, to wu:

And the aforesaid plaintiff, on the day of prosecuting and suing forth of the aforegoing writ, declared against the said defendant in the plea aforesaid, in the form following, to wit:—

District of Columbia, Washington County, to wit:

David Taylor, late of the county aforesaid, was attached to answer unto Thomas Ewing, Jr., in a plea of trespass on the case, and so forth. And whereupon the said plaintiff, by Charles S. Wallach, his attorney, complains that, whereas the defendant, on the first day of September, in the year eighteen hundred and fifty-two, at the county aforesaid, was indebted to the plaintiff in the sum of four thousand nine hundred and seventy dollars, current money of the United States, for sundry matters and articles, properly chargeable in an account, as by a particular account thereof herewith into court exhibited, appears. And being so indebted, the defendant, in consideration thereof, afterwards, to wit, on the day and year aforesaid, of the county aforesaid, undertook, and faithfully promised to the said plaintiff, to pay him the aforesaid sum of money, when he should be thereto afterwards required.

And whereas, also, the defendant, on the first day of September, in the year eighteen hundred and fifty-two, at the county aforesaid, was indebted to the plaintiff in the further sum of four thousand nine hundred and seventy dollars, for work and labor done and performed by the plaintiff for the defendant, at his special request; and in the further sum of four thousand nine hundred and seventy dollars, for money received by the defendant for the use of the plaintiff; and in the further sum of four thousand nine hundred and seventy dollars, for money lent and advanced by the plaintiff to the defendant, at his, the defendant's, request; and in the further sum of four thousand nine hundred and seventy dollars, for money paid, laid out, and expended, by the plaintiff for the use of the defendant, at his, the defendant's, request; and being so indebted, the defendant afterwards, that is to say, on the day and year aforesaid, at the county aforesaid, in consideration thereof, undertook, and then and there faithfully promised to the said plaintiff, that he the defendant, the said several sums of money, when required, would well and truly pay to the plaintiff.

And whereas, the defendant afterwards, that is to say, on the first day of September, in the year aforesaid, at the county aforesaid, accounted with the plaintiff, of and concerning divers sums of money, from the said defendant to the plaintiff due, owing, then in arrear and unpaid; and upon such accounting, the said defendant was then and there found in arrear, and indebted to the said plaintiff the further sum of four thousand nine hundred and seventy dollars; and being so found in arrear and indebted, the said defendant afterwards, that is to say, on the day and year last mentioned, at the county aforesaid, in consideration thereof, undertook, and then and there faithfully promised to pay to the plaintiff, when thereto afterwards required, the said last-mentioned sum of money.

Nevertheless, the defendant said promises in nowise regarding, the said several sums of money, or any part thereof, though often required, to the plaintiff has not paid, but the same to pay has always refused, and still refuses, to the damage of the plaintiff, in the sum of ten thousand dollars, and therefore he brings suit, &c.   CHARLES S. WALLACH,
For the Plaintiff.

The said plaintiff, by his attorney aforesaid, at the time of prosecuting and suing forth the said writ, also filed the following affidavit to hold to bail, to wit: —

District of Columbia, Washington County, to wit:

THOMAS EWING, JR. ⎫
     v.   ⎬
DAVID TAYLOR. ⎭

On this fourth day of October, 1852, personally appeared before me, the subscriber, a justice of the peace, in and for the county and district aforesaid, Joseph T. Coombs, of the county and district aforesaid, agent for the plaintiff in the above cause, and made oath on the Holy Evangely of Almighty God, that David Taylor, a resident of the State of North Carolina, defendant in the above cause, is indebted to the said plaintiff in the full and just sum of four thousand nine hundred and seventy dollars, for moneys due upon a certain agreement or contract herewith filed, and for work and labor done at his, the said David Taylor's, special instance and request, in the district and county aforesaid, a particular account whereof is herewith filed. And that the said Taylor, being now in the said county and district, is about to remove from and go out of said county and district, and remove his property, rights, and credits from said county and district, with a view and in order to avoid the payment of the said debt, as this affiant verily believes, and that said debt was contracted in said county and district by the said David Taylor; and that said work and labor were done and performed in the said county and district by the said plaintiff, between the 8th day of March, 1850, and the first day of September, 1852, at his, the said David Taylor's, special instance and request.

J. T. COOMBS.

Subscribed and sworn before me.   H. NAYLOR, *J. P.*
4th October, 1852.

Agreement referred to in the aforegoing Affidavit.

Contract made and concluded on the twenty-eighth day of March, A. D. 1851, by and between Thomas Ewing, Junior, formerly of Ohio, and David Taylor, formerly of North Carolina, in behalf of himself and his wife and childien, in these words: ——

The said party of the first part, covenants and agrees to prosecute before Congress, or before the public departments of the general government, the claim of the said party of the second part, and that of his wife and children, under the Cherokee treaty of 1835-6, to the appraised value of a reservation of 640 acres of land, lying in the State of Tennessee, which said claim was before the Committee of Indian Affairs of the Senate at the last session of Congress; and further, that the said party of the first part, will use proper diligence in the prosecution of the said claim, and at no time will let the interests of the said party of the second part suffer by want of a proper degree of attention to the claim, on his part, unless prevented from rendering it by sickness or some other unavoidable and unforeseen necessity.

And the said party of the second part, in consideration of the valuable services which the said party of the first part has already rendered in the prosecution of the said claim; and in further consideration of the agreement which the said party of the first part herein makes, to continue to prosecute the claim until it is finally allowed and paid, hereby covenants and agrees to pay unto the said party of the first part the sum of twenty per centum upon the amount of said claim, whenever the same may be allowed; and if at any time a part of it only is allowed then the said party of the second part covenants and agrees to pay unto the said party of the first part, a like per centage upon the sum allowed.

And for the true and faithful performance of all the agreements above mentioned, the parties to these presents bind themselves, each unto the other, in the penal sum of five thousand dollars, as fixed and settled damages, to be paid by the failing party.

In testimony whereof, the parties to these presents have hereunto set their hands and affixed their seals, the day and year first above written.   THO. EWING, Jr.   [SEAL.]

his
DAVID X TAYLOR [SEAL.]
mark.

The within .contract was read by me to Mr. Taylor, before signing it, and he declared himself fully satisfied with the conditions herein expressed.

Signed, sealed, and delivered in my presence, this 28th day of March, A. D. 1851.   W. H. COLLEDGE.

A copy of which said affidavit was made, and sent with the writ aforesaid to the marshal of the district aforesaid, thereon indorsed, to wit, "To be served on the defendant with the writ."

Account referred to in the foregoing Affidavit, to wit :

Washington, Sept. 1st, 1851.
Mr. David Taylor, Dr. to Thomas Ewing, Jr.

To commission, 20 per cent., on $24,853.04, amount allowed on your claim against United States, under Cherokee Trea y of 1835, for work and labor done and performed in obtaining said allowance, and as per agreement   .   .   . $4,970.00

At which mentioned third Monday of October, in the year eighteen hundred and fifty-two, and the day of the return of the aforegoing writ, comes again into the Circuit Court here, the said plaintiff, by his attorney aforesaid; and the marshal of the district aforesaid, to whom the said writ was in form aforesaid directed, makes return thereof to the court thus indorsed, to wit, "Cepi in jail. R. Wallach, Marshal."

And now, to wit, on the   day of November, A. D. 1852, in open court, appears David Taylor, in custody of the marshal of the district aforesaid, and moves the court here that he be permitted to enter a common appearance to the said writ of the said Thomas Ewing, Jr.; and at the same time the said David Taylor, by his attorney, Robert J. Brent, Esq., offered to appear to said writ, and to defend the same; but the court refused to allow the said David Taylor to appear to said writ until he should give special bail, to the amount of indebtedness sworn to in the affidavit of said Thomas Ewing, Jr., filed in this cause. And thereupon the said David Taylor, so being in open court, prayed the court to take special bail for him in this action, to the amount of one hundred and thirty-three dollars thirty-three and one third cents. And at the same time appeared in open court John Frederick May and Joseph L. Williams, residents of the District of Columbia, who, with the consent of the said David Taylor, offered to enter themselves as special bail for the said David Taylor, and to justify in double the said last amount; but the court, in nowise denying the sufficiency of said bail as offered, refused to accept or take special bail for any amount less than the amount sworn to by said Thomas Ewing, Jr., as aforesaid; and the said David Taylor declining to give or offer bail to the amount required by the court, he is thereupon ordered and remanded by the court to the custody of the marshal of the District of Columbia.

Test. JOHN A. SMITH, Clerk.

District of Columbia, Washington County, to wit :

I, John A. Smith, Clerk of the Circuit Court of the District of Columbia, for the county of Washington, hereby certify that the aforegoing is a full and perfect transcript of all the proceedings had in the said court, in the said case of Thomas Ewing, Jr., against David Taylor, as appears from the minutes of the proceedings of said court.

In testimony whereof, I have hereunto subscribed my name, and affixed the seal of said court, this 10th December, 1852.

[SEAL.] JNO. A. SMITH, Clerk.

It appears, in this case, that a suit was brought in the Circuit Court of the United States for Washington County, in the District of Columbia, by Thomas Ewing, Jr., against David Taylor, to recover a sum of money which he alleged to be due to him, upon a contract which is set forth in the proceedings, and also for services rendered to Taylor at his instance and request.

The writ issued on the 4th of October, 1852, returnable to the October term, which began on the third Monday of the same month. And at the time of issuing the writ, the plaintiff filed his declaration containing the usual money counts, and also an affidavit stating the amount due, and the nature of his claim; that the debt was contracted in Washington county, in the District of Columbia, and that Taylor, being then in said county and district, was about to remove from it, and remove his property, rights, and credits, in order to avoid the payment of this debt.

The marshal arrested Taylor, and made his return upon the writ " Cepi in jail ; " and thereupon Taylor appeared in court, in the custody of the marshal, and, by his counsel, moved for leave to appear on common bail. But the court refused to permit him to appear and to discharge him from custody, until he should give bail to the amount of the debt sworn to in the affidavit of the plaintiff. Taylor then moved for leave to appear, upon giving bail in the sum of one hundred and thirty-three dollars thirty-three and a third cents, claiming that he was entitled to be discharged upon giving bail to that amount, under the act of Assembly of Maryland of 1715, which act, together with the other laws of Maryland in force when the United

States assumed jurisdiction over this district, were adopted by Congress as the laws of Washington county.

But the Circuit Court adhered to its decision, and refused to permit the party to appear, without giving bail to the amount claimed in the plaintiff's affidavit.

Upon this state of the case, Taylor moves for a rule on the Judges of the Circuit Court to show cause why a *mandamus* shall not be issued from this court, commanding the Judges of the Circuit Court to permit Taylor to appear to the above-mentioned suit on common bail, in order that he may be discharged from the custody of the marshal; and failing that motion, then to show cause why he should not be permitted to appear, upon giving bail to the amount of one hundred and thirty-three dollars and thirty-three and one third cents, under the provisions of the Maryland law.

According to the established practice of this court, a rule of this kind is not granted as a matter of course, and the inferior court is never called on to show cause, unless a case is presented which *primâ facie* requires the interposition of this court. It was so settled in the case of the Postmaster-General *v.* Trig, Administrator of Rector, 11 Pet. 173.

We proceed, then, to inquire whether such a case has been presented to support this motion.

The proceedings by which Taylor was arrested and held in custody, were under the act of Congress of August 1st, 1842, (5 Stat. at Large, 498.) This act provides that no person shall be held to bail in any suit in the District of Columbia, unless upon such an affidavit as is described in the law, which must be filed previously to the issuing of the writ.

It is insisted, on behalf of Taylor, that he was entitled to his discharge from custody upon entering an appearance by his attorney to the suit, because, as he alleges, the affidavit filed in the suit does not conform to the provisions of the act of Congress, and therefore was not sufficient, under that law, to justify the court in demanding bail.

But that is a question which this court cannot consider. The act of Congress provides that the sufficiency of the affidavit to hold to bail, and the amount of bail to be given shall, upon application of the defendant, be decided by the court in term time, and by a single judge in vacation. In deciding upon the application to discharge Taylor from the custody of the marshal, the court must necessarily have considered and interpreted the act of Congress, as well as the affidavit, and determined whether the affidavit was sufficient or not. And certainly, even in England, the King's Bench never claimed or exercised the power to issue a *mandamus* to an inferior court of record, commanding it to reverse its judgment, in a matter where the law authorized it to judge. In the case before us, the power of deciding on the sufficiency of the affidavit, and the amount of bail, is a part of the judicial power of the court. It has exercised this power, and passed its judgment. We do not mean to say that this judgment is in any respect erroneous. But, assuming it to be so, this court cannot, by *mandamus*, command them to reverse it. The writ has never been extended so far, nor ever used to control the discretion and judgment of an inferior court of record acting within the scope of its judicial authority. There is no ground, therefore, for the rule under the act of Congress.

The application under the Maryland act of 1715, is equally untenable. The provision in that act relied on in support of the motion, was never held in Maryland to apply to any thing but the bail-bonds to be taken by the sheriff in certain cases, and never influenced the decision of the courts as to the amount of bail to be required when the defendant was brought into court. But it is unnecessary to speak of that act, or of the construction it received in the courts of Maryland; because the right of the plaintiff in the Circuit Court to demand bail depends altogether upon the act of Congress. And if there is any discrepancy between this act and the act of Assembly of 1715, the act of Congress must govern, and is a repeal *pro.tanto* of the Maryland law.

The rule to show cause is therefore refused.

THOMAS MOORE, EXECUTOR OF RICHARD EELS, PLAINTIFF IN ERROR, *v.* THE PEOPLE OF THE STATE OF ILLINOIS.

A State, under its general and admitted power to define and punish offences against its own peace and policy, may repel from its borders an unacceptable population, whether paupers, criminals, fugitives, or liberated slaves; and, consequently, may punish her citizens and others who thwart this policy, by harboring, secreting, or in any way assisting such fugitives.

It is no objection to such legislation that the offender may be liable to punishment under the act of Congress for the same acts, when injurious to the owner of the fugitive slave.

The case of Prigg *v.* The Commonwealth of Pennsylvania. (16 Peters, 539,) presented the following questions, which were decided by the court:

1. That under and in virtue of the Constitution of the United States, the owner of a slave is clothed with entire authority in every State in the Union, to seize and re-capture his slave, wherever he can do it without illegal violence or a breach of the peace.

2. That the government of the United States is clothed with appropriate authority and functions to enforce the delivery, on claim of the owner, and has properly exercised it in the act of Congress of 12th February, 1793.

3. That any State law or regulation which interrupts, impedes, limits, embarrasses, ·delays, or postpones the right of the owner to the immediate possession of the slave, and the immediate command of his service, is void.

This court has not decided that State legislation in aid of the claimant, and which does not directly nor indirectly delay, impede, or frustrate the master in the exercise of his right under the Constitution, or in pursuit of his remedy given by the act of Congress, is void.

THIS case was brought up from the Supreme Court of the State of Illinois, by a writ of error issued under the 25th section of the Judiciary Act.

The section of the law of Illinois, under which Eels was indicted in 1842, and the facts in the case are set forth in the opinion of the court, and need not be repeated. The court before which he was tried, fined him four hundred dollars, and the Supreme Court of Illinois affirmed the judgment. The case is reported in 4 Scammon's Rep. 498.

It was argued, in this court, by *Mr. Chase*, for the plaintiff in error, and a printed argument filed by Mr. Dixon on the same side ; and by *Mr. Shields* for the defendant in error, who filed a printed argument prepared by Mr. McDougall, Attorney-General of Illinois.

The arguments urged by the counsel for the plaintiff in error, in order to show that the law of Illinois was void, were, —

1. That the act of Congress, passed in 1793, was constitutional; that the power of legislating upon the subject of fugitive slaves, ought to be vested in Congress; that the act had been declared to be constitutional by the following authorities : 16 Peters, 620 *et seq.*; 9 Johns, 67 ; 12 Wendell, 311 ; 2 Pick. 11 ; 5 Sergeant & Rawle, 62 ; 2 Wheeler's Crim. Cases, 594.

2. That the power was vested exclusively in Congress, and if there was an omission to legislate, silence was as demonstrative of its will as express legislation. 5 Wheat. 1, 21, 22 ; 16 Pet. 617 *et seq.*

3. That admitting the power to be concurrent, its exercise by Congress supersedes all State legislation. 1 Kent, 380, 391 ; 1 Story, Com. on Con. § 437 to 443 ; 12 Wend. 316, 325 ; 1 Pet. Con. Rep. 429 ; 4 Id. 414–5 ; 2 Wheel. Crim. Cas. 594 ; 5 Wheat. 21, 24, 36, 70, 75 ; 14 Wend. 532–6 ; 16 Pet. 617–8.

4. The act of Congress of 1793, and the law of Illinois, conflict with each other.

5. Two laws legislating over the same offence, cannot exist at the same time.

6. If so, the law of Illinois must give way

It was particularly pressed upon the court by Mr. Chase, that this court had decided, in the case of Prigg v. Pennsylvania, (16 Pet. 539,) that all State legislation upon the subject of fugitive slaves, was void, whether professing to be in aid of the legislation of Congress, or independent of it, was void; and he claimed the benefit of that decision.

The counsel for the defendant in error, commented on the various positions above mentioned; and the following extract from the brief, shows the principal ground relied upon to vindicate the State law.

The case just cited, (Houston v. Moore, 5 Wheaton,) leads directly to the question, What is the particular power exercised by the State in the present instance; whence derived, and what the design and mode of its operation? And it may be as well here to remark, that it is not alone in the light of an act in aid of the legislation of Congress, that this law is to be considered. The question before this court is one of power — of power in the State to legislate in the particular manner. If the power exists in the State, no matter from whence derived, the validity of the law cannot be questioned.

It is now contended that the power in question belongs to the States in virtue of their original and unsurrendered sovereignty; in virtue of those great conservative powers which all governments must have, exercise, and maintain for their own protection and preservation; powers which, in the language of Mr. Madison, (Federalist, No. 45,) "extend to all the objects which, in the ordinary course of affairs, concern the lives, liberties, and properties of the people; and the internal order, improvement, and prosperity of the State."

In the City of New York v. Miln, (11 Pet. 139,) the court say, "that a State has the same undeniable, and unlimited jurisdiction over all persons and things within its territorial limits as any foreign nation, when that jurisdiction is not surrendered or restrained by the Constitution of the United States," &c.

It has been before remarked, that slavery exists to a limited extent in the State of Illinois; nevertheless, it is the settled policy of the State to discourage the institution, as also a free negro population. By numerous acts of legislation, before and since the present constitution, it has been made penal to introduce negroes from other States, except upon severe conditions. Negroes have been and continue to be regarded as constituting a vagabond population; and to prevent their influx into the State, restrictive laws have been from time to time passed. In connection with this regulation is to be found the law in question, prohibiting persons within the State from harboring or secreting fugitive negro slaves. The question whether a State may not prohibit its citizens from harboring or protecting felons, fugitives from other countries, is the same with this. It is possible that some new State might become a country of refuge for the accused and convicted outcasts of older and stronger governments; would that State be compelled to receive and welcome the moral pestilence? Certainly not; the right of self-preservation, necessary to all governments, would justify any act required to repel them from her borders.

It was upon this principle, as a sovereign power in the State, that this court sustained the law of New York, intended to prevent the influx of a pauper and vagabond population at the port of New York. City of New York *v.* Miln, (11 Pet. 142.) In which case the court say, " We think it as competent and as necessary for a State to provide precautionary measures against the moral pestilence of paupers and vagabonds, and possibly convicts, as it is to guard against the physical pestilence which may arise from unsound and infectious articles imported, or from a ship the crew of which may be laboring under an infectious disease."

It was in favor of this same power that the court, in Prigg *v.* Pennsylvania, (16 Pet. 625,) qualify the general terms of their opinion, — " To guard, however, against any possible misconstruction of our views, it is proper to state that we are by no means to be understood, in any manner whatsoever, to doubt or to interfere with the police power belonging to the States, in virtue of their general sovereignty," &c.

The State may arrest, restrain, and even remove from its borders, the fugitive slave, and so long as the rights of the owner are not interfered with, it is a constitutional exercise of power. If, then, the greater power exists, that over the person of the slave, for the purpose of police, certainly the lesser power, that over the citizen, preventing him from harboring, secreting, or protecting the slave, for like purposes of police, will not be denied.

It will be perceived that this view of the case settles the point made in the opposing argument, that the law of Illinois is a violation of the Federal and State Constitutions, which prohibit two punishments for one offence. A legal offence is the breach of a law. Eels, in harboring a fugitive slave, violated a law of this State, by interfering with its internal policy. He also violated a law of Congress, by interfering with the rights of the slave-owner secured by the Constitution. The one act constitutes two distinct offences against the several laws of distinct jurisdictions. Within the same jurisdiction one act frequently constitutes several offences, as in the familiar cases of assaults, libels, and other personal injuries, which are offences against the persons injured, and at the same time offences against the government; and the different offences may be separately tried,

·and separately punished. The constitutional provision is not, that no person shall be subject, for the same act, to be twice put in jeopardy of life or limb; but for the same offence, the same violation of law, no person's life or limb shall be twice put in jeopardy.

Mr. Justice GRIER delivered the opinion of the court.

The plaintiff in error was indicted and convicted under the criminal code of Illinois for " harboring and secreting a negro slave." The record was removed by writ of error to the Supreme Court of that State; and it was there contended, on behalf of the plaintiff in error, that the judgment and conviction should be reversed, because the statute of Illinois, upon which the indictment was founded, is void, by reason of its being in conflict with that article of the Constitution of the United States which declares " that no person held to labor or service in one State, under the laws thereof, escaping into another, shall, in consequence of any law or regulation therein, be discharged from such service or labor, but shall be delivered up on claim of the party to whom such labor may. be due." And, also, because said statute is in conflict with the act of Congress on the same subject.

That this record presents a case of which this court has jurisdiction under the twenty-fifth section of the judiciary act, is not disputed.

The statute of Illinois, whose validity is called in question, is contained in the 149th section of the Criminal Code, and is as follows: " If any person shall harbor or secrete any negro, mulatto, or person of color, the same being a slave or servant owing service or labor to any other persons, whether they reside in this State or in any other State or territory, or district, within the limits and under the jurisdiction of the United States, or shall in any wise hinder or prevent the lawful owner or owners of such slaves or servants from retaking them, in a lawful manner, every such person so offending shall be deemed guilty of a misdemeanor, and fined not exceeding five hundred dollars, or imprisoned not exceeding six months."

The bill of indictment, framed under this statute, contains four counts. The first charges that " Richard Eels, a certain negro slave, owing service to one C. D., of the State of Missouri, did unlawfully secrete, contrary to the form of the statute," &c.

2. That he harbored the same.

4. For unlawfully secreting a negro owing labor in the State of Missouri to one C. D., which said negro had secretly fled from said State and from said C. D.

4. For unlawfully preventing C. D., the lawful owner of said

2*

slave, from retaking him in a lawful manner, by secreting the said negro, contrary to the form of the statute, &c.

In view of this section of the Criminal Code of Illinois, and this indictment founded on it, we are unable to discover any thing which conflicts with the provisions of the Constitution of the United States or the legislation of Congress on the subject of fugitives from labor. It does not interfere in any manner with the owner or claimant in the exercise of his right to arrest and recapture his slave. It neither interrupts, delays, or impedes the right of the master to immediate possession. It gives no immunity or protection to the fugitive against the claim of his master. It acts neither on the master nor his slave; on his right or his remedy. It prescribes a rule of conduct for the citizens of Illinois. It is but the exercise of the power which every State is admitted to possess, of defining offences and punishing offenders against its laws. The power to make municipal regulations for the restraint and punishment of crime, for the preservation of the health and morals of her citizens, and of the public peace, has never been surrendered by the States, or restrained by the Constitution of the United States. In the exercise of this power, which has been denominated the police power, a State has a right to make it a penal offence to introduce paupers, criminals, or fugitive slaves, within their borders, and punish those who thwart this policy by harboring, concealing, or secreting such persons. Some of the States, coterminous with those who tolerate slavery, have found it necessary to protect themselves against the influx either of liberated or fugitive slaves, and to repel from their soil a population likely to become burdensome and injurious, either as paupers or criminals.

Experience has shown, also, that the results of such conduct as that prohibited by the statute in question are not only to demoralize their citizens who live in daily and open disregard of the duties imposed upon them by the Constitution and laws, but to destroy the harmony and kind feelings which should exist between citizens of this Union, to create border feuds and bitter animosities, and to cause breaches of the peace, violent assaults, riots, and murder. No one can deny or doubt the right of a State to defend itself against evils of such magnitude, and punish those who perversely persist in conduct which promotes them.

As this statute does not impede the master in the exercise of his rights, so neither does it interfere to aid or assist him. If a State, in the exercise of its legitimate powers in promotion of its policy of excluding an unacceptable population, should thus indirectly benefit the master of a fugitive, no one has a right to complain that it has, thus far at least, fulfilled a duty assumed or imposed by its compact as a member of the Union.

But though we are of opinion that such is the character, policy, and intention of the statute in question, and that for this reason alone the power of the State to make and enforce such a law cannot be doubted, yet we would not wish it to be inferred, by any implication from what we have said, that any legislation of a State to aid and assist the claimant, and which does not directly nor indirectly delay, impede, or frustrate the reclamation of a fugitive, or interfere with the claimant in the prosecution of his other remedies, is necessarily void. This question has not been before the court, and cannot be decided in anticipation of future cases.

It has been urged that this act is void, as it subjects the delinquent to a double punishment for a single offence. But we think that neither the fact assumed in this proposition, nor the inference from it, will be found to be correct. The offences for which the fourth section of the act of 12th February, 1793, subjects the delinquent to a fine of five hundred dollars, are different in many respects from those defined by the statute of Illinois. The act of Congress contemplates recapture and reclamation, and punishes those who interfere with the master in the exercise of this right — first, by obstructing or hindering the claimant in his endeavors to seize and arrest the fugitive ; secondly, by rescuing the fugitive when arrested ; and, thirdly, by harboring or concealing him after notice.

But the act of Illinois, having for its object the prevention of the immigration of such persons, punishes the harboring or secreting nego slaves, whether domestic or foreign, and without regard to the master's desire either to reclaim or abandon them. The fine imposed is not given to the master, as the party injured, but to the State, as a penalty for disobedience to its laws. And if the fine inflicted by the act of Congress had been made recoverable by indictment, the offence, as stated in any one of the counts of the bill before us, would not have supported such an indictment. Even the last count, which charges the plaintiff in error with "unlawfully preventing C. D., the lawful owner, from retaking the negro slave," as it does not allege notice, does not describe an offence punishable by the act of Congress.

But admitting that the plaintiff in error may be liable to an action under the act of Congress, for the same acts of harboring and preventing the owner from retaking his slave, it does not follow that he would be twice punished for the same offence. An offence, in its legal signification, means the transgression of a law. A man may be compelled to make reparation in damages to the injured party, and be liable also to punishment for a breach of the public peace, in consequence of the same act.; and may be said, in common parlance, to be twice punished for the same offence. Every citizen of the United States is also a citizen of a State or territory. He may be said to owe allegiance to two sovereigns, and may be liable to punishment for an infraction of the laws of either. The same act may be an offence or transgression of the laws of both. Thus, an assault upon the marshal of the United States, and hindering him in the execution of legal process, is a high offence against the United States, for which the perpetrator is liable to punishment; and the same act may be also a gross breach of the peace of the State, a riot, assault, or a murder, and subject the same person to a punishment, under the State laws, for a misdemeanor or felony. That either or both may (if they see fit) punish such an offender, cannot be doubted. Yet it cannot be truly averred that the offender has been twice punished for the same offence; but only that by one act he has committed two offences, for each of which he is justly punishable. He could not plead the punishment by one in bar to a conviction by the other; consequently, this court has decided, in the case of Fox v. The State of Ohio, (5 How. 432,) that a State may punish the offence of uttering or passing false coin, as a cheat or fraud practised on its citizens; and, in the case of the United States v. Marigold, (9 How. 560,) that Congress, in the proper exercise of its authority, may punish the same act as an offence against the United States.

It has been urged, in the argument on behalf of the plaintiff in error, that an affirmance of the judgment in this case will conflict with the decision of this court in the case of Prigg v. The Commonwealth of Pennsylvania, 16 Pet. 540. This, we think, is a mistake.

The questions presented and decided in that case differed entirely from those which affect the present. Prigg, with full power and authority from the owner, had arrested a fugitive slave in Pennsylvania, and taken her to her master in Maryland. For this he was indicted and convicted under a statute of Pennsylvania, making it a felony to take and carry away any negro or mulatto for the purpose of detaining them as slaves.

The following questions were presented by the case and decided by the court: —

1. That, under and in virtue of the Constitution of the United States, the owner of a slave is clothed with entire authority, in every State in the Union, to seize and recapture his slave, wherever he can do it without illegal violence or a breach of the peace.

2. That the government is clothed with appropriate authority and functions to enforce the delivery, on claim of the owner, and has properly exercised it in the act of Congress of 12th February, 1793.

3. That any State law or regulation which interrupts, impedes, limits, embarrasses, delays, or postpones the right of the owner to the immediate possession of the slave, and the immediate command of his service, is void.

We have in this case assumed the correctness of these doctrines; and it will be found that the grounds on which this case is decided were fully recognized in that. " We entertain," say the court, (page 625,) " no doubt whatsoever, that the States, in virtue of their general police power, possess full jurisdiction to arrest and restrain runaway slaves, and remove them from their borders, and otherwise to secure themselves against their depredations and evil example, as they certainly may do in cases of idlers, vagabonds, and paupers. The rights of the owners of fugitive slaves are in no just sense interfered with or regulated by such a course; and, in many cases, the operations of the police power, although designed essentially for other purposes, — for the protection, safety, and peace of the State, — may essentially promote and aid the interests of the owners. But such regulations can never be permitted to interfere with or to obstruct the just rights of the owner to reclaim his slave, derived from the Constitution of the United States, or with the remedies prescribed by Congress to aid and enforce the same."

Upon these grounds, we are of opinion that the act of Illinois, upon which this indictment is founded, is constitutional, and therefore affirm the judgment.

Mr. Justice McLEAN.

In the case of Prigg v. The Commonwealth of Pennsylvania, the police power of the States was not denied, but admitted. This court held, in Fox v. The State of Ohio, (5 How. 410;) that a person might be punished under a law of the State for passing counterfeit coin, although the same offence was punishable under the act of Congress, and, consequently, that the conviction and punishment under the State law would be no bar to a prosecution under the law of Congress. In that case I dissented, and gave at large the grounds of my dissent.

As the case now before us involves the same principle as was ruled in that case, I again dissent for the reasons then given, and I deem it unnecessary now to repeat them.

It is contrary to the nature and genius of our government, to punish an individual twice for the same offence. Where the jurisdiction is clearly vested in the Federal Government, and an adequate punishment has been provided by it for an offence, no State, it appears to me, can punish the same act. The assertion of such a power involves the right of a State to punish all offences punishable under the acts of Congress. This would practically disregard, if it did not destroy, this important branch of criminal justice, clearly vested in the Federal Government. The exercise of such a power by the States would, in effect, be a violation of the Constitution of the United States, and the Constitution of the respective States. They all provide against a second punishment for the same act. It is no satisfactory answer to this, to say that the States and Federal Government constitute different sovereignties, and, consequently, may each punish offenders under its own laws.

It is true, the criminal laws of the Federal and State Governments emanate from different sovereignties; but they operate upon the same people, and should have the same end in view. In this respect, the Federal Government, though sovereign within the limitation of its powers, may, in some sense, be considered as the agent of the States, to provide for the general welfare, by punishing offences under its own laws within its jurisdiction. It is believed that no government, regulated by laws, punishes twice criminally the same act. And I deeply regret that our government should be an exception to a great principle of action, sanctioned by humanity and justice.

It seems to me it would be as unsatisfactory to an individual as it would be illegal, to say to him that he must submit to a second punishment for the same act; because it is punishable as well under the State laws, as under the laws of the Federal Government. It is true he lives under the *ægis* of both laws; and though he might yield to the power, he would not be satisfied with the logic or justice of the argument.

Order.

This cause came on to be heard on the transcript of the record from the Supreme Court of the State of Illinois, and was argued by counsel. On consideration whereof, it is now here ordered and adjudged by this court, that the judgment of the said Supreme Court in this cause be, and the same is hereby, affirmed, with costs.

CORNELIUS KANOUSE, PLAINTIFF IN ERROR, *v.* JOHN M. MARTIN.

Where a motion was made, under the 12th section of the Judiciary Act, to remove a cause from a State Court to the Circuit Court of the United States, notwithstanding which the State Court retained cognizance of the case, and it was ultimately brought to this court under the 25th section of the Judiciary Act, a motion to dismiss it for want of jurisdiction cannot be sustained. The question will remain to be decided upon the full hearing of the case.

A MOTION was made by *Mr. Martin,* to dismiss this case, which was argued by himself and *Mr. Garr.*

The circumstances, upon which the motion was based, are stated in the opinion of the court.

Mr. Chief Justice TANEY delivered the opinion of the court.

This is a writ of error, directed to the Superior Court of the City of New York, and a motion has been made by the defendant in error to dismiss it for want of jurisdiction.

The record shows that a suit was brought by the defendant in error against the plaintiff, in the State Court above mentioned; the former being a citizen of New York, and the latter a citizen of New Jersey. The plaintiff in error, at the time of entering his appearance in the State Court, filed his petition, stating the citizenship of the parties, and praying for the removal of the cause for trial into the next Circuit Court, to be held in the district where the said suit was pending; and, at the same time, offered good and sufficient security for his entering in such court, on the first day of the session, copies of the process against him, and also for his then appearing and entering special bail in the cause.

The State Court, however, refused to permit the cause to be removed; and after the petition was filed and the bond given, proceeded in the case, and finally gave judgment against the plaintiff in error for the sum of money mentioned in the record. Various proceedings, it appears, were afterwards had in the appellate courts of the State, in relation to this judgment, but the decision in these courts was also against the plaintiff in error; and the judgment rendered in the Superior Court of the City of New York, still remains there and is in full force, if that court had jurisdiction of the case after the application to remove it.

The case then, as it stands on the motion, is this: The plaintiff in error claimed the right to remove this cause from the State Court to the Circuit Court of the United States, under the 12th section of the Judiciary Act of 1789. The right claimed was denied by the State Court, which retained the case, and proceeded to give a final judgment against him.

It is therefore precisely one of the cases enumerated in the 25th section of the act of 1789, in which jurisdiction is conferred upon this court, and in which the judgment of the State Court may be reviewed upon writ of error. For the construction of an act of Congress was drawn in question, and the decision of the court was against the right claimed under it, by the plaintiff in error.

As to the authority of the Superior Court of the City of New York to retain the case, and the validity or invalidity of its proceedings and judgment, after the motion to remove; that question, according to the practice of the court, will stand for hearing when the case is reached in the regular call of the docket. But the motion to dismiss, for want of jurisdiction in this court, is overruled.

Order.

On consideration of the motion, made on a prior day of the present term of this court, to dismiss this writ of error, and of the argument of counsel thereupon had, as well in support of as against the motion, it is now here ordered by the court that the said motion be, and the same is hereby, overruled.

Ex parte William Many.

Where there was a blank in the record of the Circuit Court in the taxation of the costs recovered by the plaintiff, and the judgment being affirmed by this Court, a mandate with the same blank went down to the Circuit Court; and a motion was there made to open the original judgment for the purpose of taxing the costs, which motion was refused by the court, such refusal cannot be reached by a *mandamus* from this court.

The refusal of the court was not a ministerial act, but an exercise of judicial discretion. This court could issue a. *mandamus* for the Circuit Court to proceed to judgment, but such a writ would not be appropriate to the present case.

Mr. Chief Justice TANEY delivered the opinion of the court.

A motion has been made for a rule on the District Judge of the Massachusetts District, to show cause why he should not proceed to adjudicate and allow the petitioner's costs in an action at law in the Circuit Court. The rule is moved for upon the District Judge, because he alone was holding the Circuit Court when the decision was made which has given rise to this application.

The case is this: Many recovered a judgment in the Circuit

Court for the District of Massachusetts against Sizer and others, for the infringement of a patent right. The judgment was entered in the following words :—

" It is thereupon considered by the court, that the said William V. Many recover against the said George W. and Henry Sizer the sum of seventeen hundred and thirty-three dollars and seventy-five cents damages and costs of suit taxed at   "

The judgment was rendered in 1848 ; and upon writ of error brought by the defendants, it was affirmed in this court at December term, 1851. The costs were not taxed in the Circuit Court before the removal, and the blank left for them remained unfilled when the judgment was affirmed. The usual mandate issued to the Circuit Court to carry the judgment into execution, and the blank space for costs was necessarily left in the mandate, in order to conform to the judgment of the court below, as it appeared in the transcript transmitted to this court.

Upon the return of the case to the Circuit Court, the counsel for the plaintiff moved that his costs be taxed by the clerk as and for the October term, 1848, and that an order be made amending the record of the judgment of the Circuit Court so as to insert therein the amount of the taxation, and that an execution on the judgment so amended be issued.

The court refused to allow the amendment to be made, and overruled the motion. And we think its judgment, whether it be correct or not, cannot be revised in the form of proceeding moved for on behalf of the plaintiff. The decision of the Circuit Court was not a mere ministerial act. It was the decision of a court of competent jurisdiction made in the exercise of judicial authority and discretion. This court might unquestionably issue a *mandamus* to the court below to proceed to judgment. But in this case the court has proceeded to judgment, upon the question submitted for its decision. And whether that judgment be erroneous or not, this court has not jurisdiction to reëxamine it in a proceeding by *mandamus*.

The motion for a rule to show cause must therefore be overruled for want of jurisdiction.

JOHN A. BROWN, ADMINISTRATOR OF JOHN ASPDEN, DECEASED, ET AL., APPELLANTS, v. MATHIAS ASPDEN'S ADMINISTRATORS, ET AL.

A reargument of a case decided by this court will not be granted, unless a member of the court, who concurred in the judgment, desires it ; and when that is the case, it will be ordered without waiting for the application of counsel.

And this is so, whether the decree of the court below was affirmed by an equally
divided court or a majority; or whether the case is one at common law or chancery.

The rules of the English Court of Chancery have not been adopted by this court.
Those which are applicable to a court of original jurisdiction, are not appropriate
to an appellate court.

THIS was an appeal from the Circuit Court of the United
States for the Eastern District of Pennsylvania, and was the
conclusion of the case of Aspden et al. *v.* Nixon et al., reported
in 4 How. 467.

It was affirmed by a divided court in December, 1852; and
in February, 1853, a petition for a rehearing was filed by the
appellants.

Upon which petition Mr. Chief Justice TANEY delivered
the opinion of the court.

A motion has been made for a rehearing in this case, and we
have been referred to the practice of the English Chancery Court
in support of the application. The argument presupposes that
this court, in cases in equity, has adopted the rules and practice
of the English chancery. But this is a mistake. The English
chancery is . court of original jurisdiction; and this court is
sitting as an appellate tribunal. It would be impossible, from
the nature and office of the two tribunals, to adopt the same
rules of practice in both.

Nothing could show this more strongly than the present application. By the established rules of chancery practice, a rehearing, in the sense in which that term is used in proceedings
in equity, cannot be allowed after the decree is enrolled. If the
party desires it, it must be applied for before the enrolment.
But no appeal will lie to the proper appellate tribunal, until
after it is enrolled, either actually or by construction of law.
And, consequently, the time for a rehearing must have gone by
before an appeal could be taken. In the House of Lords, in
England, to which the appeal lies from the Court of Chancery,
a rehearing is altogether unknown. A reargument, indeed, may
be ordered, if the house desires it, for its own satisfaction. But
the chancery rules in relation to rehearings, in the technical sense
of the word, are altogether inapplicable to the proceedings on
the appeal.

Undoubtedly this court may and would call for a reargument,
where doubts are entertained which it is supposed may be removed by further discussion at the bar. And this may be done
after judgment is entered, provided the order for reargument is
entered at the same term. But the rule of the court is this, —
that no reargument will be heard in any case after judgment is

entered, unless some member of the court who concurred in the judgment afterwards doubts the correctness of his opinion, and desires a further argument on the subject. And when that happens, the court will, of its own accord, apprise the counsel of its wishes, and designate the points on which it desires to hear them.

There is certainly nothing in the history of the English Court of Chancery to induce this court to adopt rules in relation to re-arguments, analogous to the chancery practice upon applications for a rehearing. According to the general practice of that court, one rehearing, where the application has been sanctioned by the signature of two counsel, is a matter of course. And this facility in obtaining one rehearing, has naturally led to others, and in cases of interest or difficulty, two, or even three, rehearings have sometimes been allowed, under the special leave of the court, before the decree was enrolled, and, consequently, before it could be removed to the House of Lords. The natural result of this practice is to produce some degree of carelessness in the first argument, and hesitation and indecision in the court. But the great evil is in the enormous expenses occasioned by these repeated hearings, and the delays which it produces in the decision, which often prove ruinous to both parties before the final decree is pronounced. Nor is the mischief confined to the particular suit in which such proceedings and delays are permitted to take place. A multitude of others are always behind it, waiting anxiously to be heard. And the result of the practice of which we are speaking has been such that, although the court has always been filled by men of the highest order, distinguished for their learning and industry, yet the expenses and delays of the court have become a byword and reproach to the administration of justice, and Parliament has at length been compelled to interpose.

And if this court should adopt a practice analogous to that of the English chancery, we should soon find ourselves in the same predicament; and we should be hearing over again at a second term almost all the cases which we had heard and adjudged at a former one, and upon which our own opinions would have been definitively made up upon the first argument. We deem it safer to adhere to the rule we have heretofore acted on. And no reargument will be granted in any case, unless a member of the court who concurred in the judgment desires it; and when that is the case, it will be ordered without waiting for the application of counsel.

It is true that the decree of affirmance in this court, in the case before us, was upon an equal division of the members composing the court at the time of the argument, eight being present. But the case was fully heard, more than a week being occupied in the arguments of counsel. And when, upon conference and a full interchange of opinion, it was found that the court was divided, the case was held over until the present term, in order that each member of the body might have an ample opportunity of investigating the subject for himself. This has been done. And when the court reassembled, it was found that the opinions of each member of the tribunal was unchanged, and the decree was therefore affirmed by a divided court. Further arguments would be mere waste of time, when opinions have been formed after so much argument and such deliberate examination.

Nor is the circumstance, that a decree is affirmed by a divided court, any reason for ordering a reargument before a full bench in any case. In a body as numerous as this, it must often happen, from various causes, that the bench is not full. And experience has shown, that it has rarely happened that every judge has been present every day throughout any one entire term. The case before us is certainly an important one, in its principles and in the amount in dispute. But there are many cases on the docket at every term of the court much more important in both respects. And if it is to be understood, that cases of this description are not to be finally decided without the concurrence of a majority of the whole bench, it would be an useless consumption of time to hear them in the absence of any one judge, because it would be uncertain whether a judgment could follow after the argument. And it is easy to foresee the inconvenience, delay, and expenses to which a practice of that kind would subject the parties, and the uncertainty and confusion it would produce (to the great injury of other suitors) in the order of business as it stands on the docket of the court.

Neither is there any difference between a decreee in chancery and a judgment at law, as to its affirmance on a division of the court. In both cases, the motion is to reverse; and if that fails, the judgment or decree necessarily stands, and must therefore be affirmed. And in most of the cases affirmed in this manner, a majority, in fact, of the judges, who act judicially upon the case, concur in the judgment. For the Circuit Court is composed of two members, and if both are on the bench, they must concur in the judgment or decree; otherwise it could not be passed, and the point would be certified by a divided court.

In every view of the subject, we see no sufficient ground for ordering a reargument, and the application is therefore refused.

JOHN HAGAN, SURVIVING PARTNER OF THE LATE FIRM OF JOHN HAGAN & CO., APPELLANT, *v.* LEROY P. WALKER, ADMINISTRATOR OF WILLIAM H. POPE, DECEASED, AND FRANCES ANN POPE, WIDOW AND GUARDIAN AD LITEM OF WILLIAM POPE AND JULIA ANN POPE, MINOR CHILDREN OF SAID WILLIAM H. POPE, DECEASED, AND SAMUEL BRECK, ADMINISTRATOR OF LEROY POPE, DECEASED.

A court of equity has jurisdiction of a bill against the administrator of a deceased debtor and a person to whom real and personal property was conveyed by the deceased debtor, for the purpose of defrauding creditors.

In such a case, the court does not exercise an auxiliary jurisdiction to aid legal process, and consequently it is not necessary that the creditor should be in a condition to levy an execution, if the fraudulent obstacle should be removed.

It is proper to make a prior encumbrancer, who holds the legal title, a party to the bill, in order that the whole title may be sold under the decree; for the purpose of such a decree, the prior encumbrancer is a necessary party; but the court may order a sale subject to the encumbrance, without having the prior encumbrancer before it, and in fit cases it will do so.

If the prior encumbrancer is out of the jurisdiction, or cannot be joined without defeating it, it is a fit cause to dispense with his presence, and order a sale subject to his encumbrance, which will not be affected by the decree.

THIS was an appeal from the District Court of the United States for the Northern District of Alabama.

The bill was originally filed in the names of John Hagan, of New Orleans, and a citizen of the State of Louisiana, and Thomas Barrett, of New Orleans, and a citizen of the State of Louisiana, formerly commission merchants and partners, trading under the firm, name, and style of John Hagan & Co., complainants, against William H. Pope, of Huntsville, and a citizen of the State of Alabama, Samuel Breck, of Huntsville, and a citizen of the State of Alabama, the said Breck being the administrator of the estate of Leroy Pope, who in his lifetime resided in Huntsville, and was a citizen of the State of Alabama, and Charles B. Penrose, of Washington city, and a citizen of the District of Columbia, and successor in office of Virgil Maxcy, who in his lifetime resided in Washington city, and was a citizen of the District of Columbia, and Solicitor of the Treasury of the United States.

The suit was commenced in February, 1846. The plaintiffs were judgment creditors of Leroy Pope, by a judgment rendered in April, 1834, upon which an execution in October, 1834, was returned, " No property found."

The plaintiffs sought to obtain satisfaction of this judgment, from property which they allege the said Leroy Pope conveyed fraudulently to his son William H. Pope, the defendant.

This property was conveyed, March, 1834, by Leroy Pope to

3*

William H. Pope, and upon considerations which the plaintiffs alleged to be colorable and inadequate.

The property thus conveyed, was charged to have been the whole estate of the said Leroy, and William H. Pope was charged to have been, before that time, without property, and to have had no means of payment for this.

The plaintiffs alleged that the property was never delivered to the "exclusive possession" of William H. Pope, but "remained as much in the possession of the said Leroy as the said William, and that the said Leroy and William enjoyed the proceeds and profits jointly."

They alleged that William H. Pope, in March, 1834, conveyed the land and slaves to the Solicitor of the Treasury in mortgage, to secure a debt due to the United States by the said Leroy Pope, of $29,290.90, which William H. Pope at that date assumed, and for which he gave his notes; and that at the same date he guaranteed to the United States a debt of $20,000, for which other security had been given to the United States by Leroy Pope.

They averred that the $20,000 thus mentioned, was paid from the securities deposited by Leroy Pope, and that the only debt really incurred by William H. Pope, was that for $29,-290.90. This debt the plaintiffs admitted to be a charge on the property, and they did not contest it. They charged, however, that the securities to the Solicitor of the Treasury were designed by the grantor (William H. Pope) as a fraud upon the creditors of Leroy Pope.

The death of Leroy Pope was alleged to have occurred in 1844, and the appointment of Breck, as administrator, in 1844.

The prayer of the bill was, that the conveyances of Leroy and William H. Pope should be declared null. That, after satisfying the debt of the United States, the remainder of the property should be appropriated to satisfy the debt of the plaintiffs. Process was prayed against William H. Pope and Samuel Breck, administrators of Leroy Pope, and the Solicitor of the Treasury, (Penrose,) a citizen of the District of Columbia.

The defendants, Breck and Pope, demurred to the bill; the demurrer was allowed by the District Court, and the bill was dismissed.

An appeal from this decree of dismissal brought the case up to this court. It was argued by *Mr. Johnson* for the appellant, and *Mr. J. A. Campbell* for the appellees.

As the demurrer was sustained in the court below, the points before this court to be argued were, the reasons for dismissing the bill and sustaining the demurrer. These were stated by Mr. Campbell, as follows, and it is sufficient to state the points and authorities.

I. That the jurisdiction of the Court of Chancery to set aside conveyances executed by a failing debtor to defraud creditors, is not an original and independent jurisdiction of that court, but is an auxiliary and limited jurisdiction. The creditor must show that the remedies at law have been exhausted — that there is an obstruction which can only be removed by the aid of the Court of Chancery, and that his cause is so situated at law, that, upon the interposition of the court in the manner sought, he could immediately enforce the right he claims. 3 Mylne & Craig, 407; 11 S. & M. 366; 8 Barb. N. Y. R. 593; 7 Ala. 319, 928; 1 Hill's So. Car. R. 297, 307; 20 Johns. 554; 2 Rand. 384; 1 Paige, 388.

II. The bill shows in this case three facts sufficient to have determined the lien of the judgment against Leroy Pope, under the laws of the United States, and the State of Alabama.

Five years had elapsed from the 3d of March, 1839, before the filing of the bill. The act of Congress of that date determined the lien. 5 Stat. at Large, 338.

Ten years had elapsed from the judgment and return of the last execution. Clay's Digest, 206, 207, § 28, 29; 5 Ala. R. 188; 18 Ala. 675; 19 Ala. 207.

The death of Leroy Pope put an end to the lien of the judgment and the right to issue execution. Bush v. Jones, 13 Ala. R. 167.

III. The plaintiff sets forth the conveyance of Leroy Pope to William H. Pope, to have taken place in 1834. He does not aver that the conveyance was upon any trust for Leroy Pope, nor does he aver that any title remained in Leroy Pope. The bar of the statute of limitations of six years will apply to the personal property. 7 Yerger, 222; 1 Bailey, Ch. R. 228; 1 Humph. 335; 1 Hill, Ch. R. 113; 8 Yerger, 145; 7 Wheat. 60, 117, &c.; Peck's Rep. 41.

IV. The Court of Chancery, except in cases of express trusts and fraud, follow the courts of law in the application of the statute of limitation.

In this case no trusts in favor of Leroy Pope are charged to exist; nor is there an averment that the plaintiff did not discover till within six years the fraudulent purpose and consideration upon which they were made.

In the absence of such averments, the court will presume the possession to have been consistent with the legal title, and the bar of the statute will run from the date of the title deeds. 4 How. S. C. R. 503, 560; 7 How. 234; 10 Wheat. 168.

In reference to personal property, the limitation upon personal actions is adopted in equity. 1 Dev. & B. Eq. 95; 5 Ala. R. 90, 508; 3 Ala. R. 756.

V. No averment is made by the plaintiff showing the condition of the estate of Leroy Pope, after his death. The bill contains an averment, that the crops from the lands and other profits of the estate have been large, and that Leroy Pope enjoyed them till his death.

There is nothing to show that ample means are not to be found in the hands of the administrator to pay the debt. No presentment to, nor demand of, the administrator is averred, and no refusal to pay on his part shown. A bill must show this, or it is fatally defective. 3 Ham. 287; 5 Har. & J. 381; 5 Gill & J. 432 ; 2 McCord's Ch. R. 416, 169.

VI. The court had no jurisdiction of the cause. The Solicitor of the Treasury, a citizen of the District of Columbia, is made a party. The prayer of the bill is to cancel deeds made to him, and to appropriate property in which he has a legal right. 3 Cranch, 267 ; 14 Pet. 60, 65.

Mr. Justice CURTIS delivered the opinion of the court.

John Hagan & Co. filed their bill in the District Court of the United States for the Northern District of Alabama, in which they state that, in the year 1834, they recovered a judgment at law in that court against Leroy Pope, for upwards of seven thousand dollars, which is wholly unsatisfied; that a writ of *fieri facias*, running against the lands, goods, and body of the debtor, was regularly issued, and, on the 10th day of October, 1834, was returned *nulla bona;* and from that time to the filing of the bill, there has not been, in that district or elsewhere, any property of Leroy Pope out of which the judgment-debt could be collected, except certain property afterwards mentioned. The bill further alleges that, about a month before the complainants recovered their judgment at law, Leroy Pope, intending to defraud the complainants, and to hinder them from obtaining payment, made conveyances, both of real and personal estate, to a large amount, to his son, William H. Pope, who was a party to the fraud, and is made a defendant in the bill; that Leroy Pope died in the year 1844, and Samuel Breck, who was appointed his administrator, is also a party defendant. The complainants are averred to be citizens of Louisiana, and William H. Pope and the administrator citizens of Alabama. The defendants having demurred to the bill, it was dismissed by the District Court, and the complainant, who is the surviving partner, appealed to this court.

The principal ground upon which the demurrer has been rested in this court is, that the bill does not show that the complainants are entitled to equitable relief. The argument is, that the jurisdiction of a court of equity, to aid a judgment-creditor, by removing a fraudulent encumbrance on the property of his debtor, is ancillary merely; that this aid is not given unless the creditor has obtained a lien at law upon the specific property sought for, if that be legal property upon which an execution could be levied; or if it be equitable assets, not liable to a levy by execution; that the creditor must have exhausted his legal remedy, by a return of *nulla bona* on his execution, and must also be in a condition to proceed at once at law to enforce his right, if the obstacle should be removed. That if his judgment has become ineffectual to entitle him to an execution, so that he could not levy, even if the assets were legal, and not subject to any fraudulent encumbrance, equity will not exert itself to subject equitable property to the payment of his judgment. And it is further argued, that, according to the local law of Alabama, governing these proceedings at law, the judgment-creditors had lost their lien on the personal estate of the debtor, because they had suffered more than one term to elapse without issuing an *alias* execution; and upon the real estate, because more than ten years elapsed after the return of their last execution, and before this bill was filed; and that the lien, both upon the personal and real estate, was destroyed by the death of Leroy Pope, which suspended the right to issue an execution. That, by reason of his death and the lapse of more than ten years, the right to issue an execution being suspended, equity would not subject equitable assets to the payment of this judgment.

It does not distinctly appear whether the property sought to be reached by this bill is equitable or legal. There is reason to suppose, from some allegations in the bill, that a part or the whole of the property was conveyed by Leroy Pope, in 1831, to Louis McLane, as Secretary of the Treasury, to secure a debt due to the United States by a deed of trust, and this conveyance is not impeached. If it embraced the whole or any part of the property now in question, only an equitable estate therein was left in Leroy Pope. The bill is not distinct in its allegations on this subject; but we do not deem it necessary that it should be; because we are of opinion that this case is not to be treated as an application by a judgment-creditor for the exercise of the ancillary jurisdiction of the court, to aid him in executing legal process, but comes under a head of original jurisdiction in equity. It is a bill by a creditor of a deceased debtor, against the administrator and a party who is fraudulently holding all the property of the deceased, which in equity should be applied to the payment of this debt, and the bill prays that the debt may be paid out of this fund. That a single creditor may maintain a bill against an administrator of a deceased debtor, for a discovery of assets and the payment of his debt, there can be no doubt. That, in some cases, he may join with the administrator a third person, who is in possession of property which is amenable to the payment of the debt, is also clear. The instances in which it has been actually held that such third person might be joined, are chiefly cases of collusion between the administrator and the third person possessed of assets, insolvency of the administrator, and where the third·person was the surviving partner of the deceased. Utterson *v.* Mair, 2 Ves. Jr. 95; Alsager *v.* Rowley, 6 Ves. 748; Burroughs *v.* Elton, 11 Ves. 29; Gedge *v.* Traill, 1 Russ. & M. 281; Long *v.* Majestre, 1 Johns. Ch. Rep. 306. But it will be found that the equitable right of the creditor to join a third person, and have a discovery and an appropriation of assets held by him, has never been limited to these particular cases.

For, while it is generally agreed that some special case must be made, it is also declared in all the cases, that what is to constitute it has not been limited by any precise and rigid rule. In Holland *v.* Prior, (1 My. & K. 240,) Lord Brougham applied the rule to the case of a representative of a deceased representative, without any suggestion of collusion between him and the present representative. In Simpson *v.* Vaughn, (2 Atk. 33,) Lord Hardwicke said: "It has been said at the bar, that you may make any person a defendant that you apprehend has possessed himself of assets upon which you have a lien. But this certainly cannot be laid down as a general rule; for it would be of dangerous consequence to insist that you can make any·person a defendant who has assets, unless you can show to the court he denies that he has assets, or applies them improperly." Considering, then, that some special and sufficient reasons must be shown for proceeding against a third person, jointly with the administrator, the inquiry is, whether this bill does not contain those reasons; and we are of opinion it does.

It appears, from the statements in the bill, that William H. Pope is in possession. of all the assets of the deceased debtor, both real and personal, holding them under conveyances made to him by the deceased, absolute in form, but accompanied by secret trusts in favor of the grantor, designed to defraud this particular creditor, and prevent him from obtaining payment of his judgment, and that this fraudulent design has thus far been successfully executed.

Now these conveyances are not only valid on their face, but they are really valid as between the parties; and though they are void as against creditors, and the property, both at law and in equity, is subject to the payment of the debts of the deceased, yet the embarrassments attending any attempt by the administrator to possess himself even of that part of these assets, which were personalty, at law would certainly be great, and perhaps insuperable. 2 Rand. Rep. 384; Martin v. Root, 17 Mass. Rep. 228. It is true he is the representative of creditors, as well as of the next of kin, and in the former capacity might be able to make good his claim to a sufficient amount of these personal assets to enable him to pay the debts. Holland v. Cruft, 20 Pick. 321. But the impracticability of taking an account of the debts at law, and proportioning the recovery to the amount required to pay them, would render a resort to equity indispensable to do entire justice between all parties, even if the assets were legal in their nature. If this bill had contained an allegation that the administrator had been requested to sue, and had refused, the case would be free from all doubt; and, upon the facts averred in the bill, we do not think such a request necessary; because it does appear that about two years elapsed after the death of Leroy Pope before this bill was filed, and the administrator took no step to reduce these assets to possession; because, when this bill was filed, he resists it by a demurrer, relying on the statute of limitations; because it must be admitted to have been doubtful how far he had a remedy, without the concurrence of any creditor; and chiefly, because there is no danger of interfering with the due course of administrations, or taking from administrators their proper control over suits for the recovery of assets, by holding that a creditor may file a bill against the administrator and the fraudulent grantee of deceased debtor, to subject the property fraudulently conveyed to the payment of the debt. It comes within the case put by Lord Hardwicke; for here this specific property is amenable to the claim of this creditor, and in the sense in which he employs the word, the creditor had a lien upon these assets; and it does appear to the court, that the party holding them both denies that they are assets and applies them improperly, for he claims them as his own, and is endeavoring to defeat a just creditor by an assertion of a title invalid as against him.

In this view of the case, it is not essential that the creditor cannot proceed at law until after a revival of the judgment by a scire facias. In Burroughs v. Elfon, (11 Ves. 36 – 7,) Lord Eldon had occasion to consider the force of this objection in a similar case. It was a bill to reach real assets in the hands of a surviving partner. The complainant's judgment was upwards of seventeen years old, and no step had been taken to revive it against the administrator or the heir. His decision, in accordance with two previous cases to which he refers, was, that such a creditor could sustain the bill, though it might be necessary to direct him to proceed at law to revive his judgment.

It has been argued, that the bill does not show that there are not other assets in the hands of the administrator sufficient to pay this debt, and contains no allegation that the administrator was ever requested to pay it. But the bill does expressly aver, that, aside from the property fraudulently conveyed, there is not, any where, any property of Leroy Pope, out of which the debt could be collected ; and, although it states that the fraudulent grantor and grantee both remained in possession, and took the crops jointly, and that these crops were of great value, yet, inasmuch as between themselves the crops belonged to the grantee, and as it was the object of the conveyances to prevent them from being applied to the benefit of creditors, we are of opinion there is no presumption that any thing arising from this joint possession ever came to the hands of the administrator, and, therefore, that a demand on him would have been a vain act, which the creditor was not compelled to do.

One other ground on which the demurrer has been rested, requires notice. The bill alleges that, after the fraudulent conveyances to William H. Pope had been made, he mortgaged the property to Virgil Maxcy, as Solicitor of the Treasury of the United States, to secure the debt of Leroy Pope which William H. Pope assumed to pay, and it avers that this debt has been in part paid by means described in the bill. Virgil Maxcy and, subsequently when he went out of office, his successor, Charles B. Penrose, were named as parties to the bill, but they were out of the jurisdiction, no process was served on either of them, and neither ever appeared or answered. The bill prays that William H. Pope may be compelled to pay to the United States the balance due to them, out of the property in question, and that the residue may be subjected to the payment of the complainant's debt, and for other and further relief.

Under the act of Congress of the 28th of February, 1839, (5 Stat. at Large, 321, § 1,) it does not defeat the jurisdiction of the court that a person named as defendant is not an inhabitant of or found within the district where the suit is brought ; the court may still adjudicate between the parties who are properly before it, and the absent parties are not to be concluded or affected by the decree.

It is obvious, however, that there may be cases in which the court cannot adjudicate between the parties who are regularly before it, for the reason that it cannot bind those who are absent. Where no relief can be given without taking an account between an absent party and one before the court, though the defect of parties may not defeat the jurisdiction, strictly speaking, yet the court will make no decree in favor of the complainant.

The case before us is not one of this character; for although the whole of the relief specially prayed for cannot be granted in the particular mode there indicated, because the United States not being a party, no account can be taken of the debt due to them from Leroy Pope or William H. Pope, yet, subject to the encumbrance of this debt, and without affecting it in any manner, the property may be appropriated to the payment of the complainant's debt.

It is true, that in Finley v. The Bank of the United States, (11 Wheat. R. 306,) which was a bill to foreclose a mortgage by sale, Chief Justice Marshall says: " It cannot be doubted that the prior mortgagee ought regularly to - have been a party defendant, and that had the existence of his mortgage been known to the court, no decree ought to have been pronounced in the cause until he was introduced into it." But it could not have been intended by this to say, that a prior encumbrancer was absolutely a necessary party without whose presence no decree of sale could be made, because in that very case the court refused to treat the decree as erroneous, after it had been executed.

In Delabere v. Norwood, (3 Swanst. R. 144, n.) in a bill to obtain payment of an annuity charged on land, prior annuitants were held not to be necessary parties. In Rose v. Page, (2 Sim. 471,) the same rule was applied to a prior mortgagee; and in Wakeman v. Grover, (4 Paige, R. 23,) and Rundell v. Marquis of Donegal, (1 Hogan, 308,) and Post v. Mackall, (3 Bland, 495,) to prior judgment creditors; and in Parker v. Fuller, (1 Russ. & My. 656,) persons having encumbrances on real property, which the bill sought to subject to the payment of debts of the deceased owner, were held not to be necessary parties to the bill. See also Hoxie v. Carr, 1 Sum. R. 173; Calvert on Parties, 128.

On the other hand there are cases in which it has been declared that all encumbrancers are necessary parties. Many are collected in Story's Eq Pl. 178, n. But we consider the true rule to be, that, where it is the object of the bill to procure a sale of the land, and the prior encumbrancer holds the legal title, and his debt is payable, it is proper to make him a party in order that a sale may be made of the whole title. In this sense, and for this purpose, he may be correctly said to be a necessary party, that is, necessary to such a decree. But it is in the power of the court to order a sale subject to the prior encumbrance, a power which it will exercise in fit cases. And when the prior encumbrancer is not subject to the jurisdiction of the court, or cannot be joined without defeating its jurisdiction, and the validity of the encumbrance is admitted, it is fit to dispense with his being made a party. To such a case the 47th rule for the equity practice of the Circuit Courts of the United States is applicable, and by force of it, this cause may proceed without making the United States, or the Solicitor of the Treasury a party to the decree.

The decree of the District Court must be reversed, and the case remanded, with directions to overrule the demurrer and order the defendants, other than the representative of the United States, to answer the bill.

Order.

This cause came on to be heard on the transcript of the record from the District Court of the United States for the Northern District of Alabama, and was argued by counsel. On consideration whereof it is now here ordered, adjudged, and decreed, that the decree of the said District Court in this cause be, and the same is hereby, reversed with costs, and that this cause be, and the same is hereby, remanded to the said District Court, with directions to overrule the demurrer, and to order the defendants, other than the representative of the United States, to answer the bill.

John Kennett, Ezekiel S. Haines, Eden B. Reeder, George Graham, Jr., John McCarty, Joshua Yorke, and Robert B. Bowler, Appellants, v. Thomas J. Chambers.

t belongs exclusively to the political department of the government to recognize or to refuse to recognize a new government in a foreign country, claiming to have displaced the old and established a new one.

Until the political department of the government acknowledged the independence of Texas, the Judiciary were bound to consider the old order of things as having continued.

While the government of the United States acknowledged its treaty of limits and of amity and friendship with Mexico as still subsisting and obligatory, no citizen of the United States could lawfully furnish supplies to Texas to enable it to carry on the war against Mexico.

A contract, made in Cincinnati, after Texas declared itself independent, but before its independence was acknowledged by the United States, whereby the complainants agreed to furnish, and did furnish money to a General in the Texan army, to enable him to raise and equip troops to be employed against Mexico, was illegal and void, and cannot be enforced in a court of the United States.

The circumstance that the Texan officer agreed, in consideration of these advances of money, to convey to them certain lands in Texas, of which he covenanted that he was then the owner, will not make the contract valid when it appears upon the face of it, and by the averments in the bill, that the object and intention of the complainants in advancing the money was to assist Texas in its military operations.

A contract made in the United States at that time for the purchase of land in Texas, would have been valid even if the money was afterwards used to support hostilities with Mexico. But in this case it was not an ordinary purchase, but the object of the complainants, as avowed in the contract and the bill, was to aid Texas in its war with Mexico.

The contract being absolutely void by the laws of the United States at the time it was made, the circumstance that it was valid in Texas, and that Texas has since become a member of the Union, does not entitle the complainants to enforce it in the courts of the United States.

No contract can be enforced in the courts of the United States, no matter where made or where to be executed, if it is in violation of the laws of the United States, or is in contravention of the public policy of the government or in conflict with subsisting treaties.

In this cause *Mr. Justice Catron* was absent, because of indisposition, during the hearing before the court, and took no part in the decision.

This was an appeal from the District Court of the United States for the District of Texas.

The facts in the case are stated in the opinion of the court.

There were several causes of demurrer filed in the court below, but it is necessary to notice only the following, because the decision in this court turned entirely upon them.

1. The said bill, if the facts therein were true, which is in no sort admitted, contains no matter or thing of equity upon which to ground any decree, or give the complainants any aid or relief.

2. The complainants' said bill shows no legal or valid agreement upon which to ask the aid or decree of the court; but, to the contrary, sets out and shows an agreement which was in violation of the neutrality of the United States towards the Republic of Mexico in her contest with Texas.

3. The complainants' said bill seeks the aid or assistance of the court to enforce the specific execution of an agreement made in the State of Kentucky, between citizens thereof and this defendant, in violation of the policy of the government of the United States in her intercourse with foreign governments.

The demurrer was sustained generally by the court below, and therefore all the points were open to argument in this court; but it is not necessary to notice any except those upon which the judgment of the court rested.

It was argued by *Mr. Snethen*, for the appellants, and there was also a brief filed upon that side by *Mr. L. Sherwood.* On the part of the appellee it was argued by *Mr. Volney E. Howard.*

Mr. Snethen contended that the neutrality and foreign policy of the United States towards Mexico were regulated entirely by law, which was found in the 6th section of the act of Congress of the 20th of April, 1818, (3 Stat. at Large, 449.)　There is an entire absence, in the contract, of all declaration or indication of the place or country where the proposed military expeditions were to be begun, or of the place whence they were to be carried on.　It will not be denied that, to subject an offender to the pains and penalties of this section, it must be incontestably and directly shown and proved that the "military expedition or enterprise" which he may "begin or set on foot," or "provide or prepare the means for," was begun or set on foot "within the territory or jurisdiction of the United States," and was "to be carried on from thence" against a nation with whom they were at peace.　So obvious a proposition hardly needs the weight of authority to support it.　Now the contract proves no such offence. The defendant may have done, and intended to have carried on, all the acts which the complainants enabled him to do, within and from some other country than the United States.　The place or country where the forbidden acts were done and whence they were to be carried on, cannot be inferred from the language of the contract with any degree of certainty, and the omission cannot be supplied by any known rule of construction.

The 6th section of the act of 1818, is a penal enactment and must be construed strictly, and the proof to sustain an offence against it must.be direct and positive.　The contract affords not only no such proof, but no proof at all, that the forbidden acts were done within the United States, and to be carried on from thence.　No such offence, therefore, as that denounced by the act, when strictly construed, having been proved against the parties to the contract, the contract itself consequently was not, when made, in violation of the neutrality or foreign policy of this country towards Mexico and other nations, as established and defined by said section and act.

The same course of argument was pursued by *Mr. L. Sherwood* in his brief for the appellants.

1. Texas, at the time of this contract, was an independent government.　And in making the contract the complainants did not violate the laws of the United States, enacted to preserve our neutrality with nations with whom we were at peace, nor did they violate our treaty of amity with Mexico.　Hence, the contract was legal, under the laws of the United States.

The people of Texas, represented by delegates, met in general convention at Washington, in Texas, on the 2d day of March, 1836, and declared themselves a "Free and Independent Republic."　And then and there set themselves at work to organize and establish a government.　And on the 17th day of the same month, had fully organized a government by the name of " The Republic of Texas," under a written Constitution. (Laws of Republic of. Texas, vol. 1, page 1 to 25.)

Then a new nation was born. An independent nation, that maintained her independence and freedom among the nations of the earth, and was subsequently recognized by them as possessing all the sovereignty and attributes of other nations. As such Republic, she maintained her independence in fact and in name, until she became incorporated into the government of the United States, December 29, 1845.

The first question to be determined by this court is, whether Texas, at the time before stated; had the right to become, and whether she did become an independent government?

That she had the right so to become, will not be doubted by any man, nor by any court, who " hold these truths to be self evident, that all men are created equal; that they are endowed by their Creator with certain unalienable rights; that among these are life, liberty, and the pursuit of happiness. That to secure these rights, governments are instituted among men, deriving their just powers from the consent of the governed. That whenever any form of government becomes destructive of these ends, it is the right of the people to alter or abolish it, and to institute a new government, laying its foundation on such principles, and organizing its powers in such form, as to them shall seem most likely to effect their safety and happiness.'

Such right your honors will not doubt. It was happily incorporated in the first principles of the first truly written international law; — in America, the first law that is learned by the courts or by the bar — learned generally, ere professional studies are commenced, and imbibed almost with the first nourishment of the American child.

That Texas, at the time to which I have referred, became entirely severed from the Republic of Mexico, is fully shown by the reference I have made to the first volume of her laws. That she maintaineu her independence, and was never again subjected to the dominion of Mexico, is a fact, sustained by the history of her struggles, as well as by the history of our own government, and other governments in their negotiations. with her.

Although our government had not officially recognized the independence of Texas, at the date of this contract, yet, shortly after that period, official correspondence and intercourse commenced between the United States and the Republic of Texas, and we find a treaty negotiated between th~ two governments, as early as April, 1838. 8 Stat. at Large, 510.

It is claimed that this contract is void, as being in violation of the laws of the United States, provided for the punishment

4 *

of persons who shall, within the territory or jurisdiction of the United States, " begin or set on foot, or provide or prepare, the means for any military expedition or enterprise, to be carried on from thence against the territory or dominions of any foreign prince or State, with whom the United States are at peace."

This is a penal statute, and must be construed strictly. And I respectfully insist, that, while it is the policy of the United States government, to preserve her neutrality between belligerent nations, there is nothing in this law to prevent one of her citizens entering into a contract with a citizen of another independent government for the purchase of land lying in that government, even though it be recited in the contract, that it is the intention of the person selling his lands to use the money he receives for them in raising and equipping volunteers to maintain and advance the independence of his country.

It does not appear, from the bill, that the contract was for the advancement of funds to raise and equip volunteers within the United States, or to carry on war from thence against Mexico. For aught that appears, the design of General Chambers was to raise his volunteers in Texas. And it might as well be presumed that they were to be raised in Europe, as in the United States.

Besides, Texas was an independent government. And the purpose of General Chambers, as declared, was, to maintain her independence; and not to make incursions from the United States, or even from Texas, into Mexico.

There is nothing in this statute inhibiting a citizen of the United States from volunteering in the service of another government to maintain her independence, already declared; and uphold her government, fully instituted; nor declaring it unlawful for a citizen of the United States to contribute means for such purposes.

Again, it is insisted by the defendant, that this contract is in violation of the treaty of amity, commerce and navigation between the United States of America and the United Mexican States, of April 5, 1832.

The 1st article of that treaty is in these words: " There shall be a firm, inviolable, and universal peace, and a true and sincere friendship between the United States of America and the United Mexican States, in all the extent of their possessions and territories, and between their people and citizens respectively, without distinction of persons or places."

In revolutions, there must be a time when an old government ends and a new one begins. And when a new one begins, it must embrace a certain portion of the earth of which it has possession. Now with regard to this provision of the Treaty, I respectfully insist, that, by a revolution, a portion of what was before Mexico, ceased to be any part of the possessions or territory of Mexico, and became the possessions and territory of the new government; and that this provision in the treaty could no longer bind the United States to regard the revolted territory as any part of the Mexican territory.

In regard to the obligations of this Treaty, and its binding force upon the United States, in September, 1836, the question is not, whether the United States had recognized the independence of Texas; but whether Texas had, in fact, achieved her independence.

If Texas had not achieved her independence in 1836, when this contract was executed, then she had not achieved it at a subsequent period, when the United States government did officially recognize her independence. And if these citizens of Ohio, in September, 1836, violated this treaty of amity with Mexico, then the United States government violated the same treaty in March, 1837, by recognizing, and in April, 1838, by treating with the Republic of Texas. For when this contract was made, the revolted colony had already achieved her independence, established her government, and had never relinquished any part of her territory acquired by the revolution.

The question whether Texas had achieved her independence in September, 1836, was a historic and governmental fact — a fact not depending upon any question of recognition by other and different nations.

It is true that other governments might or might not, as they should choose, send to and receive from Texas diplomatic agents. But whether they did or not, could not alter the fact of Texan independence, so long as Mexico never repossessed herself of the revolting territory. And so far as the fact of Texan independence was concerned, it was no more the province of our government than of any other to determine when that fact transpired. And, as I conceive, no more the province of any government, than of the citizens, except so far as concerns the relations of diplomacy.

The recognition of the independence of Texas, by the United States, in no way determined the fact as to when she became independent, any more than did the acknowledgment of the independence of the United States by the British government, determine the fact as to when the United States became independent. If the time or date of the independence of revolting colonies depends on the decision of neutral nations, and not upon the fact whether the revolting colony has established a civil government which is continued in successful operation, performing all the functions of an independent power, then we are all mistaken in the date of our national existence; and instead of celebrating the anniversary of the 4th of July, 1776, we should ascertain the different days of the recognition of our independence by other nations, and celebrate them. And thus, instead of having one national holiday, we would have as many as there are nations with whom we have diplomatic relations. By such a decision our boys would be delighted, and the interests of pyrotechnists greatly benefited.

Mr. Volney E. Howard, for the appellees.

We insist that the bill in this case cannot be maintained, because, —

1. It is shown, on the face of the contract and the bill, that the obligation was given to enable General Chambers to raise and equip volunteers, to carry on a war in Texas against the republic of Mexico, and was therefore in violation of our neutrality laws with Mexico. The contract was entered into in Ohio, in September, 1836, before this government had acknowledged the independence of Texas. Contracts to furnish money to carry on war by revolted subjects, against a government with whom we are at peace, are void. 1 Kent, 116, 118, 123; Dewentz *v.* Hendricks, 9 Moore, C. B. 586. If the government does not interfere, it is illegal for citizens to do so. 1 Kent, 24, note A, 25, note. And, until the government acknowledges the independence of the revolted province, the courts recognize the ancient condition of things, under which this contract would be illegal. 1 Kent, 25; 9 Ves. 347; 4 Cranch, 272; 13 J. R. 561, 587; 3 Wheat. 324, 610; Wheaton's Elements, 453.

2. It appears from the contract, and the allegations of the bill, on page 8 of the record, that the contract in this case was entered into, not only for the purpose of furnishing money to equip volunteers to carry on a war in Texas against Mexico, in aid of the revolutionists, but for the further illegal purpose of raising volunteers to proceed from this country. The contract was therefore void, as against the laws of the United States and our treaty of amity and friendship with Mexico. The contract was executed in Cincinnati, on the 16th September, 1836, and recites that General Chambers "is *now* engaged in raising, arming, and equipping volunteers for Texas," &c. Act of Congress, 1836, p. 53; Senate Journal, 1837, pp. 110, 310; Act of March 10, 1838, 5 Stat. at Large, 212; Ex. Doc. 1835, p. 183; Vol. 6, Doc. 256; Doc. 38, p. 36.

Mr. Chief Justice TANEY delivered the opinion of the court.

This is an appeal from the decree of the District Court of the United States for the District of Texas.

The appellants filed a bill in that court against the appellee, to obtain the specific execution of an agreement which is set out in full in the bill; and which they allege was executed at the city of Cincinnati, in the State of Ohio, on or about the 16th of September, 1836. Some of the complainants claim as original parties to the contract, and the others as assignees of original parties, who have sold and assigned to them their interest.

The contract, after stating that it was entered into on the day and year above mentioned, between General T. Jefferson Chambers, of the Texan army, of the first part, and Morgan Neville and six others, who are named in the agreement, of the city of Cincinnati, of the second part, proceeds to recite the motives and inducements of the parties in the following words: —

" That the said party of the second part, being desirous of assisting the said General T. Jefferson Chambers, who is now engaged in raising, arming, and equipping volunteers for Texas, and who is in want of means therefor; and, being extremely desirous to advance the cause of freedom and the independence of Texas, have agreed to purchase of the said T. Jefferson Chambers, of his private estate, the lands hereinafter described."

And after this recital follows the agreement of Chambers, to sell and convey to them the land described in the agreement, situated in Texas, for the sum of twelve thousand five hundred dollars, which he acknowledged that he had received in their notes, payable in equal instalments of four, six, and twelve months, and he covenanted that he had a good title to this land, and would convey it with general warranty. There are other stipulations, on the part of Chambers, to secure the title to the parties, which it is unnecessary to state, as they are not material to the questions before the court.

After setting out the contract at large, the bill avers, that the notes given, as aforesaid, were all paid; and sets forth the manner in which the complainants, who were not parties to the original contract, had acquired their interest as assignees; and charges that, notwithstanding the full payment of the money, Chambers, under different pretexts, refuses to convey the land, according to the terms of his agreement.

It further states, that they are informed and believe that he received full compensation, in money, scrip, land, or other valuable property, for the supplies furnished by him, and in arming and equipping the Texan army referred to in the said contract, and which it was in part the object of the said parties of the second part to assist him to do, by the said advances made by them, as before stated, and which said advances did enable the said Chambers so to do.

To this bill the respondent (Chambers) demurred, and the principal question which arises on the demurrer is, whether the contract was a legal and valid one, and such as can be enforced by either party in a court of the United States. It appears on the face of it, and by the averments of the appellants in their bill, that it was made in Cincinnati, with a general in the Texan army, who was then engaged in raising, arming, and equipping volunteers for Texas, to carry on hostilities with Mexico; and that one of the inducements of the appellants, in entering into this contract and advancing the money, was to assist him in accomplishing these objects.

The District Court decided that the contract was illegal and void, and sustained the demurrer and dismissed the bill; and we think that the decision was right.

The validity of this contract depends upon the relation in which this country then stood to Mexico and Texas; and the duties which these relations imposed upon the government and citizens of the United States.

Texas had declared itself independent a few months previous to this agreement. But it had not been acknowledged by the United States; and the constituted authorities charged with our foreign relations, regarded the treaties we had made with Mexico as still in full force, and obligatory upon both nations. By the treaty of limits, Texas had been admitted by our government to be a part of the Mexican territory; and by the first article of the treaty of amity, commerce, and navigation, it was declared, "that there should be a firm, inviolable, and universal peace, and a true and sincere friendship between the United States of America and the United Mexican States, in all the extent of their possessions and territories, and between their people and citizens respectively, without distinction of persons or place." These treaties, while they remained in force, were, by the Constitution of the United States, the supreme law, and binding not only upon the government, but upon every citizen. No contract could lawfully be made in violation of their provisions.

Undoubtedly, when Texas had achieved her independence, no previous treaty could bind this country to regard it as a part of the Mexican territory. But it belonged to the government, and not to individual citizens, to decide when that event had taken place. And that decision, according to the laws of nations, depended upon the question whether she had or had not a civil government in successful operation, capable of performing the duties and fulfilling the obligations of an independent power. It depended upon the state of the fact, and not upon the right which was in contest between the parties. And the

President, in his message to the Senate, of December 22, 1836, in relation to the conflict between Mexico and Texas, which was still pending, says: "All questions relative to the government of foreign nations, whether of the old or the new world, have been treated by the United States as questions of fact only, and our predecessors have cautiously abstained from deciding upon them until the clearest evidence was in their possession, to enable them not only to decide correctly, but to shield their decision from every unworthy imputation." Senate Journal of 1836, 37, p. 54.

Acting upon these principles, the independence of Texas was not acknowledged by the Government of the United States until the beginning of March, 1837. Up to that time, it was regarded as a part of the territory of Mexico. The treaty which admitted it to be so, was held to be still in force and binding on both parties, and every effort made by the government to fulfil its neutral obligations, and prevent our citizens from taking part in the conflict. This is evident, from an official communication from the President to the Governor of Tennessee, in reply to an inquiry in relation to a requisition for militia, made by General Gaines. The despatch is dated in August, 1836; and the President uses the following language: " The obligations of our treaty with Mexico, as well as the general principles which govern our intercourse with foreign powers, require us to maintain a strict neutrality in the contest which now agitates a part of that republic. So long as Mexico fulfils her duties to us, as they are defined by the treaty, and violates none of the rights which are secured by it to our citizens, any act on the part of the Government of the United States, which would tend to foster a spirit of resistance to her government and laws, whatever may be their character or form, when administered within her own limits and jurisdiction, would be unauthorized and highly improper. Ex. Doc. 1836, 1837, Vol. 1, Doc. 2, p. 58.

And on the very day on which the agreement of which we are speaking, was made, (September 16, 1836,) Mr. Forsyth, the Secretary of State, in a note to the Mexican Minister, assured him that the government had taken measures to secure the execution of the laws for preserving the neutrality of the United States, and that the public officers were vigilant in the discharge of that duty. Ex Doc. Vol. 1, Doc. 2, page 63 – 64.

And still later, the President, in his message to the Senate of December 22, 1836, before referred to, says: " The acknowledgment of a new State as independent, and entitled to a place in the family of nations, is at all times an act of great delicacy and responsibility; but more especially so when such a State has forcibly separated itself from another, of which it formed an integral part, and which still claims dominion over it." And, after speaking of the policy which our government had always adopted on such occasions, and the duty of maintaining the established character of the United States for fair and impartial dealing, he proceeds to express his opinion against the acknowledgment of the independence of Texas, at that time, in the following words : —

" It is true, with regard to Texas, the civil authority of Mexico has been expelled, its invading army defeated, the chief of the republic himself captured, and all present power to control the newly organized Government of Texas annihilated within its confines. But, on the other hand, there is, in appearance at least, an immense disparity of physical force on the side of Mexico. The Mexican republic, under another executive, is rallying its forces under a new leader, and menacing a fresh invasion to recover its lost dominion. Upon the issue of this threatened invasion, the independence of Texas may be considered as suspended ; and, were there nothing peculiar in the relative situation of the United States and Texas, our acknowledgment of its independence at such a crisis would scarcely be regarded as consistent with that prudent reserve with which we have heretofore held ourselves bound to treat all similar questions."

The whole object of this message appears to have been to impress upon Congress the impropriety of acknowledging the independence of Texas at that time ; and the more especially as the American character of her population, and her known desire to become a State of this Union, might, if prematurely acknowledged, bring suspicion upon the motives bv which we were governed.

We have given these extracts from the public documents not only to show that, in the judgment of our government, Texas had not established its independence when this contract was made, but to show also how anxiously the constituted authorities were endeavoring to maintain untarnished the honor of the country, and to place it above the suspicion of taking any part in the conflict.

This being the attitude in which the government stood, and this its open and avowed policy, upon what grounds can the parties to such a contract as this, come into a court of justice of the United States and ask for its specific execution? It was made in direct opposition to the policy of the government, to which it was the duty of every citizen to conform. And, while they saw it exerting all its power to fulfil in good faith its neutral obligations, they made themselves parties to the war, by furnishing means to a general of the Texan army, for the avowed purpose of aiding and assisting him in his military operations.

It might indeed fairly be inferred, from the language of the contract and the statements in the appellants' bill, that the volunteers were to be raised, armed, and equipped within the limits of the United States. The language of the contract is : " That the said party of the second part, (that is the complainants,) being desirous of assisting the said General T. Jefferson Chambers, who is now engaged in raising, arming, and equipping volunteers for Texas, and is in want of means therefor." And as General Chambers was then in the United States, and was, as the contract states, actually engaged at that time in raising, arming, and equipping volunteers, and was in want of means to accomplish his object, the inference would seem to be almost irresistible that these preparations were making at or near the place where the agreement was made, and that the money was advanced to enable him to raise and equip a military force in the United States. And this inference is the stronger, because no place is mentioned where these preparations are to be made, and the agreement contains no engagement on his part, or proviso on theirs, which prohibited him from using these means and making these military preparations within the limits of the United States.

If this be the correct interpretation of the agreement, the contract is not only void, but the parties who advanced the money were liable to be punished in a criminal prosecution, for a violation of the neutrality laws of the United States. And certainly, with such strong indications of a criminal intent, and without any averment in the bill from which their innocence can be inferred, a court of chancery would never lend its aid to carry the agreement into specific execution, but would leave the parties to seek their remedy at law. And this ground would of itself be sufficient to justify the decree of the District Court dismissing the bill.

But the decision stands on broader and firmer ground, and this agreement cannot be sustained either at law or in equity. The question is not whether the parties to this contract violated the neutrality laws of the United States or subjected themselves to a criminal prosecution; but whether such a contract, made at that time, within the United States, for the purposes stated in the contract and the bill of complaint, was a legal and valid contract, and such as to entitle either party to the aid of the courts of justice of the United States to enforce its execution.

The intercourse of this country with foreign nations, and its policy in regard to them, are placed by the Constitution of the

United States in the hands of the government, and its decisions upon these subjects are obligatory upon every citizen of the Union. He is bound to be at war with the nation against which the war-making power has declared war, and equally bound to commit no act of hostility against a nation with which the government is in amity and friendship. This principle is universally acknowledged by the laws of nations. It lies at the foundation of all government, as there could be no social order or peaceful relations between the citizens of different countries without it. It is, however, more emphatically true in relation to citizens of the United States. For as the sovereignty resides in the people, every citizen is a portion of it, and is himself personally bound by the laws which the representatives of the sovereignty may pass, or the treaties into which they may enter, within the scope of their delegated authority. And when that authority has plighted its faith to another nation that there shall be peace and friendship between the citizens of the two countries, every citizen of the United States is equally and personally pledged. The compact is made by the department of the government upon which he himself has agreed to confer the power. It is his own personal compact as a portion of the sovereignty in whose behalf it is made. And he can do no act, nor enter into any agreement to promote or encourage revolt or hostilities against the territories of a country with which our government is pledged by treaty to be at peace, without a breach of his duty as a citizen, and the breach of the faith pledged to the foreign nation. And if he does so he cannot claim the aid of a court of justice to enforce it. The appellants say, in their contract, that they were induced to advance the money by the desire to promote the cause of freedom. But our own freedom cannot be preserved without obedience to our own laws, nor social order preserved if the judicial branch of the government countenanced and sustained contracts made in violation of the duties which the law imposes, or in contravention of the known and established policy of the political department, acting within the limits of its constitutional power.

But it has been urged in the argument that Texas was in fact independent, and a sovereign state at the time of this agreement; and that the citizen of a neutral nation may lawfully lend money to one that is engaged in war, to enable it to carry on hostilities against its enemy.

It is not necessary, in the case before us, to decide how far the judicial tribunals of the United States would enforce a contract like this, when two states, acknowledged to be independent, were at war, and this country neutral. It is a sufficient answer to the argument to say that the question whether Texas had or had not at that time become an independent state, was a question for that department of our government exclusively which is charged with our foreign relations. And until the period when that department recognized it as an independent state, the judicial tribunals of the country were bound to consider the old order of things as having continued, and to regard Texas as a part of the Mexican territory. And if we undertook to inquire whether she had not in fact become an independent sovereign state before she was recognized as such by the treaty-making power, we should take upon ourselves the exercise of political authority, for which a judicial tribunal is wholly unfit, and which the Constitution has conferred exclusively upon another department.

This is not a new question. It came before the court in the case of Rose v. Himely, 4 Cr. 272, and again in Hoyt v. Gelston, 3 Wheat. 324. And in both of these cases the court said, that it belongs exclusively to governments to recognize new states in the revolutions which may occur in the world; and until such recognition, either by our own government or the government to which the new state belonged, courts of justice are bound to consider the ancient state of things as remaining unaltered.

It was upon this ground that the Court of Common Pleas in England, in the case of De Wutz v. Hendricks, 9 Moore's C. B. Reports, 586, decided that it was contrary to the law of nations for persons residing in England to enter into engagements to raise money by way of loan for the purpose of supporting subjects of a foreign state in arms against a government in friendship with England, and that no right of action attached upon any such contract. And this decision is quoted with approbation by Chancellor Kent, in 1 Kent's Com. 116.

Nor can the subsequent acknowledgment of the independence of Texas, and her admission into the Union as a sovereign State, affect the question. The agreement being illegal and absolutely void at the time it was made, it can derive no force or validity from events which afterwards happened.

But it is insisted, on the part of the appellants, that this contract was to be executed in Texas, and was valid by the laws of Texas, and that the District Court for that State, in a controversy between individuals, was bound to administer the laws of the State, and ought therefore to have enforced this agreement.

This argument is founded in part on a mistake of the fact. The contract was not only made in Cincinnati, but all the stipulations on the part of the appellants were to be performed there and not in Texas. And the advance of money which they agreed to make for military purposes was in fact made and intended to be made in Cincinnati, by the delivery of their promissory notes, which were accepted by the appellee as payment of the money. This appears on the face of the contract. And it is this advance of money for the purposes mentioned in the agreement, in contravention of the neutral obligations and policy of the United States, that avoids the contract. The mere agreement to accept a conveyance of land lying in Texas, for a valuable consideration paid by them, would have been free from objection.

But had the fact been otherwise, certainly no law of Texas then or now in force could absolve a citizen of the United States, while he continued such, from his duty to this government, nor compel a court of the United States to support a contract, no matter where made or where to be executed, if that contract was in violation of their laws, or contravened the public policy of the government, or was in conflict with subsisting treaties with a foreign nation.

We therefore hold this contract to be illegal and void, and affirm the decree of the District Conrt

Mr. Justice DANIEL and Mr. Justice GRIER dissented.

Order.

This cause came on to be heard on the transcript of the record from the District Court of the United States for the District of Texas, and was argued by counsel. On consideration whereof it is now here ordered, adjudged, and decreed by this court, that the decree of the said District Court in this cause be, and the same is hereby, affirmed with costs.

JOSEPH WISWALL, PLAINTIFF IN ERROR, v. DAVID SAMPSON, LESSEE OF EDWARD HALL AND EDWARD S. DARGAN.

Where real estate is in the custody of a receiver, appointed by a court of chancery, a sale of the property under an execution issued by virtue of a judgment at law, is illegal and void.

The proper modes of proceeding pointed out, to be pursued by any person who claims title to the property, either by mortgage, or judgment, or otherwise.

THIS case was brought up, by writ of error, from the Circuit Court of the United States for the Southern District of Alabama.

Wiswall v. Sampson.

It was an ejectment for the following lot, in the city of Mobile, bounded south by St. Francis street, and lying between Water and Commerce and Planters streets of the said city, having a front of thirty-live feet on St. Francis street, and extending to Planters street, with the same breadth; bounded east by lands formerly belonging to M. D. Eslava, and west by a lot of Beach, Ela & Co.

The declaration contained three counts; two upon a demise from Edward Hall, a citizen of the State of Maryland, and the third a demise from Edward S. Dargan.

Although the decision of the court turned upon a single point it is necessary to connect it with the other circumstances of the case which are somewhat complicated.

The following table contains a reference to the principal facts bearing upon the respective titles of the plaintiff and defendant.

1840, April 28. Ticknor, being in possession, conveyed the property to Day

Plaintiff's Title.	Defendant's Title.
1840.	1840.
Dec. 28. Fowler and others obtained a judgment against Ticknor for $4,991. Dec. 31. Crouch and Sneed obtained a judgments against Ticknor for $7,176.25.	
1842.	1842. June 14. Wiswall obtained judgment against Ticknor for $2,233.17. July 1. *Fi. fa.* issued on it, returned "no property found.'
1843.	1843. Feb. 7. Bill filed by Wiswall to set aside the deed from Ticknor to Day as fraudulent.
1845. Feb. 24. *Alias fi. fa.* on Crouch and Sneed's judgment. April 7. *Alias fi. fa.* on Fowler's judgment. July 7. Lot sold to Dargan under the executions. August 13. Marshal executed a deed to Dargan.	1845. April Term. Deed from Ticknor to Day set aside as fraudulent. June 27. Receiver appointed by the chancellor, took possession. Nov. 26. Dargan applied to the chancellor to have the property delivered over to him, or for leave to bring an ejectment. Both refused.
1847.	1847. March 1. Lot sold by the master in chancery to Wiswall, and deed made.
1848. April Dargan brought an ejectment against Wiswall.	1848.

5*

Upon the trial, the following bill of exceptions was taken:

Be it remembered, that on the trial of this cause on this 4th day of January, 1849, before the Honorable William Crawford, Judge, the plaintiffs, to show title in their lessors, offered in evidence a judgment rendered in this court on the 28th December, 1840, in favor of C. S. Fowler & Co., against John Ticknor, for $4,991, besides costs; also a judgment rendered in this court, on the 31st December, 1840, in favor of Crouch and Sneed against John Ticknor, $7,176.25 and costs; upon each of which judgments *fi. fas.* were issued within a year and returned by the marshal, No property found; no other executions or process issued upon either of these judgments, except the following: Upon the judgment of Crouch and Sneed an *alias fi. fa.* was issued on the 24th February, 1845, and levied on the property sued for, upon which the marshal returned, Levied — and " the sale of the property levied on postponed by Judge E. S. Dargan, until further order." And on the 17th May, 1845, a *pluries fi. fa.* issued on this judgment and was levied on the same property. Upon the judgment of C. S. Fowler & Co. an *alias fi. fa.* was issued on the 7th of April, 1845, and levied on the same property, and returned, For want of time to sell. And on the first day of May, 1845, a *venditioni exponas* issued, upon which and the execution on the Crouch and Sneed judgments, issued the 17th May, the property was sold by the marshal on the 7th July, 1845, to Edward S. Dargan, for $7,500 and a deed was made by the marshal to said Dargan, bearing date the thirteenth of August, 1845. The plaintiff further offered in evidence a deed of release and quitclaim of the same premises, from Edward S. Dargan to Edward Hall, one of the lessors, bearing date the 3d of April, 1848, a copy of which is hereto attached, marked X; to the reading of which the defendant, by his attorney, objected, on the ground that it was neither acknowledged nor recorded; but the objection was overruled by the court, and the deed admitted in evidence upon the proof of the handwriting of Dargan, and the defendant excepted. The plaintiff further offered evidence to show that John Ticknor was in possession of the property sued for from 1838 or 1839 claiming title, and that he remained in possession until about 1845; but whether, after 1840, Ticknor claimed it as his own, or held possession as the tenant of some one else, witness did not know. It further appeared that Ticknor built the store; that in 1839 or 1840, he became embarrassed, and that he owed a large sum of money to one James L. Day, and from some time in 1840 carried on business in the store as the agent of said Day. Day was often there and had the control, but Ticknor managed all the details. It was further proved that McCoy and Johnson, the tenants served with the declaration, were in possession of the premises in April, 1848, and had been in possession since November, 1847.

The defendant then offered in evidence a judgment obtained in the Circuit Court of Mobile County, on the 14th day of June, 1842, in favor of Joseph Wiswall against John Ticknor, for the sum of $2,233.17, besides costs; and a *fi. fa.* issued thereon the 1st July, 1842, returnable to the fall term of said court, which was returned by the sheriff, No property found; also the transcripts from the records, duly certified, of a deed made by John Ticknor to James L. Day, bearing date the 28th of April, 1840, a copy of which is annexed, marked A; also the exemplification of a decree and proceedings in a suit in chancery, filed the 7th of February, 1843, by Joseph Wiswall, as a judgment creditor of John Ticknor, against said Ticknor and James L. Day; a copy of which bill, answers, and decrees, are hereto annexed, marked B; also a decree and proceedings in the same court of chancery upon a bill filed March 1st, 1845, by the president, directors, and company of the Bank of Mobile, James Stewart, and Henry Lazarus, several judgment creditors of said Ticknor, and against said Ticknor and James S. Day, which bill was similar in its form and object to the bill of Wiswall, and was served on the defendant, Ticknor, on the 1st March, 1845; a copy of the answer of Day, and the decree, is annexed, marked C. The defendant then proved that Waring, the receiver of the Court of Chancery in the above two suits, went into the possession of the property sued for on St. Francis street, as such receiver, on the 27th day of June, 1845, and remained in possession as such receiver until the same was sold by him on the first Monday of March, 1847; that notice was given at the marshal's sale, when the property was bid off by Dargan, of the pendency of the above-named suits in chancery, and the claims of the complainants there asserted, and that he was, as receiver aforesaid, then in possession of said property under the decrees in chancery in the above suits. The property was duly sold by the receiver on the 1st day of March, 1847, to K. B. Sewall for six thousand five hundred dollars, and a deed of the same made to him by the said receiver and master in chancery; and on the tenth day of May, 1847, the same was conveyed by said Sewall to the defendant, Joseph Wiswall; it was also shown that the purchaser from the receiver went into possession, and that the whole amount of the purchase-money was paid and appropriated under the directions of the Court of Chancery.

The defendant then offered in evidence the transcript of a decree and proceedings had in a court of chancery, in Mobile, upon the petition of Edward S. Dargan against Moses Waring, receiver, Joseph Wiswall, John Ticknor, and James L. Day, a copy of which is hereto annexed, marked Exhibit D; which decree had been affirmed by the Supreme Court; C. Cuyler, the deputy marshal who made the sale to Dargan, testified that no money whatever was paid upon said sale, but that Dargan gave his note to the marshal for the costs.

John F. Adams testified that he acted as the attorney of C. S. Fowler & Co. in recovering their judgment in this court, and had ever since represented said judgment; and that E. S. Dargan, from some time prior to the marshal's sale, represented the judgment of Crouch and Sneed; that it was agreed between said attorneys, Adams and Dargan, representing said judgments, that the land should be sold upon them, and bid off in the name of Dargan, and that if the title' thus acquired should enable Dargan to recover the property, the judgment of C. S. Fowler & Co. should be paid out of it; but that if the property should not be recovered by such title, then the sale was to be considered a nullity, and no money to be paid whatever on account of it; and that this was the understanding of Adams, but that after the sale he yielded to the views of Dargan, and signed a memorandum to the effect that Dargan should be a trustee for the parties. It was further in evidence that with the arrangements between Dargan and Adams there was no connection on the part of Ticknor, the defendant in the judgment. and no assent was given by him to them.

Adams also testified that, as the representative of the judgment of C. S. Fowler & Co., he entered a motion in this court at the spring term, 1847, to amend the marshal's return made upon the execution in that case, to show that no money was in fact paid on said bid of Dargan; and said motion was produced and read to the jury, and is still pending and undetermined

Defendant then offered to read a bill filed in the Chancery Court of Mobile, on the 18th February, 1847, in the name of David A. Hall, assignee in bankruptcy of C. S. Fowler & Co., against John Ticknor, James L. Day, Moses Waring, receiver, Joseph Wiswall, Bank of Mobile, James Stewart, and Henry Lazarus, the object of which bill was to reach and have appropriated to the payment of said judgment of C. S. Fowler & Co. the proceeds of the sale of the property to be made in that' court upon the bill of said Wiswall and others; said bill was filed by J. F. Adams, as solicitor of the parties, and sets forth, among other things, the following: "That the said premises were sold on the 1st of July, 1845, by the marshal, to Edward S. Dargan, for the nominal sum of $7,500, and the marshal executed to said Dargan his formal deed for the same, and thereupon made return upon the process that the premises were sold for the sum above named. And your orator now averreth, that in fact neither the sum of $7,500, nor any other sum, was paid by said Dargan to the' plaintiffs in execution, or to any person for them, but his said bid was made upon his stipulation made with the plaintiffs' attorney, and on the distinct understanding and intent on his part, that in case his title under the said sale should prove to be valid and effectual in law, he would pay to the said plaintiffs or your orator so much money upon his said bid as he might thereafter be able to realize by a sale; but if the said title should not prove to be available nor enable him to obtain possession, that in that case he should pay nothing." Said bill is not sworn to, and is still pending in the Court of Chancery: to the introduction of this bill as evidence, the plaintiffs objected on the ground that it was not connected with the plaintiffs in this suit, and as being the statement of counsel merely, and not evidence against C. S. Fowler & Co.; and the objection was sustained, and the said bill excluded; to which the defendant, by his counsel, excepted. This was all the evidence offered in the case, and thereupon the court charged the jury —

That the deed from Ticknor to Day, of April 28th, 1840, was, upon its face, in connection with the answers of Ticknor and Day, fraudulent as to creditors, and void; to which, the defendant excepted.

The court further charged, that the title of Dargan, derived from the marshal's sale, under the judgment of C. S. Fowler & Co. and of Crouch & Sneed, was superior to the title of Wiswall, derived from the sale under the chancery proceedings, and entitled the plaintiffs to recover; to which the defendant, by his counsel, excepted.

The court further charged the jury, that the proceedings and decree in the Court of Chancery, upon the petition of Dargan, was not binding or conclusive upon the parties in this suit; that it was not necessary for Dargan to go into the Court of Chancery for aid, that his remedy was at law, and the proceedings there upon his petition had no effect whatever upon his title, and must be wholly disregarded in this suit; to which the defendant, by his counsel, also excepted, and requested the court to give the following charges to the jury :—

1. That, if the jury believe the deed from the marshal to Dargan was made without any pecuniary consideration, it could pass no title; which the court refused; but charged that, under the evidence before them, it was valid if no money was paid by the purchaser, to which the defendant excepted.

2. That the filing of Wiswall's bill in chancery, and the pro-

ceedings thereon, to a final decree in his favor, gave him a specific lien upon the property of Ticknor, from the commencement of his suit, which could not be divested by any subsequent proceedings upon the older judgments under which the plaintiffs here claim; which was refused, and the defendant excepted.

.3. That the receiver of the Court of Chancery, in the suits of Wiswall and others, being in possession of the property under the order of that court at the time of the marshal's sale, and notice thereof being given at that sale, affected the purchaser, and invalidated his title; which was refused; and the court charged that such possession and notice in no manner affected the marshal's sale. or the purchaser under it; and the defendant excepted.

4. That the proceedings in the Court of Chancery, upon he petition of Dargan, the purchaser at the marshal's sale, was conclusive upon the parties and his title thus acquired; which was refused; and the defendant excepted.

5. That, under the statutes and decisions of Alabama, it is not the oldest judgment, but the judgment lien, that has been kept alive by the oldest execution, regularly issued, without the loss of a term, that has the priority as between judgment creditors; which was refused; and the defendant excepted.

6. That, if neither Dargan nor Edward Hall were in possession of the property on the 3d of April, 1848, the deed of that date, from Dargan to Hall, was void and conveyed no title; this was also refused; and the court charged that, under the evidence before the jury, this deed was valid; to all which the defendant excepted.

And the defendant tenders the above as his bill of exceptions in the case, and prays the court to sign and seal the same, which is done accordingly.

WILLIAM CRAWFORD. [SEAL.]

All the exceptions were argued in this court; but it is only necessary to refer to the above charge, viz., that the title of Dargan was superior to that of Wiswall, and that the decree in chancery, on the petition of Dargan, was not conclusive upon the rights of the parties; that he was not bound to go into that court for relief, as his remedy was at law.

It was argued by *Mr. Seward*, for the plaintiff in error, with a brief of Mr. Sewall, and by *Mr. Chilton*, for the defendant in error, with a brief of Mr. John A. Campbell.

It was contended, by the counsel for the plaintiff in error, that the court erred in refusing to instruct the jury, " that the receiver of the Court of Chancery, in the suits of Wiswall and others, being in possession of the property, under the order of the court, at the time of the marshal's sale, and notice thereof being give 1 at that sale, affected the purchase by Dargan and invalidated his title, and in charging, on the contrary, that such possession and notice in no manner affected the marshal's sale, or the purchase under it." Because, —

1. The levy, under the judgments of C. S. Fowler & Co. and Crouch & Sneed, invested neither the marshal with any title nor the Federal Court with any jurisdiction over the land, nor could it divest any title, if the defendant Ticknor was in possession, unless followed by an actual sale by the marshal, and payment of the purchase-money by the purchaser. Forrest & Lyon v. Camp, 16 Ala. 647.

And then, not until the sale took place and the money was paid. The sale took place in July; the deed was made in August. 1 Rich. Eq. Rep. 340.

2. But Ticknor was not in possession. The Court of Chancery, by its receiver, was in possession on the 25th June previous; and held, not for Ticknor, but for Wiswall and the other parties claiming against Ticknor. 3 P. Wms. R. 379; 2 Story, Eq. § 833. The Court of Chancery was not holding the property in safe custody, until the right should be determined between Wiswall on the one side, and Ticknor & Day on the other; for it had already determined the right in favor of Wiswall, and ordered a sale, and the proceeds to be applied to his judgment. Ticknor & Day v. Wiswall, 6 Ala. 178. Its jurisdiction was complete, and adverse to all third parties. 10 Paige, 43.

Where different courts have concurrent jurisdiction, that before which proceedings are first had, and whose jurisdiction first attaches, has authority paramount to the others, and cannot be ousted by subsequent proceedings in those courts. The Court of Chancery took jurisdiction to decide upon the right and title to this land, when Wiswall filed his bill on the 7th February, 1843, and it continued its jurisdiction over it until it was sold under its decree. No jurisdiction as to the premises attached to the Federal Court before the sale to Dargan, if then. Hagan v. Lucas, 10 Pet. 400; Smith v. McIver, 9 Wheat. 532; Corning v. White, 2 Paige, 567; The Robert Fulton, 1 Paine, 621; P. & M. Bank v. Walker, 7 Ala. 945; Parker v. Browning, 8 Paige, 389.

The counsel for the defendant in error thus noticed this point: —

We deny that the Court of Chancery could prevent the execution of the levy made by the marshal, by placing a receiver in possession. The Court of Chancery insists upon no such power.

The rule of chancery is stated in 7 Paige, 513. The headnotes are: " When property is rightfully in the hands of a receiver, it is in the custody of the court, and cannot be distrained upon for rent without permission of the court by whom the receiver was appointed; and any person who takes the property out of the possession of the receiver.without such permission, after he has notice of the character in which possession is holden, is guilty of a contempt."

The same principles are applicable to any interference with the possession of a receiver, sequestrator, committee, or custodee, who holds the property as the officer of the Court of Chancery; as his possession is the possession of the court itself. Noe v. Gibson, 7 Paige, 513.

" Where a receiver is in possession of real estate which is subject to the lien of a judgment, the sale of the premises by the sheriff, upon an execution on such judgment, does not disturb the possession of the receiver; and the sheriff cannot, therefore, be proceeded against for a contempt in making such a sale. But the purchaser cannot disturb the possession of the receiver, when he obtains his conveyance from the sheriff, without the permission of the court. 9 Paige, 373.

This subject is discussed at large in a late case before Lord Truro, reported in 3 Gordon & Macnaghten R. 104, from which we extract.

" I am of opinion, that it is not competent for any one to interfere with the possession of a receiver, or to disobey an injunction or any other order of the court, on the ground that such orders were improvidently made. Parties must take a proper course to question their validity; but while they exist they must be obeyed. I consider the rule to be of such importance to the interests and safety of the public, and to the due administration of justice, that it ought on all occasions to be inflexibly maintained. I do not see how the court can expect its officers to do their duty, if they do it under the peril of resistance, and of that resistance being justified on grounds tending to the impeachment of the order under which they are acting. In the present case, it would have been perfectly open to the plaintiffs in the execution to have applied to this court, to be heard *pro interesse suo*, or to have been heard on a summary application for leave to levy under their execution, notwithstanding the posssesion of the receiver. There is no instance in which justice may not be readily obtained by persons who are supposed to have their rights interfered with by an order or process issued by this court. Thus, I find, in one case, where a party wished to distrain for rent on property in the possession of a receiver, that the court, being satisfied that the legal right of distress was paramount to the title of the party for whose benefit the receiver was appointed, allowed the distress to be made. In another case, where property liable to distress had been sold, and the receiver had received the proceeds and paid them into court, the landlord having claimed a right to distrain while the receiver was in possession, this court ordered the receiver to pay out of those proceeds, to the landlord, the rents that were due to him, the receiver being in possession for the benefit of the tenant for life, who was liable for the payment of that rent which was so sought to be distrained for on the property in the possession of the receiver. I apprehend, then, it may be taken as a rule that, though this court may have issued a process, or have made an order which may interfere with the supposed rights and interests of other parties, not parties to the cause, it is always competent for such parties to make an application to the court for relief; and it is not to be presumed or doubted, but that justice will be duly administered to them on that application."

Mr. Justice NELSON delivered the opinion of the court.

This is a writ of error to the Circuit Court of the United States for the Southern District of Alabama.

The suit in the court below was an action of ejectment against Wiswall to recover the possession of a lot of land situated in the city of Mobile.

The lessors of the plaintiff gave in evidence two judgments against John Ticknor — one in favor of Fowler & Co. for $4,491, rendered 28th December, 1840 — the other in favor of Crouch & Sneed for $7,167.25, rendered 31st December of the same year, each of them in the Circuit Court of the United States. Executions were issued upon each of the judgments within the year, and returned by the marshal "no property found."

An *alias fi. fa.* was issued on the judgment in favor of Crouch & Sneed on the 24th February, 1845, and the lot in question levied on; *an alias fi. fa.* was also issued on the judgment in favor of Fowler & Co. on the 7th April, 1845, and a levy made on the same; and on the 7th July the lot was sold on both executions, and bid off by Dargan, one of the lessors of the plaintiff, for the sum of $7,500, and a deed executed to him by the marshal on the 13th August of the same year. Dargan quitclaimed the premises to Hall, the other lessor. The lessors of the plaintiff claim title under this sale.

Wiswall v. Sampson.

The defendant, Wiswall, gave in evidence a judgment in his favor against Ticknor in the Circuit Court of the State for $2,233.17, rendered 14th June, 1842; an execution issued 1st July of the same year, which was returned by the sheriff " no property found;" also a deed of the lot in question from Ticknor to one James L. Day, bearing date 28 April, 1840; and the exemplifi- cation of a decree and the proceedings in chancery on a bi'' filed 7th February, 1843, by Wiswall against Ticknor and Day, setting aside the deed to Day as fraudulent and void against creditors. The decree was rendered April term, 1845. Also the appointment of a receiver by the court, to whom possession of the property was delivered on the 27th June of the same year. The receiver remained in the possession till the lot was sold by the master, 1st March, 1847, under the decree in chancery, and was purchased in for the defendant Wiswall for the sum of $6,500.

The defendant claims under this title.

Notice was given, on the day of sale, by the marshal, under the two judgments, of the pendency of this suit in chancery, and of the appointment of a receiver, and that he was in the possession of the property.

It appeared, also, that the lot was bid off by Dargan at the marshal's sale, by an arrangement between the attorneys repre- senting the two judgments, Dargan being the attorney for the one in favor of Crouch & Sneed, that if the title thus acquired should enable him to recover the property, the judgment in favor of Fowler & Co. should be paid out of it; but, if he should fail to recover it, then the sale was to be considered a nullity, and no money was to be paid.

It further appeared, that an application had been made by the attorney in the judgment in favor of Fowler & Co. to the court to amend the marshal's return so as to set forth the fact that no money had been paid, and that the motion was then pending in court And further, that a bill had been filed in chancery by the assignee in bankruptcy of the judgment of Fowler & Co. against the defendant and others, to have the proceeds of the sale of the property on the decree applied to the payment of that judgment, and in which bill it is insisted that the sale under the two judgments was inoperative, on account of the agreement between the attorneys under whom it was made, and that this suit was then pending.

It further appeared, that Dargan applied to the Court of Chan- cery on the 26th November, 1845, by petition, setting out his title under the two judgments to have the possession of the lot by the receiver delivered up to him, or if that should not be ordered, then that he might be at liberty to bring an action of eiectment against the receiver to recover the same.

That the defendant Wiswall put in his answer, setting up the same matters now relied on to invalidate the sale to Dargan, and also claiming a paramount lien upon the property by virtue of his judgment, and bill in chancery and decree setting aside the fraudulent conveyance to Day, directing a sale and application of the proceeds to the payment of his judgment, the appointment of a receiver, &c.

That the chancellor overruled the application, and dismissed the petition on the 10th December, 1845. From which order an appeal was taken to the Supreme Court, and the decree or order affirmed.

After the evidence was closed, the court charged the jury, that the title of Dargan under the marshal's sale upon the two judgments was superior to that of the defendant under the sale upon the decree in chancery, and directed a verdict for the plaintiff. And further, that the decree in chancery on the petition of Dargan was not conclusive upon the rights of the parties — that he was not bound to go into that court for relief, as his remedy was at law.

The case is now before us on exceptions to this charge.

It was made a question, on the argument, whether or not the lien of the judgments, under which the marshal's sale took place, had not been postponed to that of Wiswall, on account of laches in the enforcement of them by execution. But in the view we have taken of the case, the validity of the liens, at the time of sale, will be conceded, without, however, intending to express any opinion upon the question.

Wiswall filed his bill in chancery against Ticknor and Day to set aside the fraudulent conveyance to the latter, and have the property applied to the satisfaction of his judgment, on the 7th February, 1843. In that bill he prayed for a sale of the real estate, and for the appointment of a receiver to take charge of it with other assets of the judgment debtor; and, also, for an injunction. A temporary injunction was granted. On the coming in of the answers of the defendants, the complainant, on the 11th April of the same year, moved for the appointment of a receiver, and the defendants, at the same time, moved to dissolve the injunction. The court denied the motion to appoint the receiver, and dissolved the injunction, expressing the opinion that the answers so far explained the circumstances under which the deed to Day was given, as to remove the charge of fraud against it. An appeal was taken to the Supreme Court, and, on the 10th April, 1844, that court reversed the order of the court below, and remanded the cause for further proceedings: and on the 15th April, 1845, the Chancellor made a decree, that the deed was fraudulent and void, as against the complainant, and referred the case to a master, to take. and state the account between the parties. He further ordered and decreed that a receiver should be appointed to take possession of all the property embraced in the fraudulent conveyance, and, particularly, that possession should be delivered to him of the premises in question; and further, that the receiver, under the direction of the master, should sell the same and apply the proceeds to the payment of the complainant's judgment, with costs, &c.

The receiver was appointed on the 27th June, 1845, and on the same day Ticknor, who was in possession of the premises, attorned to him, who held possession until the sale was made in pursuance of the decree. It will be recollected that the execution on the judgment in favor of Crouch & Sneed, was issued, and levied on the 24th February, 1845; and on that in favor of Fowler & Co. 7th April of the same year, and that the sale took place under which the lessors of the plaintiff claim, 7th July, 1845.

At the time, therefore, of this sale, the receiver was in the possession of the premises, under the decree of the Court of Chancery — in other words, the possession and custody of them were in the Court of Chancery itself, (as the court is deemed the landlord,) to abide the final decree to be thereafter rendered in the suit pending.

The appointment of a receiver is a matter resting in the discretion of the court; and, as a general rule, in making the appointment on behalf of a complainant seeking to enforce an equitable claim, or a claim which is the subject of equitable jurisdiction, against real estate, it will take care not to interfere with the rights of a person holding a prior legal interest in the property. Thus, where there is a prior mortgagee having the legal estate, the court will not, by the appointment of a receiver, deprive him of his right to the possession; but, at the same time, it will not permit him to object to the appointment by any act short of a personal assertion of his legal rights, and the taking of possession himself. 1 J. & W. 648; 2 Swanst. 108, 137; 3 Id., 112, n. 115; 3 Daniel's Pr. 1950, 1951.

If the person holding the legal interest is not in possession, the equitable claimant against the property is entitled to the interference of the court, not only for the purpose of preserving it from waste, but for the purpose of obtaining the rents and profits accruing, as a fund in court to abide the result of the litigation. For until the person holding the legal interest takes possession, or asserts his right to the possession, the accruing rents and profits present a question simply between the parties to the litigation. And the court will also appoint a receiver, even against a party having possession under a legal title, if it is satisfied such party has wrongfully obtained that interest in the property. Thus, where fraud can be proved, and immediate danger is likely to result, if possession, pending the litigation, should not be taken by the court in the mean time. 13 Ves. 105; 16 Id. 59; 3 Daniel's Pr. 1955.

The effect of the appointment is not to oust any party of his right to the possession of the property, but merely to retain it for the benefit of the party who may ultimately appear to be entitled to it; and when the party entitled to the estate has been ascertained, the receiver will be considered his receiver, (T. & R. 345; Daniel's Pr. 1982); and the master will usually be directed to inquire what encumbrances there are affecting the estate, and into the priorities respectively. 10 J. R. 521, Codwise v. Gelston.

When a receiver has been appointed, his possession is that of the court, and any attempt to disturb it, without the leave of the court first obtained, will be a contempt on the part of the person making it. This was held in Angel v. Smith, 9 Ves. 335, both with respect to receivers and sequestrators. When, therefore, a party is prejudiced by having a receiver put in his way, the course has either been to give him leave to bring an ejectment, or to permit him to be examined *pro interesse suo*. 1 J. & W. 176, Brooks v. Greathed; 3 Daniel's Pr. 1984. And the doctrine that a receiver is not to be disturbed, extends even to cases in which he has been appointed expressly, without prejudice to the rights of persons having prior legal or equitable interests. And the individuals having such prior interests must, if they desire to avail themselves of them, apply to the court either for liberty to bring ejectment, or to be examined *pro interesse suo;* and this, though their right to the possession is clear. Cox, 422; 6 Ves. 287.

The proper course to be pursued, says Mr. Daniel, in his valuable treatise on Pleading and Practice in Chancery, by any person who claims title to an estate or other property sequestered, whether by mortgage or judgment, lease or otherwise, or who has a title paramount to the sequestration, is to apply to the court to direct the plaintiff to exhibit interrogatories before one of the masters, in order that the party applying may be examined as to his title to the estate. An examination of this sort is called an examination *pro interesse suo*, and an order for such examination may be obtained by a party interested, as well where the property consists of goods and chattels, or personalty, as where it is real estate.

And the mode of proceeding is the same in the case of the receiver. 6 Ves. 287; 9 Id. 336; 1 J. & W. 178; 3 Daniel's Pr. 1984.

A party, therefore, holding a judgment which is a prior lien upon the property, the same as a mortgagee, if desirous of enforcing it against the estate after it has been taken into the care and custody of the court, to abide the final determination of the litigation, and pending that litigation, must first obtain leave of the court for this purpose. The court will direct a master to inquire into the circumstances, whether it is an existing unsatisfied demand, or as to the priority of the lien, &c., and take care that the fund be applied accordingly.

Chancellor Kent, in delivering the opinion of the court in Codwise. *v.* Gelston, as Chief Justice, observed, " that if a fund for the payment of debts be created under an order or decree in chancery, and the creditors come in to avail themselves of it, the rule of equity then is, that they shall be paid *in pari passu*, or upon a footing of equality. But when the law giv* a priority, equity will not destroy it, and especially where legal assets are created by statute, as in case of a judgment lien. they remain so, though the creditors be obliged to go into equity for assistance. The legal priority will be protected and preserved in chancery."

The settled rule, also, appears to be, that where the subject-matter of the suit in equity is real estate, and which is taken into the possession of the court pending the litigation, by the appointment of a receiver, or by sequestration, the title is bound from the filing of the bill; and any purchaser, *pendente lite*, even if for a valuable consideration, comes in at his peril. 3 Swanst. 278, n., 298, n.; 2 Daniel's Pr. 1267; 6 Ves. 287; 9 Id. 336; 1 J. & W. 178; 3 Daniel's Pr. 1984.

It has been argued, that a sale of the premises on execution and purchase, occasioned no interference with the possession of the receiver, and hence no contempt of the authority of the court, and that the sale therefore, in such a case, should be upheld. But, conceding the proceedings did not disturb the possession of the receiver, the argument does not meet. the objection. The property is a fund in court, to abide the event of the litigation, and to be applied to the payment of the judgment creditor, who has filed his bill to remove impediments in the way of his execution. If he has succeeded in establishing his right to the application of any portion of the fund, it is the duty of the court to see that such application is made. And, in order to effect this, the court must administer it independently of any rights acquired by third persons, pending the litigation. Otherwise, the whole fund may have passed out of its hands before the final decree, and the litigation become fruitless.

It is true, in administering the fund, the court will take care that the rights of prior liens or encumbrances shall not be destroyed; and will adopt the proper measures, by reference to the master or otherwise, to ascertain them, and bring them before it. Unless the court be permitted to retain the possession of the fund, thus to administer it, how can it ascertain the interest in the same to which the prosecuting judgment creditor is entitled, and apply it upon his demand?

There can be no difficulty in ascertaining the prior liens and encumbrances, as all of them are matters of record. Several of the judgment creditors came in, in this case, and received their share in the distribution.

These two judgment creditors had notice of the suit before the sale, and might have made themselves parties to it, and claimed application of the fund according to the priority of their liens.

They were also before the court, pending the litigation, on the petition of Dargan, who had purchased for their benefit, to have the possession of the receiver delivered up to the purchaser. There is no pretence, therefore, for saying that they have not had notice of the proceedings in the equity suit. The prayer of the petition was denied, among other grounds, because their appropriate remedy was a motion to the court, founded on their judgments to have the proceeds of the sale under the decree applied to them according to priority.

We agree, that the person holding the prior legal lien or encumbrance, must have notice, and an opportunity to come in and claim his prior right to the property or interest in the fund before his legal right can be affected; and the proper way is by summons or notice upon the order or direction of the court.

This notice can be readily given on the report of the master, of the prior liens or encumbrances resting upon the estate.

But it is not necessary to go this length in the case before us, as it is sufficient to say, that the sale under the judgment, pending the equity suit, and while the court was in possession of the estate without the leave of the court, was illegal and void. We do not doubt but that it would be competent for the court, in case the judgment creditor holding the prior lien had not come in and claimed his interest in the equity suit, to decree a sale in the final disposition of the fund subject to his judgment. The purchaser would then be bound to pay it off. But this disposition of the legal prior encumbrance is a very different matter, and comes to a very different result, from that of permitting the enforcement of it, *pendente lite*, without the leave of the court. The rights of the several claimants to the estate or fund is then settled, and the purchase under the decree can be made with a full knowledge of the condition of the title, or charges to which it may be subject.

Neither do we doubt but that it is competent, and might, in some cases, be fit and proper for the court, where the property in dispute is ample, and the litigation protracted, to permit the execution to issue, and compel the prosecuting creditor to pay off the judgment. 3 Beav. 428. But it is manifest that these proceedings, on behalf of the prior encumbrancer, should be under the control of the discretion of the court, as the condition of the title to the property may frequently be so complicated and embarrassed, that unless the sale was withheld until the title was cleared up by the judgment of the court, great sacrifice must necessarily ensue to the parties interested.

This case affords an apt illustration of the remark. The marshal's sale was made under an arrangement that no money was to be paid by the purchaser, unless he succeeded in obtaining a title to the property under it. It is obvious, therefore, if the purchase had been unconditional, and at the risk of the purchaser, it must have been bid off for a nominal consideration.

As we have already said, it is sufficient, for the disposition of this case, to hold, that while the estate is in the custody of the court, as a fund to abide the result of a suit pending, no sale of the property can take place either on execution or otherwise, without the leave of the court for that purpose. And upon this ground, we hold that the sale by the marshal on the two judgments was illegal and void, and passed no title to the purchaser.

We are, also, inclined to think, that the question of title to the property under the marshal's sale is concluded between these parties by the judgment of the court in the proceedings on the petition by the purchaser for the removal of the receiver, and to be let into the possession. This, we have seen, is the appropriate remedy on behalf of a person claiming a paramount legal right to an estate which has been brought into the possession and safe keeping of the Court of Chancery, pending the litigation in respect to it.

This proceeding was explained by Lord Eldon in Angel v. Smith, (9 Ves. 335), speaking of the rule in respect to sequestrators, and which he held was equally applicable in the case of receivers. "Where sequestrators," he observed, "are in possession under the process of the court, their possession is not to be disturbed, even by an adverse title, without leave: upon this principle, that the possession of the sequestrators is the possession of the court, and the court being competent to examine the title, will not permit itself to be made a suitor in a court of law, but will itself examine the title. And the mode is, by permitting the party to come in to be examined *pro interesse suo;* the practice being, to go before the master to state his title, and there is the judgment of the master, and afterwards, if necessary, of the court upon it. See also 10 Beav. 318; 2 Daniel's Pr. 1271; 2 Mad. 21; 1 P. Wms. 308.

An appeal to the House of Lords will lie from the order or decree of the Chancellor upon exceptions to the master's report in the matter. 2 Daniel's Pr. 1273; 3 Id. 1633, 1634.

In the petition to the Chancellor in the case before us, the purchaser set out his title at large under the marshal's sale, and claimed the possession of the property by virtue of his title, that the receiver might be removed, and the possession delivered to the petitioners.

The answer of Wiswall set up his right to the property under the decree in the suit against Ticknor and Day.

The right of the petitioner, therefore, under his title to the possession of the property as against the right of Wiswall under the proceedings in equity and the decree in his favor, would seem to be a question directly involved. The court so understood the issue and passed upon it, holding, as we hold in this case, that the sale was illegal and void, having been made while the estate was in the possession and safe keeping of the Court of Chancery. From this decision an appeal was taken to the Supreme Court, where the order or decree of the court below was affirmed. 11 Ala. R. 938, Dargan v. Waring and others.

The question is one depending very much upon the local law of Alabama, and the judgment, therefore, in the matter, by the highest court of the State, is entitled to the highest respect.

For these reasons we are of opinion that the judgment of the court below was erroneous and must be reversed, and the case remitted for further proceedings.

Order.

This cause came on to be heard on the transcript of the record from the Circuit Court of the United States for the Southern District of Alabama, and was argued by counsel. On consideration whereof, it is now here ordered and adjudged by this court, that the judgment of the said Circuit Court in this cause be, and the same is hereby, reversed with costs, and that this cause be, and the same is hereby, remanded to the said Circuit Court for further proceedings to be had therein, in conformity to the opinion of this court.

SAMUEL SAMPLE, ISRAEL W. PICKINS, AND BURWELL SCOTT, APPELLANTS, v. SHADRACH BARNES.

Where there was a judgment at law against a defendant in Mississippi, and he sought relief in equity, upon the ground that the consideration of the contract was the introduction of slaves into the State, and consequently illegal; a court of equity will not grant relief, because the complainant was in *pari delicto* with the other party.

Moreover, such a defence would have been good at law, and the averments, that deception was practised to prevent the complainant from making the defence, are not sustained by the evidence in the case. And, further, after the judgment, the complainant gave a forthcoming bond, thus recognizing the validity of the judgment.

THIS was an appeal from the Circuit Court of the United States for the Southern District of Mississippi.

The facts are all stated in the opinion of the court.

It was argued, in a printed brief, for the appellants, by *Messrs. Walker, Freeman,* and *Volney E. Howard.* No counsel appeared for the appellee.

The argument consisted chiefly in comments upon the testimony, and contending that giving a forthcoming bond did not recognize the validity of the judgment.

The giving and forfeiture of the forthcoming bond did not deprive the party of his right to a decree for a new trial at law. It is, in legal effect, little more than the ordinary bond of replevin. There was no judicial proceedings on the forfeiture, and no right, under the laws of Mississippi, to inquire into the irregularities, errors, or frauds of the original judgment. The giving of the bond therefor did not operate a delay in presenting his defence at law. He could only make it in equity.

It has been decided, in Mississippi, that the giving and forfeiting of a forthcoming bond operates as an extinguishment of the original judgment. But this has been held with reference to judgment liens and process. The courts would not, of course, permit an execution on the original judgment, and on the statutory judgment on the forthcoming bond, or sustain liens on both judgments. The courts of that State, however, have fully recognized the principle, that the statutory judgment rested entirely on the judicial judgment, and have held that the former could not be supported without the latter, and became void on its reversal. Hoy v. Couch, 5 How. Miss. Rep. 188. If, therefore, the appellant had a good cause for a new trial in chancery, he did not lose it by giving the forthcoming bond. So far as the merits and the equity is concerned, both proceedings are but one judgment. The statutory proceeding is only held a judgment, as a mere legal fiction, and cannot stand in the way of a court of equity.

Mr. Justice DANIEL delivered the opinion of the court.

In their bill, filed in the Circuit Court, it is alleged by the appellants that, in the month of October, 1836, the appellee, Barnes, in conjunction with one Dunett, introduced from other States of the Union into the State of Mississippi, and in violation of her constitution and laws, a number of negro slaves, for the purpose of being sold as merchandise. That, in execution of the design for which they were introduced, a number of those slaves were sold by the appellee to one Thomas B. Ives, from whom he took, in payment, a bill of exchange, bearing date in October, 1836, drawn by Ives on N. and J. Dicks, of New Orleans, and indorsed by the appellant, Sample, and one G. A. Thompson. That this bill, being presented first for acceptance and subsequently for payment, was, in each instance, refused by the drawees, but was not protested either for non-acceptance or non-payment. That, after these transactions, upon some agreement between Barnes and Ives, a second bill of exchange was, in 1837, drawn by the latter upon the firm of Ford, Markham, & Co., for $5,916.66, at ten months after date, and was indorsed by the appellant, Sample, and by George A. Thompson, the indorsers of the previous bill, and was substituted in lieu thereof. That this second bill was not paid; but whether it was protested, or whether notice of its dishonor was ever given, the appellant, Sample, states that he was unable to recollect. That Barnes, being urged by Sample to sue Ives immediately for the amount of the second bill, instead of complying with this direction, took a deed of trust on certain property of Ives, stipulating in this deed to give further time for the payment of the bill; and that this deed of trust, and the agreements therein contained, were made without the knowledge and against the consent and directions of the appellant, Sample, and in fraud of his rights as a surety. That a suit having been instituted in the Circuit Court of the United States for the Southern District of Mississippi, against Sample, as the last indorser of the bill of exchange drawn on Ford, Markham, & Co.; the said Ives, upon information being given him of that fact by Sample, assured him that he need not feel any uneasiness on that account, as he, Ives, had employed able counsel to defend him in that suit. That, subsequently to this assurance from Ives, in a conversation of the appellant, Sample, with Barnes, the latter promised him, that, if Ives would confess a judgment in the State court for the amount of the bill, he, Barnes, would dismiss the suit he had instituted against the appellant as indorser of that bill That, upon communicating to Ives the proposition of the appellee, Ives professed his perfect readiness to comply with that proposal, and Barnes then parted with the

appellant, with the professed purpose of obtaining from Ives
a confession of judgment, and at the same time agreed with
the appellant, Sample, that, in the event of a failure by Ives to
give such confession, he would inform Sample thereof, in order
that they, conjointly, might endeavor to obtain from Ives a fulfilment of his promise. That Barnes omitted to give information of the refusal on the part of Ives; but permitted the
appellant, Sample, to remain under the impression that a confession of judgment had been given by Ives, until after the
commencement of the Circuit Court, in the month of May,
1839, when the appellant, Sample, was informed by Barnes that
Ives was insolvent. That, by these circumstances, and especially by the conduct of Barnes, Sample was thrown off his
guard, and a judgment by default was, in consequence thereof,
rendered against him at the May term of the Circuit Court, in
1839, for the sum of $6,822.62, and the costs of suit. That, exe-
cution having been sued out on this judgment, the appellant,
Sample, in conformity with advice given him, had, with the other
appellants, Pickins and Scott, as his sureties, executed a forthcoming bond for the delivery to the marshal of the property therein
named; which bond, having been forfeited, operated as a judgment, and execution thereon had been sued out, and had been
levied on the slaves and other personal property of Sample.

Upon the foregoing statements, the appellants prayed, that
the original contract for the sale of the slaves by Barnes, and
all the undertakings and liabilities growing out of that sale,
might be declared to be void as having been in violation of the
constitution and laws of Mississippi; and that for this cause,
affecting the character of the contract, and by reason too of the
fraud and deception imputed by the bill to the appellee, Barnes,
with reference to Sample, the judgments and executions obtained for his benefit might be perpetually enjoined.

Upon the 24th of April, 1840, an injunction was awarded the
appellants by the Judge of the District Court of the United
States for the Southern District of Mississippi.

To that portion of the bill which charges the introduction of
slaves in violation of the constitution and laws of Mississippi,
the appellee declines to answer, as that charge included the liability to a criminal prosecution. To this refusal of the appellee
no exception was taken, either in the pleadings or at the hearing
of the cause. To every other charge in the bill the answer is
directly responsive, and fully denies every material allegation.
And with respect to all the charges, inclusive of the first, the
testimony adduced by the complainant below, falls far short of
sustaining any one of them. It is deemed loose, vague, and
immaterial. Nay, the very contract with Ives, filed as an exhibit

with the bill, and which is alleged to have been an agreement for indulgence to Ives, to the prejudice of the rights of Sample, absolutely overthrows this assertion, and is shown upon its face, and by its terms and object, to have been simply an additional security from Ives, operating, if at all, for the advantage of Sample; a security too, which the grantee, in that instrument had the right to enforce immediately upon failure to pay the bill of exchange drawn on Ford, Markham, & Co.

Upon the hearing of this cause before the Circuit Court at the November term of 1848, the injunction which had been awarded the appellants was dissolved, and the bill dismissed with costs. For the examination of that decree upon appeal, this cause is now before us.

This case is then left to be decided upon its features, as disclosed in the bill and answer; and the application to these of a few settled and familiar principles of equity jurisprudence, will at once determine its fate. And first with respect to the intrinsic merits of the appellant's original claim to exemption from liability; and secondly, as to the degree or extent in which such claim, if ever existing, has been affected by his own conduct, as evincing either the assertion or the surrender of that claim. The bill commences by charging the introduction and sale of slaves within the State of Mississippi, in violation of the constitution and laws of that State, as the essential ground of impeachment of the original contract and of Sample's exemption from liability accruing therefrom. Yet it is somewhat singular, that whilst urging this objection and whilst admitting his participation in the sale, by giving it the sanction of his name and credit, he is entirely silent as to any knowledge by him as to the illegality of a transaction in which he bore so important a part. He certainly possessed, at some period of time, knowledge of the character of that transaction; and if his knowledge reached back to its origin and purposes, or to the date of his own participation therein, he must be viewed as standing *in pari delicto* with all similar actors therein — a position which, however it might shield him against attempts from associates in wrong, so far as these should be urged through the instrumentality of courts of justice, can invest him with no rights, either at law or in equity as against advantages acquired by his confederates. The appellant, Sample, was certainly bound to show himself clear of the taint of a transaction which he denounces as illegal and fraudulent, but in which he shows that he has mingled from its inception, and which he deliberately ratified at an interval of six months after his first participation in it. His failure to do this, if his denunciation of the transaction be taken as true, must be decisive of his fate before a tribunal which lends its

aid or countenance to those only who can present themselves
with pure hands, and who are free from suspicion.

The rule, as applicable to the position of this party, a rule believed to be without exception, has been distinctly announced
by this court in a case very similar in most of its features to the
one now before us; for that, like the present, was a case in which
the contract was impeached for precisely the same reason for
which the interposition of equity was here invoked; and in that,
too, as in this instance, after the omission to set up a defence at
law. We allude to the case of Creath's Administrator *v.* Sims,
in the 5th of Howard, where this court, on page 204, have thus
announced the rule by which courts of equity are governed.
" Whosoever," say they, " would seek admission into a court
of equity must come with clean hands, and such a court will
never interfere in opposition to conscience or good faith. The
effect of these principles upon the statements of the complainant is obvious upon the slightest consideration. The complainant alleges that the obligation to which he had voluntarily
become a party was intentionally made in fraud of the law,
and for this reason he prays to be relieved from its fulfilment.
This prayer, too, is addressed to a court of conscience, to a court
which touches nothing which is impure. The condign and appropriate answer from such a tribunal to such a prayer is this,
that, however unworthy may have been the conduct of your
opponent, you are confessedly *in pari delicto;* you cannot be
permitted here to plead your own demerits: precisely therefore,
in the position in which you have placed yourself, in that
position we must leave you." The attitude of the appellant,
Sample, in connection with this aspect of the case, would of
itself alone be conclusive against his application to equity for
relief; but as this party has adduced other reasons upon which
he has supposed himself entitled to equitable interposition, it
may not be out of place to show their utter inconsistency with
the very rudiments of equity jurisprudence; with principles
so familiar to the courts and to the profession as to render their
particular annunciation scarcely necessary. The defence now
attempted to be set up by Sample, viz.: the illegality under the
constitution and statutes of Mississippi of the consideration for
which the two bills of exchange were given, if true, was a legal
defence, to be availed of in the action at law by plea or demurrer. Of this principle he seems to be aware, and therefore
he endeavors to escape from its operation by attempting to fix
upon Barnes certain practices by which he, Sample, was prevented from making a proper defence in the action against him
in the Circuit Court; but with respect to the testimony adduced
to establish such alleged practices, it may be remarked in the

first place, that it does not make them out as they are averred by the bill to have occurred, and in the next place, admitting the averments in the bill, with respect to the practices objected against Barnes after the institution of the suit at law, supposing them to have occurred as stated in the bill, they could have formed no valid obligation upon Barnes to surrender, without consideration or equivalent, his legal rights, nor any dispensation to the appellant, Sample, from his duty to guard his interests in the pending litigation in which he was a party. Barnes had no power to compel a confession of judgment by Ives; and even if such confession had taken place, there could be no propriety in requiring Barnes to substitute for his demand, upon a solvent debtor, a judgment against another who was not solvent.

The appellant, Sample, appears to have been guilty of the grossest neglect and disregard of that diligence which the law requires at the hands of all suitors, and from the consequences of which they cannot be rescued consistently with the rights of others or the order of society. The law, as applicable to such neglect, is plainly declared in the case of Creath v. Sims, already quoted, in which this court have said that "a court of equity will never be called into activity to remedy the consequences of laches or neglect, or the want of reasonable diligence. Whenever, therefore, a competent remedy or defence shall have existed at law, the party who may have neglected to use it, will never be permitted here to supply the omission, to the encouragement of useless and expensive litigation, and perhaps to the subversion of justice."

How, then, shall the conduct of the appellant, Sample, be reconciled with the principles by this court so emphatically announced? He not only omits to insist upon his legal defence in the suit at law against him in the Circuit Court, but, after the judgment in that court by default, he executes a delivery bond, with the other appellants as his sureties; thus, after the first judgment against himself by default, the procures a second judgment against himself and his sureties as it were by confession. This party has, by his conduct, four times recognized the claim against him by Barnes — twice by his indorsement upon the bills drawn on N. and J. Dicks & Co , and on Ford, Markham, & Co.; in the third instance by permitting the judgment by default; and fourthly, by executing the forthcoming bond, which he knew was tantamount to a confession of judgment for the demand.

Upon these grounds, solely, and independently of the original consideration on which the undertaking by Sample was founded and supposing that consideration to have been invalid, if inquired into at the proper time, this appellant must, by his conduct, be regarded as having waived all right of inquiry into that consideration, nay, rather as having repeatedly admitted its validity. To permit him, after so doing, to contradict all that he has repeatedly and formally declared, would be to allow him to falsify his solemn acts, to trifle with the settled rules of law and the practice of the courts, and would lead to endless litigation. We therefore order that the decree of the Circuit Court, dissolving the injunction and dismissing the bill in this case, be, and the same is hereby, affirmed.

Order.

This cause came on to be heard on the transcript of the record from the Circuit Court of the United States for the Southern District of Mississippi, and was argued by counsel. On consideration whereof, it is now here ordered, adjudged, and decreed by this court, that the decree of the said Circuit Court in this cause be, and the same is hereby, affirmed with costs.

WILLIAM F. RAYMOND's LESSEE *v.* NICHOLAS LONGWORTH.

IN the State of Ohio, it is not a sufficient description of taxable lands to say, " Cooper, James, 5 acres, section 24, T. 4, F. R. 1." A deed made in consequence of a sale for taxes under such a description is void. The courts of Ohio have so decided, and this court adopts their decision.

THIS case was brought up, by writ of error, from the Circuit Court of the United States for the District of Ohio.

It was an ejectment, brought by Raymond, for the following property, viz.: — All that certain tract of land in the western part of, Cincinnati, commencing thirty feet north of Nicholas Longworth's individual property, on the west side of Mill Creek road, thence north, on the line of said road, five hundred feet, and extending back, the same width, at right angles with said road, four hundred feet.

The facts are set forth in the opinion of the court.

It was argued by *Mr. Chase*, for the plaintiff in error, and submitted, on printed argument, by *Mr. Stanberry*, for the defendant in error.

·The bill of exceptions brought up other points besides the one upon which the judgment of this court rested; but it is not necessary to notice them.

The following authorities were cited by *Mr. Stanberry*, in support of the ruling of the Circuit Court.

The entire record having been admitted .in evidence, the defendant requested the court to instruct the jury, "that the description of the lot upon the . duplicate, as appears by the abstract aforesaid," (Exhibit D,) "was not a pertinent description of the lot, such as the statute required; and, therefore, that the forfeiture to the State of Ohio was illegal and void, and the subsequent sale, by the auditor of Hamilton county, to Charles Phelps, was also void."

This instruction, as prayed by the defendant, was given by the court; and the plaintiff excepted to this opinion of the court also.

On the validity of this exception turns the principal question in the case.

In behalf of the defendant, and in support of the ruling of the court on this point, we deem it unnecessary to do more than point out the utter want of certainty in the description of the land, as contained upon the duplicate for taxation, and in the advertisements for sale and returns, as exhibited throughout the abstract from the record (Exhibit D, aforesaid); and, having done so, refer the court to the uniform course of decision in Ohio upon the subject, — invariably holding such descriptions invalid, and forfeitures and sales under them void. Indeed, all this is fully and sufficiently done in the circuit report of the present case. 4 McLean's Rep. 481; and in the case of Miner's Lessee *v.* McLean's Assignee, 4 McLean's Rep. 138.

We shall, therefore, only briefly state, that the description of the lands, as shown by this record, upon the duplicate of taxes, and in the various returns and advertisements, is thus throughout:

" Cooper, James, 5 acres, S. 24, T. 4, fr. R. 1, Cincinnati. Value $830. Amount due, $———.''

This is to be read substantially thus: — " Five acres *in* section 24, fractional range 1, Cincinnati, valued at 830 dollars," &c.

The uncertainty of description, which renders the title void, consists in its being wholly impossible to know in what part of the section this particular lot of five acres is located. Entire sections contain 640 acres, and these five acres, so far as appears, may as readily be in one part as another.

Such descriptions have been holden void by the Supreme Court of Ohio, in the following cases: Lessee of Massie's Heirs *v.* Long et al., 2 O. R. 287; Lessee of Treon *v.* Emerick, 6 O. R. 391; Lessee of Laferty *v.* Byers, 5 O. R. 458. See also, 15 O. R. 134; 16 O. R. 24.

Mr. Justice CATRON delivered the opinion of the court.

Raymond sued Longworth, in the Circuit Court of Ohio, for a piece of land, containing about five acres, lying in the western part of the city of Cincinnati. The plaintiff claimed title, under a sale for State taxes, for the years 1837 and 1838, made by the Auditor of Hamilton county, to Charles Phelps, for eighty dollars.

The land had been listed for taxation, as the property of James Cooper. The description on the tax-list, and in the subsequent return to the State Auditor, and in the advertisements of the property for sale, was as follows: — " Cooper, James, 5 acres, sec. 24, T. 4, F. R. 1." The taxes not having been paid, and the land being advertised and offered for sale, by the Auditor of Hamilton county, and no bid being made for it, it was returned to the General Auditor, as forfeited to the State, and he again ordered the land to be advertised and sold. On the trial below, it was insisted that the description of the premises was vague on the tax-list, and in the duplicate returned to the State Auditor, and in the advertisements offering the land for sale; that no forfeiture could be founded on such description, nor a valid sale be made. And so the Circuit Court instructed the jury, pronouncing the County Auditor's deed to Charles Phelps void. And the question presented is, whether the description was sufficient.

The uncertainty consists in not setting forth in what part of section 24 the five acres are situated.

It is settled, by the Supreme Court of Ohio, that the tax-list, and the duplicate transmitted to the State Auditor, as well as the advertisement, must describe the land so that its identity may be ascertained from the description, either by the owner, who wishes to pay the taxes before it is offered for sale, or that he may redeem after a forfeiture is pronounced; or that the public may be assured what is offered for sale

We refer to the description in the leading cases, where the sales were pronounced void for want of sufficient certainty. In Mathews v. Thompson, 5 Ohio, the description was, " 100 acres, sec. 4 township 7, range 4." In 5 Ohio, 458, " Haines, John, No. entry, 4401; original quantity, 170 acres; quantity taxed, 70 acres." In 6 Ohio, 399, " Sixty acres, part of the N. half of S. 13." In 16 Ohio, 25, there had been listed 333 acres, as part of an original survey for 1,000 acres, without specifying in what part of the 1,000 acres the 333 acres lay. In each of the cases cited, it was held, that the description was vague and the sale void. Here, the five acres are listed, and advertised as part of section 24, and the description is equally vague as any of the foregoing. And, as the State courts have settled what certainty is required, it is our duty to follow their decisions on the State laws, regulating proceedings in cases of tax-sales. We accordingly order the judgment of the Circuit Court to be affirmed.

Order.

This cause came on to be heard on the transcript of the record from the Circuit Court of the United States for the District of Ohio, and was argued by counsel. On consideration whereof, it is now here ordered and adjudged by this court, that the judgment of the said Circuit Court in this cause be, and the same is hereby, affirmed, with costs.

DAVID B. HERMAN, PLAINTIFF IN ERROR, v. JAMES PHALEN; SAME v. SAME.

The case of League v. DeYoung and Brown, (11 Howard, 185,) considered and again established.

THESE two cases were brought up, by writ of error, from the Circuit Court of the United States for the Eastern District of Louisiana, and were argued together by *Mr. Allen* and *Mr. Ovid F. Johnson* for the defendant in error. No counsel appeared for the plaintiff in error.

The points in the case were argued in the case of League v. DeYoung, 11 Howard, 188, to which the reporter refers.

Mr. Chief Justice TANEY delivered the opinion of the court.

These two cases have been argued together and depend upon the same principles. They were decided in the Circuit Court, before the opinion of this court was pronounced in the case of League v. DeYoung and Brown, reported in 11 Howard, 185. In that case, all of the questions which arise in the cases before us were fully considered and decided; and that decision is adverse to the doctrines now contended for by the defendant in error. Upon reviewing the opinion in League v. DeYoung and Brown, we see no reason for changing it in any respect; and these two cases must therefore be reversed, and a mandate issued to the Circuit Court, directing the judgment in each of them to be reversed, and the judgment entered for the plaintiff in error.

Order.

This cause came on to be heard on the transcript of the record from the Circuit Court of the United States for the

Eastern District of Louisiana, and was argued by counsel. On consideration whereof, it is now here ordered and adjudged by this court, that the judgment of the said Circuit Court in this cause be, and the same is hereby, reversed, with costs, and that this cause be, and the same is hereby, remanded to the said Circuit Court, with directions to enter judgment for David B. Herman, the plaintiff in error.

GEORGE RUNDLE AND WILLIAM GRIFFITHS, TRUSTEES OF THE ESTATE OF JOHN SAVAGE, DECEASED, PLAINTIFFS IN ERROR, v. THE DELAWARE AND RARITAN CANAL COMPANY.

By the law of Pennsylvania, the River Delaware is a public navigable river, held by its joint sovereigns in trust for the public.

Riparian owners, in that State, have no title to the river, or any right to divert its waters, unless by license from the States.

Such license is revocable, and in subjection to the superior right of the State, to divert the water for public improvements, either by the State directly, or by a corporation created for that purpose.

The proviso to the provincial acts of Pennsylvania and New Jersey, of 1771, does not operate as a grant of the usufruct of the waters of the river to Adam Hoops and his assigns, but only as a license, or toleration of his dam.

As, by the laws of his own State, the plaintiff could have no remedy against a corporation authorized to take the whole waters of the river for the purpose of canals, or improving the navigation, so, neither can he sustain a suit against a corporation created by New Jersey for the same purpose, who have taken part of the waters.

The plaintiffs being but tenants at sufferance in the usufruct of the water to the two States who own the river as tenants in common, are not in a condition to question the relative rights of either to use its waters without consent of the other.

This case is not intended to decide whether a first licensee, for private emolument, can support an action against a later licensee of either sovereign or both, who, for private purposes, diverts the water to the injury of the first.

THIS case was brought up, by writ of error, from the Circuit Court of the United States for the District of New Jersey.

The facts in the case are set forth in the opinion of the court.

It was argued in print by *Mr. Ashmead* and *Mr. Vroom* for the plaintiffs in error, and by *Mr. John M. Read* orally, for the defendants in error. There was also a printed argument upon the same side, submitted by himself and *Mr. Green*.

The arguments, upon both sides, contained historical accounts of the legislation of Pennsylvania and New Jersey on the subject of the River Delaware, and the various compacts and negotiations between them. It is impossible, in the report of a law case, to give an explanation of these transactions, commencing before the Revolution. Those who may have occasion to investigate the matter minutely, would do well to obtain from the counsel their respective arguments. All that will be attempted, in this report, will be to give an account of the points which were made.

The declaration charged the Canal Company with having,

1. Erected a dam in the River Delaware, above the works of the plaintiffs, and, by means of it, obstructed and penned up the waters of the river.

2. With digging a canal, and diverting the waters of the river into it, and so leading them into the State of New Jersey.

3. With cutting off the streams and brooks which theretofore had been tributary to the said River Delaware, and preventing them from flowing into it.

4. With using the waters, taken from the river, to supply the said canal, and to create a water power, from which they supply various mills, manufactories, and other establishments, with water, for the sake of gain.

The judgment of the court upon the demurrer being that the plaintiffs had no right of action, the counsel for the plaintiffs in this court assumed the following as the grounds upon which the court below founded its decision, which grounds they severally contested.

The points ruled in the court below, and of which the plaintiffs complain as being erroneous, are:

1. That the authority under which the dam of Adam Hoops has been kept and maintained in the River Delaware, since the year 1771, was not a grant, but a license, revokable at the pleasure of New Jersey alone, and, at best, impunity for a nuisance.

2. That the plaintiffs, who claim as the assignees of Adam Hoops, for the diversion of the water from their mills, cannot recover, because their works are situated in the State of Pennsylvania, and not in New Jersey, and that the claim for damages must be regulated by the rule established by the Pennsylvania courts, which rule is opposed to the one recognized in the State of New Jersey, and applied by the Supreme Court to these defendants in error in a similar case.

3. That it is not competent for the plaintiffs to question the authority of New Jersey, to take the waters of the Delaware for her public improvements, without the consent of Pennsylvania.

First Point. With respect to the first point, the counsel for the plaintiffs in error contended,

1. That the said acts were, in form, substance, and legal effect, a grant, and not a license. They then commented on the acts, and cited the following authorities:

An authority given, will operate by way of license or grant, according to its nature and the intention of the parties. Thus, in 15 Viner's Ab. Tit. Lease, (N.) Pl. 1, it is said, " That if a man license me to enter into his land, and to occupy it for a year, half year, or such like, this is a lease and shall be so pleaded." A confirmation of a title by act of Congress, (which was the least effect to be given to the acts of 1771 and 1804,) not only renders it a legal title, but furnishes higher evidence of that fact than a patent, inasmuch as it is a direct, whereas a patent is only the act of its ministerial officer. Grignon's Lessee v. Astor, 2 Howard, 319; Sims v. Irvine, 3 Dallas, 425; Patton v. Easton, 1 Wheaton, 476; Strother v. Lucas, 12 Peters, 410. In this latter case, at page 454, it is said by Judge Baldwin, delivering the opinion of the court, "that a grant may be made by a law, as well as a patent pursuant to a law, is undoubted, 6 Cr. 128; and a confirmation by a law, is as fully, to all intents and purposes, a grant, as if it contained in terms a grant *de novo*."

2. If the acts of 1771 are to be regarded as a technical license, such license is not revocable by the parties granting it, or either of them, it being a license not executory, but executed, on the faith of which large expenditures had been incurred, previous to the alleged revocation by the State of New Jersey, in 1830, by the passage of the act chartering the Delaware and Raritan Canal.

The authorities are clear and conclusive, that a license by one man to another, to make use of his land for purposes requiring expenditures of money, and contemplating permanence, is, in effect a grant, and is not revocable in its nature. Thus, in Rerick v. Kern, 14 S. & Rawle, 267, it is said that, "permission to use water for a mill, or or any thing else that was viewed by the parties as a permanent erection, will be of unlimited duration and survive the erection itself, if it should be destroyed, or fall into a state of dilapidation." Although a license executory may be revoked, yet a license executed cannot be. Winter v. Brockwell, 8 East, 308. Lord Ellenborough says, in this case, "that he thought it unreasonable, that, after a party had been led to incur expense, in consequence of having obtained a license from another to do an act, and that the license had been entered upon, that either should be permitted to recall his license." In Taylor v. Waters, 7 Taunton, 374, it is decided that a license granted on consideration cannot be revoked Liggins v. Inge, 7 Bingham, 682, (20 English Com. Law. 287,) decides that where the plaintiff's father, by oral license, permitted the defendant to lower the bank of a river, and to make a weir above the plaintiff's mill, whereby less water than before flowed to the plaintiff's mill, the plaintiff could not sue the defendants for continuing the weir; the court holding that the license in that case, being executed, was not countermandable by the party who gave it. So, in Wood v. Manly, 11 Adol. & Ellis, 34, (39 Eng. Com. Law 19,) it was held that a license to enter upon land to take away property purchased thereon, was part of the consideration of the purchase, and could not be revoked. The case of Webb v. Paternosier, (Palmer, 151,) asserts the general principle, that an executed license is not countermandable. Rerick v. Kern, (14 S. & Rawle, 267,) was the case of a license to use a water power, given without any consideration, and held not revocable. The court said the license " was a direct encouragement to spend money," and " it would be against all conscience to annul it," and further, that " the execution of it would be specifically enjoined; and that the party to whom the license was granted would not be turned round to his remedy for damages." " How very inadequate it would be. in a case like this," says the court, " is perceived by considering that a license, which has been followed by the expenditure of ten thousand dollars, as a necessary qualification. for the enjoyment of it, may be revoked by an obstinate man who is not worth as many cents." Again, it is remarked — " having had in view an unlimited enjoyment of the privilege, the grantee has purchased, by the expenditure of money, a right indefinite in point of duration."

3. If the joint acts of 1771 and 1804, are ever to be regarded as a revocable license, and not as a grant, such license has never been actually revoked by both or either of the State legislatures. The act of 1830, by which the Delaware and Raritan Canal Company was chartered by the State of New Jersey, contains no such provision, and a revocation by implication will not be inferred where so great a wrong would be perpetrated on an individual.

4. Admitting that the State of New Jersey, by the act chartering the Delaware and Raritan Canal Company, intended to revoke the grant or executed license made to Adam Hoops, and those claiming under him, it was incompetent for that State to do so.

If the joint act of the legislatures of the two States be a grant, or, what is the same in legal effect, an executed license, then that grant or executed license is a contract within the meaning of the constitution, and cannot be impaired by subsequent legislation. Fletcher v. Peck, 6 Cranch, 87; Terret v. Taylor, 9 Cranch, 43. Where a legislature has once made a grant, it is as much estopped by it as is an individual. Such a grant amounts to an extinguishment of the right of the grantor, and a contract not to reassert that right. Id. It is a principle applicable to every grant that it cannot effect preëxisting titles. Although a grant is conclusive on its face, and cannot be controverted, yet if the thing granted is not in the grantor, no right passes to the grantee. City of New Orleans v. Armas, 9 Peters, 224; New Orleans v. United States, 10 Peters, 662; Lindsey Lessee of Miller, 6 Peters, 666.

Again: If the franchise and privileges, secured to the plaintiffs by the joint acts of 1771, are the subject of legislative revocation, the revocation must certainly be as extensive as the license accorded. It must, to be effectual, be the joint act of both legislatures, and not the separate act of either. Pennsylvania was no party to the charter granted by New Jersey to the defendants. Indeed, she refused to become such, on the terms proposed by her. In many respects, this case resembles that of the Chesapeake and Ohio Canal Company v. The Baltimore and Ohio Railroad Company, 4 Gill & Johns. 1. This was the case of a contest between the plaintiffs, who claimed under the joint acts of the States of Maryland and Virginia and the United States, and the defendants, who claimed part of the same franchise under a separate act of the State of Maryland. It was held, that neither Maryland nor Virginia, without the consent of the other, could impair a charter granted by their previous joint legislation, nor could they do so even jointly.

Second Point. The second proposition ruled by the learned Judge below, was, that the plaintiffs, who claim as the assignees of Adam Hoops, for the diversion of the water from their mills, cannot recover, because their works are situated in the State of Pennsylvania, and not in New Jersey, and that the claim for damages must be regulated by the Pennsylvania courts, which rule is opposed to the one recognized in the State of New Jersey, and applied by the Supreme Court to these defendants in error in a similar case.

1. The accuracy of this position is denied; because, the action, having been instituted in the Circuit Court of New Jersey, against a New Jersey corporation, to recover damages consequent upon the erection of a public work exclusively within her own soil, the laws of New Jersey and the decisions of its Supreme Court, must furnish the rule of decision as to the extent of the liability of this corporation for the act complained of, and not the laws and decisions of Pennsylvania, as to the liability of Pennsylvania corporations.

2. If the plaintiffs' claim for damages is to be regulated by the decisions in Pennsylvania, there is no case of binding authority in the adjudications of Pennsylvania, which rules this point against them; the doctrine not going to the extent supposed by the learned Judge.

Third Point. The third point ruled by the learned Judge below, is, "that it is not competent for the plaintiffs to question the authority of New Jersey to take the waters of the Delaware River for her public improvements, without the consent of Pennsylvania, the chennel and waters of this river being vested in the two States, as tenants in common, and no one can question the authority of either to divert the water, but the other."

(These points were examined and contested.)

It has been before mentioned, that the briefs of the counsel contained references to numerous historical documents. That filed on the part of the defendants in error was very elaborate, and *Mr. Read* referred to them in his oral argument. The summing up was as follows:

We have thus presented a chronological detail of the history of the Delaware, and of the legislative negotiation, and executive action of both States in relation to the river, its navigation, and the various uses of its water for canal or mill purposes; and we think it can leave no doubt, in any dispassionate mind, that the plaintiffs in error have no title whatever to claim damages from the Delaware and Raritan Canal Company, for taking water from the river for the use of its canal, under a direct and positive authority granted by the legislature of New Jersey.

Adam Hoops's dam, uniting the main land with Bird's Island, and extending from the head of it into the main channel of the river, and perhaps one other dam on the Pennsylvania side, were erected by the owners of the fast land, prior to 1771, without any authority whatever, either from the crown, or the provincial government. Now, these erections being in the river, and beyond the low-water mark, whether the tide ebbed and flowed there or not, or whether the river was then vested in the crown or the proprietaries, were, by the unquestioned law of Pennsylvania, nuisances, and could have been abated by individuals, and certainly by the authorized agents of the government.

The law of Pennsylvania is well stated by Mr. Justice Grier, in this case. "But the law of Pennsylvania," says the learned Judge, "by which the title and rights of the plaintiffs must be tested, differs materially from that of England and most of the other States of the Union. As regards her large fresh-water rivers, she has adopted the principles of the civil law, in p ;ference to that of England." Rundle v. Delaware and Raritan Canal Company, Wallace, Jr. 297.

In the case of Carson v. Blazer, the Supreme Court of that State, decided that the large rivers, such as the Susquehanna and Delaware, were never deemed subject to the common law of England applicable to fresh-water streams; but they are to be treated as "navigable rivers;" that the grants of William Penn, the proprietary, never extended beyond the margin of the river, which belonged to the public; and that the riparian owners have, therefore, no exclusive right to the soil or water of such river, *ad filum medium aquæ.*

These principles are fully sustained by all the Pennsylvania cases down to the present time, which are cited below, and which also exemplify the doctrine that mere tolerations or licenses on navigable streams, are always in the power of the sovereign, and can be withdrawn, at any moment, without any violation of the constitutional provision.

These nuisances were in existence at the passage of the act of 9th March, 1771, and, under its general terms, the commissioners named in it, would have been obliged to abate them at once, as artificial obstructions to the navigation, except for the proviso in the 7th section, which prohibits the commissioners, therein appointed, from removing or altering the same. The same observation applies to the New Jersey act of the same year.

"But," to use again the language of the learned Judge below, "we can discover nothing in the nature of a grant in the words of this proviso. It amounts to no more than the present toleration of a nuisance, previously erected, or, at most, to a license revocable at pleasure. The doctrine of the cases which we have just quoted, applies to it with full force and conclusive effect; nor can the plaintiff claim by prescription against the public for more than the act confers on him, which, at best, is but an impunity for a nuisance." 2, Binn. 475; Brown v. Commonwealth, 3 S. & R. 273; Shrunk v. Schuylkill Navigation Co. 14 S. & R. 71; Bacon v. Arthur, 4 Watts, 437; Couvert v. O'Connor, 8 Watts, 470; Ball v. Slack, 2 Wharton, 508, 538; Monongahela Nav. Co. v. Coons, 6 W. & S. 101; Susquehanna Canal Co. v. Wright, 9 Id. 9; Commonwealth v. Church, 1 Barr, 105; Fisher v. Carter, 1 Wallace, Jr. 69; Mayor v. Commissioners of Spring Gardens, 7 Barr, 348; Reading v. Commonwealth, 1 Jones, 201; M'Kinney v. Monongahela Nav. Co. 2 Harris, 66; Henry v. Pittsburg, 8 W. & S. 85; O'Connor v. Pittsburg, Sept. 1851, MS.; Wallace, Jr. 300, 301.

But if there be any doubt on this subject, it is removed by a reference to the agreement of 26th April, 1783, between the two sovereign States of New Jersey and Pennsylvania, then recognizing no common superior, and not affected by any provision afterwards contained in the Constitution of the United States.

The acts of 1771 were temporary in their character, and all operations under them ceased from the commencement of the Revolutionary War. The compact of 1783, which is perpetual in its operation, declared "the River Delaware, from the station point, or north-west corner of New Jersey northerly, to the place upon the said river where the circular boundary of the State of Delaware toucheth upon the same, in the whole length and breadth thereof, is, and shall continue to be and remain a common highway, equally free and open for the use, benefit, and advantage of the said contracting parties."

Such language admits of no dispute. It is a complete and total revocation of all license or toleration, or grant of any kind to any dams or works erected on the Pennsylvania or Jersey side of the river, which were nuisances *ab origine.*

It cannot be supposed that two or more original nuisances were saved out of the general and comprehensive terms of the compact, and that they are to subsist to all future time as obstacles to any use of the river, by either or both States, which may in any manner affect the works thus placed on the soil and in the waters of the public.

This view is supported by the unbroken legislation of Pennsylvania particularly — by the ground taken by her commissioners in 1817, and virtually recognized by those of New Jersey, and by the subsequent agreements of 1829 and 1834, entered into by the commissioners of both States, which treated these works as nuisances, and as not to be regarded in any disposition to be made of the waters of the river, whether by the erection of dams, or for the supply of canal or water power.

They were in fact treated as if they had no legal existence. Can such a title give a claim for damages upon a company incorporated by a sovereign State of the confederacy?

It is also clearly " not competent for the plaintiffs to question the authority of New Jersey to take the waters of the Delaware for her public improvements, without the consent of Pennsylvania. The channel and waters of this river are vested in the two States, as tenants in common, as we have already seen; and no one can question the authority of either to divert its waters but the other. Pennsylvania was the first to seize on a portion of their joint property, for her separate use, and is estopped by her own act from complaint against New Jersey, who has but followed her example. Besides this, mutual consent may be presumed from mutual acquiescence. At all events, the plaintiff, who is shown to have no title to the river, or any part of it, and whose toleration or license could at best only protect him from a prosecution, is not in a situation to dispute the rights of either, or claim compensation for a diversion of its waters, for the purpose of the public improvements of either of its sovereign owners."

Mr. Justice GRIER delivered the opinion of the court.

The plaintiffs in error, who were plaintiffs below, are owners of certain mills in Pennsylvania, opposite to the city of Trenton, in New Jersey. These mills are supplied with water from the Delaware River, by means of a dam extending from the Pennsylvania shore to an island lying near and parallel to it, and extending along the rapids to the head of tide water.

The plaintiffs, in their declaration, show title to the property under one Adam Hoops, who had erected his mill and built a dam in the river previous to the year 1771. In that year, the Provinces of Pennsylvania and New Jersey, respectively, passed acts declaring the River Delaware a common highway for purposes of navigation up and down the same, and mutually appointing commissioners to improve the navigation thereof, with full power and authority to remove any obstructions whatsoever, natural or artificial; and subjecting to fine and imprisonment any person who should set up, repair, or maintain any dam or obstruction in the same, provided, " that nothing herein contained shall give any power or authority to the commissioners herein appointed, or any of them, to remove, throw down, lower, impair, or in any manner to alter a mill-dam erected by Adam Hoops, Esq., in the said River Delaware, between his plantation and an island in the said river, nearly opposite to Trenton; or any mill-dam erected by any other person or persons in the said river, before the passing of this act, nor to obstruct, or in any manner to hinder the said Adam Hoops, or such other person or persons, his or their heirs and assigns, from maintaining, raising, or repairing the said dams respectively, or from taking water out of the said river for the use of the said mills and waterworks erected as aforesaid, and none other."

The declaration avers, that by these acts of the provincial legislatures, the said Hoops, his heirs and assigns, became entitled to the free and uninterrupted enjoyment and privilege of the River Delaware for the use of the said mills, &c., without diminution or alteration by or from the act of said Provinces, now States of Pennsylvania and New Jersey, or any person or persons claiming under them or either of them. Nevertheless, that the defendants erected a dam in said river above plaintiffs' mills, and dug a canal and diverted the water, to the great injury, &c.

The defendants are a corporation, chartered by New Jersey, for the purpose of " constructing a canal from the waters of the Delaware to those of the Raritan, and of improving the navigation of said rivers." They admit the construction of the canal, and the diversion of the waters of the river for that purpose, but demur to the declaration, and set forth as causes of demurrer —

" That the act of the legislature of the then Province of Pennsylvania, passed March ninth, in the year of our Lord one thousand seven hundred and seventy-one, and the act of the then Province.of New Jersey, passed December twenty-first, in the year of our Lord one thousand seven hundred and seventy-one, as set forth in said amended fifth count, do not vest in the said Adam Hoops, or in his heirs or assigns, the right and privilege to the use of the water of the River Delaware without diminution or alteration, by or from the act of the then Province, now State, of Pennsylvania, or of the then Province, now State, of New Jersey, or of any person or persons claiming under either of them, or of any person or persons whomsoever, as averred in the said amended fifth count of the said declaration. And also, for that it does not appear, from the said amended fifth count, that the same George Rundle and William Griffiths are entitled to the right and privilege to the use of the water of the River Delaware, in manner and form as they have averred in the said amended fifth count of their declaration.

" And also that, as it appears from the said amended fifth count, that the said River Delaware is a common highway and public navigable river, over which the States of Pennsylvania and New Jersey have concurrent jurisdiction, and a boundary of said States, these defendants insist that the legislative acts of the then Province of Pennsylvania and New Jersey, passed in the year of our Lord seventeen hundred and seventy-one, as set forth in the said amended fifth count, were intended to declare the said River Delaware a common highway, and for improving the navigation thereof, and that the provision therein contained, as to the mill-dam erected by Adam Hoops, in the said River Delaware, did not and does not amount to a grant or conveyance of water power to the said Adam Hoops, his heirs or assigns, or to a surrender of the public right in the waters of the said river, but to a permission only to obstruct the waters of the said river by the said dam, without being subjected to the penalties of nuisance ; that the right of the said Adam Hoops was, and that of his assigns is, subordinate to the public right at the pleasure of the legislature of Pennsylvania and New Jersey, or either of them."

On this demurrer the court below gave judgment for the defendants, which is now alleged as error.

It is evident, that the extent of the plaintiff's rights as a riparian owner, and the question whether this proviso operates as the grant of a usufruct of the waters of the river, or only as a license or toleration of a nuisance, liable to revocation or subordinate to the paramount public right, must depend on the laws and customs of Pennsylvania, as expounded by her own courts. It will be proper, therefore, to give a brief sketch of

8 *

the public history of the river and the legislative action connected with it, as also of the principles of law affecting aquatic rights, as developed and established by the courts of that State.

The River Delaware is the well known boundary between the States of Pennsylvania and New Jersey. Below tide water, the river, its soil and islands, formerly belonged to the crown; above tide water, it was vested in the proprietaries of the coterminous provinces — each holding *ad medium filum aquæ*. Since the Revolution, the States have succeeded to the public rights both of the crown and the proprietaries. Immediately after the Revolution, these St   , entered into the compact of 1783, declaring the Delaware a common highway for the use of both, and ascertaining their respective jurisdiction over the same. For thirty years after this compact, they appear to have enjoyed their common property without dispute or collision. When the legislature of either State passed an act affecting it, they requested and obtained the concurrence and consent of the o her. Their first dispute was caused by an act of New Jersey, passed February 4, 1815, authorizing Coxe and others to erect a wing dam, and divert the water for the purpose of mills and other machinery. The consent of the State of Pennsylvania was not requested; it therefore called forth a protest from the legislature of that State. This was followed by further remonstrance in the following year. A proposition was made to submit the question of their respective rights to the Supreme Court of the United States, which was rejected by New Jersey. After numerous messages and remonstrances between the governors and legislatures, commissioners were mutually appointed to compromise the disputes. But they failed to bring the matter to an amicable conclusion. The dispute was never settled, and the wing dam remained in the river.

In 1824, New Jersey passed the first act for the incorporation of the Delaware and Raritan Canal Company, for which the company gave a bonus of $100,000. This act requires the consent of the State of Pennsylvania; and on application being made to her legislature, she clogged her consent with so many conditions, that New Jersey refused to accept her terms, returned the bonus to the company; and so the matter ended for that time.

Both parties then appointed commissioners to effect, if possible, some compact or arrangement by which each State should be authorized to divert so much water as would be necessary for these contemplated canals. After protracted negotiations, these commissioners finally (in 1834) agreed upon terms, but the compact proposed by them was never ratified by either party.

In the mean time, each State appropriated to itself as much of the waters of the river as suited its purpose. In 1827 and 1828, Pennsylvania diverted the River Lehigh, a confluent of the Delaware, and afterwards, finding that stream insufficient, took additional feeders for her canal, out of the main stream of the Delaware. On the 4th February, 1830, the legislature of New Jersey passed the act under which the defendants were incorporated, and in pursuance of which, they have constructed the dam and feeder, the subject of the present suit.

The canals in both States, supplied by the river, are intimately and extensively connected with their trade, revenues, and general property — while the navigation of the river above tide water, and the rapids at Trenton, is of comparatively trifling importance, being used only at times of the spring freshets, for floating timber down the stream, when the artificial diversions do not affect the navigation. The practical benefits resulting to both parties, from their great public improvements, appear to have convinced them that further negotiations, complaints, or remonstrances, would be useless and unreasonable; and thus, by mutual acquiescence and tacit consent, the necessity of a more formal compact has been superseded.

The law of Pennsylvania, by which the title and rights of the plaintiffs must be tested, differs materially from that of England, and most of the other States of the Union. As regards her large fresh-water rivers, she has adopted the principles of the civil law. In the case of Carson v. Blazer, the Supreme Court of that State decided, that the large rivers, such as the Susquehanna and Delaware, were never deemed subject to the doctrines of the common law of England, applicable to fresh water streams, but that they are to be treated as navigable rivers; that the grants of William Penn, the proprietary, never extended beyond the margin of the river, which belonged to the public, and that the riparian owners have therefore no exclusive rights to the soil or water of such rivers *ad filum medium aquæ.*

In Shrunk v. The Schuylkill Navigation Company, the same court repeat the same doctrine; and Chief Justice Tilghman, in delivering the opinion of the court, observes: " Care seems to have been taken, from the beginning, to preserve the waters of these rivers for public uses, both of fishery and navigation; and the wisdom of that policy is now more striking than ever, from the great improvements in navigation, and others in contemplation, to effect which, it is necessary to obstruct the flow of the water, in some places, and in others to divert its course. It is true that the State would have had a right to do these things for the public benefit, even if the rivers had been private property; but then, compensation must have been made to the owners, the amount of which might have been so enormous as to have frustrated, or at least checked these noble undertakings."

In the case of The Monongahela Navigation Company v. Coons, the defendant had erected his mill under a license given by an act of the legislature (in 1803) to riparian owners to erect dams of a particular structure, "provided they did not impede the navigation," &c. The Monongahela Navigation Company, in pursuance of a charter granted them by the State, had erected a dam in the Monongahela, which flowed back the water on the plaintiff's mill, in the Youghiogany, and greatly injured it. And it was adjudged by the court, that the Company were not liable for the consequential injury thus inflicted. The court, speaking of the rights of plaintiff, consequent on the license granted by the act, (of 1803,) observe: "That statute gave riparian owners liberty to erect dams of a particular structure, on navigable streams, without being indictable for a nuisance, and their exercise of it was, consequently, to be attended with expense and labor. But was this liberty to be perpetual, and forever tie up the power of the State? Or, is not the contrary to be inferred, from the nature of the license? So far was the legislature from seeming to abate one jot of the State's control, that it barely agreed not to prefer an indictment for a nuisance, except on the report of viewers to the Quarter Sessions. But the remission of a penalty is not a charter, and the alleged grant was nothing more than a mitigation of the penal law."

The case of the Susquehanna Canal Company v. Wright, confirms the preceding views, and decides, "that the State is never presumed to have parted with one of its franchises in the absence of conclusive proof of such an intention. Hence a license, accorded by a public law to a riparian owner, to erect a dam on the Susquehanna River, and conduct the water upon his land for his own private purposes, is subject to any future provision which the State may make, with regard to the navigation of the river. And if the State authorize a company to construct a canal which impairs the rights of such riparian owner, he is not entitled to recover damages from the company. In that case, Wright had erected valuable mills, under a license granted to him by the legislature; but the court say,—" He was bound to know that the State had power to revoke its license whenever the paramount interests of the public should require it. And, in this respect, a grant by a public agent of limited powers, and bound not to throw away the interests confided to it, is different from a grant by an individual who is master of the subject. To revoke the latter, after an expenditure in the prosecution of it, would be a fraud. But he who accepts a license from the legislature, knowing that he is dealing with an agent bound by duty not to impair public rights, does so at his risk; and a voluntary expenditure on the foot of it, gives him no claim to compensation."

The principles asserted and established by these cases, are, perhaps, somewhat peculiar, but, as they affect rights to real property in the State of Pennsylvania, they must be treated as binding precedents in this court. It is clear, also, from the application of these principles to the construction of the proviso under consideration, that it cannot be construed as a grant of the waters of a public river for private use, or a fee-simple estate in the usufruct of them, "without diminution or alteration." It contains no direct words of grant, which would operate by way of estoppel upon the grantor. The dam of Adam Hoops was a nuisance when it was made; but, as it did little injury to the navigation, the commissioners, who were commanded to prostrate other nuisances, were enjoined to tolerate this. The mills of Hoops had not been erected on the faith of a legislative license, as in the cases we have quoted, and a total revocation of it would not be chargeable with the apparent hardship and injustice which might be imputed to it in those cases. His dam continues to be tolerated, and the license of diverting the water to his mills is still enjoyed, subject to occasional diminution from the exercise of the superior right of the sovereign. His interest in the water may be said to resemble a right of common, which by custom is subservient to the right of the lord of the soil; so that the lord may dig claypits, or empower others to do so, without leaving sufficient herbage on the common. Bateson v. Green, 5 T. R. 411.

Nor can the plaintiff claim by prescription against the public for more than the act confers on him, which is at best impunity for a nuisance. His license, or rather toleration, gives him a good title to keep up his dam and use the waters of the river, as against every one but the sovereign, and those diverting them by public authority, for public uses.

It is true, that the plaintiff's declaration in this case, alleges, that the waters diverted by defendants' dam and canal are used for the purpose of mills, and for private emolument. But as it is not alleged, or pretended, that defendants have taken more water than was necessary for the canal, or have constructed a canal of greater dimensions than they were authorized and obliged by the charter, to make, this secondary use must be considered as merely incidental to the main object of their charter. We do not, therefore, consider the question before us, whether the plaintiff might not recover damages against an individual, or private corporation, diverting the water of this river to their injury, for the purpose of private emolument only, with or without license, or authority of either of its sovereign owners. The case before us requires us only to decide, that by the laws of Pennsylvania, the River Delaware is a public, navigable river, held by its joint sovereigns, in trust, for the public; that riparian owners of land have no title to the river, or any right to divert its waters, unless by license from the State. That such license is revocable, and in subjection to the superior right of the State, to divert the water for public improvements.

It follows, necessarily, from these conclusions, that, whether the State of Pennsylvania claim the whole river, or acknowledge the State of New Jersey, as tenant in common, and possessing equal rights with herself; and whether either State, without consent of the other, has or has not, a right to divert the stream, it will not alter or enlarge the plaintiff's rights. Being a mere tenant at sufferance to both, as regards the usufruct of the water, he is not in a condition to question the relative rights of his superiors. If Pennsylvania chooses to acquiesce in this partition of the waters, for great public improvements, or is estopped to complain by her own acts, the plaintiff cannot complain, or call upon this court to decide questions between the two States, which neither of them sees fit to raise. By the law of his own State, the plaintiff has no remedy against a corporation authorized to take the whole river for the purpose of canals or improving the navigation; and his tenure and rights are the same as regards both the States.

With these views, it will be unnecessary to inquire whether the compact of 1783, between Pennsylvania and New Jersey, operated as a revocation of the license or toleration implied from the proviso of the colonial acts of 1771, as that question can arise only in case the plaintiffs' dam be indicted as a public nuisance.

Nor is it necessary to pass any opinion on the question of the respective rights of either of these co-terminous States to whom this river belongs, to divert its waters, without the consent of the other.

The question raised is not without its difficulties; but being bound to resolve it by the peculiar laws of Pennsylvania, as interpreted by her own courts, we cannot say that the court below has erred in its exposition of them, and therefore affirm the judgment.

Mr. Justice McLEAN and Mr. Justice DANIEL dissented.
Mr. Justice CATRON gave a separate opinion; and Mr. Justice CURTIS dissented from the judgment of the court, on the merits, but not from its entertaining jurisdiction.

The following are the opinions of Mr. Justice CATRON and Mr. Justice DANIEL.

Mr. Justice CATRON.

My opinion is, and long has been, that the mayor and aldermen of a city corporation, or the president and directors of a bank, or the president and directors of a railroad company, (and of other similar corporations,) are the true parties that sue and are sued as trustees and representatives of the constantly changing stockholders. These are not known to the public, and not suable in practice, by service of personal notice on them respectively, such as the laws of the United States require. If the president and directors are citizens of the State where the corporation was created, and the other party to the suit is a citizen of a different State, or a subject or citizen of a foreign government, then the courts of the United States can exercise jurisdiction under the third article of the Constitution. In this sense I understood Letson's case, and assented to it when the decision was made; and so it is understood now.

If all the real defendants are not within the jurisdiction of the court, because some of the directors reside beyond it, then the act of February 28, 1843, allows the suit to proceed, regardless of this fact, for the reasons stated in Litson's case. 2 How. 597.

If the United States courts could be ousted of jurisdiction, and citizens of other States and subjects of foreign countries be forced into the State courts, without the power of election, they would often be deprived, in great cases, of all benefit contemplated by the Constitution; and, in many cases, be compelled to submit their rights to judges and juries who are inhabitants of the cities where the suit must be tried, and to contend with powerful corporations, in local courts, where the chances of impartial justice would be greatly against them; and where no prudent man would engage with such an antagonist, if he could help it. State laws, by combining large masses of men under a corporate name, cannot repeal the Constitution; all corporations must have trustees and representatives, who are usually citizens of the State where the corporation is created; and these citizens can be sued, and the corporate property charged by the suit; nor can the courts allow the constitutional security to be evaded by unnecessary refinements, without inflicting a deep injury on the institutions of the country

Mr. Justice DANIEL.

In the opinion of the court, just announced in this cause, I am unable to concur.

Were the relative rights and interests of the parties to this controversy believed to be regularly before this court, I should have coincided in the conclusions of the majority; for the reason, that all that is disclosed by the record, either of the traditions or the legislation of the States of Pennsylvania and New Jersey, shows an equal right or claim on the part of either of those States to the River Delaware, and to the uses to which the waters of that river might be applied. From such an equality in each of those States, it would seem regularly to follow, that no use or enjoyment of the waters of that river could be invested in the grantees of one of them, to the exclusion of the like use and enjoyment by the grantees of the other. The permission, therefore, from Pennsylvania to Adam Hoops, or his assignees, to apply the waters of the Delaware in the working of his mill, whatever estate or interest it might invest in such grantee, as against Pennsylvania, could never deprive the State of New Jersey of her equal privilege of applying the waters of the same river, either directly, in her corporate capacity, or through her grantee, the Delaware and Raritan Canal Company. My disagreement with my brethren in this case has its foundation in a reason wholly disconnected with the merits of the parties. It is deducible from my conviction of the absence of authority, either here or in the Circuit Court, to adjudicate this cause; and that it should therefore have been remanded, with directions for its dismission, for want of jurisdiction.

The record discloses the fact, that the party defendant in the Circuit Court, and the appellee before this court, is a corporation, styled in the declaration, " a corporation created by the State of New Jersey." It is important that the style and character of this party litigant, as well as the source and manner of its existence, be borne in mind, as both are deemed material in considering the question of the jurisdiction of this court, and of the Circuit Court. It is important, too, to be remembered, that the question here raised stands wholly unaffected by any legislation, competent or incompetent, which may have been attempted in the organization of the courts of the United States; but depends exclusively upon the construction of the 2d section of the 3d article of the Constitution, which defines the judicial power of the United States; first, with respect to the subjects embraced within that power; and, secondly, with respect to those whose character may give them access, as parties, to the courts of the United States. In the second branch of this definition, we find the following enumeration, as descriptive of those whose position, as parties, will authorize their pleading or being impleaded in those courts; and this position is limited to " controversies to which the United States are a party; controversies between two or more States,—between citizens of different States,—between citizens of the same State, claiming lands under grants of different States,—and between the citizens of a State and foreign citizens or subjects."

Now, it has not been, and will not be, pretended, that this corporation can, in any sense, be identified with the United States, or is endowed with the privileges of the latter; or if it could be, it would clearly be exempted from all liability to be sued in the Federal courts. Nor is it pretended, that this corporation is a State of this Union; nor, being created by, and situated within, the State of New Jersey, can it be held to be the citizen or subject of a foreign State. It must be, then, under that part of the enumeration in the article quoted, which gives to the courts of the United States jurisdiction in controversies between citizens of different States, that either the Circuit Court or this court can take cognizance of the corporation as a party; and this is, in truth, the sole foundation on which that cognizance has been assumed, or is attempted to be maintained. The proposition, then, on which the authority of the Circuit Court and of this tribunal is based, is this: The Delaware and Raritan Canal Company is either a citizen of the United States, or it is a citizen of the State of New Jersey. This proposition, startling as its terms may appear, either to the legal or political apprehension, is undeniably the basis of the jurisdiction asserted in this case, and in all others of a similar character, and must be established, or that jurisdiction wholly fails. Let this proposition be examined a little more closely.

The term *citizen* will be found rarely occurring in the writers upon English law; those writers almost universally adopting, as descriptive of those possessing rights or sustaining obligations, political or social, the term *subject*, as more suited to their peculiar local institutions. But, in the writers of other nations, and under systems of polity deemed less liberal than that of England, we find the term *citizen* familiarly reviving, and the character and the rights and duties that term implies, particularly defined. Thus, Vattel, in his 4th book, has a chapter, (cap. 6th,) the title of which is: "The concern a nation may have in the actions of her citizens." A few words from the text of that chapter will show the apprehension of this author in relation to this term. "Private persons," says he, "who are members of one nation, may offend and ill-treat the citizens of another; it remains for us to examine what share a state may have in the actions of her citizens, and what are the rights and obligations of sovereigns in that respect." And again: "Whoever uses a citizen ill, indirectly offends the state, which is bound to protect this citizen." The meaning of the term *citi-*

zen or *subject*, in the apprehension of English jurists, as indicating persons in their natural character, in contradistinction to artificial or fictitious persons created by law, is further elucidated by those jurists, in their treatises upon the origin and capacities and objects of those artificial persons designated by the name of *corporations.* Thus, Mr. Justice Blackstone, in the 18th chapter of his 1st volume, holds this language: " We have hitherto considered persons in their natural capacities, and have treated of their rights and duties. But, as all personal rights die with the person; and, as the necessary form. of investing a series of individuals, one after another, with the same identical rights, would be inconvenient, if not impracticable; it has been found necessary, when it is for the advantage of the public to have any particular rights kept on foot and continued, to constitute artificial persons, who maintain a perpetual succession, and enjoy a kind of legal immortality. These artificial persons are called *corporations.*"

This same distinguished writer, in the first book of his Commentaries, p. 123, says, " The rights of persons are such as concern and are annexed to the persons of men, and when the person to whom they are due is regarded, are called simply rights; but when we consider the person from whom they are due, they are then denominated, duties," And again, cap. 10th of the same book, treating of the PEOPLE, he says, " The people are either aliens, that is, born out of the dominions or allegiance of the crown; or natives, that is, such as are born within it." Under our own systems of polity, the term, citizen, implying the same or similar relations to the government and to society which appertain to the term, subject, in England, is familiar to all. Under either system, the term used is designed to apply to man in his individual character, and to his natural capacities; to a being, or agent, possessing social and political rights, and sustaining, social, political, and moral obligations. It is in this acceptation only, therefore, that the term, *citizen*, in the article of the Constitution, can be received and understood. When distributing the judicial power, that article extends it to controversies between citizens of different States. This must mean the natural physical beings composing those separate communities, and can, by no violence of interpretation, be made to signify artificial, incorporeal, theoretical, and invisible creations. A corporation, therefore, being not a natural person, but a mere creature of the mind, invisible and intangible, cannot be a citizen of a State, or of the United States, and cannot fall within the terms or the power of the above-mentioned article, and can therefore neither plead nor be impleaded in the courts of the United States. Against this position it may be urged, that the converse thereof has been ruled by this court, and that this matter is no longer open for question. In answer to such an argument, I would reply, that this is a matter involving a construction of the Constitution, and that wherever the construction or the integrity of that sacred instrument is involved, I can hold myself trammelled by no precedent or number of precedents. That instrument is above all precedents; and its integrity every one is bound to vindicate against any number of precedents, if believed to trench upon its supremacy. Let us examine into what this court has propounded in reference to its jurisdiction in cases in which corporations have been parties; and endeavor to ascertain the influence that may be claimed for what they have heretofore ruled in support of such jurisdiction. The first instance in which this question was brought directly before this court, was that of the Bank of the United States v. Deveaux, 5 Cranch, 61. An examination of this case will present a striking instance of the error into which the strongest minds may be led, whenever they shall depart from the plain, common acceptation of terms, or from well ascertained truths, for the attainment of conclusions, which the subtlest ingenuity is incompetent to sustain. This criticism upon the decision in the case of the Bank v. Deveaux, may perhaps be shielded from the charge of presumptuousness, by a subsequent decision of this court, hereafter to be mentioned. In the former case, the Bank of the United States, a corporation created by Congress, was the party plaintiff, and upon the question of the capacity of such a party to sue in the courts of the United States, this court said, in reference to that question, "The jurisdiction of this court being limited, so far as respects the character of the parties in this particular case, to controversies between citizens of different States, both parties must be citizens, to come within the description. That invisible, intangible, and artificial being, that mere legal entity, a corporation aggregate, is certainly not a citizen, and consequently cannot sue or be sued in the courts of the United States, unless the rights of the members in this respect can be exercised in their corporate name. If the corporation be considered as a mere faculty, and not as a company of individuals, who, in transacting their business, may use a legal name, they must be excluded from the courts of the Union." The court having shown the necessity for citizenship in both parties, in order to give jurisdiction; having shown farther, from the nature of corporations, their absolute incompatibility with citizenship, attempts some qualification of these indisputable and clearly stated positions, which, if intelligible at all, must be taken as wholly subversive of the positions so laid down. After stating the requisite of citizenship, and showing that a corpo-

·ration cannot be a citizen, " and consequently that it cannot sue or be sued·in the courts of the United States," the court goes on to add, " unless the rights of the members can be exercised in their corporate name." Now, it is submitted that it is in this mode only, viz. in their corporate name, that the rights of the members can be exercised ; that it is this which constitutes the character, and being, and functions of a corporation. If it is meant beyond this, that each member, or the separate members, or a portion of them, can take to themselves the character and functions of the aggregate and merely legal being, then the corporation would be dissolved ; its unity and perpetuity, the essential features of its nature, and the great objects of its existence, would be at an end. It would present the anomaly of a being existing and not existing at the same· time. This strange and obscure qualification, attempted by the court, of the clear, legal principles previously announced by them, forms the introduction to, and apology for, the proceeding, adopted by them, by which they undertook to adjudicate upon the rights of the corporation, through the supposed citizenship of the individuals interested in that corporation. They assert the power to look beyond the corporation, to presume or to ascertain the residence of the individuals composing it, and to model their decision upon that foundation. In other words, they affirm that in an action at law, the purely legal rights, asserted by one of the parties upon the record, may be maintained by showing or presuming that these rights are vested in some other person who is no party to the controversy before them.

Thus stood the decision of the Bank of the United States *v.* Deveaux, wholly irreconcilable with correct definition, and a puzzle to professional apprehension, until it was encountered by this court, in the decision of the Louisville and Cincinnati Railroad Company *v.* Letson, · reported in 2 Howard, 497. In the latter decision, the court, unable to untie the judicial entanglement of the Bank and Deveaux, seem to have applied to it the sword of the conqueror ; but, unfortunately, in the blow they have dealt at the ligature which perplexed them, they have severed a portion of the temple itself. They have not only contravened all the known definitions and adjudications with respect to the nature of corporations,·but they have repudiated the doctrines of the civilians as to what is imported by the term *subject* or *citizen*, and repealed, at the same time, that restriction in the Constitution which limited the jurisdiction of the courts of the United States to controversies between " citizens of different States." They have asserted that, " a corporation created by, and transacting business in a State, is to be deemed an inhabitant of the State, capable of being treated as a citizen, for all the purposes of suing and being sued, and that an averment of the facts of its creation, and the place of transacting its business, is sufficient to give the circuit courts jurisdiction."

The first thing which strikes attention, in the position thus affirmed, is the want of precision and perspicuity in its terms. The court affirm that a corporation created by, and transacting business within a State, is to be deemed an inhabitant of that State. But the article of the Constitution does not make inhabitancy a requisite of the condition of suing or being sued; that requisite is citizenship. Moreover, although citizenship implies the right of residence, the latter by no means implies citizenship. Again, it is said that these córporations may be treated as citizens, for the purpose of suing or being sued. Even if the distinction here attempted were comprehensible, it would be a sufficient reply to it, that the Constitution does not provide that those who may be treated as citizens, may sue or be sued, but that the jurisdiction shall be limited to citizens only; citizens in right and in fact. The distinction attempted seems to be without meaning, for the Constitution or the laws nowhere define such a being as a *quasi* citizen, to be called into existence for particular purposes; a being without any of the attributes of citizenship, but the one for which he may be temporarily and arbitrarily created, and to be dismissed from existence the moment the particular purposes of his creation shall have been answered. In a political, or legal sense, none can be treated or dealt with by the government as citizens, but those who are citizens in reality. It would follow, then, by necessary induction, from the argument of the court, that as a corporation must be treated as a citizen, it must be so treated to all intents and purposes, because it is a citizen. Each citizen (if not under old governments) certainly does, under our system of polity, possess the same rights and faculties, and sustain the same obligations, political, social, and moral, which appertain to each of his fellow-citizens. As a citizen, then, of a State, or of the United States, a corporation would be eligible to the State or Federal legislatures; and if created by either the State or Federal governments, might, as a native-born citizen, aspire to the office of President of the United States —or to the command of armies, or fleets, in which last example, so far as the character of the commander would form a part of it, we should have the poetical romance of the spectre ship realized in our Republic. And should this incorporeal and invisible commander not acquit himself in color or in conduct, we might see him, provided his arrest were practicable, sent to answer his delinquencies before a court-martial, and subjected to the penal-

9*

ties of the articles of war. Sir Edward Coke has declared, that a corporation cannot commit treason, felony, or other crime; neither is it capable of suffering a traitor's or felon's punishment; for it is not liable to corporeal penalties — that it can perform no personal duties, for it cannot take an oath for the due execution of an office; neither can it be arrested or committed to prison, for its existence being ideal, no man can arrest it; neither can it be excommunicated, for it has no soul. But these doctrines of Lord Coke were founded upon an apprehension of the law now treated as antiquated and obsolete. His lordship did not anticipate an improvement by which a corporation could be transformed into a citizen, and by that transformation be given a physical existence, and endowed with soul and body too. The incongruities here attempted to be shown as necessarily deducible from the decisions of the cases of the Bank of the United States *v.* Deveaux, and of the Cincinnati and Louisville Railroad Company *v.* Letson, afford some illustration of the effects which must ever follow a departure from the settled principles of the law. These principles are always traceable to a wise and deeply founded experience; they are, therefore, ever consentaneous, and in harmony with themselves and with reason; and whenever abandoned as guides to the judicial course, the aberration must lead to bewildering uncertainty and confusion. Conducted by these principles, consecrated both by time and the obedience of sages, I am brought to the following conclusions: 1st. That by no sound or reasonable interpretation, can a corporation — a mere faculty in law, be transformed into a citizen, or treated as a citizen. 2d. That the second section of the third article of the Constitution, investing the courts of the United States with jurisdiction in controversies between citizens of different States, cannot be made to embrace controversies to which corporations and not citizens are parties; and that the assumption, by those courts, of jurisdiction in such cases, must involve a palpable infraction of the article and section just referred to. 3d. That in the cause before us, the party defendant in the Circuit Court having been a corporation aggregate, created by the State of New Jersey, the Circuit Court could not properly take cognizance thereof; and, therefore, this cause should be remanded to the Circuit Court, with directions that it be dismissed for the want of jurisdiction.

Order.

This cause came on to be heard on the transcript of the record from the Circuit Court of the United States for the

District of New Jersey, and was argued by counsel. On consideration whereof, it is now here ordered and adjudged by
this court, that the judgment of the said Circuit Court in this
cause be, and the same is hereby, affirmed with costs.

In re Thomas Kaine, an alleged Fugitive from Great Britain.

Under the tenth article of the treaty of 1842. between the United States and Great
  Britain, a warrant was issued by a commissioner, at the instance of the British
  Consul, for the apprehension of a person who, it was alleged, had committed an
  assault, with intent to murder, in Ireland.
The person being arrested, the Commissioner ordered him to be committed, for the
  purpose of abiding the order of the President of the United States.
A *habeas corpus* was then issued by the Circuit Court of the United States, the Dis-
  trict Judge presiding, when, after a hearing, the writ was dismissed, and the prisoner
  remanded to custody.
A petition was then presented to the Circuit Judge, at his chambers, addressed to the
  Justices of the Supreme Court. and praying for a writ of *habeas corpus*, which was
  referred by the Circuit Judge, after a hearing, to the Justices of the Supreme
  Court. in bank, at the commencement of the next term thereof.
At the meeting of the court, a motion was made, with the papers and proceedings
  presented to the Circuit Judge annexed to the petition. for writs of *habeas corpus*
  and *certiorari* to bring up the defendant and the record from the Circuit Court, for
  the purpose of having the decision of that court examined.
The motion was refused; the writs prayed for denied, and the petition dismissed.

On the 14th of June, 1852, Anthony Barclay, the British Consul at New York, addressed to Samuel R. Betts, Judge of the District Court of the United States for the Southern District of New
York, and to any commissioners authorized to perform judicial
duties in the matter, a requisition and complaint. It set forth,
that it had been represented to Mr. Barclay, and was believed by
him, that one Thomas Kane, or Kaine, or Cain, then of Cooleen,
in Ireland, did, on or about the 5th of April, 1851, fire a pistol
at one James Balfe, with intent to murder him; that a warrant
to apprehend him was issued by a justice of the peace, but that
said Kaine had absconded and fled to the United States. The
requisition further stated, that the crime of which he had been
guilty would have justified his apprehension and commitment
if it had been committed within the United States. It then
asked that a warrant for his apprehension might be issued, to
the end that the evidence of criminality may be heard and considered; and if, on such hearing, the evidence should be deemed
sufficient, that it should be certified to the proper executive
authority, in order that a warrant might issue for the surrender
of such fugitive, under the treaty between the United States
and Great Britain.

The truth of this complaint was sworn to by Mr. Barclay.

Kaine was arrested and brought before Joseph Bridgham, a Commissioner of the United States, at New York.

The case was heard before the Commissioner, who decided, on the 23d of June, that the evidence was sufficient in law to justify the commitment of Kaine, upon the charge of assault with intent to commit murder; and ordered that the prisoner should be committed, to abide the order of the President of the United States.

A writ of *habeas corpus* was sued out, and allowed by Judge Betts. The writ was returnable to the Circuit Court of the United States; and, on the 3d of July, Judge Betts, the District Judge, then sitting alone in the Circuit Court, decided that the writ should be dismissed and the prisoner be remanded to the custody of the marshal.

On the 17th of July, the Acting Secretary of State issued a warrant, directing the marshal to deliver up Kaine to the British Consul.

On the 22d of July, Kaine presented a petition to Mr. Justice Nelson, at his chambers, praying for a writ of *habeas corpus*. The petition, although handed to Mr. Justice Nelson, was addressed to the Justices of the Supreme Court of the United States, which was not then in session.

On the 3d of August, Mr. Justice Nelson allowed the writ, and made it returnable on the 11th.

The marshal, in his return, stated the above facts, when, on the same day, Mr. Justice Nelson ordered as follows:

" The marshal having made the within return, Ordered that, in consequence of the difficult and important questions involved in the case, it be heard before all the Justices of the Supreme Court in bank, at the commencement of the next term thereof; and that, in the mean time, the prisoner remain in the custody of the said marshal."

A motion was made in this court for a *certiorari*, to bring up the proceedings of the Circuit Court, when holden by Judge Betts, which were printed, and ready to be used if the writ should be ordered.

In this condition of the case, the court passed the following order.

On consideration of the petition filed in this cause yesterday, and of the arguments of counsel thereupon had, as well in support of the application as against it, it is now here ordered by the court, that counsel have leave to argue the following questions, to wit:

1. Has this court jurisdiction upon the case, as certified by Judge Nelson ?

2. Can a. *certiorari* issue to bring up the proceedings in the Circuit Court?

3. Assuming the court to have jurisdiction, and the proceedings in the Circuit Court to be legally before this court, is the party entitled to be discharged?

And it is further ordered by the court, that the same be, and hereby are, set down for argument on the first Monday of January next.

The unusual length of the opinions delivered by the Judges prevents the Reporter from inserting the arguments of counsel, which he would wish to do.

The case was argued by *Mr. Busteed* and *Mr. Brady*, for the petitioner, no counsel appearing on the other side.

As the opinions refer to a particular part of the proceedings and evidence below, it is necessary to insert the following.

Warrant.   *To John M. Higginson, Esq., Sub-Inspector, and his Assistants, this to execute.*

COUNTY OF WESTMEATH, *to wit:*

Whereas, complaint on oath has been made before her majesty's justices of the peace, of and for the said county of Westmeath, at Ballinlober, on this day, that one Thomas Kane did, at Cooleen, in said county of Westmeath, on this fifth day of April, instant, feloniously and maliciously fire a pistol, loaded with powder and lead, at one James Balfe, with the intent to murder him, and did then and there wound the aforesaid James Balfe:

These are, therefore, in her majesty's name, to charge and command you, immediately on receipt thereof, to apprehend and bring before some of her majesty's justices of the peace, of and for said county, the body of the aforesaid Thomas Kane, to answer the complaint, and to be further dealt with according to law.

Given under my hand and seal, this 5th day of April, 1851.

JAS. FEATHERSTON, *J. P.* [SEAL.]

To Sub-Constable Martin Meagher and his lawful assistants, this warrant legally to execute.

J. M. HIGGINSON, 3*d S. I.*

MOATE, 5th April, 1851.

Endeavored to execute same on the 11th and 12th of April, '51, at Liverpool, without effect.

MARTIN MEAGHER, *A. C.*

Endeavored to execute this warrant on the night of the 29th instant, with J. M. Higginson, Esq., S. I., and party; did not succeed.   James Green, *Head Constable.*

Do. do. on the 7th June, 1851.
J. G., *H. C.*
Endeavored to be executed on the 6th July, '51, by
Jas. Moore, *C.*
Do. Oct. 16. } J. G., *H. C.*
Do. do. 28. }
Do. Nov. 10, '51. M. M., *A. C.*
Do. Nov. 25, '51. J. Malon, *S. C.*
Do. No. 29, '51. A. C. Meagher and party.
Do. Dec. 21st. M. Costigan, *C.*
Do. do. 27th.
Do. do. 12th Jan'y, '52.
A. C. Meagher and party.
Do. 22d Feb., '52. By Sub-Inspr. and party.

Moate, May 30th, '51. This warrant endeavored to be executed on the morning of the 16th November, '51, without effect.
Endeavored to execute this warrant on Thos. Kane, night of the 29th Feb., '52, without effect.
M. Costigan, *Const.*
Endeavored to execute this warrant, night of the 13th March, '52, without effect.
M. Costigan, *Const.*

Borough of Liverpool, *to wit:*

Whereas, proof upon oath hath this day been made before me, one of her majesty's justices of the peace for the said borough, that the name, James Featherston, to the within warrant subscribed, is of the handwriting of the justice of the peace within mentioned. I do hereby authorize Martin Meagher, who bringeth to me this warrant, and all other persons to whom it was originally directed, or by whom it may lawfully be executed, and also all constables and other peace officers of the said borough of Liverpool, to execute the same within the said late mentioned borough.

Given under my hand, this 11th day of April, 1851.
R. E. Harvey.

County of Westmeath, *to wit:*

The information and complaint of James Balfe, of Shurock, farmer, taken 5th day of April, in the year of our Lord 1851, before the undersigned, one of her Majesty's justices of the peace in and for said county of Westmeath, who saith, that on this day, (the 5th day of April,) I was ploughing near that part of the land of Cooleen, in said county of Westmeath, which land a man named William Stones had lately been dispossessed of, and about which he had frequently threatened me, and told me a few days since that I might sow it, but that I should not

In re Kaine.

live to reap it. Saith, about the hour of 12 o'clock at noon, on said day, a man named Thomas Cain, or Kain, came up to me when I was ploughing, armed with a case of pistols. On coming up to me he said to me, ' God save you; are you Peter Balfe ? ' I said, don't you know well I am not, Tom. He then asked, is that Stones' land ? I said not; that it was the other side of the ditch. He then asked me, was I warned to have nothing to do with it, (Stones' land,) and I said not, except what I heard from Stones. He then said he came to warn me, and asked had I a prayer-book. I said not. Well, I have one myself; and he took both pistols in one hand, and took a prayer-book out of his pocket and threw it on the ground towards me. I stooped to take it up, and while stooping he fired one of the pistols at me; and on examining my person, I found the mark of ·a bullet and twenty-seven grains of shot in my side, just under my left arm. He was so close that the powder discolored my coat, and some of the said shot marks was on my left arm. I then jumped up and ran away, and he followed me some distance; he then turned back towards the horses, and I went into John Mularney's house, and sent for the horses. I saw no more of him. I knew him well for some years back, and I kept his prayer-book.

his
JAMES ·X· BALFE.
mark.

Sworn before me the day and year first mentioned, at Ballentubbe, in said county of Westmeath, this 5th day of April, 1851.
JAMES FEATHERSTON, H.

I certify that the information, copied on the other side hereof, is the original deposition upon which the original warrant has been issued by me for the apprehension of Thomas Kain, charged with shooting at James Balfe, of Shurock, in the county of Westmeath, with intent to murder him, the said James Balfe; and I further certify, that the said copy at the other side hereof is a true copy of said original deposition.
Dated the 25th day of May, 1852.

JAS. FEATHERSTON, H.
*One of her Majesty's Justices of the Peace
of the county of Westmeath, in Ireland.*

Witness present—MARTIN MEAGHER, A. C.

The following opinion was delivered by Mr. Justice CATRON, in which Mr. Justice McLEAN, Mr. Justice WAYNE, and Mr. Justice GRIER, coincided. Mr. Justice CURTIS delivered a separate opinion, and Mr. Chief Justice TANEY, Mr. Justice DANIEL, and Mr. Justice NELSON, dissented.

Mr. Justice CATRON.

The facts adduced on the part of Kaine, the applicant for our interference, show that a complaint was made out in due form by counsel, at the instance of the British government, through its agents, to secure the surrender of the fugitive; and that Mr. Barclay, the British Consul at New York, was specially employed, by direct authority of the British Minister, accredited to this government, to take the proper steps, according to the tenth article of the treaty of 1842; and furthermore, an officer of the Irish constabulary, who was able to identify Kaine, had been sent to Mr. Barclay, with letters from the British Home Department, to assist in the prosecution.

In pursuance of this authority, Mr. Barclay made the necessary affidavit, and caused Kaine to be arrested and brought before Joseph Bridgham, Esquire, a commissioner appointed by the Circuit Court of the United States, for the Southern District of New York; who reports the principal facts presented to him, as having occurred in Ireland, as follows: " The original warrant in this case was issued by James Featherstonhaugh, Esq., a justice of the peace of the county of Westmeath, Ireland, in which county the alleged crime was committed. The warrant was produced before me, together with a copy of the information or affidavit upon which said warrant was issued, said copy being certified according to the act of Congress, by the justice of the peace, who issued the warrant, and attested by the oath of the witness to be a true copy. James Balfe, the witness who made the information or affidavit, states, among other things, 'that on the 5th day of April, 1851, he was ploughing some land in the county of Westmeath, when Thomas Kaine came up to him, armed with a case of pistols, and after some conversation respecting some land, of which a man named Stone had lately been dispossessed, and respecting which the witness had been threatened, said, that he came to warn the witness Balfe about it, and asked if he, witness, had a prayer-book; witness said that he had not; Kaine then said that he had one himself, and threw it on the ground before the witness, who stooped to pick it up; that while stooping, Kaine fired one of the pistols at him, and that on examining his person he found marks of a bullet and twenty-seven shot in his side, just under his left arm; that he then fled, and that Kaine pursued him some distance, but finally turned back, and witness saw no more of him.'

" Upon this information the said Featherstonhaugh, justice of the peace for the county of Westmeath, granted his warrant, for the apprehension of Thomas Kaine, the prisoner, upon complaint on oath, made before him, that the prisoner had feloniously and maliciously fired a pistol, loaded with powder and lead at the said James Balfe, with intent to murder him. This warrant, dated April 5, 1851, was immediately put into the hands of one Martin Meagher, constable of Westmeath, who made search for the prisoner and was unable to find him, or to execute the warrant. The said Meagher was produced before me, as a witness, and testified, among other things, that he was acting constable of the Irish constabulary, of the county of Westmeath, in Ireland, and had been such constable for several years; that he knew Thomas Kaine, the prisoner, and had known him for three years and upwards; that he had received, as such constable, the warrant before mentioned, to execute against the prisoner; that it was the original warrant; that he saw James Featherstonhaugh, the magistrate, execute it, and that he knew said Featherstonhaugh to be a justice of the peace of the county of Westmeath, in Ireland."

The case presented to us shows that the facts here stated are correctly made. Nothing is found in the proceedings before us, from which it appears that our government took any step to aid the British authorities in arresting and committing Kaine. And the Attorney-General declined to appear, on the part of the United States in this court, in opposition to this motion; nor did counsel appear on behalf of the British government, the argument before us being on behalf of the fugitive only.

On the foregoing state of facts the question arises, whether the United States Commissioner had power and jurisdiction to proceed without the previous authority of his own government.

Several obscurities in our extradition treaties with Great Britain and France were supposed to require legislation, on the part of Congress, to secure their due execution, and accordingly the act of August 12, 1848, was passed. By its provisions, the Judges of the Supreme Court, and those of the District courts of the United States, the Judges of the several State courts, and also Commissioners appointed for the purpose by any of the courts of the United States, are severally vested with power and jurisdiction to act, on complaint made under oath, charging a person with having committed any of the crimes enumerated within the foreign jurisdiction; and to issue a warrant for the apprehension of the person charged, so that he may be brought before such Judge or Commissioner, to the end that the evidence of criminality may be heard and considered; and if it be deemed sufficient to sustain the charge, under the provisions of the treaty, then it is made the duty of the Judge or Commissioner, to certify the fact of sufficiency, together with a copy of all the testimony taken before him, to the Secretary of State, so that a warrant may issue by the Executive, on the requisition of the foreign government, through its proper authorities, for the surrender of the fugitives. And the person charged shall be committed to jail, and there remain under the warrant of the Judge or Commissioner until the surrender shall be made.

That an Executive order of surrender to a foreign government is purely a national act, is not open to controversy; nor can it be doubted that this executive act must be performed through the Secretary of State by order of our Chief Magistrate representing this nation. But it does not follow that Congress is excluded from vesting authority in judicial magistrates to arrest and commit, preparatory to a surrender.

The treaty with Great Britain is equally binding on us as the act of Congress, and it likewise confers jurisdiction and authority on the judges and magistrates of the respective governments, to issue warrants for the apprehension of fugitives; and for hearing and considering the evidence produced against them; and also provides, that the committing magistrate shall certify as to the sufficiency of the evidence, to the executive authority, so that a warrant of surrender may issue. But we are here more particularly considering the first and third sections of the statute; they are merely explanatory of the treaty, and altogether consistent with it. Congress was scrupulously careful, neither to limit or extend the treaty stipulations. According to the terms of the statute, no doubt is entertained by me, that the judicial magistrates of the United States, designated by the act, are required to issue warrants and cause arrests to be made, at the instance of the foreign government, on proof of criminality, as in ordinary cases when crimes are committed within our own jurisdiction, and punishable by the laws of the United States.

But it is insisted that, as these acts, in cases of fugitives, must be done in conformity to a treaty of one nation with another, and as a nation can only act through the supreme Executive authority, representing the nation, the Judges and Commissioners have no power to take the first step without being authorized to do so by the President, who represents the nation; and that the agents of the foreign nation have no right to call on our judicial officers to act, in advance of authority from the President.

On the other hand, it is supposed that the judicial magistrate proceeds in obedience to the treaty and act of Congress, by which he is invested with power to determine, independent of the President's commands, on the authority of those who apply to prosecute the fugitive; and that he must decide for himself, before the warrant issues, whether the prosecutor has the authority of his nation to demand the warrant, either from official

In re Kaine.

station, or by special deputation, in some satisfactory form, so that oppression of the party accused will be avoided.

That the British Consul in this instance had the authority of his government to demand the arrest and commitment, cannot be doubted; nor that the British government was, and now is, seeking the surrender.

Two acts of Parliament have been passed to carry the treaty of 1842 into effect in the British dominions; one in 1843, and the other in 1845; the authority of which is invoked as expressing the true construction of the treaty. They require one of the principal secretaries of state in England, if the fugitive is found in England, or the chief Secretary of the Lord-Lieutenant of Ireland, if the fugitive is found there, or if found in a colony abroad, the officer administering the government of the colony, to signify that the requisition has been made, and to require all magistrates and officers of justice within the jurisdiction where the requisition is made, to aid in apprehending the person accused, and committing him for the purpose of being delivered, according to the provisions of the treaty.

The British acts confer authority to arrest and commit, on judges of courts, and also on justices of the peace, and inferior police magistrates. Our act of Congress excluded justices of the peace and inferior magistrates, and limits the power to the Judges of the United States courts, and to Commissioners appointed for the purpose by them; and to the respective State Judges. And these, as already declared, are, in my opinion, authorized to proceed without a previous mandate from the executive department. Nor can I see any good reason why it should be otherwise. The judicial magistrate is bound to decide on the sufficiency of the affidavits on which the warrant of arrest is founded, and compelled to determine on the right to further prosecute, in every step of the proceeding; and why he should not have power to decide on the prosecutor's authority to institute the proceeding, it is difficult to perceive.

The people of this country could hardly be brought to allow an interference of the President with the Judges in any degree. The experiment was made during Mr. Adams's administration, in 1799, and signally failed. Jonathan (or Nathan) Robbins had been arrested as a fugitive, under the 27th article of Jay's treaty, for murder in the British fleet. He was imprisoned at Charleston under a warrant of the District Judge of South Carolina, and had been confined six months, when the Secretary of State addressed a letter to the Judge, mentioning that application had been made by the British Minister to the President, for the delivery of Robbins, according to the treaty. The letter said—"The President *advises and requests* you to deliver him up." On this authority the prisoner was brought before the District Court on *habeas corpus,* and his case fairly enough heard, to all appearance, from the accounts we now have of it; and the Judge ordered the surrender in ˙the following terms: " I do therefore order and command the marshal, in whose custody the prisoner now is, to deliver the . body of said Nathan Robbins, *alias* Thomas Nash, to the British Consul, or such person or persons as he shall appoint to receive him."

The prisoner was accordingly delivered to a detachment of federal troops stationed there, to aid in the surrender; and they delivered him to an officer of the British navy, who was ready to receive him on board of a vessel of war, in which he was carried away.

That the Judge˙acted by order of the President, and in aid of the executive department, was never disputed; and the then administration was defended on the ground that the treaty was a compact between nations, and might be executed by the President throughout; and must be thus executed by him, until Congress vested the courts or judges with power to act in the matter; which had not been done in that instance. 5 Pet. Ap. 19; 7 Am. Law Jour. 13.

The subject was brought to the notice of the House of Representatives in Congress, by resolutions impeaching the President's conduct in Robbins's case, and where Mr. Marshall (afterwards Chief Justice of this court) made a speech in defence of the President's course, having much celebrity then and since, for its ability and astuteness. But a great majority of the people of this country were opposed to the doctrine that the President could arrest, imprison, and surrender, a fugitive, and thereby execute the treaty himself; and they were still more opposed to an assumption that he could order the courts of justice to execute his mandate, as this would destroy the independence of the judiciary, in cases of extradition, and which example might be made a precedent for similar invasions in other cases; and from that day to this, the judicial power has acted in·cases of extradition, and all others, independent of executive control.

That the eventful history of Robbins's case had a controlling influence on our ,distinguished negotiator, when the treaty of 1842 was made; and especially on Congress, when it passed the act of 1848, is, as I suppose, free from doul .. The assumption of power to arrest, imprison, and extrude, on executive warrants, and the employment of a judicial magistrate to act in obedience to the President's commands, where no independence existed, or could exist, had most materially aided to overthrow the administration of a distinguished revolutionary patriot, whose honesty of purpose no fair-minded man at this day doubts. Public opinion had settled down to a firm resolve, long before the treaty of 1842 was made, that so dangerous an engine of oppression as secret proceedings before the executive, and the issuing of secret warrants of arrest, founded on them, and long imprisonments inflicted under such warrants, and then, an extradition without an unbiased hearing before an independent judiciary, were highly dangerous to liberty, and ought never to be allowed in this country.   Congress obviously proceeded on this public opinion, when the act of 1848 was passed, and therefore referred foreign powers to the judiciary when seeking to obtain the warrant, and secure the commitment of the fugitive; and which judicial proceeding was intended to be independent of executive control, and in advance of executive action on the case.   And such has been the construction, and consequent practice, under the act of Congress and treaty by our executive department, as we are informed, on application to that department.   What aid the executive will afford to a foreign government through its prosecuting attorneys, in cases arising under treaties, rests with itself, and not with us, as it acts altogether independent of the judiciary.

In my judgment, the law is as it should be.   The treaty of 1842 settled the dividing line of jurisdiction between the United States and the British possessions in America, from the Atlantic ocean to the Rocky Mountains.   On either side of the line, in great part, there is an extensive population ; escapes of criminals from the jurisdiction where the crime was committed, to the other, must often occur; and if criminals are taken at all, they must be arrested in hot pursuit, when fleeing from justice. To do so, a magistrate must be at hand to issue the warrant, cause the arrest, and adjudge the criminality.   If Congress had delared that the President should first be applied to through the British Minister, and then issue his mandate to the judges to proceed in each case, the treaty would become nugatory in most instances ; and in the entire range of country west of the Rocky Mountains, and for more than five hundred miles on this side of it, throughout the great western plains, no arrests could be made, nor would they be attempted.

What Great Britain has done by its legislation, cannot control our decision; we must abide by our own laws.   If theirs are inconvenient, or supposed to violate the spirit of the treaty, it is the duty of our government to complain, and ask that they be reformed.

There is another striking consideration that must have had weight with our government, when the act of 1848 was passed. Judges and State magistrates arrest and commit our own citi-

10*

zens, without exception, in all instances, and for every grade of crime and offence against our State and Federal laws; they determine on the rights of the prosecutor to commence the proceeding; on the sufficiency of the affidavit on which the warrant of arrest is founded; on the evidence of criminality after the arrest is made; and imprison or take bail preparatory to a trial in court. Of this there is no complaint, nor any supposed danger of oppression, as the writ of *habeas corpus* promptly corrects all irregularities. Why, then, should a foreign criminal be more tenderly dealt by? He, too, has every benefit of the writ of *habeas corpus;* and furthermore can only be arrested by the authority of his own government; whereas, our citizens can be arrested at the instance of any person making the proper affidavit that the crime had been committed within our jurisdiction.

This country is open to all men who wish to come to it. No question, or demand of a passport meets them at the border. He who flees from crimes committed in other countries, like all others, is admitted; nor can the common thief be reclaimed by any foreign power. To this effect we have no treaty. But it is certainly due to our own citizens that they should be protected against murderers, and those who attempt to murder; and against pirates, house-burners, robbers, and forgers. That these should be extruded, on the demands of a foreign government where the crime was committed, and there punished, is due to humanity. Such wicked and dangerous men ought not to remain here. The case before us furnishes a striking instance of our dangerous condition in this respect. The prisoner successfully resisted and evaded execution of process on him by the civil authority in England, to which he fled from Ireland, for nearly a year, and in various instances, as the official returns on the original warrant show. And when the Circuit Court heard his case, the Judge tells us that it was to be deplored that, during the argument, the manifestations by the crowd thronging the court, to resist the detention of the prisoner, should be such that the marshal reported to the court he could not venture to remove him from the prison, in obedience to the writ, without an armed force; and therefore his case was heard, from necessity, in the prisoner's absence, for fear " that he would be rescued from the custody of the law by a mob."

It also appears, that when the warrant of the Secretary of State was delivered to the British consul and agent, he had to delay, and could not ship the prisoner, " on account of the expressed belief of the marshal, of the necessity of an armed, or powerful police force, to counteract outward excitement and threats of rescue."

This case is embarrassed with some other considerations. It

is urged that the Commissioner who committed Kaine had no power, because he had not been specially appointed for that purpose. The Circuit Court held, that the order of appointment covered the case of fugitives. That the order conferred on this special magistrate authority to commit in all other criminal cases, to the full extent that the United States Judges have authority, is admitted; and that he was a magistrate of the United States government, within the direct term of the treaty, cannot be denied, as I think. If there was a doubt, however, as to the meaning of the order of appointment, it was quite easy to remedy the defect in several ways. The order might have been amended, and a new commitment made, as one of the clerks of the Federal Court at New York was acting as Commissioner; or either of the Judges might have committed the defendant in the exercise of the original jurisdiction. But the Circuit Court has construed its own order, nor will I interfere with that construction.

It is proper, however, to. say, that Commissioners, acting under orders of appointment, couched in general terms, as this is, in its concluding part, have executed the act of 1848, without any one supposing they wanted power, until now; nor has any special appointment been made, to the mere end of executing the act, by any court of the United States, so far as I know. I feel quite safe in saying, that it has not been done in any judicial circuit in the United States.

The proof that Kaine shot Balfe, with an intent to commit murder, is conclusive, beyond controversy, if competent; and the only question that can arise on the merit, is, whether the copy of Balfe's deposition, received by Commissioner Bridgham, was admissible.

It is objected, " that there was no evidence what the authority of the foreign magistrate was; whether to issue warrants, or to take cognizance of offences, and of what grade of offences."

The Commissioner held, that it was not necessary to produce the commission under which the Irish magistrate held office, and acted, nor to prove its contents, proof that he publicly discharged the duties being *primâ facie* evidence of his official character; the presumption being, that if a man regularly acts in a public office, he has been rightfully appointed. Meagher proves that the Irish magistrate thus acted, and his proof is fortified by the original warrant produced by him. It is official and authentic on its face.

There was sufficient evidence, in my opinion, before the Commissioner, to establish the official character of the magistrate, before whom Balfe's deposition was taken; and that the copy proved to be a true copy, by Meagher, was properly received, under the 2d section of the act of 1848. It requires, that copies shall be certified under the hand of the person issuing the warrant, and proved to be true copies, by the oath of the party producing them. And I think it is doubtful whether Congress did not mean to say, that the official character of the magistrate should be *primâ facie* established by the deposition and certificate, without further proof of his authority.

After Kaine had been committed by the Commissioner, the Circuit Court was applied to, by petition, for writs of *habeas corpus* and *certiorari*, to bring up the prisoner and proceedings before that court. The writs were issued, and a very thorough examination had of the law and the facts. The court decided that the commitment was, in all respects, legal and proper, concurred with the Commissioner's decision, and ordered the prisoner to be remanded to the custody of the marshal, under the commitment of the Commissioner.

The opinion and judgment of the District Judge, who presided, are before us, and form part of the proceedings presented here; and it is due to that able jurist to say, that he brought to the consideration of the case a degree of patience, learning, and capacity rarely met with, and which no other Judge can disregard without incurring the risk of error.

After this careful consideration of the case, in open court, the Circuit Judge granted a second writ of *habeas corpus*, and thereby stayed the warrant for Kaine's extradition, awarded by the Secretary of State, and which had been delivered to the British authorities; and the matter was again brought before that Judge, at chambers, but not deeming it proper to act, he adjourned the proceeding, as presented to him, into this court; and of the case thus presented, we are called on to take jurisdiction. Cognizance could only be taken of the matter, on the assumption that original jurisdiction existed in the Circuit Judge to act, but on which he did not act; and the case comes here as one of original jurisdiction, which we are called on to exercise; and as the Constitution declares that this court shall only have appellate powers, in cases like this, it follows that the transfer made by the Circuit Judge is of no validity, and must be rejected. Foreseeing that we might thus hold, the counsel for the prisoner, Kaine, also moved this court, on petition, with the papers and proceedings presented to the Circuit Judge annexed thereto, for writs of *habeas corpus* and *certiorari*, to bring up the defendant, and the record from the Circuit Court, to the end of having the decision of that court examined here.

The case has been carefully and ably argued before us, on behalf of the prisoner; and anxiously considered by this court, on every ground presented, and especially on its merits; and I am authorized to say, that Judges McLean, Wayne, and Grier, agree with the views above given, and that we refuse the motion for the writ, on the merits. We are not disposed, under the circumstances, to exercise the jurisdiction of this court in the case.

Mr. Justice CURTIS.

To state intelligibly the grounds on which I rest my judgment in this case, it is necessary to advert to the proceedings by means of which it comes before us.

On the 14th day of June, 1852, a complaint, on oath, was presented to Joseph Bridgham, Esq., one of the commissioners to take affidavits, &c., appointed by the Circuit Court of the United States, in the Southern District of New York, charging, that Thomas Kaine, in that part of the dominions of Her Britannic Majesty, called Ireland, had feloniously assaulted one John Balfe, and inflicted upon him a wound with a pistol, with intent to murder him; that a warrant to arrest Kaine, for this felony, was issued by a justice of the peace, duly authorized for this purpose, but Kaine having fled from justice, took refuge in the United States, and was then in the Southern District of New York; and the complainant, who describes himself as the Consul of Her Britannic Majesty in New York, prays that a warrant may be issued to apprehend Kaine, to the end that such proceedings may take place for his surrender to the authorities of Great Britain, as are required by the treaty between the United States and Great Britain, and the act of Congress, passed to carry that treaty into effect.

A warrant did issue, Kaine was arrested, and a hearing took place, the result of which was, that the Commissioner ordered Kaine to be committed, pursuant to the treaty, to abide the order of the President of the United States, in the premises.

In this stage of the proceedings, a writ of *habeas corpus* was issued by the Circuit Court of the United States, for the Southern District of New York. Kaine was brought before that court, in which the District Judge then presided, and after a hearing, upon all the objections raised by the Prisoner, the writ of *habeas corpus* was dismissed, and Kaine was remanded and continued in the custody of the marshal, under his arrest and commitment by the process of the Commissioner. On the 22d day of July, 1852, Kaine presented to Mr. Justice Nelson, at chambers, a petition addressed to the Justices of the Supreme Court of the United States, in which he sets forth, that he is detained in custody by an order made by Judge Betts, on the 9th day of July, 1852, that his detention is illegal, and praying for a writ of *habeas corpus* to inquire into the cause of his commitment.

Upon this petition, Mr. Justice Nelson made an order, under which a writ issued, which is as follows:

The President of the United States of America, to the United States Marshal for the Southern District of the State of New York, or to any other person, or persons, having the custody of Thomas Kaine, greeting:—·

{ Seal of the Circuit Court of the Southern District of New York. }

We command you, that you have the body of Thomas Kaine, by you imprisoned and detained, as it is said, together with the cause of such imprisonment and detention, by whatsoever name the said Kaine me   ,e called or charged, before our Justices of our Supreme Co   ;t of the United States, at his chambers, in Cooperstown, New York, on the 11th day of August, instant, to do and receive what shall then and there be considered, concerning the said Thomas Kaine.

Witness, SAMUEL NELSON, Esq., one of our Justices of our said Court, this third day of July, eighteen hundred and fifty-two.

RICHARD BUSTEED, *Attorney for petitioner.*

Upon the return of the marshal to this writ, a hearing was had, which resulted in the following order, made by Mr. Justice Nelson:

COOPERSTOWN, August 11, 1852. *At Chambers.*

The marshal having made the within return, Ordered, that in consequence of the difficult and important questions involved in the case, it be heard before all the Justices of the Supreme Court, in bank, at the commencement of the next term thereof; and that, in the mean time, the prisoner remain in the custody of the said marshal.   S. NELSON.

These are the proceedings which have brought this case here, and the first question which arises is, whether, under these proceedings, we have any power to act?

In my opinion, we have not. Passing over the question, whether the court itself could rightfully issue a writ of *habeas corpus* upon the case made before Mr. Justice Nelson, which I shall consider hereafter, I think a Judge of the court in vacation, at his chambers, has no·power to grant a writ of *habeas corpus* out of this court, or to make such a writ returnable before himself, and then adjourn it into term; and, that if he had such power, it has not been exerted in this case, the writ actually issued not being a writ out of this court, or upon which, as process, this court can take any action.

It is not to be doubted, that whatever jurisdiction belongs to the Supreme Court, under any writ of *habeas corpus ad subjici-*

endum, is appellate. It is equally clear that no part of the appellate jurisdiction of this court can be exercised by a single Judge, at his chambers. It is also well settled, that the question, whether such a writ of *habeas corpus* shall issue from this court, is one upon which the court ought to pass, before the writ issues; the allowance of the writ being an exercise of its limited appellate jurisdiction, which only the court itself has the power to exert. Ex parte Milburn, 9 Peters, 704.

From these premises it also follows, that if such a writ be issued from this court, it cannot be made returnable before a Judge, at chambers, for the reason, that he cannot there exercise any appellate power under it. And, finally, this writ does not bear the seal of the Supreme Court, is not tested by the Chief Justice, or signed by the clerk, as is required by the act of Congress, (1 Stat. at Large, 93,) but bears the seal of the Circuit Court of the Southern District of New York, is tested by Mr. Justice Nelson, is not signed by any clerk, and therefore cannot be considered process issuing out of this court, or upon which we can take jurisdiction.

I concur with my brethren in the opinion, that under this writ the court can pass no order whatever.

It remains to consider the application made by the counsel of Kaine, to have another writ of *habeas corpus* allowed by this court.

The first question is, whether we have jurisdiction to act under the writ, if allowed in the case shown by the petitioner. There are some principles, bearing on this question, which are settled. That this court has no original jurisdiction to issue a writ of *habeas corpus ad subjiciendum*, and can grant such a writ only in the exercise of its appellate jurisdiction, and consequently, by means of it, can revise only the proceedings of those tribunals over which, and in respect to which, it has an appellate control, have been so repeatedly and uniformly decided here, that they must be considered as finally settled. Marbury *v.* Madison, 1 Cr. 175; Ex parte Bollman, 4 Cr. 100, 101; Ex parte Kearney, 7 Wheat. 38; Ex parte Watkins, 3 Peters, 193, S. C. 7 Peters, 568; Cohens *v.* State of Virginia, 6 Wheat. 264; Osborn *v.* Bank of the United States, 9 Wheat. 738; Ex parte Madraza, 7 Peters, 627; Ex parte Barry, 2 Howard, 65. That no such control, by means of an appeal, writ of error, or other proceeding, can be exercised by this court over a Commissioner, acting under the authority of an act of Congress, or under color of such an authority, and that this court has no power in any way to revise his proceedings, I consider equally clear. In Ex parte Metzger, (5 Howard, 176,) it was determined that a writ of *habeas corpus* could not be allowed, to examine a commitment by a District Judge, at chambers, under the treaty between the United States and France, for the reason that the Judge, in ordering the commitment, exercised a special authority, and the law had made no provision for the revision of his judgment. The same reason applies to the action of this Commissioner. Not only has the law made no provision for the revision of his acts by this court, but, strictly speaking, he does not exercise any part of the judicial power of the United States. That power can be exerted only by Judges, appointed by the President, with the consent of the Senate, holding their offices during good behavior, and receiving fixed salaries. (Constitution, art. 3, sec. 1.) The language of Mr. Chief Justice Taney, in United States v. Ferreira, (13 Howard, 48,) in speaking of the powers exercised by a District Judge, and the Secretary of the Treasury, under the treaty with Spain, of 1819, describes correctly, the nature of the authority of such a Commissioner as acted in the case before us. " The powers conferred by Congress upon the Judge, as well as the Secretary, are, it is true, judicial in their nature. For judgment and discretion must be exercised by both of them. But it is not judicial, in either case, in the sense in which judicial power is granted by the Constitution to the courts of the United States."

Since, then, the Commissioner did not, in this case, exercise any part of the judicial power of the United States, and no mode has been provided by law to transfer the case on which he acted into any court of the United States, and thus bring that case under the judicial power, this court can have no appellate control over it; because its appellate power cannot extend beyond the action of the inferior courts, established by Congress to take, original jurisdiction under the Constitution, and which exercise judicial power therein conferred. As it is plain, then, that to revise the proceedings of the Commissioner by a writ of *habeas corpus*, would be an exercise of original, and not of appellate jurisdiction, the inquiry recurs whether we can grant the writ for the purpose of revising the decision of the Circuit Court, made upon the writ of *habeas corpus* issued by that court.

This court has appellate power only in the cases provided for by Congress. United States v. Moore, 3 Cr. 159; Durousseau v. United States, 6 Cr. 307.

We must therefore find, in some act of Congress, power to review the decision of a circuit court simply remanding a prisoner on a writ of *habeas corpus;* otherwise this writ cannot be allowed. The only grant of power, supposed to be applicable to such a case, is contained in the fourteenth section of the Judiciary Act, (1 Stat. at Large, 81,) which authorizes this

In re Kaine.

court to issue writs of *habeas corpus;* and the question is, whether a grant of power to issue a writ of *habeas corpus* "to examine into the cause of commitment," is a grant of power to review this particular decision of the Circuit Court.

As the only jurisdiction conferred arises from the authority to issue the writ, and the consequent authority to proceed under it, the exigency of the writ must necessarily limit the jurisdiction. So far as the subject-matter involved in this writ extends, the jurisdiction exists, and no further.

That subject-matter is "the cause of the commitment." So that we must ascertain whether the decision of the Circuit Court is the cause of the commitment. If it is, we have jurisdiction to inquire into it; if it is not, then that decision is not within the exigency of this writ, forms no part of its subject-matter, and is not within our appellate control.

To determine whether the decision of the Circuit Court is the cause of the commitment in this case, it is necessary to have distinctly before us the precise acts which have been done, and then to consider their legal effect.

On the 29th day of June, 1852, the Commissioner, after the previous proceedings which have been mentioned, made the following warrant to the Marshal of the Southern District of New York:

UNITED STATES OF AMERICA,
Southern District of New York, *ss.*
In the matter of Thomas Kaine.

This case having been heard before me, on requisition, through Anthony Barclay, Esquire, Her Britannic Majesty's Consul at the Port of New York, that the said Kaine be committed for the purpose of being delivered up as a fugitive from justice, pursuant to the provisions of the treaty made between the United States and Great Britain, August 9th, 1842, I find and adjudge that the evidence produced against the said Kaine, is insufficient in law to justify his commitment on the charge of assault with intent to commit murder, had the crime been committed within the United States. Wherefore, I order that the said Thomas Kaine be committed, pursuant to the provisions of the said treaty, to abide the order of the President of the United States in the premises.

Given under my hand and seal, at the city of New York, this 29th day of June, 1852.

(Signed,) JOSEPH BRIDGHAM, [L. S.]
United States Commissioner for the Southern District of New York.

Directed to the Marshal of the Southern District of New York.

Under this warrant Kaine was held by the marshal, at the time the writ of *habeas corpus* was issued by the Circuit Court; and upon the return of that writ, several questions of law were raised and argued, touching the jurisdiction of the Commissioner, and the regularity and validity of his proceedings; and on the 9th day of July, 1852, the Circuit Court gave its decision, to the effect that the Commissioner had jurisdiction, and had proceeded regularly, and concluded by passing the following order :

" The court accordingly adjudges that the commitment and imprisonment of the prisoner for the causes in the return to the *habeas corpus* in the case set forth, are sufficient cause and warrant in law for his detention by the marshal.

" Therefore, it is ordered by the court, that the writ of *habeas corpus* allowed in this case be dismissed, and that the prisoner be remanded and continued in the custody of the marshal, under such his arrest and commitment by the aforesaid process."

Is this order " the cause of the commitment" of Kaine within the meaning of a writ of *habeas corpus?* With the utmost respect for the opinions of those of my brethren who have so considered it, I cannot come to that conclusion. It seems to me, that it is not the cause of the commitment; either in substance or in form.

In substance, it is merely a refusal to discharge the prisoner from an existing commitment, because the cause of that existing commitment is found sufficient in law. It creates no new cause; it simply declares the existing cause to be sufficient. It makes no new commitment, and issues no new process as an instrument for it, but only pronounces the old process valid, and consequently the continuance of the commitment under it legal. . The custody was at no time changed. Certainly, when a prisoner is brought into court upon the return of a *habeas corpus ad subjiciendum,* he is then in the power and under the control of the court; but until the court makes some order changing the custody, it remains. The court may, in some cases, admit to bail, and may also take order for the future production of the prisoner, without bail; but in all cases, until the court makes some order changing the custody, either for the care or security of the prisoner, or founded on the illegality of his commitment, the original custody continues. In this case, no such order was made.

If, then, this order of the Circuit Court created no new cause of commitment, made no new commitment, and only pronounced the existing cause sufficient, and the existing custody lawful, I cannot perceive how that order can, in substance, be treated as the cause of the commitment of Kaine.

Nor, in my apprehension, is it so, even in form. In form, the court first adjudges that the causes set forth in the return, are sufficient, and, " therefore, it is ordered, by the court, that the writ of *habeas corpus* allowed in this case, be dismissed, and that the prisoner be remanded, and continued in the custody of the marshal, under such his arrest and commitment by the aforesaid process."

This clearly expresses, in words, precisely what would be the legal effect of dismissing the writ of *habeas corpus*, without those words. And I do not perceive how it can be more plainly expressed than by the language of this order, that the process of the Commissioner, being found sufficient, the commitment by that process is not interfered with.

It is true, the order contained the word, remanded, but in the context, where it stands, it means only that the command of the writ is no longer operative, and that the court would exercise no further control over the body of the prisoner, and not that, being out of the custody of the marshal, he is recommitted to him anew, for the words are " remanded and continued in the custody of the marshal, under such his arrest and commitment by the aforesaid process."

In point of form, the same order would have been passed if it had been found by the Circuit Court, on the return of the writ, that the prisoner was not held under, or by color of the authority of the United States, and therefore that, under the Judiciary Act, the court had no power to relieve him by *habeas corpus*. It could not be contended that, after such an order, the prisoner was confined by order of the Circuit Court, and that its order was the cause of his commitment, yet in such a case the writ must have been dismissed, and the prisoner remanded.

But whatever literal interpretation might be put upon the precise words employed in the order, I should be unable to find " the cause of the commitment " in an act of the court dismissing a writ of *habeas corpus*, because the cause of the commitment shown by the return is found sufficient. The cause of the commitment is to be looked for in the warrant under which it began, and has been continued, and not in the decision of a court pronouncing that warrant valid.

I have thus far considered this question of jurisdiction upon those principles which seem to me applicable to it. It remains to examine the former decisions of this court, to ascertain whether the question is determined by authority.

There are two cases which have been chiefly relied on at the bar. The first is Ex parte Burford, 3 Cr. 448. As this case has many facts in common with the case at bar, it is necessary carefully to examine it. Without detailing the preliminary proceedings, it will be sufficient to say, that Burford was committed to the jail of the county of Washington, in the District of Columbia, by a warrant of certain justices of the peace, which was defective,.because it did not state " some good cause certain, supported by oath." That he was brought before the Circuit Court for the District of Columbia, upon a writ of *habeas corpus*, and, after a hearing, that court passed the following order, which, as it is not given in the report of the case by Judge Cranch, and as its terms seem to me to be important, I have procured from the original record in this court.

" *January 8th*, 1806. John A. Burford was brought into court by the Marshal of the District of Columbia, agreeably. to the *habeas corpus* issued by this court, on the 4th instant, with the cause of his commitment annexed thereto, (which *habeas corpus* and cause of commitment are hereunto annexed,) whereupon, all and singular the premises being heard, and by the court have been fully understood, the court order, that the said John A. Burford, enter into a recognizance, himself in $1,000, and one or more sureties in the like sum, for his good behavior for one year from this day, and that he be remanded to jail, there to remain until such recognizance be entered into."

This case is relied upon as a decision to show, that although this court cannot, as was held in Metzger's case, issue a writ of *habeas corpus* to examine the validity of the warrant of the Commissioner; yet, if the Circuit Court has, by such a writ, examined its validity, pronounced it valid, and therefore dismissed the writ, and ordered the prisoner to be continued in the custody of the marshal, this court may, upon a writ of *habeas corpus*, examine that decision, and reverse it, if found erroneous

Before considering whether the decision in Burford's case, goes this length, I think it consistent with the profoundest respect for the very eminent judges who sat in that case, to say, that it does not appear that the question now made, was by them examined and considered, or that they themselves would have deemed it foreclosed by that decision. Indeed, that they would not have so considered, seems to me from the fact that, at the term of the court following this decision, when a writ of *habeas corpus* was moved for, to bring up the body of James Alexander, Marshall, C. J., said :— " The whole subject will be taken up *de novo*, without reference to precedents. It is the wish of this court to have the motion made in a more solemn manner to-morrow, when you may come prepared to take up the whole ground." 4 Cr. 75, note. Further proceedings upon this motion became unnecessary, in consequence of the discharge of the prisoner by another tribunal; but a few days after, upon motions in behalf of Bollman and Swartwout, committed by the Circuit Court under a charge of treason, the court proceeded to hear arguments upon its jurisdiction to issue the writs, and in an elaborate judgment affirmed the jurisdiction to examine a cause of commitment by the Circuit Court. I cannot doubt, therefore, that if at that time the further question had arisen whether the court had also jurisdiction to examine a cause of commitment by a Commissioner, after the Circuit Court had reviewed that cause, and pronounced it sufficient, the court would have thought it necessary to consider that question also *de novo*, upon all its grounds, and would not have treated Burford's case as a sufficient basis on which to rest their decision. But, as I understand Burford's case, it is clearly distinguishable from the case at bar. The Circuit Court, in that case, did not dismiss the writ of *habeas corpus;* they made an order under it, to imprison Burford. That order was, tha, he be remanded to jail, there to remain until he should enter into a recognizance, with surety, in the sum of $1000, for his good behavior for one year. This order was the cause of commitment, and under this order he was held when the writ of *habeas corpus* issued from this court. It necessarily superseded the order made by the justices of the peace, which was, that Burford should be imprisoned until he should recognize in the sum of $4000, with surety, to be of good behavior indefinitely.

It is true the Circuit Court did not proceed *de novo*, and that for this reason their order was held invalid. But the question of jurisdiction did not depend upon the validity of the order, or the causes of its invalidity, but simply upon the fact that the Circuit Court caused the commitment; and when it issued an order, complete in itself, that Burford should be imprisoned, and by that order superseded the former order of the Justices, the Circuit Court did an act which caused his commitment, and this court might inquire, by a writ of *habeas corpus*, into its validity. The distinction between such a case, and one where the Circuit Court merely dismissed the writ of *habeas corpus*, is to my mind clear.

And it must be observed that the question now is, not whether this court treated the act of the Circuit Court as the cause of commitment. I have no doubt they did so treat it, and it seems to have been so considered in subsequent cases. In Ex parte Watkins, (7 Peters, 573,) Mr. Justice Story, in reviewing the cases on the subject of *habeas corpus*, says:—" In Ex parte Burford, the prisoner was in custody under a commitment by the

11*

Circuit Court, for want of giving a recognizance for his good behavior, as awarded by the court." So in Metzger's case, (5 How. 189,) Mr. Justice McLean says :—" Ex parte Burford was a *habeas corpus*, on which the prisoner, who had been committed by the Circuit Court in this district, was discharged, there being no sufficient cause for the commitment."

It is undoubtedly true, that the imprisonment of Burford was considered to be under a commitment by the Circuit Court, and the case is an authority to prove that when a writ of *habeas corpus* is returned in the Circuit Court, and that court makes an order imprisoning the party, this court may review that order. But it is not, in my judgment, an authority to show that the Circuit Court of the Southern District of New York did make an order imprisoning Kaine. In Burford's case, the court did not dismiss the writ, nor refuse to discharge the prisoner from the commitment by the Justices, but made an order which constituted a new cause of commitment, and superseded the existing cause. In Kaine's case, the Circuit Court held the existing cause to be sufficient, and refused to interfere with it. In my judgment, these cases are not parallel.

Nor do I consider the case Ex parte Watkins, (7 Pet. 572,) to be an authority that jurisdiction exists in this case. It is only necessary to quote a single passage, from the opinion of the court, to show that it cannot aid in solving the question which I am now considering. " The award of the *capias ad satisfaciendum*, must be considered as the act of the Circuit Court, it being judicial process issuing under the authority of the court. The party is in custody under that process. He is then in custody in contemplation of law, under the award of process by the court."

It is upon this ground the decision is rested, and I can find nothing in it tending to show that in the case at bar the act of the Circuit Court is the cause of commitment.

I shall not particularly examine the other decisions of this court, which are still more remote from the case at bar.

My opinion is, that the cause of commitment of Kaine is not the act of the Circuit Court, but of the Commissioner, and for this reason the writ must be refused.

But there is another ground, on which this refusal may be rested. The decision of the Circuit Court was made on the 9th day of July. On the 17th day of July, a warrant was issued from the Department of State, which was in the following words :

DEPARTMENT OF STATE, Washington, July 17th, 1852.

To all whom these presents shall come, greeting : —

Whereas, John F. Crampton, Envoy Extraordinary and

Minister Plenipotentiary to Her Majesty the Queen of Great Britain and Ireland, hath made requisition, in conformity with the 10th article of the treaty between the United States and Great Britain, for the mutual surrender of fugitive criminals, concluded at Washington, the 9th day of August, 1842, for the delivery up to justice of Thomas Kaine, charged with the crime of assault with an intent to commit murder, in the county of Westmeath, Ireland.

And whereas, the said Thomas Kaine hath been found in the State of New York, within the jurisdiction of the United States, and has, by proper affidavit, and in due form, been brought before Joseph Bridgham, a Commissioner duly appointed by the United States Circuit Court for the Southern District of New York, in the second circuit, for examination of said charge of assault with intent to commit murder. And whereas, the said Commissioner hath deemed the evidence sufficient to authorize the commitment of said Thomas. Kaine, and has, accordingly, committed him. All of which appears by a copy of the proceedings transmitted to this department.

Now, these presents are to require of the United States Marshal for the Southern District of New York, or of any other public officer or person having charge or custody of said Thomas Kaine, to surrender and deliver him up to Anthony Barclay, Her Britannic Majesty's Consul at the Port of New York, or to any other person or persons duly authorized to receive said fugitive, and conduct him to Great Britain for trial.

In testimony whereof, I have hereunto signed my name, and caused the seal of this Department to be affixed, at Washington, this 17th day of July, A. D. 1852, and of the independence of the United States the seventy-seventh.

[SEAL.]   Signed,   W. HUNTER,
Acting Secretary of State.

Upon its face, this warrant is perfectly regular. Its recitals set forth every fact necessary to warrant the act of extradition, according to the treaty and the act of Congress. It appears, by the return of the marshal upon the writ issued by Mr. Justice Nelson, that before he received that writ, this warrant had come to his hands, and he had, in obedience to it, tendered Kaine to Anthony Barclay, who expressed his readiness to receive him ; and while arrangements were about to be made to put Kaine on shipboard, the writ of *habeas corpus*, issued by Mr. Justice Nelson, suspended the further execution of the warrant of extradition.

This warrant of extradition is the final process under the treaty and act of Congress. When it comes to the hands of the marshal, he holds the prisoner for the purpose of executing it. Upon this process, therefore, Kaine is now held.

The act of Congress requires the Judge, or Commissioner, to certify to the Secretary of State his finding, together with a copy of all the testimony taken before him, that a warrant may issue upon the requisition of the proper authorities of the foreign government for the surrender of the fugitive, according to the stipulations of the treaty. Such a warrant having issued, and its validity not having been considered by any court of original jurisdiction, in my judgment it is not the exercise of an appellate power to examine its validity by a writ of *habeas corpus*. It may be true that, if the proceedings before the Commissioner were to be held void, this warrant must also be invalid. But the question is not, whether this warrant is valid, but whether we have jurisdiction to examine its validity. It may also be true that, if this warrant were final process, issued by the Circuit Court, and we had power to examine the legality of a judgment or order of that court, pursuant to which it issued, we should also have jurisdiction upon a *habeas corpus*, to examine the validity of such a warrant, and of the proceedings of executive officers under it. But this warrant did not emanate from the Circuit Court, nor does it depend, in any way, upon its authority, nor is it a legal consequence of the action of the Circuit Court on the writ of *habeas corpus*, or in any other proceeding. It emanates from a department of the executive, which rests its action upon the proceedings of the Commissioner, and over neither can this court have, under the Constitution, nor has it under the laws, any appellate jurisdiction or control. Marbury v. Madison, 1 Cr. 137.

For the reason, then, that if a writ of *habeas corpus* were allowed in this case, the validity of the warrant of extradition could not be examined here, I think the writ should be refused.

In considering the question, whether the Supreme Court of the United States has jurisdiction, under the Constitution and laws of the United States, to entertain this application, I have not felt at liberty to allow my judgment to be pressed upon by the great value of the particular writ applied for, or the propriety and expediency of a power in this court to review the judgments of the Circuit Courts, in cases affecting the liberty of the citizen. To all that has been said concerning the pre-eminent utility of the writ of *habeas corpus*, I readily assent. But it must be remembered, that the real question here is not, whether this great writ shall be freely and efficiently used, but whether our appellate power is large enough to extend to this case. The Circuit Court has power, upon its own views of the law, to inflict, not only imprisonment, but even the punishment of death, without appellate control by this court. Even when it is alleged, that the proceedings of a circuit court, by which a citizen is imprisoned, are *coram non judice* and void, its judgment is final, and no relief can be had here, by writ of error or appeal, or by *habeas corpus*. Ex parte Watkins, 3 Pet. 193; Ex parte Kearney, 7 Wheat. 38.

Undoubtedly, it would be competent for Congress to do, in cases like this, what it has done in a class of cases somewhat analogous. By the act of August 29, 1842, (5 Stat. at Large, 539,) when the subject of a foreign government is imprisoned for an act done under the authority of that government, and a writ of *habeas corpus* is issued by a Judge of this court, or by a District Judge, an appeal to the Circuit Court, and from its order to this court, is expressly given.

It is for Congress to determine, whether this class of cases requires the same privileges. Until it so determines, I must give my decision upon our jurisdiction, as, according to my judgment, it exists, unaffected by the consideration, that it might be expedient to enlarge it. My opinion is that, if the writ prayed for were issued, we should not have jurisdiction to inquire into the cause of commitment shown by the petition, and consequently the writ should be refused. I give no opinion upon the sufficiency of the cause of the commitment, not deeming it to be judicially before us.

Mr. Justice NELSON.

The application for the arrest and delivery of Thomas Kaine was originally made on the requisition of the British Consul, resident at the port of New York, before Joseph Bridgham, Esq., a United States Commissioner for the Southern District of New York. A warrant was issued and the arrest made, and, on the return before this officer, an examination took place upon a charge that the fugitive had committed an assault, with intent to murder, upon one James Balfe, in Ireland, on the 5th April, 1851· The Commissioner, upon hearing the allegation and proofs, adjudged the prisoner guilty, and ordered that he be committed, in pursuance of the treaty, to abide the order of the President of the United States. A petition was then presented to the Circuit Court for the Southern District of New York, holden by the District Judge, for a writ of *habeas corpus*, directed to the marshal, to bring up the body of the prisoner; and also a *certiorari* to the Commissioner, to bring up the proceedings that had taken place before him; and upon a full review of all these proceedings, on the 9th July, 1852, adjudged that the commitment and detention were for sufficient cause, and ordered that the writ of *habeas corpus* be dismissed, and the prisoner be remanded, and continued in the custody of the marshal, under said commitment. On the 17th July, copies of these proceedings having been forwarded to the Department of State, at Washington, the Acting Secretary issued his warrant to the marshal having the custody of the prisoner, directing that he be surrendered to Mr. Barclay, the British Consul, or to any other person or persons duly authorized to receive the fugitive and transport him to Great Britain for trial. On the 22d July, a petition was presented to me, at my chambers, in Cooperstown, on behalf of the prisoner, for a writ of *habeas corpus*, which I declined allowing until the whole of the proceedings that had already taken place in the matter were laid before me. Copies of them were subsequently furnished, and, upon an examination, being satisfied that the Commissioner had no jurisdiction over the case, I allowed the writ, on the 8d of August, returnable before me, at my chambers, on the 11th of the same month, and which return was made accordingly. As the case was one in which I entertained a different opinion from that of the tribunals before whom the proceedings had taken place, not only as to the jurisdiction of the Commissioner, but also in respect to their interpretation of the treaty, and act of Congress passed to carry it into effect; and, as the questions involved were of considerable interest of themselves, and concerned deeply the two nations who were parties to the treaty, on the return to the writ I entered an order, directing that the case be heard before all the Judges, at the commencement of the next term of this court. The case has now been heard in full bench, and I am inclined to concur with my brethren, that we cannot entertain jurisdiction of it upon my allowance of the writ and adjournment of the proceedings to be heard in this court. The practice is a familiar one, in the proceedings under this writ, before the King's Bench, in England. 1 Burr. R. 460, 542, 606; Comyn's Digest, *Habeas Corpus*, 3d ed.; Bl. Com. 131; 9 Ad. & Ell. 731, Leonard Watson's case, and which furnished the precedent for that adopted by me in this case. That, however, is an original proceeding; and, in cases where the court has original jurisdiction to hear and determine the matters upon the return, and where the hearing may be had either before one of the Justices, at chambers, or in full bench. But, according to the settled course of decisions in this court, we can only issue the writ, and entertain jurisdiction of the matters set forth on the return, in the exercise of our appellate power. United States *v.* Hamilton, 3 Dall. 17; Ex parte Burford, 3 Cr. 448; Ex parte Bollman and Swartwout, 4 Id.; Ex parte Kearney, 7 Wheat. 38; Ex parte Watkins, 3 Pet. 193; 7 Id. 568; Ex parte Metzger, 5 How. 189. And, as the power cannot be exercised by one of the

In re Kaine.

Justices, at chambers, there may be ground for a distinction between the proceedings, under the writ, in this court and in the King's Bench. The issuing of the writ, and proceedings before me, at chambers, under it, must undoubtedly be regarded as an original proceeding, and not in the exercise of an appellate power. If this conclusion be a sound one, the remedy for the defect in the law must be sought in Congress, who can make provision for the issuing of the writ in vacation as well as in term, in all cases where this court possesses jurisdiction to entertain proceedings under it. The right of the citizen to appeal to the court for the benefit of this great writ, in case of an illegal restraint of his liberty, ought not to be restricted to the time of its sitting; but, as in all other cases where its jurisdiction may be exercised, provision should be made for instituting the proceeding in vacation. The prisoner has now presented to this court a petition, praying for a writ of *habeas corpus* to be directed to the marshal, that he may be brought up, together with the ground of his commitment; and, also, for a *certiorari* to the Circuit Court, to bring up the proceedings that have taken place in that court, which disembarrasses the case of all exceptions to the form of the application; and the return of the marshal and the proceedings before the Circuit Court being now before us, on this preliminary motion, by the agreement of the counsel, the case is in a situation to enable us to express an opinion upon the merits. It is objected, that this court cannot entertain jurisdiction of the case, even upon the petition, return of the marshal, and of the proceedings before the Circuit Court to the *certiorari*, for the reason, it appears, as supposed, that the prisoner is held in confinement under the warrant of the Commissioner, and not under the decision and order of the Circuit Court; that this court cannot reach and review the proceedings before the Commisioner, by virtue of this writ, in the exercise of its appellate power, but can only reach and review the proceedings and order of the Circuit Court; and, as the confinement of the prisoner is not under or in pursuance of the order of that court, the proceedings under the writ here would be a nullity. The first case in which this question was discussed at large by counsel and by the court, was that of Ex parte Bollman and Swartwout. They were in confinement in this district, under a warrant from the Circuit Court, upon a charge of treason against the United States. Two objections were taken to the power of this court to issue the writ to bring up the prisoners: 1st, that it involved the exercise of an original jurisdiction, not given by the Constitution; and, 2d, that, if it was the exercise of an appellate power, it was not within the 14th section of the Judiciary Act, which alone conferred the authority to issue this writ. Chief Justice Marshall, who delivered the opinion in that case, admitted the power could not be exercised as a part of the original jurisdiction of the court; but held, that it possessed jurisdiction, as an appellate power, under this 14th section. After answering the argument, that the power to award the writ was limited by that section to causes pending in this court, in which it was necessary, in order to enable it to make a final decision in the case, he observed that the proviso to the section extended to the whole of it; that proviso is as follows:

That writs of *habeas corpus* shall in no case extend to prisoners in jail, unless where they are in custody under or by color of the authority of the United States, or are committed for trial before some court of the same, or are necessary to be brought into court to testify.

And that, construing the section with reference to this proviso, the power of the court to issue the writ extended to all cases where the prisoner was restrained of his liberty, under the authority of the federal government. The same principle is derived from that section, as stated by Mr. Justice McLean in Ex parte Dorr, 3 How. 103–105. " The power given to the courts," he observes, " in this section to issue writs of *scire facias, habeas corpus*, &c.; as regards the writ of *habeas corpus*, is restricted by the proviso to cases where a prisoner is in custody under or by color of the authority of the United States, or has been committed for trial before some court of the same, or is necessary to be brought into court to testify. This is so clear," he observes, "from the language of the section, that any illustration of it would seem to be unnecessary. The words of the proviso are unambiguous. They admit of but one construction." If this construction of the section is to be maintained, (and the case Ex parte Bollman and Swartwout was very fully and deliberately considered,) then it is manifest the power to issue this great writ for the security of the liberty of the citizen, is much broader than has been contended for on behalf of the prisoner in the case before us. Hamilton's case, decided in 1795, led the way to the decision in Bollman and Swartwout. That case repudiates the idea, that the power to issue the writ is limited to instances where the proceeding is ancillary to the determination of a suit pending. Hamilton was in jail on a warrant issued by the District Judge, at chambers, upon a charge of treason. Chief Justice Marshall, in Ex parte Tobias Watkins, (3 Peters, 208,) observes that in the case of Bollman and Swartwout, the *habeas corpus* was awarded on the same principle on which it was awarded in Hamilton's case; and, in Ex parte Kearney, Mr. Justice Story, in stating the points in the case, observes, "the first is whether or not this court has authority to issue a *habeas corpus* where a person is in jail under the warrant or order of any other court of the United States." And then says, " that it is unnecessary to say more than that the point has already passed in *rem judicatam* in this court. In the case of Bollman and Swartwout, it was expressly decided, upon full argument, that this court possessed such authority, and the question has ever since been considered at rest." In the case of Ex parte Watkins, reported in 7 Peters, 568, there is a still stronger exercise of the power to issue this writ. In that case the prisoner was in custody of the marshal under three executions regularly issued out of the Circuit Court, but their efficacy had expired by the neglect of the marshal to bring in the body on the return day. The error or wrongful detention lay wholly with the marshal, and yet this court issued the *habeas corpus*, and discharged the prisoner. The case stands upon the principle decided in Hamilton's case, and in Bollman and Swartwout, that the writ may issue in all cases where the prisoner is in custody under and by color of the authority of the United States. In the case Ex parte Metzger, the prisoner was committed to the custody of the marshal by the District Judge, at his chambers, under the French treaty of extradition. This court held that they possessed no power to issue the writ of *habeas corpus*, inasmuch as the order of commitment had been made at chambers and not in court. This case undoubtedly stands alone, and has very much narrowed the power of the court in issuing this great writ in favor of the liberty of the citizen, from that repeatedly asserted in previous cases. But I do not propose to disturb it. For the case before us is within the doctrine of this case, and of every other that has heretofore been passed upon by the court, as I shall proceed briefly to show. The *habeas corpus*, which was issued in the case before us, by the court below, to the marshal, brought up the body of the prisoner, and also the warrant of commitment, into that court, and the *certiorari* to the Commissioner brought up the record, or tenor of the record of the proceedings before him, upon which the warrant had issued. The whole case, therefore, was in that court. And pending the examination or hearing, the prisoner, in all cases, on the return of the writ, is detained, not on the original warrant, but under the authority of the writ of *habeas corpus*. He may be bailed on the return *de die in diem*, or be remanded to the same jail whence he came, or to any other place of safe keeping under the control of the court, or officer issuing the writ, and by its order brought up from time to time, till the court or officer determines whether it is proper to discharge or remand him absolutely. The King's Bench may, pending the hearing, remand to the same prison or to their own, the Marshalsea. The efficacy of the original commitment is superseded by this writ while the proceedings under it are pending, and the safe keeping of the prisoner is entirely under the authority and direction of the court issuing it, or to which the return is made. Bacon, title *Habeas Corpus*, B. 12; 5 Mod. 22, The King *v.* Bethel; Comyn, title *Habeas Corpus*; 1 Vent. 330, 346; 3 East, 156; 1 B. & Cr. 358; 4 B. & A. 295. Holt, Chief Justice, observed, in the King *v.* Bethel, when a man comes in by *habeas corpus*, by the power of the court, he may be bailed to appear *de die in diem*, till the case is determined, and then he may be remanded to the same prison. "By the petition of right," he again remarks, " we are to bail or discharge in three days, but when we bail (that is, *de die in diem*) and afterwards remand him, it is no escape, for the entry is '*remittitur*,' and that is a commitment grounded on the old one."

The Circuit Court, in the case before us, after reviewing the proceedings on the return of the writ, and also to the *certiorari*, arrived at the conclusion that they were regular and legal; and, to use its own words, —

" Accordingly adjudges that the commitment and imprisonment of the prisoner, for the causes in the return to the *habeas corpus*, in the case set forth, are sufficient cause and warrant in law for his detention by the marshal. Therefore, it is ordered by the court that the writ, &c., be dismissed, and that the prisoner be remanded, and continued in the custody of the marshal, under such his arrest and commitment by the aforesaid process," meaning the original warrant of the Commissioner.

The question here is, whether, upon the law governing the writ of *habeas corpus*, and to which I have referred, and upon this judgment of the court, the prisoner is or is not held in confinement under the order of the Circuit Court. If he is, it is admitted by all that this court has jurisdiction of the case, and is bound to revise that decision. That court not only adjudges the commitment and imprisonment lawful, but directs the prisoner to be remanded, which, says Holt, Chief Justice, is a commitment grounded on the old one; and, further, (which was superfluous,) the order directs that he shall be continued in the custody of the marshal, under the old commitment. How it can be said, in view of the law governing this writ, and of the form of the judgment of the court below, that the prisoner is not in confinement under that judgment, but simply under the process of the Commissioner, without dependence upon that judgment, I admit I am incapable of comprehending. But if any further authority is wanting upon this question, I will refer to an early case in this court, Ex parte Burford, 3 Cranch, 448. That was a commitment by magistrates in this district. The case was reviewed on writ of *habeas corpus* by the Circuit Court, and the prisoner remanded; afterwards, a writ, issued from this court, bringing up the prisoner, and also th proceedings which were before the court below. This court discharged the prisoner, saying that the warrant of commitment by the magistrates was illegal, for not stating the cause of commitment — that the Circuit Court had revised the proceedings and corrected two of the errors of the magistrates and left the rest. The case, in principle, is not distinguishable from the one before us. Here the Circuit Court has corrected none of the errors of the Commissioner, if any, but confirmed all of them, and recommitted the prisoner to the custody of the marshal. It has been argued that great inconvenience would arise, if the writ of *habeas corpus* could issue from this court into any part of the Union to bring up a prisoner on a petition that he was illegally restrained of his liberty under the authority of the United States, as the proceeding must be attended with delay and expense, by reason of the great extent of our territory. But, it must be remembered that, in the case of a right of property involved, dependent upon the laws of the Union, and a decision against it, the party against whom a decision has been made in a State court, however small the amount in controversy, is entitled to a writ of error to this court, to bring up the case for review, by tne 25th section of the same act in which this 14th section is found. And I am yet to learn that the right of the liberty of the citizen is not as dear to him, and entitled to be guarded with equal care by the Constitution and laws, as the right of property, notwithstanding the supposed inconvenience. Such has heretofore been, as we have seen, the opinion in this court, when dealing with the writ in question; and I will simply add, in the language of Chief Justice Denman, in the case of the Canadian prisoners, "that it seems to me that we would be tampering with this great remedy of the subject, the writ of *habeas corpus*, if we did not say that we would abide by the practice we find, and deal with this as it has been formerly dealt with." I am satisfied, therefore, that this court has jurisdiction to issue the writ of *habeas corpus*, to inquire into the legality of the commitment below; and, as the whole case is before us on this motion, by the stipulations of the parties, shall proceed to an examination of the questions raised upon the merits.

It may, I think, be assumed, at this day, as an undoubted principle of this government, that its judicial tribunals possess no power to arrest, and surrender to a foreign country, fugitives from justice, except as authorized by treaty stipulations, and acts of Congress passed in pursuance thereof. Whether Congress could confer the power independently of a treaty, is a question not necessarily involved in this case, and need not be examined. If it was, as at present advised, I am free to say that I have found no such power in any article or clause of the Constitution, delegated to that body by the people of the States. It belongs to the treaty-making power, and to that alone, and its exercise is dependent upon the executive department, with the concurrence of two thirds of the Senators, and such I think has been the practical construction given to the Constitution since the foundation of the government. We must look, therefore, to the provisions of the treaty with Great Britain, and the act of Congress passed in pursuance thereof, for the authority to be exercised by the judiciary in the surrender of the alleged fugitive in question, and by these provisions and act, ascertain and determine whether or not the proceedings in the tribunals below, who have ordered a surrender, are in conformity with them, and warranted by law. By the treaty, " it is agreed, that the United States and Her Britannic Majesty, shall, upon mutual requisitions by them, or,their ministers, officers, or authorities, respectively made, deliver up to justice, all persons who, being charged with the crime of murder," &c.; " and the respective judges and other magistrates of the two governments shall have power, jurisdiction, and authority, upon complaint, made under oath, to issue a warrant for the apprehension of the fugitive," &c.

In the case before us, Her Britannic Majesty's Consul at the port of New York made a requisition and complaint, before one of the United States Commissioners, against the fugitive in question — upon which, a warrant was issued and the arrest made, and, after an examination into the charge, committed, for the purpose of being surrendered. No demand was made upon this government, by the government of Great Britain, claiming the surrender. This government was passed by, and the requisition made by the Consul, directly upon the magistrate, on the ground, as contended for, namely, that the consent or authority of the Executive is unnecessary to warrant the institution of the proceedings ; and, in support of their propriety and regularity, the position is broadly taken, and without which the proceedings cannot be upheld, that, according to the true interpretation of the treaty, any officer of Great Britain, however inferior, properly represents the sovereign of that country, who may choose to prosecute the alleged fugitive in making the requisition, and is entitled to the obedience of the judicial tribunals for that purpose, and if sufficient evidence is produced before them, to arrest and commit, that a surrender may be made ; and, that in this respect, such officer is put on the footing of any of the prosecuting officers of this government, who are authorized to institute criminal proceedings for a violation of its laws; that the country is open to him, throughout the limits of the Union, and the judicial tribunals bound to obedience on his requisition and proofs, to make the arrest and commitment. This is the argument. Now, upon recurring to the terms of the treaty it will be seen, I think, that no such stipulations were entered into, or intended to be entered into, by either government, or any authority conferred to justify such a proceeding. The two nations agree, that upon " mutual requisition by them, or their officers or authorities respectively made " — that is, on a requisition made by the one government, or by its ministers or officers properly authorized, upon the other — the government, upon whom the demand is thus made, shall deliver up to justice all persons charged with the crimes, as provided in the treaty. who shall have sought an asylum within her territories. In other words, on a demand, made by the authority of Great Britain upon this government, it shall deliver up the fugitive; and so in respect to a demand by the authority of this government upon her. This is the exact stipulation entered into, when plainly interpreted. It is a compact between the two nations in respect to a matter of national concern — the punishment of criminal offenders against their laws — and where the guilty party could be tried and punished only within the jurisdiction whose laws have been violated. The duty or obligation entered into, is the duty or obligation of the respective nations, and each is bound to see that it is fulfilled, and each is responsible to the other in case of a violation. When the *casus fœderis* occurs, the requisition or demand must be made by the one nation upon the other. And upon our system of government, a demand upon the nation must be made upon the President, who has charge of all its foreign relations, and with whom only foreign governments are authorized, or even permitted, to hold any communication of a national concern. He alone is authorized, by the Constitution, to negotiate with foreign governments, and enter into treaty obligations binding upon the nation; and, in respect to all questions arising out of these obligations, or relating to our foreign relations, in which other governments are interested, application must be made to him. A requisition or demand, therefore, upon this government, must, under any treaty stipulation, be made upon the Executive, and cannot be made through any other department, or in any other way. Judge Marshall, in his celebrated argument in the case of Jonathan Robbins, who was demanded by Great Britain, under the treaty of 1795, and from which this part of the treaty of 1842, was taken almost *verbatim*, speaking of the requisition in that case, observes :

" That the case was, in its nature, a national demand, made upon the nation. The parties were the two nations. They cannot come into court to litigate their claims, nor can a court decide on them. Of consequence, the demand is not a case of judicial cognizance." He further observes, that " the President is the sole organ of the nation, in its external relations, and its sole representative with foreign nations. Of consequence, the demand of a foreign nation can only be made on him." Again, he says : " The department, which is intrusted with the whole foreign intercourse of the nation, with the negotiations of all treaties, with the power of demanding a reciprocal performance of the article, which is accountable to the nation for the violation of its engagements with foreign nations, and for the consequences resulting from such violation, seems the proper department to be intrusted with the execution of a national contract, like that under consideration."

The idea of a requisition of a foreign nation upon the judiciary of another, much more upon the humble magistrate of another, demanding, as of right, the fulfilment of treaty obligations, is certainly novel, and one that I would not willingly attribute to the distinguished men who negotiated this one, nor to the governments that ratified it. So extraordinary an interpretation ought not to be given to the instrument, unless upon the plainest and most imperative terms. It does great injustice to both nations. The proceedings, consequent upon it, compromit the character and dignity of the one making the demand, and are disrespectful to the other, and may be dangerous to the liberty of the citizen. The record before us shows, that a requisition, with due solemnity, was made upon the Commissioner, in this case, by Her Britannic Majesty's government, through her Consul, and seems to imply, that the magistrate is to act under the power and authority of that government, rather than in obedience to the laws of his own ; and that a refusal to act would be a contempt of that authority, and of the *casus foederis* of a treaty obligation. If any further argument was wanting for the interpretation of the treaty for which I am contending, I might refer to that given by the authority of Great Britain, in providing by act of Parliament for carrying it into execution on her part.

By the 6th and 7th Victoria, chapter 76, it is enacted, " That, in case a requisition shall at any time be made by the authority of the United States, in pursuance of, and according to the said treaty, for the delivery of any person charged with the crime of murder, &c., it shall be lawful for one of Her Majesty's principal Secretaries of State, or, in Ireland, for the Chief Secretary of the Lord-Lieutenant of Ireland, and in any of Her Majesty's colonies or possessions abroad, for the officer administering the government of any such colony or possession, by warrant under his hand and seal, to signify that such requisition has been so made, and to require all justices of the peace, and magistrates and officers of justice, within the several jurisdictions, to govern themselves accordingly, &c.; and thereupon it shall be lawful for any justice of the peace, &c., to examine upon oath any person or persons, touching the charge," &c.

Now, it will be seen that, according to the interpretation given to the treaty by Great Britain, the requisition for the delivery of the fugitive must be made by the President upon that government, and its warrant obtained, before any magistrate within her dominion is authorized to act in the matter. The act of Parliament deals with the treaty as regulating a matter of national concern, and in respect to which both nations must act in carrying into execution its stipulations; and it is only after both have acted, and an authority obtained for the surrender, that the power of the judiciary can be called into requisition. I am satisfied this is a sound interpretation of its provisions, and is one, while it secures the punishment of the offender, guards the citizens and subjects of the respective countries against any abuse of the power. While its exercise is thus kept under the supervision and control of the two governments, there can be no danger of its being perverted, to the purposes of private malice and revenge, which might justly be apprehended, if left to the unrestrained discretion of the subordinate officers of either. The construction, against which I am contending, would refer the execution of the treaty to the subordinate and inferior agents of both governments, so far as the surrender of the fugitive, on our part, is concerned; for, as I understand that construction, any subordinate officer of Great Britain may make the requisition directly upon the magistrate, for the apprehension and committal; and, upon such commitment being communicated to the government, the Secretary of State issues his warrant that the prisoner be delivered to the British authorities. And, as I am advised, that department decided, in the case before us, that the government would not go behind the decision of the Commissioner, adjudging the prisoner guilty. Thus, the whole of the proceeding in the exercise of this high and delicate power, if the requisition of the President, in the first place, is dispensed with, would pass out of the hands and beyond the control of the government. This seems to be the result of the American interpretation of the treaty, sought to be established. It has been argued that, in Metzger's case, in which demand was made by the French government, under the treaty of November 9, 1843, the Executive declined to act until an application had been made to the judiciary, and that this construction was sanctioned by the court in that case. The treaty, in express terms, requires the requisition to be made through the diplomatic agents of the respective governments; but that the surrender shall not be made until the crime is established according to the laws of the country in which the fugitive is found. In that case, the requisition was made upon the Executive by the diplomatic agent of France, who was referred to the judiciary. The application to the judiciary, therefore, was with the approbation of this government. How formal it was given, does not appear in the case. The same practice was adopted by the Executive, in the case of Jonathan Robbins. There, on the requisition made by Great Britain upon the President, he referred the case to a Judge of the District Court of the United States, to inquire into the facts and determine whether or not he was guilty of the offence charged against him. And it is upon this construction, given to the treaty of 1795, upon which all our subsequent treaties of extradition seem to have been drafted. The power to surrender is not confided exclusively to the Executive under the treaty in question, nor was it under the treaty of 1795. On the requisition being made, if the President is satisfied, upon the evidence accompanying it, that a proper case is presented for an inquiry into the crime charged, the authorities claiming the fugitive are referred to the judiciary; and then, it is the duty of the courts or judges to act and to take the proper steps for the arrest and inquiry. The Executive alone possesses no authority, under the Constitution and laws, to deliver up to a foreign power any person found within the States of this Union, without the intervention of the judiciary. The surrender is founded upon an alleged crime, and the judiciary is the the appropriate tribunal to enquire into the charge. It has also been urged that great inconvenience may exist in the pursuit and apprehension of fugitives upon the construction contended for, in consequence of the extended frontier line between the two countries, as much time will be consumed in making the requisition upon the President. This may be so; but I cannot agree that a sound construction of the treaty, and one which affords nothing more than a just protection to the personal liberty of the citizen against the abuse of power, shall be made to yield to the suggestions of convenience; for, although the prisoner before us may be a foreigner, and even may be a fit subject to be given up to the subordinate and irresponsible agents of the government claiming him, still, it is not to be denied that the same power, thus attempted to be exercised by them, in this instance, is equally applicable to any citizen of the country, upon a like complaint; and besides, under our system of laws and principles of government, so far as respects personal security and personal freedom, I know of no distinction between the citizen and the alien who has sought an asylum under them. I will simply add, that, according to the act of 6th and 7th Victoria, already referred to, carrying into effect this treaty, the indulgence of any such convenience in its execution, is regarded as too dangerous to the subjects of that government residing within its dominions, on the other side of this extended boundary. The treaty, after providing for the requisition of the one government upon the other, for the surrender, then provides that the respective judges and other magistrates of the two governments shall have power, jurisdiction, and authority, upon complaint made under oath, to issue a warrant for the apprehension of the fugitive. After the requisition has been made upon the President, the organ of the government as regards our foreign relations, and his authority obtained, the means are thus provided for procuring the surrender. An application is then made to the judiciary of the country, not upon the requisition of the foreign government, but, as in all other cases, upon the authority of its own — and the warrant issued in pursuance of such application, runs in the name of the President of the United States. The act of Congress, passed to carry our treaties of extradition into effect, and of course this one among others, takes up the subject at this stage of the proceedings, and designates the judicial officers who are authorized to act, and prescribes, in general terms, the steps to be pursued in the arrest, the examination of the criminal charge, and final commitment for the surrender, if evidence of the criminality is found sufficient. There is no necessary discrepancy between the provisions of this act and the treaty, as the requisition of the one government upon the other is not attempted to be regulated or defined, but is left as regulated by the terms of that instrument. The provisions of the treaty must, therefore, be resorted to for the purpose of ascertaining how that requisition shall be made. I have already explained my interpretation of them, and need not repeat it. The judicial officers designated in the treaty, and upon whom jurisdiction is conferred, are "the respective judges and other magistrates of the two governments." The act of Congress, in carrying out this provision, designates the Justices of the Supreme Court, the Judges of the several District Courts of the United States, the Judges of the several State Courts, and Commissioners specially authorized so to do, by any of the courts of the United States. The terms "other magistrates of the two governments," are quite indefinite and difficult in their application by judicial construction. In an enlarged sense, they might embrace all the United States Commissioners appointed by the Circuit Court, who, under the act of Congress of the 23d of August, 1842, are authorized to arrest persons for crimes against the United States, and imprison or bail the same; and, also, all the justices of the peace of the several States, upon whom like power is conferred by the 33d section of the Judiciary Act of 1789. I can hardly suppose that the distinguished citizen who represented this government in the negotiation of the treaty, or the President, under whose supervision it was entered into, contemplated the exercise of so high and delicate a power over the rights and liberty of the citizen, by so numerous a body of the magistracy of the country. But, be this as it may, Congress, in providing for the execution of the treaty, has declared who shall constitute those " other magistrates," before whom the application may be made for the arrest and examination, and have confined the jurisdiction, in this respect, to the Judges of the several State courts, and Commissioners specially authorized by the courts of the United States, for the performance of that duty. The provision necessarily excludes the great body of the State magistrates and of United States Commissioners, possessing general power to arrest and commit for offences against the United States, and is in no respect in conflict with any clause in the treaty, but in harmony with it, and in furtherance of a proper and discreet execution of its stipulations.

It has been argued that, admitting the State magistrates to possess no power under the act of Congress passed to carry the treaty into effect, yet that act confers the power upon the body of United States Commissioners, authorized to arrest and commit for crimes against the United States, under the act of 1842. A slight attention to the provisions of the act, I think, will refute any such conclusion. The 1st section confers the exercise of the power under the treaty, upon the Judges of the Federal courts, and of the State courts, and upon " Commissioners authorized so to do by any of the courts of the United States ; " and the 6th section provides—" That it shall be lawful for the courts of the United States, or any of them, to authorize any person or persons to act as a Commissioner or Commissioners under the provisions of this act ; and the doings of such person or persons so authorized in pursuance of any of the provisions aforesaid, shall be good and available to all intents and purposes whatever."

Taking these two provisions together, and construing them as part of a regulation prescribed by law for carrying the treaty into effect, I think it plain that a Commissioner, competent to act in the matter, must be specially appointed, or authorized by the Federal courts for that purpose. The first section confines the exercise of the power to Commissioners thus specially authorized to perform this duty; and the sixth provides for the appointment of them, and declares that their doings in the premises, in conformity with law, shall be good and valid. How it can be said that the exercise of a power thus guarded and restricted, both in the grant and in the appointment, is conferred, also, upon a body of officers appointed under a different act, and for other special and limited duties, I admit is beyond my comprehension. But it is urged that if the act of Congress cannot be construed as conferring the power, it may be derived from the appointment of this Commissioner, under a rule of the Circuit Court of the United States, adopted in January, 1851. That rule provides that the clerk of the Circuit Court and of the District Court, and their deputies, (the Commissioner in question being a deputy of the Clerk of the District Court,) shall be *ex officio* Commissioner of the Circuit Court; and shall be authorized to execute all the powers, and perform all the duties conferred by several acts of Congress, enumerating them, but of which the act of 1848, the one in question, is not included, " or of any act of Congress having relation to such Commissioners, and their duties or powers." These officers, thus appointed by the Circuit Court, are authorized, by the several acts enumerated, to take affidavits and bail in civil cases; and to arrest and commit for offences against the United States, and the latter clause of the rule provides for the performance of any other duties that may be conferred upon them by any other acts of Congress. Now it is apparent, unless it can be shown that the act of 1848 confers the power to act under the treaty in the extradition of fugitives upon these officers, this clause in the rule has no application to the case; and that no such power has been conferred by that act, if I am not greatly mistaken, has been already demonstrated. The rule of the court adds nothing to the argument in favor of the power, as that depends upon the act of Congress which provides for carrying the treaty into effect, and which confers the power only upon Commissioners, specially appointed by the Federal courts for this purpose. The treaty provides that the arrest of the alleged fugitive, and commitment for the purpose of a surrender, shall be made, "upon such evidence of criminality as, according to the laws of the place where the fugitive or person so charged shall be found, would justify his apprehension and commitment for trial, if the crime or offence had there been committed."

The act of Congress makes no provision on this subject, except as it respects the admissibility of a species of evidence which will be noticed hereafter. The laws of New York, therefore, arc to govern and regulate the Judge or Commissioner in hearing and determining the criminality of the prisoner, as he was found in that jurisdiction. This would be so even without the specific provision of the treaty, as the only mode of proceeding, in summary criminal proceedings before the Federal magistrates, is according to the practice before the State magistrates, is according to the practice before the State magistrates, is according to the practice before the State magistrates, in analogous cases. The thirty-third section of the Judiciary Act of 1789, expressly provides that summary proceedings against persons for crimes committed against the United States, shall be agreeably to the usual mode of process against offenders in the State in which he may be found. I am not aware of any other act of Congress on the subject. This accords with the construction given to the treaty in the act of Parliament, 6th and 7th Victoria, which requires the production of such evidence as, according to the laws of that part of her Majesty's dominions where the prisoner is found, would justify his apprehension and committal for trial, if the crime had been there committed. According to the laws of New York, regulating these summary proceedings, in criminal cases, evidence is heard, as well on behalf of the accused as against him, and should have been so heard in this case. The 2d section of the act of Congress, to carry into effect the treaty, provides that on the hearing upon the return of the warrant of arrest, "copies of the depositions upon which an original warrant in any such foreign country may have been granted, under the hand of the person or persons issuing such warrant, and attested upon the oath of the party producing them, to be true copies of the original depositions, may be received in evidence of the criminality of the person so apprehended."

This species of evidence is exceedingly loose and unsatisfactory, in any aspect in which it can be viewed; but certainly it cannot be characterized as evidence of any description, unless it appears that the magistrate in the foreign country taking the depositions and issuing the warrant, had jurisdiction of the case, and was competent to perform these acts. Unless the authority exists, the acts are *coram non judice*, and void. And the rule is universal, that in the case of magistrates, or other persons of limited or special jurisdiction, any party setting up a right or title under, and by virtue of, their acts or proceedings, must first show affirmatively that they possessed jurisdiction or authority to act in the matter. The jurisdiction is never presumed. These are principles too familiar to require a reference to authorities. It was proved, in this case, that the person taking the depositions in Ireland, and issuing the warrant, acted as a justice of the peace; and, it has been contended, that affords

In re Kaine.

evidence not only of his appointment to that office, but also of the competency of his jurisdiction. I cannot assent to this doctrine. I admit that evidence of a person exercising the duties of a public officer, and even reputation of the fact, may dispense with the proof of a regular appointment, and if there is no question as to the extent of his power or authority, the proof will be sufficient. But if, in addition to the appointment, it becomes necessary to give evidence of his jurisdiction, neither his acting in the office, or reputation, furnishes any evidence of the fact. 1 Phillips, Ev. 432, 433, 450; C. & Hill's Notes, 280, 281; 3 Wend. 267. If a contrary principle can be found in the law, it is a little remarkable that the rule should ever have obtained that, in an action founded upon the adjudication or decision of a magistrate, or any other officer of special and limited jurisdiction, the party claiming a right under it, must aver and prove jurisdiction in the particular case, for the very adjudication, or decision, would afford all the necessary evidence of the officer acting as such within the principle contended for. In other words, the judgment would afford evidence *per se* of the jurisdiction, and in all cases dispense with further proof, and thus every inferior magistrate would be placed upon the footing of courts of general jurisdiction. I do not think it necessary to pursue this branch of the argument further, and am satisfied that the Commissioner acted, in the arrest and commitment of the prisoner, without any competent evidence of his guilt of the crime alleged against him. To permit the copies as evidence, without proof of the jurisdiction of the magistrate, would be against all principle, and might lead to the most scandalous abuses in carrying into execution the stipulations of the treaty. This species of evidence is very differently guarded, in the act 6th and 7th Victoria. There, copies of the depositions laid before the government, and upon which the proper officer issued his warrant to the magistrates, authorizing them to institute proceedings to arrest and commit the fugitive, are those only permitted to be given in evidence. In other words, copies of the depositions upon which the government acted in the matter, are admissible as evidence of the criminality. The original of these are those upon which our government make the requisition; and, of course, the good faith of the nation is pledged that they were taken before competent officers, and that the facts stated in them were true. But, in the case before us, the copy was taken by a police officer of the foreign country, and produced here before the Commissioners, without the sanction of either government, and without any competent evidence of the authority of the person before whom it was taken. There was no evidence of the authority of this magistrate, or of any authority under the treaty, for the arrest of the accused, before the Commissioner, but what depended upon the oral testimony of this officer, and the statement of the Consul, of what had been represented to him in the matter. The Consul does not aver that any of the facts stated by him, in what he calls his requisition upon the Commissioner, were within his own knowledge. Even the authority attempted to be derived from the Under Secretary of State in Ireland, depends upon the oral statement of this police witness; and I assert, and do so upon the responsibility that I know belongs to my place and the occasion, that there is not one word or scintilla of evidence in the record of the Commissioner, upon which the accused in this case has been tried and adjudged guilty, but depends entirely and exclusively upon the oral examination of this foreign police officer, who does not pretend that he had any personal knowledge of the commission of the crime. His knowledge only extends to the verification of the copy of the deposition taken before a person in Ireland, of whose authority to take it we know nothing. To those familiar with the criminal laws of this country, I need not say that such evidence, against any person charged with an offence against our laws, would be inadmissible and utterly worthless, and especially so, under the laws of the State of New York, which must govern in this case, unless otherwise regulated by act of Congress ; and equally so, in my judgment, within a sound construction of the act providing for the admissibility of these copies of a deposition, taken before the foreign magistrate.

I have thus gone over the case much more at large than I should have deemed it necessary, were it not for the very great diversity of opinion in respect to it among my brethren. I have regarded it as a case of considerable importance, not only from the delicacy of the power involved in the treaty, the provisions of which we are called upon to interpret, but also from the principles lying at the foundation, which concern the rights and liberty of every citizen of the United States. I cannot but think the denial of the power to grant the writ of *habeas corpus*, in this case, is calculated to shake the authority of a long line of decisions in this court, from Hamilton's case, decided in 1795, down to the present one. That case, as understood and expounded in the case of Bollman and Swartwout, in 1807, which received the most deliberate consideration of the court, and to which the doctrine in Hamilton's case was applied, held that this great writ was within the cognizance of the court, under the 14th section of the Judiciary Act, in all cases where the prisoner was restrained of his liberty, " under, or by color of the authority of the United States," and no case has held the contrary since that decision, with the exception of that of Metzger, decided in 1847, which, I have already stated, stands alone, but which distinctly admits the power and jurisdiction of the court in the case before us. This writ has always been justly regarded as the stable bulwark of civil liberty; and undoubtedly, in the hands of a firm and independent judiciary, no person, be he citizen or alien, can be subjected to illegal restraint, or be deprived of his liberty, except according to the law of the land. So essential to the security of the personal rights of the citizen was the uninterrupted operation and effect of this writ, regarded by the founders of the Republic, that even Congress cannot suspend it, except when, in cases of rebellion or invasion, the public safety may require it. I cannot, therefore, consent to cripple or limit the authority conferred upon this court by the Constitution and laws to issue it, by technical and narrow construction; but, on the contrary, prefer to follow the free and enlarged interpretation always given, when dealing with it by the courts of England, from which country it has been derived. They expound the exercise of the power benignly and liberally in favor of the deliverance of the subject from all unlawful imprisonment; and, when restrained of his liberty, he may appeal to the highest common-law court in the kingdom, to inquire into the cause of it. So liberally do the courts of England deal with this writ, and so unrestricted is its operation in favor of the security of the personal rights of the subject, that the decision of one court or magistrate upon the return to it, refusing to discharge the prisoner, is no bar to the issuing of a second, or third, or more, by any other court or magistrate having jurisdiction of the case, and it may remand or discharge, according to its judgment, upon the same matters. 13 M. & Welsby, 679; 9 Ad. & Ellis, 731; 1 East, 314; 14 Id. 91; 2 Salk. 503; 5 M. & Welsby, 47. Upon the whole, I am satisfied, that the prisoner is in confinement under the treaty and act of Congress, without any lawful authority. I am of opinion, therefore, that the writ of *habeas corpus* should issue in the case, to bring up the prisoner.

1. On the ground that the judiciary possesses no jurisdiction to entertain the proceedings under the treaty for the apprehension and committal of the alleged fugitive, without a previous requisition, made under the authority of Great Britain, upon the President of the United States, and his authority obtained for the purpose.

2. That the United States Commissioner, in this case, is not an officer within the treaty or act of Congress, upon whom the power is conferred, to hear and determine the question of criminality, upon which the surrender is to be made.

3. That there was no competent evidence before the Commissioner, if he possessed that power, to issue the warrant. And

4. Upon these grounds, the Circuit Court ought to have discharged the prisoner, instead of remanding him into custody, and its decision in the case is a proper subject of review by this court, by virtue of the writ of *habeas corpus*.

Mr. Chief Justice TANEY.

I concur in opinion with my brother Nelson. The questions involved in this application are very grave ones; and I should have felt it to be my duty to state the grounds on which my opinion has been formed, had not the whole subject been so fully and, to my mind, satisfactorily discussed by him. But, concurring, as I do, in all that he has said, I shall forbear any discussion on my part, and content myself with expressing my entire assent to the opinion he has just delivered.

Mr. Justice DANIEL.

The question just disposed of by the court, involving the lives and liberties, not only of those who from abroad may seek protection under our laws, but the lives and liberties of our own citizens, is undoubtedly one of the most important which can claim the vigilance of our government in every department. Having deliberately compared my own views of this vital question with what has been so well expressed by my brother Nelson, and concurring, as I do, in all that he has said upon it, I deem it unnecessary to do more than thus solemnly to attest my adherence to the great principles of law, justice, and liberty vindicated by him.

Order.

On consideration of the petitions for writs of *habeas corpus* and of *certiorari*, filed in this case, and of the arguments of counsel thereupon had, — It is now here considered, ordered, and adjudged by this court, that the writs prayed for be, and the same are hereby, denied; and that the said petitions be, and the same are hereby, dismissed.

DAVIS B. LAWLER, TIMOTHY WALKER, STEPHEN S. L'HOMME-
DIEU, GEORGE GRAHAM, JOHN S. HARRISON, AND JACOB BUR-
NET, PLAINTIFFS IN ERROR, v. JAMES H. AND JOHN WALKER.

Where the Supreme Court of a State certified that there was "drawn in question
the validity of statutes of the State of Ohio," &c., without naming the statutes, this
was not enough to give jurisdiction to this court, under the 25th section of the
Judiciary Act.
Nor, in this case, would the court have had jurisdiction if the statutes had been
named, because, —
In 1816, the Legislature of Ohio passed an "Act to prohibit the issuing and circulation of unauthorized bank paper," and in 1839, an act amendatory thereof; and
the question was, whether or not a canal company, incorporated in 1837, was subject to these acts. In deciding that it was, the Supreme Court of Ohio only gave
a construction to an act of Ohio, which neither of itself, nor by its application,
involved in any way a repugnancy to the Constitution of the United States, by
impairing the obligation of a contract.
The case of the Commercial Bank of Cincinnati v. Buckingham's Executors, (5
How. 317,) examined and sustained.

THIS case was brought up, by writ of error, from the Supreme
Court of the State of Ohio, under the 25th section of the Judiciary Act.

As the case was decided upon the point of jurisdiction, it
will be necessary to state only so much of it as to show what
the question was which came before this court. See 18 Ohio
Rep. 151.

James H. Walker and Jóhn Walker, partners in trade, under
the name of J. H. and J. Walker, brought a writ against the
plaintiffs in error in the Hamilton Court of Common Pleas, in
Ohio. The action was brought to recover $2,000 from the
plaintiffs in error, as directors, stockholders, or otherwise interested in an association known as the Cincinnati and Whitewater Canal Company. The evidence upon the trial was, that
the plaintiffs had become the holders of a large amount of such
notes as the following :

No. 18667.   D.
      1   1
The Cincinnati & Whitewater Canal Co. promise to pay one
dollar to R. McCurdy, or order, twelve months after date, for
value received, at their office, Cincinnati, 9th Nov. 1840.
    SAM. E. FOOTE, Sec'y.   J. BONSALL Pres't.
    No. 1.   Indorsed " R. McCurdy."

The court charged the jury as follows : —
That, if the paper was issued under the directions or orders
of the defendants, and intended to circulate as currency, they
would be liable in this action, whether issued for the individual
benefit of the defendants or for the benefit of the Cincinnati

13 *

and Whitewater Canal Company; that if the company had issued notes not intended to circulate as a currency, as bank paper generally does, in the ordinary form, but merely to pay off their creditors, the defendants would not be liable; that if the defendants, in issuing said notes, acted merely as directors of the Cincinnati and Whitewater Canal Company, and within the limits of their corporate powers, they would not be personally liable; but that said charter of said company did not authorize the issuing of notes designed or calculated to circulate as money, and therefore would not protect the defendants, if the jury should be satisfied that they issued such notes; that although, in ordinary cases, where notes are made payable to order, it may be necessary for a plaintiff to prove the indorsement, yet, if the jury find, in this case, that these notes were issued and intended to circulate as a currency, it is not necessary to prove the handwriting of the indorser, and the mere fact of the plaintiffs having the notes in their possession is *primâ facie* evidence of ownership.

The jury found a verdict for the plaintiffs, for $3,452.10.   ui

The Supreme Court of Ohio affirmed the judgment of the Court of Hamilton County, and gave the following certificate:

In this cause, the judgment of the Court of Common Pleas having been affirmed, it is now certified that this is the highest court of law in the State of Ohio, in which a decision of this suit could be had; and that there is drawn in question the validity of statutes of the State of Ohio, in which it is claimed by plaintiffs in error, those statutes are in violation of the Constitution of the United States; and which statutes have been held valid and binding by this court, notwithstanding such objections.   And this certificate is ordered to be made part of the record.

The defendants brought the case up to this court.

It was argued upon printed briefs by Messrs. *Fox, Walker,* and *Grosbeck* for the plaintiffs in error, and by *Mr. Chase,* with whom was *Mr. Rockwell,* for the defendants in error.

The question of jurisdiction was thus stated by one of the counsel for the plaintiffs in error, *Mr. Walker.*

This case comes before this court under that clause of the 25th section of the Judiciary Act, (1 U. S. Stat. at Large, 85,) which authorizes a writ of error to a State court in the case of " a final judgment in any suit in the highest court of law of a State in which the decision in the suit could be had, where is drawn in question the validity of a statute of a State, on the ground of its being repugnant to the Constitution of the United States, and the decision is in favor of such its validity."

This state of fact appears on the face of the record. The validity of the statute of Ohio, of March 18, 1839, " further to amend the act entitled ' an act to prohibit the issuing and circulating of unauthorized bank paper,' " (Swan's Stat. 140,) was drawn in question. It was drawn in question upon the ground that it was repugnant to the Constitution of the United States, because it impaired the obligation of the contract made by the State of Ohio with the Whitewater Canal Company, in the act incorporating the latter; and the decision of. the State court — the highest court of law in the State in which the decision could be had — was in favor of the validity of that statute.

The case therefore arises where this court may entertain jurisdiction. Commonwealth Bank of Kentucky v. Griffith, 14 Peters, 56.

On the other hand, the counsel for the defendant in error contended that this court has no jurisdiction. It is not a case in which was drawn in question the validity of a statute of a State, on the ground of its being repugnant to the Constitution of the United States, and in which the decision was in favor of such its validity.

1. The case is within the decision of the court in the case Commercial Bank v. Buckingham, 5 Howard, 317.

The defendants below did not claim that the acts of Ohio were unconstitutional; their claim was that those statutes imposed a penalty for their violation, and that thus the action was barred in four years under the general statute of limitation of the State. The Supreme Court of Ohio decided otherwise; and as they claim erroneously, and they *now* claim on account of that erroneous decision to give this court jurisdiction.

2. It does not appear from the record that the question was raised at the trial as to the constitutionalty of the Ohio statutes of 1816 and 1839.

Nothing of the kind is shown, o. to be inferred, from the pleadings in the case.

From the bill of exceptions it appears that the plaintiffs in error excepted, on three grounds, to the admission of testimony and claimed the charge of the Judge to the jury on nine points but no one of them has any reference to, nor in any manne involves this question.

The charge itself presents no such question; no reference whatever is made to any such question in the assignments of errors in the Court of Common Pleas or Supreme Court of Ohio.

The only thing on the record, showing that the constitutional validity of any law was in question, is found in the certificate ordered by the court to be entered on the record, (p. 19,) " that there is drawn in question the validity of statutes of the State of

Ohio," &c., without saying what statutes, or on what ground the decision was made, or in what manner statutes of Ohio were connected with the subject-matter of the case before the court; nor is there any thing in any part of the record showing that these statutes of 1816 and 1839 were in question, nor any reference made to them.

Mr. Justice WAYNE delivered the opinion of the court.

We do not think that this court has jurisdiction of this case We cannot find in the record, nor can it be inferred from any part of it, (the certificate of the Supreme Court included) which of the statutes of Ohio were declared to be valid, which has been alleged to be in conflict with the Constitution of the United States.

The 25th section of the act to establish the judicial courts of the United States, requires something more definite than such a certificate, to give to this court jurisdiction.

The conflict of a State law with the Constitution of the United States, and a decision by a State court in favor of its validity, must appear on the face of the record, before it can be reëxamined in this court. It must appear in the pleadings of the suit, or from the evidence in the course of trial, in the instructions asked for, or from exceptions taken to the ruling of the court. It must be, that such a question was necessarily involved in the decision, and that the State court would not have given a judgment without deciding it.

The language of the section is, that no other cause can be assigned, or shall be regarded as a ground of reversal, than such as appears on the face of the record.

This certificate is, that the Supreme Court of Ohio held that certain statutes of Ohio were valid, which had been alleged to be in violation of the Constitution of the United States, without naming what those statutes were. This is neither within the letter nor spirit of the act.

If permitted, it would make the State courts judges of the jurisdiction of this court, and might cause them to take jurisdiction in cases in which conflicts between the State laws and the Constitution and the laws of the United States did not exist.

The statutes complained of in this case should have been stated. Without that, the court cannot apply them to the subject-matter of litigation, to determine whether or not they violated the Constitution or laws of the United States.

This court has already passed upon a certificate of a like kind from Ohio, in the case of the Commercial Bank and Eunice Buckingham's Executors, 5 How. 317. That was more to the purpose than this, but it was declared to be insufficient to give jurisdiction to this court. In that case it was certified that the plaintiffs in error relied upon the charter granted them in February, 1829, and the 4th section of it was given; and they claimed, if a section of an act of 1824 was applied in the construction of their charter, that it would be a violation of the Constitution of the United States, because it impaired the obligation of a contract. It was also stated tha the objection had been overruled, and that a decision had been given in favor of the validity of the act of 1824. When the case was considered here, we first examined our jurisdiction under the 25th section, and determined against it. Not because we did not think that the certificate was a part of the record, or that it did not show sufficiently the act which the plaintiffs in error alleged could not be applied in that case without impairing the obligation of a contract, but because we thought, from our view of the entire record, that the only question which was raised on the trial of the case in the State court, was one of construction of two Ohio statutes. And that was, whether or not the bank was legally liable to pay on account of its refusal to pay its notes in specie, the six per cent. imposed by the act of 1824. as a penalty for such refusal, in addition to the twelve per cent. imposed by its charter. The constitutionality of the act of 1824 was not denied. Indeed, it was admitted. But it was urged that the application to make the bank pay the penalty imposed by it, and twelve per cent. besides, would impair the obligation of a contract which the State had made with the corporation in their charter. Here, then, the validity of the act of 1824 was not drawn in question, on the ground of its being repugnant to the Constitution, treaties, or laws of the United States, nor was a point raised for the construction of any clause of the Constitution, of a treaty, or of a statute of the United States. The admission of the constitutionality and validity of the act of 1824, only raised a question of construction of two State statutes, one of which it was said would be repugnant to the other, if its penalty should be applied to the bank, in addition to that imposed by its charter, without words implying that the bank would not be liable to an universal statute, passed before the bank was chartered, which imposes six per cent. upon all banks which should refuse to pay their notes in specie. The court decided, that the bank was liable to the penalty of the act of 1824, but it erroneously supposed, because a constitutional point had been made in the argument, that it was one which necessarily arose from the case itself, and that it could not give a judgment in the case upon its merits without deciding that it involved the question of a conflict with the Constitution of the United States.

It was in that view of the case that this court said, in its opinion, — "It is not enough that the record shows that the plaintiff contended and claimed, that the judgment of the court impaired the obligation of a contract and violated the provision of the· Constitution of the United States, and that this claim was overruled by the court, but it must appear by clear and necessary intendment, from the record, that the question must have been raised and must have been decided in order to induce the judgment." And it was also in this view, when one State statute was said to be repugnant to another, both being admitted to be constitutional, that it was said in that case, " It is the peculiar province and privilege of the State courts to construe their own statutes," and when they did so, "it was no part of the functions of this court to review their decisions," or, in such cases, "to assume jurisdiction over them, on the pretence that their judgments have impaired the obligation of contracts."

Having said that this court had not jurisdiction in this case on account of the insufficiency of the certificate, we now say, if it could be made as definite as that in the case of Buckingham's Executors, by inserting in it the statutes of Ohio, which the court supposed involved a constitutional question, that it would not give this court jurisdiction. Then the cases would be so much alike that the Buckingham case would rule this as to the question of jurisdiction. In the Buckingham case it was urged that the penalty, in a general statute upon banks, for refusing to pay their notes in specie, could not be imposed upon a bank subsequently chartered, in addition to the penalty imposed by its charter, without a violation of the Constitution of the United States. It is urged, in argument in this case, that a statute passed in 1816, entitled " an act to prohibit the issuing and circulating of unauthorized bank paper," which was amended in 1839, could not be applied to make the defendants liable to pay notes which were issued in 1840 by a canal company, in its corporate name, and which notes were meant for circulation in the community as bank paper. It was not contended that the canal company could legally issue such paper for circulation as money, though it was said they could give notes payable to order in payment of its debts.

It was not denied that the company could give notes in payment of debts, but it was said, that they could not make them for that purpose and for circulation, as bank paper. The point then raised for decision, was, whether the canal company could do so, without making its stockholders and directors liable to pay them to the holders of the notes, under the statute of 1816, amended in 1839. The Supreme Court decided that the defendants in this case, being directors and stockholders of the canal company were liable, by the statutes of 1816 and 1839, to pay such notes. It seems to us, that the statement gives its own answer, and that the Supreme Court, in making its decision, only gave a construction to an act of Ohio, which neither of itself, nor by its application, involved in any way a repugnancy to the Constitution of the United States, by impairing the obligation of a contract. Whether the construction of the act and the charter of the canal company was correct, or not, we do not say. We do not mean to discuss that point, or to give any opinion upon it; but we mean to say, that the construction does not violate a constitutional point under the 25th section of the Judiciary Statute, so as to give this court jurisdiction of this cause.

If more was wanting in aid of our conclusion, it is to be found in the pleadings in the case, in the evidence given on the trial, the objections made to the admissibility of certain parts of it, in the prayers of the defendant to the court to instruct the jury, and in the charge which the court gave. By no one of them is a constitutional question raised. It was only suggested, in argument, and on that account it was, that the court certified that the "validity of statutes of Ohio was drawn into question, which were said to be in violation of the Constitution of the United States, and not because the court considered, that such a point had been rightly raised before it, under the 25th section of the Judiciary Act of 1789."

We do not think it necessary to repeat any thing which this court has hitherto said, from an early day to the present, concerning the 25th section. Its interpretation will be found in the case of Crowell v. Randall, 10 Peters, 308; in other cases, cited in that case; and in Armstrong v. The Treasurer of Athens County, 16 Peters, 281. We shall direct this suit to be dismissed for want of jurisdiction.

Order.

This cause came on to be heard on the transcript of the record from the Supreme Court of the State of Ohio, and was argued by counsel. On consideration whereof, it is now here ordered and adjudged by this court, that this cause be, and the same is hereby, dismissed, for the want of jurisdiction.

THOMAS OTIS LE ROY, AND DAVID SMITH, PLAINTIFFS IN ER-
ROR, *v.* BENJAMIN TATHAM, JUNIOR, GEORGE N. TATHAM,
AND HENRY B. TATHAM.

In a patent for improvements upon the machinery used for making pipes and tubes
from lead, or tin, when in a set, or·solid state, by forcing it under great pressure,
from out of a receiver, through apertures, dies, and cores, the claim of the patentees
was thus stated : " What we claim as our invention, and desire to secure by letters-
patent, is the combination of the following parts, above described, to wit, the core
and bridge, or guide-piece, the chamber, and the die, when used to form pipes of
metal, under heat and pressure, in the manner set forth, or in any other manner
substantially the same."
The Circuit Court charged the jury, " that the originality did not consist in the
novelty of the machinery, but in bringing a newly discovered principle into practical application, by which an useful article of manufacture is produced, and wrought
pipe made as distinguished from cast pipe."
This instruction was erroneous.
Under the claim of the patent, the combination of the machinery must be novel.
The newly discovered principle, to wit, that lead could be forced, by extreme
pressure, when in a set or solid state, to cohere and form a pipe, was not in the
patent, and the question whether it was or was not the subject of a patent, was not
in the case.

Mr. Justice Curtis, having been of counsel for the defendants
in error, upon the letters-patent drawn in question in this case,
did not sit at the hearing.

This case was brought up, by writ ·of error, from the Circuit
Court of the United States for the Southern District of New
York.

The declaration was filed by the defendants in error, on the
8th of May, 1817, to recover damages in a plea of trespass
upon the·case, from the plaintiffs in error, and Robert. W. Lowber, for the alleged infringement of their patent, for new and
useful improvements in machinery, or apparatus for making
pipes and tubes from metallic substances.

The declaration alleged, that John and Charles Hanson, of
Huddersfield, England, were the inventors of the alleged improvements, on or before the 31st of August, 1837.

That on the 10th of January, 1840, the Hansons, assigned. in
writing, to H. B. and B. Tatham, (two of the defendants in error,) the full and exclusive right to the said improvements.

That on the 29th of March, 1841, letters-patent of the United
States were granted to H. B. & B. Tatham, as assignees of the
Hansons, for the said improvements.

That on the 12th of October,·1841, H. B. & B. Tatham,
assigned to G. N. Tatham, (the remaining defendant in error,)
one undivided third part of the said letters-patent.

That, on the 14th of March, 1846,·the said letters-patent having been surrendered, on account of the defective specifications

of the said improvements, new letters-patent were issued therefor, on an amended specification, whereby there was granted to
the plaintiffs below, their heirs, &c., for the term of fourteen
years from the 31st of August, 1837, the full and exclusive right
of making, vending, &c., the said improvements; a description
whereof was annexed to and made a part of such patent.

That the letters-patent were of the value of $50,000; and that
the defendants below had wrongfully and unlawfully made, used,
and vended the said improvements, and made lead pipe to the
amount of 2,000 tons, thereby to the injury of the plaintiffs;
$20,000.

To this declaration, the defendants, Le Roy and Smith, pleaded not guilty; the defendant, Lowber, making no defence, and
permitting a default to be taken against him.

The cause was tried at the April Term, 1849, and a verdict
rendered by the jury in favor of the plaintiffs, for $11,394, and
costs, and a bill of exceptions was tendered by the defendants
below.

On the trial of the cause below, the plaintiffs produced,—

1. Their patent of 1846, and the specification referred to
therein, and making a part of the same.

2. They read in evidence certain agreements between the defendant, Lowber, and the defendants, Le Roy and Smith.

3. They gave evidence, tending to prove that J. & C. Hanson were the original and first inventors of the improvement;
that the invention was a valuable one, &c.

4. That lead, recently become set, under heat and pressure,
in a close vessel, would reunite perfectly after a separation of
its parts; that, in the process described in the said patent, pipe
was so made; that the Hansons were the first and original discoverers thereof; and that such discovery, and its reduction to
a practical result, in the mode described in the patent, was useful and important.

5. That the defendants, Smith and Leroy, had been jointly
engaged with Lowber in making lead pipe upon the plan described in the letters-patent, and selling the same, and had thus
made and sold large quantities of pipe; that the agreement between them, relative to the manufacture of pipe, was colorable
only, and was made as a cover to protect Le Roy and Smith,
and throw the responsibility on the defendant, Lowber, who
was insolvent.

6. That the improvement described in the said letters-patent
was the same invention for which letters-patent had been granted
to the Hansons, in England, and to H. B. & B. Tatham, here,
as their assignees.

7. That the plaintiffs had been ready, and had offered to sell

the said invention, and had sold the same for a large portion of the United States, within the last eighteen months.

The defendants below then read in evidence, —

1. The description of the English patent to the Hansons.

2. The patent to H. B. & B. Tatham, of 1841, and the specification thereof.

3. The specification of an English patent, granted to Thomas Burr, of 11th April, 1820.

4. The patent and specification of Burroughs Titus, granted in 1831.

5. The patent granted to George W. Potter, in 1833.

6. The evidence of George Fox, tending to show the invention and use by him of a similar machine, in 1830.

7. The specification of a patent to John Hague, in 1822.

8. The specification of a patent granted to Busk & Harvey, in 1817.

9. The specification of a patent granted to Ellis & Burr, in 1836.

10. The specification of a patent granted to Joseph Bramah, in 1797.

11. The defendants then gave evidence tending to prove that J. & C. Hanson were not the original and first inventors of the combination of machinery described in the letters-patent.

12. That the invention was not useful, nor the lead pipe, made upon the plan described, good.

13. That the combination of machinery described in public works, as having been invented by Titus, Potter, Fox, Hague, Bramah, and Busk & Harvey, were substantially the same as that described in the plaintiffs' patent.

14. That lead, when recently become set, under heat and extreme pressure, in a close vessel, would not reunite perfectly after a separation of its parts; and that, in the process as described in the plaintiffs' patent, it was not in a set, but in a fluid state when it passed the bridge.

15. That the defendants, Le Roy & Smith were not concerned in the manufacture of the pipe, or in making or using the machinery; that it was made for them by the defendant, Lowber, at a certain price per hundred pounds; and that they had not infringed upon the patent of the plaintiffs.

16. That the improvement described in the plaintiff's patent, of 1846, was not the same invention as that for which letters-patent had previously been granted to the Hansons, and to H. B. & B. Tatham.

17. That, for the space of eighteen months, from the date of the patent of 1841, the plaintiffs had neglected to put and continue on sale to the public, on reasonable trust, the invention or discovery for which the said patent issued.

The evidence being closed, the case was argued before the jury, after the court had given the charge, which will be presently stated. The jury found a verdict for the plaintiffs, which, when increased by the court, amounted to. $11,748.60. The following bill of exceptions brought up the rulings of the court upon the several points made:

The evidence being closed, the Judge charged the jury

That the first question which it was material to determine was, what was the invention or discovery of John and Charles Hanson, for which their patent had issued, as the precise character of that invention had been the subject of controversy on the trial.

The patentees state in their specification, that the invention consists in certain improvements upon, and additions to, machinery for making pipes of metal, capable of being pressed, as described in Burr's patent, dated April 11, 1820. They then describe Burr's apparatus, and the process by which the pipe was made by it, and state the defects of that plan, in consequence of which, they say, it failed to go into general use.

These defects they claim to have overcome and remedied; and state that they had found that lead, and some of its alloys, when just set, or short of fluidity, and under heat and great pressure, in a close vessel, would reunite, after a separation of its parts, as completely as if it had not been separated, or, in other words, that, under these circumstances, it could be welded.

That, on this discovery, and in reference to and in connection with it, they made a change in the machinery of Burr, by which they succeeded in making perfect pipes, and were enabled to use a bridge at the end of the cylinder and short core, and thus surmount the difficulty of the Burr machine.

They also state, that they do not claim any of the parts — the cylinder, core, die, or bridge; but that they claim the combination when used to form pipes of metal, under heat and pressure, in the way they have described.

There can be no doubt that, if this combination is new, and produces a new and useful result, it is the proper subject of a patent. The result is a new manufacture.

And even if the mere combination of machinery in the abstract is not new, still, if used and applied in connection with the practical development of a principle, newly discovered; producing a new and useful result, the subject is patentable. To which last opinion and decision, the counsel for the defendants did then and there except.

In this view, the improvement of the plaintiffs is the application of a combination of machinery to a new end, — to the development and application of a new principle, resulting in a new and useful manufacture.

That the discovery of a new principle is not patentable; but it must be embodied and brought into operation by machinery, so as to produce a new and useful result.

Upon this view of the patent, it is an important question, for the jury to determine, from the evidence, whether the fact is established on which the alleged improvement is founded, that lead, in a set or semi-solid state, can thus be reunited or welded after separation.

The Judge here commented briefly upon the testimony, referring to the experiments which were testified to, and the results of which were exhibited to the jury, on the part of the plaintiffs and defendants, and, in continuation, stated:

That there was one experiment which was testified to by Mr. Keller, and the result of which was shown to the jury, which was made under circumstances that seem not to be subject to any misapprehension, and which, if he is not mistaken, and his testimony is correct, would seem to settle the question. But this was a question of fact, to be decided by the jury on the evidence. Hereupon, the counsel for the defendants excepted to this part of the charge of the Judges. — That it had been objected, that the improvement described in the patent of March 14, 1846, was different from that of March 29, 1841. The act only authorized a reissue for the same invention, the first specification being defective. — That he had compared the descriptions contained in the two patents; and, though the language was in some parts different, it would be found that the improvement was substantially the same, and that he therefore apprehended they would have no great difficulty in this branch of the case; to which the defendants' counsel excepted. — That it was also objected, that the plaintiffs' patent was invalid, for want of originality; that the invention had been before described in public works, and Bramah, Hague, Titus, Fox, and Potter, were relied on by the defendants. — That, in the view taken by the court, in the construction of the patent, it was not material whether the mere combinations of machinery referred to were similar to the combination used by the Hansons; because the originality did not consist in the novelty of the machinery, but in bringing a newly-discovered principle into practical application, by which a useful article of manufacture is produced, and wrought pipe made, as distinguished from cast pipe. Hereupon the defendants' counsel excepted.

That in the patents referred to, from the year 1797 to 1832, the combination which was claimed to be identical, was confessedly used for making pipe, by casting with fluid lead in a mould, and after it was set by the application of water, forcing it out.

And the question is, whether any of these inventions are substantially the same as the plaintiffs'; whether, even if by these modes pipe had been successfully made for common use, it would have been made in the same manner as the Hansons'; to which opinion the counsel for the defendants excepted.

That it was further objected that the patentees have forfeited their rights, on account of having omitted to put and continue the invention on sale within eighteen months after the patent was granted, upon reasonable terms. The Judge here commented upon the testimony on this part of the case, and in continuation said:

That it was not essential, under the section of the statue referred to, that the patentees should take active means for the purpose of putting their invention in market, and forcing a sale, but that they should at all times be ready to sell at a fair price, when a reasonable offer was made.

That it was for the jury to say whether it was put and continued on sale, under this view of the law; to which opinion the counsel for the defendants excepted.

That the defendants, LeRoy, and Smith, contend that they have not infringed the plaintiffs' patent; that they were but the purchasers of the pipe, and that Lowber was the manufacturer, under the agreement which has been read.

The Judge here referred to the evidence on this branch of the case, and said:

That if the contract made by the defendants with Lowber, was *bonâ fide*, and they had no connection with the manufacture of the articles, except to furnish lead and pay him a given price, deducting the expenses; and if the contract was in fact carried out and acted upon in that manner, then the defendants would not be liable. But if the agreement was only colorable, and was entered into for the purpose of deriving the benefit and profits of the business, without assuming the responsibility for the use of the invention, and for the purpose of throwing the responsibility on Lowber, who was insolvent, then they were as responsible as he was.

That aiding and assisting a person in carrying on the business and in operating the machinery, would implicate the parties so engaged. If, therefore, these defendants participated actively in conducting the machine, directing and supervising its operations; if the evidence establishes that position, then, as aiding and assisting, they are as responsible as Lowber, (to which last opinion and decision the defendants' counsel excepted.)

14*

Prior to the giving of the preceding charge to the jury, the defendants' counsel requested the court to instruct them according to the following written proposition submitted; and his honor, after he delivered the said charge, took up the said propositions in their order, and gave the instructions to the jury, which are respectively subjoined thereto.

Proposition I. If the jury believe that the agreements executed on the 13th of April and 13th of May, 1846, by which Lowber, as manufacturer, was to make the pipe for LeRoy & Co., on his machine, at 55 cents the 100 pounds, was real and *bona fide*, on an actual dissolution of the partnership of Lowber & LeRoy, and not colorable to throw the responsibility of working the machine on Lowber alone, then the plaintiffs cannot recover.

Upon which, his honor said that he had already given all the instructions he deemed necessary on that point; the proposition was correct, and it was for the jury to decide that fact.

Proposition II. That even if the Tathams first introduced the pipe in question in this country, as an article of commerce, that does not give them any right to recover, unless the patents under which they claim were good and valid, for an invention not before known, used, or described in a public work.

Upon which his honor instructed the jury, as requested by the defendants' counsel.

Proposition III. That if the jury believe that the combination patented by the plaintiffs was before patented by Burroughs Titus, or any one else in this country, or patented and described in a well known public work abroad, the plaintiffs cannot recover, although such machines thus patented were not actually put in operation, so as to make pipe for the public.

Upon which his honor instructed the jury that he had already stated to them that the plaintiffs' invention did not consist in the mere combination of machinery, and, therefore, if those patents were for casting lead pipe, the point was not material; that it was not necessary that they would have made pipe for public use to defeat a subsequent patent. To which instruction, and refusal to instruct the jury as requested, the defendants' counsel excepted.

Proposition IV. That the Tatham patent is void on its face, the Burr machine having the entire combination, including heat and pressure, and the lead in a set state. The patent is void for claiming too much; should only have been for the improvement, viz. substituting the bridge and short core for the long core, and not for the whole combination.

His honor declined to give this instruction, to which the defendants' counsel excepted.

Proposition V. That the bridge and short core having been before patented in this country by Burroughs Titus, and also before used in other machines, no claim could be made for introducing into Burr's combination such bridge.

Upon which his honor instructed the jury as follows: Undoubtedly that is so, but that is not the plaintiffs' claim.

Proposition VI. That the state of the lead, when used as described in the plaintiffs' specification, being a principle of nature, is not the subject of a patent, either alone or in combination with the machine mentioned in that specification.

To which his honor stated, the first part of the proposition was correct, and the latter part not; and the defendants' counsel excepted.

Proposition VII. That the using of a metal in a certain state, or at a certain temperature, alone, or in combination with a machine, was not the subject of a patent.

To which his honor stated, I have already instructed the jury that the invention, as described by the Hansons, is a patentable subject; to which the defendants' counsel excepted.

Proposition VIII. That if the jury believe that the combination of cylinder, piston, bridge, short core, die, and chamber, under heat and pressure, was before patented in this country, by Burroughs Titus, then the plaintiffs cannot recover.

Whereupon, his honor instructed the jury, that novelty in the mere combination of the machinery was not essential to the plaintiffs' right to recover, except as connected with the development and application of the principle before mentioned; to which the defendants' counsel excepted.

Proposition IX. That if the jury believe that the same combination of cylinder, piston, bridge, short core, die, and chamber, under heat and pressure, had before been patented in England, by Bramah, and published in a well known work, then the plaintiffs cannot recover.

His honor instructed the jury, that Bramah's patent and the Tathams' were not identical, and declined to instruct them as requested; to all which the defendants' counsel excepted.

Proposition X. That if the jury believed that the Burr, Bramah, Titus, and Hague machines, or either of them, were published to the world in well known public works, and had the same combination, in whole or in part, as the Hanson machine, up to a certain point, the Tathams' patent is void, for claiming too much, viz. the whole combination.

His honor instructed the jury, that he had explained to them his views on that part of the case, and declined to instruct them as requested, in the form of which the proposition was stated; and to which the defendants' counsel excepted.

Proposition XI. That the reissue of the patent of 1846, on which alone the plaintiffs can claim, was not warranted by the patent of 1841, it being for a different, and not the same invention, misdescribed by inadvertence, accident, or mistake; and, in fact, was a new patent, under color of a reissue.

That if the jury believe that the reissue of 1846 was for a different invention from the patent of 1841, and not for the same invention, misdescribed by inadvertence, accident, or mistake, then the plaintiffs cannot recover.

His honor declined to instruct the jury according to the first branch of this proposition, to which the defendants' counsel excepted; but did instruct them in the affirmative, upon the last branch thereof.

Proposition XII. That if the jury believe that the combination patented, was before described in some well known public work, either in this country or in England, the plaintiffs cannot recover, although such machine, or the pipe made by it, was never introduced in this country.

Upon which his honor instructed the jury in the affirmative.

Proposition XIII. If the jury believe that the combination claimed was before known or used, to make lead pipe, by others than the Hansons or the Tathams, the plaintiffs are not entitled to recover, no matter how limited such knowledge or use was, if the invention was not kept secret.

Upon which his honor instructed the jury in the affirmative.

Proposition XIV. That if the Maccaroni machine, or the Busk and Harvey clay-pipe machine, contained the same combination as the plaintiffs' machine, that the plaintiffs cannot recover, by reason of applying the same combination to a new use.

Which instructions his honor declined to give, and stated that he had explained to them his views on that subject; and the defendants' counsel excepted.

Proposition XV. That if the jury believe that Mr. Lowber's machine was used by his men when the lead was in a fluid, and not in a set, or solid state, then there was no infringement, and the plaintiffs cannot recover, if the plaintiffs' patent were valid.

Upon which his honor instructed the jury in the affirmative.

Proposition XVI. That the jury are the sole and exclusive judges, as questions of fact, whether the combination and process were the same in plaintiffs' machine as was in Bramah's, or in any other of the machines proved on the trial.

Upon which his honor charged the jury that this was so undoubtedly, subject, however, to the principles of law, as laid down in his preceding charge and instructions; to which the defendants' counsel excepted.

Proposition XVII. That if the jury believe that the lead, when it may be successfully used to make pipe with plaintiffs' machine, must not be in a set or solid state, as described in their specification, and that it can only be thus used in a fluid or pasty state, then that the patent is void, and the jury should find for the defendants, on the ground that the specification does not fairly and fully describe the nature of the invention claimed, nor the condition in which the lead should be used, so as to enable the public to ascertain the true nature of the invention, the manner of using the machine, and the condition in which the lead ought to be used.

Which instruction his honor answered in the affirmative.

The jury then retired to consider their verdict, under the said charge and instructions; and subsequently, on the 25th day of May, 1849, returned into court with a verdict for the said plaintiffs for $11,394 damages, and six cents costs.

And, inasmuch as the said several matters aforesaid, do not appear by the record of the said verdict, the said defendants' counsel did then and there request his honor, the said Judge, to put his seal to this bill of exceptions, containing the said several matters aforesaid; and his honor, the said Judge, did, in pursuance of the said request, and of the statute in such case made and provided, put his seal to this bill of exceptions, containing the said several matters aforesaid, at the city of New York, aforesaid, the same 25th day of May, 1849.   S. NELSON.

The case was argued by *Mr. Gillett* and *Mr. Noyes*, with whom was *Mr. Barbour*, for the plaintiffs in error, and by *Mr. Cutting* and *Mr. Staples*, for the defendants in error.

The points made by the counsel for the plaintiffs in error, were the following.

1. In construing a patent, and deciding what are the inventions patented thereby, the summing up is conclusive. Nothing is patented but what is expressly claimed. Moody v. Fiske, 2 Mason, 112, 118; Rex v. Cutler, 1 Starkie, R. 354; Davies on Patents, 398, 404; Bovil v. Moore, 2 Marsh. R. 211; Wyeth v. Stone, 1 Story, R. 285; Hovey v. Stevens, 3 W. & M. 17.

2. What is described in a patent, and not claimed, whether invented by the patentee or not, is dedicated to the public, and cannot be afterwards claimed, as a part of his patent, in a reissue, or otherwise. Battin v. Taggart, Judges Kane and Grier, September 10, 1851; 6th section of act of 1836; Mellus v. Silsbee, 4 Mason, 111; Grant v. Raymond, 6 Pet. 218; Shaw v. Cooper, 7 Pet. 292, 322, 323; Pennock v. Dialogue, 2 Pet. 1, 16.

3. A patent void in part, is void in whole, except when other-

wise provided by statute. Wyeth v. Stone, 1 Story, R. 285, 273 – 293 – 4; Moody v. Fiske, 2 Mason, 118, 119; Woodcock v. Parker, 1 Gall. 438; Evans v. Eaton, 7 Wheat. 356; 5 Cond. R. 302, 314; Bovil v. Moore, Davies's Patents, 398; Id. 2 Marshall, 211; Hill v. Thompson, 3 B. Moore, 244; Bevinton v. Hawks, 4 B. & Ald. 541; Saunders v. Aston, 3 B. & Ald. 881; Kay v. Marshall, 5 Bing. N. C. 492; Gibson v. Brand, 4 M. & Gr. 178; McFarlane v. Price, 1 Starkie, 199; Minton v. Moore, 1 Nev. & P. 595; Rex v. Cutler, 1 Starkie, R. 359.

4. The Judge was bound to present to the consideration of the jury, as a question of fact, in the words of the statute, whether the patentee, being an alien, " had failed and neglected, for the space of eighteen months from the date of the patent, to put and continue on sale to the public, on reasonable terms, the invention for which the patent issued." Tatham and others v. Loring, decision by Judge Story on this patent, cited on brief.

5. It was error in the Judge to instruct the jury that he had examined the surrendered and reissued patent, and found the improvement the same. He should have submitted the question, as one of fact, to the jury, for them to determine, upon the evidence, of the weight of which they were the exclusive judges. It was also error to instruct them that Bramah's and Tatham's patent were not identical. That was a question for the jury. Curtis, sec. 381; Carver v. Braintree, 2 Story, R. 432; Stimpson v. West Chester Railroad Co. 4 Howard, 381.

6. The question, whether the combination had been previously patented, or described in a printed publication, was one of fact, which should have been submitted to the jury.

7. Applying an old machine to a new use, or to produce a new result, is not the subject of a lawful patent. Boulton v. Bull, 2 H. Bl. 487; Lash v. Hague, Web. Pat. 207; Crane v. Price, 4 Mann. & Grang. 580; Huddart v. Grainshaw, Web. Pat. 8; Howe v. Abbott, 2 Story, R. 190, 193; Bean v. Smallwood, 2 Story, R. 408, 410; Hovey v. Stevens, 1 Wood. & M. R. 290, 297, 298; Kay v. Marshall, 5 Bing. N. C. 492, (35 Com. Law R. p. 194, 197, 198); Gibson v. Brand, 4 Mann. & Grang. 179, (43 Com. Law, 100, 110); Hotchkiss v. Greenwood, 11 Howard, 248, 266; Curtis, § 26, 27.

8. Making an addition to an old combination does not authorize a patent for the whole combination. Such a patent would be broader than the invention, and void.

Act 1836, sec. 6. Hindmarch on Pat. 184, 190, and cases cited; Basil v. Gibbs, Davies's Pat. 398, 413; Whittemore v. Cutler, 1 Gall. 478; Barrett v. Hall, 1 Mason, 447, 474; Moody v. Fiske, 2 Mason, 117; Prouty v. Draper, 1 Story, R. 568; Howe v. Abbott, 2 Story, R. 190; Brooks v. Jenkins, 3 McLean, 433;

Evans v. Eaton, 1 Pet. C. C. R. 322; Curtis, sect. 8, 9, 10, 11; Brooks v. Bicknell, 4 McLean, 64, 73; Root v. Ball, 4 McLean, 177, 180; Parker v. Haworth, 4 McLean, 370, 373; Prouty v. Ruggles, 16 Pet. 336, 341; Evans v. Eaton, 7 Wheat. 356; 5 Cond. R. 302, 314.

9. The plaintiffs, Henry B. and Benjamin Tatham, not being inventors, were not authorized to surrender the patent granted to them as assignees, and receive a reissued patent thereon. Patent act of 1837, sec. 6.

10. The reissued patent is void, because issued to a party who was neither an original inventor, nor his assignee. Act of 1837, sec. 6.

11. Neither a principle nor an effect can be patented, but a patent must be for a mode of embodying the former to produce the latter, invented by the patentee. Kemper's case, by Chief Justice Cranch, in Curtis on Pat. 500; Wyeth v. Stone, 1 Story, R. 285; Hill v. Thompson, 8 Taunton, 375; S. C. 4 Com. L. R. 151; Brunton v. Hawks, 4 Barn. & Ald. 541; S. C. 6 Com. L. R. 509; Moody v. Fiske, 2 Mason, 118; Whittemore v. Cutler, 1 Gall. 478, 480; Stone v. Sprague, 1 Story, R. 270. 272; Blanchard v. Sprague, 3 Sumner, 535, 540; S. C. 2 Story, R. 164, 194; Howe v. Abbott, 2 Story, R. 194; Smith v. Downing, decided in 1850 by Judge Woodbury; Detmould v. Reeves, Grier and Kane, Judges, 1851; Boulton v. Watt, 2 H. Bl. 453; S. C. Davis on Pat. 162, 192.

The counsel for the defendants in error made the following points:

No exception was taken to the admission or exclusion of testimony; but solely to the Judge's charge.

The invention for which the patent was granted consisted in the discovery, that, under certain conditions, and by the use and application of certain methods, lead, and some of its alloys, while in a set state, could, after being separated into parts, be re-united and welded, and thus formed into pipe; and also of the mode of doing this; producing thereby a new article of manufacture, wrought lead pipe — avoiding the objections which had always prevented success in casting pipe; and by this discovery overcoming the defects of Burr's method, on which this was an improvement.

The patentees, in describing the invention, say that they "have found from experience that lead and some of its alloys, when recently become set, or in a condition just short of fluidity, being still under heat and extreme pressure, in a close vessel, will reunite perfectly after a separation of its parts," and that, therefore, they construct their machinery as follows — and then proceed to describe the machinery or apparatus, as adapted by them to this discovery, and by which they produce the practical result above stated.

After describing the apparatus and the modes of using it, the patentees repeat, "that the remarkable feature of their invention is, that soft metals, when in a set state, being yet under heat can be made, by extreme pressure, to reunite perfectly, around a core after a separation, and thus be formed into strong pipes or tubes."

And "that the essential difference in the character of this pipe, distinguishing it from all others before made, was, that it was wrought under heat by pressure and constriction from set metal; and that it is not a casting formed in a mould."

And they close by claiming, as their invention, "the combination described by them, when used to form pipes of metal under heat and pressure in the manner set forth."

The Judge, in his charge, in commenting on the patent, states the invention to be substantially as above stated; and to this construction and view of the patent, no exception was taken by the defendants.

The court then proceed further to instruct the jury, and in answer to certain propositions submitted by the plaintiffs in error for the consideration of the court.

I. The first proposition laid down by the court, is, that the mere combination of machinery, not new, in the abstract, when combined with and applied to the practical development of a new principle, to produce a new and useful result, may be the subject of a valid patent. This principle is repeated several times, in different connections, in the course of the charge to the jury; and as often excepted to by the counsel for the defendants.

The counsel for the defendants in error, insist that the above position is correct, and supported by principle, by precedent, and by practice.

1. The position is supported by principle, founded on the statutes giving patents to inventors. He who discovers a new principle, and points out the means of applying it, to produce a new and useful result, comes within the settled construction of the English act, giving a patent for the sole working of any manner of new manufactures. See 6th section of the act 21 James 1, (1623.) By our patent law, any person, having invented or discovered any new manufacture, &c., is entitled to a patent. See 6th section of the act 4th July, 1836. The term new manufacture includes not only the thing produced, but the means of producing it.

2. This principle is supported by authority. Curtis, Pat. § 9. §§ 71 to 91; also chap. 2, pp. 57 to 94, and cases there cited

Earl Dudley's patent for the use of pea or pit coal, in the manufacture of iron. 1 Carpmael, 15; Webster's Patent Cases, 14, S. C. — Nielson's patent for the hot air blast, in connection with common bituminous pit coal, in the manufacture of iron. 8 Mees. & Welsb. 806 to 825; A. D. 1841; Nielson v. Hartford, &c., Web. Pat. Ca. 295, 328, and 328 to 373; A. D. 1841; S. C. 374. — Crane's patent for the hot air blast, in connection with anthracite coal. Crane's patent, Web. Pat. Cas. 375; date 1836. Crane v. Price, &c.; Webs. Pat. Cas. 377, 393; A. D. 1842, S. C. 4 Mann. & Grang. 380; S. C. 43 Eng. Com. L. R. 301; S. C. 2d vol. Frank. J. for year 1851, p. 388; French, &c. v. Rogers, &c. 394 to 397, and cases there cited by the court. 6 Eng. Law and Equity Rep. 536, overruling 2 Carrington & Kirwan, cited vs. Leon. 43, 47, 52; Curtis, 81 a.; Webster, 229, note.

II. The second exception by the defendants' counsel is to the charge of the court, in relation to Mr. Keller's evidence.

It is difficult to see upon what ground this exception of the defendants to the charge of the court is founded. After remarking upon the character and weight of the fact testified to, the whole is submitted to the jury for their decision.

III. The third exception taken to the charge of the court is found in the next two paragraphs on the same page, and relates to the reissued patent. The same is repeated in the call of the defendants, in their eleventh proposition, upon which they ask the court to instruct the jury.

The substance of the charge, as given in both instances, is, that the language in one patent was in some parts different from that in the other, but the meaning was substantially the same in both. That the reissued patent must be for the same invention as the first; and the matter of fact was left to the jury.

IV. The next exception is to the charge of the court, as found at the top of the 42d page of the case, and is as follows:

" That in the patents referred to, from the year 1797 to 1832, the combination which was claimed to be identical, was confessedly used for making pipe, by casting with fluid lead in a mould, and after it was set, by the application of water, forcing it out.

" And the question is, whether any of these inventions are substantially the same as the plaintiffs'; whether, even, if by these modes, pipe had been successfully made for common use, it would have been made in the same manner as the Hansons'; to which opinion, the counsel for the defendants excepted."

Whether the modes referred to by the court, of manufacturing pipe, were the same or different, was a question of fact left to the jury; and the court did not, by the manner of stating the point, withdraw it from the consideration of the jury.

V. The fifth exception relates to the charge of the court, as to the duty of the plaintiffs to put and keep the invention on sale on reasonable terms, and they say that it was not essential that the patentees should take active means for the purpose of putting their invention in market, and forcing a sale; but that they should at all times be ready to sell at a fair price, when a reasonable offer was made.

That it was for the jury to say whether it was put and continued on sale, under this view of the law — to which the counsel for the defendants excepted.

We insist that the court took a correct view of the statute, and properly submitted the question of fact to the jury; and that the exception is not well taken.

VI. The next exception in the order in which the defendants in error have noticed them, relates to the instructions of the court, in relation to the liability of Le Roy and Smith jointly, with the other defendant, Lowber.

It seems, to the counsel for the defendants in error, that the question was properly submitted. to the jury, as a question of fact, how far Le Roy and Smith had made themselves liable with Lowber. The defendants in error insist that the exception to this part of the charge is not well taken.

VII. In answer to the fourth proposition, on which the court was requested to instruct the jury that Tatham's patent was void on its face, &c. We say that the charge of the court was correct. The patentees in Tatham's patent have pointed out clearly what they claim, and what they do not claim.

VIII. In their ninth proposition, the defendants requested the court to instruct the jury —

"That if they believed the same combination of cylinder, piston, bridge, short core, die, and chamber, under heat and pressure, had before been patented in England by Bramah, and published in a well known work, then the plaintiffs cannot recover."

Upon this proposition the court instructed the jury, that Bramah's patent and the Tathams' were not identical; and declined to instruct the jury as requested. To which the counsel for the defendants excepted. This request by the defendants for the above instruction was based on the assumption of a fact not proved and not true, and was correctly refused.

IX. The defendants requested the court to instruct the jury according to their tenth proposition, which is as follows — "That if the jury believe that the Burr, Bramah, Titus, and Hague machines, or either of them, were published to the world in well known public works, and had the same combination, in whole or in part, as the Hanson machine, up to a certain point, the Tathams' patent is void for claiming too much, viz., the whole combination; and the court thereupon instructed the jury, that they had explained their views on that part of the case, and declined to instruct them as requested in the form in which the proposition was stated." To which the counsel for the defendants excepted, and the defendants in error insist that this exception is not well taken.

X. The sixteenth proposition, on which the court was requested to instruct the jury, is in the following words, namely,—

" That the jury are the sole and exclusive judges as to the questions of fact, whether the combination and process were the same in the plaintiffs' machine as was Bramah's, or in any other of the machines proved on the trial. And thereupon the court instructed the jury, that this was so undoubtedly; subject, however, to the principles of law as laid down in the preceding charge and instructions." To which the counsel for the defendants excepted.

The defendants in error insist that none of the exceptions aforesaid are well taken; and that said judgment should be affirmed, with costs and damages.

Mr. Justice McLEAN delivered the opinion of the court.

This is a case on error, from the Circuit Court of the Southern District of New York.

The action was brought in the Circuit Court, to recover damages for an alleged infringement of a patent for new and useful improvements in machinery for making pipes and tubes from metallic substances.

The declaration alleged that John and Charles Hanson, of England, were the inventors of the improvements specified, on or prior to the 31st of August, 1837; that on the 10th of January, 1840, the Hansons assigned to H. B. and B. Tatham, two of the defendants in error, the full and exclusive right to said improvements; that, on the 29th of March, 1841, letters-patent were granted for the improvements to the Tathams, as the assignees of the Hansons; that, afterwards, H. B. and B. Tatham assigned to G. N. Tatham, the remaining defendant in error, an undivided third part of the patent.

On the 14th of March, 1846, the said letters-patent were surrendered, on the ground that the specifications of the improvements claimed were defective, and a new patent was issued, which granted to the patentees, their heirs, &c., for the term of fourteen years, from the 31st of August, 1837, the exclusive right to make and vend the improvements secured. The declaration states, the patent was of the value of fifty thousand dollars; and that the defendants below had made and vended lead pipe to the amount of two thousand tons, in violation of the patent, and to the injury of the plaintiffs twenty thousand dollars.

The defendants pleaded not guilty; the defendant Lowber did not join in the plea, but permitted judgment to be entered against him by default. On the trial, certain bills of exceptions were taken to the instructions of the court to the jury, on which errors are assigned.

The schedule, which is annexed to the patent, and forms a part of it, states that the invention consists " in certain improvements upon, and additions to, the machinery used for manufacturing pipes and tubes from lead or tin, or an alloy of soft metals capable of being forced, by great pressure, from out of a receiver, through or between apertures, dies, and cores, when in a set or solid state, set forth in the specification of a patent granted to Thomas Burr, of Shrewsbury, in Shropshire, England, dated the 11th of April, 1820." After describing Burr's machine, its defects, and the improvements made on it as claimed, the patentees say, " Pipes thus made are found to possess great solidity and unusual strength, and a fine uniformity of thickness and accuracy of bore is arrived at, such as, it is believed, has never before been attained by any other machinery."

" The essential difference in the character of this pipe, which distinguishes it, as well as that contemplated by Thomas Burr, from all other heretofore known or attempted, is that it is wrought under heat, by pressure and constriction, from set metal; and that it is not a casting formed in a mould."

And they declare, " We do not claim as our invention and improvement, any, of the parts of the above-described machinery, independently of its arrangement and combination above set forth. What we do claim as our invention, and desire to secure, is, the combination of the following parts above described, to wit: the core and bridge, or guide-piece, with the cylinder, the piston, the chamber and the die, when used to form pipes of metal, under heat and pressure, in the manner set forth, or in any other manner substantially the same."

The plaintiffs gave in evidence certain agreements between the defendants, showing the manufacture of lead pipe by the defendant Lowber, for the defendants Le Roy and Smith. And also evidence tending to prove that the said John Hanson and Charles Hanson were the original and first inventors of the improvement described in the said letters-patent; that the invention and discovery therein described was new and useful; that the lead pipe manufactured thereby, was superior in quality and strength, capable of resisting much greater pressure, and more free from defects than any pipe before made ; that in all the modes of making lead pipe, previously known and in use, it could be made only in short pieces, but that by this improved mode it could be made of any required length, and also of any required size ; and that the introduction of lead pipe, made in the mode described, had superseded the use of that made by any of the modes before in use, and that it was also furnished at a less price."

"And the plaintiffs also gave evidence tending to prove that lead, when recently become set, and while under heat and extreme pressure in a close vessel, would reunite perfectly, after a separation of its parts; and that in the process described in the said patent, lead pipe was manufactured by being thus separated and reunited; and that the said John and Charles Hanson were the first and original discoverers thereof; and that such discovery, and its reduction to a practical result in the mode described in said letters-patent, was useful and important."

"And the plaintiffs also gave evidence, conducing to prove that the improvement, described in the letters-patent, was the same invention and discovery which had been made by the said John and Charles Hanson, and for which letters-patent had been granted to them in England, and subsequently in this country, to the Tathams, as recited in the letters-patent."

"And the plaintiffs also gave evidence conducing to prove that they had been ready and willing, and had offered to sell the said invention, within eighteen months succeeding the issuing of said letters-patent to them, and also since; and had, within the said eighteen months, sold the same for a large portion of the United States."

The defendants' counsel then read in evidence from the "Repertory of Arts," vol. 16, page 314, the description of the patent to the Hansons, dated August 31, 1837. They also read in evidence the patent issued upon the application of the plaintiffs to the Patent Office, containing another specification, which was annexed to the patent surrendered. And also they read the specification of Thomas Burr's patent, of April 11, 1820. Also a patent granted to George W. Potter, described in the 12th "Franklin Journal of Arts," published in 1833; they also read the specification of a patent granted in England, to Bush and Harvey, on December 5th, 1817; and also the specification of a patent granted in England to Joseph Bramah, October 31st, 1797.

Evidence was also given, to show that the combination of machinery for making lead pipe, described in public works as

15*

having been invented by Burroughs Titus, by George W. Potter, by Jesse Fox, by John Hague, and by Joseph Bramah, were substantially the same as that used by the plaintiffs; that the combination of machinery, patented as herein before stated, by Bush and Harvey, for making pipes of clay, and that used for making maccaroni, were substantially the same as that described in the plaintiffs' patent.

In their charge to the jury, the court said, " They, the plaintiffs, also state, that they do not claim any of the parts of the machinery, the cylinder, core, die, or bridge, but that they claimed the combination when used to form pipes of metal, under heat and pressure, in the way they have described. There can be no doubt that if this combination is new, and produces a new and useful result, it is the proper subject of a patent." " The result is a new manufacture. And even if the mere combination of machinery in the abstract is not new, still, if used and applied in connection with the practical development of a principle, newly discovered, producing a new and useful result, the subject is patentable. In this view, the improvement of the plaintiffs is the application of a combination of machinery to a new end ; to the development and application of a new principle, resulting in a new and useful manufacture. That the discovery of a new principle is not patentable, but it must be embodied and brought into operation by machinery, so as to produce a new and an useful result. Upon this view of the patent, it is an important question for the jury to determine, from the evidence, whether the fact is established, on which the alleged improvement is founded, that lead in a set, or semi-solid state, can thus be reunited or welded, after separation." To this instruction the defendants excepted.

It was also objected, that the plaintiffs' patent was invalid for want of originality ; that the invention had been before described in public works, and Bramah, Hague, Titus, Fox, and Potter, were relied on by the defendants.

To this it was replied, by the court, " That in the view taken by the court in the construction of the patent, it was not material whether the mere combinations of machinery referred to were similar to the combination used by the Hansons, because the originality did not consist in the novelty of the machinery, but in bringing a newly discovered principle into practical application, by which a useful article of manufacture is produced, and wrought pipe made as distinguished from cast pipe." To this charge there was also an exception.

The word *principle* is used by elementary writers on patent subjects, and sometimes in adjudications of courts, with such a want of precision in its application, as to mislead. It is admitted, that a principle is not patentable. A principle, in the abstract, is a fundamental truth; an original cause; a motive; these cannot be patented, as no one can claim in either of them an exclusive right. Nor can an exclusive right exist to a new power, should one be discovered in addition to those already known. Through the agency of machinery a new steam power may be said to have been generated. But no one can appropriate this power exclusively to himself, under the patent laws. The same may be said of electricity, and of any other power in nature, which is alike open to all, and may be applied to useful purposes by the use of machinery.

In all such cases, the processes used to extract, modify, and concentrate natural agencies, constitute the invention. The elements of the power exist; the invention is not in discovering them, but in applying them to useful objects. Whether the machinery used be novel, or consist of a new combination of parts known, the right of the inventor is secured against all who use the same mechanical power, or one that shall be substantially the same.

A patent is not good for an effect, or the result of a certain process, as that would prohibit all other persons from making the same thing by any means whatsoever. This, by creating monopolies, would discourage arts and manufactures, against the avowed policy of the patent laws.

A new property discovered in matter, when practically applied, in the construction of a useful article of commerce or manufacture, is patentable; but the process through which the new property is developed and applied, must be stated, with such precision as to enable an ordinary mechanic to construct and apply the necessary process. This is required by the patent laws of England and of the United States, in order that when the patent shall run out, the public may know how to profit by the invention. It is said, in the case of the Househill Company v. Neilson, Webster's Patent Cases, 683, "A patent will be good, though the subject of the patent consists in the discovery of a great, general, and most comprehensive principle in science or law of nature, if that principle is by the specification applied to any special purpose, so as thereby to effectuate a practical result and benefit not previously attained." In that case, Mr. Justice Clerk, in his charge to the jury, said, "the specification does not claim any thing as to the form, nature, shape, materials, numbers, or mathematical character of the vessel or vessels in which the air is to be heated, or as to the mode of heating such vessels," &c. The patent was for "the improved application of air to produce heat in fires, forges and furnaces, where bellows or other blowing apparatus are required."

In that case, although the machinery was not claimed as a part of the invention, the jury were instructed to inquire, " whether the specification was not such as to enable workmen of ordinary skill to make machinery or apparatus capable of producing the effect set forth in said letters-patent and specification." And, that in order to ascertain whether the defendants had infringéd the patent, the jury should inquire whether they, " did by themselves or others, and in contravention of the privileges conferred by the said letters-patent, use machinery or apparatus substantially the same with the machinery or apparatus described in the plaintiffs' specification, and to the effect set forth in said letters-patent and specification." So it would seem that where a patent is obtained, without a claim to the invention of the machinery, through which a valuable result is produced, a precise specification is required; and the test of infringement is, whether the defendants have used substantially the same process to produce the same result.

In the case before us, the court instructed the jury that the invention did not consist " in the novelty of the machinery, but in bringing a newly discovered principle into practical application, by which a useful article of manufacture is produced, and wrought pipe made as distinguished from cast pipe."

A patent for leaden pipes would not be good, as it would be for an effect, and would, consequently, prohibit all other persons from using the same article, however manufactured. Leaden pipes are the same, the metal being in no respect different. Any difference in form and strength must arise from the mode of manufacturing the pipes. The new property in the metal claimed to have been discovered by the patentees, belongs to the process of manufacture, and not to the thing made.

But we must look to the claim of the invention stated in their application by the patentees. They say, " We do not claim as our invention and improvement any of the parts of the above described machinery, independently of their arrangement and combinaʹ on above set forth." " What we claim as our invention, and desire to secure by letters-patent, is, the combination of the following parts above described, to wit, the core and bridge or guide-piece, the chamber, and the die, when used to form pipes of metal, under heat and pressure, in the manner set forth, or in any other manner substantially the same."

The patentees have founded their claim on this specification, and they can neither modify nor abandon it in whole cr in part. The combination of the machinery is claimed, through which the new property of lead was developed, as a part of the process in the structure of the pipes. But the jury were instructed, " that the originality of the invention did not consist in the novelty of the machinery, but in bringing a newly discovered principle into practical application." The patentees claimed the combination of the machinery as their invention in part, and no such claim can be sustained without establishing its novelty — not as to the parts of which it is composed, but as to the combination. The question whether the newly developed property of lead, used in the formation of pipes, might have been patented, if claimed as developed, without the invention of machinery, was not in the case.

In the case of Bean v. Smallwood, 2 Story, R. 408, Mr. Justice Story said, "He (the patentee) says that the same apparatus, stated in this last claim, has been long in use, and applied, if not to chairs, at least in other machines, to purposes of a similar nature. If this be so, then the invention is not new, but at most is an old invention, or apparatus, or machinery applied to a new purpose. Now I take it to be clear, that a machine, or apparatus, or other mechanical contrivance, in order to give the party a claim to a patent therefor, must in itself be substantially new. If it is old and well known, and applied only to a new purpose, that does not make it patentable."

We think there was error in the above instruction, that the novelty of the combination of the machinery, specifically claimed by the patentees as their invention, was not a material fact for the jury, and that on that ground, the judgment must be reversed. The other rulings of the court excepted to, we shall not examine, as they are substantially correct.

Mr. Justice Nelson, Mr. Justice Wayne, and Mr. Justice Grier dissented.

Mr. Justice NELSON—dissenting.

The patent in this case, according to the general description given by the patentees, is, for improvements upon, and additions to, the machinery or apparatus of Thomas Burr, for manufacturing pipes and tubes from metallic substances. They declare, that the nature of their invention, and the manner in which the same is to operate, are particularly described and set forth in their specification. In that, they refer to the patent of Burr of the 11th April, 1820, for making lead pipe out of set or solid lead by means of great pressure, the product being wrought pipe, as contradistinguished from cast, or pipe made according to the draw-bench system. The apparatus, as described by Burr, consisted of a strong iron cylinder, bored sufficiently true for a piston to traverse easily within it. This cylinder was closed at one end by the piston, and also closed at the other, except a small aperture for the die which formed the external diameter of the pipe. The core or mandril, which determined the inner diameter, was a long cylindrical rod of steel, one end of which was attached to the face of the piston, extending through the centre of the cylinder, and passing also through the centre of the die at the opposite end, leaving a space around the core and between it and the die for the formation of the pipe. The metal to form the pipe was admitted into the cylinder in a fluid state, and when it become set or solid, the power of a hydraulic press was applied to the head of the piston, which, moving against the body of solid lead in the cylinder, drove it through the die, the long core advancing with the piston and with the body of lead through the die, and thus forming the pipe. The cylinder usually holds from three to four hundred pounds of lead, and continuous pipe is made till the whole charge is driven out.

This plan, though one of deserved merit, and of great original- ity, failed, when reduced to practice, except for the purpose of making very large pipe, larger than that usually in demand, and consequently passed out of general use. The long core attached to the face of the piston, advancing with it in the solid lead un- der the great pressure required, was liable to warp and twist out of a straight line, and out of centre in the die, which had the effect to destroy the uniformity of the thickness and centrality of the bore of the pipe.

The old mode, therefore, of making pipe by the draw-bench system, continued down to 1837, when the patentees in this case discovered, by experiment, that lead, when recently set and solid, but still under heat and extreme pressure, in a close vessel, would reunite after a separation of its parts, and " heal " (in the language of the patentees) " as it were by the first intention," as completely as though it had not been divided.

Upon the discovery of this property of lead, which had never before been known, but, on the contrary, had been supposed and believed, by all men of science skilled in metals, to be im- possible, the patentees made an alteration in the apparatus of Burr, founded upon this new property discovered in the metal, and succeeded completely in making wrought pipe out of solid lead by means of the hydraulic pressure. The product was so much superior in quality to that made according to the old mode, that it immediately wholly superseded it in the market. The pipe was also made much cheaper.

The patentees, by their discovery, were enabled to dispense with the long core of Burr, and to fix firmly a bridge or cross bars at the end of the cylinder near the die, to which bridge they fastened a short core extending into and through the die. By this arrangement they obtained a firm, immovable core, that always preserved its centrality with the die, and secured the manufacture of pipe of uniformity of thickness of wall and accuracy of bore, of any dimension. The lead after being admitted into the cylinder in a fluid state, was allowed to remain till it became solid, and was then driven by the piston through the apertures in the bridge into the chamber between it and the die, where the parts reunited, after the separation, as completely as before, and, passing out at the die around the fixed short core, formed perfect pipe.

The patentees state, that they do not intend to confine themselves to the arrangement of the apparatus thus particularly specified, and point out several other modes by which the same result may be produced, all of which variations would readily suggest themselves, as they observe, to any practical engineer, without departing from the substantial originality of the invention, the remarkable feature of which, they say, is, that lead, when in a set state, being yet under heat, can be made, by extreme pressure, to reunite perfectly around a core after separation, and thus be formed into strong pipes or tubes. Pipes thus made are found to possess great solidity and unusual strength, and a fine uniformity, such as had never before been attained by any other mode. The essential difference in its character, and which distinguishes it from all other theretofore known, they add, is, that it is wrought under heat, by pressure and constriction, from set or solid metal.

They do not claim, as their invention or improvement, any of the parts of the machinery, independently of the arrangement and combination set forth.

" What we claim as our invention, they say, is, the combination of the following parts above described, to wit : the core and bridge or guide-piece, with the cylinder, the piston, the chamber, and die, when used to form pipes of metal under heat and pressure, in the manner set forth, or in any other manner substantially the same."

It is supposed that the patentees claim, as the novelty of their invention, the arrangement and combination of the machinery which they have described, disconnected from the employment of the new property of lead, which they have discovered, and by the practical application and use of which they have succeeded in producing the new manufacture. And the general title or description of their invention, given in the body of their letters-patent, is referred to as evidence of such claim. But every patent, whatever may be the general heading or title by which the invention is designated, refers to the specification annexed for a more particular description ; and hence this court has heretofore determined, that the specification constitutes a part of the patent, and that they must be construed together when seeking to ascertain the discovery claimed. Hogg et al. v. Emerson, 6 How. 437.

The same rule of construction was applied by the Court of Exchequer, in England, in the case of Neilson's patent for the hot air blast.   Webster's Cases, 373.

Now, on looking into the specification, we see, that the leading feature of the invention consists in the discovery of a new property in the article of lead, and in the employment and adaptation of it, by means of the machinery described, to the production of a new article, wrought pipe, never before successfully made. Without the discovery of this new property in the metal, the machinery or apparatus would be useless, and not the subject of a patent.   It is in connection with this property, and the embodiment and adaptation of it to practical use, that the machinery is described, and the arrangement claimed.   The discovery of this new element or property led naturally to the apparatus, by which a new and most useful result is produced.   The apparatus was but incidental, and subsidiary to the new and leading idea of the invention.   And hence, the patentees set forth, as the leading feature of it, the discovery, that lead, in a solid state, but under heat and extreme pressure in a close vessel, will reunite, after separation of its parts, as completely as though it had never been separated.   It required very little ingenuity, after the experiments in a close vessel, by which this new property of the metal was first developed, to construct the necessary machinery for the formation of the pipe.   The apparatus, essential to develop this property, would at once suggest the material parts, especially in the state of the art at the time. Any skilful mechanic, with Burr's machine before him, would readily construct the requisite machinery.

The patentees, therefore, after describing their discovery of this property of lead, and the apparatus by means of which they apply the metal to the manufacture of pipe, claim the combination of the machinery, only when used to form pipes under heat and pressure, in the manner set forth, or in any other manner substantially the same.   They do not claim it as new separately, or when used for any other purpose, or in any other way ; but claim it, only, when applied for the purpose and in the way pointed out in the specification.   The combination, as machinery, may be old ; may have been long used ; of itself, what no one could claim as his invention, and may not be the subject of a patent.   What is claimed is, that it never had been before applied or used, in the way and for the purpose they have used and applied it, namely, in the embodiment and adaptation of a newly-discovered property in lead, by means of which they are enabled to produce a new manufacture — wrought pipe — out of a mass of solid lead.   Burr had attempted it, but failed.   These patentees, after the lapse of seventeen years, having discovered this new property in the metal, succeeded, by the use and employment of it, and since then, none other than wrought lead pipe, made out of solid lead, has been found in the market, having superseded, on account of its superior quality and cheapness, all other modes of manufacture.

Now the construction, which I understand a majority of my brethren are inclined to give to this patent, namely, that the patentees claim, as the originality of their invention, simply, the combination of the machinery employed, with great deference, seems to me contrary to the fair and reasonable import of the language of the specification, and also of the summary of the claim. The tendency of modern decisions is to construe specifications benignly, and to look through mere forms of expression, often inartificially used, to the substance, and to maintain the right of the patentee to the thing really invented, if ascertainable upon a liberal consideration of the language of the specification, when taken together. For this purpose, phrases standing alone are not to be singled out, but the whole are to be taken in connection. 1 Sumn. 482–485.

Baron Parke observed, in delivering the opinion of the court in Neilson's patent, " That, half a century ago, or even less, within fifteen or twenty years, there seems to have been very much a practice with both judges and juries to destroy the patent-right, even of beneficial patents, by exercising great astuteness in taking objections, either as to the title of the patent, but more particularly as to the specifications, and many valuable patent rights have been destroyed in consequence of the objections so taken. Within the last ten years or more, the courts have not been so strict in taking objections to the specifications, and they have endeavored to hold a fair hand between the patentee and the public, willing to give the patentee the reward of his patent."

Construing the patent before us in this spirit, I cannot but think, that the thing really discovered, and intended to be described, and claimed by these patentees, cannot well be mistaken. That they did not suppose the novelty of their invention consisted, simply, in the arrangement of the machinery described, is manifest. They state, distinctly, that the leading feature of their discovery consisted of this new property of lead, and some of its alloys, — this, they say, is the remarkable feature of their invention, — and the apparatus described is regarded by them as subordinate, and as important only as enabling them to give practical effect to this newly-discovered property, by means of which they produce the new manufacture. If they have failed to describe and claim this, as belonging to their invention, it is manifest, upon the face of their specification, that they have failed to employ the proper words to describe and claim what they intended; and that the very case is presented, in which, if the court, in the language of Baron Parke, will endeavor to hold a fair hand between the patentee and the public, it will look through the forms of expression used, and discover, if it can, the thing really invented. Apply to the specification this rule of construction, and all difficulty at once disappears. The thing invented, and intended to be claimed, is too apparent to be mistaken.

The patentees have certainly been unfortunate in the language of the specification, if, upon a fair and liberal interpretation, they have claimed only the simple apparatus employed; when they have not only set forth the discovery of this property in the metal, as the great feature in their invention, but, as is manifest, without it the apparatus would have been useless. Strike out this new property from their description and from their claim, and nothing valuable is left. All the rest would be worthless. This lies at the foundation upon which the great merit of the invention rests, and without a knowledge of which the new manufacture could not have been produced; and, for aught we know, the world would have been deprived of it down to this day.

If the patentees had claimed the combination of the core and bridge or guide-piece, with the cylinder, the chambers, and the die, and stopped there, I admit the construction, now adopted by a majority of my brethren, could not be denied; although, even then, it would be obvious, from an examination of the specification as a whole, that the draughtsman had mistaken the thing really invented, and substituted in its place matters simply incidental, and of comparative insignificance. But the language of the claim does not stop here. The combination of these parts is claimed only when used to form pipes of lead, under heat and pressure, in the manner set forth, — that is, when used for the embodiment and adaptation of this new property in the metal for making wrought pipe out of a solid mass of lead. This guarded limitation of the use excludes the idea of a claim to the combination for any other, and ties it down to the instance, when the use incorporates within it the new idea or element which gives to it its value, and by means of which the new manufacture is produced. How, then, can it be consistently held, that here is a simple claim to the machinery, and nothing more, when a reasonable interpretation of the words not only necessarily excludes any such claim, but in express .terms sets forth a different one, — one not only different in the conception of the invention, but different in the practical working of the apparatus, to accomplish the purpose intended?

I conclude, therefore, that the claim, in this case, is not simply for the apparatus employed by the patentees, but for the embodiment or employment of the newly-discovered property in the metal, and the practical adaption of it, by these means, to the production of a new result, namely, the manufacture of wrought pipe out of solid lead.

Then, is this the proper subject-matter of a patent?　　　m

This question was first largely discussed by counsel and court in the celebrated case of Boulton v. Bull, (2 Hen. 31, 463,) involving the validity of Watts's patent, which was for "a new invented method for lessening the consumption of fuel and steam in fire-engines." This was effected by inclosing the steam vessel or cylinder with wood, or other material, which preserved the heat in the steam vessel; and by condensing the steam in separate vessels. It was admitted, on the argument, that there was no new mechanical construction invented by Watt, and the validity of the patent was placed on the ground that it was for well-known principles, practically applied, producing a new and useful result. On the other hand, it was conceded, that the application of the principles in the manner described was new, and produced the result claimed; but it was denied, that this constituted the subject-matter of a patent. Heath and Buller, Justices, agreed with the counsel for the defendant. But Lord Chief Justice Eyre laid down the true doctrine, and which, I think, will be seen to be the admitted doctrine of the courts of England at this day. "Undoubtedly," he observed, "there can be no patent for a mere principle; but for a principle, so far embodied and connected with corporeal substances as to be in a condition to act, and to produce effects in any art, trade, mystery, or manual occupation, I think there may be a patent. Now, this," he continues, "is, in my judgment, the thing for which the patent stated in the case was granted; and this is what the specification describes, though it miscalls it a principle. It is not that the patentee conceived an abstract notion, that the consumption of steam in fire-engines may be lessened; but he has discovered a practical manner of doing it; and for that practical manner of doing it he has taken this patent. Surely," he observes, "this is a very different thing from taking a patent for a principle. The apparatus, as we have said, was not new. There is no new mechanical construction, said the counsel for the patentee, invented by Watt, capable of being the subject of a distinct specification; but his discovery was of a principle, the method of applying which is clearly set forth." Chief Justice Eyre admitted that the means used were not new, and that if the patent had been taken out for the mechanism used, it must fail.

He observed, " When the effect produced is some new substance or composition of things, it should seem that the privilege of the sole working or making ought to be for such new substances or composition, without regard to the mechanism or process by which it has been produced, which, though perhaps also new, will be. only useful as producing the new substance." Again, " When the effect produced is no new substance, or composition of things, the patent can only be for the mechanism, if new mechanism is used ; or for the process, if it be a new method of operating, with or without old mechanism, by which the effect is produced." And again, he observes, " If we wanted an illustration of the possible merit of a new method of operating with old machinery, we might look to the identical case before the court." p. 496, 493, 495.

This doctrine, in expounding the law of patents, was announced in 1795, and the subsequent adoption of it by the English courts, shows, that Chief Justice Eyre was considerably in advance of his associates upon this branch of the law. He had got rid, at an early day, of the prejudice against patents so feelingly referred to by Baron Parke in Neilson v. Harford, and comprehended the great advantages to his country if properly encouraged. He observed, in another part of his opinion, that " The advantages to the public from improvements of this kind are beyond all calculation important to a commercial country ; and the ingenuity of artists, who turn their thoughts towards such improvements, is, in itself, deserving of encouragement."

This doctrine was recognized by the Court of King's Bench in the King v. Wheeler, 2 B. & Ald. 340, 350.

It is there observed, that the word " manufactures," in the patent act, may be extended to a mere process to be carried on by known implements or elements, acting upon known substances, and ultimately producing some other known substance, but producing it in a cheaper or more expeditious manner, or of a better or more useful kind.

Now, if this process to be carried on by known implements acting upon known substances, and ultimately producing some other known substance of a better kind, is patentable, a fortiori will it be patentable, if it ultimately produces not some other known substance, but an entirely new and useful substance.

In Forsyth's patent, which consists of the application and use of detonating powder as priming for the discharge of firearms, it was held that whatever might be the construction of the lock or contrivance by which the powder was to be discharged, the use of the detonating mixture as priming, which article of itself was not new, was an infringement. Webster's Pat. Cas. 94, 97, (n) ; Curtis on Pat. 230.

This case is founded upon a doctrine which has been recognized in several subsequent cases in England, namely, that where a person discovers a principle or property of nature, or where he conceives of a new application of a well-known principle or property of nature, and also, of some mode of carrying it out into practice, so as to produce or attain a new and useful effect or result, he is entitled to protection against all other modes of carrying the same principle or property into practice for obtaining the same effect or result.

The novelty of the conception consists in the discovery and application in the one case, and of the application in the other, by which a new product in the arts or manufactures is the effect; and the question, in case of an infringement, is, as to the substantial identity of the principle or property, and of the application of the same, and consequently the means or machinery made use of, material only so far as they affect the identity of the application.

In the case of Jupe's patent for " an improved expanding table," Baron Alderson observed, speaking of this doctrine, " You cannot take out a patent for a principle; you may take out a patent for a principle coupled with the mode of carrying the principle into effect. But then, you must start with having invented some mode of carrying the principle into effect; if you have done that, then you are entitled to protect yourself from all other modes of carrying the same principle into effect, that being treated by the jury as piracy of your original invention." Webster's Pat. Cases, 147. The same doctrine was maintained also in the case of Neilson's patent for the hot air blast, in the K. B. and Exchequer in England. Webster's Pat. Cases, 342, 371; Curtis, § 74, 148, 232; Webster's Pat. Cases, 310.

This patent came also before the Court of Sessions in Scotland; and in submitting the case to the jury, the Lord Justice remarked, " That the main merit, the most important part of the invention, may consist in the conception of the original idea — in the discovery of the principle in science, or of the law of nature, stated in the patent; and little or no pains may have been taken in working out the best mode of the application of the principle to the purpose set forth in the patent. But still, if the principle is stated to be applicable to any special purpose, so as to produce any result previously unknown, in the way and for the objects described, the patent is good. It is no longer an abstract principle. It becomes to be a principle turned to account, to a practical object, and applied to a special result. It becomes, then, not an abstract principle, which means a principle considered apart from any special purpose or practical operation, but the discovery and statement of a principle for a special purpose, that is, a practical invention, a mode of carrying a principle into effect. That such is the law," he observes, " if a well-known principle is applied for the first time to produce a practical result for a special purpose, has never been disputed, and it would be very strange and unjust to refuse the same legal effect, when the inventor has the additional merit of discovering the principle, as well as its application to a practical object."

Then he observes, again, " Is it an objection to the patent that in its application of a new principle to a certain specified result, it includes every variety of mode of applying the principle according to the general. statement of the object and benefit to be attained? This," he observes, "is a question of law, and I must tell you distinctly, that this generality of claim, that is, for all modes of applying the principle to the purpose specified, according to, or within a general statement of the object to be attained, and of the use to be made of the agent to be so applied, is no objection to the patent. The application or use of the agent for the purpose specified, may be carried out in a great variety of ways, and only shows the beauty and simplicity, and comprehensiveness of the invention."

This case was carried up to the House of Lords on exceptions to the charge, and among others, to this part of it, which was the sixth exception, and is as follows : " In so far as he (the Judge) did not direct the jury, that on the construction of the patent and specification, the patentee cannot claim or maintain that his patent is one which applies to all the varieties in the apparatus which may be employed in heating air while under blast; but was limited to the particular described in the specification." And although the judgment of the court was reversed in the House of Lords on the eleventh exception, it was expressly affirmed as respects this one. Lord Campbell at first doubted, but after the decision of the courts in England on this patent, he admitted the instruction was right. Webster, Pat. Cases, 683, 684, 698, 717.

I shall not pursue a reference to the authorities on this subject any further. The settled doctrine to be deduced from them, I think, is, that a person having discovered the application for the first time of a well-known law of nature, or well-known property of matter, by means of which a new result in the arts or in manufactures is produced, and has pointed out a mode by which it is produced, is entitled to a patent; and, if he has not tied himself down in the specification to the particular mode described, he is entitled to be protected against all modes by which the same result is produced, by an application of the same law of nature or property of matter. And *a fortiori*, if he has discovered the law of nature or property of matter, and applied it, is he entitled to the patent, and aforesaid protection.

And why should not this be the law? The original conception — the novel idea in the one case, is the new application of the principle or property of matter, and the new product in the arts or manufactures — in the other, in the discovery of the principle or property, and application, with like result. The mode or means are but incidental, and flowing naturally from the original conception; and hence of inconsiderable merit. But, it is said, this is patenting a principle, or element of nature. The authorities to which I have referred, answer the objection. It was answered by Chief Justice Eyre, in the case of Watts's patent, in 1795, fifty-seven years ago; and more recently in still more explicit and authoritative terms. And what if the principle is incorporated in the invention, and the inventor protected in the enjoyment for the fourteen years. He is protected only in the enjoyment of the application for the special purpose and object to which it has been newly applied by his genius and skill. For every other purpose and end, the principle is free for all mankind to use. And, where it has been discovered, as well as applied to this one purpose, and open to the world as to every other, the ground of complaint is certainly not very obvious. Undoubtedly, within the range of the purpose and object for which the principle has been for the first time applied, piracies are interfered with during the fourteen years. But any body may take it up and give to it any other application to the enlargement of the arts and of manufactures, without restriction. He is only debarred from the use of the new application for the limited time, which the genius of others has already invented and put into successful practice. The protection does not go beyond the thing which, for the first time, has been discovered and brought into practical use; and is no broader than that extended to every other discoverer or inventor of a new art or manufacture.

I own, I am incapable of comprehending the detriment to the improvements in the country that may flow from this sort of protection to inventors.

To hold, in the case of inventions of this character, that the novelty must consist of the mode or means of the new application producing the new result, would be holding against the facts of the case, as no one can but see, that the original conception reaches far beyond these. It would be mistaking the skill of the mechanic for the genius of the inventor.

Upon this doctrine, some of the most brilliant and useful inventions of the day by men justly regarded as public benefactors, and whose names reflect honor upon their country — the successful application of steam power to the propulsion of vessels and railroad cars — the application of the electric current for the instant communication of intelligence from one extremity of the country to the other — and the more recent, but equally brilliant conception, the propulsion of vessels by the application of the expansibility of heated air, the air supplied from the atmosphere that surrounds them. It would be found, on consulting the system of laws established for their encouragement and protection, that the world had altogether mistaken the merit of their discovery; that, instead of the originality and brilliancy of the conception that had been unwittingly attributed to them, the whole of it consisted of some simple mechanical contrivances which a mechanician of ordinary skill could readily have devised. Even Franklin, if he had turned the lightning to account, in order to protect himself from piracies, must have patented the kite, and the thread, and the key, as his great original conception, which gave him a name throughout Europe, as well as at home, for bringing down this element from the heavens, and subjecting it to the service of man. And if these simple contrivances, taken together, and disconnected from the control and use of the element by which the new application, and new and useful result may have been produced, happen to be old and well known, his patent would be void; or, if some follower in the tract of genius, with just intellect enough to make a different mechanical device or contrivance, for the same control and application of the element, and produce the same result, he would, under this view of the patent law, entitle himself to the full enjoyment of the fruits of Franklin's discovery.

If I rightly comprehend the ground upon which a majority of my brethren have placed the decision, they do not intend to controvert so much the doctrine which I have endeavored to maintain, and which, I think, rests upon settled authority, as the application of it to the particular case. They suppose that the patentees have claimed only the combination of the different parts of the machinery described in their specification, and therefore, are tied down to the maintenance of that as the novelty of their invention. I have endeavored to show, that this is a mistaken interpretation; and that they claim the combination, only, when used to embody and give a practical application to the newly-discovered property in the lead, by means of which a new manufacture is produced, namely, wrought pipe out of a solid mass of lead; which it is conceded, was never before successfully accomplished.

For these reasons, I am constrained to differ with the judgment they have arrived at, and am in favor of affirming that of the court below

Order.

This cause came on to be heard on the transcript of the record from the Circuit Court of the United States for the Southern District of New York, and was argued by counsel. On consideration whereof, it is now here ordered and adjudged, by this court, that the judgment of the said Circuit Court in this cause be, and the same is hereby, reversed, with costs, and that this cause be, and the same is hereby, remanded to the said Circuit Court, with directions to award a *venire facias de novo.*

THE UNITED STATES, APPELLANTS, *v.* THE HEIRS OF VINCENT RILLIEUX, DECEASED.

This court again decides, as in 11 Howard, 580, that under the acts of Congress of 1824 and 1844, the District Court had no power to act upon evidence of mere naked possession, unaccompanied by written evidence conferring, or professing to confer, a title of some description.

By the treaty of 1763, the land in question passed from France to Great Britain; and the certificate of two French officers in 1765, certifying that the claimant had been for a long time in possession, furnished no evidence of title. No application was made to the British government for a grant.

A purchase from the Indians, whilst the province was under French authority, conveyed no title unless sanctioned by that authority.

In this case, also, there is no proof that the claimants are the heirs of the party originally in possession.

THIS was an appeal from the District Court of the United States, for the Eastern District of Louisiana. The petition was filed in that court by the heirs of Rillieux, under the act of June 17th, 1844, (5 Stat. at Large, 676,) which court decreed in favor of the petitioners. The United States appealed to this court, where it was argued by *M.. Bibb* and *Mr. Crittenden,* (Attorney-General,) for the appellants. No counsel appeared for the appellees.

Mr. Justice CATRON delivered the opinion of the court.

The petitioners aver, that they are the lawful heirs of Vincent Rillieux and Marie Tronquet his wife; and as such heirs, are the true and lawful owners of a tract of land in the parish of St. Tammany, State of Louisiana, "bounded on the South side by Lake Ponchartrain; on the East by Pearl River; on the West by the bayou Bonfouca; and on the North by a line running from the western source of said bayou, and from the head waters of the same to Pearl River"—containing an extent of about one hundred thousand acres.

It is alleged, that this tract of land was purchased in part by

Vincent Rillieux and his wife, the ancestors of the petitioners, from the Biloxi Indians residing thereon, in 1761, by consent of the French government, as appears from a copy of the title annexed to the petition, given by C. P. Aubry and D. N. Foucault, bearing date March 16th, 1765. The said tract of land, at the time the title was given, and before, having been in the possession of Vincent Rillieux, and so continued to be possessed by him and those claiming under him, with consent of the French, Spanish, and American governments, without interruption; and which was used, inhabited and cultivated as private property."

The District Court gave a decree for the land, to the extent claimed by the petition.

Occupancy and cultivation, from an early date, of comparatively small portions of the land claimed, is established by proof; and, also, that the land was claimed by Rillieux's heirs, as property derived by descent from their ancestors; but the extent of claim was indefinite.

Several considerations present themselves in advance of the paper title set up. In the first place, the District Court was exercising a special jurisdiction, created by the act of 1824, where none existed before, and could only take cognizance of such description of claims as the statute allowed. It embraced those who claimed by virtue of any French or Spanish grant, concession, warrant, or order of survey. And the act of June 17th, 1844, added similar claims originating with the British authorities. Jurisdiction to adjudicate written evidences of title, was alone conferred by Congress on the district courts. It follows, that no decree can be founded on mere possession; we so held in the case of Power's heirs, 11 Howard, 580. Congress reserved to itself the power to provide for actual settlers. The act of March 3, 1819, for adjusting claims to lands East of the Island of New Orleans, provided for such claimants as the widow and heirs of Rillieux were; and which act with its various amendments, continued in force until after the act of 1824 expired, and the district courts ceased to have jurisdiction by virtue thereof. The various acts of Congress, bearing on claims founded on occupancy and cultivation, are enumerated in the case of the United States v. Power's heirs, 11 Howard, 580.

In the next place: By the treaty of 1763, between France and Great Britain, there was ceded to Great Britain all the country east and north of a line running through the River Iberville, Lakes Maurepas and Pontchartrain to the sea; and as the land claimed lies to the left of this line, the jurisdiction of France over it, ceased with the treaty of peace. And the King of Great Britain having, by his proclamation of 1763, established the government of West Florida, the colonial Governor exercised the King's power; and therefore, on the 18th of March, 1765, the widow of Vincent Rillieux addressed the Governor, saying, that she had ascertained what the necessary proceedings and submissions on her part were, in order that she might remain in the peaceable enjoyment of her property, situate in the part of the Province where she resided; and therefore, prayed the Governor to accept that letter as her oath of fidelity and submission to the British authority; she being advised by Captain Cambell, that the letter would suffice in her case. She further proceeds to state: " I have the honor to annex hereto a certificate from Messieurs, the Commandant and Intendant-Commissary of this Province, as a title, which proves the peaceable enjoyment and possession of my said property, believing it to be necessary: my widowed state and my numerous family, give me ground to hope from your goodness all the protection of which I have need, and for which I shall always feel the deepest gratitude."

The certificate of Aubry and Foucault, the Commandant and Intendant, bears date two days earlier than the widow Rillieux's letter, to which the certificate purports to be annexed; and these two papers furnish the only written evidence of title presented to the District Court. These French officers state, that Madame Rillieux had been in peaceable possession and enjoyment for twenty-four years preceding, of lands " situate in the direction north of Lake Pontchartrain, between the bayou Bonfouca and Pearl River; a great portion of which tract consists of *prairies tremblantes*, (trembling prairies,) quite valueless; and not having a sufficient extent in front, she, Mrs. Rillieux, was compelled in 1761, to purchase from the Biloxi Indians, all that part of the good lands belonging to that nation, lying between the land which she owned and Pearl River, in order to procure the necessary pasturage for at least one hundred cows, so that the land the said lady was in possession, as well by her late husband, as by her, for the last twenty-four years; also what she acquired by purchase from the Biloxi Indians in 1761, as explained above, form to-day a peninsula, (Presque Isle,) bounded by the trembling and immediate lands which border lake Pontchartrain, bayou Bonfouca, and Pearl River. In faith of which (say Aubry and Foucault) we have delivered the foregoing certificate to the said widow Rillieux, to be used by her in such manner as she may think proper."

The certificate is not addressed to the Governor of West Florida, but " to all whom it may concern." No power to grant land is assumed by the certificate; neither was application made to the British Governor for a grant. Nor does Madame Rillieux's letter, or the certificate of these French officers at New Orleans, assert that any paper title had ever issued to Vincent Rillieux, or to his widow, for the land claimed, but only that they had been in peaceable possession and enjoyment for twenty-four years preceding.

That portions of the land had been purchased from the Biloxi Indians, amounted to nothing, unless the purchase had been made with the assent of the French colonial government.

This is the true state of the case, admitting that the foregoing certificate was competent evidence for any purpose. But, as it was given by individuals having no more authority to act in the premises than any other third person, it can have no validity or credit attributed to it; and this reduces the case to a naked statement in the petition, with proof of great length of possession and continual claim.

That the District Court had no power to decree on such proof, we have already stated.

The petitioners claim as heirs of Vincent Rillieux and his wife. No proof was introduced to establish the heirship. This of course was necessary before a decree could be made to these individual claimants, as was held by this court in the case of the United States v. LeBlanc et al. 12 Howard, 436.

It has also been urged, on the part of the United States, that no decree could be made for any specific tract of land, as no description was given in the certificate of Aubry and Foucault, from which boundaries could be ascertained. But as that paper is of no value, we do not deem it necessary to examine this question.

For the reasons above stated, we order that the decree of the District Court be reversed, and that the petition be dismissed.

Order.

This cause came on to be heard on the transcript of the record from the District Court of the United States for the Eastern District of Louisiana, and was argued by counsel. On consideration whereof, it is now here ordered, adjudged, and decreed by this court, that the decree of the said District Court in this cause be, and the same is hereby, reversed and annulled, and that this cause be, and the same is hereby, remanded to the said District Court, with directions to dismiss the petition of the claimants.

THE UNITED STATES, APPELLANTS, v. JOHN GUSMAN.

THIS, like the preceding case of The United States v. The Heirs of Rillieux, was an appeal f.om the District Court of the United States for the Eastern District of Louisiana. In fact, it was a part of it, because Gusman claimed under th title of Rillieux.

Mr. Justice CATRON delivered the opinion of the court.

Gusman claims under the heirs of Rillieux, and relies on the same evidences of title that they do; and his vendors having had no title when they assumed to convey the land, it is ordered, that the decree in this case be also reversed, and the petition dismissed

Order.

This cause came on to be heard on the transcript of the record from the District Court of the United States for the Eastern District of Louisiana, and was argued by counsel. On consideration whereof, it is now here ordered, adjudged, and decreed by this court, that the decree of the said District Court in this cause be, and the same is hereby, reversed and annulled, and that this cause be, and the same is hereby, remanded to the said District Court, with directions to dismiss the petition of the claimant.

THE TROY IRON AND NAIL FACTORY, APPELLANT, v. ERASTUS CORNING, JOHN F. WINSLOW, AND JAMES HORNER.

In 1834, Burden obtained a patent for a new and useful improvement in the machinery for manufacturing wrought nails and spikes, which he assigned to the Troy Iron and Nail Factory, and also covenanted that he would convey to that company any improvement which he might thereafter make.

In 1840, he made such an improvement, for making hook and brad-headed spikes, with a bending lever, which he assigned to the Troy Iron and Nail Factory in 1848.

Before this last assignment, however, viz, in 1845, Burden made an agreement with Corning, Horner, and Winslow, in which, amongst other things, it was agreed, that both parties might thereafter manufacture and vend spikes of such kind and character as they saw fit, notwithstanding their conflicting claims.

wing to the peculiar attitude of the parties to each other at the time of making this agreement, and the language used in it, it cannot be construed into a permission to Corning, Horner, and Winslow, to use the improved machinery patented by Burden in 1840; and the right to use it, having passed to the Troy Iron and Nail Factory, a perpetual injunction upon Corning, Horner, and Winslow will be decreed.

THIS was an appeal from the Circuit Court of the United States for the Northern District of New York.

The facts are all stated in the opinion of the court.

The bill was filed in the Circuit Court, by the Troy Iron and Nail Factory against Corning, Winslow, and Horner, to restrain them from violating a patent issued to Henry Burden on the 8th of September, 1840, for new and useful improvements in the machinery for making hook, or brad-headed spike, which patent had been assigned to them; and also to account for the profits.

After the proceeding, mentioned in the opinion of the court, the Circuit Court passed the following decree:

This cause having heretofore been brought to a hearing upon the pleadings and proofs, and counsel for the respective parties having been heard, and due deliberation thereupon had, and it appearing to the said court that the said Henry Burden was the first and original inventor of the improvement on the spike-machine in the bill of complaint mentioned, and for which a patent was issued to the said Henry Burden, bearing date the 2d of September, 1840, as in said bill of complaint set forth, and that the said complainants have a full and perfect title to the said patents for said improvements, by assignment from the said Henry Burden, as is stated and set forth in the said bill of complaint.

But it also further appearing to the court, on the pleadings and proofs, that the instrument in writing, bearing date the 14th of October, 1845, stated and set forth in the said bill of complaint, and also in the answer of the said defendants thereto, entered into upon a settlement and compromise of certain conflicting claims between the said parties, and among others of mutual conflicting claims to the improvements in the spike machine in said bill mentioned, and when said instrument was executed by the said Henry Burden of the one part, and the said defendants of the other; the said Henry Burden, at the time, being the patentee and legal owner of the said improvements, and fully authorized to settle and adjust the said conflicting claims, did, in legal effect, and by just construction, impart, and authorize, and convey, a right to the defendants to use the said improvements in the manufacture of the hook-headed spike, without limitation as to the number of machines so by them to be used, or as to the place or district in which to be used.

Therefore, it is ordered, adjudged, and decreed, that the said bill of complaint be, and the same is hereby, dismissed, with costs to be taxed, and that the defendants have execution therefor.

From this decree, the complainants appealed to this court.

It was argued by *Mr. Johnson* and *Mr. Stevens*, for the appelants, and *Mr. Seward* and *Mr. Seymour*, for the appellees.

As the case turned mainly upon the construction of the agreement of October 14th, 1845, (which is inserted in the opinion of the court,) only such of the arguments of counsel will be given as relate to that construction.

The counsel for the appellants contended,

Third. It is respectfully submitted, that the instrument of the 14th of October, 1845, does not convey to the defendants any right or title to said invention, or give them any authority to use it in manufacturing hook-headed spikes. Such was not the object or intention of the parties.

This instrument was executed under the following circumstances :

At the June term of the Circuit Court, 1843, Mr. Burden recovered a judgment for $700, against the defendants, for violating this patent.

On the 2d of October, 1840, Mr. Burden filed his bill in equity in said Circuit Court, to restrain the defendants from further infringing the patent, and for an account.

After this bill was filed, the defendants ceased using the invention, for a short time; and then commenced using it again, as Mr. Burden was informed. Mr. Burden, therefore, on the 13th November, 1844, made a new affidavit, to obtain an injunction upon his bill previously filed; and, on the 20th of November, obtained an order for an injunction by default.

On the 25th of November, 1844, the defendant Winslow, and two men by the name of Osgood and Blanchard, made affidavits in said cause, for the purpose of moving the court to open the order granting an injunction; in which affidavit, they all swear that defendants did not use Mr. Burden's invention, in making hook-headed spikes, but made them with machinery entirely different in principle and mode of operation.

The machinery, by which defendants claimed to make the hook-headed spike, after the bill was filed, is described in two patents, granted to the defendants, or some of them.

Prior to these legal proceedings, in November, 1844, the parties had been endeavoring to settle, but did not succeed; subsequently, negotiations for a settlement of the suit were renewed. Mr. Burden claimed that he had the exclusive right to manufacture the hook-headed spikes by machinery, and insisted that defendants should cease making such spikes by machinery. Defendants insisted they had a right to make such spikes by their own machinery, which they insisted, in their affidavits, made November 25th, 1844, was entirely different, in principle and mode of operation, from that patented to Mr. Burden.

Mr. Burden claimed, that defendants had violated his patent for machinery for making horseshoes, and told defendants, if they did not immediately desist from using his horseshoe machine, he would prosecute them, and they did desist and stop, six months before the settlement was made.

It is necessary and proper to take these facts and circumstances into consideration, in giving a construction to the agreement of the 14th of October, 1845.

"It is well settled, that in the construction of all contracts, the situation of the parties, and the subject-matter of their transactions, may be taken into consideration, in determining the meaning of any particular sentence or provision. Extraneous evidence is admissible, so far as to ascertain the circumstances under which the writing was made, and the subject-matter to be regulated by it." Sumner *v.* Williams, 8 Mass. R. 214; Fowle *v.* Bigelow, 10 Mass. R. 384; Wilson *v.* Troup, in the Court for the Correction of Errors of N. Y. 2 Cow. 228–9; Nesmith *v.* Calvert, 1 Wood. & Min. 40.

I. This agreement does not, by its terms, convey, or purport to convey, or in any manner to give or invest the defendants with any interest in, or right or authority to use the machinery patented in September, 1840, to make hook-headed spike.

1st. It was contended by the defendants, (and, as we understand the decree, so decided,) that the 2d clause in the agreement, in legal effect, did impart, authorize, and convey to the defendants a right to use the said improvements, without limitation as to the number of machines used by them, or as to the place or territory where they might be used.

The 2d clause of the agreement is in these words: "And it is further agreed, that the said parties may each, hereafter, manufacture and vend spike of such kind and character as they see fit, notwithstanding their conflicting claims to this time."

After the judgment at law, in 1843, there was no conflict as to the right of defendant to use Mr. Burden's improvement in manufacturing hook-head spike. That had been fully settled against the defendants, by the suit at law, and conceded by them.

The defendants did not claim the right to use Burden's invention; but only the right to make said spike by machinery, which they claimed was different from Mr. Burden's, both in principle and operation. Mr. Burden denied this right claimed by the defendants, and claimed that he had the exclusive right to make such spike by machinery. This was the only conflicting claim, as to the right to make spike at the time of the settlement. By this clause in the agreement, Mr. Burden relinquished his pretensions to the exclusive right to make hook-headed spike by machinery; but he gave no right to the defendants to use his improvement in manufacturing such spike.

Whether Mr. Burden was right or wrong in his pretension to the exclusive right to make such spike by machinery, can in no manner affect the construction of the agreement.

The intention of the parties, as expressed in the agreement, taken in connection with the state of facts and circumstances under which it was executed, and the subject-matter intended to be regulated by it, must control the construction of this clause. Mr. Burden supposed he had such exclusive right, and simply relinquished it, without the most remote idea that he was conveying to the defendants any right to use his improvement, much less, that he was conveying an interest in his patent equal to one half of it.

The settlement of the equity suit, — the relinquishment by Mr. Burden of his pretension to exclude' the defendants from making hook-headed spike by machinery, — and the settlement, by defendants, of Mr. Burden's claim against them, for infringing his horseshoe patent, for which he had threatened them with a suit, — fully satisfies every clause in the agreement; and it cannot be stretched to the enormous extent claimed by defendants, without interpolating other important provisions, which cannot at law be accomplished by parol evidence. An assignment, or any other conveyance of any part of a patent, or of any interest in or under it, must be in writing. Contracts, which by law are required to be in writing, cannot rest partly in writing and partly in parol. Is it not most extraordinary that the defendants did not have this agreement recorded in the Patent-Office until the 21st of August, 1848, if they had had the least idea that it conveyed to them such an important right as they now claim? Patent Act of 1836, § 11; Curtis on Patents, p. 478.

This instrument has neither the form nor substance of a license or assignment, or any other conveyance of an interest in a patent heretofore in use or known.

If the parties had intended this instrument as a conveyance of any interest in Mr. Burden's improvement, it would have been very easy to have said so. Nesmith v. Calvert, 1 Wood. & Min. 40; Iggulden v. May, 7 East, 242.

The court below fell into the mistake, that the cause depended upon the question, whether the agreement authorized the defendants to make hook-headed spike.

The opinion of the court, after stating the 2d clause in the agreement, proceeds: " Why stipulate that the defendants may thereafter manufacture and vend spikes of any character and description, without regard to previous claims to the contrary

if it was not intended to admit or concede the right to manufacture hook-headed spikes? and how can we say that this particular spike is not embraced in the stipulation?

" What is meant by the agreement, that the defendants may
manufacture spikes of such a kind and character as they see
fit, notwithstanding their (the parties) conflicting claims to this
time, if it was intended to exclude hook-headed? The argument
is quite as strong and well founded, to exclude spikes of any other
description. Indeed, stronger, if it were possible, as this particular spike was the principal item in controversy at the time
of the compromise or settlement, and a suit was pending in
respect to it.

" The language of the instrument is certainly most remarkable,
if it was intended by the parties to exclude the defendants from
the right to make this particular spike, as there are not only no
words of exclusion or prohibition, but an express admission of
the right, in terms so full and specific, that no argument can
make it clearer. We are asked to interpret a stipulation, to
make any kind of spike the parties see fit, to mean any kind
except hook-headed; and spikes, too, in the case of a compromise of a disputed right to manufacture spikes of this character
and description, among other matters, this being regarded as the
principal one. We think it impossible to come to any such
conclusion, without a disregard to the clear import of the agreement."

The counsel for the appellant in the court below must have
been exceedingly unfortunate, if his language presented any
such idea. The bill does not claim it, and the written points
handed to the court do not pretend it. On the contrary, it was
conceded, that Mr. Burden relinquished his pretensions to the
exclusive right to make those spike by machinery, but insisted
that he had given no right to defendants to use his improvements
for that purpose.

2d. The decree assumes that, among the conflicting claims
settled by the agreement of 14th October, 1845, were the mutual
conflicting claims to the improvements in the spike-machine,
patented by Mr. Burden.

This is mere assumption, founded wholly in mistake. No
such conflicting claim is stated in the instrument, and none such
was proved to exist at the time of the settlement. The very
reverse was sworn to the year before, by the defendant, Winslow,
himself, and by two other witnesses, by his procurement. The
correspondence which took place before the settlement, shows
that no such claim was set up or pretended by the defendants.
The judgment at law had fully and definitely settled and determined that the defendants had no such right.

But if such conflicting right to Mr. Burden's improvement had existed at the time of the settlement, the terms of the agreement would not confer any right upon the defendants to use it.

The agreement concedes the defendants' right to make any kind of spike they see fit, which of course embraces hook-headed spike ; but it does not, directly or indirectly, give or concede the right to defendants to use Mr. Burden's improvement for that purpose. " The said parties may each, hereafter, make and vend spike of such kind and character as they see fit." But how manufacture? The agreement does not specify how,; but the plain construction is, that it should be done as it had been done from the recovery of·the judgment at law, up to the time of the settlement — that Mr. Burden should manufacture the spike with his machine, and the defendants with their machine, which they claimed and swore was totally different from Mr. Burden's in principle and mode of operation. Can it be pretended, that the defendants gave Mr. Burden any right to use their machine? Had Mr. Burden ever claimed any such right? Had it been shown, that hook-headed spike could not be made without the use of Mr. Burden's improvement, it might have furnished some ground for an argument that, by implication, such right was given by the agreement.

But such was not the fact. Hook-headed spike could be made, and were made by hand, prior to Mr. Burden's invention ; and the defendants show that, as early as the fall of 1844, that they had machinery by which they made hook-headed spike, which was wholly different, both· in principle and mechanical operation, from Mr. Burden's improvement ; and the only right they claimed, after the judgment at law up to and at the item of the settlement, was to make such spike by that machinery, and disclaimed all right or desire to use Mr. Burden's improvement.

3. Mr. Burden could not have intended to convey such an interest to the defendants.

It would have been a violation of his duty to, and his contract with, the appellant; and would have deprived him of the benefit of a contract from which he received more than $10,000 annually.

4. There was no adequate consideration for the conveyance of such an extensive interest in this patent.

The defendants allege, in their answer, that the purchase by them of the appellant, of half of a dock, was a part of ·the same transaction, and a part of the consideration for this agreement.

This pretence is fully disproved. The evidence clearly shows, that the agreement to purchase the dock, although made at the same time with the other agreement, had no connection with it, and that the one half of said dock was worth more than the $15,00 which defendants paid for it.

The defendants also set up in their answer, that their agreement not to make horseshoes, was a part of the consideration of the agreement on the part of Mr. Burden.

The evidence shows the facts to be, that prior to this settlement, the defendants had been infringing Mr. Burden's patent for a machine to make horseshoes — were threatened with a suit if they did not desist, and they did desist six months before the settlement.   The defendants had a patent for machinery to make horseshoes, but it was worthless.

Mr. Burden did not claim that the defendants should not make horseshoes with the machinery they had patented, but that they should not use the machinery he had patented for that purpose.   If horseshoes could have been made by the machinery patented by defendants, the agreement gives neither Mr. Burden nor the appellant any right to use that machinery, nor does it restrict the defendants from selling to others the right to make horseshoes, with the machinery patented by them.   There is nothing in the agreement which would prohibit the defendants, or their assignees, from maintaining a suit against the appellant, or any other person, for infringing defendants' patent, should the appellant or any other person use the invention thereby patented.

The defendants also allege, in their answer, that they had used the improvement in question, to make hook-headed spike since said settlement, and appellant never requested them to cease using the same, or to account for any profits for such use.

The fact thus alleged, the defendants insisted in the court below, was a circumstance to show that the appellant and Mr. Burden understood and considered the said agreement, as conveying to the defendants the right to use said improvement.

The answer to this is:

1. The answer does not allege, that the appellant, or any of its officers or agents, knew that said defendants were using said improvement.

2. It is proved, that neither Mr. Burden, nor any other of the officers or agents of the appellant, knew that defendants were using said improvement, until August, 1847.

Defendants also insist, that Mr. Burden, by his letters, bearing date between the 9th of March, 1846, and 29th December, 1846, both inclusive, requesting defendant Winslow, to agree upon the price for which they would sell hook-headed and other spike, recognizes the defendants' right to use said improvement.

The answer to this position is, that just such an arrangement, as requested in those letters, had existed between the appellant and defendant, for nine years before the settlement of 14th October, 1845, and at the time Mr. Burden wrote those letters, he did not know that defendants were using his improvement to manufacture hook-headed spike.

The letters were also written by Mr. Burden, before he knew defendants were using his improvement in making hook-headed spike.

Indeed, none of the letters, in any manner intimate, that the defendants were using, or had any right to use the improvement.

The counsel for the defendants in error contended, that the decree of the Circuit Court should be affirmed, because,

I. The agreement of October 14th, 1845, was a valid agreement, binding upon the parties.

1. It was made by parties fully competent to contract in reference to the subject-matter of the contract.

Burden was patentee, and as such, could contract for himself as the owner of the patent. He was also at the time a large stockholder in the complainants' corporation, and their agent, and as such, could contract for them.

The allegation, made by the complainants in their bill of complaint, that Henry Burden "had no power or authority to give such license, your orator having been the legal and equitable owner of the said last-mentioned patent, and the rights and privileges granted and secured thereby, from the time said patent was granted," is not sustained by the proof.

The only proof tending to show that on the 14th October, 1845, the complainants were the owners of this improvement of the bending lever, and that therefore Burden had no authority to grant a license, or make a contract as to the use of the same, is to be found in the agreement between Burden and complainants as to the patents for the spike machine and the horseshoe, and dated 2d December, 1836.

In reference to this agreement, the defendants insist as follows :

1. The agreement between the plaintiffs and Henry Burden, of December 2d, 1836, did not even purport to convey to the plaintiffs any interest or right to the patent of 1840, or to the bending lever, the thing patented. It first gives the right to use the machines for manufacturing wrought nails or spikes, then on the premises of the company ; and secondly, the exclusive right to construct other machines for the manufacturing wrought nails or spikes, after the method invented by Burden, with all the improvements which he had made, or should make, in the same, in any other part of the United States ; and thirdly, a

covenant that he, Burden, would obtain a patent for any improvements which he should afterward make in his nail and spike machine; and then provides that "the license hereby g.a ited to the party of the second part, shall be deemed to extend to all such improvements." It only contemplates the granting of a license; and the statement in the assignment of June 19, 1848, that Burden had agreed to transfer and assign the improvement, is not true.

The bending lever, patented by the patent of 1840, was not then in existence. It was a mere contingent possibility, and therefore was not susceptible of being conveyed. There was nothing to convey. Phillips on Patents, 354; Curtis on Patents, sec. 189.

The privilege of assigning, given by the eleventh section of the Patent Act of July 4, 1836, implies that the thing assigned shall be then in existence, and the subsequent requirement in the same section, as to recording the assignment, supports the same idea.

2. Even if this agreement did purport to grant and assign a future improvement thereof, such grant could not apply to the bending lever, for the reason that the bending lever is not an improvement upon either of the patented machines mentioned in the agreement of December 2d, 1836, but is a distinct and independent article, or invention, equally applicable to any spike machine, and in fact, used upon various other machines.

The plaintiffs consider the agreement of December 2d, 1836, as merely a covenant to convey the improvement alleged to have been patented on the 2d of September, 1840, and have accordingly resorted to a special assignment of it, which was made on the 19th of June, 1848, and which, in terms, refers to the agreement of December, 1836, as merely a covenant to convey subsequent improvements, and purports to have been given in performance of such covenant.

The right of the plaintiffs to this improvement of the bending lever is based in their bill upon the assignment of the 19th June, 1848. This right is therefore subject to any rights that were acquired by the defendants by the agreement of October 14, 1845.

But if the complainants had, previous to the 14th October, 1845, become the owners of the improvement called the bending lever, and the patent therefor, still, as general agent of the corporation, Burden had a right to enter into the agreement of October 14, 1845, and it binds his principals.

3. The agreement of October 14, 1845, was founded upon a good and valuable consideration, as between the parties—1st, the settlement of the suit then pending between them; and

2d, the relinquishment by the defendant, Winslow, in behalf of himself and his copartners, of the right to manufacture the patent horseshoe, an advantage worth to the other contracting party, $10,000 per annum.

3. The agreement, too, was carried out by the parties; first, by the conveyance of the dock property by the plaintiffs, and its occupation by the defendants; second, by the payment of the consideration of the dock property by the defendants; thirdly, by the relinquishment by the defendants, of the horseshoe business, from that time to the present, and the enjoyment of it as a monopoly ever since by the plaintiffs; fourth, by the continued use by the defendants, of the bending lever in making hook-headed spikes, from the 14th of October, 1845, to the 8th July, 1848, two years and about nine months, without objection, they having made, during that period, hook-headed spikes to the value of over $137,000.

III. The agreement of October 14, 1845, was a contract for the settlement of conflicting claims to two patented machines, one for the bending lever, and the other for the horseshoe machine, and it not only gives rights to make the spikes and the horseshoes, but to use the respective patented machines in making them.

The agreement of October 14, 1845, does not, in terms, give the right to the defendants to use the machines patented by Burden, by his patent of 1840, but it does give it by the strongest implication. It releases all claims for violation of patent-rights, up to that date, and gives the right to both parties, thereafter, to manufacture and vend spike of such kind and character as they see fit, notwithstanding their conflicting claims to that time.

Defendants' exhibits show that those conflicting claims related only to the use of the patented machinery. This is also shown by Burden's letters. The subject-matter of this general settlement was, therefore, their conflicting claims to the use of the patented machinery. The agreement gives the right to make the spike, which could be made for sale in market only by the use of the bending lever, or of some analogous device. 1 Washington's C. C. Rep. 168, Rutger v. Kanowrs & Grant; Phillips on Patents, 346.

A construction of the agreement of October 14, 1845, which would allow the defendants only the privilege of making the hook-headed spikes, and would deny them the use of the bending lever in making them, would render the instrument senseless, absurd, and inoperative.

For, if it is held, that the defendants obtained under the agreement only the privilege of making hook-headed spikes, either by hand, or by the use of any machinery which they might choose, other than that which should infringe upon Burden's patent, then it results that the defendants relinquish the patent horse-shoe business, worth, as is proved by the testimony of Mr. Davidson, $10,000 per annum, for the privilege of doing just what they had a right to do before, and what every body else had the right of doing, that is, making those spikes by hand, or with any machinery not infringing on Burden's patent. Such a construction would be contrary to the well-settled rule in the interpretation of contracts, that, when a clause is capable of two significations, it should be understood in that in which it will have some operation, rather than in that which it will have none, " *ut res magis valeat quam pereat.*" Pothier, cited in 2 Comvn on Contracts, 533; Parkhurst *v.* Smith, Willes's Reports, 332; Archibald *v.* Thomas, 3 Cowen, 290. An agreement or contract must have a reasonable construction, according to the intent of the parties, as if a man agree with B. for twenty barrels of ale, he shall not have the barrels after the ale is spent. Comyns's Digest, Title Agreement, C. So if a man promise payment, without saying to whom, it shall be intended to him from whom the consideration comes. Cro. Eliz. 149. And upon a promise of payment, according to the rate of forty shillings per ton, it shall be intended that payment will be made for the odd pounds, according to the same rate. Yelverton, 124.

The practical construction of both parties has been in conformity to the interpretation on which the defendants insist. " *Contemporanea expositio est fortissima lex.*"

If the construction were a doubtful one, it should, under the circumstances, be held to be against that set up by the plaintiffs, whose grantor, Henry Burden, is the contractor. In a case of doubt, the words of a promise, or covenant, are to be taken most strongly against the promisor or contractor. Coke Lit. 183, a. This rule should be applied, in this case especially, for two very apparent reasons: First, because it was well understood, by both parties, with what machinery alone these hook-headed spikes could be successfully made for sale in market, and that the defendants were then using that machinery in their works; and, secondly, because Burden had a strong pecuniary motive to deal in generalities, and not to grant, specifically and clearly, a license to use the bending lever. He feared he might jeopard the thirty per cent., secured to him by the agreement of December 2d. 1836, and which was afterwards in controversy, and was claimed by the plaintiffs to have been forfeited by him; and yet he desired to obtain the monopoly of the horseshoe business.

The contemporaneous exposition of the agreement, by Burden,

is in accordance with the position of the defendants. See his letter of December 15th, 1845, and his letter of December 11th, 1846. In this latter letter, Burden speaks of his intention to share the spike business with defendants. He very well knew that could not be done, except by uniform prices, and that we could have no uniform price with him, unless we used the bending lever.

But there was an actual sharing between appellant and respondents, of contracts for spikes. Burden declared that it was his intention to share with respondents the spike business, and this was done, as is shown by his letters. Such was the practical contemporaneous construction of the agreement, and it appears, by Burden's letter of February 10th, 1848, that not only was there to be an uniform price for hook-headed spikes, but that the whole field was to be occupied by the parties in common, and to the exclusion of all others. The whole object of this letter was to tell respondents what he had been doing to protect their common rights. Can there be any thing more needed to show that it was the understanding of both parties, that by the agreement of October 14th, 1845, respondents had the right to use the bending lever?

Winslow's letters, written in January, 1845, show that respondents were using the bending lever at that time, and that Burden then knew it. In Burden's letter of January 10th, 1845, and in Winslow's reply to it, of January 13th, 1845, they both refer to "the machinery in question," which can only mean the bending lever.

IV. But whatever might have been the construction which a court would, under other circumstances, have put upon this agreement—a Court of Equity will not now grant an injunction, as is prayed for in the complainants' bill, after an acquiescence in the use of the patented machinery, under this agreement of October 14th, 1845, for near three years before the commencement of this suit. Wyeth v. Stone, 1 Story, 273; Rundle v. Murray, Jacob's R. 311; Williams v. the Earl of Jersey, 1 Craig & Phil. 91; Warwick v. Hooper, 3 Eng. Law and Eq. Rep. 233, cited; U. S. Dig. Appendix, vol. 5, 1851, title *Patent.*

Mr. Justice WAYNE delivered the opinion of the court.

This is an appeal from the Circuit Court of the United States for the Northern District of New York.

The appellants are a manufacturing company, incorporated by the laws of the State of New York. They aver, that Henry Burden was the inventor of a new and useful improvement in the machinery for manufacturing wrought nails and spikes, for which letters-patent were granted to him, on the 2d of December, 1834. They allege that it was assigned to them, for a valuable consideration, and also, that Burden covenanted with them, if he should thereafter make any improvement upon his invention, that he would convey the same to them. Burden afterwards did make a new and useful improvement in machinery for making hook or brad-headed spikes, for which a patent was granted to him, on the 2d of September, 1840. He assigned it to the complainants, in virtue of his covenant, whereby they became the exclusive owners of the patent. They then complain that the defendants had infringed the same, by having erected and put in use, in their iron and nail works, in the city of Troy, four or five machines for the manufacture of hook, or brad-headed spikes, containing the improvements in their assigned patent, and had used them for manufacturing hook, or brad-headed spikes, since the 15th of October, 1845.

It is also stated, that Burden brought an action at law against the defendants, for an infringement, secured by the patent of September 2d, 1840. The defendants resisted a recovery, upon the ground that Burden was not the first inventor of the improvements for which that patent had been obtained. A trial of this case, upon the merits, resulted in a verdict for Burden, for seven hundred dollars, which was carried into a final judgment against the defendants, after a motion which they made for a new trial had been overruled.

The defendants are then charged with again using the improvements in the patent of 1840, under the pretence that they have a license from Burden to do so. This is denied by the complainants; and they say, if such license had been given by Burden, that it was in contravention of his assignment to them of his patent, by which they became the legal and equitable owners, from the time it was granted, on September 2d, 1840.

The bill is then concluded, with a prayer that the court would enjoin the defendants, Corning, Horner, and Winslow, their attorneys, and agents, and workmen, to desist from making, using, or vending, any machine containing the improvements, for which letters-patent were granted to Burden, on the 2d of September, 1840; and, from selling or using any spikes which they then had on hand, which had been manufactured by their machines containing the improvements of that patent. An account of the profits, which they had derived from the use of such patented improvements, is also called for.

The letters-patent granted to Burden, on the 2d day of September, 1834, and that of the 2d of September, 1840, describing an improvement called a bending lever, in the machinery for making hook or brad-headed spikes, are made exhibits to the bill.

This bill was answered by the defendants.

It admits that the complainants were an incorporated body, under the style of the Troy Iron and Nail Factory Company; also, that Henry Burden was the inventor of the improvements in the machinery for making nails and spikes, for which letters-patent were granted to him in December, 1834, and that he assigned the same to the complainants two years thereafter. But they deny that there was any covenant in the assignment, or in any other agreement then recorded in the Patent-Office, or any agreement between Burden and the complainants, obliging him to convey to them any improvement which he might make upon his invention. And they insist, if such an agreement was made, that, as it was only a covenant to convey a contingent possibility, which would be inoperative and void, and could not affect them. The defendants also admit that Burden obtained the patent of 2d September, 1840; but they deny its validity. They declare that the bending lever, described in the specification of it, or one similar to it in form and principle of construction and operation, had been invented and had been used by several persons in making spikes for several years before the patent had been obtained by Burden for his improvement of the bending lever. They state that it was invented by Thomas and William Osgood, and used by them in the years 1835, '36, '37, '38, upon one of their spike machines, to make hook or brad-headed spikes, which they sold during those years in Philadelphia. It is also stated by the defendants, that the bending lever, patented by Burden, was the invention of one Ebenezer Hunt, whilst he was in the employment of the former. It is then admitted that Burden assigned to the complainants his patent for the bending lever, in June, 1848; but it is said to have been fraudulently done, and that the appellants have no right, legal or equitable, to that improvement, under that assignment, or by that of the agreement between the complainants of Burden, of December, 1836. And, it is added, should they have any right or interest in the patent for Burden's bending lever, that the defendants have also the right to use the same under an agreement with Burden of the 14th October, 1845, which was made for himself, and in behalf of the appellants, as their agent, before he had assigned it to them in 1848.

The defendants then aver, that this agreement of the 14th October was made with the understanding of both parties; that it would finally settle all differences between themselves and Burden and the complainants, which had arisen out of counter claims by both parties to a patent for making horseshoes, and also to a patent-right for making hook or brad-headed spikes, each party claiming the right to manufacture and vend such horseshoe: and such spikes, under their respective counter claims and patents, without the permission of either to the other, and to use, in the manufacture of the brad-headed spike, Burden's bending lever.

The consideration of the agreement is said to have been a purchase by the defendants from the complainants, of an undivided half part of a dock on the Hudson River, for $1,500, — a grant by the defendants to them for the exclusive manufacture of patent horseshoes, — and a mutual relinquishment of their counter claim to the patents for making hook-headed spikes by a bending lever. It is averred, that they had used Burden's bending lever in the manufacture of such spikes, from the date of the agreement, with his knowledge, without objection by him or by the appellants, and that Burden had discontinued the suit against them. It is not necessary to state more of the pleadings. The abstract given discloses what had been the relations between these parties for several years before this suit was brought, and their views and conduct respecting the patent for the bending lever.

We will now turn to the evidence in the case. It shows, first, that every allegation in the bill has either been proved or admitted by the answer of the defendants, excepting such as they respectively make concerning the agreement of the 14th October, 1845, which will hereafter have our attention.

The letters-patent obtained by Burden, in 1834, which describes a machine for making nails and spikes, is annexed as an exhibit to the bill, and so is that afterwards granted to them, in 1840, for his improvement on the first, for making hook or brad-headed spikes. The answer admits that he was the inventor of the first, and that he had a patent for it. It also admitted that he obtained a patent for the other; but it is denied that he was the inventor of it. This the defendants have failed to prove; and, in our opinion, the evidence given by them on that point rather serves to establish the originality of the invention than to impair it. We think so, because it is uncertain and conflicting, and, as our learned brother said concerning it in the court below, is irreconcilable. The appellants stand upon that patent as the first which was granted for the bending lever, and they may well do so, until other evidence than that in this record shall be given to disprove its originality. It is admitted that Burden assigned that patent also to the appellants; but it is said to have been fraudulently done, and that it was not made, because Burden had covenanted, in his assignment to them of his first patent, to convey to the appellants any improvements he might thereafter make upon that machine during the time that the patent had to run. The assignment by Burden to the appellants of his patent for making wrought nails or spikes is dated in December, 1836, just two years after it was obtained. It contains, after the transferring clause, and in connection with it, these words, " with all the improvements which he hath made or shall make in the same, in any other part of the United States, as the said parties of the second part shall deem expedient, during the term for which the same are or may be patented by the said party of the first part." The assignment itself being admitted by the defendants, this, as a part of it, must also be included in the admission. It is, in our opinion, a covenant which bound Burden to convey to the appellants his improvement upon his machine of the bending lever. Though the assignment of it was not made until several years after it was patented, the appellants were equitably entitled to it before. Without something besides to sustain them, than the delay in making the assignment, the defendants had no ground for stating that it was a fraudulent device to overreach and defeat the agreement between themselves and Burden, of the 14th October, 1845. The defendants also admit that they were sued by Burden in 1842, for an infringement of the rights secured to him by his patent for the bending lever. That, though they had resisted it, upon the ground that Burden was not the inventor, the jury, who tried the case upon its merits, had returned a verdict against them for the infringement, with $700 damages; and that it was carried into judgment. This was in the year 1843.

In November, 1844, Burden, believing that the defendants were again using his bending lever, for making brad-head spikes, brought against them a bill, to enjoin them from doing so, and asking for an account. They had notice of it; but, from some accidental cause, they did not appear to resist the application, and an injunction was granted until the further order of the court.

In a few days, with the view to be released from it, Mr. Winslow, in behalf of himself and his associates, filed an affidavit, with another made by Thomas Osgood and Israel Blanchard. In each of them, they swear that the defendants were not using Burden's invention in their manufacture of hook or brad-headed spikes, but that they made them with machinery altogether different in principle and mode of operation from that which they were using when Mr. Burden sued them in 1842 for an infringement of his patent, and when he obtained a judgment against them. Mr. Winslow states, that the machinery they were then using, is entirely different in principle and operation from the machine used by Burden in making hook and brad-headed spikes. Osgood and Blanchard, after stating that they had been in the employment of the defendants

18*

for several years, say that they were well· acquainted with the process used by the defendants in making hook-headed spikes, and with that which they were using, when the defendants were prosecuted for an infringement of Mr. Burden's patent, and that they were well acquainted with the improvement claimed to have been invented by Burden; that the machinery then used by the defendants not only differed from that which they used when they were prosecuted for an infringement of Burden's patent, but also that the process then in use by the defendants, by which the hook-head is formed, is entirely new and different, in principle and use, from the bending lever described by Burden in his patent. They proceed to say, that Burden's patent, in their opinion, is in no manner violated by the manufacture of 'hook-headed spikes in the mode in which they are now made by the defendants. The process mentioned, by them, and by Mr. Winslow, is not stated in their affidavits. What it was, we do not know with certainty.

These affidavits show the attitude in which the defendants put themselves, on the 25th of November, 1844, in the suit then pending with Burden.

It was this, that as a defence against that suit, they claimed the right to manufacture hook or brad-headed spikes, by machinery entirely differing, in principle and operation, from Burden's bending lever for the same manufacture.

So it continued, until the agreement of the 14th of October, 1845, was made. Then, and the day after, all of the new processes mentioned in the affidavits of Winslow, Osgood, and Blanchard, for making brad-headed spikes, and such as are described in the patents obtained by the defendants, were set aside in their factory, for Burden's more manageable and efficient bending lever.

This brings us to the consideration of the agreement. We give it, *totidem verbis.*

Agreement, made this fourteenth day of October, 1845, between Henry Burden of the one part, and Erastus Corning, James Horner, and John F. Winslow, of the other part. Whereas, a suit is now pending in the Circuit Court of the United States, in the Northern District of New York, in favor of the said Henry Burden, against the said Corning, Horner, and Winslow, arising out of the alleged violation and infringement of a patent-right, claimed by said Burden for making of spike, both parties claiming the right to make said spike : It is now agreed, between the said parties, that the said suit shall be, and is hereby, discontinued, each party paying their own costs. And it is further agreed, that the said parties may each hereafter manufacture and vend spikes, of such kind and character as they see fit, notwithstanding their conflicting claims to this time. And the said John F. Winslow, claiming as patentee, to have the right for the benefit of the said Corning, Horner, and himself, to manufacture the patent horseshoe. And the said Henry Burden also claiming such right exclusiv ly. It is severally agreed, by said Corning, Horner, and Win low, that said Burden may manufacture said patent horseshoes, and that said Corning, Horner, and Winslow, will not manufacture them. And each party, in consideration of the premises, hereby releases to the other, or others, all claim, demand, and cause of action, by reason of any violation of the patent-rights claimed by them, as aforesaid, to the date hereof.

Dated October 14th, 1845.   H. BURDEN.

It contains, besides its premises, which will be seen are not unimportant for the construction of it, four substantive clauses.

First, the discontinuance of the suit then pending between the parties, each party to pay their own costs. Next, that each party might, thereafter, manufacture spike of such kind and character as they see fit, notwithstanding their conflicting claims to that time. Then the concession by the defendants to Burden, that he may manufacture the patent horseshoes, and that they will not do so, though they had claimed the right to make them, notwithstanding Burden's exclusive claim for that purpose. And this is followed by releases by each party to the other, of all claim, demand, and causes of action, by reason of any violation of the patent-rights claimed by them, as aforesaid, to the date hereof.

The defendants contend that, in virtue of this agreement, they have a right to use the Burden bending lever, upon their spike machines. That it was made for the settlement and compromises of all differences and claims then existing between themselves and Burden, on account of their counter claims for making patent horseshoes and brad-headed spike. And that the consideration of the agreement on their part, was, that they had given to these appellants fifteen hundred dollars, for an undivided half part of a dock on the Hudson River; had conceded to them an exclusive privilege to make patent horseshoes; and that each party had relinquished to the other their patents for making hook-headed spikes by a bending lever, so that both might use that of the other. It is further stated, by the defendants, that they had fully performed their obligations of the agreement, and that they had, from the date of it, used Burden's bending lever, in making spike, with the knowledge of Burden and the appellants, without any objection by either of them.

From the premises of the agreement, it appears that the suit to be discontinued was one which Burden had brought against Corning, Horner, and Winslow, for an alleged infringement of his patent for making spike. each party in the suit claiming the right to do so.   What their counter claims were, are not given in the agreement.   They are, however, distinctly recited in the bill, and in the answer of the defendants, as they say they existed at the date of the agreement.   Each party, at that time, claimed a right to make brad-headed spikes by different machines.   Burden's claim is put upon his patent for the bending lever.   The defendants denied that they had infringed it by the machine which they had in use, and swear that it was different, in principle and operation, from Burden's patent bending lever. It is also said by them, in their answer, that there were differences between them as to a patent for making the horseshoe. The differences, however, on that account, were never litigated by the parties, and the subject is only before us because it is mentioned in the agreement, and in the answer of the defendants in this suit.

Having ascertained, from the agreement itself, and from the pleadings in this suit, what were the conflicting claims between the parties when the agreement was made, we are prepared to give our construction to that clause of it, from which the defendants claim the right, or a license, to use Burden's bending lever for making brad-headed spikes.

It is in these words: " And it is further agreed, that the said parties may each hereafter manufacture and vend spike of such kind and character as they see fit, notwithstanding their conflicting claims to this time"—that is, up to the date of the agreement.

The limitation as to time, clearly indicates, as the existing litigation between them in the suit had been the rights claimed by both in it, to manufacture brad-headed spike, with a bending lever, operating differently in the machines which they were respectively using in their factories, that each thereafter could make and vend them, notwithstanding the claim made by Burden, in his bill, that he had, by his patent, the exclusive right to make them.   The words are, " that the said parties may each hereafter manufacture and vend spike, of such kind and character as they see fit."   Burden had obtained at law one verdict against the defendants, for a violation of his patent, and the suit then pending was another, which he had brought in equity, to restrain the parties from continuing the infringement.   They deny that the judgment against them, in the suit at law, had settled the validity of Burden's patent.   That that question was still open in the second suit, as they say it is in this, the third suit; but in no one of them did they ever claim the right to use Burden's invention as such, or as they now claim to do, under the agreement, but they claimed, in all of them, only a right to make brad-headed spikes, by machinery which was different, in principle and operation, from Burden's patent. When the parties were adjusting a compromise of the second suit, and up to the time when it was done, Burden had claimed an exclusive right, from his patent, to make brad-headed spike with a bending lever. The defendants claimed also that right, and it was because they exercised it, that Burden sued them for an infringement of his patent. Both parties were making brad-headed spike; Burden, under an unquestioned right, growing out of his patent; the defendants under a controvertible claim, which the suit was brought to settle judicially. They had already almost obtained a monopoly for the supply of such spike for the railroads of the country. It was with the hope of doing so entirely, and with the expectation of dividing the spike business of the United States between them, notwithstanding the threatening competition of other persons, who claimed the right to make brad-headed spike, and were making them with a bending lever, that Mr. Burden and these defendants were induced to compromise their litigation. It was a mere matter of interest, which actuated them, without any other sympathies between them than the disinclination of all persons to have the relations of social life and of business broken up by protracted litigation. But each party, business-like, alive to his own interest, did not mean to make any sacrifice to the other, except such as their common object might require; that was, to drive all others out of the brad-headed spike trade. Burden had obtained one verdict against the defendants, for infringing his patent. He was suing them for doing so again, and had obtained no injunction *nisi*, to restrain them from continuing it. They continued to make spike with a machine, alleging it to be no infringement of their competitor's patent. That was the point of controversy. It was believed, by both of them, that their common interest required a relinquishment of it by Mr. Burden, and he made it, intending that each might thereafter make brad-headed spike himself, as he had a right to do, from his patent, and the defendants, as they represented themselves to be doing, by the machine which they swear was different, in principle and operation, from his, and no infringement of it. Brad-headed spike could be made with either of them, and that being the case, it was agreed that each might thereafter manufacture and vend spike of such kind and character as they might " see fit" to do.

It was admitted, in the argument of this case, and had it not been, it is certain that the agreement of October 14, 1845, does not, in terms, give to the defendants the right to use the machines patented by Burden in 1840. But, it is said, it does give that right by implication; that such was the understanding and intention. And that is inferred from matters in the agreement and from a circumstance out of it, which are said to determine its construction in favor of the claim made by the defendants to use Burden's patent. We proceed to examine it.

In the agreement it is said, " Each party, in consideration of the premises, releases to the other all claim, demand, and cause of action, by reason of any violation of the patent-rights claimed by them, as aforesaid, to the date hereof." Those are its words.

By the premises, of course, in its use here, is meant all of the deed which precedes the releases, making every part or clause the consideration for which the releases are given. The release is a relinquishment by both parties of all claim, demand, and cause of action, for the violation of patent-rights claimed by them, to that date. It is imperfectly expressed, as to the subject-matters in controversy, which were then to be compromised as they appear in the suit. That such was the intention, appears from the language of the release, it being for any violation of the patent-rights claimed by them. The defendants never charged Burden with any violation of any patent of theirs in their pleadings. They make but two claims: The first, that they had as good a right to make brad-headed spikes as Burden had, notwithstanding his suit against them for infringing his patent; and, as patentee, that they had the right to manufacture the patent horseshoe, against the exclusive claim of Burden, under his patent, to make them. Now, though the release, as it is expressed, may imply that there had been between the parties other claims than such as we find in the suit and in the agreement, we think the words in the release, " claimed by them, as aforesaid," fix its meaning to what is expressed. And if this was not so, we should say, without these words, " claimed by them, as aforesaid," that the general words would be restrained by the particular occasion of using them; and that its meaning is, that Burden releases to the defendants, for the considerations of the agreement, all claim and causes of action up to that date, for any violation of his patent-rights for the horseshoe and bending lever, for which they asserted a claim as well as himself. T. Raymond, 399; 3 Mod. 277; 1 Lev. 235; 3 Id. 273; 2 Shower, 47.

Besides, the releases being operative only up to that date, it is very difficult to admit that it was meant to provide prospectively for the defendants to use a particular machine, for any previous violation for which they were then to be released. It is a bar to any right of action for the past for the causes stated, and not a limitation upon the releases for any thing of a like kind which may be done thereafter.

But it was also urged, that the rights of the defendants, under the agreement, to use Burden's bending lever, might be inferred from their relinquishment to the appellant of their right to make the horseshoe. The proofs in the case disclose, that Burden had obtained, in November, 1835, a patent for a new and useful improvement in the machine for making horseshoes, and that he also patented another improvement upon that in 1843. In May, 1844, Mr. Horner and Mr. Winslow bought from Elisha Tolles and Nathaniel B. Gaylord, for $1,000, a patent for making or bending horseshoes, claimed by Tolles as his invention, of which Gaylord became the owner of an undivided half, by assignment from Tolles, before the latter obtained his patent, in 1834. In the agreement for the purchase it is recited that, the patent having been lost, a new patent was issued to Tolles, in May, 1844. The view taken by Winslow and Horner of their purchase of that patent is shown by covenants in the agreement. It is that, in case it shall at any time appear, by the decision of any court having competent jurisdiction, that the patents conveyed to Winslow and Horner were not valid and effectual to secure to them the exclusive privileges thereby granted, whether for the reason that Tolles was not the original inventor of the machine, or otherwise, then, that the purchase-money was to be returned to Horner and Winslow, with interest from the time it was received, both Tolles and Gaylord being only responsible for the portions of the money that they might receive, Gaylord guaranteeing to the purchasers one hundred dollars of the three hundred and seventy-five dollars, which it appears he did receive from Mr. Winslow, Gaylord having, on the same day, received from him six hundred and seventy-five dollars. Such was the claim of the defendants for a patent for bending horseshoes, and no more. The defendants had the right to buy such a patent, with an undertaking to pay the expenses of a law suit, if they pleased to do so. And they had a right to use the patent which they bought, if it had really been obtained, and was not an infringement of another patent. But, having shown their own apprehension of its invalidity, and provided that they were to lose nothing by it, in case it should prove to be the right, which they asserted under it in the agreement of 14th October, 1845, can only be viewed by us as a relinquishment of a very doubtful claim to make the patent horseshoe, to the exclusive claim made by Burden, to make them under his patent, which formed an inducement with the latter to enter into the release contained in that agreement. As to the circumstance out of the agreement, upon which the defendants state formed in fact the consideration, it is only necessary to say, it sufficiently appears that the undivided half of the dock, which they bought from the appellants, was fully worth the sum paid for it when the purchase was made, and, therefore, the price given cannot be a consideration for any thing else.

We have so far construed the agreement from what is expressed in it, in connection with the claims made by the parties in the suit which Burden agreed to discontinue. There are other reasons which would bring us to the same conclusion:

Though no form has been prescribed, either for assignments of patents or for licenses to use them, we have judicial decisions concerning both which are to determine what language will make either, and how they are to be distinguished from each other. The clause of the agreement from which the defendants wish it to be inferred that they have the right to use Burden's bending lever, gives nothing definitely. The claim made by them in their answer is uncertain. It is difficult to distinguish whether they mean to claim by assignment or by a license; and when it was urged, in the argument, that they did so by license, it was equally uncertain whether they did so upon a claim which they might assign or use for others who might become owners in their factory, or which they could only personally use without being transmissible by them to others. The difference is well understood. A mere license to a party, without having his assigns or equivalent words to them, showing that it was meant to be assignable, is only the grant of a personal power to the licensees, and is not transferable by him to another. Curtis on Patents, sec. 198; 2 Story's Reports, 525, 554. It is true that, in the argument, the claim was for a license to use Burden's bending lever; but to what extent, or where, or for what time, was not said; nor can it be collected from their answer. Such uncertainties we cannot affirm of an agreement which definitely states wha, they may do. Further, we cannot adopt the construction of the agreement contended for by the defendants, because they gave no such consideration for such an interest in Burden's patent. We do not say an inadequate one, but no consideration. We can find none in the agreement, nor any in what is said in their answer to have been a consideration. It has already been shown, that the dock bought by them from the appellants could not have been any part of a consideration, because the proofs in the cause show that their use of it is a convenience in their business, and that the interest which they acquired in that property was fully worth the price given by them for it. In addition to what has already been said concerning the relinquishment of the horseshoe manufacture, or that Burden might manufacture them, and that they would not, we cannot see how that, as a part of the agreement, can be made by any implication to mean more than this, — that it was a surrender to the exclusive claim of Burden to make them of a very equivocal right upon their part to do so, for the discontinuance of the pending suit, for the allowance to them to make brad-headed spike, which it was the purpose of the suit to prevent, and for the releases, mutually given against any future claim for past violations of the patent-rights claimed by them in their pleadings. We think, from the agreement, that such was the intention of the parties to it, notwithstanding the declaration of the defendants that it was otherwise. We do so, because there is no proof of it in the case, and because it is not permitted to a party to control a written agreement by parol testimony of declarations or conversation, at the time it was completed or before, which would contradict, add to, or alter the written agreement, either in the case of a latent or patent ambiguity, though in either, collateral facts, and the circumstances in which the parties were placed when the agreement was made, may be given in evidence. In the first case, to ascertain something extrinsic or matter out of the instrument where there is no ambiguity from the language of it, and in the other when, from defective terms, the intention of the parties may not be collected from them. In this agreement, we can see no such ambiguity of expression to make it doubtful, or any thing extrinsic connected with it to make it uncertain.

The proofs in this case disclose, that Burden's bending lever is a valuable invention. So much so, that the appellants gave to him for the assignment of it, with its improvements and for the assignment of the horseshoe patent, thirty per cent. upon the net gains of the manufacture of both, with a like interest in the value of all the machinery of both which might be on hand when the contract shall be at an end — and with the same interest in all the real estate, the additions and improvements of it, which shall be bought and made out of the earnings of the assigned machinery, with this further stipulation upon the part of the appellant, that his interest, as they have been stated, should commence six months before the date of his assignments. With such advantages, it cannot be supposed that it was understood by the parties to the agreement of 14th October, 1845, that Burden meant to put a rival establishment in possession of an interest in his patent equal to that of the appellants, for making brad-headed spike, and that for nothing.

Before concluding, we will remark, that there is no proof in the cause to maintain the averment in the answer of the defendants, that they used the bending lever of Burden with his knowledge and that of the appellants, from the date of the agreement until the suit was brought, without any objection or complaint from either of them.

In every point of view which we can take of this case, we think that the defendants have infringed the patent for making hook or brad-headed spike with Burden's bending lever. We shall direct the decree of the court below to be reversed, and hall order a perpetual injunction to enjoin the defendants from using the machine with Burden's bending lever in the manufacture of brad-headed spike, and shall remand the case to the court below, with directions for an account to be taken as is prayed for by the appellants.

Mr. Chief Justice TANEY, and Mr. Justice NELSON dissented.

Order.

This cause came on to be heard on the transcript of the record from the Circuit Court of the United States for the Northern District of New York, and was argued by counsel. On consideration whereof, it is now here ordered, adjudged, and decreed by this court, that the decree of said Circuit Court in this cause be, and the same is hereby, reversed, with costs, and that this cause be, and the same is hereby, remanded to the said Circuit Court, with instructions to enjoin the defendants perpetually from using the improved machinery with the bending lever for making hook and brad-headed spikes, patented to Henry Burden, the 2d September, 1840, and assigned to the complainant as set forth in complainant's bill, and to enter a decree in favor of the complainants, for the use and profits thereof, upon an account to be stated by a master, under the direction of the said Circuit Court, as is prayed for by the complainant, and for such further proceedings to be had therein in conformity to the opinion of this court, as to law and justice may appertain.

HORACE C. SILSBY, WASHBURN RACE, ABEL DOWNS, HENRY HERRION, AND CHARLES D. THOMPSON, v. ELISHA FOOTE.

Upon a trial in New York, a juror became ill, and was discharged before any evidence was given, and before the plaintiffs' counsel had concluded his opening address. The court ordered another juror to be sworn, and proceeded with the trial. The defendant cannot object to this. It is the practice in New York, and the Circuit Court had a right to follow it.

The court having erroneously refused to allow the plaintiff to offer a paper in evidence as a disclaimer of part of a patent, afterwards refused to allow the defendants to offer the same paper in evidence for the purpose of prejudicing the plaintiffs' rights. This last refusal was correct. The reason given was erroneous, but this is not a sufficient cause for reversing the judgment.

The courts of the United States have not the power to order a non-suit against the wishes of the plaintiff.

Under a notice given by the defendant, that the invention claimed by the plaintiff was described in Ure's Dictionary of Arts, Manufactures and Mines, and had been used by Andrew Ure, of London, it was not competent to give in evidence a very large book. The place in the book should have been specified.

Nor, under the notice, was the book competent evidence that Andrew Ure, of London, had a prior knowledge of the thing patented. The notice does not state the place where the same was used.

One of the specifications of the patent being for a combination of certain parts of mechanism necessary to produce the desired result, it was proper for the court to instruct the jury that the defendants had not infringed the patent, unless they had used all the parts embraced in the plaintiffs' combination; and the jury were to find what those parts were, and whether the defendants had used them.

When a claim does not point out and designate the particular elements which compose a combination, but only declares, as it properly may, that the combination is made up of so much of the described machinery as effects a particular result, it is a question of fact which of the described parts are essential to produce that result, and to this extent, not the construction of the claim, strictly speaking, but the application of the claim, should be left to the jury.

THIS case was brought up, by writ of error, from the Circuit Court of the United States for the Northern District of New York.

The facts are stated in the opinion of the court.

It was argued by *Mr. Seward*, for the plaintiffs in error, and by *Mr. Foote*, in proper person, for the defendant in error.

Mr. Justice CURTIS delivered the opinion of the court.

This is an action on the case for the violation of a patent-right granted to the defendant in error on the 26th day of May, 1842, for "a new and useful improvement in regulating the draft of stoves." On the trial in the Circuit Court for the Northern District of New York, the defendants took exceptions to the rulings of the District Judge, who presided at the trial, and have brought the case here by a writ of error.

The first exception shows the following facts: After the counsel for the plaintiff had begun his opening address to the jury, a juror became ill, applied to the court to be discharged, and was discharged from the panel on account of physical inability to sit on the residue of the trial. Thereupon the court ordered another juror to be drawn and sworn, and the panel being thus full, the trial proceeded, and the plaintiffs' counsel concluded his address. The plaintiff assented to this proceeding: the defendant objected, and excepted to the order of the court.

We think it was not erroneous for the presiding Judge to treat the physical inability of the juror as simply creating a vacancy on the panel, and proceeding to fill it in the usual way by having a twelfth juror drawn and sworn. We understand it to have been the practice of the courts of the State of New York so to treat such a withdrawal of a juror, when the presiding Judge in his discretion has thought proper to do so, and under the act of July 20, 1840, (5 Stat. at Large, 394,) the Circuit Court might properly conform to that practice. Of course it must be confined to cases like the present, in which it is apparent the party objecting received no injury. The defendant cannot be supposed to have been prejudiced by the failure of the twelfth juror to hear a part of the opening argument for the plaintiff, r. evidence having been given, and he did not make known to the court that he desired to attempt to exercise any right of challenge of the other eleven jurors, to which he might have been restored if any cause existed, and the panel had been treated as broken up. Rex v. Edwards, 4 Taunt. 309 ; Green v. Norville, 3 Hill, (S. C.) 262. In such a case we think it rested in the discretion of the court whether the withdrawal of a juror should be treated simply as occasioning a vacancy on a still existing panel, or as breaking up the panel altogether, and it being a matter of discretion, no error could be assigned upon it, even if there were reason to believe, what in this case there is not, that the discretion was not wisely exercised.

The next exception was to the refusal of the Judge to allow the defendant to put in evidence to the jury an indorsement on the original letters-patent. The plaintiff had previously offered in evidence a duly certified copy of the following disclaimer:

To the Commissioner of Patents, the petition of Elisha Foote, of Seneca Falls, in the county of Seneca, and State of New York, respectfully represents :

That your petitioner obtained letters-patent of the United States for an improvement in regulating the draught of stoves, which letters-patent are dated on the 26th day of May, 1842. That he has reason to believe that, through inadvertence and mistake, the claim made in the specification of said letters-patent, in the following words, to wit: " What I claim as my invention and desire to secure by letters-patent, is the application of the expansive and contracting power of a metallic rod, by different degrees of heat, to open and close a damper which governs the admission of air into a stove, or other structure in which it may be used, by which a more perfect control over the heat is obtained than can be by a damper in the flue," is too broad, including that of which your petitioner was not the first inventor.

Your petitioner, therefore, hereby enters his disclaimer to so much of said claim as extends the application of the expansive and contracting power of a metallic rod, by different degrees of heat, to any other use or purpose than that of regulating the heat of a stove, in which such rod shall be acted upon directly by the heat of the stove or the fire which it contains; such disclaimer is to operate to the extent of the interest in said letters-patent vested in your petitioner, who has paid ten dollars into the treasury of the United States, agreeably to the act of Congress in that case made and provided.   ELISHA FOOTE.

Witnesses — Morris Newton, Edwin L. Baltink.

The defendants objected upon the ground that the instrument did not state "the extent of his interest in such patent." 5 Stat. at Large, 193, sec. 7.   The court sustained the objection, and refused to permit the instrument to be read by the plaintiff as a disclaimer.   At a subsequent stage of the trial the defendant offered to read to the jury a copy of this instrument indorsed on the original letters-patent, not as a disclaimer under the act of Congress above referred to, but as a confession by the plaintiff that he was not the original and first inventor of a part of the thing patented.   The plaintiff objected, because the indorsement on the letters-patent was not in his handwriting, nor signed by him, and the defendants had already caused a duly certified copy of the same instrument to be rejected.   The court sustained the objection.

We are of opinion the court erred in not allowing the plaintiff to put this instrument in evidence as a disclaimer, under the 7th section of the act of March 3, 1837.   5 Stat. at Large, 193. This section authorizes not only the patentee, but his executors, administrators, and assigns, whether of the whole or of a sectional interest in the patent, to make disclaimer, "stating therein the extent of his interest in such patent."   This instrument states that the plaintiff was himself the patentee, and having thus shown a grant to himself of the whole interest, it is silent respecting a transfer of any part of it.   The fair implication is that he still owns the whole; and this implication is sufficient without an express declaration that he had parted with no interest.   It has been argued that the words "such disclaimer is to operate to the extent of the interest vested in your petitioner," imply that he had not the whole title.   But the interest previously described as vested in him was the entire title as patentee, and this reference to that interest, accompanied by a declaration that the disclaimer was intended to operate upon it to its whole extent, strengthens, rather than weakens the implication that he owned the whole patent.   This being so, it follows, that when the defendants offered to put a copy of the instrument in evidence, not as a disclaimer, but as a confession of the defendant, to prejudice his rights, it was properly rejected. It is true the rejection of the evidence was placed on a different

19*

ground by the Judge below. But if the defendants were not deprived of any right by the rejection of the evidence, it is not cause for reversing the judgment that an erroneous reason was given for rejecting it; and they were not deprived of any right, if the paper was not legal evidence upon the particular point for which alone it was offered, or if its reception, accompanied by proper instructions to the jury concerning its legal effect, must necessarily have assisted the opposite party.

The next exception is to the refusal of the Judge to order a nonsuit. But, as it has been repeatedly decided that the courts of the United States have no power to order a peremptory nonsuit, against the will of the plaintiff, it is not necessary to examine the grounds of the motion. Doe v. Grymes et al. 1 Pet. 469; D'Wolf v. Rabaud et al. 1 Pet. 476; Crane v. Morris et al. 6 Pet. 598.

In the course of the trial, the defendants offered to put in evidence two articles contained in Ure's Dictionary of Arts, Manufactures, and Mines, to prove that the patent declared on was not valid. The plaintiff objected, and the evidence was excluded. It is incumbent on the defendants to show their right to introduce this evidence. To do so, they rely on the fifteenth section of the act of July 4th, 1836. 5 Stat. at Large, 123· This section enables the defendant, in any action on the case founded on letters-patent, to give in evidence, under the general issue, any special matter of which notice in writing may have been given to the plaintiff, or his attorney, thirty days before the trial, tending to prove, among other things, that the patentee was not the original and first inventor of the thing patented, or of some substantial and material part thereof claimed as new, or that it had been described in some public work anterior to the supposed discovery thereof by the patentee; and whenever the defendant relies, in his defence, on the fact of a previous invention, knowledge, or use of the thing patented, he is required to state, in his notice of special matter, the names and places of residence of those whom he intends to prove possessed a prior knowledge of the thing, and where the same had been used. The notice given in this case was as follows:

"The patentee was not the original and first inventor or discoverer of a substantial and material part thereof, claimed as new. That it had been described in a public work, called 'Ure's Dictionary of Arts, Manufactures, and Mines,' anterior to the supposed invention thereof by the patentee; and also. had been in public use and known before that time, and used by Andrew Ure, of London, the late M. Bonnemair, of Paris, and George H. McClary, of Seneca Falls, New York."

Ure's Dictionary contains upwards of thirteen hundred pages, and the articles which the defendants offered to read were entitled " Thermostad" and " Heat Regulator." The first question is, whether this was a sufficient notice of the special matter, tending to prove that the thing patented, or some substantial part thereof, claimed as new, had been .described in a printed publication. We are of opinion it was not. The act does not attempt to prescribe the particulars which such a notice shall contain. It simply requires notice. But the least effect which can be allowed to this requirement, is, that the notice should be so full and particular as reasonably to answer the end in view. This end was not merely to put the patentee -on inquiry, but to relieve him from the necessity of making useless inquiries and researches, and enable him to fix with precision upon what is relied on by the defendants, and to prepare himself to meet it at the trial. This highly salutary object should be kept in view, and a corresponding disclosure exacted from the defendant of all those particulars which he must be presumed to know, and which he may safely be required to state, without exposing him to any risk of losing his rights. Less than this would not be reasonable notice, and, therefore, would not be such a notice as the act must be presumed to have intended.

Now, we do not perceive that the defendants would be exposed to the risk of losing any right, by requiring them to indicate, in their notice, what particular things, described in the printed publication, they intended to aver were substantially the same as the thing patented. This they might have done, either by reference to pages, or titles, and perhaps in other ways, for the particular manner in which the things referred to are to be identified, must depend much upon the contents of the volume, and their arrangement. It has been urged that a defendant may not have access to the book in season for the notice. But it must be remembered that, some considerable time before it is necessary to give such a notice, the defendant has begun to use the thing patented, which, *primâ facie*, he has no right to use, and it would seem to be no injustice, or hardship, to expect him, before he begins to infringe, to ascertain that the patentees' title is not valid, and if its invalidity depends on what is in a public work, that he should inform himself what that work contains, and, consequently, how to refer to it. We do not think it necessary so to construe this act, designed for the benefit of patentees, as to enable the defendant to do, what we fear is too often done, to infringe first, and look for defences afterwards.

Nor does a notice, that somewhere, in a volume of thirteen hundred pages, there is something which tends to prove that the thing patented, or some substantial and material part thereof claimed as new, had been described therein, relieve the patentee from the necessity of making fruitless researches, or enable him to fix with reasonable certainty on what he must encounter at the trial. Upon this ground, therefore, the exception cannot be supported.

But, it is further urged that the book ought to have been admitted as evidence; that Andrew Ure, of London, had a prior knowledge of the thing patented. This view cannot be sustained. For, although the name of Andrew Ure, of London, is contained in the notice of persons who are alleged to have had this prior knowledge, yet the defendants have not brought themselves within the act of Congress, because the notice does not state " where the same was used," by Andrew Ure. Besides, inasmuch as the same section of the statute provides that a prior invention in a foreign country shall not avoid a patent, otherwise valid, unless the foreign invention had been described in a printed publication, the defendants are thrown back upon that clause of the act which provides for that defence, arising from a printed publication, which has already been considered.

The next exception was to the charge of the presiding Judge to the jury. The defendants requested the Judge to charge the jury, 3d, that it was erroneous to consider as constituent parts of the combination claimed by the plaintiff only those points which were requisite to the operation of opening and closing the damper; but that, on the contrary, the jury must consider as constituent parts of the combination all the parts of the machine, as described in the specification, by which the regulation of the heat of a stove, or the other structures, is effected.

4. That the index is a constituent part of the combination patented by the plaintiff.

5. That the detaching process of the lever is a constituent part of the combination patented by the plaintiff.

6. That the pendulum is a constituent part of the combination.

And, in this connection,

7. That if the defendants do not use all the constituent parts of the combination patented by the plaintiff, a verdict must be rendered for the defendants.

As to the 2d, 3d, 4th, 5th, 6th, and 7th of the instructions prayed for by the defendants, the Judge charged the jury, that it was true as insist~' by the defendants' counsel, that the third article of the summary of the plaintiff's specification, on which alone, if at all, he was entitled to recover, was for a combination; and unless it appeared by the evidence that the defendants had used all the parts of the plaintiff's stove embraced in such combination, he was not entitled to recover. That the combination claimed in the article in question was of such parts of the mechanism described in the specification as are necessary to regulate the heat of the stove. And unless it appeared by the evidence that some parts of the mechanism, not shown to have been used by the defendants, were necessary to perform that office, or that, according to the just construction of the specification, such parts were intended to be claimed by the plaintiff as a part of such combination, they are not to be considered as embraced within it. That inasmuch as by the fourth article of the plaintiff's summary, he made a distinct and separate claim to what had been called the detaching apparatus, there seemed to be good reason to infer that it was not his intention to claim this in the third article as a part of the combination therein mentioned. But the Judge observed, that the question relative to the extent of the combination, had been treated by the defendants' counsel as a question of fact, and he had no disposition to withdraw it from the consideration of the jury; and he therefore submitted it to the jury to decide, from the evidence, whether the parts of the mechanism described in the specification, which were not shown to have been used by the defendants, were necessary to regulate the heat of the stove; and instructed the jury that if they should so find, the defendants would be entitled to a verdict. And the Judge refused to charge otherwise in relation to such instructions, or any of them.

To this charge and refusal of the Judge, as the 2d, 3d, 4th, 5th, 6th, and 7th of the instructions prayed by the defendants, the defendants' counsel then and there excepted.

The substance of the charge is, that the jury were instructed by the Judge, that the third claim in the specification was for a combination of such parts of the described mechanism as were necessary to regulate the heat of the stove; that the defendants had not infringed the patent, unless they had used all the parts embraced in the plaintiff's combination; and he left it to the jury to find what those parts were, and whether the defendants had used them.

We think this instruction was correct. The objection made to it is, that the court left to the jury what was matter of law. But an examination of this third claim, and of the defendants' prayers for instruction, will show that the Judge left nothing but matter of fact to the jury. The construction of the claim was undoubtedly for the court. The court rightly construed it to be a claim for a combination of such of the described parts as were combined and arranged for the purpose of producing a particular effect, viz., to regulate the heat of a stove. This was in accordance with the defendants' third prayer. But the defendants also desired the Judge to instruct the jury that the index, the detaching process, and the pendulum, were constituent parts of this combination. How could the Judge know this as matter of law? The claim is in these words : " I also claim the combination, above described, by which the regulation of the heat of the stove, or other structure in which it may be used, is effected." The writing which the Judge was to construe, calls for all such elements of the combination as are actually employed to effect the regulation of the heat, according to the plan of the patentee, described in the specification, and it therefore became a question for the jury, upon the evidence of experts, or an inspection by them of the machines, or upon both, what parts described did in point of fact enter into, and constitute an essential part of this combination. When a claim does not point out and designate the particular elements which compose a combination, but only declares, as it properly may, that the combination is made up of so much of the described machinery as effects a particular result, it is a question of fact which of the described parts are essential to produce that result ; and to this extent, not the construction of the claim, strictly speaking, but the application of the claim, should be left to the jury. The defendants themselves so treat this matter in their third prayer, and we are satisfied the Judge did not err in so treating it.

The defendants' counsel exhibited to the court the models of the machines of the defendants and the plaintiff, for the purpose of satisfying the court the jury must have understood they were at liberty to construe the claim, and that they did in truth so construe it, as to exclude from the combination claimed by the plaintiff, what is called the detaching process. But we can draw no such inference from an examination of those models. And while we do not think it proper to express any opinion on what is really a matter of fact, yet we think it pertinent to say, that an examination of the models has satisfied us that a jury might fairly come to the conclusion that the defendants did use a detaching process, not substantially different from the plaintiff's, and occupying in their combination the same place, and answering substantially the same purpose, as the plaintiff's detaching process does in his combination ; and therefore we can draw no inference such as is contended for.

We have examined all the exceptions, and no one being found tenable, the judgment is affirmed.

Mr. Justice McLEAN dissented.

Order.

This cause came on to be heard on the transcript of the record from the Circuit Court of the United States for the Northern

District of New York, and was argued by counsel. On consideration whereof, it is now here ordered and adjudged, by this court, that the judgment of the said Circuit Court in this cause be, and the same is hereby, affirmed, with costs and interest until the same is paid, at the same rate per annum that similar judgments bear in the courts of the State of New York.

E. P. CALKIN AND SAMUEL JONES, TRADING UNDER THE FIRM AND STYLE OF E. P. CALKIN AND COMPANY, PLAINTIFFS IN ERROR, *v.* JAMES H. COCKE.

The State of Texas was admitted into the Union on the 29th of December, 1845, (9 Stat. at Large, 108,) and from that day the laws of the United States were extended over it.

Consequently, on the 30th of January, 1846, the revenue laws of Texas were not in force there, and goods seized for a non-compliance with those laws, were illegally seized.

THIS case was brought up by writ of error from the Supreme Court of Errors and Appeals for the State of Texas, under the 25th section of the Judiciary Act.

Calkin and Company were merchants of the county of Galveston, Texas, and Cocke was collector of Galveston under the Republic of Texas.

By a joint resolution of Congress, approved on the 1st of March, 1845, the President of the United States was authorized to submit one of two alternative propositions to·the Republic of Texas, as an overture for her admission as a State into the Union. One of these contemplated the completion of this measure and the adjustment of its terms, by legislation, and the other by negotiation. The President selected the former, and presented to Texas the proposals contained in the first and second sections of the said resolutions. The first section declared " that Congress doth consent that the Territory of Texas may be. erected into a State, to be called the State of Texas, with a republican form of government, to be adopted by the people of said Republic, by deputies in convention assembled, with the consent of the existing government, in order that the same may be admitted as one of the States of this Union."

And the second section declares that this consent, on the part of the United States, was given upon several conditions, one of which required the constitution, which was to be framed by the Convention, to be transmitted, with the proper evidences of its adoption by the people of the said Republic of Texas, to the President of the United States, to be laid before the Con-

gress of the Union for its final action, on or before the first day
of January, one thousand eight hundred and forty-six. This
consent, with the conditions on which it was given, was communicated to the Republic of Texas, and in the course of the
following summer and autumn the people of Texas, by deputies
in Convention assembled, with the consent of the then existing
government, erected it into a new State, with a republican form
of government, as shown by the constitution then adopted by
them for its government, and declared and ordained that they
accepted the proposal contained in the resolutions just spoken.
of, and assented to the conditions on which it was made. The
constitution adopted by the people of Texas, with the evidence
of its adoption, and of their acceptance of the proposal made
by Congress, and their assent to the conditions with which it
was accompanied, was laid before Congress at the opening of
the session of 1845–6, and on the 29th of December, 1845, the
Congress of the United States, after taking cognizance of the
acceptance of the proposal and of the conditions annexed to it
by the people of Texas, and of the constitution adopted by
them, declared that the State of Texas "shall be one, and is.
hereby declared to be one, of the United States of America," &c.

This constitution of Texas, thus adopted by that State and
laid before Congress, contained, amongst others, the following
provisions. By the first section of the twelfth article of the said
constitution, it was declared that "all process which' shall be
issued in the name of the Republic of Texas, prior to the organization of the State government under this constitution, shall
be as valid as if issued in the name of the State of Texas."
In the second section of the same article it was provided, that
"all criminal prosecutions or penal actions which shall have
arisen prior to the organization of the State government under
this constitution, in any of the courts of the Republic of Texas,
shall be prosecuted to judgment and execution in the name of
the State," &c. The sixth section contained a provision that
if it should appear, on the second Monday of November, 1845,
from the returns, that a majority of the votes polled of the people of Texas were given for the adoption of the constitution,
the President should make proclamation of that fact, and thenceforth the constitution was ordained and established as the
constitution of the State, to go into operation, and be of force
and effect, from and after the organization of the State government under the said constitution. By section ten, it was declared
"that the laws of this Republic relative to the duties of officers,
both civil and military, of the same, shall remain in full force,
and the duties of their several offices shall be performed in conformity with the · existing laws, until the organization of the

government of the State under this constitution, or until the first day of the meeting of the legislature," &c.

On the same day that Congress declared that Texas shall be and is hereby declared to be one of the United States, viz. on the 29th of December, 1845, (9 Stat. at Large, 108,) Congress passed an act extending the laws of the United States over Texas, and declaring them to have full force and effect within the State. It provided also for the establishment of a court of the United States, with its necessary officers. And on the 31st of December, 1845, another law was passed, constituting Texas a collection district, and making Galveston a port of entry.

The Legislature of Texas did not meet, nor was the State government completely organized under its new constitution, until the 16th of February, 1846.

On the 30th of January, 1846, Calkin and Company imported into Galveston, from New Orleans, a large amount of merchandise, principally the growth and manufacture of the United States.

These goods were seized by Cocke, claiming one thousand dollars as duty, under the revenue laws of Texas. Calkin and Company protested against this, and demanded that the goods should be delivered to them in accordance with an act of Congress of the United States, of the 31st December, 1845, and of a circular of the Secretary of [the] Treasury of the United States, of 9th January, 1846, declaring that " vessels and their cargoes arriving in any port of the State of Texas, either from a foreign port, or a port in any other State or Territory of the United States, are to be placed on a similar footing with vessels and their cargoes arriving at ports in any of the States of the Union."

On the trial of the case in the District Court of the State of Texas, on the 5th of January, 1847, a judgment was rendered therein in favor of plaintiffs, restraining the defendant from claiming any duties on the merchandise, and condemning him to pay to the plaintiffs the sum of two hundred and fifty dollars, the damages assessed by the jury, as damages for the unlawful detention of the merchandise, and the costs of the suit. From this judgment a writ of error was prosecuted to the Supreme Court of Texas, and by that tribunal the judgment was reversed, and one given in favor of the defendant for the sum of nine hundred and sixteen dollars, the amount of duties unpaid, and the amount of costs expended in and about the suit.

A writ of error brought this judgment up to this court.

The case was argued, in printed arguments, by *Mr. Miles Taylor*, for the plaintiff in error, and *Mr. Harris*, for the defendant in error.

Mr. Taylor, after reciting the laws and other proceedings relative to annexation, continued:

Now it is an undoubted truth, that when a proposition, made by one party to another, is accepted as made, there is, from the instant of the acceptance, a valid contract, which from that moment is obligatory upon both, and must, to the full extent of its provisions, thereafter regulate the respective rights and obligations of the respective parties. Here the proposition was, that Texas should be admitted a member of the Union, on her compliance with certain terms and conditions. She complied with the terms and conditions, and accepted the proposition, and the Congress, in which the power to admit was vested, admitted her as a State into the Union, and on the 29th day of December, 1845, declared that she " is one of the United States." Was she not so ? I believe she was, and that whilst this necessarily results from the terms of the proposition to admit her into the Union, and of its acceptance, it is further shown by the action of Texas herself.

Texas regarded the contract for her admission into the Union as complete, when she had given her assent to the proposition submitted to her in relation to it, and had acceded to the specified conditions. This is at once evident from the fact that immediately after her assent was given, she called on the Executive of the United States to employ the military force of the nation to protect her from hostilities threatened by Mexico, I have not the public documents before me, so as to be able to refer to the precise date of this application. It was made, however, some time before the meeting of Congress, in the autumn of 1845, and was based upon the obligation imposed on the national government by the Constitution, of exercising its power to protect every member of the confederacy from invasion. That this construction given by Texas to the effect of her acceptance of the proposition submitted to her is correct, cannot be doubted. The contract was complete from the time of her acceptance. She was entitled, from that moment, to all the advantages growing out of it, and was subject to all the burdens resulting from it. It is true, there was a new state of things created, not contemplated by the existing laws, and that some action on the part of Congress was necessary to give effect to the new rights and obligations, and to extend the laws of the nation over Texas. That was the case with respect to the judiciary, the revenue system, the operations of the post-office, &c. But whilst something was necessary for these purposes on the part of the Congress of the United States, there was nothing which was required to be done by Texas. The Constitution of the United States, and the laws made in pursuance thereof, is the supreme law of the land, and when Congress exercised the power delegated to it by the Constitution, on the 29th day of December, 1845, by act of Congress, and said that all the laws of the United States were thereby " declared to extend to and over, and to have full force and effect within the State of Texas, admitted at the present session of Congress into the confederacy and Union of the United States," the revenue and other laws were extended *proprio vigore*, and not because of any thing contained in the constitution of Texas, which had just been adopted, for " the Constitution of the United States, and the laws made in pursuance thereof," being the supreme law of the land, if any thing had been contained in the constitution of Texas, which conflicted with them, it would have been absolutely null and void, and have no more force or effect than if not written.

The pretensions set up by the defendant, in his pretended capacity of collector, under the authority of the revenue laws of the late Republic of Texas, are understood to be based on the 10th section of the twelfth article of the constitution of Texas, in which it is declared " that the laws of this Republic, relative to the duties of officers, both civil and military, of the same, shall remain in full force, and the duties of their several offices shall be performed in conformity with the existing laws, until the organization of the government of the State under this constitution, or until the first day of the meeting of the legislature."

An attentive consideration of this section, and of the other sections embraced in the same article of the constitution of Texas, will, I think, make it apparent that no such consequence as that now contended for, was contemplated, or could legitimately flow from it. The different sections contained in that article were designed to provide for the transition from an independent government to one adapted to the new order of things, and were not intended or designed to limit or restrain the rightful authority of the Constitution or laws of the United States, within the territory of Texas, or to fix a time when the independent authority of Texas should yield and give place to the national authority of the United States. By the first section of this article, it was declared, that " all process that should be issued in the name of the Republic of Texas, prior to the organization of the State government under the constitution, should be as valid as if issued in the name of the State of Texas." The second section provided, " that all criminal prosecutions or penal actions" which should have arisen prior to the organization of the State government under the constitution, in any of the courts of the Republic of Texas, should " be prosecuted to judgment and execution in the name of the State," &c.

The sixth section directed, that "if it should appear on the second Monday of November, 1845, from the returns, that a majority of the votes polled of the people of Texas, were given for the adoption of the constitution, the President should make proclamation of that fact, and thenceforth the constitution was ordained and established as the constitution of the State, to go into operation and be of force and effect from and after the organization of the State government under the constitution. And then in the tenth section of the same article, is found the provision before recited, to the effect that the laws of the Republic relative to the duties of officers, both civil and military, of the same, should remain in full force, and the duties of the several offices be performed "in conformity with the existing laws, until the organization of the government of the State," under the constitution, or " until the first day of the meeting of the legislature," &c.

These various provisions were introduced into the constitution of Texas, not, as I before remarked, to bind or restrain the rightful authority of the Constitution and laws of the United States within the territory of Texas, or fix a time when the independent authorities of Texas should yield to and give place to the national authorities of the United States, but to obviate the inconveniences which might otherwise have grown out of the change from one constitution to another. In the absence of any declaration to the contrary, it cannot be presumed that any limitation or condition, on the contract just completed by their formal assent, was intended by these general expressions, because full effect can be given to them without adopting such a construction. But if it were otherwise, and it were the design of the people of Texas to impose such a limitation, the provision would have produced no such effect. If Texas ever has been an integral part of the Union, she was so when Congress declared her to be so, on the 29th day of December, 1845, after her acceptance of the proposition submitted to her in relation to it. If she were so at that time for any purpose, she was so for all purposes; and then it would of necessity follow, that as the Constitution of the United States, and the laws adopted under its authority, are the supreme laws of the land, the constitution and laws of the Republic of Texas, wherever they conflicted with them, were at once abrogated, and that the people of Texas could not at any future time give validity or binding force to any new constitutional or legal provision which conflicted with it.

Mr. Harris, for the defendant in error.

It is obvious that the main question presented by the record is, whether Texas was annexed to the United States, on the 26th of December, 1845, or on the 16th of February, 1846; and, as a consequence, at which of these periods the right of the late Republic to collect import duties terminated. It is contended by the plaintiffs, that this right ceased on the 29th of December, 1845, when the joint resolution of Congress was passed for the admission of Texas as one of the States of the Union; while it is contended, on the part of the defendant, that it did not cease until the 16th day of February, 1846, the day on which the State government was organized.

For the settlement of this question, resort must be mainly had to the terms of the joint resolution "for the annexation of Texas," &c., approved March 1, 1845; to those of the constitution of the State of Texas, and of the joint resolution of the 29th of December, mentioned above.

It is submitted that the first of these amounts to nothing more than a proposition, on the part of Congress, for the annexation of Texas, and this resolution may be said to be only preliminary to that object. The first and second sections, it is contended, clearly show that it was not the intention of Congress to concede to Texas the power to consummate annexation by any act of her own; for it provides that the constitution of the proposed State, "with the proper evidence of its adoption by the people of the said Republic of Texas, shall be transmitted to the President of the United States, to be laid before Congress, for its final action, on or before the first day of January, one thousand eight hundred and forty-six." This is entirely consistent with the preamble of the joint resolution "for the admission of the State of Texas into the Union."

The last section of the constitution of Texas, provides that "the ordinance passed by the convention on the fourth day of July, assenting to the overtures for the annexation of Texas to the United States, shall be attached to the constitution, and form a part of the same." They were transmitted to the President, to be laid before Congress together, and the meaning of the ordinance was restrained and limited, not only by the intention of the first joint resolution, but also by the spirit and terms of the constitution itself.

This constitution, containing the conditions upon which Texas consented to be annexed, and having been accepted by Congress, must, with all its terms and conditions, be regarded as a part of the contract, or treaty of annexation. It having been adopted by Congress, it is supposed that its provisions became a portion of the laws of the United States, and that the constitution of Texas, and the joint resolution of the 29th of December, 1845, should be taken and construed together.

20*

Under this view, attention is most respectfully invited to several articles of that instrument.

The first section of the 12th article of the constitution provides, that " all process which shall be issued in the name of the Republic of Texas, prior to the organization of the State government under this constitution, shall be as valid as if issued in the name of the State of Texas." In the second section, it is provided, " that all criminal prosecutions, or penal actions, which shall have arisen prior to the organization of the State government, under this constitution, in any of the courts of the Republic of Texas, shall be prosecuted to judgment and execution, in the name of the State," &c. The sixth section, under the same article, among other things, provides, that if the constitution be adopted by the people, it shall " go into operation, and be of force and effect, from and after the organization of the State government, under said constitution," &c.

By the 10th section it is declared, " that the laws of the Republic relative to the duties of officers, both civil and military, of the same, shall remain in full force, and the duties of their several offices shall be performed in conformity with the existing laws until the organization of the government of the State under this constitution, or until the first day of the meeting of the legislature."

It is most respectfully submitted, that these provisions furnish cumulative and convincing evidence, that the people of Texas (one of the contracting parties) intended and stipulated that the government of the Republic of Texas and all its laws should remain in full force until the 16th of February, 1846, " the first day of the meeting of the legislature." It is also submitted, that the other party, by accepting this constitution, became bound by all its terms and stipulations, as portions of the contract of annexation.

For the convenience of the argument, it may be supposed that Texas proposed to be annexed upon the terms and conditions contained in her State constitution, and that this proposition was accepted by the government of the United States. Had such been the case, it is easy to see that the effect of the contract would not be changed. If it had been so consummated, it is equally obvious that no diversity of opinion would have arisen in regard to its construction.

Then the condition, that the sovereignty and laws of the Republic should remain unimpaired until the 16th of February, 1846, was proposed by Texas and assented to by Congress.

It may be further remarked, that Congress must have understood this to be one of the stipulations of the contract. By reference to the act of Congress, of the 29th of May, 1846, (see acts of 1845, '46, page 23,) it will be seen, that the 3d section provides that the Postmaster-General was not authorized to pay the expenses incurred for carrying the mail in Texas, prior to the 16th of February, 1846. When the contract of annexation was one and indivisible, was it the intention of Congress to receive its benefits from the 29th of December, 1845, and to postpone its burdens to the 16th of February, 1846?

Mr. Justice NELSON delivered the opinion of the court.

This is a writ of error to the Supreme Court of the State of Texas. The suit was originally brought by the plaintiffs in error before the District Court of Galveston county, to recover the possession of a stock of goods from the defendant, who had seized them at Galveston, as collector of that port, under the authority of the Republic of Texas, for non-payment of duties They recovered a judgment in that court; but, on a writ of error from the Supreme Court, the judgment was reversed, and the goods held liable to the duties.

The case was this: The plaintiffs shipped from New Orleans into Galveston the stock of goods, on the 30th January, 1846, and the defendant, claiming to act as collector under the Republic of Texas, and also that the revenue laws of that government were then in force, charged them with a rate of duty in conformity with those laws, and for the non-payment by the plaintiffs, they insisting that the goods were not liable to any rate of duty since the admission of Texas into the Union, he seized and took possession of, and detained them, until they were redelivered to the plaintiffs, by the order of the District Court.

The question in the case is, whether the revenue laws of this government were in force in the State of Texas at the date of the importation, or those of the former government of that country. The Supreme Court held the latter were in force, and charged the goods with the customary duties.

The State of Texas was admitted into the Union on the 29th December, 1845, on an equal footing with the original States, in all respects whatever. 9 Stat. at Large, p. 108. And by the 1st section of an act of Congress, passed the same day, all the laws of the United States were declared to be extended over, and to have full force and effect within, the State. And, by the 2d section, the State was declared to constitute one judicial district, called the District of Texas, for which a judge should be appointed, and should hold the first term of his court at Galveston, on the first Monday of February then next. The remaining part of the section confers upon the court the usual powers belonging to a district court, and also of a circuit court of the United States. The 3d section provides for the appointment of a district attorney, and marshal for the district, and for a clerk of the court. Id. p. 1, 2.

On the 31st December, 1845, the next day after the admission into the Union, Congress passed an act declaring the State to be one collection district, and making the city of Galveston a port of entry, and to which was annexed several other places, as ports of delivery. The 2d section provides for the appointment of a collector for the port of Galveston, and the 3d section for the appointment of a surveyor for each port of delivery.

Now it is quite apparent, from the joint resolution of Congress, admitting the State of Texas into the Union, and the acts passed, organizing the Federal courts and revenue system over it, that the old system of government, so far as it conflicted with the federal authority, became abrogated immediately on her admission as a State. This is clearly so, unless some provision is found in the act of admission postponing the time when it shall take effect, and, as applied to the case before us, postponing it until after the 31st January, 1846, when these goods were shipped to the port of Galveston.

This has been attempted on the part of the defendant in error.

We have been referred to the 1st section of the 13th article of the constitution of Texas, which provides, "that all process which shall be issued in the name of the Republic of Texas, prior to the organization of the State government under this constitution, shall be as valid as if issued in the name of the State of Texas." And also to the 2d section of the same article, which provides that "all criminal prosecutions or penal actions, which shall have arisen prior to the organization of the State government under this constitution, in any of the courts of the Republic, shall be prosecuted to judgment and execution in the name of the State." And also, to the 6th section, which provides, upon its appearing that a majority of the votes of the people given is for the adoption of the constitution, "it shall be the duty of the President (of the Republic of Texas) to make proclamation of the fact, and thenceforth this constitution shall be ordained and established as the constitution of the State, to go into operation, and be of force and effect, from and after the organization of the State government." And also, to the 10th section, which declares, "that the laws of the Republic, relative to the duties of officers, both civil and military, of the same, shall remain in full force, and the duties of the several offices shall be performed in conformity with the existing laws, until the organization of the government of the State under this constitution, or until the first day of the meeting of the legislature."

It is supposed that these several provisions of the constitution of Texas, and which is the one accepted, when she was admitted into the Union by Congress, have the effect to postpone and fix the period of admission to the time of the first meeting of the legislature of the State and organization of the government under the constitution, which was on the 16th February, 1846 ; and, of course, to postpone the operation of the laws of the Union over her till that period.

But the obvious answer to this view is, that these several provisions in the constitution were designed and intended, and had the effect, to organize a government at once, on the adoption of the constitution by the people, and thereby to avoid an interregnum between the abrogation of the old and the erection of the new system, and until the legislative body could meet, and put the government in operation in conformity with the requirements of the organic law.

The whole of the 10th section, a part of which has been already referred to, affords an illustration of the design of the framers of the constitution. It is as follows: " That no inconvenience may result from the change of government, it is declared, that the laws of the Republic, relative to the duties of officers, both civil, and military, of the same, shall remain in full force, and the duties of the several offices shall be performed in conformity with existing laws, until the organization of the government of the State under this constitution, or until the first day of the meeting of the legislature." This section, taken in connection with the 3d section of the same article, completed an organization which effectually prevented any interval between the old and new systems, when the laws did not operate, or an organized government was not in force. That section provides, that " all laws and parts of laws, now in force in the Republic of Texas, which are not repugnant to the Constitution of the United States, the joint resolutions for annexing Texas to the United States, or to the provisions of this constitution, shall remain in force, as the laws of this State, until they expire by their own limitation or repealed by the legislature.

This section, as it will be seen, also negatives the idea, that the Constitution and laws of the Union were not in force within the State as soon as her admission into the Union took place.

This subject was very fully considered in Benner et al. v. Porter, (9 How. 235,) which involved an inquiry into the affect of the admission of Florida into the Union as a State. Some of the questions there were very similar to those raised in this case, as the machinery of the territorial government had been adopted by an ordinance in the constitution until the organization was effected under the constitution by the legislature.

We there said, "that, on the admission of Florida as a State into the Union, the organization of the government under the new constitution became complete; as every department became filled, at once, by the adoption of the territorial laws, and the appointment of the territorial functionaries for the time being." That "the convention being the fountain of all political power, from which flowed that embodied in the organic law, were, of course competent to prescribe the laws and appoint the officers under the constitution, by means whereof the government could be put into immediate operation, and thus avoid an interregnum that must have intervened, if left to an organization according to the provisions of that instrument. This was accomplished in a few lines, adopting the machinery of the territorial government for the time being, and until superseded by the agency and authority of the constitution itself."

An argument is attempted to be drawn against the conclusion that the laws of the Union were extended over Texas as soon as she was admitted into it, founded upon certain acts of Congress concerning the establishment and regulation of the post-office system over the State. On the 6th February, 1846, various post routes were established in Texas, and the Postmaster-General was authorized to contract for conveying the mail on them as soon as could be conveniently done, after the passage of the act. A joint resolution was also passed on the 20th May, 1846, authorizing the Postmaster-General to continue the mail service existing in the State under the laws and authority of Texas, or such part as, in his judgment, the public interest required, from the time that Texas became a State in the Union, and until contracts could be made, and the mail service put in operation on post routes established by Congress at its then session. And on the 29th of the same month, another act was passed establishing several post routes, and repealing the act of the 6th February, referred to. The second section of this act authorizes the Postmaster-General to continue in operation the existing mail service in Texas, established under its former laws, upon any of the routes mentioned, as he may deem expedient, not to extend, however, beyond the 30th June, 1850. And the third section provides for the payment of mail contractors in Texas for service performed by them since the 16th February, 1846, and also, the officers employed in superintending the mail service, with a proviso, that such payment shall in no case exceed the compensation agreed upon with the late authorities of Texas. The act then provides, that the several postmasters in Texas, appointed by the late government, shall account to the Postmaster-General for all balances accruing at their offices respectively, after the 16th February, 1846.

Calkin and Company v. Cocke.

We perceive nothing in these several acts expressing or implying that Congress possessed no power to extend the system of mail service over the State from the time of its admission into the Union, or that the date of the admission is to be limited to the 16th February, 1846.

There was necessarily some delay in putting the system into practical operation; and to avoid any inconvenience in the mean time, the existing system under the laws of the former government was recognized and adopted, until the several post routes were designated by Congress, and contracts made for the performance of the service in the usual way. The period fixed when the payment of the old contractors and superintendents of the service should commence; and, also, when the existing postmasters should begin to account to the Postmaster-General for the money collected, and the allowance of compensation, to wit, the 16th February, 1846, relate simply to the arrangement as to compensation; and as to the adjustment of the accounts of these several officers. The system, as established under the Republic of Texas, was recognized, and not interfered with in the adjustment down to the period mentioned; after that it was placed under the laws and regulations of the Post-Office Department of the general government.

That these acts do not admit the want of powers in Congress to extend the post-office laws over Texas until the 16th of February, 1846, is shown by the act passed the 5th of that month, designating several post routes, and conferring the power upon the Postmaster-General to enter into contracts for conveying the mail over them. This act continued in force until repealed on the 29th of May following, when a new and somewhat different arrangement of mail routes was provided for.

Without pursuing the case farther, our opinion is, that the admission of Texas into the Union is to take date from the 29th of December, 1845, the time of its admission by Congress, and that the laws of the Union extended over it from that time; and, consequently, the seizure of the stock of goods in question by the defendant under the revenue laws of the Republic, on the 30th of January, 1846, was without authority of law.

The judgment of the Supreme Court below, must therefore be reversed with costs; and that the proceedings be remitted to that court with directions that the judgment of the District Court be affirmed with costs in Supreme Court and District Court.

Order.

This cause came on to be heard on the transcript of the record from the Supreme Court of Errors and Appeals for the

State of Texas, and was argued by counsel. On consideration whereof, it is now here ordered and adjudged, by this court, that the judgment of the said Supreme Court of Errors and Appeals in this cause be, and the same is hereby, reversed, with costs, and that this cause be, and the same is hereby, remanded to the said Supreme Court of Errors and Appeals, with directions to affirm the judgment of the District Court for the county of Galveston in said cause, with costs in said Supreme and District Courts.

JAMES W. DOWNEY, EXECUTOR OF SAMUEL S. DOWNEY, DECEASED, PLAINTIFF IN ERROR, *v.* MARY M. HICKS, EXECUTRIX OF JOSEPH T. HICKS, DECEASED.

Where the declaration, in an action of assumpsit, contained the following counts:—
1. On a promissory note; 2. *Indebitatus assumpsit* for the hire of slaves; 3. An account stated; 4. *Quantum valebat* for the services of slaves; 5. Work and labor, goods sold and delivered, and money lent and advanced; 6. Money had and received; 7. An account stated; 8. A special agreement for the hire of slaves· And the defendant pleaded.—1. The general issue; 2. Statute of limitations; 3. Payment;—and the jury found a verdict for "the defendant upor th: issue joined as to the within note of four hundred and fifty-six dollars, and the w.:.:in account"—this verdict, although informal, was sufficient to authorize to enter a general judgment for the defendant.

An objection cannot be made in this court to a release under which a witness was sworn, unless the objection was made in the court below, and an exception taken.

Where a certificate of deposit in a bank, payable at a future day, was handed over by a debtor to his creditor, it was no payment, unless there was an express agreement on the part of the creditor, to receive it as such; and the question, whether there was or was not such an agreement, was one of fact to be decided by the jury.

The bank being insolvent when the certificate of deposit became due. there was no ground for imputing negligence in the collection of the debt by the holder, as no loss occurred to the original debtor.

If the evidence showed that, after the maturity of the certificate, the original debtor admitted his liability to make it good, the jury should have been .'structed that this evidence conduced to prove that the certificate was not taken in payment.

Mr. Chief Justice Taney did not sit in this cause.

THIS case was brought up, by writ of error from the Circuit Court of the United States for the Southern District of Mississippi.

There were three bills of exceptions taken upon the trial in the Circuit Court, which extended over more than one hundred pages of the printed record. The last one included the whole of the evidence. The substance of the case is given in the opinion of the court, to which the reporter refers the reader.

It was argued by *Mr. Badger*, with whom was *Mr. William A. Graham,* for the plaintiff in error, and *Mr. Volney E. Howard,* with whom was *Mr. Walker,* for the defendant in error.

The argument of the counsel for the plaintiff in error, was so intermingled with their statement of the facts in the case, that it will be necessary to insert the whole.

The declaration of the plaintiff in error, who was the plaintiff in the court below, is an assumpsit, and contains eight counts.

The first is on the promissory note of testator, in the name of Hicks & Arnold, for $456; the second is *indebitatus* assumpsit for hire of forty slaves; the fourth a *quantum valebat* for the services of forty other slaves; the third and seventh, each upon an account stated; the fifth for work and labor, goods sold and delivered, and money lent and advanced, and the seventh for money had and received; the eighth and last count is upon a special agreement of testator to hire from the plaintiff certain slaves mentioned in the count, and to pay the same rates of hire as the testator had agreed to pay Williams & Mills for the same slaves, &c.

The defendant pleaded 1st, the general issue; 2d, the statute of limitations; 3d, payment, upon which plea issues were joined, and the cause tried. The jury found a verdict in these words: " That they find for the defendant upon the issues joined, as to the within note of four hundred and fifty-six dollars, and the within account," and upon this finding, the court gave a general judgment for the defendant.

It is insisted, on the part of the plaintiff in error, that the verdict is imperfect, irresponsive to the issues, and does not dispose of the whole matter submitted by the pleadings; that upon the most favorable interpretation which can be given of it, it passes only on the first count on the note, and the third and seventh upon accounts stated, and leaves the matters arising upon the five other counts entirely undisposed of. That this verdict being thus imperfect, partial, and irresponsive to the issue, and consequently illegal, does not support the judgment, which is therefore erroneous.

The first bill of exceptions states, that the plaintiff objected to the reading of the deposition of Andrew Arnold, taken for the defendant, on the ground of his incompetency, but the objection was overruled, and the deposition read to the jury. Arnold was at one time plainly interested and incompetent.

In order to meet the objection, the defendant, by his 16th interrogatory, asks the witness, "Are you interested in this case? if you have any release from the executrix of Joseph T. Hicks, please mark it, and inclose it." To which the witness answers, " I am not interested in this case; I have a release from Mary M. Hicks, the surviving executrix of Joseph T. Hicks, deceased, which is marked with the letter A, and is hereto attached." By reference to the paper set out in the second, it appears to have been attested as a witness by one John Curan.

It is insisted, for the plaintiff in error, that the deposition ought not to have been read, because there was no legal evidence of the execution of the release.

1. The subscribing witness ought to have been produced, or his absence accounted for, and his handwriting proved, or other proper matter shown, to let in secondary evidence of the execution of the deed. This rule is of general application to all instruments attested, or appearing to have been attested, by a witness, whether produced to support the action, or used collaterally in evidence, and that no acknowledgment of the party, however solemn, though made on oath, will supply the want of evidence as to the subscribing witness. 2 Phillips, Ev. ch. 6, p. 201 to 203 ; Call v. Dunning, 4 East, 53.

The rule is very well and forcibly stated by Mr. Starkie. 1 Stark. on Ev. Part 2, sec. 139, p. 330.

In order to render a witness competent by a release, it must be produced and proved as in other cases. 2 Stark. Ev. Part 4, p. 759 ; Corking v. Jarrard, 1 Camp. 37 ; and it is then evidence in the cause for all purposes. Starkie, *ut supra;* Gibbons v. Wilcox, 2 Stark. Cas. 39.

2. There is no evidence of the execution of the release at all. The witness says, " I have a release," which I annex. He does not swear to the execution, or the handwriting, or the acknowledgment of it. Suppose it a forgery, how could he be indicted for perjury ?

Another bill of exceptions, is to the admission by the Judge, of A. W. Brien as a witness for the defendant. Brien, in his *voir dire*, stated that he was the husband of a daughter of Sarah Curan, to whom, by the will of defendant's testator, a legacy was given ; that he and his wife had received $1500 in full of his share of the estate, and had released to the defendant.

It is insisted that the witness was liable to refund to the defendant, and without her release was not competent. Moffit v. Lane, 2 Ired. 254.

The same bill states that the defendant produced an account-book, kept by the testator, and the said witness having deposed that a certain portion of the book was in the handwriting of John R. Hicks, that portion of the account was allowed by the Judge to be read to the jury, notwithstanding objection taken thereto by plaintiff's counsel.

It is insisted, on the part of the plaintiff, that this account was not competent evidence, because the said John R. Hicks was not a general agent of plaintiff, nor his agent to state the account, nor in any other manner so connected with the plaintiff as to make his statement evidence against plaintiff.

By the third bill of exceptions, it appears that the defendant's testator was, in 1836, the agent of plaintiff to receive the hires of certain slaves, owned by him in Mississippi; that he collected large sums on account thereof; that he afterwards took the slaves into his own employment, as hirer, to execute a contract on the Mississippi Railroad; that subsequently, in 1838, having formed a partnership with one Arnold, he continued the slaves in the employment of this firm of " Hicks & Arnold."

The said testator, and Hicks & Arnold, being thus indebted to the plaintiff in a large amount, Dr. John R. Hicks, a neighbor of plaintiff's in North Carolina, and a brother of the testator, visited Mississippi, in June, 1839, to collect hires due for his own negroes, and took with him a letter from plaintiff, desiring the testator to send him whatever was due him, to the amount of $12,000, if possible. An account was then stated, showing a balance due plaintiff, 1st January, 1839, of nearly $10,000. The testator thereupon drew a check upon the Mississippi Railroad Bank, for the amount, which the witness Arnold deposes was received by John R. Hicks, as plaintiff's agent, in payment, but Hicks himself deposes that he had no authority to bind the plaintiff, merely acting as his friend. The said testator and John R. Hicks then went to Natchez, to make further arrangements respecting the business, where the check was converted into a certificate of deposit for the same amount, dated 10th January, 1849, and payable with eight per cent. interest, on the 1st of November following. This certificate is copied in the record.

It was proved, by the deposition of Eli Montgomery, president of the bank, that this certificate was not issued upon any deposit, but in settlement of a debt due to Hicks & Arnold, and made payable on the 1st of November, by which day it was supposed the bank would have funds to meet it; that, in March, 1840, it was admitted by the testator, Andrew Arnold, and the plaintiff, that " Hicks & Arnold" owed plaintiff a large debt, for the hire of negroes, and had sent this certificate to him on account of their debt, and that plaintiff had refused to accept it in payment or satisfaction of any part of the debt; that Hicks & Arnold were bound to plaintiff to pay the debt (if the bank did not pay the certificate) in the same manner and to the same extent as if the certificate had not been sent. It was proved that the credit of the bank had greatly sunk at the maturity of the certificate, became continually worse, and by April, 1840, it had stopped payment; that a suit was brought, by concert between Hicks & Arnold and plaintiff, against the bank, Hicks & Arnold admitting their own liability, and no satisfaction was ever obtained from the bank.

The plaintiff's counsel prayed the Judge to instruct the jury: —(See the substance of the prayer in the opinion of the court.)

These instructions the Judge refused to give, as prayed, and, by the instructions actually given, he manifestly erred, by substantially repudiating proper instructions, and by leaving to the jury to decide questions of law which he ought to have decided himself.

The acceptance of the certificate by plaintiff, was not in law an extinguishment of the debt, unless there was an express agreement so to accept it; and the burden of proof, that the certificate was given and received as a satisfaction or extinguishment of the preceding debt, was upon the defendant.

A bill, or note, given for a preceding debt, is not deemed payment, unless so expressly agreed, or it has been negotiated, and is outstanding against the defendant. Burden v. Halton, 4 Bing. 454; Rott v. Watson, Ibid. 273; Raymond v. Merchant, 3 Cam. 147; Owenson v. Morse, 7 T. R. 64; Hickly v. Hardy, 7 Taunt. 312; Mussen v. Price et al. 4 East, 147. See also Greenwood v. Curtis, 6 Mass. 358; Johnson v. Johnson, 11 Mass. 361; Murray v. Governeur, 2 Johns. Ca. 438; Johnson v. Weed, 9 Johns. 310.

Nor is the receipt of a note as cash, evidence that it was taken as an absolute payment. Tobey v. Barber, 5 Johns 68.

It is but a suspension of the right of action, until the maturity of the note. Putnam v. Lewis, 8 Johns. 389.

In the absence of proof that a draft or check was received in absolute payment, it is regarded but as a means whereby the creditor may obtain payment — as payment provisionally, until dishonored; and if dishonored, it is no payment. The People v. Howell, 4 Johns. 296; Cromwell v. Lovett, 1 Hall, N. Y. Rep. 56; Olcott v. Rathbone, 5 Wend. 490; Everett v. Collins, 2 Camp. 515; Puckford v. Maxwell, 6 T. R. 52.

What is true of notes, checks, and bills, is true also of the certificate; and yet the Judge refused the instructions prayed to this effect.

The Judge, after some general and immaterial statements of the duty of an agent, proceeds to leave to the jury to decide what was reasonable diligence on the part of the plaintiff in endeavoring to obtain payment of the certificate from the bank.

But what diligence is reasonable, is a question of law, (the facts of the case being ascertained,) to be decided by the Judge, and not by the jury. 1 Stark. Part 3, sec. 27, page 414; Battle v. Little, 1 Dev. Rep. 387.

Besides, the rule as to the kind of diligence necessary, on the part of the plaintiff, is erroneous.

The bank, at the maturity of the certificate, was failing; shortly after, stopped payment. Hicks & Arnold paid nothing for the certificate, but took it on account of a debt which the bank could not pay. All the facts were fully known to them, but not to the plaintiff. Under these circumstances, nothing but such gross and long-continued negligence, on the part of the plaintiff, as would amount to a fraud, would discharge Hicks & Arnold, considered as guarantors. Goring v. Edmonds, 6 Bing. 94, 19 E. C. L. 14.

This case is to be tested, not by the rules applying to negotiable instruments. If no loss was sustained for want of notice or suit, want of notice or suit does not affect the plaintiff's right. See Shewell v. Knox, 1 Dev. 412, and cases there cited.

Again, the Judge informs the jury that the plaintiff was bound by the act of Hicks, his agent, "if ratified" by him; whereas, he should have informed the jury what acts or declarations of plaintiff would amount to a ratification, and left them to decide, as their proper function, whether those acts or declarations had been proved.

The Judge ought to have told the jury, as prayed by the plaintiff, that bringing suit on the certificate to the first court after it became due, &c., was reasonable diligence. But to leave a matter of law to the jury, is itself error. Panton v. Williams, in Error; 2 Adolph. & Ellis, N. S. 169; Beale v. Roberson, 8 Ired. 276.

The Judge ought to have instructed the jury that the acknowledgment of Hicks & Arnold, after the certificate fell due, if made by them, was evidence that it was not taken as absolute payment, &c., as prayed by the plaintiff.

The counsel for the defendant in error made the following points.

1. Joseph T. Hicks was the agent of Downey, and even if he took the certificate of deposit in good faith, exercising the care which a prudent man should do in the management of his own affairs, he could not be held liable for the subsequent failure of the bank. He had reason to believe the bank was solvent; and as the certificate bore interest, it was considered better than specie as a remittance.

2. The proof on the record is sufficient to show, that John R. Hicks was the agent of Downey at the time of the settlement in 1839, but the subsequent reception of the certificate from Dr. John Hicks, by Downey, was an ample satisfaction of all he had done, even if he had no power to make the settlement in the first instance, and equivalent to an original authority. Story on Agency, § 539; Dunlap's Pailey, 171, note O.; Lawrence v. Taylor, 5 Hill, 107, 113.

3. It was the duty of Downey to have dissented from the ar-

21 *

rangement, and refused the certificate of deposit at the time it was tendered to him; but at all events, it was gross negligence, and not a reasonable time, to wait three or four years without notifying J. T. Hickey that he could not receive it as a payment. Pailey's Arg. 172, note; 2 Kent, 127; Caines v. Bleeker, 12 J. R. 300.

4. John Hicks proves that Downey took the certificate as absolute payment; and being thus accepted, was a good discharge of the debt; especially as it was in the name of Downey. Story on Contracts, § 998; 2 Greenleaf, Ev. § 523; Whitbeck v. Van Ness, 11 J. R. 409; 15 Ib. 241.

Whether it was accepted in satisfaction, was a question for the jury. 15 S. & R. 162; 9 J. R. 310.

5. The rulings of the court, it is submitted, were correct. It will be seen that the questions are not leading, if he apply to them the test which the rules of evidence establishes as a criterion. Greenleaf's Ev. § 434.

It will be admitted that several of the instructions, asked for by plaintiff, did not apply to the proof in the record, especially the first. It is submitted that the instructions given covered every legal proposition asked for by the plaintiffs.

Mr. Justice McLEAN delivered the opinion of the court.

This case was brought before us by a writ of error to the Circuit Court for the Southern District of Mississippi.

An action of assumpsit was commenced by the plaintiff, on a note for four hundred and fifty-six dollars, and a large sum for the hire of slaves.

The declaration contained ten counts, to which the defendant pleaded *non assumpsit*, the statute of limitations, and payment, on all o which issues were joined. The jury "found for the defendant upon the issues joined as to the within note of four hundred and fifty-six dollars, and the within account." This finding, it is contended, is imperfect, irresponsive to the issues, and does not dispose of the whole matter submitted by the pleadings.

A verdict is bad if it varies from the issue in a substantial matter, or if it finds only a part of that which is in issue; and, though the court may give form to a general finding, so as to make it harmonize with the issue, yet if it appears that the finding is different from the issue, or is confined to a part only of the matter in issue, no judgment can be rendered upon the verdict. Patterson v. United States, 2 Wheat. 221. The verdict rendered was informal, but there was sufficient to authorize the court to enter it in form. The matter in controversy was the note stated and the hire of the negroes, the amount claimed for which, was stated in an account; and on both these the jury found for the defendant, on the issues joined. We think this was sufficient.

Andrew Arnold, a copartner of the testator, was offered as a witness, and being objected to on the ground of interest, a release was given in evidence, which, on its face, appeared to be duly executed; on which the witness was sworn. Objection is made that the execution of the release was not proved. The answer to this is, that there was no exception taken to the paper on that ground.

From the facts, it appears that Joseph T. Hicks, now represented by his executrix, was indebted to the plaintiff on the 10th January, 1839, on a settlement, nine thousand seven hundred and ninety-nine dollars and eighty nine cents, for the hire of negroes, which John R. Hicks, the friend of Downey, received in a certificate of deposit from the Mississippi Railroad Bank, situated at Natchez, payable on the 1st of November ensuing, for which he executed a receipt. He was not authorized to act as the agent of Downey, but he acted as his friend in the business. Being assured by his brother, Joseph T. Hicks, and others, that the bank was good, (and as a reason for this opinion it was stated that wealthy men had an interest in the bank,) and as eight per cent. interest was paid for deposits, the certificate was preferred, believing it would be satisfactory to the plaintiff. At the time of this transaction the bank was indebted to Joseph T. Hicks and Arnold, for labor on the railroad, a sum exceeding twenty thousand dollars. The mode of payment was by drawing a check on the bank for several claims, and then crediting on the books of the bank, as a deposit, the sum due to each claimant.

In February ensuing, when John R. Hicks returned to North Carolina, where he and the plaintiff resided, he handed over to Downey the certificate of deposit, who received it, saying he would have preferred the gold and silver; but said nothing further in repudiation or confirmation of the act of Hicks. In a letter dated the 3d of March, 1839, from J. T. Hicks and Arnold, to the bank, they say, "We have ever entertained the kindest feeling towards your institution, and every disposition of indulgence to the utmost of our ability. The time has now arrived when ruin awaits us, from a total inability to use your postnotes to meet our engagements;" and they proposed to take some money and negroes for the money due them from the bank, or to take the whole in negroes, if the money could not be paid.

For a short time after the date of the certificate of deposit, the bank continued to pay small notes in specie, but evidence was given conducing to show it was unable to meet its engagement of a district attorney, and marshal for the district, and for a clerk of the court.   Id. p. 1, 2.

On the 31st December, 1845, the next day after the admission into the Union, Congress passed an act declaring the State to be one collection district, and making the city of Galveston a port of entry, and to which was annexed several other places, as ports of delivery.   The 2d section provides for the appointment of a collector for the port of Galveston, and the 3d section for the appointment of a surveyor for each port of delivery.

Now it is quite apparent, from the joint resolution of Congress, admitting the State of Texas into the Union, and the acts passed, organizing the Federal courts and revenue system over it, that the old system of government, so far as it conflicted with the federal authority, became abrogated immediately on her admission as a State.   This is clearly so, unless some provision is found in the act of admission postponing the time when it shall take effect, and, as applied to the case before us, postponing it until after the 31st January, 1846, when these goods were shipped to the port of Galveston.

This has been attempted on the part of the defendant in error.

We have been referred to the 1st section of the 13th article of the constitution of Texas, which provides, "that all process which shall be issued in the name of the Republic of Texas, prior to the organization of the State government under this constitution, shall be as valid as if issued in the name of the State of Texas."   And also to the 2d section of the same article, which provides that "all criminal prosecutions or penal actions, which shall have arisen prior to the organization of the State government under this constitution, in any of the courts of the Republic, shall be prosecuted to judgment and execution in the name of the State."   And also, to the 6th section, which provides, upon its appearing that a majority of the votes of the people given is for the adoption of the constitution, "it shall be the duty of the President (of the Republic of Texas) to make proclamation of the fact, and thenceforth this constitution shall be ordained and established as the constitution of the State, to go into operation, and be of force and effect, from and after the organization of the State government."   And also, to the 10th section, which declares, "that the laws of the Republic, relative to the duties of officers, both civil and military, of the same, shall remain in full force, and the duties of the several offices shall be performed in conformity with the existing laws, until the organization of the government of the State under this constitution, or until the first day of the meeting of the legislature."

It is supposed that these several provisions of the constitution of Texas, and which is the one accepted, when she was admitted into the Union by Congress, have the effect to postpone and fix the period of admission to the time of the first meeting of the legislature of the State and organization of the government under the constitution, which was on the 16th February, 1846 ; and, of course, to postpone the operation of the laws of the Union over her till that period.

But the obvious answer to this view is, that these several provisions in the constitution were designed and intended, and had the effect, to organize a government at once, on the adoption of the constitution by the people, and thereby to avoid an interregnum between the abrogation of the old and the erection of the new system, and until the legislative body could meet, and put the government in operation in conformity with the requirements of the organic law.

The whole of the 10th section, a part of which has been already referred to, affords an illustration of the design of the framers of the constitution. It is as follows: " That no inconvenience may result from the change of government, it is declared, that the laws of the Republic, relative to the duties of officers, both civil, and military, of the same, shall remain in full force, and the duties of the several offices shall be performed in conformity with existing laws, until the organization of the government of the State under this constitution, or until the first day of the meeting of the legislature."   This section, taken in connection with the 3d section of the same article, completed an organization which effectually prevented any interval between the old and new systems, when the laws did not operate, or an organized government was not in force.   That section provides, that " all laws and parts of laws, now in force in the Republic of Texas, which are not repugnant to the Constitution of the United States, the joint resolutions for annexing Texas to the United States, or to the provisions of this constitution, shall remain in force, as the laws of this State, until they expire by their own limitation or repealed by the legislature.

This section, as it will be seen, also negatives the idea, tnat the Constitution and laws of the Union were not in force within the State as soon as her admission into the Union took place.

This subject was very fully considered in Benner et al. v. Porter, (9 How. 235,) which involved an inquiry into the affect of the admission of Florida into the Union as a State.   Some of the questions there were very similar to those raised in this case, as the machinery of the territorial government had been adopted by an ordinance in the constitution until the organization was effected under the constitution by the legislature.

his authority, or acts without authority, the principal is not bound, unless he ratify such acts. But the jury are not informed what amounts to a ratification. They are told, where acts are done, c˝ which the principal is informed if he does not in a reasonable time object thereto, he is presumed to ratify the acts, and is bound thereby.

This, in all probability, misled the jury. Doctor Hicks, in receiving the certificate of deposit, did not pretend that he was authorized to receive it — much less that he was authorized to receive it as payment. The receipt of the certificate, under such circumstances, by Downey, without any express agreement on the subject, could not operate as payment. In this respect, therefore, unless such an agreement was shown and connected with this part of the charge, it was erroneous.

The jury were instructed that, if the certificate was received on condition the deposit, if paid by the bank, should be appli xd as payment, Downey was bound to use reasonable diligence. But the jury were not informed what that kind of diligence was, except, " that it consisted in such exertions as a prudent man would use in his own case in the collection of the certificate." Where a note is received as collateral security, and this certificate of deposit is only the obligation of the bank, and does not, in principle, in this respect, differ from a note, the holder is not bound to active diligence. If the note have an indorser, and it matures in his hands, he may be bound to take such steps as shall charge the indorser as a bank is bound, where a note is sent to it for collection. But he is not bound to bring suit. He is only chargeable with a negligence, which shall operate to the injury of the owner of the paper.

As, in less than three months from the date of the certificate of deposit by the showing of the defendant, the post-notes of the bank answered him no valuable purpose in satisfying the demands against him, there is no ground to allege that the defen tant suffered by any want of diligence in the plaintiff. The ba. k was insolvent, if not when the certificate was given, before it became due. The above instruction was erroneous.

We think the court erred, also, in refusing to give the third instruction, as prayed by the plaintiff. If the evidence showed, after the maturity of the certificate, that Hicks & Arnold, or Hicks, admitted their liability to make it good, the jury should have been told by the court, that if they believed such an admission was made, it conduced to prove that the certificate was not taken in payment.

For the above reasons, the judgment of the Circuit Court is reversed, and the cause is remanded for further proceedings.

Mr. Justice DANIEL and Mr. Justice GRIER dissented.

Mr. Justice DANIEL, (Mr. Justice GRIER concurring.)

It is my opinion, that the judgment of the Circuit Court, in this case, should be affirmed, upon the questions raised in the argument, 1st, upon the sufficiency of the finding by the jury, as being responsive to all the issues, or otherwise; — 2dly, as to the admissibility in evidence of the release to Arnold, in the absence of the subscribing witness to that release, there is an entire concurrence amongst the Judges. But with the views announced as those of the court with respect to the authority and the acts of Doctor Hicks, as the agent of Downey, and as to the consequences deducible from those acts, I am constrained to disagree.

And here I must remark, that, according to my apprehension of the evidence upon the record, as to the authority vested in Doctor Hicks, as agent, and his acts under that authority, and with respect to the conduct of Downey, as principal, in confirmation of those acts, — that evidence has not been accurately stated. It is said by the court, that Doctor Hicks did not act as the agent, but merely as the friend of Downey. There seems to be some difficulty, and even confusion, in this attempt to discriminate between these two characters. True it is, that the agent, however confided in, does not always prove the best friend of his principal; but it is equally true, that the principal would rarely select, as his agent, one whom he regarded in any other light than that of a friend. But the record, according to my apprehension of the evidence, discloses the most ample and explicit authority to Doctor Hicks, to settle the claims of Downey upon the firm of Hicks & Arnold, and exhibits instructions equally clear to Doctor Hicks, to transmit to Downey the amount which this agent, upon the settlement made by him, should ascertain to be owing from Hicks & Arnold to Downey. The record discloses these further facts: 1. The settlement made by Doctor Hicks with Hicks & Arnold; 2. The drawing of a check by these persons in favor of Doctor Hicks, the agent, upon the bank at Natchez, for the amount ascertained to be due to Downey; 3. The presentation of that check by the agent, at the bank at Natchez; 4. The proffer by the bank, of payment in specie of the amount of the check; and the express agreement of the agent with the bank, to commute that check and proffer of immediate payment in money for a certificate of deposit, or post-note, payable at a deferred period, bearing an interest of 8 per centum. So much, then, for the acts of the agent in virtue of the authority originally vested in him; and if there could arise a doubt as to their validity, that doubt could apply only to the transmutation of the demand for the money into a certificate of deposit, or deferred payment, bearing interest. But, supposing there had been room for doubt in this respect, on the ground that the agent had transcended his power, that doubt must be entirely dispelled when the conduct of the principal is considered. Upon being informed, by the agent, of the measure he had taken, and upon having the certificate transmitted to him, the principal said, in reply, that although he would have preferred a payment down in money, yet as the agent had acted for himself as he had done for his principal, he could not find fault with the arrangement. He expressed no apprehensions as to the prudence or safety of the arrangement, but ratified it expressly; and in fact the proof is clear, that at the time, and for some months after, the bank was paying specie; and that its certificates, like the one in question, commanded a premium in the market. In this mode was the entire proceedings of the agent explicitly ratified.

If this apprehension of the testimony be correct, then it is difficult to conceive how the jury could have been misled by the instructions which were given them by the court. Indeed this court, so far as those instructions covered the relation of principal and agent, have not questioned the correctness of those instructions. But it is said, that the court erred in the opinion it expressed upon the subject of the diligence requisite in the application for payment of the certificate of deposit. Let it be conceded that this opinion of the court upon the subject of reasonable diligence was not the law; still it should not affect the decision in this case, because that opinion had no connection with the true character of the case, which depended upon a phase of the evidence to which that instruction had no application, and could not influence. If the agent of Downey was authorized to settle, and had settled with the debtors of Downey, and the latter had accepted from his debtors what he acknowledged was payment, at this point the transaction closed; and unless the parties making payment could be affected by showing fraud or bad faith, the whole matter was terminated by the agreement between the parties. Downey had an indisputable right to receive payment in any medium he might choose, and it is not in the power of a court to control his first choice and give him the right to a second, or to visit, upon those who have applied their means to his satisfaction, and by so doing prevented them being available to themselves to any other possible purpose, the mischiefs resulting from his choice.

But it is said by the court, that Hicks & Arnold, subsequently to the failure of the bank, admitted their liability to Downey for this demand. Here, again, I conceive that the evidence in this cause has been greatly misapprehended, and that a correct understanding of the testimony will show that the

De Lane e: al. v. Moore et al.

admission which has been brought to bear upon this transaction, related to a posterior and wholly different liability of the same parties — to a transaction in which Hicks and Arnold had deposited a certificate of deposit of this bank as collateral security for a debt from Arnold, and that security turning out not to be available, they held themselves bound to satisfy the demand it was designed to secure. This subsequent transaction had no connection whatever with that in which the check in question was given, and on which payment in money was proffered, but for which the certificate of deposit was, by express agreement of the agent, ratified by his principal, taken in full satisfaction.

Order.

This cause came on to be heard on the transcript of the record from the Circuit Court of the United States for the Southern District of Mississippi, and was argued by counsel. On consideration whereof, it is now here ordered and adjudged, by this court, that the judgment of the said Circuit Court in this cause be, and the same is hereby, reversed with costs, and that this cause be, and the same is hereby, remanded to the said Circuit Court, with directions to award a *venire facias-de novo*.

PHILIP H. DE LANE, JOHN M. CHILES, MARTHA C. CHILES, JOHN E. LYKES, AND GRACE A. LYKES, APPELLANTS, *v.* ANDREW B. MOORE, AND JAMES L. GOREE, EXECUTORS OF JAMES L. GOREE, DECEASED.

Where an antenuptial contract was alleged to have been made, and the affidavits of the parties claiming under it alleged that they never possessed or saw it; that they had made diligent inquiry for it, but were unable to learn its present existence or place of existence; that inquiry had been made of the guardian of one of the children, who said that he had never been in possession of it, and did not know where it was; that inquiry had been made at the recording offices in vain, and that the affiants believed it to be lost; secondary proof of its contents ought to have been admitted.

Whether recorded or not, it was binding upon the parties. If recorded within the time prescribed by statute, or if reacknowledged and recorded afterwards, notice would thereby have been given to all persons of its effect.

If it was regularly recorded in one State, and the property upon which it acted was removed to another State, the protection of the contract would follow the property into the State into which it was removed.

But where no suit was brought until eight or nine years after the death of the husband, and then the one which was brought was dismissed for want of prosecution; another suit against the executors who had divided the property, comes too late.

THIS was an appeal from the District Court of the United States for the Middle District of Alabama.

The case is fully stated in the opinion of the court.

It was argued by *Mr. Johnson* and *Mr. Butler*, for the appellants, and *Mr. Bradley* and *Mr. Davidge*, for the appellees.

The counsel for the appellants, after stating the case, proceeded:

It appears, from the record, that the defendants objected to the reading of the papers of the marriage settlement, because the affidavits of the complainants did not make out such a case of the loss or destruction as would dispense with the production of the original. The objection was sustained by the presiding Judge. By the ruling of the Judge, the complainants' bill was ordered to be dismissed.

It is submitted, that the ruling of the Judge was erroneous; and if it should be sustained here, the complainants must fail in any attempt to recover their rights, because they cannot be allowed to introduce the only evidence on which they rest.

The evidence offered by the complainants, and rejected by the court, was both competent and sufficient to satisfy a Judge, when discretion must, on such questions, regulate his judgment; and especially so in the chancery jurisdiction of the court, where it is usual to receive with a liberal latitude, *sub modo* at least, all evidence that can lead to a competent judgment on the rights of the parties. The bill was filed by those who were seeking their rights by discovery, and against the acts of those who had a temptation to destroy the evidence against them. But it is submitted, that the question has been authoritatively ruled by the court; and, according to the adjudged cases on the same subject in Alabama, where this case was tried, the evidence rejected should have been admitted. Tayloe *v.* Riggs, 1 Pet. 591, 596; S. C. 9 Wharton, 483; Winn *v.* Patterson, 9 Pet. 663, 676; S. C. 5 Pet. 233, 240, 242; Sturdevant *v.* Gaines, 5 Ala. 435; Slerge *v.* Clapton, 6 Ala. 589.

If the evidence rejected by the Judge, as to the reading of the marriage settlement, should have been received, as we think it should, then it may become necessary to bring in review the questions made by the defendants' answer.

Was the marriage settlement duly and legally recorded in South Carolina. By the laws of South Carolina (see act of 1786 and 1823) marriage settlements, according to the first act, are required to be recorded in the office of the Secretary of State, and by the second act, also, in the office of Register of Mesne Conveyances, within three months after their execution, otherwise they will be regarded as void at law. The marriage settlement, in this case, was executed on the 20th May, and if recorded before the 20th of August, would have been duly recorded, according to the requirements of the act of 1786. It appears from Guiguard's official certificate, that the paper was recorded in the Register of Mesne Conveyances, on the 31st day of July, 1816, the day on which it was proved by Young, one of the witnesses to it.

The certificate of Arthar, the deputy Secretary of State, is not definite as to the time when the paper was recorded in the office of the Secretary of State. There is no doubt, however, that it had been first recorded in that office, as such should have been done, according to the act of 1786, (which is the only act affecting this case.) We think such must be the conclusion of the court, as scarcely any other fair inference could be drawn from the premises. If such should be the holding of the court, a second proposition arises, was it necessary that it should have been recorded in Alabama?

According to the tenor of the decisions of this court, it was not necessary that there should be such a recording to protect the rights of the complainants against the claims of a subsequent purchaser.

"A marriage settlement or deed, in favor of the wife, duly executed and recorded in Virginia, will be good against the creditors in the District of Columbia, although they may have had no express notice. Bank v. Lee, 13 Peters, 119, 120. Such has been the current of decisions in South Carolina and Alabama?

But the complainants have a right, from the proof in the record, to take refuge in the equity of their rights.

According to the evidence of W. R. Hamilton, Goree, the testator of defendants, who seems to have been a shopkeeper, purchased the slave in question, with express notice of complainants' title, by the marriage settlement of their mother with Yancey. The testimony of Hamilton was duly taken; for, if defectively taken in the first instance, the defendants had an opportunity, and were required, to retake it, if they chose, by an express agreement of the parties.

Such being their condition — that is, purchasers with express notice — he, Goree, took the property subject to the acknowledged claims of the complainants, and having taken under their title, he should not be allowed to claim against it.

The doctrine of notice is well established. He who acquires a legal title, having notice of the prior equity of another, becomes a trustee for that other to the extent of his equity. 1 Cranch, 100.

If a man will purchase, with notice of another's right, giving a consideration will not avail him. 2 Bridgman's Digest, Vendors and Purchasers, IX. 691.

With respect to the operation of the statute of limitations upon cases of trust in equity, the distinction is, if the trust be constituted by act of the parties, the possession of the trustee is the possession of the *cestui que trust*, and no length of such possession will bar; but if a party is constituted a trustee by the decree of a court of equity founded on fraud, or the like, his possession is adverse, and the statute of limitations will run from the time that the circumstances of the fraud were discovered. 2 Bridgman's Digest, 252.

In the case of Miller *v.* Kershaw, marriage settlement was held void at law; in equity, however, the party claiming under the settlement, would be protected where the purchaser had actual notice of the settlement. Bayley's Equity, 481.

If the foregoing propositions can be sustained, another question arises, and that is, can the defendants claim to be protected by the statute of limitations? The complainants allege, in their bill, that they were minors at the death of their mother, and could not assert their rights, under the marriage settlement, as remaindermen, after the death of Yancey, their step-father. They aver, furthermore, that they were ignorant as to the time of Yancey's death, from their distant and separated situations. It is also stated expressly in their bill, (and it is a bill of discovery,) that they were not informed as to the time when a fraud had been committed upon their rights, to wit, when Yancey sold, and Goree purchased, with a full disclosure and knowledge of their title. This reduces the parties to the relation of trustee and *cestui que trust*, and exempts the complainant from the operation of the statute of limitations.

Purchaser from mortgagor, with notice, cannot claim by possession against a mortgage. Thayer *v.* Craner, 1 McCord, 395.

Court of Equity, bound by statute, upon legal title and demands, except in cases which are excepted upon purely equitable principles, such as trust, fraud, &c. Van Rhyn *v.* Vincent, 1 McCord, 314.

In cases of fraud, it runs from the time the fraud has been discovered. Id. 4 Dess. Rep. 480.

If one intrudes upon the rights of an infant, and takes the profits, he will be treated as guardian. His character is fiduciary; the statute of limitations is inapplicable; and lapse of time will not bar account. Goodhue *v.* Barnwell, Rice, Equity, 239.

The ruling of the Judge below was evidently in reference to a single question, in which he clearly was in error. But, independently of his decision, it may become the plaintiffs to satisfy this court that, if he had all these questions before him, the defendants, in any point of view, would have been entitled to a decree in their favor.

Therefore, it becomes the complainants to show that they were entitled to a decree in their favor, upon the entire merits of their case.

The counsel for the appellees made the following points :
First point omitted.

II. The court was right in rejecting the copy of the marriage contract.

1. The affidavits of the complainants were insufficient to prove the loss of the original, which they had never seen, and which had never been seen by any witness in the cause.

The foundation that is the existence of an original, was not laid, unless it is shown by the copy.

This distinguishes it from the case of Winn v. Patterson, (9 Pet. 663,) and all the other cases; 5 Pet. 233, et al.

2. If this foundation was laid, they do not show a search for the original such as is required by the court.

They state where they have searched; but Yancey removed from South Carolina to Alabama, carrying the personal property with him. His right, according to the theory of complainants, depended upon this agreement. He would have carried it with him. It would have been among his papers. There was no search there. See the cases cited on appellant's brief.

3. The copy from the records in South Carolina, cannot rest on the principle of an ancient deed. The possession and acts of Yancey, as represented by complainants, were inconsistent with any limitation on his title, and therefore with this deed. Nor does the rule apply to copies, unless some other proof of the existence of the deed is given. There must be proof *aliunde* that there was an original. Winn v. Patterson, 9 Pet. 675–6, and the cases cited by appellant.

4. The affidavit of Lykes and wife was properly rejected by the court; and, in order to lay the foundation for the secondary proof, all the complainants should have purged themselves from any concealment or laches.

III. The copies could only be admitted on the ground of their having been duly and lawfully recorded in South Carolina.

1. The title is set up in a married woman residing in Alabama, in personal property, openly under the control of her husband, which title depends on a marriage contract made in South Carolina. The case of Lee v. The Bank of the United States, (13 Pet.) shows that such a title may be supported, not-

22 *

withstanding there is no record in Alabama, nor any badge or token to distinguish it from the general property of the husband.

If the action had been in the State Court, the law of South Carolina must have been proved, as any other fact in the cause. But this court has said, in Leland v. Wilkinson, (6 Pet.) and Owings v. Hull, (9 Pet.) that the general laws of the several States will be judicially noticed in the courts of the United States.

We are, then, to inquire what the law of South Carolina was in 1816? It required the record to be made within three months after the date of the deed, and after the execution had been proved according to law, in the office of the Secretary of State only.

This disposes of the copy from the Richland district.

2. No statute of South Carolina is produced, showing how the deed was to be proved. But, admitting that this deed was executed and proved according to law, the proof of the recording does not sustain the claim.

The law of South Carolina will be found in James's Dig. 275–6; 2 Brev. Dig. 45–6; 6 Stat. at Large, App. 636–7; and 5 Stat. at Large, 203.

That law required the record to be made within three months, or the deed was void.

One of these copies appears to have been recorded on the 31st of July, 1816, in the Richland office; the other, between the 30th of July and the 14th of November, in the Secretary's office. The presumption, then, is, that the former was first recorded; for it could hardly be that it was recorded in this last office on the 30th, and in the former on the 31st.

Again; the law authorizing the record in the Register's office, was not passed until 1823. How, then, came this deed to be recorded there seven years in anticipation of such a law? Is it not evident that the parties placed it there first, by mistake, and, discovering their error, afterwards had it placed in the Secretary's office? Then, when was it put there? They must show it was within three months after its date. They have failed to do so.

So that whether the affidavits were, or not, sufficent to admit the secondary proof, the secondary proof itself is wholly insufficient, by reason of the failure of complainants to show the record under the statute.

IV. The defendants have pleaded the statute of limitations of six years.

It would be a complete bar, in any action at law. Aik. Dig. tit. Limitation, p. 270, 271.

The disabilities are coverture, infancy, *non compos*, and absence of defendant beyond seas.

In this case, the slave was sold in 1821; the coverture terminated in 1823; the husband survived to 1834, with the right of possession and enjoyment only. In 1834, complainants' right was complete, if they had any. The youngest must have been of full age in, or before, the year 1837. They are all children of the widow DeLane, before her marriage with Yancey, in 1816. A suit in Equity against these defendants was pending in 1843, for this very property, and dismissed for want of prosecution. It was as if it had never existed. In 1847, when this suit began, more than twice the period of limitation had elapsed since the right, if any, accrued.

Courts of Equity will not encourage such demands. There must be some diligence, some activity, some movement, by the party. Piatt v. Vattier, 9 Pet. 405; McKnight v. Taylor, 1 How. 161.

V. Such activity was peculiarly necessary in this case. It is a suit against executors, bound to close their office with reasonable despatch. A suit pending against them in 1843, had been dismissed. They had gone on to settle their trust; the debts had been paid, and the assets distributed, when this suit was brought, and courts of equity will protect them. The claim should have been presented within eighteen months. Aik. Dig.; Clay's Dig. 195, § 17.

VI. Finally, the presumptions of fact are all against the claim set up.

The marriage contract authorizes a sale by the husband, with the consent of the wife. They are residing together, apparently in not a very prosperous condition, and both purchase, for their own support and the support of their family, (of these very complainants,) the goods of the defendants' testator. They are unable to pay for them, and one or both of them sell the slave to him for these very things. Honesty and fair dealing required that the wife should out of her means aid the husband in supporting the children of her prior marriage, and this court will presume that she did what common honesty required of her, and that she did unite in the sale. At all events, it was a sale and delivery of possession made in her lifetime for her benefit, and this court could compel her to ratify it now if she had not done so before.

This contract was made in South Carolina in 1816; the parties removed to Alabama before 1820. It is to be interpreted by the laws then in force in South Carolina.

In 1811, (Ewing v. Smith, 3 Dess. 417, 455, 457, 462, 463,) the Court of Appeals of that State declared the common law of England was not applicable to cases of married women having separate estates in that State. This was followed by Carter v. Eveleigh, 4 Dess. 19, and James v. Maysant, Ib. 591.

De Lane et al. v. Moore et al.

From these cases it appears — 1st. That a married woman, having a separate estate, can only change, encumber, or dispose of it, strictly according to the provisions of the settlement. 2d. That an estate limited to the joint use of husband and wife during coverture, with power to her to dispose of it by deed or will, and to go to her sole and absolute use in case of her surviving him, is a separate estate. 3d. The separate estate will be liable for debts contracted for the purposes for which it was created.

In this case the conditions necessary to raise a separate estate to her out of the joint estate, do not exist.

1. There is no power of disposition given to her, but it is given to the husband only with her consent.

2. There is no sole and absolute use reserved to her; but the right of survivorship, without any power of disposal, is mutual.

3. The debt in this case was contracted for the purposes of the trust, and on the credit of the trust estate.

The cases of Cooke v. Kennedy and Smith, (12 Ala. 42) ; Bender v. Reynolds, (15 Ala. 446,) are directly in point, that such an estate, with the property in the possession of the husband, is subject to the husband's debts. See also Moss v. McCall, 12 Ala. 630.

Here acquiescence may be inferred. Square v. Dean, 4 Bro. C. C. 326 ; Beresford v. Ar. Bis. Armagh, 13 Sim. 643.

Mr. Justice DANIEL delivered the opinion of the court.

·· The appellants, in the year 1847, filed their bill in the court aforesaid against the appellees, seeking of them a discovery as to certain slaves charged to have come to the possession of their testator, and also an account and a recovery of ·the value, increase, hires, and profits of those slaves, and claiming by name a negro woman named Linda or Linder, together with her children.

The bill charges that in the year 1816, Mrs. Ann Wood De Lane, a widow lady residing in the State of South Carolina, and possessed of valuable real estate, and of sundry slaves, being about to intermarry with one John Yancey, an antenuptial contract was entered into and executed between these parties. The stipulations in this contract, which is made an exhibit with the bill, are to the following effect: That " all the estate of the said Ann, real and personal, should be and remain for the joint use, support, and enjoyment of the said John and Ann during their joint lives, and to the survivor of them during his or her life; that the same should be free from any debts, dues, demands, or contracts of said Yancey, unless it should be under the following restrictions: That the said John Yancey should not have the right to dispose of any portion of the estate or property, real or personal, unless the said Ann should consent thereto. That the said John should have the right to dispose of the property upon his obtaining such consent. That the said Ann should have the right of granting or withholding her consent without resorting to the aid of a court of equity, or to the intervention of a trustee. That all transfers by the said John of any portion of the property with the consent of the said Ann, should be valid, whether made for his separate use and benefit, or for the joint use of himself and wife; and that the said John should not be compellable to settle any equivalent for property so transferred, unless there should be a stipulation between the parties to that effect. That all of the estate, real or personal, which should remain undisposed of during the joint lives of the parties, should be for the use and benefit of the survivor; and at his or her death should be equally divided amongst all the children of the said Ann, both of this and of the former marriage. That none of the aforesaid estate, real or personal, should be liable for any debts, judgments, or executions, that might be in existence at the date of the contract, or at any time thereafter against the said John, unless by mutual consent of the parties. The bill further charges that the marriage having taken place between the said Ann Wood De Lane and John Yancey, they removed to the State of Alabama, where the said Ann having died, the said Yancey, who survived her, sold to James L. Goree, deceased, either during the lifetime or after the death of the said Ann, but without her consent, and in violation of the antenuptial agreement, several of the slaves mentioned in that agreement. That the said Philip H. De Lane, Martha Chiles, and Grace Lykes, who are the children of Ann W. De Lane, by her first marriage, and her only heirs, were, at the date of the sale aforesaid by Yancey, infants of tender years.

The bill makes no persons defendants, and seeks relief against none others, except the said Andrew B. Moore, and James L. Goree, the executors of James L. Goree, deceased.

The respondents deny all personal knowledge of a purchase of slaves by their testator, of Yancey, but state that they have been informed, and believe, that the decedent did, in his lifetime, and in the lifetime of Ann W. Yancey, obtain from the said John Yancey, in the year 1822, a negro woman slave, named Lindy, and her child Becky, in payment of a store account contracted with the decedent, whilst a merchant in Alabama, by said John and Ann Yancey, for sugar, coffee, pork, butter, clothing, and other necessaries for the support of the said John and Ann, and of the complainants, the children of the said Ann, and of the slaves conveyed in the marriage settlement. The respondents deny that any slave mentioned in that agreement, except the woman Lindy, ever came to the possession of their testator, and after naming the offspring of Lindy, they aver that this female slave and her offspring were never held by the respondents in any other right than as the executors of James L. Goree, deceased; that long before the institution of this suit, the respondents, as such executors, had delivered over to the distributees of their testator, all the slaves held by them, had settled their account as executors, and received a discharge, viz., on the 2d day of January, 1846. Having made the above statements in answer to interrogatories put by the bill, the respondents propound these separate averments, and claim to be allowed the benefit of them as if specially pleaded.

1. That their testator was a *bonâ fide* purchaser of the slave Lindy for valuable consideration, without notice of the alleged marriage settlement.

2. That more than six years had elapsed between the death of Yancey, who survived his wife, and the commencement of this suit, and therefore the suit is barred by the statute of limitations.

3. That the said marriage settlement was made in the State of South Carolina, and was not recorded according to the laws of that State, and is therefore void, both as to the respondents and to their testator, who was a *bonâ fide* purchaser without notice.

4. That if the marriage settlement had been properly recorded, or was otherwise valid the sale of the slave Lindy was made with the assent of the said Ann Yancey.

5. That the respondents received the said slaves as the executors of the last will and testament of decedent, as a part of his estate, and had, before this suit was commenced, disposed of them according to the provisions of said will, by distribution and delivery to the legatees of said estate, and that long before the commencement of this suit, had made a final settlement of said estate, and had been discharged from said executorship.

To the answer of the respondents, the complainants filed a general replication, and upon the pleadings and proofs in the cause, the District Court, on the 7th of December, 1849, pronounced a decree, dismissing the bill of the complainants, with costs. The correctness of that decree we will proceed to consider.

The first question which presents itself, in the natural order of investigation of the proceedings of the District Court, is that which was raised upon the admissibility in evidence, of an authenticated copy of the antenuptial contract, upon the suffi-

ciency of the cause assigned for the non-production of the
original. The cause so assigned, was this. The three children
of Mrs. De Lane, with the husbands of the two daughters,
depose that they never possessed, nor ever saw the original contract; that they have made diligent inquiry for it, but have been
unable to learn either its present existence, or place of existence—
and believe that it has been lost or destroyed. And the son,
Philip De Lane, states farther, that he had made inquiry for it,
first of John Partridge, his guardian, who informed him that he
had never been in possession of it, and did not know where it
was; that deponent had also made inquiry for it at the Office
of Mesne Conveyances, and at the Office of the Secretary of
State, of South Carolina, but upon search and inquiry it could
not be found at either of those places; and he believes that this
instrument was either destroyed by said Yancey, or by fire when
the court house in Monroe county, in Alabama, was burned in
1833—that the subscribing witnesses to the agreement, he
believes, after diligent inquiry, are dead. That Yancey died in
1836, in Mississippi, utterly insolvent, and no person ever administered on his estate. In disregard of these affidavits, the
District Court refused to consider the copy of the antenuptial
contract as legal or admissible in the absence of the original,
and in this refusal, we think that court has erred. Upon the
most obvious principles of reason and justice, we think, that
the complainants could not have laid a stronger foundation for
the introduction of the secondary proof. The custody of the
original document, or the duty of preserving it, could in no view
be brought home to them. And its absence, therefore, over
which they could have had no control, and produced by no default
of theirs, should not have deprived them of the effect of that
document to avail for whatever it might be worth. This view
of the question before us, is strengthened by the obvious considerations, that no suspicion justly attaches to the complainants
from the non-production of the original agreement, and that its
exhibition was calculated rather to corroborate, than to weaken
their claims. The instances in which secondary evidence is to
be admitted, and the requisites demanded by the courts to warrant its introduction, are treated of in the elementary works on
evidence, as for instance, in 2 Saunders on Pleading and
Evidence, 833, et seq. But in a decision of this court, this
subject has been dealt with in a manner so strikingly appo-
site to the question now before us, as to warrant particular
notice thereof, as being in all respects, decisive of that question.
We allude to the decision of Tayloe v. Riggs, reported in 1
Peters, 591. That case presented by no means so strong a
a claim for the introduction of secondary evidence as does the

one now under consideration, for that was an application for leave to substitute parol for written evidence, and not for the substitution of an authenticated copy of a written and recorded document in lieu of the original. In Tayloe v. Riggs, the Chief Justice lays down the law as follows:

" The rule of law is, that the best evidence must be given of which the nature of the thing is capable; that is, that no evidence shall be received which presupposes greater evidence behind in the party's possession or power. The withholding of that better evidence raises a presumption, that if produced, it might not operate in his favor.. For this reason, a party who is in possession of an original paper, or who has it in his power, is not permitted to give a copy in evidence, or to prove its contents. When, therefore, the plaintiff below offered to prove the contents of the written contract on which this suit was instituted, the defendant might very properly require the contract itself. It was itself superior evidence of its contents to any thing depending on the memory of a witness. It was once in his possession, and the presumption was that it was still so. It was necessary to do away this presumption, or the secondary evidence must be excluded. How is it to be done away? If the loss or destruction of the paper can be proved by a disinterested witness, the difficulty is at once removed. But papers of this description, generally remain in possession of the party himself, and their loss can, in most instances, be known only to himself. If his own affidavit cannot be received, the loss of a written contract, the contents of which are well known to others, or a copy of which can be proved, would amount to a complete loss of his rights, at least in a court of law. The objection to receiving the affidavit of the party is, that no man can be a witness in his own cause. This is undoubtedly a sound rule, which ought never to be violated. But many collateral questions arise in the progress of a cause, to which the rule does no apply. Questions which do not involve the matter in controversy, but matters auxiliary to the trial, which facilitate the preparation for it, often depend on the oath of the party. An affidavit of the materiality of a witness, for the purpose of obtaining a continuance, or a commission to take a deposition, or an affidavit of his inability to attend, is usually made by the party, and received without objection. So affidavits to support a motion for a new trial are often received. These cases, and others of the same character, which might be adduced, show that in many incidental questions that are addressed to the court, and which do not affect the question to be tried by the jury, the affidavit of the party is received. The testimony which establishes the loss of the paper is addressed to the court, and does not relate to the contents of the paper. It is a fact which may be important as letting the party in to prove the justice of the cause, but does not of itself prove any thing in the cause. As this fact is generally known only to the party himself, there would seem to be a necessity for receiving his affidavit in support of it."

The law, as thus clearly declared by this court in Tayloe v. Riggs, is in strictest accordance with the rule prevailing in the Supreme Court of the State within which the case before us was decided. Thus, in the case of Sturdevant v. Gaines, (reported in the 5th vol. Alabama Reports, p. 435,) that court thus announces the rule by which they are governed with respect to the introduction of secondary evidence. "In the recent case of Jones v. Scott, (2 Alabama R. 61,) it is stated, that no fixed rule can be laid down as applicable to this class of cases; that, in general, search must be made where the lost paper was last known to be. These remarks are quite applicable to this case. Search was made where the paper was last known to be only three days before." Again: "We cannot say that half an hour's search in a lawyer's office, was not sufficient to ascertain whether the paper was not where it was left, nor, in the absence of any fact indicating that it might be found elsewhere, can we perceive that there was any necessity to search elsewhere for it. If the admission that the paper, on further search where it was last known to be, or elsewhere, might still be discovered, would preclude the secondary evidence, it would annihilate the rule in all cases where the lost paper was not proved to be destroyed as well as lost, as otherwise there must always be a possibility that it may be found." With regard to the position insisted upon in the answers, that the antenuptial contract was void for the failure to record it within three months from its date, in conformity with the law of South Carolina; that position, however maintainable it might be, so far as the instrument was designed to operate by mere legal or constructive effect on creditors and purchasers, becoming such before it was recorded, or, in the event of its never being recorded, cannot be supported to the extent, that by the failure to record it within the time prescribed by the statute, the deed would thereby be void to all intents and purposes. Such a deed would, from its execution, be binding at common law *inter partes*, though never recorded; and if, after expiration of the time prescribed by statute, it should be reacknowledged and then recorded, either upon such reacknowledgment, or upon proof of witnesses, it would, from the period of that reacknowledgment and admission to record, be restored to its full effect of notice, which would, by construction, have followed from its being recorded originally within the time prescribed by law. These conclusions are sustained by numerous decisions. We refer, in support of them, to the cases of Turner *v.* Stip, 1 Wash. 319; Currie *v.* Donald, 2 Wash. 58; Eppes *v.* Randolph, 2 Call, 125; Guerrant *v.* Anderson, 4 Ran. 208; Roanes *v.* Archer, 4 Leigh, 550; Woods *v.* Owings & Smith, 1 Cranch, 239; Lessee of Sicard *v.* Davis, 6 Peters, 124.

The antenuptial agreement between Ann Wood De Lane and John Yancey, is proved to have been executed on the 20th day of May, 1816; if it was admitted to record at any time before the 20th of August, in the same year, it operated as notice to all creditors and purchasers becoming such subsequently to the execution of that agreement; if it was not recorded until the 14th of November, in the year 1816, it could by construction operate as notice from the latter period only, but as between the parties, and with regard to subsequent creditors and purchasers with notice, it operated from the period of its execution. The sole purpose of recording the deed, is, that those who n ight deal with the parties thereto, or with the subjects it comprised, should have knowledge of the true condition of both, and if such knowledge is presumed, nay, established by legal inference from the fact that the deed has been recorded, *a fortiori*, it must be established by actual notice.

It has been made a ground of defence, in the answers in the court below, and it has also been insisted upon in argument here, that admitting the antenuptial contract to have been recorded in the State of South Carolina, and, in consequence thereof, to have been so operative as to affect with notice creditors and purchasers within that State, yet, that upon the removal of the parties, carrying with them the property into another State or jurisdiction, the influence of the contract, for the protection of the property, would be wholly destroyed, and the subject attempted to be secured, would be open to claims by creditors or purchasers subsequently coming into existence. The position here advanced is not now assumed for the first time in argument in this court. It has, upon a former occasion, been pressed upon its attention, and has been looked into with care, and unless it be the intention of the court to retrace the course heretofore adopted, this may be now, as it formerly was, called an adjudged question. The case of the United States Bank *v.* Lee et al., (reported in the 13th of Peters, p. 107,) brought directly up for the examination of this court, the effect of a judgment and execution, obtained by a subsequent creditor in the District of Columbia, upon property found within that district, but which had been settled upon the wife of a debtor, by a deed executed and recorded in Virginia, according to the laws of that State, the husband and wife being, at the time of making the instrument, inhabitants of the State of Virginia. The question was, by Mr. Justice Catron, who delivered the opinion of the court, elaborately investigated, and the cases from the different States, founded upon their registry acts, carefully collected. The cases of Smith v. Bruce's Administrator, from 2d of Harris & Johnson, and of Crenshaw v. Anthony, from Martin & Yerger's Reports, p. 110, cited by the learned Judge, fully sustain his reasoning upon the point. This court come unhesitatingly and clearly to the conclusion, that the deed of settlement, executed and recorded in favor of Mrs. Lee, in conformity with the laws of Virginia, protected her rights in the subject settled, against the judgment of the subsequent creditor, in the District of Columbia. We should not be disposed to disturb the doctrine laid down in the case of the Bank of the United States v. Lee, and in the decisions of the State courts of Maryland and Tennessee, above mentioned, if the rights of the parties turned upon the operation of the contract as constituting notice; or upon the proof of knowledge on the part of Goree, the purchaser from Yancey, of the existence of the marriage contract. But we think that the rights of the parties to this controversy should not be made to depend upon any such incident as the existence of notice of the contract, either actual or constructive.

It has been premised, in the statement of the pleadings in this case, that the only defendants in the court below, were the executors of James L. Goree, deceased, called upon in their representative character, and in no other. The marriage contract between Ann W. De Lane and John Yancey, was executed in 1816. It is proved that Yancey died in 1833, or 1834. The complainants are the children of Mrs. Yancey, by her first marriage; so that, at the time of the death of Yancey, the youngest of those children, if born immediately preceding the second marriage, could not have been younger than seventeen years; the elder children were then probably nearly or fully at majority. After the death of Yancey, the record discloses no claim on the part of the complainants, nor any effort by them to recover the property settled by the contract, earlier than 1842, eight or nine years after Yancey's death; at which last period, it is said, there was a suit pending in one of the State courts, against the testator of the appellees, but which suit, after being revived against the appellees, subsequently to the death of their testator, was, in the year 1843, dismissed for the want of prosecution. The bill in this suit was filed in January, 1847, at an interval of thirty-one years after the execution of the marriage agreement, and of fourteen years after the death of Yancey; from which last event, the complainants had an undoubted and unobstructed power to seek their rights under that contract, whatever they were.

If mere tardiness in asserting their pretensions, were all that could be imputed to the appellants, this, of itself, would place them in a position which could not commend them the countenance of courts of justice; but, this delay is by no means the only or the least imputation, resting upon the course of the appellants; for we see that, after calling upon the appellees for satisfaction of their demand, the appellants abandoned that demand, proclaiming thereby to the representatives of Goree (if indeed they were then in possession of the subject,) permission to apply it in conformity with the will of their testator. The appellants, it is not pretended, ever held or claimed the subject in dispute, except in their representative capacity, and in trust for the creditors and legatees of their testator. In the interval between the abandonment of their first and the institution of their second demand by the complainants, those executors have, in fulfilment of their trust, handed over the subject to those for whom they held it under the will; have accounted with the authorities to whom they were responsible, and have received from those authorities a full acquittance. Under these circumstances, to hold them liable to the demands of the appellants, would in effect be to render penal the regular discharge of their duty.

This aspect of the cause we regard as fully warranting the decree of the District Court, dismissing the bill of the complainants — that decree is therefore affirmed.

Order.

This cause came on to be heard on the transcript of the record from the District Court of the United States for the Middle District of Alabama, and was argued by counsel. On consideration whereof it is now here ordered, adjudged, and decreed by this court, that the decree of the said District Court in this cause be, and the same is hereby, affirmed with costs.

THE BOARD OF TRUSTEES FOR THE VINCENNES UNIVERSITY, PLAINTIFFS IN ERROR, *v.* THE STATE OF INDIANA.

In 1804, Congress passed an act, (2 Stat. at Large, 277,) "making provision for the disposal of the public lands in the Indiana Territory, and for other purposes," in which it reserved from sale a township in each one of three districts, to be located by the Secretary of the Treasury, for the use of a seminary of learning.

In 1806, the Secretary of the Treasury located a particular township in the Vincennes district, for the use of that district; and when, in 1806. the territorial government incorporated a "Board of Trustees of the Vincennes University," the grant made in 1804 attached to this Board, although, for the two preceding years, there had been no grantee in existence.

Under the ordinance of 1787, made applicable to Indiana by an act of Congress, the territorial government of Indiana had power to pass this act of incorporation.

The language of the act of Congress, by which Indiana was admitted into the Union, did not vest the above township in the legislature of the State.

The Board of Trustees of the University was not a public corporation, and had no political powers. The donation of land for its support was like a donation by a private individual; and the legislature of the State could not rightfully exercise any power by which the trust was defeated.

THIS case was brought up from the Supreme Court of the State of Indiana, by a writ of error, issued under the 25th section of the Judiciary Act.

The manner in which the case arose, and the laws relating to it, are stated in the opinion of the court.

It was argued by *Mr. Judah*, with whom was *Mr. Dunham*, for the plaintiffs in error, and *Mr. O. H. Smith*, for the State of Indiana.

The counsel for the plaintiff in error contended:

1. That the effect of the reservation in the act of Congress passed in 1804, was a grant.

The defendant, and Judge Smith, of the Supreme Court of Indiana, assert that this is not a grant, because there was not a grantee in *esse;* and that the reservation could only become effectual to pass the title by an appropriation, to be made by Congress, or under its authority.

In Wilcox *v.* Jackson, (13 Peters, 498,) this court, at page 512, define "appropriation" as follows: "That is nothing more nor less than setting apart the thing for some particular use." And afterwards, in the same case, (page 513,) the court say: "But we go further, and say, that, whensoever a tract of land shall once have been legally appropriated to any purpose, from that moment, the land thus appropriated becomes severed from the mass of public lands, and that no subsequent law, or proclamation, or sale, would be construed to embrace it, or operate upon it, although no reservation was made of it."

Was the Gibson township so appropriated? It was reserved for a special purpose. It was located in pursuance to the reservation. Was there any thing more necessary to set it apart for the particular use?

But, say the counsel for the State and Judge Smith, though

23*

appropriated, it was not granted, because there was no grantee in *esse.*

If, as a general rule, it is true, that there cannot be a grant without a grantee in *esse*, it is as true that there are exceptions.

A grant, in case of a charity, or of the dedication of land to a public use, is good without a grantee in *esse.*   Town of Paulet *v.* Clark, 9 Cr. 292; Beaty *v.* Kurtz, 2 Pet. 566; Cincinnati *v.* White, 6 Pet. 435; and in Vidal *v.* Girard's Executors, 2 How. 127; at pages 192, 193, it is stated, that donations given to the establishment of colleges, &c., are charities in the sense of the common law.

2. That the territorial legislature had the power to apply to use the township appropriated by Congress, and did apply it by the act of incorporation.

The counsel for the State of Indiana made the following points:

First. The complainants have no such corporate existence as would authorize and empower them to sue.   2 B. A. 482, note a, last edition; and see the extracts from their records in evidence.

Second. The suit is barred by the statute of limitations. R. S. 1843, pp. 795, 799; Act of 1845 – 6, explanatory of Rev. Stat.

Third. The suit is barred by twenty years adverse possession, as the State, and those claiming under the State by purchase and lease, had held adversely more than twenty years before any suit was brought by the University to recover the possession, even if the former actions which were dismissed could aid this suit, which is denied.

Fourth. The case does not come within the principles of an executory devise, and would not avail the complainants even if it were an executory devise.   17 Serg. & Rawle, 88; 5 H. & J. 392; 9 Ohio, 203; 12. Mass. 537; 16 Pick. 107; 3 Pet. 101; 4 Dana, 355; 3 Pet. 146; 9 Ves. 399; 9 Mass. 419; 7 Ves. 69; 9 Ves. 399; 10 Ves. 522.

Fifth. The act of Congress of 1804, was a mere reservation from sale, to be afterwards appropriated to educational purposes, and neither vested the same in the complainants, nor divested the United States of the legal title.   P. L. L. 104; 2 McLean R. 416; P. L. L. 2d part, 69; 1 Johns. R. 303; 9 Johns. R. 74; Wright's Ohio R. 144.

Sixth. The case does not embrace the principles of a dedication to public or pious uses, so as to sustain this claim.   2 Pet. 566; 6 Pet. 431, 498; 6 Paige, 639; 6 Wend. 667; 4 Paige, 510; 7 Ohio, 219.

Seventh. The act of Congress of 1816, vested the legal title to these lands in the State of Indiana, as a trustee, with power to direct to what object or institution, being "a seminary of learning," the trust fund shall be applied ; and the State, having designated the State University, at Bloomington, as the "seminary of learning" to which the trust fund shall go, the complainants have no claim whatever, either in law or equity, against the State, the trustee of the fund. See act of Congress of 1816, act of 1818, and the several acts for the admission of the other new States into the Union.

Eighth. The doctrines of estoppel, in their most rigid application, can only permit the complainants to retain what they have already received, and for this the State will not contend.

Ninth. In any and all events, the funds were public funds, and the legislature of the State had competent authority to change their direction to any other seminary of learning at will. Had the funds been the private funds of the complainants, and had they been vested with them, there might have been some pretext for the assumption, that the acts of the Indiana legislature, endowing the State University, were unconstitutional. 4 Wheat. 430 ; 4 Pet. Con. Rep. 536.

Mr. Justice McLEAN delivered the opinion of the court. ɪɪɪ

This case is before us on a writ of error to the Supreme Court of the State of Indiana, under the 25th section of the Judiciary Act of 1789.

The bill was filed under an act of the legislature of Indiana, of 1846, which authorized the trustees of the Vincennes University to file a bill in chancery, in the nature of an act of disseisin against the State, to try their right to the seminary township in Gibson county. The facts stated in the bill are substantially as follows :

The Indiana Territory was organized by the act of Congress of the 7th of May, 1800, with the powers to legislate given by the ordinance of 1787. On the 26th of March, 1804, an act of Congress was passed, for the survey and disposal of the public lands, by which three land districts were established, and an entire township in each was reserved for the use of a seminary of learning, to be located by the Secretary of the Treasury. The boundaries of the Vincennes land district were the same as designated in a late treaty with the Wabash Indians. The Secretary of the Treasury, by letter of the 10th of October, 1806, located township No. 2 south range, No. 11 west, in Gibson county, for the use of a seminary in that district.

The act of the 29th November, 1806, and the supplement thereto, passed the 17th of September, 1807, established the

Vincennes University, and incorporated the same by the name of " The Board of Trustees of the Vincennes University." The corporation was duly organized at Vincennes, on the 6th of December, 1806, under the act, and has since continued. The second section of the act of incorporation, after reciting the seminary lands under the act of Congress, provided, " that the trustees, in their corporate capacity, or a majority of them, should be legally authorized to sell, transfer, convey, and dispose of any quantity, not exceeding four thousand acres, of said land, for the purpose of putting into immediate use the said university; and to have on rent the remaining part of said township to the best advantage, for the use of said public school or university."

In virtue of the above acts, the complainants became possessed of the said township of land, and so continued during the territorial government. The same rights and powers in the corporation, as they existed under the territorial government, were secured by the 1st section of the 12th article of the constitution of Indiana. Between the years 1806 and 1820, complainants sold 4,000 acres of the land, and rented a part of the residue. A college building was constructed by them at Vincennes.

On the 22d January, 1820, a joint resolution of the legislature of Indiana was approved, appointing a superintendent for the seminary township, with power to rent the improved lands, to collect the rents, and to account to the State. And, on the 2d of January, 1822, the legislature appointed commissioners to sell the lands in that township. This seems to have been done, on the assumption that the board of trustees had expired through their own negligence. The lands were sold, and the money received was paid into the State Treasury. A part of the consideration money on this sale had not been collected when this bill was filed.

The complainants pray that an account may be taken of the proceeds, and interest of the sales of the lands and the rents received by the state; and that the same may be paid to the complainants, &c.

The defendant's answer denies the equity of the bill, and relies upon the statute of limitations. It also denies that the territorial government had any power to incorporate the plaintiffs; that the title remained in the United States, it never having been appropriated to any special grantee; that under the act of Congress of the 19th of April, 1816, for the admission of the State of Indiana into the Union, the title to the land in question became vested in the State.

The act of Congress, which organized the territory of Indiana, provided, that so much of the ordinance of 1787 for the government of the territory of the United States north-west of the

Ohio River, as relates to the generally assembly therein, and prescribes the powers thereof, shall be in force, and operate in the Indiana Territory, &c. The ordinance declares, " that the Governor and Judges, or a majority of them, shall adopt and publish in the district, such laws of the original States, criminal and civil, as may be necessary, and best suited to the circumstances of the district, and report them to Congress, from time to time ; which laws shall be in force in the district until the organization of the general assembly therein, unless disapproved of by Congress." Provision is made in the ordinance for the appointment of a legislative council, and it is then provided, that " the Governor, legislative council, and house of representatives, shall have authority to make laws, in all cases, for the good government of the district, not repugnant to the principles and articles in this ordinance."

Under the ordinance, the legislature of the territory was vested with general legislative powers, restricted only by the articles contained in that instrument. It had power to grant an act of incorporation, with all the functions necessary to effectuate its objects. There can be no question, therefore, that the corporate powers vested in the plaintiffs, by the legislature of the territory, were legitimately conferred. And these powers were not affected, and could not be affected by the constitution of the State. It provided that " all rights, contracts, and claims, both as respects individuals and bodies corporate, shall continue as if no change had taken place in this government."

If the Board of Trustees, by a failure to elect when vacancies occurred, or through any other means, became reduced to a less number than was authorized to act by the charter, the corporation was not thereby dissolved. In such a case, its franchises would be suspended only, until its functions were restored by legislative action. This was done by the act of the legislature of the 17th of February, 1838. In that act the territorial act of incorporation is recognized, the existence of six of the trustees admitted, the vacancies supplied, and the board, thus constituted, was organized. If, therefore, the corporation by *non user* had become liable to a judicial process of forfeiture, after this act, such a procedure could not be instituted.

The proviso in the act of 1838, could only operate, so as to secure any rights which the State might be supposed to have, in the Gibson township.

The reservations for the seminaries of learning and for schools, are made in the same terms, and in some respects, must rest on the same principles. In all the Western States, north of the Ohio, similar reserves for schools and seminaries of learning have been made. In the case of Wilcox v. Jackson, (13 Peters,

498,) this court held, that a reservation set apart the thing reserved for some particular use; and that " whensoever a tract of land shall once have been legally appropriated to any purpose, it becomes separated from the public lands."

In the States where school lands have been reserved, the legislatures have enacted laws to carry out and effectuate the benign policy of the general government. Special authority has been given to individuals elected, in the respective townships, to lease the lands, sue for rents, &c., exercising, to some extent, corporate powers. The citizens within the township are the beneficiaries of the charity. The title to these lands has never been considered as vested in the State; and it has no inherent power to sell them, or appropriate them to any other purpose than for the benefit of schools. For the exercise of the charity under the laws, the title is in the township. No patent has been issued by the Federal government, in such cases, as it has not been considered necessary. For the sale of school lands, the consent of Congress has been obtained, as that changes the character of the fund.

The title to the seminary lands, it is contended, did not vest in complainants, as they are not named in the reservation, and had no existence for two years afterwards.

This question is not to be decided, on the principles which apply to an ordinary grant, from one individual to another. The title partakes of the nature of an executory devise, or a dedication of property to public use. In the case of Inglis v. The Sailors' Snug Harbor, (3 Peters, 126,) this court say, " What objection can there be to this as a valid executory devise, which is such a disposition of lands, that thereby no estate vests at the death of the devisor, but only on some future contingency?" If the words, " reserved for the use of a seminary of learning," were indorsed on a town plat when made, there is no doubt that the title would vest in a corporation created afterwards for the establishment and government of such an institution. If it be reserved for the public use, the title would vest in the public, so soon as a public should exist in the town. Trustees of the McIntyre Poor School v. The Zanesville Canal Company, 9 Ohio Rep. 203; Cincinnati v. The Lessee of White, 6 Peters, Rep. 435; Barclay et al. v. Howell's Lessee, 6 Peters, Rep. 498; New Orleans v. the United States, 10 Peters, Rep. 662.

Land, at common law, may be granted to pious uses, before there is a grantee in existence competent to take it; and in the mean time, the fee will be in abeyance. The Town of Pawlet v. Clark et al. 9 Cranch, 292; Witman v. Lex, 17 Serg. & Rawle, 88.

" When a corporation is to be brought into existence by some future acts of the corporators, the franchises remain in abeyance, until such acts are done; and when the corporation is brought into life, the franchises instantaneously attach to it. There is no difference between the case of a grant of lan l or franchises to an existing corporation, and a grant to a corporation brought into life for the very purpose of receiving the grant. As soon as it is in esse, and the franchise and property become vested and executed in it, it is as much an executed contract, as if its prior existence had been established for a century." Dartmouth College v. Woodward, 4 Wheat. 518.

There was no uncertainty in this appropriation. The township was designated, and the purpose stated, for which it was reserved. And there can be no doubt, from the authorities, that the right vested, so soon as a capacity was given to the corporation to receive it; prior to this it remained in the federal government. This is the settled doctrine on that subject.

If, on general principles, the title to this township cannot be considered as vested in the State of Indiana, it is contended it so vested by the provision in the sixth section of the act of the 19th of April, 1816, which admitted the State into the Union. The provision is, "That one entire township, which shall be designated by the President of the United States, in addition to the one heretofore reserved for that purpose, shall be reserved for the use of a seminary of learning, and vested in the legislature of the said State, to be appropriated solely to the use of such seminary by the said legislature."

The words of the act seem to be so clear as to admit of but one construction. A township, in addition to the one formerly reserved, is appropriated and vested in the legislature. The former township is only referred to, to show that the one then appropriated was in addition to it. The Gibson township had before been appropriated. A part of it had been sold, and a part was held under leases. Whether we regard the words used, or their grammatical arrangement, the intention of Congress seems to be clearly expressed.

In the act of the 18th of April, 1818, for the admission into the Union, of the State of Illinois, a different phraseology is used in giving an additional township to the State. " That thirty-six sections, or one entire township, shall be designated by the President of the United States, together with the one heretofore reserved for that purpose, shall be reserved for the use of a seminary of learning, and vested in the legislature of the State," &c. Here both townships are as clearly vested in the State, as that one only is vested under the act admitting Indiana into the Union.

By this latter act, the Gibson Township Seminary was recognized, and its present government sanctioned.

It is argued that this is a public corporation, and that, consequently, the legislature of Indiana have a right to modify its charter, or abolish it, at its discretion. If the position assumed be sustainable the consequence stated will not be controverted.

In the case of Dartmouth College v. Woodward, (4 Wheat. 629,) Chief Justice Marshall says: "If the act of incorporation be a grant of political power, if it create a civil institution to be employed in the administration of the government, or if the funds of the college be public property, or if the State of New Hampshire, as a government, be alone interested in its transactions, the subject is one in which the legislature of the State may act, according to its own judgment, unrestrained by any limitation of its power, imposed by the Constitution of the United States." Again, he says, (634,) " So far as respects its funds, it is a private corporation. Do its objects stamp on it a different character? Are the trustees and professors public officers, invested with any portion of political power, partaking in any degree in the administration of civil government, and performing duties which flow from the sovereign authority?" He continues: " The character of civil institutions does not grow out of their incorporation, but out of the manner in which they are formed, and the objects for which they are created." " The right to change them is not founded on their being incorporated, but on their being the instruments of government, created for its purposes." " The trustees are not public officers, nor is it a civil institution, participating in the administration of the government; but a charity school, or a seminary of education, incorporated for the preservation of its property, and the perpetual application of that property to the objects of its creation."

In the same case, Mr. Justice Story says: " Public corporations are generally esteemed such as exist for public political purposes only, such as towns, cities, parishes and counties; and, in many respects, they are so, although they involve some private interests; but, strictly speaking, public corporations are such only as are founded by the government for public purposes, where the whole interests belong to the government."

The seminary township in question, was not a donation from the State, but from the United States. It was reserved and designated out of the public lands, before they were offered for sale, and consequently so munificent an endowment for a literary institution must have increased the value of the public lands, in that part of the State, and made them more desirable. And this consideration, no doubt, induced Congress to have designated, for seminary purposes, a township of land in each land district. Every purchaser of the public lands, in each district, acquired an interest in the reservation. And if these reservations had been judiciously managed, they would have constituted a fund, at this time, of at least two hundred thousand dollars each. This would have afforded the means of educating, in each land district, as many students, free of charge, as would ordinarily desire classical instruction. Such an advantage was too obvious to be overlooked, or not to be appreciated, by the purchasers of the public lands in these districts.

The legislative power of the Territory and State, in advancing the public interests, was bound to afford all the facilities necessary to carry out and secure the benign objects of Congress, in making these township reservations. This was done by a wise and liberal act, in regard to the Gibson township. The corporators were vested with all the necessary powers to carry out the trust. And for the purposes of the trust, the title became vested in them, as soon as they acquired a capacity to receive it. This corporation had no political powers, and could, in no legal sense, be considered as officers of the State. They were not appointed by the State. Their perpetuity depended upon the exercise of their own functions; and they were no more responsible for the performance of their duties, than other corporations established by the State to execute private trusts.

So far as regards the trust confided to the complainants, there is nothing which, by construction, can make it a public corporation. The donation in no sense proceeded from the State. It was made by the Federal government, and is no more subject to State power, than if it had been given by an individual for the same purpose. An act of incorporation being necessary, would not be withheld to give effect to a private donation of land, for the purpose of establishing a literary institution. Its benefits would be enjoyed by the public generally, but this would not make it a public corporation.

The complainants, by accepting and exercising their corporate powers, acquired certain rights, and made certain contracts, which could not be impaired by the legislature. They constituted an eleemosynary corporation, in which the State has no property, and can exercise no power to defeat the trust. But this has been done by the legislature, not only by appointing an agent to collect the funds due to the corporation, and paying them into the State treasury; but, by selling the lands, they have diverted the fund, for the preservation and management of which, the corporation was instituted. This was an extraordinary proceeding, and was wholly without authority. The result is, that the complainants are stript of their powers, and the University which they established, with the sanction of the legislature, is left without revenue.

power to seek their rights under that contract, whatever they were.

If mere tardiness in asserting their pretensions, were all that could be imputed to the appellants, this, of itself, would place them in a position which could not commend them the countenance of courts of justice; but, this delay is by no means the only or the least imputation, resting upon the course of the appellants; for we see that, after calling upon the appellees for satisfaction of their demand, the appellants abandoned that demand, proclaiming thereby to the representatives of Goree (if indeed they were then in possession of the subject,) permission to apply it in conformity with the will of their testator. The appellants, it is not pretended, ever held or claimed the subject in dispute, except in their representative capacity, and in trust for the creditors and legatees of their testator. In the interval between the abandonment of their first and the institution of their second demand by the complainants, those executors have, in fulfilment of their trust, handed over the subject to those for whom they held it under the will; have accounted with the authorities to whom they were responsible, and have received from those authorities a full acquittance. Under these circumstances, to hold them liable to the demands of the appellants, would in effect be to render penal the regular discharge of their duty.

This aspect of the cause we regard as fully warranting the decree of the District Court, dismissing the bill of the complainants — that decree is therefore affirmed.

Order.

This cause came on to be heard on the transcript of the record from the District Court of the United States for the Middle District of Alabama, and was argued by counsel. On consideration whereof it is now here ordered, adjudged, and decreed by this court, that the decree of the said District Court in this cause be, and the same is hereby, affirmed with costs.

THE BOARD OF TRUSTEES FOR THE VINCENNES UNIVERSITY, PLAINTIFFS IN ERROR, v. THE STATE OF INDIANA.

In 1804, Congress passed an act, (2 Stat. at Large, 277,) "making provision for the disposal of the public lands in the Indiana Territory, and for other purposes," in which it reserved from sale a township in each one of three districts, to be located by the Secretary of the Treasury, for the use of a seminary of learning.

In 1806, the Secretary of the Treasury located a particular township in the Vincennes district, for the use of that district; and when, in 1806. the territorial government incorporated a "Board of Trustees of the Vincennes University," the grant made in 1804 attached tó this Board, although, for the two preceding years, there had been no grantee in existence.

Under the ordinance of 1787, made applicable to Indiana by an act of Congress, the territorial government of Indiana had power to pass this act of incorporation.

The language of the act of Congress, by which Indiana was admitted into the Union, did not vest the above township in the legislature of the State.

The Board of Trustees of the University was not a public corporation, and had no political powers. The donation of land for its support was like a donation by a private individual; and the legislature of the State could not rightfully exercise any power by which the trust was defeated.

THIS case was brought up from the Supreme Court of the State of Indiana, by a writ of error, issued under the 25th section of the Judiciary Act.

The manner in which the case arose, and the laws relating to it, are stated in the opinion of the court.

It was argued by *Mr. Judah*, with whom was *Mr. Dunham*, for the plaintiffs in error, and *Mr. O. H. Smith*, for the State of Indiana.

The counsel for the plaintiff in error contended:

1. That the effect of the reservation in the act of Congress passed in 1804, was a grant.

The defendant, and Judge Smith, of the Supreme Court of Indiana, assert that this is not a grant, because there was not a grantee in *esse;* and that the reservation could only become effectual to pass the title by an appropriation, to be made by Congress, or under its authority.

In Wilcox *v.* Jackson, (13 Peters, 498,) this court, at page 512, define "appropriation" as follows: "That is nothing more nor less than setting apart the thing for some particular use." And afterwards, in the same case, (page 513,) the court say: "But we go further, and say, that, whensoever a tract of land shall once have been legally appropriated to any purpose, from that moment, the land thus appropriated becomes severed from the mass of public lands, and that no subsequent law, or proclamation, or sale, would be construed to embrace it, or operate upon it, although no reservation was made of it."

Was the Gibson township so appropriated? It was reserved for a special purpose. It was located in pursuance to the reservation. Was there any thing more necessary to set it apart for the particular use?

But, say the counsel for the State and Judge Smith, though

23*

capable of taking the title as grantee, and administering the trust.

It is not necessary to this opinion to discuss the doctrine of abeyance, upon which so much learning and talent has been displayed by Mr. Fearne, in his treatise on Contingent Remainders. It is sufficient to state under what circumstances the title, in the eye of the law, is said to be in abeyance. And Comyns, in his Digest, tells us, that "when the fee or freehold of the land is not vested in any one, but stands solely in consideration of law, it is said to be in abeyance, or *in nubibus*."

I cannot regard the title to lands reserved from sale by Congress, for the purposes of education, as standing in this condition. A reservation is not a grant. It does not pass the title out of the United States, but leaves it where it was before. The uniform practice of the government, and of judicial decision also, appears to have proceeded on the ground that the title remained in the United States, until it was afterwards transferred by the authority of Congress. It is not usual, it is true, to issue patents for these lands, but they have been granted by acts of Congress, which the courts have always recognized as valid conveyances. And I am not aware of any case in which the validity of these conveyances of reserved lands has been doubted by the court; or in which it has been suggested that the title was out of the United States, and in abeyance from the time of the reservation. If such be the result of a reservation, the subsequent conveyance of Congress is of no value. And who is to protect the reserved lands from trespasses and depredations, while the title is in abeyance?

In the case of Gaines and others v. Nicholson and others, reported in 9 Howard, 356, the title to a section reserved for schools, was the matter in dispute. It did not, it is true, involve the question now before us. But it appears, in that case, that the section was one of those reserved for schools in the different townships in the Territory of Mississippi, by an act of Congress passed in 1803; and that afterwards, as late as the year 1815, another act was passed, authorizing the County Court of each county in the territory to lease the sections so reserved, in order to improve them, and to apply the rents to purposes of education within the township; and also to proceed and recover damages against any persons found trespassing upon them. And this law contains an express provision that every lease, in virtue of this act, shall cease to have any force or effect after the first day of January next, succeeding the establishment of a State government. The trustees of the schools, who were parties to this suit, were appointed under a law of the State, and claimed under that appointment. The point in dispute, was whether the opposing party had not a right prior and superior to the State, by virtue of an Indian reservation, made in the treaty by which the territory had been ceded to the United States. And in deciding the question, this court treated the acts of Congress granting the land to the State, and also the law of the State appointing the Commissioners, as valid and constitutional; and it is not suggested, in the opinion, that the inhabitants of the township had a legal title to the school section, or any right to appoint Commissioners to control and administer the fund, unless authorized to do so by a law of the State. In the case before us, therefore, if the act of 1816 does not vest the title in the State, it still remains in the United States, and not in the trustees.

8. If, however, these lands were conveyed to the trustees, by virtue of the act of the territorial legislature of 1806, yet they were but agents of the State, without any private individual interests, and have no ground therefore for this proceeding in equity against the State. The whole fund was created by the public for public purposes. And in the case of the Dartmouth College, (4 Wheat. 629,) the court said, " If the act of incorporation be a grant of political power, if it create a civil institution to be employed in the administration of the government, or if the funds of the college be public property, or if the State of New Hampshire, as a government, be alone interested in its transactions, the subject is one in which the legislature of the State may act according to its own judgment, unrestrained by any limitation of its power imposed by the Constitution of the United States." Here the funds are contributed entirely by the public for a public purpose, and these appellants have no private individual interest, and allege none in their bill in behalf of themselves or others, which entitles them to maintain a suit against the State. They are public agents for a public purpose, and nothing more, and so describe themselves. The laws of the State, which directed the appropriation of the fund to the uses for which it was dedicated, are therefore constitutional and valid, under the decision above referred to, and in my opinion the decree of the Supreme Court of the State ought to be affirmed.

Order.

This cause came on to be heard on the transcript of the record from the Supreme Court of the State of Indiana, and was argued by counsel. On consideration whereof, it is now here ordered, adjudged, and decreed by this court, that the decree of the said Supreme Court in this cause be, and the same is hereby, reversed, with costs, and that this cause be, and the same is hereby, remanded to the said Supreme Court, in order that such further proceedings may be had therein, in conformity to the opinion of this court, as to law and justice may appertain.

WILLIAM CHRISTY, PLAINTIFF IN ERROR, *v.* WILLIAM T. SCOTT; WILLIAM CHRISTY *v.* JAMES D. FINLEY; WILLIAM CHRISTY *v.* WILLIAM YOUNG; WILLIAM CHRISTY *v.* HIRAM HENLY.

In Texas, the technical forms of pleading, fixed by the common law, are dispensed with, but the principles which regulate the merits of a trial by ejectment and the substance of a plea of title to such an action, are preserved.

Therefore, where the plaintiff filed a petition alleging that he was seised in his demesne as of fee of land from which the defendant had ejected him, and the defendant pleaded, that if the plaintiff had any paper title, it was under a certain grant which was not valid, this plea was bad.

So also was a plea denying the right of the plaintiff to receive his title, because he was not then a citizen of Texas. These pleas would have been appropriate objections to the plaintiff's title when produced upon the trial.

So also where, under a plea of the statute of limitations, the defendant claimed certain land by metes and bounds, and disclaimed all not included within them. There is nothing to show that the land so included, was part of the land claimed by the plaintiff.

So also where the plea was in substance that the plaintiff had no good title against Texas, no title in the defendant being shown. For the action may have been maintainable, although the true title was not in the plaintiff.

THESE four cases were brought up, by writ of error, from the District Court of the United States for the District of Texas.

They all involved the same principles, and were covered by the decision in Scott's case. It is necessary, therefore, to set out the pleadings in that case.

Christy filed his petition, alleging that he was seised in his demesne as of fee, in a certain tract or parcel of land, (which he described by metes and bounds,) from which Scott ejected him; and praying judgment for damages, and for the recovery of the lands.

Scott filed the following answer: And now comes the said defendant, and answering the petition of the plaintiff, says, that he denies all and singular the allegations in the said petition, and prays that the plaintiff be held to strict proof of the same.

2. And as to the trespasses and ejectments, or either or any of them, complained of by [the] plaintiff in his petition, the defendant says he is not guilty, and puts himself upon the country, &c.

3. And the defendant further says, that as to the pretended grant or title of the plaintiff to the land described in his petition, (if any paper title he has) the same bears date, to wit, the twentieth day of September, A. D. 1835, and the land described

in said pretended grant or title, and in said petition, is, and was at the date of said grant, situated in the twenty frontier leagues bordering on the United [States] line, and said pretended grant was made without the approbation or assent of the executive of the national government of Mexico.

4. And the said defendant further answers, and says, that if any such grant or title was made, as by said plaintiff is pretended; the same was made, (as by said plaintiff's pretended grant appears,) on, to wit, the twentieth day of September, A. D. 1835, and was not made by any public officer, commissioner, or authority, then, to wit, at the date of said pretended grant or title, existing in the State of Coahuila and Texas, competent to make the same.

5. And the said defendant further says, that the plaintiff claims the land sued for under and through a pretended grant from the government of the State of Coahuila and Texas, made to one Miguel Arceniega, as a Mexican and purchaser, and purporting to have been procured for the said Arceniega by one William G. Logan, as his agent. And the defendant says, that the said pretended grant or title of the plaintiff to the land sued for is not valid in law, because the same was procured from the government of the State of Coahuila and Texas by fraud, in this, that the said Miguel Arceniega and the said William G. Logan combined and confederated together for the purpose of evading the law, then in force, allowing the sale of lands to Mexicans, and to them only; and falsely and fraudulently represented to the said government that the application by said Arceniega for the said grant of land was really and *bonâ fide* made for him by the said Logan, and that the said Arceniega was to be the real purchaser of said land, and to hold and enjoy the same as a Mexican citizen; while, in truth, the said Arceniega fraudulently permitted the said Logan to use his name, and in his name procure the said grant solely for the use and benefit of him, the said Logan, who was not, at the time of procuring said grant, a Mexican citizen; and who, by the false and fraudulent practices aforesaid, procured the said grant, and appropriated the land granted to his (the said Logan's) own use and benefit.

6. And the said defendant says, that the plaintiff claims the premises described in his petition by a pretended grant, purporting to have been made by authority of the government of the State of Coahuila and Texas to Miguel Arceniega, bearing date, to wit, the twentieth day of September, A. D. 1835; and that the said pretended grant was made upon the conditions that the said Arceniega, or the person or persons to whom he might alienate the land in said grant described, should cultivate the same within six years from the acquisition thereof by said

pretended title, and pay for said land the price established by law. And the defendant says, that the said Arceniega, and those claiming said land under him, wholly failed to comply with said conditions.

7. And the said defendant says, that the said plaintiff claims the land described in his petition under and through a pretended grant purporting to have been made to one Miguel Arceniega by authority of the government of the State of Coahuila and Texas, bearing date, to wit, the twentieth day of September, A. D. 1835, and under and through a pretended claim of transfers from said Arceniega to plaintiff; and that within six years from the date of said pretended grant, and before the annexation of Texas to the United States, the said pretended transfers were made to said plaintiff; and that the plaintiff was not, at the date of said pretended grant to him, and previous thereto had never been, a resident citizen of Texas or Mexico, but was then, and thence hitherto continued to be, a resident and citizen of the United States of America, owing and paying allegiance to the government thereof.

8. And the said defendant further answering says, that he is the owner of the following tracts or parcels of land, to wit : (setting out a tract of land by metes and bounds, but without saying whether or not it was the land claimed by the plaintiff) and the defendant says that his possession of the said land is by virtue of the authority and title of the said John Graves, and as claimant under said Graves; and the said defendant says, that he and the said Graves, under whom he claims as to the said last-mentioned tract of land, and that he, in his own right and those under whom he claims, as to the several parcels of land above described, have had peaceable adverse possession of said several tracts of land, claiming the same by virtue of the certificates and files aforesaid, and the surveys aforesaid, with chains of legal transfers from the government down to this defendant, and to those under whom he claims, for more than three years next before the commencement of this suit; and the defendant disclaims ownership and possession of any portion of the land described in plaintiff's petition, not included in the metes and bounds of the several tracts and parcels above set forth.

9. Said defendant further says, that the land claimed by plaintiff in his petition is located within the territory designated as the twenty frontier leagues, bordering on the United States of the North, in the act of the Congress of the Republic of Texas, approved January 9th, 1841, and entitled "An act to quiet the land titles within the twenty frontier leagues bordering on the United States of the North," and is claimed by plaintiff by virtue of said location made prior to the seventeenth day of

March, A. D. 1836; and that said plaintiff, and those under whom he claims said land, did not commence an action to try the validity of said claim within twelve months from the passage of the act aforesaid.

And the defendant suggests to the court that he has had adverse possession in good faith of the said several tracts or parcels of land, for more than one year next before the commencement of this suit; and that, during said possession, he has made permanent and valuable improvements in the same, consisting of, to wit, one thousand acres, cleared and fenced, and divers good dwelling-houses, gin-houses, barns, corn-cribs, orchards, outhouses, &c., of great value, to wit, of the value of ten thousand dollars.

The plaintiff then filed the following replications and demurrers:

2. And the plaintiff, by attorney, comes, and as to the plea by the defendant, secondly by him in his answer pleaded, whereof said defendant puts himself upon the country, he, said plaintiff, doth the like.

Demurrer [to 3d plea.]

And the said plaintiff, by attorney, comes and says, *precludi non*, by reason of any thing in the defendant's third plea, in his said answer pleaded; because he says the said plea, and the matters and things therein contained, are not sufficient in law to bar and preclude him from having and maintaining his action aforesaid, and this he is ready to verify; wherefore, he prays judgment, &c.

And for cause of demurrer, according to the form of the statute in such case made and provided, the said plaintiff sets down and shows the following, to wit:

1. The said plea in bar of plaintiff's action attempts to set up the want of the approbation or assent of the executive of the national government of Mexico, to the issuance of a grant within the twenty border leagues, when the national colonization law, under which is sought the benefit of this bar, contains no prohibition to the issuance of said grant; but if, at the time of the issuance of said grant, there was any such prohibition, it only extended to making settlements within said border leagues.

2. The said plea in bar of plaintiff's action attempts to set up the issuance of a grant under which the plaintiff claims, dated 20th September, 1835, without the approbation of the supreme executive of Mexico, within the border leagues; but does not show the nature or kind of said grant, so as to enable the court to judge of its validity.

3. And the said plea is in other respects defective, informal, and insufficient, &c.

Replication [to 4th plea.]

4. And for replication to the fourth plea by the said defendant in his said answer pleaded, the said plaintiff says, *precludi non*, because he says the grant under which the plaintiff claims was issued by an authority, at the time of the issuance of the same, in the State of Coahuila and Texas, existing and competent to issue the same, and this, he prays, may be inquired of by the country.

Replication [to 5th plea.]

5. And for replication to the fifth plea, by the said defendant in his said answer pleaded, the said plaintiff says, *precludi non*, because he says that the said grant, under which the said plaintiff claims, was not obtained or procured to be issued by fraudulent misrepresentations, as in the said plea alleged, and this, he prays, may be inquired of by the country.

Demurrer [to 6th plea.]

6. And as to the sixth plea, by the said defendant in his said answer pleaded, the said plaintiff says, *precludi non*, because he says the said plea, and the matters and things therein contained, are not sufficient in law to bar and preclude said plaintiff from having and maintaining his action aforesaid, and this he is ready to verify; wherefore he prays judgment, &c.

And for cause of demurrer, according to the form of the statute in such case made and provided, the said plaintiff sets down and shows the following, to wit:

1. The conditions set forth in the said plea, as those upon which said grant was issued, as is manifest by the said plea, were conditions subsequent, of which the defendant cannot take advantage upon a failure in their performance.

2. A failure to perform the conditions in said plea set out, might have been cause of the forfeiture of the estate passed by said grant in said plea, set out on a proceeding in behalf of the State; but this is no reason why the defendant, before forfeiture declared, should, against the plaintiff, retain possession of the estate in said grant mentioned.

3. And the said plea is, in other respects, defective, informal, and insufficient, &c.

Demurrer [to 7th plea.]

7. And as to the seventh plea, by the said defendant in his said answer pleaded, the said plaintiff says, *precludi non*, because he says the said plea, and the matters and things therein

contained, are not sufficient in law to bar and preclude him from having and maintaining his action aforesaid, and this he is ready to verify ; wherefore he prays judgment, &c.

And for cause of demurrer, according to the form of the statute in such case made and provided, the said plaintiff sets down and shows the following, to wit:

1. The said plea in bar avers, that the estate in the premises, in the said petition mentioned, was transferred to said plaintiff while and during the time he was a citizen of the United States of America, and owing allegiance to the same, and an alien to the Republic of Texas; yet shows no forfeiture declared, on office found, so as to divest the estate vested by said transfer.

2. And the said plea is in other respects defective, informal, and insufficient, &c.

Replication [*to 8th plea*]

Withdrawn, and the following demurrer substituted:

And now, at this term, comes the plaintiff, by his attorney, and, by leave of the court first had and obtained, withdraws his replication to the eighth plea, by the defendant in this behalf pleaded, and says, *precludi non,* by reason of any thing in the said defendant's eighth plea in this behalf pleaded, because he says the said plea, and the matters and things therein contained, are not sufficient in law to bar and preclude him from having and maintaining his action aforesaid, and this he is ready to verify ; wherefore he prays judgment, &c.

And for causes of demurrer, according to the form of the statute in such case made and provided, the said plaintiff sets down and shows the following, to wit:

1. The said plea avers, that the said defendant, and a certain John Graves, under whom he, the said defendant claims, as to a part of the land in said plea mentioned, had and still held peaceable possession of the same, for more than three years next before the commencement of this suit under color of title; when, to produce a bar within the statute in such case made and provided, a possession, under the circumstances, and within the time prescribed by said statutes, by said defendant alone, should have been set up.

2. The said defendant, by said plea, avers that, as to a part of the lands in said plea specified, the title is yet outstanding in a certain John Graves ; yet the said defendant, by his said plea as to said land, attempts to set up in bar, by reason of possession of the same for three years, under color of title, next before the commencement of plaintiff's action.

3. The said defendant, by his said plea, avers, that a portion of the land in said plea specified, and of which he, said defendant,

claims to be the owner, by virtue of his, said defendant's, own head-right certificate, has not been surveyed, as by law required, to vest title in the same in said defendant; yet said defendant, as to the same, by his said plea, attempts to set up in bar an adverse possession, for three years next before commencement of plaintiff's action, under color of title.

4. The said defendant, by his said plea, does not aver, that he, said defendant, was ever an actual settler upon the said land, of which, by his said plea, he claims to be in adverse possession.

5. Though the said defendant, by his said plea, attempts to set up in bar an adverse possession, under color of title, for three years next before commencement of plaintiff's action herein, yet he does not show that said color of title was duly proven and recorded.

6. The said defendant, by his said plea, attempts to set up in bar of plaintiff's action adverse possession, under color of title, for three years next before the commencement of said plaintiff's said action, when, by the purview of the statutes in such case made and provided, there can be no such bar; but if any, the bar must be by such adverse possession, under such color of title, for three years next after cause of action accrued, and before commencement of action.

7. The said plea, though in bar, does not make any case by which the plaintiff is barred of his action, by reason of any possession adverse, within the terms of the statute in such case made and provided.

8. And the said plea, is, in other respects, defective, informal, and insufficient, &c.

Demurrer [*to 9th plea.*]

9. And as to the ninth plea, by the said defendant in his said answer pleaded, the said plaintiff says, *precludi non*, because he says the said plea, and the matters and things therein contained, are not sufficient in law to bar and preclude him, said plaintiff, from having and maintaining his action aforesaid, and this he is ready to verify; wherefore he prays judgment, &c.

And for cause of demurrer, according to the form of the statute in such case made and provided, the said plaintiff sets out and shows the following, to wit:

1. The act of Congress, referred to in said plea, at the time of the approval thereof, since, and now, was not, and is not, the law of the land.

2. The said act of Congress was made and intended to impair the obligation of contracts.

3. And the said plea is, in other respects, defective, informal, and insufficient. &c.

In this state of the pleadings, the cause was called for trial, when the following judgment was rendered :

This day came the parties aforesaid, by their attorneys, and the questions of law, arising upon the demurrers of the plaintiff to the third, sixth, seventh, eighth, and ninth pleas, by the defendant in his answer pleaded, having been argued and submitted, because it seems to the court that the law is for the defendant; it is therefore considered by the court, that the said demurrers be overruled, and the plaintiff stating that he intended to abide by his demurrers, it is further considered by the court, that the defendant go hence without day, and that he recover of the plaintiff his costs, by him about his defence in this behalf expended, to be taxed by the clerk, &c.

The counsel for the plaintiff then filed the following argument of errors :

1. The defendant's third plea, by him in his answer pleaded, attempts to set up, in bar of plaintiff's action, the issuance of the grant under which the plaintiff claims, without the approbation of the executive of the Republic of Mexico, when, by the law of the State of Coahuila and Texas, under which said grant was issued, there was no prohibition to the issuance of said grant without such approbation, and the said fact pleaded is no bar; yet the said court overruled the plaintiff's demurrer to said plea, and gave judgment for defendant, when said demurrer, according to the rules of law, should have been sustained.

2. The said defendant, by his sixth plea in his said answer pleaded, attempts to set up, in bar of the plaintiff's action aforesaid, the non-performance of conditions subsequent, without showing reëntry, or other mode of enforcing a forfeiture of the estate granted; yet the court overruled the plaintiff's demurrer to said plea, when, according to the rules of law, the same should have been sustained.

3. The said defendant, by his seventh plea in his answer pleaded, attempts to set up, in bar of plaintiff's action, the fact, that the lands claimed and sued for by the plaintiff, in his petition described, were sold and transferred to the said plaintiff while and during the time he was a citizen of the United States of America, owing allegiance to the same, and an alien to the Republic of Texas, without showing any office found, or forfeiture declared in any manner whatever; yet the court overruled the plaintiff's demurrer to said plea, when, according to the rules of law, the same should have been sustained.

4. The said defendant, by his eighth plea in his said answer pleaded, insists upon a bar, by and under the fifteenth section of an act of Congress of the Republic of Texas, entitled "An Act of Limitations," approved February 5th, 1841; but, by said

plea, does not show or allege that he was a settler on the land in question, having had and held continuous adverse possession of the same, under title duly proven and recorded, or under color of title, for three years next after cause of action accrued, and before action brought, as by the rules of law he should have done; yet the said court overruled the plaintiff's demurrer to said plea, when, according to the rules of law, it should have been sustained.

5. The said defendant, by his ninth plea in his answer pleaded, attempts to set up, in bar of plaintiff's action, the failure to commence action within twelve months after the passage of an act by the Congress of the Republic of Texas, entitled "An act to quiet land-titles within the twenty frontier leagues bordering on the United States of the North," to try the validity of the grant under which plaintiff claims, when it is apparent that said grant, under which plaintiff claims, was a perfect, and not an imperfect or inchoate title, and as to which the government of the Republic of Texas had no legitimate power or authority to require or prescribe the commencement of any suit in the form or manner the same was prescribed, to try the validity of the title vested by said grant, or create a bar in consequence of a failure to commence said suit; yet the demurrer to said plea was overruled by said court, when the same, according to the rules of law, should have been sustained.

The plaintiff then sued out a writ of error, and brought the case up to this court.

It was argued by *Mr. Bibb* and *Mr. Crittenden*, (Attorney-General,) with whom was *Mr. Hughes*, for the plaintiff in error, and *Mr. Hill*, with whom was *Mr. Henderson*, for the defendant in error.

The argument, of course, turned entirely upon the validity or invalidity of the plea; but the discussion was so much involved with the laws and facts in the case, that a report of it is postponed until the record shall be brought up again in the shape suggested by the court.

Mr. Justice CURTIS delivered the opinion of the court.

This is a writ of error to the District Court of the United States for the District of Texas.

The plaintiff in error filed a petition, in which he avers, that on the 1st day of June, 1839, he was seised in his demesne as of fee of three tracts of land, described in the petition by metes and bounds, and that the defendant, with force of arms, ejected him therefrom, and has thenceforward kept him out of possession thereof; and he prays judgment for damages and costs, and for the lands described. The defendant filed what is styled an answer, containing nine distinct articles, or pleas, each of which seems to have been intended, and has been treated, as a substantive defence. The plaintiff demurred to the third, sixth, seventh, eighth, and ninth, of these pleas. There was no joinder in demurrer by the defendant, but the District Court treated the demurrers as raising issues in law, and gave judgment thereon for the defendant. The plaintiff has brought the record here by a writ of error.

Upon this record, questions of great difficulty, and understood to affect the titles to large quantities of land, have been elaborately argued at the bar. These questions involve and depend upon the interpretation of the Colonization Laws of the Republic of Mexico, and their practical administration; the relative rights and powers of the central government, and of the State of Coahuila and Texas, in reference to the public domain; the modes of declaring and vindicating those rights, and exercising those powers under the constitution of the Mexican Republic; the effect of the separation of the State of Coahuila and Texas from México, by the revolution of 1836, upon titles made by the State authorities before the revolution, and alleged to be defective for want of the sanction of the central government; as well as several important laws of the Republic of Texas, framed for the protection of the public domain, and for the repose of titles in that country.

It is impossible that the court should approach an adjudication of a case, involving elements so new and difficult, without much anxiety, lest they should have failed entirely to comprehend and fitly to apply them. And it is obvious, that before it is possible to do so, all the facts constituting the title of each party, and essential to a complete view of the case, and especially the documentary evidences of those titles, should be placed before us, in a determinate form.

This record is far from being sufficient in these substantial, and, indeed, necessary particulars. The petition avers a seisin in fee, on a particular day, and an ouster by the defendant. The defendant shows no title in himself to the land demanded, but asserts that the plaintiff claims title by a pretended grant, made on the 20th day of September, 1835; that the land was within the twenty frontier leagues bordering on the United States; that the approbation of the executive of the national government of Mexico was not given; and, in other pleas, avers other facts, to show that if any such grant had been made it would not have been valid. But no grant, under which either party claims, appears on the record, nor is the court informed, through an exhibition of any title papers, by what authority, or through what instrument, or for what consideration, or upon what conditions the title to these lands, originally passed from the State; or, whether more than one title thereto has, in fact, been made by the State; nor how, or when, if at all, any title came from the State to either of the parties.

Having thus stated what the record fails to show, we proceed to declare our judgment on each of the issues in law raised by the demurrers.

The first plea which is demurred to, is in the following words: " 3. And the defendant further says, that as to the pretended grant or title of the plaintiff, to the land described in his petition, (if any paper title he has,) the same bears date, to wit, the twentieth day of September, A. D. 1835, and the land described in said pretended grant or title, and in said petition, is, and was, at the date of said grant, situated in the twenty frontier leagues bordering on the United States line, and said pretended grant was made without the approbation or assent of the executive of the national government of Mexico."

According to the settled principles of the common law, this is not a defence to the action. The plaintiff says he was seised in fee, and the defendant ejected him from the possession. The defendant, not denying this, answers, that if the plaintiff had any paper title, it was under a certain grant which was not valid. He shows no title whatever in himself. But a mere intruder cannot enter on a person actually seised, and eject him, and then question his title, or set up an outstanding title in another. The maxim that the plaintiff must recover on the strength of his own title, and not on the weakness of the defendant's, is applicable to all actions for the recovery of property. But if the plaintiff had actual prior possession of the land, this is strong enough to enable him to recover it from a mere trespasser, who entered without any title. He may do so by a writ of entry, where that remedy is still practised, (Jackson *v.* Boston & Worcester Railroad, 1 Cush. 575,) or by an ejectment, (Allen *v.* Rivington, 2 Saund. R. 111; Doe *v.* Read, 8 East, 356; Doe *v.* Dyboll, 1 Moody & M. 346; Jackson *v.* Hazen, 2 Johns. R. 438; Whitney *v.* Wright, 15 Wend. 171,) or, he may maintain trespass, (Catteris *v.* Cowper, 4 Taunt. 548; Graham *v.* Peat, 1 East, 246.)

Nor is there any thing in the form of the remedy, in Texas, which renders these principles inapplicable to this case.

By the act of February 5th, 1840, (Hartley's Digest, 909,) it is proved, that the method of trying titles to lands shall be by action of trespass, and that the action shall be tried on its merits, conformably to the principles of trial by ejectment; and where the defendant sets up title to the land, he is required to plead the same. We understand that the technical forms of pleading, fixed by the common law, are dispensed with, but the principles which regulate the merits of a trial by ejectment, and the substance of a plea of title to such an action, are preserved. Tested by these principles, this plea is bad.

Without setting up any title in the defendant, it pleads certain evidence or source of title, which, it avers, the plaintiff relies on, and then states facts, to show that such title is invalid. This is not admissible.

The office of a plea is, to state on the record the answer of the defendant to the allegations of the plaintiff, but not to the evidence by which the defendant conjectures the plaintiff will endeavor to support those allegations. We cannot conceive that such a mode of pleading could be admissible under any system. At the common law, if the allegation that the plaintiff's paper title is under a grant mentioned in the plea, had been traversed, it would have led to an issue which, if found for the plaintiff, would determine nothing, and, therefore, the plaintiff cannot be required to answer such a plea. And where pleadings are so conducted as not to terminate in issues, as in Texas, such an answer neither confesses and avoids, nor denies the seisin, or trespass, alleged in the declaration. United States v. Girault, 11 How. 22.

There are cases in which such allegations, showing the source or nature of the plaintiff's title, are a necessary part of a defence. Whenever the defendant must plead specially any matter which is a good defence to one title, and not good to others, and the declaration does not show on what particular title the plaintiff relies, the defendant must, by proper averments, set out the plaintiff's title and the answer to it; these averments then become material and traversable as part of the defence, and if found for the plaintiff, the defence fails. An instance of this is the defence of a statute of limitations,. barring only particular titles. In such a plea, it would be necessary to show, if it did not appear in the declaration, that the plaintiff had only such a title. But this rule has no application to the defence under consideration. If the plaintiff really relies on such a title as is alleged, whenever he shows it in support of his petition, the defendant will have opportunity to object to it, and to give in evidence any collateral facts bearing upon it. He has no occasion, nor is it regular, to plead specially, for his general denial of the plaintiff's title compels the plaintiff to produce his title, and thus opens to the defendant all legal objection to it. Moreover, this article in the answer does not admit, or deny, that the plaintiff had any grant, or any paper title whatever, but says, if he had any, it was of a certain description. If it was intended to make the case turn on the validity of a particular grant, its existence ought

25 *

to be admitted; for why should the court be called upon to determine the sufficiency in law of such a grant, when it does not appear it exists?

These objections are equally applicable to the sixth plea, which is therefore also insufficient.

The next plea is as follows:

" 7. And the said defendant says, that the said plaintiff claims the land described in his petition under and through a pretended grant purporting to have been made to one Miguel Arceniega, by authority of the government of the State of Coahuila and Texas, bearing date, to wit, the twentieth day of September, A. D. 1835, and under and through a pretended chain of transfers from said Arceniega to plaintiff, and that within six years from the date of said pretended grant, and before the annexation of Texas to the United States, the said pretended transfers were made to said plaintiff, and that this plaintiff was not, at the date of said pretended grant to him, and previous thereto, had never been a resident citizen of Texas or Mexico, but was then, and thence hitherto, continued to be a resident and citizen of the United States of America, owing and paying allegiance to the government thereof."

This plea also, is subject to the same objections as the others so far as it attacks the plaintiff's title; and if it was intended as a plea to the action of the alienage of the plaintiff, it is manifestly bad, for the plaintiff, being a citizen of the United States, is capable of maintaining an action to recover lands in the State of Texas, to which he has title.

The eighth plea sets up a statute of limitations. In order to bring himself within it, the defendant avers, "that he is the owner of the following tracts or parcels of land, to wit;" and he then gives the metes and bounds of sundry tracts of land, and makes certain other averments as to his possession, and concludes, "And the defendant disclaims ownership and possession of any portion of the land described in plaintiff's petition, not included in the metes and bounds of the several tracts and parcels above set forth."

The court cannot treat this plea as an answer to the declaration. It is not averred therein, nor is there any thing on the record to show, that the tracts of land described in it are parcel of the demanded premises. The defendant says he disclaims ownership and possession of any portion of the land described in the petition, and not included in the bounds he sets out. For aught we can know, this disclaimer may cover the whole of the land described in the petition. And as it does not appear, by any direct traversable averment, that the disclaimer does not apply to all the lands demanded, or that the defence applies to any, or if any, to what part of them, the court cannot know for what to give judgment, or whether it should be for the one party or the other.

The ninth plea is as follows:

"9. Said defendant further says, that the land claimed by plaintiff in his petition, is located in the territory designated as the twenty frontier leagues, bordering on the United States of the North, in the act of the Congress of the Republic of Texas, approved January 9th, 1841, and entitled 'An act to quiet the land titles within the twenty frontier leagues bordering on the United States of the North,' and is claimed by plaintiff by virtue of said location, made prior to the seventeenth day of March, A. D. 1836, and that said plaintiff, and those under whom he claims said land, did not commence an action to try the validity of said claim within twelve months from the passage of the act aforesaid."

Assuming what we do not decide, that this plea shows, that if the plaintiff claims under such a location as is mentioned, his title is not good as against the State of Texas, still it is not a defence, because no title in the defendant is shown. If the plaintiff, as his petition avers, was actually seised, and the defendant being a mere intruder, ejected him, it was an unlawful act, and the action is maintainable, notwithstanding the State of Texas may have the true title, or may have granted it to another.

For these reasons, we are of opinion the demurrer to each of these pleas must be sustained, the judgment of the District Court reversed, and the cause remanded; and as it will undoubtedly become necessary to amend the pleadings, we think it proper to suggest, that in a case involving questions so new and of so much magnitude and importance, it would be more satisfactory, and more conducive to a just decision, for the parties to exhibit fully their respective titles, and all collateral facts bearing upon them, and have them placed upon the record, either by bill of exceptions, or a special verdict, to the end that the court may consider their title papers in connection with the extraneous facts, and not be required to decide upon partial or abstract views, which may occasion substantial injustice, not only to the one party or the other, but possibly to third persons having similar titles.

Order.

This cause came on to be heard on the transcript of the record from the District Court of the United States for the District of Texas, and was argued by counsel. On consideration whereof, it is now here ordered and adjudged, by this court, that the judgment of the said District Court in this cause be, and the same is hereby, reversed, with costs, and that this cause be, and the same is hereby, remanded to the said District Court for further proceedings to be had therein, in conformity to the opinion of this court, and as to law and justice shall appertain.

WILLIAM CHRISTY, PLAINTIFF IN ERROR, *v.* JAMES D. FINDLEY.

Mr. Justice CURTIS.

The amended pleas in this case, being five in number, are demurred to, and the demurrers are sustained for the reasons assigned in the opinion in the case of Christy *v.* Scott. The judgment of the District Court is reversed, and the case remanded for further proceedings.

Order.

This cause came on to be heard on the transcript of the record from the District Court of the United States for the District of Texas, and was argued by counsel. On consideration whereof, it is now here ordered and adjudged by this court, that the judgment of the said District Court in this cause be, and the same is hereby, reversed, with costs, and that this cause be, and the same is hereby, remanded to the said District Court, for further proceedings to be had therein, in conformity to the opinion of this court, and as to law and justice shall appertain.

WILLIAM CHRISTY, PLAINTIFF IN ERROR, *v.* WILLIAM YOUNG.

Mr. Justice CURTIS.

In this case, the sixth, eighth, ninth, and tenth pleas, are demurred to, and the demurrers are sustained, for the reasons assigned in the opinion in the case of Christy *v.* Scott. The tenth plea in this case of the ten years' limitation law of Texas, is bad, for the same reasons as the plea of the three years' statute pleaded in that case. The judgment of the District Court is reversed, and the case remanded for further procedings.

Order.

This cause came on to be heard on the transcript of the record from the District Court of the United States for the District of Texas, and was argued by counsel. On consideration whereof, it is now here ordered and adjudged by this court, that the judgment of the said District Court in this cause be, and the same is hereby, reversed, with costs, and that this cause be, and the same is hereby, remanded to the said District Court for further proceedings to be had therein, in conformity to the opinion of this court, and as to law and justice shall appertain.

WILLIAM CHRISTY, PLAINTIFF IN ERROR, v. HIRAM HENLEY.

Mr. Justice CURTIS.

In this case, the fourth, sixth, seventh, eighth, ninth, and tenth pleas, are demurred to, and the demurrers are sustained for the reasons assigned in the opinion in the cases of Christy v. Scott, and Christy v. Young. The judgment of the District Court is reversed, and the case remanded for further proceedings.

Order.

This cause came on to be heard on the transcript of the record from the District Court of the United States for the District of Texas, and was argued by counsel. On consideration whereof, it is now here ordered and adjudged by this court, that the judgment of the said District Court in this cause be, and the same is hereby, reversed, with costs, and that this cause be, and the same is hereby, remanded to the said District Court for further proceedings to be had therein, in conformity to the opinion of this court, and as to law and justice shall appertain.

STEPHEN W. DOSS AND STEWART NEWELL, APPELLANTS, v. WILLIAM TYACK AND LINDLEY MURRAY.

A court has a right to set aside its own judgment or decree, dismissing a bill in chancery, at the same term in which the judgment or decree was rendered, on discovering its own error in the law, or that the consent of the complainants to such dismissal was obtained by fraud.

A verdict on an issue to try whether a sale was fraudulent, finding the same to be fraudulent, will not be set aside on a certificate or affidavit of some of the jurors, afterwards made, as to what they meant.

A Chancellor does not need a verdict to inform his conscience, when the answer denies fraud in the abstract, whilst it admits all the facts and circumstances necessary to constitute it, in the concrete.

THIS was an appeal from the District Court of the United States for the State of Texas.

A statement of the facts is contained in the opinion of the court.

It was argued by *Mr. Allen* and *Mr. O. F. Johnson*, with whom was *Mr. Hale*, for the appellant, and *Mr. Sherwood*, for the appellee.

m

The points, raised by the counsel for the appellant, were he following:

I. The complainants having utterly failed to make out their case, by proving the material allegations and charges contained in the original and amended bills of complaint, the defendants were entitled to a decree of dismissal.

II. The property of the copartnership confided to Newell, and especially the goods sold to Edgar, were not misapplied, but disposed of in conformity with the intendment of the co-partnership agreement. By this it is manifest that the partnership was not intended as a pure mercantile establishment, but one for the transaction of a " commission, general, and auction business." Part. Agree't. Art. 1, P. R. 2 ; of a business " new and experimental in its nature "— Id. Art. 9 ; a business connected with the operations of the " Galveston Company," which Newell, by more than two years' labor and great expense, had "paved the way for ;" and which the fifth article of the said agreement refers to (there being nothing else in the case to which it could by possibility refer,) in express terms, viz. : that, in consideration of " the expense and labor heretofore incurred by Stewart Newell, in paving the way for the contemplated business, he shall be entitled to one quarter of the net profits, before division."

III. The creditors, in their instructions, refer to " agreements and understandings " of Newell, with his partners and themselves ; thereby, admitting themselves to be privy to the said partnership agreement, and that they gave credit to the co-partners, in the business thereby contemplated. The case contains no proof of any other agreement or understanding, to which they could pretend to refer.

IV. The creditors obtained, by a species of moral coercion, which their position enabled them to use, the primary concurrence of Tyack & Murray with themselves, in the appointment of William E. Warren as their mutual agent, and in their instructions, which Tyack approved, prescribing the management to be used by Warren, in his interviews with Newell, and in conducting the business confided to him, after his arrival in Texas. The suit was manifestly the result of a conspiracy between the creditors and complainants; the object being to obtain a dissolution of the partnership, a distribution of the assets in Newell's hands, or to cause him " to place the merchandise in the hands " of Warren, " as trustee for the creditors, or Captain Tyack;" the creditors, on their part, agreeing not to proceed against the firm of " William Tyack & Co.," in New York, for the space of sixty days; and, that the interests of Tyack should be protected, and his instructions, touching the suit against Newell, strictly followed.

V. The purchase of the goods by Doss, was for a valuable and adequate consideration, without notice of any intended fraud, on the part of Newell, made for the benefit of all the partners, and within the scope of the " new, experimental, and general " business, described in the partnership agreement. The verdict does not find the purchaser guilty of any fraud, and the jurors depose that they did not intend to charge him with fraud. It declares the " sale," but not the purchase, fraudulent as to the complainants. Anderson & Wilkins v. Tompkins et al. 1 Brock. 456. This finding did not authorize the annulling of the sale.

VI. Referring to the direction of the creditors, requiring their agent to be governed by the instructions of Captain Tyack, the several letters of Tyack & Murray to Newell, advising and urging him to sell the goods; their subsequent approval of the sale, after ample time to judge, and referring to their confederacy against Newell, before mentioned; the sale was authorized before, sanctioned at the time, and confirmed, after it was consummated, in the most deliberate manner by both the complainants and the creditors.

VII. All matters of complaint, embraced in the bill in this cause, excepting the said sale, were included and adjudicated in the suit of these complainants against Newell, commenced and tried in the State Court. The judgment decides the merits of the cause, is conclusive of all the said matters, and remains in full force. It directed a restoration of the goods to Newell — they having been taken out of his hands by process in the cause. After such restoration, the said goods were sold to Doss, and this judgment was a full authority for him to purchase them.

VIII. The price paid by Doss for the goods, was near $2,000

more than their value as estimated by the complainants, and near $4,000 more than that estimated by the witnesses. It consisted of $4,000 equivalent to cash advanced, and the remainder in lands, amounting to 6,485 acres, and worth much more than $7,753, as testified by the witnesses. One of the tracts, containing 177 acres, is estimated by Mr. Thompson, a witness well qualified to judge, as worth $30 per acre. Newell, in the exercise of a sound discretion, arising from his business connections with the complainants, and expressly devolved upon him by their advice and directions, and acting in conformity with the professed desire of the creditors contained in this 5th instruction, declaring that they wished " no wanton sacrifice of property for the immediate payment of the whole or a portion of their claims," could not have made a sale of the goods more-beneficial to all the parties interested, than the one negotiated with Mr. Doss.

IX. It is respectfully insisted, that the issue directed by the court " to determine whether the sale of the goods was or was not fraudulent as to the complainants," was defective and immaterial, and, for this cause, improperly granted.

The verdict must conform to, and correspond with, the issue — that is, find its affirmative or negative, and nothing else. If the jury find the former, viz., that the sale was fraudulent as to the complainants, it would be incompetent for them, under this issue, to go further, and determine also which of the defendants perpetrated the fraud, or whether they combined together, and were jointly chargeable. Such a finding could not authorize a decree setting aside the sale, nor in any way properly influence the conscience of the court. Such a decree would have to rest on proof in the cause, *dehors* the verdict, that the purchaser was a party to the fraud; and whether such proof existed or not, the verdict could be of no possible service or utility to the court.

Hence the court will reverse or disregard the order directing the issue, and determine itself the character of the sale. Nichol v. Vaughan, 2 Dow & Clark, 420; Townsend v. Graves, 3 Paige, 457; Belknap v. Trimble, 3 Paige, 601; Gardiner v. Gardiner, 22 Wendell, 526.

X. The verdict, viz., " In this case, we, the jury, find the sale fraudulent," does not determine or satisfy the issue, and is for this cause void. It does not find as to whom the sale was fraudulent, and may as reasonably be construed to apply to the creditors or to one of the defendants as to the complainants.

XI. If the verdict could be so interpreted as to charge either or both of the defendants with fraud against the complainants, which we deem impossible, it would be contrary to the entire body of evidence adduced at the trial, and is void at law.

XII. No effect can be given to the verdict prejudicial to the interests of Mr. Doss, without disregarding or inverting what the jury solemnly intended its effect to be, as appears by their affidavit. An application and construction of a verdict, opposed to the intention and moral sense of the jurors who found it, cannot quiet the conscience of a court of equity.

XIII. The issue, as tried, does not answer the purpose for which it was intended. Indeed, it was so framed that the verdict throws no light upon the question for the determination of which it was directed. The whole matter is before the court with sufficient precision, and all the proofs to enable it to come to a decision, without another reference to a jury. The court, under these circumstances, will decide the matter at once, unless in its discretion some new issue or issues be deemed expedient in order to attain substantial justice. Armstrong v. Armstrong, 3 M. & K. 45; Blackbourn v. Gregson, 1 Bro. C. C. 423, 424; Dan. Chan. 1316.

XIV. The court below erred in setting aside the decree of the 3d of August, 1849, dismissing the cause. The decree was made by consent, and is not subject to appeal or review. Webb v. Webb, 3 Swanst. Ch. R. 658; French v. Shotwell, 5 Johns. Ch. 564; Atkinson v. Manks, 1 Cowen, 691; Kane v. Whittick, 8 Wend. 219.

1. Notwithstanding the position taken by counsel, viz., that the powers of attorney, by the complainants and creditors appointing William E. Warren their mutual agent, the agreement and expenditures of money by the creditors in the prosecution of the cause, were sufficient to prevent the complainants, without the assent of the creditors, from dismissing the bill; and whether the suit be treated as a creditor's suit or not, under the authority of Williamson v. Wilson, 1 Bland, 418; still the complainants, until the final decree, retained absolute dominion over the suit, and might dismiss the bill at pleasure. Handford v. Story, 2 Sim. & Stu. 196.

2. The complainants, by their several powers of attorney, revocations, and other instruments under seal, emphatically required and obtained the dismissal of said cause, through solicitors specially employed and instructed for that purpose, and for reasons fully declared. The decree of dismissal was a mere execution of those powers. At the moment of its rendition it became a vested right of the defendants, granted and confirmed by the respective deeds of the complainants. A power executed by decree is no more revocable than one executed by grant or conveyance of land.

3. The decree was opened upon motion, founded on the application of Murray alone — it was error to open it as to Tyack.

The order could not properly vacate the decree generally; besides, it was a regular decree on the merits, and could not be set aside by a motion. Radley v. Shaver, 1 Johns. Ch. 200.

4. Murray, excepting by his petitions, does not attempt to revoke his prior deeds. This is no revocation. He prays the court to restore the suit, and to declare those deeds null and void, alleging that the same were obtained by fraud practised by Newell and others.

We respectfully insist that the court could not, so long as those deeds remained in force as executed powers, vacate the decree of dismissal or restore the suit; and that the deeds themselves, and the manner in which they were obtained or executed, could not be inquired into or pronounced void by the court, except by regular suit against the parties charged, whereby the alleged frauds could be put in issue, and the whole matter fairly tried.

The petitions of Murray and Tyack, and the supposed revocation of the latter, filed on the 7th of January, 1850, cannot obviate any objections to the said order of the previous term vacating the decree of dismissal.

6. The affidavits of Messrs. McGreal and Andrews, filed by the defendants in opposition to the said petitions of Murray, contradict all the essential statements therein contained, and effectually impeach their veracity, showing them untrue and not entitled to credit.

XV. The effect of the solemn admissions and declarations, deliberately made by both of the complainants in their several letters and instruments under seal, before referred to as evidence in favor of the defendants, is not affected or weakened by the last-mentioned petitions of the same parties contradicting and garbling these said admissions and declarations.

1. Because their said admissions and statements were opposed to their interests as complainants; whereas the contents of their said petitions tend to aid their recovery in this cause, and are justly liable to the suspicion of having been manufactured in order to accomplish their own purposes.

2. Because they are disingenuous and prevaricating in their character, and were manifestly made under influence which they, in their former statement, pronounced compulsory, coercive, and such as they were unable to resist.

3. Because they are not entitled, in law, to any weight or credit, as evidence for the complainants, who are estopped from denying or averring any thing in contradiction to what they had before solemnly and deliberately acknowledged. Sprigg v. Bank of Mount Pleasant, 10 Peters, 257; Lajoye v. Priman, 3 Miss. 529.

XVI. By the master's report, $4,473.62 were allowed Tyack on account of capital paid in by him; whereas the amount he advanced did not exceed $2,200. Nothing was allowed Newell on account of the $7,000 standing to his credit on the books of William Tyack & Co. The report further finds him indebted to the firm on account of partnership property received and not accounted for by him. Exceptions filed by him for these causes were overruled, and in this and in the final decree in this behalf there are, as we conceive, error and injustice.

XVII. The master ought to have reported fully and correctly, the proof on which the several items contained in it are found, and the claims of the alleged creditors ascertained and allowed, as suggested in the exceptions taken by Mr. Doss. The items making up the amount found against Newell cannot be gathered from the report. There can be no doubt, however, although it does not definitely appear that Newell was charged with the $2,000 he paid in goods to Edgar under the authority of the complainants, and in due course of the partnership business. These errors affect the final decree, and render it fatally erroneous and unjust. Williamson v. Wilson, 1 Bland, 418.

XVIII. The bill contains no prayer for ascertaining the names of the creditors or the amounts due them severally. It prays merely that the receiver be directed by the final decree to apply the property to the payment of the said copartnership debts. This is deemed an insufficient basis for the specific provisions in favor of the alleged creditors embraced in the decree.

XIX. The decree annuls the sale made to Stephen W. Doss, as fraudulent against the complainants. But the restoration of the money and property paid by him for the goods, as sought by his motion, (P. R. 324,) is wholly denied. The copartners, by virtue of the decree, not only keep the goods they sold to Doss, but keep also the price or consideration they received for them, amounting to eleven thousand seven hundred and fifty-three dollars, ($11,753,) without the possibility of his obtaining the slightest compensation or reimbursement at their hands, if the decree be affirmed.

Relying upon the points suggested, the appellants respectfully ask for a reversal of the decree and a dismissal of the cause; or, instead of an absolute dismissal, that the cause may be restored to the same condition that it was placed in by the procuration of the complainants themselves, under the decree of the 3d of August, 1849, dismissing the same. If this be done, the appellees cannot be prejudiced, since they would retain the right to bring suit by original bill, as they might at first, to vacate their powers of attorney, and the decree obtained in execution

of them, on account of the pretended mistakes and frauds averred in their petitions subsequently filed, in order to attain their
object in a too summary manner.

The counsel for the appellee made the following points:

1. So far as the question of fraud is concerned, the answers
of both defendants, and the depositions used on the trial, are
replete with the evidence of it. After putting forth the matters
stated and admitted in the defendants' answers, and the exhibits
made a part of them, no proof would have availed them, on the
hearing, to escape the conclusion of fraud. The bad complexion
of the whole transactions between Newell and Doss's agent,
McGreal, is only equalled by the recklessness with which they
attempted to take the property of the firm, divert it from its
proper direction, and to place the proceeds of it beyond the
reach of the copartners and creditors. The property, as copartnership property, was in the nature of trust property, and the
principles declared in the case of Wormley v. Wormley, (8
Wheat. 422,) apply fully to this case.

2. The contracts between Newell and McGreal were individual contracts. It was incompetent for them to vary them, as
evidence, or their complexion by parol proof, or their sworn answers. They were estopped from setting up the pretence, that
they fairly intended to create a *bona fide* trust in favor of complainants. The complainants might have brought the aspect of
a trust over the property to be conveyed by McGreal, had they
elected to take the lands agreed to be sold by McGreal to
Newell. The character of the transactions, however, between
Newell and McGreal, must be evidenced by the contracts they
made. The same rule would hold in reference to the absolute
assignment to Franklin, and the draft in favor of Knight. Under the circumstances, they will bear no other construction than
intention, on the part of Newell and McGreal, to place the copartnership property beyond the reach of complainants and the
creditors.

3. So far as Newell was concerned, the payment of his individual debt, of $1,400, to Edgar, out of the store of Stewart,
Newell, & Co., and his offering to mortgage the whole of the
goods to Edgar, as security for his individual indebtedness,
would have been sufficient cause for dissolving the copartnership.

4. Should the question be raised, whether his Honor, the District Judge, erred in setting aside the decree dismissing the bill,
and in reinstating the cause, it may be replied, that the court
below had power over the decree at any time during the term
at which it was entered. The order, entered on the suggestion

of complainants, on motion, was a mere voluntary dismissal of the suit, under a delusion created by defendants, without trial on its merits, and without the effect of prejudicial laches. It was not in its nature *res adjudicata*, or final, as to the rights of the parties. No enrolment had taken place, nor had the minutes of the court been signed by the Judge, at the time he vacated the order of dismissal.

5. No decree can be regarded in its effect as final, that has been obtained by fraud, practised by one of the litigating parties on the other. Fraud will vitiate the judgment or decree of any court; and the court will set it aside, and allow a party to come in at any time, where the subject-matter has not passed beyond the reach or control of the court. The proper way of applying to the court is by motion, where the order sought to be vacated has been obtained on motion.

6. It was entirely evident, in this case, at the time of the order dismissing the bill, that the complainants had been imposed upon, or that they were in collusion with the defendants. In either case, it was proper for the court to vacate its order, and reinstate the cause the moment the complainants requested it.

7. Should it be urged, that the complainants and defendants were in collusion on the application to dismiss the bill, it may be answered, that it matters not as to the extent of collusion or degree of turpitude, between parties *in pari delictu*, where one comes in and asks the court to take jurisdiction for the protection of creditors or innocent persons. In such case, it has been well said, " The fraudulent party is not entitled to a standing in court on his own account, but to subserve the purposes of justice towards those he has attempted to injure."

8. The best reason, perhaps, for setting aside the decree dismissing the bill is, that the Judge erred in listening to the application and granting the order to dismiss it. At the time of the application it had been fully shown by the bill, answers, affidavits, and depositions taken, what the character of the transactions were between Newell and McGreal. In addition to this, the complainants had asked, in the bill, that the property of the firm might be given to the creditors. They had asked for the appointment of a receiver, and prayed that the property might be delivered over to him. They had executed an assignment on their part to the receiver, that he might the better collect the assets. The creditors had paid a consideration for the protection of their interest through this suit. It was too late, therefore, for the complainants to recall what they had done. Hunt *v.* Rousmanier's Administrators, 5 Cond. Rep. 401.

9. What the complainants had done was equivalent to the execution of a power of attorney, coupled with an interest;

26*

and had all the effect of a contract or deed, with a trust ingrafted on the instrument. It was not revocable even by the death of the party. The trust had been created; the trust-fund had been placed in the hands of the receiver under the order of the court; and no imposition on the complainants, nor collusion on their part, should have been permitted by the court to work a *devastavit* on the property placed in the custody of the court for the benefit of the creditors. The doctrine implied in the language of the court, in the case of Williamson *v.* Wilson, (1 Bland. 418,) well applies to this case.

In aid of this would also come the rule, "That a naked license is not revocable where it has been once acted on, or where an encouragement to spend money has been given, and the expenditure has taken place."

Even in an action at law, where one man says to another, "Bring the suit in my name; let the property recovered be applied to the discharge of my indebtedness to you," has always been held to operate as an equitable assignment, not revocable. Canfield *v.* Munger, 12 Johns. Rep. 346. The creditor has also, in such case, the right to continue the name of the assignor as a party to the suit, notwithstanding the nominal plaintiff should attempt to countermand the license.

10. In general, persons not parties to a suit in equity, cannot come in and ask for relief or protection. There are exceptions, however, to this rule. Creditors are *quasi* parties to a suit brought for the dissolution of a copartnership, an accounting, and the distribution of the partnership property. They are entitled to come in under the decree for distribution, and prove up their demands before the master; and they thus become incidentally the objects of protection by the court. In the case of a creditor's bill suit, it is not necessary that all the creditors should be made parties complainants. It is sufficient that one creditor files the bill, with the suggestion that others who voluntarily come in and share the expenses, may participate of the proceeds on distribution. All the creditors, thus contributing, are entitled to equal favor, and it would not be insisted that collusion, between the complainant and defendants on the record, would be allowed by the court to work a defeat of the objects of the bill, by hastily dismissing the cause.

11. The bill in this case sets forth the names of the creditors prayed to be made the beneficiaries, and the respective amounts due each. The answer of the defendant, Newell, admitted them as stated in the bill. It is insisted, that this alone gave the demands of the creditors the effect of a judgment and lien on the assets in the hands of the receiver, the same as on a decree for an accounting, and the report of a master as to amounts due

creditors, in a case where they had not been in form made parties to the suit. In such case, after decree for accounting, and the establishment of the demands of creditors on reference to a master, the suit cannot be dismissed by the consent of complainants and defendants. Lashley v. Hogg, 11 Vesey, Jr. 602. What the creditors were entitled to by way of decree, as shown by the bill and answer, it is urged, could not be defeated by the fraud or collusion of the parties named as complainants and defendants on the record.

12. There is a large class of suits in equity where the power of the court must of necessity extend far beyond the immediate parties named as complainants and defendants. Of this class, are the bill for dissolution and accounting—the creditor's bill; bills against insolvent corporations, and others, where the proceedings are attended with the distribution of assets that have assumed the aspect and nature of trust property. The parties named in such suits as complainants, are considered as the representatives of all the interests that may be beneficially affected by the decree. After they have brought the matters into court, and invoked its aid and power, it would be too late to withdraw the subject-matter of litigation from the court. Were it otherwise, there would often be no remedy, from the impossibility to make parties. The most a court of equity could possibly do, under a sound discretion, would be, to allow a complainant, acting in bad faith, to retire from the suit on terms, in the mean time retaining the fund, and allowing others to come in, whose fidelity could be better depended upon, in carrying the trust property to a fair distribution.

13. Copartnership property (more especially in cases of insolvency) is strictly regarded as trust property, and the creditors of the copartnership, the *cestuis que trust*, or beneficiaries; and this, independent of any instrument or agreement making an assignment, or declaring the trust; hence the uniform practice of courts of equity in extending protection to their interests.

14. In the case at bar, it will be seen that the copartnership property had been placed, and tied up, on the application of complainants, for more than one year, in the hands of the receiver, in a condition that made it invulnerable to the creditors, except through distribution by the court. It was in the custody of the law, and could not be levied on. The remedy of the creditors against the property was suspended. The dismissal of the bill and delivery of the copartnership property to Doss, would have given the effect of having used the court to delay the creditors, and then, of prostituting its powers to defeat them. It is believed that courts of equity have power to exempt themselves from being used as instruments for such purposes.

15. It may be said, perhaps, that the case at bar is *sui generis;* that there is no precedent, in all respects, applicable to the questions involved in the motion to dismiss this cause in the court below. If so, it is respectfully submitted whether principles, applicable to the circumstances of this case, should not be declared, as well for the benefit of courts of original jurisdiction, as for the instruction of solicitors and counsel respecting their rights, duties, and responsibilities.

Mr. Justice GRIER delivered the opinion of the court.

A short history of the facts of this case, extricated from the numerous allegations of the pleadings and the mass of testimony contained in the record, will better exhibit its merits than a more formal abstract of the pleadings and proofs.

The appellees, who were complainants below, entered into articles of agreement with Samuel Newell, one of the respondents below, on the 25th of September, 1847, in which they engaged to form a copartnership under the form and style of William Tyack & Co., in New York, and Stewart, Newell & Co., in Galveston, Texas. " The nature of the business to be transacted by said firm to be a commission, general, and auction business." The parties each to contribute towards the capital stock the sum of five thousand dollars, within ninety days ; the capital to be augmented as the business required ; Newell, " in consideration of his expense and labor in paving the way for the contemplated business, as well as his influence in the State of Texas, to be entitled to one fourth of the profits, and the balance to be equally divided between the three partners. Tyack and Murray to take charge of the business in New York, and Newell in Galveston.

At the time these parties entered into this contract of partnership, their several ability to perform their agreement of advancing capital and supporting the credit of the firm, as shown by the pleadings and evidence, would appear to be as follows : Tyack was worth, in all, probably twenty thousand dollars ; Murray had nothing, and owed about five thousand dollars; Newell, while resident in Texas, " had become interested in a claim belonging to Alexander Edgar, to a league of land," on which it was supposed that the city of Galveston was built. He had come to New York, at this time, with a power of attorney from Edgar, to form a stock company of persons, who were to have an interest in this litigated claim. He had divided it into one thousand shares, to be sold at one hundred dollars each, payable in instalments. He was to have half of all the money received for the stock, over twenty thousand dollars. A few persons had been persuaded to subscribe for some of this stock, and among others, Tyack and Murray had each agreed to take a few shares; and Tyack was appointed treasurer of the company under the name of "The Galveston Land Company." Newell's property or capital consisted in the anticipated profits of this speculation, and some stock in another company, called the "Wilson Joint Stock Land Company."

The partners soon afterwards commenced business on about four or five thousand dollars, advanced by Tyack. Murray had nothing, and Newell's stocks would produce nothing in the market; those who had before subscribed for it, refusing to pay, on the plea or suspicion that it was good for nothing, as the citizens of Galveston had probably a better title to the land than the company. Thus the source from which Newell's capital was anticipated, wholly failed.

In the mean time a stock of goods was purchased for the house in Texas, costing about twenty thousand dollars, for the payment of which Newell had drawn bills on Tyack & Co. for some seventeen thousand dollars, which Tyack had accepted, in expectation of remittances of cotton or other produce from Texas, by Newell, to meet the bills at maturity. The business expected to be transacted by Tyack & Co. in New York, was the disposal of these consignments from the Texas house — of cotton and other merchandise purchased with the funds of the firm in Texas.

In March, 1848, the acceptances in New York being near maturity, and the consignments received from Newell to meet these large liabilities, amounting only to about eight hundred dollars, Tyack, to avoid impending bankruptcy, if possible, called together the creditors of the firm and made a statement of its situation. In consideration of the creditors agreeing to give further time on the acceptances about to mature, Tyack & Murray executed a power of attorney to William E. Warren, an agent chosen by the creditors, authorizing him to take possession of the property and effects of the firm in Texas, and secure them for the benefit of the creditors. Warren was authorized by the creditors to act for them, and to collect, secure, or compromise their claims, in any way he thought best; with instructions to proceed to Texas, and examine into the state of the firm, and if it was found that there was any probable prospect that the firm could eventually pay their debts, to make any reasonable arrangement for that purpose, and suffer Newell to continue the business: on the contrary, if Newell could hold out no such prospect, or if he was found to be wasting the goods of the firm, and appropriating them to any other purpose than the regular mercantile business of the firm, the agent was instructed to get possession, by all legal means, of the partnership assets, and hold them or dispose of them in the best manner for the interests of the creditors and all concerned.

In pursuance of this authority, Warren proceeded to Galveston. He there found the assets in Newell's possession insufficient to pay the debts, and that the firm was hopelessly insolvent; and moreover, that Newell had appropriated a portion of the assets of the firm to the payment of his personal debts, incurred in his land stock speculations, and was unwilling to comply with any reasonable terms of compromise, to secure the creditors, or save his partner, Tyack, from insolvency and ruin.

Warren then instituted proceedings in the State Court on behalf of Tyack and the creditors, and obtained an injunction and a writ of seizure against Newell, on which the sheriff took possession of the property of the firm. On the 10th of July, 1848, on motion of Newell's counsel, the court, for some reason, set aside the injunction and writ of seizure. The counsel for Tyack and the creditors, immediately discontinued their proceedings in the State Court, and commenced proceedings in the District Court of the United States. While the bill for that purpose was being prepared, and application being made for an injunction and the appointment of a receiver, Newell and one Peter McGreal proceeded in hot haste from the court house, got possession of the goods from the sheriff, and had the following instrument of writing executed :

" Received, Galveston, July 10, from S. W. Doss, of Brazoria, the following amounts: Two thousand dollars, in good notes, mortgages, liens, and judgments, and seven thousand seven hundred and fifty-three dollars in lands, full payment of the stock of goods, wares, and merchandise now in our store in Galveston. STEWART NEWELL.

" Recap.— Cash, $2,000; Notes, $2,000; Lands, $7,753— Total, $11,753.

" In presence of John Warrin, Isaac D. Knight."

No notes, judgments, or liens, were in fact assigned by McGreal to Newell, nor any conveyances of land made ; but McGreal gave his written promise to assign and convey securities and lands to that amount within thirty days. The production of the two thousand dollars cash, was also dispensed with, as the parties appear to have been in too great haste to be particular. The answer of Newell attempts to account for the cash as follows :

" This defendant states, that the said first payment in cash of $2,000, mentioned in said receipt, was secured and made to this defendant by Peter McGreal, Esq., the agent of said Doss ; that a portion of said sum of $2,000, to wit, about $1,200, was paid by the said McGreal, agent as aforesaid, to Benjamin C.

Franklin, Joseph A. Swett, and John B. Jones, in pursuance of, and in accordance with, an order given by this defendant to said McGreal for that purpose; that forty-two dollars and fifty cents were paid upon the order of this defendant to J. A. Sauters for rent of said store, due by said firm; and the balance, to wit, about seven hundred and fifty dollars, was directed by this defendant to be paid over or secured to Isaac D Knight, to be by him held to the use of the firm of S. N. & Co., to be paid over for the said use upon the order of this defendant, in like manner as the said book debts and other choses in action assigned to said Franklin, as above mentioned."

What right Franklin, Swett, and Jones had, to receive this money, or how, or why it was paid to them, (if it was paid,) or how Knight, the brother-in-law of Newell, became a trustee for the creditors of the firm, the answer does not disclose.

McGreal appears also to have treated Newell with the same unbounded confidence which Newell had reposed in him. He took the goods on trust, as to quantity and quality; required no invoice or schedule, being content with one which the sheriff had made; and immediately commenced to pack them up and seek for assistance and means for carrying them off. The transaction commenced after twelve o'clock in the day, and by twelve o'clock at night, a large portion of the goods were put on board the sloop Alamo, which set sail before morning. In the mean time the bill in this case had been filed, and a receiver appointed, who, on the following day, (11th July,) was enabled by means of a writ of assistance, to arrest the sloop and get possession of the goods.

It is unnecessary to enumerate all the charges of the bill, and the answers thereto, as it is amply sufficient for the purposes of the decision in this case, that the facts we have already stated were either admitted by the answers, or undeniably proved.

The plaintiff in error, Stephen W. Doss, who claims to be the owner of the goods, thus alleged to have been purchased by Peter McGreal, was made a party to the suit. Both he and Newell deny, in their answer, all fraud in the transaction, and Doss avers, " that the said transaction was made in the regular mode of conducting such business, and at a time when there was no lawful restraint existing to prevent the sale and delivery of the goods."

On this case the court below, at the March term, 1850, rendered a decree for the complainants, dissolving the partnership, setting aside the sale to McGreal, or Doss, as fraudulent, and ordering the receiver to pay over the proceeds of the goods, (which had been previously sold by order of the court,) to the creditors of the firm.

But, in order rightly to apprehend the points relied on by the counsel for appellants, in claiming a reversal of the decree, it will be necessary to state some of the intermediate proceedings in the case, as exhibited by the record. During the pendency of the suit, Newell and McGreal had gone to New York, and persuaded Tyack & Murray to revoke the power of attorney given to Warren, and to execute one to the respondents' counsel, authorizing them to dismiss the bill; and a motion was made by them, for this purpose, in August, 1848. This motion was resisted, on the ground that the firm was wholly insolvent; that the power to Warren was given on a contract with the creditors, and for a valuable consideration, and was, therefore, irrevocable; as it would be a fraud in Tyack to dismiss the proceedings, for the benefit of the creditors, after the great trouble and expense incurred by them for the purpose of protecting Tyack from ruin. Notwithstanding these objections, the court ordered · the suit to be dismissed; but, some days after, at the same term, vacated and set aside this order or decree, on proof, that the revocation of the power to Warren, and the order given to discontinue or dismiss the proceedings, were obtained from the complainants by gross misrepresentation and fraud. Afterwards, an issue was ordered, on prayer of respondents' counsel, to try the question of fraud. This issue was tried before a jury, who rendered a verdict that "the sale was fraudulent." Whereupon, the respondents moved for a new trial, on the ground that the verdict was given "under a misconstruction and misunderstanding of the charge of the court." This motion was founded on an affidavit of some of the jurors that, "on their retirement, they did not, inquire into the right and power of Doss to purchase, nor of the question of fraud on Doss's part, but only into the right and power of Newell to make the sale."

We are now prepared to examine the points relied upon for the reversal of this decree.

They are, 1st. That the court had no power to set aside the order or decree, dismissing the bill, unless, on a new and original bill, filed for the purpose. 2d. That, on this certificate of the jury, the court should have granted a new trial on the question of fraud.

1. As regards the first point, we perceive no error in the action of the court, except in their first order dismissing the suit. It did not require an original bill, to authorize the court to vacate an order or decree, at the same term in which it was made, on discovering that they have committed an error, or that the consent of the complainants to such dismissal was obtained by the fraud of the respondents, or their agents. In fact, under

such circumstances, it cannot be said that the act was done by the consent or will of the complainants, at all. The court, in vacating the decree, were correcting an error both of fact and of law; and, during the term at which it was rendered, they had full power to amend, correct, or vacate it, for either of these reasons.

2. The second point is equally without foundation. It is true, that the answers of the respondents denied fraud in the abstract, but they admitted all the facts and circumstances necessary to constitute it in the concrete. The general denial of the answer, only showed that the definition of fraud was much narrower, in the estimation of the respondents, than in that of courts of law and equity. In this case, a verdict was wholly unnecessary, to inform the conscience of the Chancellor; and, the verdict being perfectly correct, the court very properly refused to set it aside, on any representation from jurors thus obtained.

Any argument to vindicate the correctness of the verdict and the decree of the court below, after the exhibition of the merits of this case, which we have given, would be entirely superfluous.

The decree of the District Court of Texas, is therefore affirmed.

Order.

This cause came on to be heard, on the transcript of the record, from the District Court of the United States for the District of Texas, and was argued by counsel. On consideration whereof, it is now here ordered, adjudged, and decreed, by this court, that the decree of the said District Court in this cause be, and the same is hereby, affirmed, with costs.

———

JOHN PERKINS, APPELLANT, *v.* EDWARD P. FOURNIQUET AND HARRIET, HIS WIFE, AND MARTIN EWING AND ANNE, HIS WIFE.

Releases given by the complainants, in the present case, decided to cover the matters in controversy, and, therefore, to put an end to all claim by them; inasmuch as there is no proof that they were obtained by fraud or circumvention.

THIS was an appeal from the Circuit Court of the United States for the Southern District of Mississippi.

The case, in some of its branches, had been before the court three times before. A motion to dismiss a case between the same parties, at January term, 1848, is reported in 6 Howard, 206. It came up again at January term, 1849, and is reported in 7 Howard, 160. Again, at December term, 1851, a dispute, growing out of the same matters, was before this court, and the judgment of the court below affirmed by a divided court. Consequently, it was not reported; but the mandate, which was issued therein, gave rise to a difficulty, which will be the subject of the succeeding case in this volume. Ewing and wife were parties, together with Fourniquet and wife, to the present suit, but the controversy cannot be distinctly understood, without a reference to the case in 7 Howard, 160. The family connection of the parties is there explained.

The present claim of Fourniquet and wife, and Ewing and wife, against Perkins, was founded on the alleged rights of the marital community of Mrs. Perkins (the mother of Harriet and Anne) with Mr. Perkins, according to the laws of Louisiana.

The bill alleges the marriage was consummated in Louisiana, where both the widow Bynum and the defendant Perkins were then citizens; and that the defendant always retained his legal and political domicil in Louisiana, though some time after the marriage, for the ostensible purpose of health, established a family residence near Natchez, in the State of Mississippi. The bill charges, that defendant, during the marriage, expended of community funds, in the State of Mississippi, in permanent investments of real estate, an amount of about $39,600, which remained in kind at the dissolution of the marriage by the death of his wife in 1824, but which he has since sold and disposed of to his own use. That defendant had no revenues or resources in Mississippi from which these investments were made; but it was all derived from the revenues of his and his wife's property and cotton estates in Louisiana, and were partnership funds, in which complainants, as heirs of their mother's community, had rights of partnership, and now have right to hold defendant to account therefor. They charge, that if defendant intended and expected to get an advantage to himself, by investing the community funds in the State of Mississippi, rather than in Louisiana, then it was a fraud on his part, for which he is liable; or, if intended in good faith, yet such investment charged defendant with a trust, for which they pray he may be held responsible.

But complainants aver, that as defendant has heretofore kept back and concealed from settlement this investment and never accounted for the same, but in settlement with them obtained their receipts and release in full, in which this matter was not included, that said releases, so far as they may be invoked to bar this claim, were obtained by fraud and circumvention. And they declare the matters of this bill were kept back by defendant, and never accounted for. And they call on defendant to produce the account and items rendered by him when he obtained these releases, and show for what they were given.

They aver, too, that Harriet's release was given while she was yet a minor.

They pray for an account of proceeds, or amount of said investment, with eight per cent. interest, and for general relief.

Answer.

Defendant, in his answer, admits the marriage in Louisiana, admits the parties, and admits substantially the investments made in the State of Mississippi. But qualifying and explaining, says: That same year of the marriage he and his wife removed to the State of Mississippi, and continued their domicil there during all the time of their married life, which terminated by the death of his wife on the 12th August, 1824. That this removal was in pursuance of an understanding had between them before marriage with a view to health, and facilities of educating the children. Admits he retained some political rights in Louisiana after his removal till 8th of June, 1821; but says his civil domicil was changed as aforesaid, and on this allegation predicates his first and principal ground of defence, viz., that by reason of this domicil "respondent has always acted under the belief that there was no community of acquets and gains of property, lying in Louisiana, between respondent and his said wife under the laws of Louisiana."

As a second ground of defence, he submits, also, that if, as alleged in said bill, the domicil was not changed, yet, as head of the community, he was entitled to the absolute disposal of the acquets and gains, without accountability to his wife, or her legal representatives.

As a third ground of defence, denies that the investments in Mississippi were made with money to which his wife had any legal or equitable title whatever. And denies they were made to gain any unjust advantage over his wife or her heirs.

Fourth point of defence is matter in abatement, in which defendant assumes, that if liable to the demand made in said bill, it is only to an administrator of his wife's estate, and not to the complainants.

Fifth ground of defence is, that he has obtained the releases of complainants for all claims on account of the estate of their father and mother, and relies upon them as if formally plead in bar, denying they were obtained by fraud or concealment.

Sixth ground of defence submits that if said investments were made with money in which his wife had an interest, yet that defendant is entitled to the property, as tenant by curtesy during his natural life; and he interposes this right as if plead in bar.

Upon the final hearing, the Circuit Court passed the following decree:

In Chancery. Final Decree.

The report of William H. Brown, Master in Chancery, made in the above-stated case, and filed herein on the 3d day of April A. D. 1850, having been confirmed on a former day of this term; and the report of said Master made herein and filed on the first day of October, A. D. 1850, having also been confirmed on a former day of this term, except as to the said sum of five hundred dollars therein stated as having been paid by defendant subsequent to the death of Mrs. Perkins, wife of said defendant: It is now thereupon further ordered, adjudged, and decreed, that the said complainants, the said Harriet J. Fourniquet, together with the said Edward P. Fourniquet, in right of his said wife, but to her sole and separate use; and the said Ann S. Ewing, together with the said Martin W. Ewing, in right of his said wife, but to her sole and separate use, do have and recover of the said defendant, John Perkins, the amount stated in said first-named report, to wit, the sum of sixteen thousand nine hundred and sixty-eight dollars and seventy-six cents ($16,968.76,) to be paid to the said complainants by the said defendant within thirty days hereafter, together with interest thereon at the rate of eight per cent. per annum, from the first day of April, 1850, or in default thereof that said complainants have execution therefor. It is further ordered, adjudged, and decreed, that said complainants do recover of the defendant all their costs hereby in this suit incurred and herein taxed.

November 20, 1850.   S. J. GHOLSON.

From this decree Perkins appealed to this court.

It was argued by *Mr. Johnson* and *Mr. Soule*, for the appellant, and *Mr. Henderson*, for the appellees.

It is not necessary to state the points and arguments of the counsel relative to the community of acquets and gains under the law of Louisiana, and how far that law would reach investments in Mississippi; but as the decision of the court turned entirely upon the validity of the releases (one of which is inserted in 7 Howard, and both in the present opinion,) the notice of the argument will be confined entirely to that subject.

The counsel for the appellant considered the releases in the following point of view:

The bill charges that these releases were obtained by concealment, fraud, &c. The answer denies the charge in the most positive terms, and not a shadow of proof has been given of its truth.

The releases themselves are as full and thorough acquittances of all responsibility on the part of the respondent, as could have been drafted, as will be seen by reference thereto.

To the release of E. P. Fourniquet and wife to J. Perkins, dated Natchez, May 27, 1834.

To the release from M. W. Ewing and wife, dated April 11, 1828.

To the release of Benjamin S. and Mary C. Bynum, (heirs, but not parties to this suit,) April 10, 1829.

Act of confirmation by Mary C. and Thomas P. Eskridge, dated April 9, 1832.

For what were these releases made? Surely not to cover the land and slaves in Louisiana of the deceased parents of the releasors, because there had been previously (in 1827) a judicial partition and distribution of their patrimonial estate, which had been homologated, and had all the force of "the thing adjudged;" and Perkins had been fully discharged before any of these releases were executed. Then, these releases must have been wholly supererogatory in reference to the land and slaves in Louisiana; and the question arises, what could they have been designed to cover and include, unless it were such personal effects as may have remained, after all the debts and expenses of the marriage and the education and maintenance of the Bynum heirs had been defrayed?

As to the validity and effect of these releases, one of them has been attested and adjudicated, not only in the Ninth Judicial District of Louisiana, and before a jury, but in the Supreme Court of the United States.

Howard's Reports, vol. 7, contains the recitals, in Mr. Justice Daniel's opinion, showing that Fourniquet and wife sued Perkins for large amounts of property, spoliations, &c., in Concordia, Louisiana, in December, 1838, and that judgment was rendered against them in December, 1840; and that, having brought suit against him in 1844, in the United States Circuit Court for Louisiana, Perkins pleaded that judgment in bar, and prevailed both in the Circuit and Supreme Courts of the United States.

True, the opinion of Judge Daniel was rejected, as evidence, in the United States Circuit Court for Mississippi; but whether the objection was well taken or not, the weight of it, as an argument and an authority directly in point, could not be destroyed, and it applies with equal force to the release of Ewing and wife. See the case at large in 7 How. 160.

" The gratuitous remission of a debt, is as valuable as a release for a valuable consideration, and may be express or implied." Civil Code, Art. 2195.

" The *pactum remissorium, pactum de non petendo*, was binding under the Roman law; and all that was required to give it validity, was a simple convention. Mouton v. Noble, 1 Annual Reports, 194.

See also the case of Morgan v. Morgan, 5 Annual Rep. 230. [An authentic MS. copy of the record in this case, is on file at the Supreme Court of the United States, showing remarkable coincidences between the release in that case and the case at bar.]

The law presumes the acceptance of the remission of a debt, and it cannot be revoked by creditors. Civil Code, 21, 97; Lee v. Ferguson, 5 Annual Rep. 533.

For the force, as testimony, of sworn answers in chancery, see 2 Story's Equity Jurisprudence, §§ 1528, 9, 30.

m   m

Mr. Henderson, for the appellees.

We come next to consider the question of the receipts and releases, interposed in bar.

The bill charges fraud and concealment in obtaining from complainants these receipts, and declares the matters sought to be recovered in this suit, were not, at the time of these receipts, or at any other time, ever accounted for, but by defendants were concealed and kept back; and they require and demand of defendant, should he offer said receipts in bar, that he produce the account, and the items thereof rendered, for which said receipts were given.

The defendant tenders the releases as exhibits, with his answer, and states that he " relies upon said releases as if formally pleaded in bar," and denies, generally, they were obtained by fraud or concealment. They are found in the record, but in no form of plea. Now, while rule 39 permits a defendant to avail himself in his answer of matters in bar, if the matter be such as could be plead in bar, yet the rule does not allow that to subserve as a bar in an answer, which could not have been plead in bar. The alleged release of Harriet Fourniquet is not good in bar, because the deed of a married woman, not proven or acknowledged on privy examination, and therefore void. Agricultural Bank v. Rice, 4 How. 241, 242; 12 Pet. 375; 10 Pet. 20 and 22.

This release is void, also, because executed by her while a minor, as charged in her bill, and admitted by defendant's answer to interrogatory 4. Her subsequent recognition of it, before a Judge in Louisiana, (not on private examination,) gave it no additional validity. Void as the deed of a married woman in its execution, it could not be validated by her subsequent recognition of it.

The receipt of Ewing and wife is not under seal, and therefore not good in plea of bar as a release. Story, Eq. Pl. § 796; Mit. Pl. marg. 263.

But complainants have impeached, by their bill, the integrity of these receipts, so far as offered by defendant to evidence a release, or settlement, of the community sued for, and call upon defendant for a disclosure of the consideration on which they were executed.

The defendant denies fraud generally in their procurement, but makes no disclosure of the matters or accounts settled by the receipts. Nor does he venture to affirm they were given on settlement of the community; yet tenders them as "releases, as if formally pleaded in bar," notwithstanding.

Such form of pleading and issue make no ground of defence, and must be overruled and disregarded, as if not in the record. Story, Eq. Pl. § 796, 797; Mit. Pl. marg. 261, 262, 263.

If it be said, however, that these receipts were executed for the meridian of Louisiana, and not intended for common-law instruments, (though both made in Mississippi,) their deficiency in this aspect is still more palpable. For, professing to evidence the settlement of Perkins's account as tutor or guardian of the Bynum heirs, they are "null and void," because they do not show, on their face, that a full account and a delivery of vouchers was rendered the wards, ten days previous to signing the receipts. O. C. 72, art. 76; 4 How. U. S. R. 561; C. C. art. 355; 4 Rob. 296, 297.

And the civil-law doctrine of "transactions" and "remission" of debts, was never extended, and will not be in equity, to settlements of guardians with their wards.

And the defendant's answer in this case is quite demonstrative, that he never settled in any way with complainants for their mother's community. He says, "By reason of their domicil being in the State of Mississippi, respondent has always acted under the belief, and now submits to the court, by way of defence to the claim of complainants, that there was no community of acquets and gains of property lying in Louisiana, between respondent and his said wife Mary, under the laws of Louisiana."

If there be any meaning in language, this surrenders the fact, and admits the community not settled for.

For, if Perkins "always acted under this belief," he so acted when he obtained these receipts. It is conclusive, therefore, he did not settle with or compensate complainants for the community. And he waives such defence in this part of his answer, by submitting the question of community or no community to the court, and to abide that issue. If he has bought out this claim, why not show the evidence of his purchase, rather than submit the issue to the court that it never existed?

But the receipt of Ewing and wife is also express and conclusive, against this pretence of defendant. It particularly and exactly enumerates what things were settled for, and what he received. And by reference to the inventories returned by Perkins himself, the eighteen slaves, specified in the receipt, are found in inventories. The cattle, mules, and tools, all are there shown, and all of the Bynum estate. There can be no mistake in this proof. And it was no such grace on Perkins's part, that he relaxed his hold on this fraction of their father's estate, as thereby to absolve himself from community.

But the record, elsewhere, abounds with evidence on this point. On pages 71 to 76, defendant sets forth the several parcels of land purchased by him chiefly in Louisiana, during the coverture; and all such are community lands, if a marital partnership existed. And Mrs. Perkins's children were jointly seised of the title with him, at the instant of her death. Now can such receipts as here exhibited, by any stretch of presumption, be regarded as transmissive of their joint title, with Perkins, to these lands? Even if intended as such, they obviously fail as relinquishments of title to real estate.

But had this been the purpose, it is incredible of belief they would have been so executed. For the title which the heirs of Mrs. Perkins have in her community, would sustain an ejectment against Perkins, or even against a third possessor under Perkins without notice. See 5 An. Rep. 389; 2 Id. 261.

Now these Mississippi investments of $29,000, were but part of the whole, and with like certainty were not accounted for in these receipts.

They do not show they included or comprehended the community, but we think on their face they reasonably show the contrary, and the defendant shrinks from the averment that they did or do include it. He offers no proof that they did, and he evades reply, when called on to show the matters and things on which they rested, and says he always acted under the belief there was no community, and submits that issue to the court. Aside from their defective execution to make them releases, and apart from the mispleading them in bar, we think it impossible to believe they did settle for community, or were intended, by those who gave them, to comprehend that subject.

The rule in equity, and of the most common justice, then applies, that these receipts shall be held valid only for the matters and things on which they computed. And this, with such legal distrust as the relations of the parties imply. 10 How. 185, 186; 8 How. 158; 4 How. 561; 16 Pet. 276, 7, 8, 9; 2 Sum. 11; 3 Story, R. 268, 9; 1 Ed. Ch. R. 38, 39; 1 Ch. & Lef. 226.

The case of Fourniquet and wife *v.* Perkins, (7 How. 160,) is referred to and relied on as deciding these receipts valid against us. But the case quoted decides no such principle. It sustained a plea of *res judicata.* And the case plead in bar, did interpose these receipts, among other matters of defence, in a suit brought exclusively to obtain against Perkins a new account of his administration of the Bynum estates, but not for community. We were defeated in that case. And Judge Daniel said, from inspection of the record, that it did not appear we were defeated merely on the receipts, but on the merits. We admitted then, and admit now, these receipts were given to close Perkins's administration of the Bynum estate, but not community in the Perkins estate. The decision of that case does not therefore touch these receipts. They have only been decided in this case below, and in the case of Perkins *v.* Fourniquet et al. (6 How. 206); and in both decisions it has been held that these receipts did not bar this action for community.

One other, and the last point, on this subject. Both these receipts recite and count on administrative settlements, by Perkins, of Benjamin Bynum's estate, or of Mrs. Perkins's separate estate, in his capacity of guardian, curator, or executor.

Now it is familiar to the jurisprudence of Louisiana, as shown in the decisions herein quoted, that the formal and official administration of the wife's estate extends only to her separate estate, and not to her community. Perkins, in this case, as surviving partner, would, and did, have the settlement of community, and not as curator of the Bynum estate, or as administrator or executor of his wife's estate. His right, power, and duty to settle the community, resulted wholly and exclusively from his being the surviving partner in community. And his accountability for the wife's share in community was directed with her heirs, and not her administrator. And this is manifest from the right of the heirs to renounce community. O. C. 338, arts. 72, 75, 82, 84.

And there is no fact or circumstance in this case that points, in the remotest degree, to any settlement made by Perkins as surviving partner of the community. No partition with the heirs is shown; no purchase from them of their undivided portion is shown; and, upon all known principles of human action, it is impossible to believe that either of these things was done, and being done, that the evidence of it was incorporated in these receipts.

Mr. Justice WAYNE delivered the opinion of the court.

This is an appeal from the Circuit Court of the United States for the District of Mississippi, the District Judge presiding.

The suit was brought in the Vice-Chancery Court of Mississippi, and was transferred to the Circuit Court, upon the application of the respondent, under the 12th section of the act of September 24th, 1789, to establish the judicial courts of the United States.

Harriet J. Fourniquet and Anne M. Ewing are the step-daughters of the respondent, from his intermarriage with their mother, Mary Bynum. She was the widow of their father, Benjamin Bynum.

The object of the suit was to recover their portion of $39,600, alleged by them to be marital community gains of the respondent and their mother, which they charge he invested in Mississippi, and was in hand at the death of their mother. The respondent is charged with having had no means of his own to make such investments; that the money was derived from the cotton estate in Louisiana; that the same, by the laws of that State, became a community of acquets and gains, one half of which, upon the death of their mother, became theirs and her other heirs; and they charge him, further, with having fraudulently taken the money derived from the Louisiana property, into Mississippi, to invest it there, in order to give him undue advantages over his wife's and their interest in the fund. It is said, that at the death of their mother there were then living four children of the first husband, and three by the respondent. Three of the four and two of the three are still living. Mary B. Eskridge, one of the survivors of the Bynum children, and John Perkins and William Perkins, adults and heirs of the complainant, do not concur with them in their suit, and for that reason are not made parties. The respondent, besides being charged generally with fraud, is especially so in reference to certain receipts and releases, which these complainants gave to him, which they now say were obtained by concealment and circumvention.

The respondent, in his answer to the bill, admits his marriage in Louisiana, at the time and place stated. That he removed to Mississippi with his wife in 1818; that their domicil was there continued to be kept during the coverture, and that their removal was not only with the consent of the wife, but in pursuance of an understanding between them before their marriage took place. He denies that any community of gains was established conventionally, or that it legally could occur under the law of Louisiana, on account of the residence of himself and wife in that State when they were married, because it was their intention, before the marriage took place, to remove into Mississippi. He denies that any money, invested by him in lands in Mississippi, belonged, either legally or equitably, to his wife in either State; and asserts, even if there was a marital community between them, he was entitled to dispose of the gains as he pleased, without any liability, under the law of Louisiana, to account for the same to his wife or her representatives. He denies the charge, that he was without productive property or available means to purchase the property in Mississippi. That property consists of several tracts of land and the improvements put upon them, as is said, by community funds. The tract upon which the improvements were put contained one hundred acres. It was bought from Arthur Mahan, on the 30th October, 1818, for $9,926. It was improved for a residence for the respondent with his family, including the children of the wife by the first husband. There was another tract, containing 2,100 acres, bought by the respondent from Elihu Hall Bay, in January, 1819, for $5,000. There were two other purchases, — one of them, a lot in Natchez, bought from Walter S. Parker, in March, 1823, for $600; and the other is a purchase from Sugar Zenor, in March, 1824, for $1,000. The aggregate sum given for these lands, and the improvements upon the first, amount to $39,600. The complainants allege, that they have a right to elect to take their interest in them in money, with interest upon the amount from the time of their mother's death.

To this answer, the complainants filed the general replication.

The case was tried, and the court below gave an interlocutory decree against the respondent. It declares that a community of gains had existed between the respondent and his wife during the marriage. That its resources were altogether in Louisiana, and that the respondent had invested from the gains large sums in the purchase and improvement of real estate in Mississippi, and that it was held by him, in 1824, when the marriage was dissolved by the death of Mrs. Perkins. The court also referred the matter to a master, to take an account conformably to its decree. In the course of the reference, the master sustained an objection to an allowance for which the complainants contended. It was submitted to the court, whether he had properly refused it. He was instructed, that it was only necessary for him to ascertain the amount of the funds vested by the respondent in Mississippi during the community; and that, as to the source from which Perkins derived them, the court would decide under all the proof. The master proceeded accordingly. He reported, without any proof of the source from which Mr. Perkins obtained the money, that $16,968.76 was due to the complainants. The report was subsequently confirmed, and the court gave a final decree for them for the sum just stated, with interest, at 8 per cent. from the 1st April, 1850.

It does not appear that the court's attention had been particularly directed to the releases which the complainants admit they gave to the respondent, and which he says were given to him with a positive denial of the statement, that he obtained them by fraud, concealment, and circumvention.

If it had been, we think that the court would have determined the effect of the releases upon the case before it gave its interlocutory decree, and that it would not have made a final decree upon the master's report.

We proceed to give our view of these releases.

The first, from Ewing and wife, was executed on the 11th April, 1828. Fourniquet and wife executed theirs on the 27th May, 1834, within a month of six years after the other.

They are as follows:

Release from E. P. Fourniquet et ux. to John Perkins.

Received, Natchez, May 27th, 1834, of John Perkins, on settlement of all accounts, debts, dues, and demands, whatever, up to the present day, one hundred dollars in full, having, on a previous occasion, received from him, as the guardian of my wife, Mrs. Harriet J. Fourniquet, late Miss Bynum, all the estate, portion, and share, which she inherited by the death of her late father, Benjamin Bynum, late of Concordia, Louisiana, deceased, or her mother, Mrs. Mary Perkins, of the county of Adams, and State of Mississippi, and brother, Benjamin S. Bynum, of the county of Clairborne, and State last aforesaid, deceased; and do, by these presents, jointly with my said wife, release and forever discharge the said Perkins, from all and every claim which she, or either of us, might or could have against him, the said Perkins, either as guardian or otherwise, growing out of the estates aforesaid, or in any other matter and shape whatsoever, and forever exonerate him, by these presents, his heirs and executors and administrators therefrom.

[In] witness whereof, we have hereunto set our hands and seals, the day and year first above written, to wit, in the year of our Lord, one thousand eight hundred and thirty-four, in the presence of Elijah Bell and John E. Maddux, whose names are hereunto subscribed, as witnesses hereunto, the said John Perkins being also personally present, and by these presents accept-

E. P. FOURNIQUET. [SEAL.]
HARRIET FOURNIQUET. [SEAL.]
JOHN PERKINS. [SEAL.]

Witnessed, signed, sealed, and delivered, in the presence of —

ELIJAH BELL,
JOHN E. MADDUX.

Release from M. W. Ewing to John Perkins.

Received of John Perkins two negro slaves, Lewis and Anderson, also his draft on A. Fisk, for four hundred and seventy dollars, thirty-four cents, in one ,hundred and twenty days, indorsed by R. M. Gaines; which, when paid, will be in full of all claims and demands, of every kind and description, which we, or either of us, may have against said Perkins individually, or against him as curator of the estates of Benjamin Bynum and Mary Perkins, in the parish of Concordia, State of Louisiana, or as executor of the will of the said Mary Perkins, dated March 30, 1822, and in full of all claims of every kind, which we or either of us, may have against said Perkins, in any way whatever; we having received from said Perkins, heretofore, the following named slaves, to wit: Judah Myers, aged 25 years; Edward, about 4 years; Harry, about 7 months; Little Daniel, about 16 years.; Patrick, 13 years; Lewis 5 years; Big Daniel, 50 years; Big Sarah Miambo, about 50 years; Ned, 16 years; Polly, 14 years; Frank, about 50 years; Maria, his wife, 37 years old; Frank, aged about 1 year; Fanny, about 7; Samuel, about 19 years. Also two mules, thirty head of cattle, and a chest of tools; and the said Perkins accepts hereof, as a full satisfaction and discharge from the said Martin W. Ewing, and Anne, his wife, in the premises.

Witness our hands, this 11th day of April, A. D. 1828.

MARTIN W. EWING,
ANNE EWING.

Att. R. M. GAINES.   JOHN PERKINS.

The operative words of these releases are as full as they can be, and they cover the subject-matter for which the complainants brought the suit.

We have carefully examined and considered this record, without finding in it any thing against the fairness of the releases. The complainants do not give any proof against it. Nothing is in proof from which it can be inferred that they were given in ignorance of their rights in the estates of Benjamin S. Bynum and Mary Bynum when the releases were made, or that they were in any way circumvented by the respondent. Their testimony in the case is exclusively upon the community of gains,

and upon the inability of the respondent to make such purchases
and improvements from his own means.

It consists of copies of conveyances for the property bought,
of depositions, in which there is not a word relating to the releases, and of answers by the respondent to other suits against
him, one of which was a suit in equity brought by these complainants in the Circuit Court of the United States, in Louisiana.

In that answer may be found a narrative of the respondent's
business connection, and dealings with the estate of Benjamin
S. Bynum and that of his widow, afterwards the wife of the
respondent. It shows that he rendered an account of both.
That it was done in an open manner and with an intention that
it should be examined by those who were interested. It is
further shown, that after the accounts had been officially filed,
that there was a partition of all the property among the heirs,
and that it was consummated by receipts and acquittances
from all of them, among them those given by Ewing and his
wife, and by Fourniquet and his wife, as they have been already
recited in this opinion. The respondent also denies in that
answer the charge there made by these complainants, as it is
repeated in this suit, that these acquittances were obtained by
fraud, misrepresentation, and concealment, and avers that they
were executed by the parties with a full knowledge of all their
rights, and for a valuable consideration. In that case, as in this,
there was no proof that those receipts or releases were fraudulently obtained. The witnesses, Henderson, Montgomery, and
Walworth, in this suit, are not questioned as to the execution
of the releases. The same interrogations were put to all of
them. The answers of each are very immaterial for any purposes in this suit. No one of them knew any thing concerning
the respondent's pecuniary situation when he married, or when
he removed into Mississippi, or of the sources from which the
money came which was invested in Mississippi. The same
may be said of Wren's testimony. Loria's testimony is as
indefinite as that of the others, and he also was not questioned
concerning the execution of the releases. On the other hand,
the evidence produced by the respondent in this suit, shows that
the releases were not precipitately made. That neither of the
complainants gave them until after they had had time to examine
his accounts, and not until they had examined them. Whatever they may have thought of the integrity of the respondent,
they did not act then as if they suspected it. We see them
receiving from him their portions of the estates, of which they
were distributees, and other property besides, as gratuities from
the respondent, and dealing with both, among themselves and
with others, and acting towards the respondents as if they were

content with what he had done, and with what they had received.

There was an interval of five years and eleven months between the releases given by the complainants to the respondent. The accounts upon which they were given, were all that time accessible to them. The proofs show that Ewing had scanned them before he gave his release. His interest in the estates were the same as Fourniquet's. It was a family business, talked of, no doubt, among themselves, as such matters always will be, and it cannot be supposed that Fourniquet took his wife's portion of the estates without knowing that Ewing had given to the respondent a release when he took his wife's part, or without having had the same means as his associate to learn the condition of the estates, and the truthfulness of the respondent's official statement of them. Their acceptance of the portions of their wives must be taken as an admission that the respondent had dealt fairly in the business, and that he meant to do so, until they shall prove that it was his design to cheat all of the heirs, including his own children, as well as the wives of the complainants. He may not have acted in his long management of the estates, with all caution and exactness, but nothing has been shown in this case, in his final settlement with the heirs, that he did not mean to act with fairness and liberality, or that any one of them did not think he had done so, when they made these releases.

With the view of these releases, we think that the court erred in giving its interlocutory order for an account to be taken. We are relieved by it from considering the points which were made in the argument concerning any community of gains between the respondent and his wife. However that may have been, the releases put an end to all controversy between these parties about it. They were fully argued by counsel, as they should have been, as they could not foresee what would be our view upon the effect of the releases. We could not add any thing to the decisions of the courts of Louisiana upon connubial or legal communities of gains between husband and wife.

We are satisfied, whether it did or did not exist, that the releases given by the complainants are conclusive against them for any claim upon the respondent on account of the estates in which they were interested. No proof having been given that these releases were obtained by any fraud or circumvention, we shall order the decree of the court below to be reversed, and that the bill of the complainants shall be dismissed.

Mr. Justice CURTIS dissented.

Order.

This cause came on to be heard on the transcript of the record from the Circuit Court of the United States for the Southern District of Mississippi, and was argued by counsel. On consideration whereof, it is now here ordered, adjudged, and decreed by this court, that the decree of the said Circuit Court in this cause, be, and the same is. hereby, reversed, with costs, and that this cause be, and the same is hereby, remanded to the said Circuit Court, with directions to dismiss the complainant's bill.

JOHN PERKINS, APPELLANT, *v.* EDWARD P. FOURNIQUET, AND HARRIET, HIS WIFE.

The sixty-second rule of this court, (13 Howard,) is as follows: "In cases where a writ of error is prosecuted to the Supreme Court, and the judgment of the inferior court is affirmed, the interest shall be calculated and levied from the date of the judgment below, until the same is paid, at the same rate that similar judgments bear interest, in the courts of the State where such judgment is rendered. The same rule shall be applied to decrees for the payment of money, in cases in Chancery, unless otherwise ordered by this court. This rule to take effect on the first day of December term, 1852.

Before this rule, interest was to be calculated at six per cent., from the date of the judgment in the Circuit Court to the day of affirmance here; and the confirmation of the report of the clerk, in the case of Mitchell *v.* Harmony, (13 Howard, 149,) was under the rules then existing.

So, also, where a case from Mississippi was affirmed at December term, 1851, the mandate from this court should have been construed to allow interest at six per cent. from the date of the decree in the court below, to the date of the affirmance in this court. Therefore, it was erroneous either to allow six per cent. until paid, or to allow the current rate of interest in Mississippi, in addition to the six per cent. allowed by this court.

The several rules upon this subject examined and explained.

THIS was an appeal from the Circuit Court of the United States for the Southern District of Mississippi.

It is stated, in the report of the preceding case, that, at December term, 1851, a case of Fourniquet and wife, against Perkins, came up from Mississippi, and the decree of the Circuit Court was here affirmed by a divided court. It was, therefore, not reported.

The proceedings under the mandate, and the questions which arose thereon, are set forth in the following opinion of the court:

Mr. Chief Justice TANEY delivered the opinion of the court.

It appears, in this case, that on the 22d of May, 1849, the Circuit Court for the Southern District of Mississippi, passed a decree in favor of the appellees, against the appellant, directing him to pay the sum of $16,496.61, within thirty days thereafter, with legal interest from the date of the said decree, or, in default thereof, the appellees to have execution against the appellant.

This decree was affirmed at the last term of this court, with costs and damages, at the rate of six per cent. per annum; and a mandate issued to the Circuit Court reciting the judgment of this court, and directing it to be carried into execution.

After this mandate was filed in the Circuit Court, the appellees obtained an execution against the appellant, by which the marshal was commanded to levy the amount of the original judgment in the Circuit Court, with the Mississippi interest of eight per cent., and damages at the rate of six per cent. in addition, making together, fourteen per cent., from the date of' the original judgment, until paid.

The appellant insisted that, under the mandate, he was bound to pay nothing more than damages at the rate of six per cent. on the original decree, from the time it was rendered. And, acting upon this construction of the judgment of this court, and supposing himself chargeable with the six per cent. damages, until the decree was satisfied, he payed the marshal, on the 12th of May, 1852, the amount he supposed to be due, calculating the interest up to that time, and, by some error in the reckoning, he paid a small sum over. -And, as the appellees still insisted upon levying the whole amount for which they had obtained process of execution, he moved the Circuit Court to refer it to a Commissioner, to report the amount due under the judgment of this court, and how much, if any, he had overpaid in his settlement with the marshal. It was admitted that the costs were all paid. The only controversy was about the interest and damages, as above stated.

The commissioner reported that, according to the basis of settlement claimed by the appellant, he had overpaid the amount due on the decree, $61.50; but that, according to the construction of the mandate insisted on by the appellees, there was still due to them a balance of $3,831.02.

Upon this report, the appellant moved the court to order satisfaction of the decree to be entered of record; or, to quash the execution then in the hands of the marshal, and order the clerk of the court to issue no furthe *fi. fa.* on the decree; and, also, for an order on the marshal, or the appellees, as might be proper to refund the money overpaid.

But the court overruled the motion, ordering, at the same time, that no further execution should issue, until the appellant had a reasonable time to present an appeal to this court. And this appeal was accordingly taken.

An objection has-been made to the manner in which this case

28 *

has been brought before the court, and a motion made to dismiss, upon the ground that an appeal will not lie from this
decision of the Circuit Court.

This objection to the form of proceeding, involves nothing
more than a question of practice. The mandate from this
court left nothing to the judgment and discretion of the Circuit
Court, but directed it to carry into execution the decree of this
court, which was recited in the mandate. And if the decree of
this court has been misunderstood, or misconstrued, by the court
below, to the injury of either party, we see no valid objection to
an appeal to this court, in order to have the error corrected.
The question is merely as to the form of proceeding which this
court should adopt, to enforce the execution of its own mandate
in the court below. The subject might, without doubt, be
brought before us upon motion, and a mandamus issued to compel its execution. But an appeal from the decision of the court
below, is equally convenient and suitable; and, perhaps, more
so, in some cases, as it gives the adverse party notice that the
question will be brought before this court, and affords him the
opportunity of being prepared to meet it at an early day of the
term. The appeal certainly would not stay proceedings. And
it would be the duty of the Circuit Court, notwithstanding the
appeal, to proceed to execute the judgment of this court, unless,
as in this case, he entertained doubts of its construction and
meaning, and deemed it, therefore, just and equitable to suspend
its execution, until the decision of this court could be had in
the premises.

In the case before us, however, there was substantially an
equity proceeding and final decree, after the mandate was filed.
It is true, they were summary, and necessarily so, as the matters
in dispute under the execution were brought before the court by
motion. But the claims of the respective parties were referred
to a Commissioner to examine and report ; he made his report,
and the court decided upon it. This decision, although briefly
stated, was, in substance, a final decree upon the matters in
controversy. It might, therefore, under the act of Congress, be
regarded as such, and revised accordingly, by an appeal to this
court. Plenary and formal proceedings are not necessary, and
never required, when the dispute is confined to matters arising
under process of execution. They are more conveniently and
as fully brought before the court, by a summary proceeding on
motion.

The questions in controversy in the Circuit Court, and its
decision upon them, are, therefore regularly before us.

The difficulty in that court, seems to have arisen from supposing that the act of 1842 applied to judgments and decrees in

this court. And this, we presume, occasioned the error it committed, in the construction and execution of the decree and mandate in question.

The act of 1842 does not embrace cases in equity; nor does it extend to either judgments or decrees, in this court. It is confined, in plain terms, to judgments at law, in the circuit and district courts. It places the judgments of these courts, in respect to interest, upon the same footing with the judgments of the State courts. And where, by the law of the State, the judgment of a court carries a certain interest until paid, the former rule and the same rate of interest is to be allowed in the circuit and district courts of the United States. And the marshall is directed to levy it on process of execution, wherever it can be so levied on a judgment in the State Court. In such cases the judgment bears interest by force of the law, although, upon the face of it, it may not purport to carry interest. Upon common-law principles a judgment does not carry interest. It is true, that damages may be recovered for the detention of the debt, in an action on the judgment. But previous to the act of 1842, neither interest nor damages, for the detention of the debt, could have been levied under process of execution, upon the judgment of a circuit or district court of the United States.

But the act of 1842, does not speak of interest or damages upon the judgments of this court, nor does it repeal the 23d section of the act of 1789. This section provides, that when a judgment or decree is affirmed here, this court is directed to adjudge or decree to the respondent in error, just damages for his delay, and single or double costs, at their discretion. Under this law there is no distinction made between cases in equity, and at law. In either of them, the damages to be allowed, in addition to the amount found to be due by the judgment or decree of the court below, is confided to the judicial discretion of this court. And the 17th, 18th, and 20th rules were adopted in pursuance of this power.

These rules have been in force, and acted on by the court, since 1807, when the 20th rule was adopted, until the new rule upon this subject was made at the close of the last term. And the change then made was not occasioned by any supposed repugnancy between them and the act of 1842. But because the court deemed it just to place the judgments in this court upon the same footing with the judgments in the circuit and district courts; and that suitors in the courts of the United States, should stand on the same ground with suitors in the State courts in its appellate, as well as in its inferior tribunals. In adopting the new rule this court exercised the same power which it had exercised in adopting the former rules, that is, the discretionary power conferred by the act of 1789, as hereinbefore mentioned.

The 17th rule provides, that when a case appears to be brought merely for delay, damages shall be awarded at the rate of ten per cent. on the amount of the judgment; and by the 18th rule, the damages are to be at the rate of six per cent. when it appears that there is a real controversy.

These two rules were passed in 1803. And as some difficulty arose as to the time for which these damages were to be computed, the 23d rule was afterwards (1807) adopted, and provides, that the damages allowed by the two former rules shall be calculated to the day of the affirmance of the judgment in this court.

The question as to the operation of the act of 1842, upon the 18th and 20th rules, was brought to the consideration of the court at the last term, in the case of Mitchell v. Harmony. The judgment brought up by the writ of error, was rendered in the Circuit Court of New York, and was affirmed in this court. The sum recovered was large, and the interest, even for a short time, was therefore important. And the counsel for Harmony, the defendant in error, moved the court to allow him the New York interest of seven per cent. upon the amount of the judgment, and that the interest should run until the judgment was paid. But as the rules above mentioned were still in force, the court held, that he was entitled only to six per cent., to be calculated from the date of the judgment in the Circuit Court, to the day of affirmance here.

The case now before us, was decided in the early part of the last term, before the case of Mitchell v. Harmony, and consequently falls within the operation of the same rules, and damages upon the affirmance of the decree must be calculated in like manner.

Indeed, in the New York case, the claim for interest stood on stronger ground than in the present one, for that was an action at law. The act of 1842, therefore, applied to the judgment in the Circuit Court, and it would have carried the State interest until paid, if it had not been brought here by writ of error. But this is a decree in equity, and not embraced in the act of 1842, and according to the settled chancery practice, no interest or damages could have been levied under process of execution, upon the amount ascertained to be due, and decreed to be paid, if there had been no appeal; 2 Ves. 157, 168, n. 1, Sumn. Ed.; 2 Dan. Chan. Plead. and Prac. 1442, 1437, 1438. Nor could any damages or interest have been given on its affirmance here, but for the discretionary power vested in this court by the act of 1789 That discretion, as we have already said, extends to decrees in equity, as well as judgments at law. And the rules have always been applied to both, unless otherwise specially ordered.

It follows, from what we have said, that the appellees, upon the affirmance of the decree, were entitled to damages at the rate of six per cent., to be calculated from the date of the decree to the date of the affirmance; and to no 'further interest or damages. The decree was passed by the Circuit Court, on the 22d day of May, 1849, for $16,496.61, and was affirmed in this court on the 24th of December, 1851. The interest from the date of the decree to the time of affirmance in this court, is $2,562.37, making together the aggregate sum of $19,058.98. This amount, together with the costs, is all that the appellees were entitled to recover under the judgment and mandate of this court. It appears, however, that the marshal has received, under the process of execution, $19,500, in addition to the costs, and paid it over to the solicitor of the appellees.

They have, therefore, received $441.02 more than they were entitled, and that sum must be refunded to the appellant.

It is proper to say, that the mandate in question was in the usual form, and the same with the mandate in Mitchel v. Harmony, and indeed the same that has been used since the adoption of the rules above mentioned. And it never has been supposed by this court to sanction the collection of State interest on the judgment; and still less the unprecedented interest and damages claimed in this case, amounting together to fourteen per cent.

The decree of the Circuit Court, overruling the motion of the appellant, must therefore be reversed, and a mandate issued, directing the court below to enter the decree satisfied, and also to order and direct the appellees to repay to the appellant the sum of $441.02, with the State interest thereon of eight per cent. from the time it was received by their solicitor from the marshal.

Order.

This cause came on to be heard on the transcript of the record from the Circuit Court of the United States for the Southern District of Mississippi, and was argued by counsel. On consideration whereof, it is ordered, adjudged, and decreed, that the decree of the Circuit Court overruling the motion of the appellant, be, and the same is hereby, reversed, with costs, and that this cause be, and the same is hereby, remanded to the said Circuit Court, with instructions to that court to enter the decree rendered by that court on the 22d day of May, A. D. 1849, for $16,496.61, with legal interest from said date, satisfied, and to order and direct the appellees to repay to the appellant the sum of $441.02, with the State interest thereon, of eight per cent. from the time it was received by their solicitor from the marshal.

BENJAMIN D. HARRIS, PLAINTIFF IN ERROR, v. WILLIAM HARDE-MAN, HENRY R. W. HILL, COTESWORTH P. SMITH, AND HENRY A. MOORE.

A statute of Mississippi directs that where the defendant cannot be found, a writ of *capias ad respondendum* shall be served, by leaving a copy thereof with the wife of the defendant, or some free white person above the age of sixteen years, then and there being one of the family of the defendant, and found at his usual place of abode, or leaving a copy thereof at some public place, at the dwelling-house or other known place of residence of such defendant, he being from home, and no such free white person being found there willing to receive the same.

The Circuit Court of the United States adopted a rule that the *capias* should be served personally, or, if the defendant be not found, by leaving a copy thereof at his or her residence, or usual place of abode, at least twenty days before the return day thereof.

The marshal made the following return to a writ of *capias:* "Executed on the defendant Hardeman, by leaving a true copy at his residence."

This service was neither in conformity with the statute nor the rule.

Therefore, when the court gave judgment, by default, against Hardeman, and an execution was issued, upon which a forthcoming bond was given, and another execution issued, and at a subsequent day the court quashed the proceedings, and set aside the judgment by default, this order was correct.

When the judgment by default was given, the court was not in a condition to exercise jurisdiction over the defendant, because there was no regular service of process, actual or constructive.

The cases upon this point, examined.

Moreover, when the proceedings were quashed, they were still in *fieri*, and not terminated; and any irregularity could be corrected, on motion.

THIS case was brought up, by writ of error, from the Circuit Court of the United States for the Southern District of Mississippi.

The facts are stated in the opinion of the court.

It was argued by *Mr. Nelson* for the plaintiff in error, and *Mr. Freeman* for the defendant.

Mr. Nelson contended that the judgment of the court below was erroneous, and referred to the following authorities.

To show that the bond was regularly taken under the Mississippi statute. Hutch. Code, 910, Art. 6, sec. 2; Howard & Hutch. 653, sec. 78.

The ground of the motion made by the defendants in error, in the court below, was, that the original judgment was void for want of notice; and that being void, the process issued upon it and the bond taken under that process, were nullities.

It may be true that the return of the service of notice was insufficient. Smith v. Cohen, 3 Howard, (Miss.) 35; Tomlinson v. Hoyt, 1 Smedes & Marsh. 515; Eskridge v. Jones, Id. 595.

But that was matter to be considered and passed upon by the court rendering the judgment. Fatheree v. Long, 5 Howard, (Miss.) 661; Smith v. Bradley, 6 Smedes & Marsh. 492.

Besides, the defendants were estopped, by the execution of the bond, from denying the validity of the judgment and the execution. Bank U. S. v. Patton, 5 Howard, (Miss.) 200; Miller v. Patten, 3 Smedes & Marsh. 463; Keringham v. Scanland, 6 Howard, (Miss.) 540; Field v. Morse, 1 Smedes & Marsh. 347; Conn v. Pender, 2 Smedes & Marsh. 386; Pender v. Felton, 2 Id. 535; Clowe v. Tharpe, 3 Id. 64; McCoul v. Ellet, 8 Id. 505.

The bond was regularly forfeited. Barker v. The Planters Bank, 5 Howard, (Miss.) 566; Puckett v. Graves, 6 Smedes & Marsh. 384; Talbert v. Melton, 9 Id. 9; Dowd v. Hunt, 10 Id. 414.

And the forfeiture of the bond extinguished the original judgment. Davis v. Dixon, 1 Howard, (Miss.) 64; Weathersby v. Proby, Id. 98; Witherspoon v. Spring, 3 Id. 60; Binny v. Stanton, 2 Smedes & Marsh. 457.

Moreover, the return was in conformity with the rule of court.

To show the validity of said rule, the plaintiff in error relied upon the act of Congress of the 24th September, 1789, sec. 34, (Laws U. S. vol. 1, 93); Act of 2d March, 1793, sec. 7, (Laws U. S. vol. 1, 335); Act of 19th May, (Laws U. S. vol. 4, 279); Wayman v. Southard, 10 Wheaton, 1; Beers v. Haughton, 9 Peters, 330, 360, 361; Fullerton v. Bank U. S. 1 Peters, Sup. Ct. Rep. 612; Williams v. Bank U. S. 2 Id. 96; Amiss v. Smith, 16 Peters, 303.

Mr. Freeman, for defendant in error.

In this case, a motion was made in the court below, to quash the forthcoming bond, and vacate the original judgment. It was sustained upon the ground of the judgment being a nullity, there having been no service of process upon Hardeman, and no appearance entered for him.

It will be conceded, that if there be no notice, actual or constructive, the judgment is a nullity. 4 Peters's Rep. 474; 2 Yerger's Rep. 484; 11 Wendell's Rep. 652; 15 Johnson's Rep. 141; 1 Smedes & Marshall's (Miss.) Rep. 351. There was no "actual service" of process on Hardeman, as is shown by the marshal's return. Did he have constructive notice? The statute of Mississippi provides, when the defendant is not found, that constructive service may be made, and points out the mode. Howard & Hutchinson's Dig. 583, sec. 27. The statute was not complied with in executing the writ in this case. It was served by leaving a copy at defendant's residence. And is not even dated. In construing this statute, the court of last resort in Mississippi, have several times held such service to be bad. As, for example, in the case of Smith v. Cohea, (3 Howard's Miss. Rep. 35,) it is held that a return on a writ "executed by leaving a copy at the boarding-house of the defendant," is insufficient. So, also, in the case of Fatheree v. Long, (5 Howard's Miss. Rep. 661,) it is held that the return "executed by leaving a copy at the defendant's house," is bad. And the court goes on to say, that when the service is not personal, the return must show that the requirements of the statute were complied with. A similar exposition of the statute was given in the cases of Tomlinson v. Hoyt, and Eskridge v. Jones, 1 Smedes & Marshall's Rep. 515 and 595.

Had this motion been made at the term next succeeding that at which the judgment was rendered, no one would doubt Hardeman's right to the relief sought by it. Does the giving and forfeiture of the forthcoming bond, and the lapse of time, bar his right?

It is believed that if the giving and forfeiture of the forthcoming bond does not bar, the mere lapse of time cannot. For there is no time limited by the statute within which such a motion may be made. That the giving and forfeiture of the forthcoming bond interpose no obstacle to the motion, is clear. It is true, the court of last resort in Mississippi, has frequently decided that a motion to quash a forthcoming bond, must be made at the term to which it is returnable. 6 Howard's Miss. Rep. 540; 1 Smedes & Marshall's Rep. 347; Id. 386. Yet the same court has held that when the judgment is absolutely void for want of jurisdiction in the court rendering it, either of the subject-matter, or over the parties, the forthcoming bond is absolutely void also, and subject to be quashed, on motion, at any time, either at, or subsequent to the return term. Buckingham v. Bailey, 4 Smedes & Marshall's Rep. 538.

A stronger reason may be added in this court. Here the forthcoming bond is treated and considered as part of the process of the court. 16 Peters's Rep. 312, 313. In this case, that process is founded upon a judgment confessedly void. The court can always control its own process; and will never permit void writs to be issued and executed, when brought to its attention. And it can make no difference whether the effort to resist the issuance and execution of such process is made within one, or after a lapse of ten years, from the date of the void judgment.

A rule of court, adopted by the District Judge, (Judge Adams,) is relied on to show that the execution of the process upon Hardeman, was sufficient. Upon this, I remark:

1. That even if the rule be valid, the service is not good, for it has no date; and it does not appear, therefore, that it was executed "fifteen days" before court, so as to give jurisdiction of the person.

2. The District Judge has no power to adopt such a rule. 16 Peters's Rep. 314. The decision of the Circuit Court should therefore be affirmed.

Mr. Justice DANIEL delivered the opinion of the court.

The defendants in error moved the Circuit Court to quash a forthcoming bond, executed by the defendants to the plaintiff; and to set aside the judgment on which the bond was founded, upon the grounds that the forthcoming bond was taken in execution of a judgment entered against the defendant Hardeman, as by default, when in truth there had been no service of original or mesne process upon him to warrant such a judgment. The facts and proceedings in this case, as disclosed by the record, are as follow: The plaintiff in error, in March, 1839, instituted in the Circuit Court an action on a promissory note against the defendant and three others; and upon the writ sued out in that action, the marshal, on the 9th of April, made a return in these words: "Executed on the defendant Hardeman, by leaving a true copy at his residence." Upon this return of the officer, at the next succeeding or return term of the court, in May, 1839, a judgment by default for want of appearance, was taken against the defendant Hardeman for the amount of the note, with interest and costs. Amongst other proceedings upon this judgment, a writ of *fieri facias* was sued out in March, 1840, was levied on sundry slaves, the property of Hardeman, and the forthcoming bond in question executed by him on the 20th of April, 1840. In pursuance of this forthcoming bond another *fieri facias* was sued out on the 11th of June, 1840, and upon this last writ was indorsed on the 8th of October, 1840, a *cessat executio* by the plaintiff's attorney.

By the statute of Mississippi regulating proceedings in courts of law, the following modes for the service of process in certain cases, are prescribed: "All writs of *scire facias* and *capias ad respondendum*, where no bail is required, may be served in the following manner: Where the defendant cannot be found, it shall be deemed sufficient service of such writ for the sheriff or other officer to whom the same is directed, to leave a copy thereof with the wife of the defendant or some free white person above the age of sixteen years, then and there being one of the family of the defendant, and found at his usual place of abode, or to leave a copy thereof at some public place at the dwelling-house, or other known place of residence of such defendant, he being from home, and no such free white person being found there willing to receive the same."

On the 18th of June, 1838, the District Judge for the Southern District of Mississippi, in the absence of the circuit or presiding Judge, caused to be entered on the minutes of the Circuit Court, as a rule of proceeding in that court, an order in the following words, viz., ." The *capias ad respondendum* shall be served by arresting the defendant, unless bail be waived ; or where bail be waived, or a summons shall issue, the same shall be served personally, or if the defendant be not found, by leaving a copy thereof at his or her residence, or usual place of abode, at least twenty days before the return day thereof, to entitle the plaintiff to á trial or judgment by default at the return term."

The action in this case was commenced by a summons, and the marshal's return of the service of that process, and the judgment thereupon by default at the return term, and the subsequent proceedings upon that judgment, were as have been already stated.

Upon the application of the defendant Hardeman, at the May term of the Circuit Court, in the year 1850, until which time the proceedings in this case had been stayed, the court quashed the forthcoming bond and *fieri facias* sued out thereon, and set aside the judgment purporting to be a judgment by default against the defendant, as being unwarranted upon the face of the proceedings, and therefore void.

In reviewing the decision of the Circuit Court, it should be borne in mind, as a rule to guide and control our examination, that the judgment impugned before that court was a judgment by default, and that in all judgments by default, whatever may affect their competency or regularity, every proceeding indeed, from the writ and indorsements thereon, down to the judgment itself, inclusive, is part of the record, and is open to examination. That such cases differ essentially, in this respect, from those in which there is an appearance and a *contestatio litis*, in which the parties have elected the grounds on which they choose to place the controversy, expressly or impliedly waiving all others. In support of the rule just stated, many authorities might be adduced ; we cite for it the cases of Nadenbush v. Lane, 4 Ran. 413, and of Wainwright v. Harper, 3 Leigh, 270.

Within the scope of this rule, two inquiries present themselves in connection with the decision of the Circuit Court. The first is this, whether the court in which the judgment by default was taken, ever had jurisdiction as to the defendant, so as to warrant the judgment entered against him by default. And the second inquiry is, whether, upon the hypothesis that the court had not jurisdiction of the person of the defendant, and that the judgment against him was not binding, it was competent for the Circuit Court, in the mode adopted by it, to set aside the judgment, and to quash the proceedings consequent thereupon.

In reference to the first inquiry, it would seem to be a legal truism, too palpable to be elucidated by argument, that no person can be bound by a judgment, or any proceeding conducive thereto, to which he never was party or privy; that no person can be in default with respect to that which it never was incumbent upon him to fulfil. The court entering such judgment by default could have no jurisdiction over the person as to render such personal judgment, unless, by summons or other process, the person was legally before it. A court may be authorized to exert its powers in reference either to persons or things — may have jurisdiction either *in personam*, or *in rem*, and the existence of that jurisdiction, as well as the modes of its exercise, may vary materially in reference to the subject-matter to which it attaches. Nay, they may be wholly inconsistent; or at any rate, so much so, as not to be blended or confounded. This distinction has been recognized in a variety of decisions, in which it has been settled, that a judgment depending upon proceedings *in personam* can have no force as to one on whom there has been no service of process, actual or constructive; who has had no day in court, and no notice of any proceeding against him. That with respect to such a person, such a judgment is absolutely void; he is no party to it, and can no more be regarded as a party than can any and every other member of the community. As amply sustaining these conclusions of law, as well as of reason and common sense, we refer to the following decisions. In Borden v. Fitch, (15 Johnson's Rep. 141,) Thompson, Chief Justice, says: " To give any binding effect to a judgment, it is essential that the court should have jurisdiction of the person and the subject-matter; and the want of jurisdiction is a matter that may always be set up against a judgment when sought to be enforced, or where any benefit is claimed under it. The want of jurisdiction makes it utterly void and unavailable for any purpose. The cases in the English courts, and in those of our sister States, are very strong to show that judicial proceedings against a person not served with process to appear, and not being within the jurisdiction of the court, and not appearing in person or by attorney, are null and void. In Buchanan v. Rucker, (9 East, 192,) the Court of King's Bench declared that the law would not raise an assumpsit upon a judgment obtained in the Island of Tobago by default, when it appeared upon the face of the proceedings that the defendant was not in the island when the suit was commenced, and that he had been summoned by nailing a copy of the declaration on the court-house door. The court said it would have made no difference in the case if the proceedings had been admitted to be valid in the Island of Tobago. In the Supreme Court of Massachusetts, Chief Justice Parsons, in Bissell v. Briggs, 9 Mass. Rep. 464, lays down the principle very clearly and distinctly, that before the adoption of the Constitution of the United States, and in reference to foreign judgments, it was competent to show that the court had no jurisdiction of the cause; and if so, the judgment, if set up as a justification for any act, would be rejected without inquiring into its merits.' After citing a number of cases, the learned Judge proceeds to say: " We have refused to sustain an action here upon a judgment in another State, where the suit was commenced by attachment, and no personal summons or actual notice given to the defendant, he not being at the time of the attachment, within the State. In such cases, we have considered the proceedings as *in rem*, and only binding the goods attached, and the judgment having no force *in personam*. This principle is not considered as growing out of any thing peculiar to proceedings by attachment, but is founded on more enlarged and general principles." It is said by the court, " that to bind a defendant personally by a judgment, when he was never personally summoned, nor had notice of the proceedings, would be contrary to the first principles of justice."

It is worthy of notice, in this place, that the cases from 9 East, and 9 Massachusetts Reports, cited by Chief Justice Thompson, were not instances in which the validity of those judgments was examined upon appeal or writ of error, but were instances in which that validity was inquired into collaterally, before other tribunals in which they were adduced as evidence to sustain other issues there pending.

In the case of Starbuck v. Murray, 5 Wendell, 156, the Supreme Court of New York say: " The courts of Connecticut, Pennsylvania, New Hampshire, New Jersey, and Kentucky, have also decided, that the jurisdiction of the court rendering a judgment, may be inquired into, when a suit is brought in the courts of another State, on that judgment;" and, after citing the cases of Thurber v. Blackburne, (1 New Hampshire Reports, 246); Benton v. Bengot, (10 Sergeant & Rawle, 240); Aldrech v. Henney, (4 Conn. Rep. 280); Curtis v. Gibbs, (Pa. Rep. 405,) they say: "This doctrine does not depend merely upon adjudged cases; it has a better foundation; it rests upon a principle of natural justice. No man is to be condemned without the opportunity of making a defence, or to have his property taken from him by a judicial sentence, without the privilege of showing, if he can, the claim against him to be unfounded." The court then proceed to say, "But it is contended, that if other matter may be pleaded by the defendant, he is estopped from asserting any thing against the allegation contained in the record. It imports perfect verity, it is said, and the parties to it cannot be heard to impeach it. It appears to me, that this proposition assumes the very fact to be established, which is the only question in issue. For what purpose does the defendant question the jurisdiction of the court? Solely to show that its proceedings and judgment are void, and, therefore, the supposed record is, in truth, no record. If the defendant had not proper notice of, and did not appear to, the original action, all the State courts, with one exception, agree in opinion, that the paper introduced as to him, is no record, but, if he cannot show, even against the pretended record, that fact, on the alleged ground of the uncontrollable verity of the record, he is deprived of his defence, by a process of reasoning that, to my mind, is little less than sophistry. The plaintiffs, in effect, declare to the defendant—the paper declared on is a record, because it says you appeared; and you appeared, because the paper is a record. This is reasoning in a circle. The appearance makes the record uncontrollable verity, and the record makes the appearance an unimpeachable fact. Unless a court has jurisdiction, it can never make a record which imports uncontrollable verity to the party over whom it has usurped jurisdiction, and he ought not, therefore, to be estopped from proving any fact which goes to establish the truth of a plea alleging the want of jurisdiction."

By the same court, this doctrine is affirmed, in the case of Holbrook v. Murray, 5 Wendell, 161. In the case of Denning v. Corwin & Roberts, 11 Wendell, 648, it was ruled, "That a judgment in partition, under the statute, where part of the premises belonged to owners unknown, was not valid, unless it appear, upon the face of the record, that the affidavit required by the statute, that the petitioner, or plaintiff in partition, is ignorant of the names, rights, or titles of such owners, was duly presented to the court, and that the notice, also, required in such cases, was duly published." And Chief Justice Savage, in delivering the opinion of the court, said: "On the part of the plaintiff, it is contended that the judgment in partition is void, for want of jurisdiction in the court, the requirements of the statute not having been complied with; and, on the part of the

defendants, it is insisted that it is conclusive until reversed o
set aside, that it cannot be attacked collaterally, and that the
defendants, being *bonâ fide* purchasers, are entitled to protection. That a judgment is conclusive upon parties and privies,
is a proposition not to be denied; but if a court has acted without jurisdiction, the proceeding is void, and if this appear on
the face of the record, the whole is a nullity." After quoting
the opinion of Chief Justice Thompson, in Borden v. Fitch,
15 Johnson, 121, Chief Justice Savage goes on to say : ". With
respect to the proceedings in partition, now the subject of consideration, there can be no doubt that the court, in which the
judgment was rendered, had jurisdiction of the subject of
partition ; but, to authorize a judgment of partition, the parties
must be before the court, or it must be shown to the court that
some of them are unknown ; and this must appear by the record,
where the proceeding is against owners unknown ; it is a proceeding *in rem*, and nothing is to be taken by intendment. There
is avowedly nothing like personal notice to the parties interested
as defendants; they are not even named; and the right of the
plaintiff depends entirely upon the fact, to be proved by affidavit,
that the owners are unknown." The Chief Justice, after showing the insufficiency, by proof of the affidavit, according to the
requisition of the statute, says : " The record then states, that at
a subsequent day the plaintiffs appear, by their attorney, and
the parties unknown being solemnly demanded, come not, but
make default. The statute gives the court no jurisdiction to
take any steps against unknown owners, until notice has been
published according to the statute. Should not the record,
therefore, show that it had been made to appear to the court, by
affidavit, that the owners were unknown to the plaintiffs, and
that such notice as the statute requires, had actually been given?
Suppose a judgment record is produced, in which the plaintiff
declares upon a promissory note, and the record does not show
that the defendant is in custody, or has been served with process, and yet the court render judgment by default, would not
such a record be an absolute nullity?" In the case of Wilson
et al. v. The Bank of Mount Pleasant, reported in the 6th of
Leigh, Tucker, President of the court, thus announces the law:
" This is an action upon a judgment of the State of Ohio,
which, it is contended, is conclusive in the courts of Virginia,
upon the principles of the Constitution of the United States.
It is unnecessary, in this case, to go into the question of the
construction of that clause of the federal compact which relates
to the, effect of judicial proceedings of the several States in
other States, for it seems to be agreed, on all hands, that the
doctrine of the conclusiveness of the judgments of the several

States, is to be taken with the qualification, that, where the court has no jurisdiction over the subject-matter, or the person, or where the defendant has no notice of this suit, or was never served with process, and never appeared to the action, the judgment will be esteemed of no validity." With this doctrine entirely agrees another doctrine of the Supreme Court of Virginia, in the case of Wynn v. Wyat's Admr', 11 Leigh, 584, in which last case the court say, "That the appearance ot the defendant, in term, and his motion to quash the attachment irregularly issued, and to set aside the proceedings at the rules, founded upon it, was not an appearance to the action, dispensing with farther and proper process; that the award of the *alias* summons was proper and necessary; and that the proceedings on that subsequent process cannot be sustained, since, confessedly, it was not duly served." But the decision which should be decisive upon the question now before us, is a decision of this court, in the case of Hollingsworth v. Barbour et al., in the 4th of Peters, p. 466. That was a case exhibiting the following features. A title had been made to land, by deed from a Commissioner, acting under a decree in Chancery, in the State Court in Kentucky, in which the "unknown heirs" of a person from whom title was deduced, were made defendants, and the decree, as against those heirs, was taken by default, after order of publication. The grantee of the Commissioner filed his bill, to obtain possession of the lands, against various persons who had taken possession thereof. The Circuit Court of the United States dismissed the bill, upon the grounds that, at the date of the proceedings in the State Court, (under which the conveyance of the Commissioner purported to have been made,) there was no law of the State authorizing those proceedings against the unknown heirs of the original owner of the land, and the decree taken upon those proceedings, by default against them, and, as they never had personal notice of the suit, the decree by default and the title made by the Commissioner, were null, as respected either those heirs, or the persons in possession of the lands. The very lucid argument of Mr. Justice Trimble, in the Circuit Court, which was adopted literally and *in extenso*, by this court, is too long for insertion here, but one or two of the conclusions reached by him, and affirmed by this court, in the words of that Judge, may be noticed. "The principle," said that Judge, and said this court in confirmation, "is too well settled, and too plain to be controverted, that a judgment or decree, pronounced by a competent tribunal, against a party having actual, or constructive notice, of the pending of the suit, is to be regarded by every other coordinate tribunal, and that, if the judgment or decree be erroneous, the erro. can be corrected only by a supreme appellate tribunal. The leading distinction is between judgments and decrees merely void, and such as are voidable only. The former are binding nowhere, the latter everywhere, until reversed by a superior authority. The suit and decree are against the unknown heirs of John Abel Hamblin. Instead of personal service of process upon the defendants in the suit, an order of publication was made against them; and, upon a certificate of the publication of this order, for eight weeks, in an unauthorized newspaper, being produced and filed in the cause, the bill was taken *pro confesso*, and, at the next succeeding term, the final decree was entered, directing the conveyance of the land to the complainant. Again, that Judge and this court speaking through him, say: " It would seem that the court acted without authority, and that the decree is void, for want of jurisdiction in the court. But if not void as being *coram non judice*, it is void and wholly ineffectual to bind or prejudice the rights of Hamlin's heirs, against whom the decree was rendered, because they had no notice, either actual or constructive. The principle of the rule, that decrees and judgments bind only parties and privies, applies to the case; for, though the unknown heirs of Hamlin are affected to be made parties in the bill, there was no service of process, nor any equivalent, to bring them before the court, so as to make them, in the eye of the law and justice, parties to the suit." Here, again, it should be borne in mind, that this is not an instance of reversal by an appellate tribunal, for error or irregularity in an inferior court, but a test, collaterally applied by an independent authority, to the character of proceedings, as void or voidable in their nature.

At this point it is proper to advert to the character and effect of the process in the suit of Harris and Hardeman, as constituting service upon the defendants in that suit, and thereby investing the court with jurisdiction over their rights. If the rule prescribed by the statute of Mississippi, already referred to, is to govern in this case, it is presumed that a doubt will, or can hardly be raised as to the insufficiency of the service, as there are not less than three instances in which the requisites of the statute have not been complied with. In the first place, it is not shown, by the return, that the defendant could not be found, which should have been shown, in order to justify the substitution of any other in lieu of personal service. Secondly, it is not shown that a copy of the process was left, either with the wife of the defendant, or with some other free white person above the age of sixteen years, being one of the family of the defendant. Thirdly, it is not stated or proved that a copy was left at some public place of the dwelling-house of the defendant,

he being from home, and no free white person, as above described, being found there, willing to receive the process. But
it has been contended, that by a rule adopted by the Judge of
the District Court, a mode for the service of process has been
prescribed, differing from that ordained by the statute of Mississippi, and dispensing with several of the requisites insisted on
by the statute, and that the service in the suit in the Circuit
Court was in conformity with the rule of the District Judge.
Forbearing, for the present, any inquiry as to the validity of the
rule made by the District Judge, under the decision of this
court, in the case of Amis v. Smith, 16 Peters, 303, we proceed to compare the proof of service as apparent upon the return of the marshal, with the requirements of the rule in question. This rule has been already quoted. The return of the
marshal has also been given *tolidem verbis*. It will be seen
that the reason assigned in the rule, as forming the justification
for dispensing with personal service, is not stated in the return
of the officer, and there is an entire omission to give the date or
time preceding the term of the court to which the process was
returnable, so as to show that the plaintiff was authorized to
take a judgment by default, in virtue of a legal constructive
notice, and a failure of appearance. Whether, therefore, the
statute of Mississippi, or the rule made by the District Judge,
be regarded as operative, there was, in the suit in the Circuit
Court, neither notice by personal service of process, nor notice
by legal construction. The judgment by default, therefore,
must be regarded as obnoxious to every impeachment of its
efficacy which can flow from its having been entered against
one who was never a party in court, with respect to the proceedings upon which that judgment was taken. But there is
another view of the questions raised in this cause, which is
equally, or even more conclusive in favor of the decision now
under review. At the time of the motion to the Circuit Court
to quash the forthcoming bond and to set aside the judgment
by default, that judgment was still unsatisfied, and was in the
progress of execution, and the forthcoming bond, filed in the
clerk's office, according to the laws of the State, was properly
a part of the process of execution, the *fieri facias* being sued
out therein from the office without any order of the court. The
proceedings then, still being as it were *in fieri*, and not terminated, it was competent for the court to rectify any irregularity
which might have occurred in the progress of the cause, and
to do this either by writ of error *coram vobis*, or by *audita querela* if the party choose to resort to the latter mode. If this
position be maintainable, then, there would seem to be an entire
removal of all exception to the judgment of the Circuit Court,

as it is believed to be the settled modern practice, that in all instances in which irregularities could formerly be corrected upon a writ of error *coram vobis* or *audita querela*, the same objects may be effected by motion to the court, as a mode more simple, more expeditious, and less fruitful of difficulty and expense. In this case the cause was still under the control and correction of the court, for the enforcement of its judgment and the supervision of its own process, and in the exercise of this function, it was competent for it to look back upon the entire progress of the case, up to the writ and indorsements thereon, under the rule already stated, as applicable to judgments by default, and to correct any irregularities which might be detected. In the present case there is less show of objection to such action, on the part of the court, as it affects the rights of no third parties, but is limited in its consequences to the parties to the suit only. We order the judgment of the Circuit Court to be affirmed.

Mr. Justice McLEAN, Mr. Justice WAYNE, and Mr. Justice GRIER, dissented.

Order.

This cause came on to be heard on the transcript of the record from the Circuit Court of the United States for the Southern District of Mississippi, and was argued by counsel. On consideration whereof, it is now here ordered and adjudged by this court, that the judgment of the said Circuit Court, on the motion to quash the forthcoming bond and to set aside the original judgment as set forth in the record of this cause, be and the same is hereby, affirmed with costs.

NATHANIEL HOYT AND JAMES BLANDIN, ADMINISTRATORS, &c., AND THE SAID JAMES BLANDIN, WILLIAM M. HUDSON, AND JOSEPHINE, HIS WIFE, HEIRS OF ANTOINE BLANDIN, DECEASED, AND ELISHA M. PEASE, APPELLANTS, *v.* GEORGE S. HAMMEKIN, AND ADELAIDE MATILDA, HIS WIFE.

Where a title to land in the State of Coahuila and Texas was obtained in 1833, by a mother for, and in the name of her daughter, and, in 1836, the father of the daughter conveyed it away by a deed executed in Louisiana, this deed was properly set aside by the District Court of Texas.
It was not executed either according to the laws of Louisiana, or those of Coahuila and Texas.

Mr. Justice Curtis was necessarily absent when this case was considered and decided.

· This was an appeal from the District Court of the United States for the District of Texas. ·

The facts are stated in the opinion of the court.

It was argued by *Mr. Allen*, for the appellant, with whom was *Mr.·Hale*, and by *Mr. Hughes*, for the appellee.

Mr. Justice McLEAN delivered the opinion of the court.

This is an appeal in Chancery, from the District Court of the United States for the District of Texas.

The bill alleges, that the States of Coahuila and Texas, on the 23d of November, 1833, granted eleven leagues of land, on the River Navasota, in the department of Nacogdoches, and of the value of fifty thousand dollars, to Adelaide Matilda Mexia; that on the 10th of February, 1836, her father, Antonio Mexia, upon some supposed necessity of having the legal title vested in a citizen of said State, and without consideration, sold and conveyed the land to John A. Merle, by authentic act before a notary public of Louisiana, and not according to any law in Texas, or in the State of Coahuila and Texas; and that the said Merle, by a like authentic act, declared that the said land was purchased by him with the funds of Antonio Blandin; that the said Antonio died intestate; that Nathaniel Hoyt and James Blandin have been appointed administrators of his succession, and that Josephine Hudson and James Blandin are his heirs at law; that the said Adelaide Matilda owns the same in her own right, but that the administrators and heirs of Blandin claim the same by descent.

An amended bill represents, that Antonio Blandin, ancestor of defendants, before his death, in order to carry out the trust created by the sale to him, and to prevent the land from being subject to his debts, and that the title might be vested in a resident of Texas, he expecting to be absent, without consideration or consent of complainants, conveyed all his right and interest in the land to Elisha M. Pease; that by reason of this convey· ance, the land did not descend to the heirs of Blandin, but the title. remains in Pease, who holds the same for the benefit of the complainants; that he does not claim title for his own benefit, but for the benefit of those for whom the trust was created. And the complainants pray that Pease may be made a party; and that the sale by Antonio Mexia be declared void, or that the heirs of Blandin may be held trustees, &c., and compelled to convey, &c.

The heirs of Blandin plead in bar to so much of the· bill as alleges the grant of the land to the said Adelaide Matilda, and a subsisting title in her, and seeks special or general relief. They allege that, in pursuance of a petition, bearing date the 27th of

January, 1830, presented to the Governor of the State of Coahuila and Texas, by, and in behalf of one Pedro Varela, a grant by way of sale, in conformity with the 24th article of the colonization law of the 24th of March, 1825, was made to him, by the said Governor, of eleven leagues of land in the vacant lands of said State. That on the 29th of March, 1832, said Varela, by notarial act, in the city of Mexico, sold and transferred said land to one Charlotte Walker, wife of said Mexia, for the use of their daughter, the said Adelaide Matilda, then a minor, unmarried, and subject to the power of her father; in order that she might enjoy or alienate said land, as absolute proprietress of the same; that by said act she became bound to pay to the government of said State, the value of the land, according to the colonization law; that the sale and transfer were founded upon a valuable consideration in money, paid by Mexia to Varela; that said act was executed by Charlotte, wife of Mexia, acting for her husband, and in his absence, by virtue of the power granted to her, according to the laws of Mexico, by Alexander Alvarez Guitian, second constitutional Alcade of the City of Mexico, on the 10th of March, 1832; and that Mexia thereby became entitled to all the benefits of said act, and was bound by the same.

That on the 23d of November, 1833, a survey having first been made, a title of possession of the land was made by the Commissioner, Vincente Aldreto, to said Adelaide Matilda; and that, on the 10th of February, 1836, said Adelaide Matilda remaining unmarried, and subject to Mexia, her father, he, by a notarial act, at the city of New Orleans, granted, sold, and transferred the land, with the consent and authorization of his said wife, to said John A. Merle, then acting as trustee for Antonio Blandin, for the consideration of $7,306.25 then paid to said Mexia by Merle, out of the funds of Blandin, in his possession. Other parts of the bill were denied in the plea.

The answer of Pease, admits, that some time in 1838, Antonio Blandin called upon him and stated, that he held the title to three eleven league grants in Texas, one, as he believes, the grant in controversy; that said land had been conveyed to him by the owners, in order that he, as a resident of Texas, might hold the same for their benefit, &c.

The other defendants admit the conveyances alleged in the bill, but do not admit the trust in their ancestor, and they allege as a reason for his conveyance to Pease, that he was embarrassed, and was apprehensive his creditors would subject the land to the payment of his debts. The land, they assert, was conveyed in trust to Pease, for the benefit of the wife and children of Blandin.

A demurrer was filed to the amended bill, which was properly overruled by the District Court. The case must be examined here on its merits.

The purchase from Varela was made by Mrs. Mexia, for the benefit of her daughter Adelaide Matilda. It was a concession to be located upon the unappropriated lands of the State. After the location and survey were made, the title of possession issued to Adelaide Matilda.

The 59th law of Toro provides, when the husband shall be absent, and no present prospect of his return, or where there be danger by reason of delay, the Justice, with a knowledge of the cause, being legitimate, or necessary, or profitable to the wife, may give the license to the wife, which the husband might give, which thus given, shall be as good as if given by the husband. 3 Novisima Recop. 404. A license thus given by the Judge, in consequence of the absence of the husband, does not authorize the wife to bind the husband, nor does it appear that she pretended to do so, in the purchase from Varela. From the conveyance, it sufficiently appears that this property did not become a part of the community property of husband and wife.

The conveyance of the land by Mexia to Merle, as trustee for Blandin, for the consideration of $7,306.25 expressed, does not contain the necessary formula for a transfer of title, under the laws of Louisiana. But those laws do not govern the right of Mexia to make the conveyance, or to make it in the form in which it was executed.

To show that this act was done by Mexia, with the consent of his wife, a letter of hers is appended to the transaction, and a part of it embodied in the conveyance. This letter bears date of November 1st, 1836, while the authentic act in which it is incorporated, is dated the 10th of February, 1836. It is not readily perceived how a letter, dated ten months after the conveyance, could constitute a part of it. From the instrument, it appears that Merle was a purchaser for himself, his heirs and assigns, when it is admitted that he purchased as the trustee of Blandin, and with his money.

But the facts in the case show that no money was paid on the purchase. The Hon. P. Soule says, the sale was made by General Mexia to John A. Merle, without consideration, and for the sole purpose of protecting the property of his children, understanding that Texian citizens only could hold lands in Texas. The witness was well acquainted with Antonio Blandin, who consulted with the witness, and stated the land was confided to his care, never speaking of it as his private property, or as having paid any consideration for it. Blandin uniformly spoke of the land as a trustee, and not as owner.

The deposition of E. M. Pease, one of the defendants, was taken by the complainants, but it was objected to by the defendants below, on the ground that Pease was a party, and that the Commissioner of the United States who had taken the same, did not appear to have been sworn.   The District Court refused to admit the deposition on both grounds.   As the deposition was not taken with the leave of the court, it was properly overruled, on the ground that the witness was a party, but the other ground in regard to the Commissioner not appearing to have been sworn, was not sustainable.   The Commissioner is an officer appointed by the courts of the United States, and his official acts are *primâ facie* valid.

Had General Mexia power to make a conveyance to Merle? Was it executed according to the laws of Louisiana, where the act was done, or the laws of Texas, where the land is situated, and which must govern the act?   The laws of Louisiana do not authorize the transfer of a child's property by parents or guardians, without an order from the Judge, granted on the advice of a family meeting.   1 Civil Code, Art. 334, 338.   No such ceremony was observed in the conveyance to Merle, as the law requires, and consequently the act was not operative by the Louisiana law.   The letter of the wife, if it were genuine and bore the proper date, is not evidence of a family meeting, and that the sale was " of absolute necessity, or of evident advantage to the minor."

It is contended that the property in question came to Adelaide Matilda, through the means of her father, and, consequently, that he had the power to convey it.   Such property under the civil law is called profectitious.

There is no evidence that the father paid any consideration for this property.   It was purchased by the mother for the benefit of her daughter; and when the concession was located and arranged, the perfect title was made in the name of the daughter. The presumption that the consideration paid was paid by the mother, arises from the facts.   Her marital rights under the civil law, as to property, were independent of her husband; and in this view it may well be presumed that she paid the consideration for the purchase.

The fact that no money was paid by Merle, although a large sum was inserted in the act of conveyance, shows the nature of that transaction; and that the step was taken, as sworn. to by Mr. Soulé, to preserve the land by a legal ownership, for the benefit of his daughter.

The mother having procured the complete title to the property in the name of her daughter, she had no power to consent to or authorize the transfer of it by her husband.   The pretence of the letter gives no validity to the act of conveyance.   The transfer of the concession to the mother, by Varela, for her daughter, was not made as a part of the marital community. The conveyance to the mother and the declared object of it, negatives such a presumption.

Acquired as the property was, the law denominates it adventitious. It came to their daughter through her mother. In this view, it is contended that the *usufruct* was in the father, "who is bound to defend and preserve it, both in court and out;" 3 Las Siate Partidas, 149, and that he had power to convey it.

From the terms of conveyance, it is clear that Mexia assumed to act, not in his own right, but in the character of father and natural tutor, and by authorization of his wife. The instrument purports to convey the title of his daughter, which admitted the right to be in her. The letter of the wife, as he supposed, was evidence of a family meeting required by law, and under which he assumed to act.

A guardian cannot dispose of the property of his ward without the permission of the judge of his domicil. 1 White's Recop. 15 and 16, Part 4, L. 14, tit. 11, p. 4. During the minority of the child, the only right of the father is, to take the *usufruct*. He has no power to sell the property of the minor, except for certain purposes, and under the sanction of the Judge. 2 Part. 1137. The conveyance to Merle was not made as the law requires, and it was therefore void. It was not valid under the laws of Louisiana, nor under the laws of Texas and Coahuila.

The decree of the District Court is affirmed.

    dm

Mr. Justice NELSON concurred in the result to which the above opinion arrived.

Order.

This cause came on to be heard on the transcript of the record from the District Court of the United States for the District of Texas, and was argued by counsel. On consideration whereof, it is now here ordered, adjudged, and decreed by this court, that the decree of the said District Court in this cause be, and the same is hereby, affirmed, with costs.

THE GENERAL MUTUAL INSURANCE COMPANY, PLAINTIFFS IN ERROR, *v.* EBENEZER B. SHERWOOD.

Under a policy insuring against the usual perils of the sea, including barratry, the underwriters are not liable to repay to the insured, damages paid by him to the owners of another vessel and cargo, suffered in a collision occasioned by the negligence of the master or mariners of the vessel insured.

A policy cannot be so construed as to insure against all losses directly referable to the negligence of the master and mariners. But if the loss is caused by a peril of the sea. the underwriter is responsible, although the master did not use due care to avoid the peril.

THIS case was brought up, by writ of error, from the Circuit Court of the United States for the Southern District of New York.

It was an action of assumpsit brought by Sherwood against the General Mutual Insurance Company, upon a policy of insurance, dated New York, 17th of· October, 1843, by which the company insured Sherwood to the amount of $8,000, for the account of whom it might concern, loss payable to him, upon the brig Emily, from the 17th October, 1843, at noon, until the 17th October, 1844, at noon, the vessel being valued in the policy at $16,000.

This policy was effected for the benefit, and to protect the interest of Frederick Sherwood and Abraham Sherwood, part owners of said vessel.

On the 13th March, 1844, the brig sailed from Charleston with a cargo of·merchandise, bound for New York, being at the time provided with a skilful and experienced master, experienced and skilful mates, and a competent crew, and was in all respects seaworthy for the voyage.

About 5 o'clock in the afternoon of Tuesday, 19th March, a licensed pilot boarded them, and took the command and management of the vessel. The wind being unfavorable, the brig ran, closehauled, heading north and north by east, until the pilot considered himself up to the point of the Romer Shoals; he then tacked and stood in for Sandy Hook, heading to the southward and westward, closehauled. Between 7 and 8 o'clock at night, the pilot gave orders to go about; in attempting to execute this order, the brig misstayed, and the pilot then gave orders to wear ship. At this time, and whilst in the act of wearing, being very close to the shore, the rigging of the vessel having become entangled, and the crew being occupied with the manœuvring of their vessel, the first mate, who was on the top-gallant forecastle, saw a schooner very close to them. Confused by this sudden appearance, his attention in keeping a sharp lookout having been distracted by his attending to the working of the vessel, he, in this sudden emergency, exclaimed, "Helm hard down! luff! luff!" The man at the wheel obeyed, and almost instantaneously the brig struck the schooner, which proved to be "The Virginian," bound from Norfolk, with a full cargo of merchandise, for New York. The order given by the mate to "luff," was erroneous.

The brig Emily was injured by the collision to the amount of $300; the schooner Virginian was so much injured that she sunk, and with her cargo was totally lost.

On the 26th March, 1844, the owners of the schooner filed their libel in the District Court of the United States for the Southern District of New York, against the brig Emily, claiming that she was specifically liable for the loss and injury occasioned by the libel.

The owners of the Emily filed their answer, denying that the collision was occasioned by the fault of those in charge of her, and imputing the blame to the crew of the Virginian. On the 12th October, 1845, the cause was brought to a hearing, and witnesses examined on both sides.

On the 22d April, 1845, Judge Betts pronounced his opinion to be, that the brig Emily was to leeward of the Virginian when the latter was first seen; that no sufficient and proper look-out was kept on board her at the time; that the intermission, for the moment, of their precautionary vigilance on board the Emily, might very naturally spring out of a confusion likely to arise from the failure of the vessel to come round to the wind, her dangerous proximity to the shore, the entanglement of some of the running rigging which impeded her manœuvre, and the distraction these circumstances were calculated to produce in the attention of the mate, who, at the moment, appeared to have been the only one acting as look-out forward; but that these circumstances did not relieve the vessel from maintaining these precautions, and from the consequences of the omission to do so; and the Judge accordingly held, that the collision occurred by the negligence or fault of the brig. He decreed in favor of the libellants for the value of the schooner Virginian, and of so much of the cargo as belonged to her owners. It was referred to the clerk to ascertain and report the amount of the loss and damage. The cause came on to be heard on the 3d of June, 1845, upon the clerk's report and exceptions thereto. The court ordered and decreed, that the libellants recover their damages by means of the premises, viz. $5,250$_{\frac{00}{100}}$, with their costs, and that the brig Emily be condemned for satisfaction thereof; the libellants' costs were taxed at 704_{\frac{00}{100}}$. On the 3d July, 1845, the owners of the Emily appealed to the Circuit Court of the United States for the Southern District of New York, and in November, 1846, the appeal was argued before Mr. Justice Nelson.

On the 6th April, 1847, Judge Nelson delivered his opinion, and found, upon the proofs, in substance, that the Virginian was not in fault; that the mistaken order of the mate of the brig to the man at the wheel, in connection with the derangement of

30 *

the running rigging of the vessel, and the confusion on board from her misstaying a few minutes before, had produced the collision. The Circuit Court affirmed the decree of the District Court, with costs. This decree was settled by compromise, and upon payment by the owners of a sum less than the decree, it was satisfied. Early notice of the pendency of the action in the District Court, and also of the appeal to the Circuit Court, was given to the Mutual Safety Insurance Company, with a request that they would unite in the defence, or take such measures as they might deem proper.

Owners of other parts of the cargo lost by the collision, filed their libels against the Virginian, which, after the decrees above mentioned, were settled by compromise; other claims were also made, and settled by compromise; in every instance, the sum paid being less than the claim. On the 23d August, 1847, the owners of the brig Emily, having previously presented to their various underwriters preliminary proofs of the loss, copies of the proceedings in the District and Circuit Courts, and of the payment and settlement of the demands aforesaid, commenced suits upon the policies of insurance, in the Circuit Court of the United States. The declaration filed in the present action contains two special counts, and the common money counts.

The special counts, set forth all the facts and circumstances with great particularity.

The defendants filed demurrers to each of the special counts, assigning as cause, that neither of the said counts showed any loss or damage by any peril covered by the policy of insurance. The plaintiff below joined in demurrer.

The cause was argued in April, 1848, before his Honor, Mr. Justice Nelson, and the Hon. Samuel R. Betts. Judgment was given upon the demurrer in favor of the plaintiff below. The defendants did not interpose any other answer to the two special counts, but to the common counts (III. IV. V. and VI.) they pleaded the general issue.

The court having decided the demurrers, ordered the damages to be assessed under the special counts. In May, 1849, the jury assessed the plaintiff's damages at $4,526$\frac{34}{100}$. Judgment was signed 5th June, 1849.

Upon the assessment of the damages, the defendant's counsel prayed the court to instruct the jury —

1. That the general objection to the recovery of the plaintiff, was, that [it] is apparent, on the face of the declaration, that the loss claimed was not occasioned by a peril insured against, but was to be attributed solely to the gross negligence of the agents of the assured; and therefore, that the loss was either an exception from the terms of the policy, or was not covered by them at all.

2. That the rule "*causa proxima non remota spectatur*," in its proper application, relieves the defendants from all liability; since the proximate cause here was, according to the decree of the District and Circuit Court, "the fault of the Emily." The collision by itself did not create the liability to pay. The want of care, skill, and vigilance on the part of the master and crew of the Emily were to be superadded to the collision.

3. That if the negligence and fault of the assured, and not the collision, were the proximate cause of the loss, such fault and negligence in this case, (without which the decree would not have been made,) should certainly excuse the underwriters.

4. That even if the insurer is liable for the amount of the claim against the Emily for the loss of the schooner, it does not follow that he is also liable for the loss of the cargo on board the schooner Virginian. No case has yet carried the liability of the underwriter to this extent.

5. That the cost of defending the suits are not chargeable upon the underwriters.

6. That the counsel fees to the advocate are clearly inadmissible.

Whereupon his honor, the Judge, charged the jury:—It appeared, from the evidence, that the brig Emily sailed from Charleston, for New York, on the thirteenth day of March, in the year 1841, with a cargo of cotton and other merchandise; that on the afternoon of the 18th day of March, aforesaid, being near Barnegat, she took aboard a licensed pilot, and proceeded towards New York, the wind being boisterous, and blowing in flaws; that between 7 and 8 o'clock in the evening she stood over for the Romer Shoals, closehauled on a wind, heading for Sandy Hook. Finding that the brig could not fetch in to the Hook upon that tack, and having run as close to the beach as he deemed prudent, the pilot gave orders to tack ship; in consequence of the maintopsail-brace being slacked the vessel did not go about, and orders were then given by the pilot to wear ship, and whilst in the act of wearing, the mate of the Emily discovered a sail close by, which proved to be the schooner Virginian, bound for New York, with a cargo on board; the mate cried out, sail ahead! but almost immediately thereafter the brig struck the schooner and sunk her, with her cargo. The owners of the schooner Virginian filed their libel in the District Court of the United States for the Southern District of New York, before referred to, against the brig Emily; alleging that the collision was occasioned by the fault and mismanagement of those having charge of the Emily. An answer was filed by the owners of the latter, denying that the collision was properly attributable to the Emily; and, on the contrary, alleging that it

was occasioned by the fault and unskilfulness of those on board
of the schooner; proofs were taken in the District Court, and
the cause having been heard upon the pleadings and proofs, an
interlocutory decree was pronounced therein on the twenty-
second day of April, in the year 1845, whereby, after reciting
that it appeared to the court that the said collision, and the
damages and loss incurred by the libellant in consequence
thereof, occurred by the negligence or fault of the said brig
Emily, it was considered that the libellants were entitled to
recover the damages by them sustained thereby; and by which
decree a reference was ordered, to ascertain the value of the
said schooner Virginian, her tackle, &c., at the time of the collision, and of the cargo then on board of her, belonging to the
libellants, and the amount of the loss in the premises sustained
by the libellants by means of such collision; and afterwards,
the said cause having again been heard upon exceptions to the
report, and the proofs and allegations of the respective parties,
a final decree was pronounced thereon on the seventh day of
June, in the year 1845, whereby it was ordered, adjudged, and
decreed, by the said District Court, that the libellants recover in
the said action their damages, by means of the premises, the
sum of five thousand two hundred and fifty-four dollars and
seventy cents, together with their costs to be taxed; and that the
said brig, her tackle and apparel, be condemned for satisfaction
thereof, which said costs of the libellants were afterwards duly
taxed at $704.96.   From this decree an appeal was taken, by
the owners of the brig Emily, to the Circuit Court of the United
States for the Southern District of New York, in the second
circuit, and after hearing the proofs and the arguments of counsel, the court affirmed the decree of the District Court, with the
costs of the respondents to be taxed.   After the decision of this
court had been pronounced, another libel was filed by the owners
of a portion of the cargo lost on board the Virginian, against
the brig Emily, and claims were made, and libels threatened by
others of the shippers of the cargo lost on board of the schooner,
against the owners of the Emily, which action and claims by
the owners of the said cargo were compromised and settled by
the owners of the Emily.   That if they should find, upon the
evidence, that, at the time of sailing from Charleston, the brig
Emily was a seaworthy vessel, properly equipped for the voyage
to New York, and that she had on board a skilful master, and a
sufficient and competent crew, the defendants are liable upon
the policy given in evidence for the one half of the loss to
the brig Emily, arising from the collision with the schooner Virginian, not exceeding the sum insured, notwithstanding that it
was occasioned by, or resulted from, the fault of the pilot, or of

the master and crew of the brig, either from want of keeping a sufficient look-out or from mismanagement of the vessel.

The direct and immediate consequence of the collision was that a lien was created on the brig, in favor of the owners of the Virginian, and of the owners of the cargo on board of her, to the extent of the value of the schooner, and of the cargo that was destroyed by the disaster, and the plaintiff is entitled to recover from the underwriters, not only the cost of the actual repairs of the injury done to the brig, but also the several sums that her owners have actually and in good faith paid to the owners of the schooner, and of the cargo lost with her, in order to discharge their vessel from the liens created by the said collision ; that the plaintiff is also entitled to recover from the underwriters on the brig the actual expenses and costs, including reasonable advocate's fees, necessarily incurred in the defence of the brig from the aforesaid claim.

The policy of insurance, in this case, is subscribed for $8,000, the vessel being valued therein at $16,000 ; it was therefore an insurance upon one half of the vessel, and the defendants are consequently liable for one half only of the loss and damage sustained by the assured in consequence of the said collision which the jury shall find, upon the evidence, was actually and properly paid by the owners of the Emily, in order to relieve their vessel.

The counsel for the defendant then and there excepted to said charge, so far as the same differed from, or did not conform to the instructions prayed for by him, as above.

The jury thereupon rendered a verdict for the plaintiff, for four thousand five hundred and thirty-six dollars and thirty-four cents damages, and six cents costs.

And because the said several matters so offered and given in evidence, and insisted upon by the defendants aforesaid, and the charge of the said Judge, and the said exceptions taken to the same, do not appear by the record of the verdict aforesaid, the said defendants have caused the same to be written on this bill of exceptions, to be annexed to such record, and have prayed the said Judge to set his hand and seal to the same. Whereupon the Hon. Samuel Nelson, the associate Justice before whom the said issues were tried, and said exceptions taken, and one of the judges of said Circuit Court, hath hereto set his hand and seal, this twenty-eighth day of November, in the year of our Lord one thousand eight hundred and fifty-one.

Upon this bill of exceptions, and the judgment of the court upon the demurrers, the case came up to this court.

It was argued by *Mr. A. Hamilton, Jr.*, for the plaintiffs in error, and *Mr. Butler*, with whom was *Mr. Cutting*, for the defendant in error.

The points made on the part of the plaintiff in error, were the following.

I. The general objection to the recovery of the plaintiff is, that it is apparent, on the face of the declaration, that the loss that is claimed was not occasioned by a peril insured against; but is to be attributed solely to the gross negligence of the agents of the assured. Hence the loss is either an exception from the terms of the policy, or is not covered by them at all. Emerigon, vol. 1, p. 429, (Ed. 1827, 329, 336); Tanner *v.* Bennett, 1 Ry & Moody, 182; Surdet *v.* Hall, 4 Bing. 607; 2 Arnold, 775, 770, 777, cases cited.

II. The rule "*causa proxima non remota spectatur*," in its proper application, relieves the defendant from all liability, since the proximate cause here was, according to the decree of the District and Circuit Courts, "the fault of the Emily." The collision, by itself, did not create the liability to pay. The want of skill, care, and vigilance on the part of the master and crew of the Emily was to be superadded to the collision. Paddock *v.* Franklin Insurance Company, 11 Pick. 227; American Insurance Company *v.* Ogden, 20 Wend. 287; Starbuck *v.* New England Marine Insurance Company, 19 Pick. 198; Robinson *v.* Jones, 8 Mass. 536.

III. If, then, the negligence and fault of the assured, and not the collision, were the proximate cause of the loss, such fault and negligence, in this case, (without which the decree would not have been made,) should certainly excuse the underwriters. Hazard *v.* New England Insurance Company, 1 Sumn. 218; 3 Kent, 5th ed. p. 176, note a. 371, 373; Copeland *v.* New England Insurance Company, 2 Metcf, 432; Cleveland *v.* Union Insurance Company, 8 Mass. 308; Bradhurst *v.* Col. Insurance Company, 9 Johns. 17–21; Potter *v.* Suffolk Insurance Company, 2 Sumn. 197; Galbraith *v.* Gracie, 1 Wash. C. C. R. 219.

IV. But even if the insurer is liable for the amount of the decree against the Emily, for the loss of the schooner, it does not follow that he is also liable for the loss of the cargo on board the schooner. No case has yet carried the liability of the underwriter to this extent.

The points made by the counsel for the defendant in error were the following.

I. The underwriters are responsible for losses by any of the perils insured against, although such losses may have been occasioned by, or have resulted from, the negligence or fault of the master or crew. If the assured has provided a seaworthy vessel, with a skilful master and a sufficient and competent crew, the underwriter takes the risks of navigation, and of the perils insured against, although caused by the negligence, carelessness or unskilfulness of the master and crew. Peters v. Warren Ins. Co. 14 Peters, 99;. Peters v. Warren Ins. Co. 3 Sumn. 389; Waters v. Merchants Ins. Co. 11 Peters, 213; Columbia Ins. Co. v. Lawrence, 10 Peters, 507; Patapsco Ins. Co. v. Coulter, 3 Peters's R. 222; Hale v. Wash. Ins. Co. 2 Story R. 176; Smith's Mercant. Law, (Amer. Edit.) 347; Sadler v. Dixon, 8 Mees. & Welsby, 895; Dixon v. Sadler, 5 M. & Welsby, 405; Bush v. The Royal Ex. Ins. Co. 2 B. & Ald. 73; Walker v. Maitland, 5 B. & Ald. 174; Bishop v. Pentland, 7 B. & C. 219; Shore v. Bentall, 7 B. & C. 798, n.; Henderson v. Western Mar. & F. Ins. Co. 10 Robinson, 164; Copeland v. N. Eng. Mar. Ins. Co. 2 Metcalf, 432; Perrins, Adm'r, v. Protect. Ins. Co. 11 Ohio R. 147; Park, Ins. 482, (Eng. Edit. of 1842, page 156.) Grim v. Phenix Ins. Co. 13 Johns. 451; in this country, and Law v. Hollingsworth, 7 Term R. 156, in England, and other cases decided about the same time, are not correct in principle, are now generally disapproved of, and are substantially overruled. Opinion of Betts, J., in this case, 1 Blatchford's R. 251.

II. A loss by collision is one of the perils insured against, as much so as loss by fire, stranding, capture, &c. If it occurs without fault.on the part of the insured vessel, it is conceded that the underwriters are bound to indemnify the assured against loss; and, upon principle and authority, the insurers are equally liable if the collision happens through the fault, mistake, error of judgment, or carelessness of the vessel insured. Peters v. Warren Ins. Co. 14 Peters's R. 99; S. C. 3 Sum. 389; Hale v. Washington Ins. Co. 2 Story, 176; 1 Phill. Ins. 636.

III. The direct and immediate consequence of the collision was that, *eo instanti*, a charge, encumbrance or lien was created on the ship to, the extent of the injury done to the Virginian and cargo. This charge caused the necessity of an expenditure by the assured, without which he could not extricate nor repossess himself of his vessel. This loss is as direct a consequence of the collision as if the Emily had been injured so as to have required repairs by carpenters to the same amount.

IV. The underwriters are liable not only for the amount of the lien or charge that was created in favor of the owners of the Virginian, but also for the lien or charge created by the destruction of the cargo, and for which the Emily was specifically liable *in rem*.

V. The defendants are responsible for all the costs, charges, and expenses, fairly and reasonably incurred by the plaintiff below, in defending the vessel from the claims made against her;. this is necessary to afford him a full indemnity; and the clause in the policy, rendering it proper and necessary to sue for labor and travel in and about the defence, safeguard and recovery of the vessel, contemplates and provides for it. See 2 Phillips on. Ins. 509, 749, 464; 1 Id. 693. Hastie v. De Peyster, 3 Caines's Rep. 190 — a case of reinsurance; suit against the first insurer defended, and a recovery with costs — principal opinion by Kent, C. J.: "Such charges are allowed, as composing part of a claim for indemnity." Per Livingston, J.: Plaintiffs gave notice to defendants, who took no steps to prevent the progress of the suit to judgment; all the costs of that suit, both plaintiffs' and defendants', are a proper charge in this: "not pretended that its defence was unnecessary or improper." 1 Story's Rep. 458; Hale v. Wash. Ins. Co. 2 Story, 176; Peters v. Warren Ins. Co. 14 Peters's Rep. 99, (p. 100, near the foot.) "Expenses of defending the suit" for a collision, included in the adjustment. Watson v. Marine Ins. Co. 7 Johns. Rep. 57 — a case of capture and recovery for a total loss, and also expenses of the captain in endeavoring to obtain the release and restoration of the ship; travelling, board, wages, and 1,105 livres left in the hands of the consignees, to prosecute an appeal to the Council of State; items were subject to opinion of court; another charge was deducted; the above allowed. Jumel v. Marine Ins. Co. 7 Johns. Rep. 412, 426 — case of capture, condemnation, appeal, compromise, sale; purchase by master; held master not bound by appeal; only to act in good faith and sound discretion, &c. Gardere v. Columbia Ins. Co. 7 J. R. 514, (same principles.) Francis v. Ocean Ins. Co. 6 Cowen, 404, affirmed, 2 Wend. 64 — seizure as for illicit trade — irregular condemnation and sale, no defence by master, &c. Expense incurred in prosecuting a claim for the proceeds of the ship. Held, "entitled to recover all the expense fairly incurred in obtaining a restoration of the proceeds of the vessel." Bridge v. Niagara Ins. Co. 1 Hall's Sup. Ct. R. 423 — salvage expenses, including costs of legal proceedings to ascertain validity and amount of salvage claims, storage of cargo, bottomry expenses, protests, surveys, wages and provisions, whilst seeking a port of refitting, and many other instances of charges and expenses, resulting from and incident to losses by perils insured against. 9 Wend. 416, Ricket v. Snyder — In an action for breach of covenant of seisin, the plaintiff is entitled to recover counsel fees as well as taxable costs incurred in defending the premises. The covenant of seisin is one of indemnity. 2 Phill. Ins. 464, 509, 749. 1 Id. 693. — The defence in the District Court, and on appeal in the Circuit Court, of the libel, by the owners of the Virginian, (owners also of some of the cargo,) and the decisions thereon, justified the plaintiff in compromising the other claims without litigation. By such compromises he greatly diminished the sum for which the defendants were liable. He was entitled to recover if he had paid the amounts without litigation. Hale *v.* Washington Ins. Co. 2 Story, 176.

Mr. Justice CURTIS delivered the opinion of the court.

This is a writ of error to the Circuit Court of the United States for the Southern District of New York.

The action was assumpsit on a time policy of insurance, subscribed by the plaintiffs in error, upon the brig Emily, during one year from the seventeenth day of October, 1843, for the sum of eight thousand dollars, the vessel being valued at the sum of sixteen thousand dollars. The policy, described in the declaration, assumed to insure against the usual sea perils, among which is barratry of the master and mariners. The declaration avers, that during the prosecution of a voyage, within the policy, while on the high seas, and near the entrance of the harbor of the city of New York, by and through the want of a proper look-out, by the mate of the said brig, and, by and through the erroneous order of the chief mate, who was stationed on the top-gallant forecastle of the said brig, who saw the schooner, hereinafter named, and cried out to the man at the wheel, "helm hard down—luff"—whereas, he ought not to have given the said order; and, by and through the negligence and fault of the said brig Emily, the said brig ran into a schooner called the Virginian, and so injured her that she sank, whereby the said brig Emily became liable to the owners of the said schooner and her cargo, to make good their damages; which liability was a charge and encumbrance on the said brig. The declaration then proceeds to aver, that the brig was libelled, by the owners of the schooner and her cargo, in the District Court of the United States; that a decree was there made, whereby it was adjudged, " That the collision in the pleadings mentioned, and the damages and loss incurred by the libellants, in consequence thereof, occurred by the negligence or fault of the said brig, and that the libellants were entitled to recover their damages by them sustained thereby;'" that the same having been assessed, a decree therefor was made by the District Court, which, on appeal, was affirmed by the Circuit Court, which found, " That the hands, on board the Emily, failed to keep a proper look-out, and, that the said brig might have avoided the collision, by the use of proper caution, skill, and vigilance." The declaration further avers, that the plaintiff has paid divers sums of money, to satisfy this decree and the expenses of making the defence, amounting to the sum of eight thousand dollars.

This statement of the substance of the declaration, presents the question which has been here argued, and sufficiently shows how it arose; for, although there was a demurrer to the first two counts in the declaration, and a trial upon the general issue pleaded to the other counts, and a bill of exceptions taken to the ruling at the trial, yet the same question is presented by each mode of trial, and that question is, whether, under a policy insuring against the usual perils, including barratry, the underwriters are liable to repay to the insured, damages paid by him to the owners of another vessel and cargo, suffered in a collision occasioned by the negligence of the master or mariners of the vessel insured.

The great and increasing internal navigation of the United States, carried on over long distances, through the channels of rivers and other comparatively narrow waters, where the danger of collisions, and the frequency of their occurrence, are much greater than on maritime voyages, renders the respective rights of underwriters and insured, growing out of such occurrences, of more moment in this than in any other civilized country; and the court has considered the inquiry presented by this case, with the care which its difficulty and its importance demand.

In examining, for the first time, any question under a policy of insurance, it is necessary to ascertain whether the contract has received a practical construction, by merchants and underwriters; not through any partial or local usages, but by the general consent of the mercantile world. Such a practical construction, when clearly apparent, is of great weight, not only because the parties to the policy may be presumed to have contracted in reference to it, but because such a practice is very high evidence of the general convenience and substantial equity of it, as a rule.. This is true of most commercial contracts; but it is especially true of a policy of insurance, which has been often declared to be an "obscure, incoherent, and very strange instrument," and, "generally more informal than any other brought into a court of justice:" (Per Buller, J., 4 T. R. 210; Mansfield, C. J., 4 Taunt. 380;· Marshal, C. J., 6 Cr. 45; Lord Mansfield, 1 Bur. 347); but which, notwithstanding the number and variety of the interests which it embraces, and of the events by which it is affected, has been reduced to much certainty, by the long practice of acute and well-informed men in commercial countries; by the decisions of courts in America and in England, and by able writers on the subject, in this and other countries.

And it should not be forgotten, that, not only in the introduction of this branch of law into England, by Lord Mansfield, but i. its progress since, both there and here, a constant reference has been had to the usage of merchants, and the science of insurance law has been made and kept a practical and convenient system, by avoiding subtle and refined reasoning, however logical it may seem to be, and looking for safe practical rules.

Now, although cases like the present must have very frequently occurred, we are not aware of any evidence, that underwriters have paid such claims, or that, down to the time when one somewhat resembling it was rejected by the Court of King's Bench, in De Vaux v. Salvador, (5 Ad. and Ellis,) decided in 1836, such a claim was ever made. And we believe that, if skilful merchants, or underwriters, or lawyers, accustomed to the practice of the commercial law, had been asked whether the insurers on one vessel were liable for damage done to another vessel, not insured by the policy, by a collision occasioned by the negligence of those on board the vessel insured, they would down to a very recent period, have answered, unhesitatingly, in the negative.

As we shall presently show, such, for a long time, was the opinion of the writers on insurance, on the continent of Europe, and in England and America. And this, alone, would be strong proof of the general understanding and practice of those connected with this subject.

But, although this practical interpretation of the contract is entitled to much weight, we do not consider it perfectly decisive. It may be, that, by applying to the case the settled principles of the law of insurance, the loss is within the policy; and, that it has not heretofore been found to be so, because an exact attention has not been given to the precise question. Or, it may be, that the weight of recent authority, and the propriety of rendering the commercial law as uniform as its necessities, should constrain us to adopt the rule contended for by the defendant in error. And, therefore, we proceed to examine the principles and authorities, bearing on this question.

Upon principle, the true inquiries are, what was the loss, and what was its cause?

The loss was the existence of a lien on the vessel insured, securing a valid claim for damages, and the consequent diminution of the value of that vessel. In other words, by operation of law, the owners of the Virginian obtained a lien on the vessel insured, as security for the payment of damages, due to them for a marine tort, whereby their property was injured.

What was the cause of this loss? We think it is correctly stated by this court, in the case of the Paragon, 14 Peters, 109.

In that case, it was said : " In the common case of an action for damages for a tort done by the defendant, no one is accustomed to call the verdict of the jury and the judgment of the court thereon, the cause of the loss to the defendant. It is properly attributable to the original tort, which gave the right to damages consequent thereon." The cases there spoken of, were claims *in personam*. But the language was used to illustrate the inquiry, what should be deemed the cause of a loss by a claim *in rem*, and is strictly applicable to such a claim. Whether the owners of the Virginian would proceed *in rem* or *in personam*, was at their election. It affected only their remedy. Their right, and the grounds on which it rested, and the extent of the defendant's liability, and its causes, were the same in both modes of proceeding. And, in both, the cause of the loss of the defendant would be the negligence of his servants, amounting to a tort. The loss consisting in a valid claim on the vessel insured, we must look for the cause of the loss in the cause of the claim, and this is expressly averred by the declaration to have been the negligence of the servants of the assured. From the nature of the case, it was absolutely necessary to make such an averment. If the declaration had stated simply a collision, and that the plaintiff had paid the damages suffered by the Virginian and her cargo, it would clearly have been bad on demurrer; because, although it would show a loss, it would state no cause of that loss. It is only by adding the fact, that the damage done to the Virginian was caused by negligence, that is, by stating the cause of damage, that the cause of payment appears, and, when it appears, it is seen to be the negligence of the servants of the assured.

We know of no principle of insurance law which prevents us from looking for this sole operative cause, or requires us to stop short of it, in applying the maxim *causa proxima non remota spectatur.* The argument is, that collision, being a peril of the sea, the negligence which caused that peril to occur is not to be inquired into; it lies behind the peril, and is too remote. This is true when the loss was inflicted by collision, or was by law a necessary consequence of it. The underwriter cannot set up the negligence of the servants of the assured as a defence. But in this case he does not seek to go behind the cause of loss, and defend himself by showing this cause was produced by negligence. The insured himself goes behind the collision, and shows, as the sole reason why he has paid the money, that the negligence of his servants compelled him to pay it. It is true that an expense, attached by the law maritime to the subject insured, solely as a consequence of a peril, may be considered as proximately caused by that peril. But where the expense is attached to the vessel insured, not solely in consequence of a peril, but in consequence of the misconduct of the servants of the assured, the peril *per se* is not the efficient cause of the loss, and cannot, in any just sense, be considered its proximate cause. In such a case the real cause is the negligence, and unless the policy can be so interpreted as to insure against all losses directly referable to the negligence of the master and mariners, such a loss is not covered by the policy. We are of opinion the policy cannot be so construed. When a peril of the sea is the proximate cause of a loss, the negligence which caused that peril is not inquired into; not because the underwriter has taken upon himself all risks arising from negligence, but because he has assumed to indemnify the insured against losses from particular perils, and the assured has not warranted that his servants will use due care to avoid them.

These views are sustained by many authorities. Mr. Arnould, in his valuable Treatise on Insurance, (vol. 2, 775,) lays down the correct rule: " Where the loss is not proximately caused by the perils of the sea, but is directly referable to the negligence or misconduct of the master or other agents of the assured, not amounting to barratry, there seems little doubt that the underwriters would be thereby discharged." To this rule must be referred that class of cases, in which the misconduct of the master or mariners has either aggravated the consequences of a peril insured against, or been of itself the efficient cause of the whole loss. Thus, if damage be done by a peril insured against, and the master neglects to repair that damage, and in consequence of the want of such repairs, the vessel is lost, the neglect to make repairs, and not the sea damage, has been treated as the proximate cause of the loss. In the case of Copeland v. The N. E. Marine Ins. Co. (2 Met. 432,) Mr. Chief Justice Shaw reviews many of the cases, and states that " the actual cause of the loss is the want of repair, for which the assured are responsible, and not the sea damage which caused the want of repair, for which it is admitted the underwriters are responsible." And the same principles were applied by Mr. Justice Story, in the case of Hazard v. N. E. Marine Ins. Co. (1 Sum. R. 218,) where the loss was by worms, which got access to the vessel in consequence of her bottom being injured by stranding, which injury the master neglected to repair. So where a vessel has been lost or disabled, and the cargo saved, a loss caused by the neglect of the master to transship, or repair his vessel and carry the cargo, cannot be recovered. Schieffelin v. N. Y. Ins. Co. 9 Johns. 21; Bradhurst v. Col. Ins. Co. 9 Johns. 17; Am. Ins. Co. v. Centre, 4 Wend. 45; S. C. 7 Cow. 504; McGaw v. Ocean Ins. Co. 23 Pick. 405. So where condemnation of a neutral vessel was caused by resistance of search; Robinson v. Jones, 8 Mass. 536; or a loss arose from the master's negligently leaving the ship's register on shore; Cleveland v. Union Ins. Co. 8 Mass. 308. So where a vessel was burnt by the public authorities of a place into which the master sailed with a false bill of health, having the plague on board; Emerigon, (by Meredith,) 348; in these and many other similar cases, the courts, having found the efficient cause of the loss to be some neglect of duty by the master, have held the underwriter discharged. Yet it is obvious that in all such cases, one of the perils insured against, fell on the vessel. And they are to be reconciled with the other rule, that a loss caused by a peril of the sea is to be borne by the underwriter, though the master did not use due care to avoid the peril, by bearing in mind that in these cases it is negligence, and not simply a peril of the sea, which is the operative cause of the loss. It may sometimes be difficult to trace this distinction, and mistakes have doubtless been made in applying it, but it is one of no small importance in the law of insurance, and cannot be disregarded without producing confusion. The two rules are in themselves consistent. Indeed, they are both but applications, to different cases, of the maxim, *causa proxima non remota spectatur*. In applying this maxim, in looking for the proximate cause of the loss, if it is found to be a peril of the sea, we inquire no further; we do not look for the cause of that peril. But if the peril of the sea, which operated in a given case, was not of itself sufficient to occasion, and did not in and by itself occasion the loss claimed, if it depended upon the cause of that peril whether the loss claimed would follow it, and therefore a particular cause of the peril is essential to be shown by the assured, then we must look beyond the peril to its cause, to ascertain the efficient cause of the loss.

The case at bar presents an illustration of both rules. So far as the brig Emily was herself injured by the collision, the cause of the loss was the collision, which was a peril insured against, and the assured, showing that his vessel suffered damage from that cause, makes a case, and is entitled to recover. But he claims to recover not only for the damages done to his vessel, which was insured, but for damages done to the other vessel, not insured. To entitle himself to recover these, he must show not only that they were suffered by a peril of the sea, but that the underwriter is responsible for the consequences of that peril falling on a vessel not insured. It is this responsibility which is the sole basis of his claim, and to make out this responsibility he does not and cannot rest upon the occurrence of a collision; this affords no ground for this claim; he must show particular cause for that collision; and aver that by reason of the existence of that cause, the loss was suffered by him, and so the underwriter became responsible for it.

This negligence is therefore the fact without which the loss would not have been suffered by the plaintiff, and by its operation the loss is suffered by him. In the strictest sense, it causes the loss to the plaintiff. The loss of the owners of the Virginia was occasioned by a peril of the sea, by which their vessel was injured. But nothing connects the plaintiff with that loss, or makes it his, except the negligence of his servants. Of his loss this negligence is the only efficient cause, and in the sense of the law it is the proximate cause.

The ablest writers of the continent of Europe, on the subject of insurance law, have distinctly declared, that, in case of damage to another vessel solely through the fault of the master or mariners of the assured vessel, the damage must be repaired by him who occasioned it, and the insurer is not liable for it. Pothier Traite d'Assurance, No. 49, 50; Boucher, 1500, 1501, 1502; 4 Boulay Paty, Droit Maritime, (Ed. of 1823,) 14, 16; Santayra's Com. 7, 223; Emerigon, (by Meredith,) 337. If the law of England is to be considered settled by the case of DeVaux v. Salvador, (4 Ad. & El. 420,) it is clear such a loss could not be recovered there. Mr. Marshall is evidently of opinion that unless the misconduct of the master and crew amounted to barratry, the loss could not be recovered. Marsh. on Ins. 495. And Mr. Phillips so states in terms. 1 Phil. on Ins. 636.

It has been urged that, in the case of the Paragon, (Peters v. Warren Ins. Co. 14 Pet. 99,) this court adopted a rule which, if applied to the case at bar, would entitle the insured to recover. But we do not so consider it. It was there determined that a collision without fault was the proximate cause of that loss. Indeed, unless the operation of law, which fixed the lien, could be regarded as the cause of that loss, there was no cause but the collision, and that was a peril insured against.

We are aware that in the case of Hall v. Washington Ins. Co. (2 Story,) Mr. Justice Story took a different view of this question; and we are informed that the Supreme Court of Massachusetts has recently decided a case in conformity with his opinion, which is not yet in print, and which we have not been able to see. But with great respect for that very eminent Judge, and for that learned and able court, we think the rule we adopt is more in conformity with sound principle, as well as with the practical interpretation of the contract by underwriters and merchants; and that it is the safer and more expedient rule.

We cannot doubt that the knowledge by owners, masters, and seamen, that underwriters were responsible for all the damage done by collision with other vessels through their negligence, would tend to relax their vigilance and materially enhance the perils, both to life and property, arising from this case.

The judgment of the Circuit Court must be reversed, and the cause remanded, with directions to render a judgment for the defendants, on the demurrer to the first two counts, and award a *venire de novo* to try the general issue pleaded to the other counts.

Order.

This cause came on to be heard on the transcript of the record from the Circuit Court of the United States for the Southern District of New York, and was argued by counsel. On consideration whereof, it is now here ordered and adjudged, by this court, that the judgment of the said Circuit Court in this cause be, and the same is hereby, reversed, with costs, and that this cause be, and the same is hereby, remanded to the said Circuit Court, with directions to enter a judgment for the plaintiff in error, on the demurrer to the two first counts, and to award a *venire facias de novo*, to try the general issue pleaded to the other counts.

ELIJAH PEALE, TRUSTEE OF THE AGRICULTURAL BANK OF MISSISSIPPI, PLAINTIFF IN ERROR, *v.* MARTHA PHIPPS, AND MARY BOWERS, WIFE OF CHARLES RICE.

Two statutes of Mississippi, one passed in 1843, and the other in 1846, provide that where the charter of a bank shall be declared forfeited, a trustee shall be appointed to take possession of its effects, and commissioners appointed to audit accounts against it.

Where these steps had been taken, and the commissioners had refused to allow a certain account, the Circuit Court of the United States had no right to entertain a bill filed by the creditors to compel the trustee to pay the rejected account. There was a want of jurisdiction.

The cases upon this point, examined.

A claim by the trustee, in re-convention, was not a waiver of the exception to the jurisdiction.

THIS case was brought up, by writ of error, from the Circuit Court of the United States for the Eastern District of Louisiana.

It will be seen, by reference to 4 Howard, 225, that Charles Rice, and Mary his wife, and Martha Phipps, recovered, in an action of ejectment against the Agricultural Bank of Mississippi, two undivided third parts of a lot of ground in the city of Natchez.

In May, 1847, they sued out a writ of *habere facias posses-* *sionem*, and entered into possession of the property.

Under the laws of Mississippi, the charter of the bank became forfeited, and Elijah Peale was appointed trustee.

In April, 1848, Martha Phipps, and Mary Bowers, wife of Charles Rice, filed their petition in the Circuit Court of the United States for the Eastern District of Louisiana, against Peale. They claimed rent of the property from 1839 to 1847, damages for injuries done to the property whilst in possession of the bank, and the costs to which they had been put by the ejectment. Peale filed exceptions, and an answer. The second exception, upon which the judgment of this court turned, was as follows.

2. Because the charter of the Agricultural Bank was declared forfeited, and the said bank put in a course of liquidation as an insolvent corporation, and this defendant appointed trustee, for the purpose of collecting the assets thereof, by the Circuit Court of Adams County, in the State of Mississippi; and said trustee is not amenable to any other court than the one that appointed him, and of which he is the officer; and this court has no jurisdiction whatever of him in his said capacity.

The following agreement of counsel was filed in the case.

It is agreed between the parties in the above-named suit, by Prentiss and Finney, attorneys for the plaintiffs, and Robert Mott, attorney for the defendant, that the following facts shall be admitted upon the trial of the cause, and the same are hereby admitted:

1. That the President, Directors, and Company of the Agricultural Bank of Mississippi, were in possession of the City Hotel, being the premises, the mesne profits of which are sued for on the 1st day of December, 1839.

2. It is admitted, that the said hotel and furniture rented, from said 1st day of December, 1839, until 1st November, 1842, for the sum of six thousand dollars per annum, and from said 1st November, 1842, until plaintiffs took possession at the rate of four thousand dollars per annum, and that said rates shall be considered as the fair annual rent of said property during said periods.

3. It is admitted, that the charter of the Agricultural Bank has been adjudged forfeited under the laws of Mississippi, and that the defendant, Elijah Peale, is the trustee appointed under, and by virtue of said laws, to represent the said corporation.

4. It is admitted, that the claim sued on, was, before the commencement of this suit, presented to the commissioners appointed in Mississippi, to audit and allow claims against said bank, to wit, to J. A. Van Dalsen and C. L. Dubuisson, and they were

requested to audit and allow the same, but that they refused to audit, allow, or in any way recognize the same.

5. It is admitted, that the claim sued on, was, before the commencement of this suit, presented to the defendant, as trustee of said Agricultural Bank, and he was requested to allow the same as a just and valid claim against said bank; but that said defendant, as trustee as aforesaid, refused to admit, recognize, or allow said claim, or any part thereof.

6. It is admitted, that the fees of counsel employed by the plaintiffs in the prosecution of the suit of ejectment against the Agricultural Bank, for the recovery of said City Hotel, in the Circuit Court and Supreme Court of the United States, exceeded in value the sum of two thousand dollars, and that said sum of $2000 dollars would be a reasonable fee for the conduct of said suit from its commencement to its termination.

It is admitted, that the furniture of house, &c., on the premises, formed part of the rent in the proportion of one fourth to three fourths thereof.

It is admitted, that the charter of the bank was declared forfeited by law, and the assets of the bank put in the possession of the defendant, who still holds the same as trustee or representative.   Ro. Mott, *Attorney.*
    Prentiss & Finney, *For Plaintiffs.*

It is further admitted, that the Agricultural Bank had stopped specie payments previous to the time of the forfeiture of the charter, and did not afterwards resume.
    Prentiss & Finney, *Plaintiffs' Attorneys.*

In January, 1849, the cause came on to be heard, when the Circuit Court decreed, that the plaintiffs do recover from Peale the sum of $20,058, with interest at 5 per cent. until paid; and that they should have execution upon the assets of the bank, which were then, or might be thereafter, in the hands of the trustee.

From this decree, Peale appealed and brought the case up to this court.

It was argued by *Mr. Lawrence,* for the plaintiff in error, and *Mr. Taylor,* for the defendants in error.

Only that point will be mentioned upon which the judgment of this court turned.

Mr. Lawrence contended, for the plaintiff in error, that the action against Peale, who was a mere officer of the Adams County Court, Mississippi, for the purpose of collecting the assets of a bank in course of liquidation, could not be maintained in the United States Circuit Court for Louisiana. If the

Peale v. Phipps et al.

plaintiff wished to bring suit, independent of the proceedings in the Adams County Court, the suit should have been brought against the corporation in its corporate name. Hutch. Dig. § 10, 11, act 1840, p. 326; § 8, act 1843, p. 328; act February 28, 1846, p. 332; 6 Howard, (Miss.) 674.

Mr. Taylor, for the defendants in error.

The second ground of exception is partly based upon the assumption that the affairs of the Agricultural Bank were administered by the trustee Peale, because of the declared insolvency of the bank. This is neither admitted, nor proved to be true; and, in fact, the affairs of the bank were taken from the management of her own officers, because those officers had violated the laws of its existence, whereby it ceased to exist. But it does not follow, as a necessary consequence, that because the charter of the bank was declared, by the Circuit Court of Adams County, to have been forfeited, or because its affairs were put in liquidation by the order of that court, or because Mr. Peale was appointed trustee by that court, no court but the Circuit Court of Adams County can entertain jurisdiction of a suit against him, as trustee. An administrator or executor is appointed to represent the estate of a person deceased, after the Probate Court has found or adjudged the fact of his death, and put his affairs into a course of liquidation in the same manner. Such executors are liable to be sued in any court whatever; and even in cases where the State laws provide expressly that they shall not be sued, except in the court by which they are appointed, they are held liable to answer to the United States Circuit Court, notwithstanding such special exemption made by the State law. See case of Dupuy v. Bemiss, where this question is fully argued, (2 Annual Rep. 509); and case of Erwin v. Lowry, (7 Howard, 172–181,) reviewing and approving the doctrines, and even the reasonings, of the Louisiana court; and also 14 Peters's Rep. 75, examining the same questions; all settling the doctrine that even where the representative of an estate is suable only in his own court by the State law, he may yet be sued in the United States Circuit Court, and there be held to answer, and compelled to pay a debt of the succession, because, in every case of a conflict between the laws made by Congress (in accordance with the Constitution of the United States) and the acts of a State Legislature, the State laws must yield. We believe, that, in Mississippi, other courts besides the Circuit Court of Adams County, could have entertained jurisdiction of a suit against this trustee, in his said capacity; and that even if it were shown that, by the positive requirement of the laws of the State of Mississippi, suit could have been brought against

Peale only in the Circuit Court of Adams County, which appointed him, we could, notwithstanding such requirement, sue Mr. Peale, as trustee, in the Circuit Court of the United States.

We also submit to the court whether the third and eighth admissions of counsel, found on the seventh page of the printed record, do not admit that the plaintiff in error, Mr. Peale, is the proper person to be sued for, and on account of, the debts due by the bank, because if, as admitted, the bank itself had ceased to exist, and Mr. Peale was in the actual possession of all its assets, and was its representative, he is the only person who can be sued on account of the liabilities of the bank. We think the admissions themselves afford good ground for overruling the exception.

Mr. Chief Justice TANEY delivered the opinion of the court.

This suit was brought by the defendants in error against the plaintiff in the Circuit Court of the United States for the Eastern District of Louisiana.

The proceeding was by petition in the usual form of Louisiana practice. It states that the plaintiff in error, in the capacity of trustee and assignee of the President, Directors, and Company of the Agricultural Bank of Mississippi, which was located, until the term of its dissolution at Natchez, in the said State, is indebted to the petitioners in the sum. of $34,000, upon the grounds set forth in the petition.

They state that they were the owners of two undivided third parts of a certain lot in Natchez, in the county of Adams, in the State of Mississippi, upon which stands the City Hotel; that they were unlawfully expelled from it by the Agricultural Bank; that they afterwards recovered back the possession by an action of ejectment in the Circuit Court of the United States for the Southern District of Mississippi; and that they are entitled to the sum above mentioned, against the bank, for damages and mesne profits while the bank held them out of possession together with the costs they incurred in the suit to recover it.

They further state, that by the decree of the Circuit Court of Adams County, a court of competent jurisdiction in the premises, the charter of the Agricultural Bank was declared forfeited, and the corporation dissolved; and that Peale, the plaintiff in error, was appointed trustee and assignee of the bank, and is the sole legal representative of the corporation; and they aver, that by operation of law all the assets of the corporation are vested in him as assignee, and that he became legally liable to the creditors to the extent of the assets which may come to his hands; and that he has assets in his possession, sufficient to pay all the debts of the corporation.

The plaintiff in error filed sundry exceptions and an answer to this petition. His 2d exception denies the jurisdiction of the court, upon the ground that, as trustee for the bank, he is not amenable to any other court than the one that appointed him. As we think this exception decisive against· the jurisdiction of the Circuit Court of Louisiana, it is not necessary in this opinion to set out the other exceptions, or to notice the claims he set up by the way of answer and reconvention, if his exceptions were overruled.

There is an agreement between the counsel of the respective parties, which admits substantially the facts stated in the petition, as respects the possession and recovery of the hotel in the suit in ejectment, and the appointment of plaintiff in error as trustee upon the forfeiture of the charter of the bank; and also that the defendants had presented this claim to the commissioners appointed in Mississippi to audit claims against the bank, and that they had refused to allow it. There are other admissions, in relation to the annual value of the lot and hotel, and the costs and expenses of the suit in ejectment, and also in relation to other things which are not material to this decision, and need not therefore be particularly stated. The case proceeded; and at the hearing of the exceptions they were all overruled, and a decree was finally passed against Peale as trustee and representative of the President, Directors, and Company of the Agricultural Bank, directing him to pay to the petitioners the sum of $20,058, with interest thereon at the rate of five per cent. until paid — and that the petitioners have execution therefor, upon the property, assets, goods and chattels, rights and credits of the said President, Directors, and Company of the Agricultural Bank of Mississippi, then in the hands of the said Peale, as trustee, or which might thereafter come to his hands.

It is to revise this judgment that the present writ of error is brought.

The power, duties, and responsibilities of the plaintiff in error, as trustee, are regulated by the laws of Mississippi.

The act of 1843 makes it the duty of every district attorney in the State, whenever he has good reason to believe that any incorporated bank, located in his district, has done any thing that would work a forfeiture of its charter, to file an information against the bank in the Circuit Court of the county in which it is situated; and if, upon the trial, the charter is adjudged to be forfeited, it is made the duty of the court to appoint one or more trustees to take charge of its books and as-acts, and to collect the debts and sell the property of the bank, and apply the proceeds in the manner which may be directed by law to the payment of the debts due from the corporation. And the trustee is required to give bond and security, to be approved by the court, for the faithful discharge of this duty.

The act of 1846 contains more detailed provisions on this subject. Among others, it directs the trustee to return, under oath, to the court by which he is appointed, an inventory of all the property and evidences of debt which shall have come into his possession; and is afterwards, under the direction of the court, to sell the same at public auction, and render an account of the sale so made to the court.

The act of 1846 also directs, that at the term at which judgment of forfeiture is rendered, the court shall appoint three commissioners to audit claims against the corporation; and it is made their duty to report their proceedings to the court at the first term after the expiration of twelve months allowed for the presentation of claims; at which time all exceptions to the report are to be heard and determined, and the court thereupon required to direct the distribution of the money in the hands of the trustee, to be made in the order prescribed by the law.

It was under these acts of the legislature of Mississippi, that the charter of the Agricultural Bank was declared forfeited, and the plaintiff in error appointed trustee. Commissioners also, it appears, were at the same time appointed to audit the accounts, who rejected this claim. Upon their refusal to allow it, the defendants in error instituted these proceedings in the Circuit Court of the United States for the Eastern District of Louisiana.

We see no ground upon which the jurisdiction of the court can be sustained. The plaintiff in error held the assets of the bank as the agent and receiver of the Court of Adams County, and subject to its order, and was not authorized to dispose of the assets, or to pay any debts due from the bank, except by the order of the court. He had given a bond for the performance of this duty, and would be liable to an action, if he paid any claim without the authority of the court from which he received his appointment, and to which he was accountable. The property, in legal contemplation, was in the custody of the court of which he was the officer, and had been placed there by the laws of Mississippi. And while it thus remained in the custody and possession of that court, awaiting its order and decision, no other court had a right to interfere with it, or to wrest it from the hands of its agent, and thereby put it out of his power to perform his duty. The case falls within the principle decided by this court in Vaughn v. Northrop, (15 Pet. 1,) in which it was held, that an administrator could not be sued in another State for a debt due from his intestate, because he is bound to account for all the assets he receives, to the proper tribunals of the government from which he derives his authority. And that decision was made in a case where the assets, by reason of which the administrator was sought to be charged, were received in the jurisdiction of the government in which the suit was brought against him, but in which he had not taken out letters of administration.

The case of Williams v. Benedict, and others, (8 Howard, 107,) is still more in point. By a law of Mississippi, if it appeared to the Orphans' Court, that the estate of a deceased person was insolvent, it was made the duty of the court to direct the property to be sold by the executor or administrator, and to appoint commissioners to audit the claims of creditors; and to distribute the proceeds of the property (after deducting the expenses of the last sickness and funeral expenses) among the creditors, in proportion to the sum due to them respectively.

The appellant was the administrator of an intestate whose estate had been declared to be insolvent by the Orphans' Court. But the appellees had obtained a judgment against the administrator in the District Court of the United States for the Northern District of Mississippi, before the adjudication of insolvency by the Orphans' Court—and issued an execution, and laid it upon property upon which his judgment was a lien, in case the estate was not insolvent. And, upon a bill filed by the appellant to obtain an injunction staying proceedings upon this execution, the appellees insisted that the estate was not insolvent, but had been wasted by the administrator, and that the proceedings in the Orphans' Court, under the law of Mississippi, were no bar to his recovery in a court of the United States. And the District Court was of that opinion, and dismissed the appellant's bill. But the decree was reversed by this court upon the ground that the jurisdiction of the Orphans' Court had attached to the assets, and that they were *in gremio legis*, and could not be seized by process from another court.

And in the case of Wiswall v. Sampson's Lessee, decided at the present term, the court held that where certain lands were in the hands of a receiver, appointed by the Chancery Court of Alabama, in a case pending before it, they could not be sold by the marshal upon process of execution, issuing out of the Circuit Court of the United States, for that district, although the judgment upon which the process issued, was a lien upon the land, and the execution was laid before the receiver obtained actual possession of the property. In the case of Erwin v. Lowry, (7 Howard, 181,) referred to in the argument of the counsel for the defendants in error, the proceedings in the Court of the United States were merely to enforce a lien created by the testator in his lifetime, and consequently could not interfere with the duties of the curator, or the authority of the State Court, under which he was acting, and to which he was bound to account.

It is suggested, also, in the argument, that the claim in reconvention made in the answer, is a waiver of the exception to the jurisdiction; because the claim in reconvention necessarily admits the jurisdiction of the court. But the article in the code of practice, and the case referred to, do not support the objection. The claim in reconvention is in express terms, made in case the exception to the jurisdiction is overruled, and not otherwise. It is made conditionally, the party at the same time denying the jurisdiction of the court in the matter in controversy.

Moreover, the facts stated in the petition of the defendants in error, show that the Circuit Court of Louisiana had no jurisdiction. And where that is the case, the general rule in all legal proceedings is, that the defendant may avail himself of the objection in any stage of the proceedings. We see nothing in the code of practice that leads us to suppose that a different rule prevails in the courts of Louisiana. And if it does, yet the exception to the jurisdiction was in this case pleaded *in limine* when the plaintiff in error appeared to the suit, and the conditional claim in reconvention cannot, by any just construction of its terms, be held to be a waiver of the plea.

The judgment of the Circuit Court must therefore be reversed, and a mandate issued directing the judgment to be entered for the plaintiff in error.

Order.

This cause came on to be heard on the transcript of the record from the Circuit Court of the United States for the Eastern District of Louisiana, and was argued by counsel. On consideration whereof, it is now here ordered, and adjudged, by this court, that the judgment of the said Circuit Court, in this cause be, and the same is hereby, reversed, with costs, and that this cause be, and the same is hereby, remanded to the said Circuit Court, with directions to enter judgment in favor of the plaintiff in error.

MATTHEW CUNNINGHAM, PLAINTIFF IN ERROR, v. MARY W. W. ASHLEY, EXECUTRIX AND SOLE LEGATEE OF CHESTER ASHLEY, DECEASED, AND WILLIAM · E. ASHLEY, FRANCES 'A. ASHLEY, (NOW FRANCES A. FREEMAN,) AND HENRY W. ASHLEY, BY MARY W W. ASHLEY, HIS · GUARDIAN, HEIRS AT LAW OF SAID CHESTER ASHLEY, DECEASED, AND ROSWELL BEEBE.

On the 25th of December, 1824, Cunningham applied to the land-office at Batesville, in Arkansas, to become the purchaser of a quarter section of land under a Cherokee certificate which had become vested in him.

This application was refused, upon the ground that two New Madrid certificates had been laid upon the land in 1820. The right under these certificates was claimed by Ashley.

In 1830, Cunningham said that Brumbach had an improvement on the same quarter section, which Brumbach assigned to Ashley. The law sanctioned the division of a quarter section, under such circumstances.

In 1831, Cunningham claimed a preëmption right under the act of 29th May, 1830. The claims under this act, and under the Cherokee float were were not inconsistent with each other.

In 1838, two floats were entered upon the same quarter section, viz.: one by Plummer, for the east half of it, under the act of 1830, and the supplemental act of 1832; the other for the west half by Jenbeau, under the act of 1834, and the circular of the General Land-Office of 1837. Patents were issued, and the title became vested in Ashley.

The title of Cunningham is better than that derived from these floats. The title under the New Madrid certificates is not decided in this case, or affected in any way by the decision. Cunningham is therefore entitled to the half of the quarter section which he claimed separately from Brumbach.

The patents obtained by Ashley and Beebe, being founded upon entries which were void, are void also, so far as they interfere with the preëmptive right of Cunningham.

THIS case was brought up from the Supreme Court of the State of Arkansas, by a writ of error issued under the 25th section of the Judiciary Act.

The facts in the case were numerous and complicated, and a statement of the principal ones is given in the opinion of the court. It would not throw light upon any general principle if the reporter were to give a more particular account of the long series of acts which the respective parties considered to be the foundation of their respective titles. Nor would it be possible to explain the arguments of counsel, commenting on contradictory testimony, without a previous and detailed history of the transactions of twenty years. One of the briefs filed in the cause was upwards of seventy printed pages. The opinion of the court has given a selection of the leading facts in the case, so that its merits upon both sides can be clearly understood.

It was argued by *Mr. Lawrence* and *Mr. Pike*, for the plaintiff in error, and by *Mr. Bradley* and *Mr. Johnson*, for the defendants in error.

32 *

Mr. Justice McLEAN delivered the opinion of the court.

A writ of error to the Supreme Court of Arkansas, brings this case in Chancery before us, under the twenty-fifth section of the Judiciary Act.

On the 25th of December, 1824, Matthew Cunningham, by his attorney, applied to the Register of the Land-Office at Bates-ville, in Arkansas, to become the purchaser of the south-east quarter of section three, in township one, north, and in range twelve, west of the fifth principal meridian, south of the Arkansas River; by virtue of a certificate (No. 23) granted by the Register of the said land district, to William Wylee, assignee of William Morrison, under the act of 26th May, 1824.

That act provided that every person, entitled to the right of preëmption by law, in the tract of country north of the Arkansas River, which was ceded to the Cherokees, should be authorized, in lieu thereof, to enter with the above Register, any tract, in the Lawrenceville district, on which he may have made improvements, previously to the passage of the act; or, on any unimproved tract, within the district, the sale of which is authorized by law

By several meshe assignments, the right of the Cherokee certificate was vested in Cunningham, and the land he proposed to enter, was, by law, authorized to be sold. The agent of the complainant informed the Register and Receiver, that he had the money, and was desirous of paying for the land; but, after consultation between the officers, he was informed the entry would not be permitted. The ground of this rejection was not stated, at the time, nor entered upon the records of either office. There can be no doubt, from the facts in the case, which appear in the correspondence of the General Land-Office, and otherwise, that the application to make the entry was rejected, on the ground that the land was covered by New Madrid locations. And it appears that two New Madrid certificates had been laid on the quarter section; one on the 19th of April, 1820, and the other on the 1st of May, of the same year.

On the 27th of May, 1831, the complainant claimed the right of preëmption to the same quarter section, under the act of the 29th of May, 1830. Being duly sworn, he stated, "that, in the year 1829, he had in cultivation about four acres, in corn and vegetables, on the land, and had been in possession of it near ten years; was in possession of it the 29th of May, 1830, and still occupied it." Several other witnesses proved the same facts, and one of them states, that he saw the complainant put down on the counter about two hundred dollars, and informed the Receiver that it was offered in payment of the land.

In the record, there is a list of the preëmptions allowed, at the Land-Office at Batesville, by H. Boswell and J. Rodman, late Register and Receiver, from the 8th of January, 1831, to the 30th of June, in the same year, as appears from the papers of that office. In that list, the name of Matthew Cunningham stands first, as having entered the south-east quarter of section three, first township, north, twelfth range, west. It is certified by Townsend Dickinson, Register. On this paper the word "rejected" is found, but by whom written, and for what purpose, does not appear on the paper. The names of H. Boswell and J. Rodman, are under the word "rejected"; and several of the witnesses state, that the word "rejected," or "allowed," was indorsed on the envelop of preëmption papers, as the decision of the land-officers was made.

In the list is the name of Nathan Cloyes, claiming the preemption right to the north-west fractional quarter of section two, in township one, north of range twelve, the claim to which was decreed to his heirs, in Lytle et al. v. the State of Arkansas et al. 9 Howard, 328.

There is, also, in the record, a certificate of Samuel W. Rutherford, Register of the Land-Office at Little Rock, where the papers of the Batesville officers are deposited, dated the 27th of December, 1837, which states, "that Matthew Cunningham was allowed, at the Land-Office at Batesville, (Lawrenceville land district,) a preëmption claim on the south-east quarter of section three, township one, north range twelve, west, as appears from the papers furnished this office from the Land-Office at Batesville, as having been allowed said Cunningham, prior to the 30th of June, of the same year." The year referred to was 1831, as stated in the above list of preëmption claims.

Various efforts were made by the complainant, at the Land-Office at Batesville, and at the General Land-Office, at Washington, to procure a full recognition of his preëmption claim. Appeals on the subject were made to the Secretary of the Treasury, and to the Attorney-General, all of which resulted in the denial of his claim, on the ground that the quarter section was not subject to a preëmptive right, by reason of the prior New Madrid locations.

It appears, from the record, that at the Land-Office at Little Rock, on the 6th of June, 1838, there was entered, by "Samuel Plummer, by virtue of his preëmption float, under the act of 1830, and the supplemental act of 1832, the east half of the south-east quarter of fractional section three, south of the Arkansas River, in township one, north of range twelve, west, containing eighty acres, &c., as per certificate granted to him, No. 3549" And that, on the same day, "Mary L. Jenbeau entered, by virtue of her preëmption float, under the act of 1834, and circular of the General Land-Office, of the 9th of June, 1837, the west half of the south-east quarter of section three, in township óne, north of range twelve, west, &c., as per certificate granted to her, No. 3554."

In their answers, the defendants say, "that they caused application to be made by legal and valid floating preëmption rights, fully authorized by law, to locate and enter said southeast quarter of section three, the same being then vacant public land, and liable, by law, to be entered by such floating rights; and this defendant, (Ashley,) in conjunction with said Beebe, caused the same to be entered, on the east half in the name of Samuel Plummer, and the west half in the name of Mary L. Jenbeau," &c. " Which said floating preëmption rights were located, entered, and transferred, according to law and all the lawful rules and regulations of the General Land-Office; and were duly patented to said Beebe, by the President of the United States, on the 25th of September, 1839."

On the 26th of December, 1838, the Commissioner of the General Land-Office, required the land-officers at Little Rock to inform him, " why entries 3549 and 3554, with two others, were permitted to be made on land already occupied by prior claims long since located, and against the validity of which this office possesses no evidence." In reply, dated 30th January, 1839, the land-officers stated, that the entries were permitted "upon the demand of Roswell Beebe, and the several allegations made by him, setting forth and showing, conclusively, that the Treasury Department had disallowed the preëmption claims under the act of 1814, upon all the lands south of the Arkansas River, ceded by the Quapaw treaties of 1818, and 1824," &c. And they say, " The original plat of survey embracing those entries, was, at the time, complete, and represented the subdivisional lines, and the number of acres corresponding respectively with those certificates of entry; and there was no evidence of record on file, in either of our offices, to show that these lands were ever regularly entered, or located, and due return made thereof, according to law, except such evidence as was exhibited by the preëmption, abstract from Batesville, under the act of 1814, and the coloring of the plat. The capitol of the State of Arkansas is built upon a portion of these lands, at a cost of some seventy thousand dollars, or more. The corporate authorities of the city of Little Rock, as well as the inhabitants, all hold under conveyances derived from, as under the preëmption claim, and against the New Madrid claims, either by a compromise made by the respective claimants about the year 1821, or, by the decision of the land-officers at Batesville, of which we are not particularl informed. All parties, within the limits of the city, we believe, are fully satisfied that these entries which embrace it will cure the defects in their titles, as no dissatisfaction is believed to exist with any one interested in the question. Those entries were therefore allowed by us upon due reflection, under the belief that we were acting correctly in the faithful discharge of our duties; and by which the individuals who supposed they rightfully claimed those lands, will be enabled to obtain a perfect title, and thereby save and protect the rights and titles of the numerous persons claiming under them, and to whom they are bound by obligation or deed."

In a letter from the Commissioner of the General Land-Office, dated the 24th of September, 1839, to the Register and Receiver at Little Rock, he says, " Your letter in reference to certain tracts of land located by floats 3549 and 3554, under the act of the 19th of June, 1834, has been received;" and he remarks, "after an attentive and careful examination of all the questions connected with the different claims preferred to the land above referred to, this office, on the 18th instant, transmitted to the Secretary of the Treasury, agreeably to his request, all the papers in reference to the case, with an opinion of this office in favor of a confirmation of these floats, regarding the bond filed by Roswell Beebe, as a sufficient compliance with the spirit of the circular of 11th of October, 1837; and I have this day received from him a communication concurring in that opinion. Patents will, therefore, issue for certificates 3549 and 3554, and two other numbers stated."

The circular referred to by the Commissioner, in the above letter of the 11th of October, 1837, contains the following sentences : " The President of the United States has directed that, until the further action of Congress thereon, the rights of preemption of eighty acres of land elsewhere, usually called floating rights, granted by the second section of the act of Congress, approved May 29th, 1830, which act was revived and continued by the act approved June 19th, 1834, and which, also, as you were informed by my circular of June 9th, 1837, is for certain purposes therein stated, still in force; shall be restricted in their location to unimproved and vacant public land."

" You are therefore instructed not to permit the entry, by virtue of a floating right, of any tract on which there is a cultivation, improvement, settlement, or occupant, unless the owner of the float shall first produce to you the written consent thereto, of the person or persons claiming the same improvement, cultivation, settlement, or occupancy, attested by two witnesses."

The second section of the act of the 29th of May, 1830, provides, " that where two persons are settled upon the same quarter section, each may receive a preëmption for eighty acres, and a right to enter eighty acres elsewhere, so as not to interfere with other settlers having a right of preference."

In his letter to the Secretary of the Treasury, "in favor of a confirmation of the above floats," the Commissioner says, "the claim of Matthew Cunningham, under the act of 26th of May, 1824, has heretofore been disposed of;" and further, "that the claims of Christian Brumbach and Matthew Cunningham, under the preëmption act of 29th May, 1830, have no validity. The report of the Register and Receiver, dated 20th July, 1839, and its accompanying papers, together with the Receiver's letter of the 25th July, 1839, with the inclosure, show that no action had been had on the claim of Christian Brumbach, by the land-officers; that no tender of the purchase-money was made by him, and no explanation can be given why his claim has been suffered to sleep from 1831 to 1839; and then only revived upon the rejection of the claim of Mrs. Backus, for the same quarter section under the act of 1838, who claims also to hold under Brumbach's claim of the act of 1830. Brumbach's own testimony shows, also, that he was living there by the permission of one of the proprietors of the town, and made the improvements for their benefit under a contract, and his deed of December 22d, 1824, accompanies those papers whereby those improvements were conveyed to Chester Ashley, one of the proprietors."

And further in relation to Cunningham's claim under the act of 1824, he says, it was rejected under the opinion of the Attorney-General; and remarks, "there is a strong point against the validity of that claim, which circumstances did not render it necessary heretofore to make, viz., that as the law of 26th May, 1824, granted the privilege of entering vacant land only, except where the preëmptor or his legal representatives was desirous of securing his own improvements made prior to the passage of the land, &c., and he argues that Cunningham should not be permitted to locate one hundred and sixty acres of land, to secure improvements on a few town lots."

On the 15th of July, 1839, it appears, by the certificate of the Receiver at Little Rock, that the complainant again tendered the sum of two hundred dollars, in payment of the quarter section in controversy.

As the legal title to the land in controversy is in the defendants, the right of the complainant can be sustained only by showing a paramount equity. This he has attempted to do. But before we enter upon this investigation, it may be proper to state, distinctly, the grounds on which the title of the respective parties will be considered. From the issue made by the pleadings, we do not consider the New Madrid locations, or any right under them, as involved in the case. They were necessarily set aside, if not abandoned, by the defendants, when they located their floating rights on the land in controversy, on which patents were obtained. The right of the complainant has, from its origin, been hostile to the New Madrid claims.

The equity of the complainant must rest upon his occupancy and improvement of the land, whether he claims under the Cherokee warrant, or a preëmption under the act of 1830. The defendant's legal title will be considered as founded, exclusively on the locations made by the floating rights, on which the patents were obtained.

The two claims, set up by the complainant in his bill, require different facts, in the order of time, to sustain them; but they are in no respect inconsistent with each other. The Cherokee float could be located only on unoccupied land, or on land improved by the holder of the warrant.

As the land-officers at Batesville would not permit the complainant to make an entry under either claim, it is therefore important to ascertain on what ground they decided; and also as to the sufficiency of the evidence to sustain the right as claimed. There can be no question that the decision of these officers was founded on the prior New Madrid locations. These were made before the complainant took possession of the land. This, under the circumstances, being an insuperable objection to the entry, no court can presume that their decision was made on any other ground, unless such ground was stated, or the evidence was defective.

The voluminous correspondence of the General Land-Office shows, that the land-officers considered the above New Madrid locations as an appropriation of the land. Was the evidence adduced by complainant sufficient to establish his right?

The authority to Samuel C. Roane to make the entry, as the agent of Cunningham, under the act of 1824, was undoubted. The application to make the entry was made in due form. The Cherokee warrant had been issued by the land-officers, who were called upon to make the entry. The assignments upon the warrant were *primâ facie* evidence of right in Cunningham, and there does not appear to have been any objection to them; they must be considered, therefore, as having been held sufficient. The money on the entry was offered to be paid to the Receiver, and the only defect in the evidence was as to the improvements and occupancy of the complainants. These, it is contended, the court may presume were within the knowledge of the land-officers, or that the facts were proved by parol, or that they were proved by affidavits, which have become mislaid or lost. As the proof in the record, in regard to these facts, applies to the preëmption claimed under the act of 1830, there is no occasion to resort to presumptions on this head.

The preëmption act of the 29th of May, 1830, in the first section, provided, "that every settler or occupant of the public lands, prior to the passage of this act, who is now in possession, and cultivated any part thereof in the year 1829, shall be, and he is hereby authorized to enter, with the Register of the land-office for the district in which the lands may lie, by legal subdivisions, any number of acres, not more than one hundred and sixty, or a quarter section to include his improvement, upon paying to the United States the then minimum price of said lands."

Under this law the applicant was a witness, and Cunningham was interrogated by the land-officers on his application. He stated that in the year 1829, he cultivated about four acres on the quarter section claimed, and that he had been in possession of said improvement for near ten years, and that he was still in possession of it. And he further stated, Christian Brumbach had an improvement on the same quarter section which he had in cultivation, in the year 1829, and has continued to hold possession of the same to this time. This statement is corroborated by the oath of C. Brumbach, and as to the occupancy and improvement of complainant, by C. H. Pelham and Richard Searcy.

It is clearly shown, that the improvements of Cunningham, up to 1831, were wholly on the quarter section claimed ; and that his cultivation and occupancy continued without interruption from the time he took possession in 1821, until the fall of the year 1831. He then removed to his present residence, the principal part of which is on the north-west quarter section, but a part, if not all, of his outbuildings, are on the south-east quarter. His former residence was south of his present one. The improvement he made at first is still cultivated by him.

As lot number one, on which the complainant's first house was built, was conveyed to Bertrand, his step-son, in 1821, by O'Harra, it is contended that the complainant had no such residence on the land, as to entitle him to preëmption. Bertrand was a minor, and lived with his step-father at the time, and it is quite clear, that a minor cannot claim a preëmptive right. But, in addition to this, as the case is now before us, it does not appear that O'Harra had any right to the lot conveyed.

It is objected that Cunningham's improvements, though on the quarter section claimed, are limited by the boundaries of a certain square, or lots, within the city of " Little Rock ;" and that, consequently, he cannot claim a preëmption for the quarter section.

On the 20th of November, 1821, certain individuals, assuming to be owners and proprietors of the north-east fractional quarter of section number three, and of fractional section number two, of township number one, north of the base line in range number twelve west, entered into a deed of assurance, in which they agreed to lay out the town of Little Rock, specifying the streets and alleys, and making certain donations of public squares and lots for public purposes. This plat appears to have been surveyed so as to embrace the quarter section in controversy. In their answers, the defendants specify a number of lots sold in the south-east quarter, and they allege the greater part of it has been sold in lots. The proprietors in their deed say, that they extended the plat to adjoining lands not owned by them.

This survey of lots in the south-east quarter of section three, if made without authority, cannot embarrass the complainant's right. The New Madrid locations being out of the case, should the right of the complainant be sustained against the legal title of the defendants, the surveys must be considered as void. The town was incorporated in 1825, and, by the act of 1827, the corporation was extended so as to embrace the whole of the town plat.

When the improvement of the complainant was commenced, the south-east quarter was in its natural state, unchanged by any improvement.

Every legal requisite appears to have been complied with under the act of 1830, to entitle the complainant to a preëmption. His improvement and occupancy under the law were clearly proved. Indeed it would seem, from the facts, that he was entitled to become the purchaser of the land under the law of 1824. But all the facts, necessary to establish his right, were before the Register and Receiver on his second application. His application to make the entry may be said to have been rejected, because it was not allowed. But no doubt can exist as to the ground of the rejection. It was not on account of any deficiency in the proof, but on the ground of the New Madrid locations. This is placed beyond question, by the parol proof in the case, and the correspondence of the General Land-Office. Other objections to the claim, after the second rejection, were stated by that officer, which alleged a want of diligence by the complainant, in failing to do what he has proved was done, in the prosecution of his right. Some of these objections showed r misapprehension of the facts, others of the law.

The offices at Batesville were loosely kept, and it appears in proof that some year or two before his death, Boswell, the Register, became intemperate, and his duties were neglected. Great labor was required from his successor to reduce to system the confused mass of papers he found in the office.

It was the practice of the office to indorse on the envelop

of the preëmption papers, the decision, of which no other entry was made. And one of the witnesses states that "rejected" was indorsed on the envelop which inclosed the papers of Cunningham. It is difficult to reconcile this .fact with two lists in the record, duly certified, of preëmptions allowed, in both of which the name of Cunningham is found. The word "rejected" is on one of the lists. There can be no doubt the claim was rejected as often as it was brought to the notice of the land department, so long as the New Madrid locations were sanctioned. No other decision could be made. But on the 6th of June, 1838, floats were permitted to be located on the quarter section in controversy, covered by the New Madrid locations. This was procured through the agency of the defendants, and for their benefit.

It was the result of a controversy of nearly twenty years' continuance. Since eighteen hundred and twenty-one, Cunningham had occupied the land, and had carried on the controversy with a commendable energy, and at no small expense of time and money. He urged his claim at the General Land-Office, personally, and by agents. The correspondence on the subject was earnest and voluminous. But the defendants, having made their entries, received the legal title. And their equity must now be compared with that of the complainants.

The New Madrid locations were controlled by the defendants. And they were not withdrawn, or the obstacle which they created removed, until the defendants' entries were made. The floats under which these entries were permitted, were issued under the act of 1830, continued in force by the act of 1834. The second section of the act declared that these floats should be so located, "as not to interfere with other settlers, having a right of preference." And the circular of the land-office directed that they "should be restricted to unimproved and vacant lands."

These stringent regulations were not sufficient to protect the rights of the complainant. His occupancy, improvements, and claim, were known to the defendants, and to all the officers of the government, who acted on the subject. They excused or justified themselves on the ground, that by permitting the entry to be made, many of the citizens of "Little Rock" would be quieted in their titles.

On the 6th of July, 1838, an instrument, under seal, was entered into between Roswell Beebe, to whom the patents were issued, of the one part, and the Mayor and Aldermen of the city of "Little Rock," in behalf of said city, as well as in behalf of the State of Arkansas, and also in behalf of any person or persons who may have in his own right a proper and regular chain of conveyance or conveyances of any town lot or lots situated in the first original town, now city of "Little Rock," derived from, by, or under, any one or more of the original owners and proprietors of the town, as represented upon the first original plan as then surveyed and laid off into town lots, of the other part, witnesseth, that whereas the said Roswell Beebe has caused to be located and entered with preëmption floating claims, at the Land-Office at "Little Rock," and upon which the city, south of the Arkansas River, and west of the Quapaw line, is now built, the following described tracts or parcels of land, to wit, the north-east fractional quarter of fractional section three, and the west fractional part of the north-west and south-west fractional quarters of fractional section two, all in township one, north of the base line of range twelve west, &c. And in all cases, where purchases of lots had been made in the above tracts, Beebe bound himself to release to the purchasers.

This arrangement induced the land-officers to permit the entries to be made, as well on the south-east quarter in controversy, as on the tracts above described. And it was considered at the General Land-Office as a sufficient compliance with the circular of that office, dated the 11th of October, 1837. The patents on this view were issued to Beebe; and on the 11th of January, 1842, Beebe conveyed one half of the south-east quarter in controversy, to Ashley.

However satisfactory the agreement of Beebe may have been to claimants of lots on the tracts specified in his agreement, as it did not embrace the land claimed by the complainant, it was not designed for his benefit. And it is unaccountable that the land-officers at "Little Rock" and at Washington, should have considered the arrangement as a compliance with the regulation which prohibited the entry of floats upon improved or occupied land. And it is worthy of remark, that these locations were permitted to be made at "Little Rock," while the claimant was at Washington, prosecuting his claim.

Has the complainant placed himself in a position to object to the defendants' equity? He did every thing he could reasonably be required to do, to locate his Cherokee warrant on the land, under the act of 1824. Had it been objected, on that application, that he did not prove his improvement and occupancy, the witnesses would, at once, have been called. With this exception, he did every thing the law required to perfect his claim.

But, under the act of 1830, his proof was in no respect defective. It was worthy of the highest credit, and full to every point; and the money was offered to be paid. But the locations of the New Madrid warrants were an obstacle then, as they had been on the first application. These locations were not in the way of defendants' floats, and it is not material to inquire by what means they were set aside. This being done, the rights of the complainant were paramount to those acquired under the new location. Those rights were founded on the settlement and improvement in 1821, and on the acts done subsequently in the prosecution of his claim. Having done every thing which was in his power to do, the law required nothing more. And the defendants who caused the floats to be located on the premises, had full notice of the complainant's rights. They are chargeable with this notice. Under the second section of the act of the 29th of May, 1830, and the circular of the Commissioner of the General Land-Office, of the 11th of October, 1847, so far as the new entries interfered with the rights of the complainant, they were void. They were in conflict with the law and the regulation.

The pretence that the agreement of Beebe, which bound him to execute deeds to the purchasers of lots, was a compliance with the above circular, so far as regards the land in controversy, was without foundation. It may have misled the officers at Washington, and in this it may have answered its purpose. The officers of the government are the agents of the law. They cannot act beyond its provisions, nor make compromises not sanctioned by it.

By the second section of the act of 1830, it is provided, "That if two or more persons be settled upon the same quarter section, the same may be divided between the two first actual settlers, if by a north and south, or east and west line, the settlement or improvement of each can be included in a half quarter section."

At the time the complainant applied for a preëmption under the act of 1830, he stated that Christian Brumbach had an improvement on the same quarter section, which he had in cultivation in the year 1829, and has continued to hold possession of the same to this time. And it was proved that Brumbach cultivated the land in 1830. The improvement occupied by complainant was commenced about the same time as the one occupied by Brumbach; and the evidence shows that they were the first settlers on the land. This we suppose, under the law, limits the preemption claimed by the complainant to one half of the quarter section. The residence and improvement of Brumbach brought him *primâ facie* within the law; whether he applied for and attained a preemption or not. It was necessary, under the regulations of the General Land-Office, that the complainant should state, in his applications, the occupancy, improvement, and cultivation of Brumbach, and whatever objection may be made to his preëmption claim by the government, cannot enlarge the right of the complainant. Brumbach applied for a preëmption in the quarter section, under the act of 1830, and established his right in every thing, except the tender of the money. His claim was rejected, no doubt, on the same ground, as was that of the complainant's.

Brumbach had conveyed his right to Ashley, in whom the legal title is vested to one half of the quarter section. This removed the objection to the location of one of the floating rights for eighty acres on the quarter, as the improvement, if not made by Ashley, was owned by him. In regard to the one half of the quarter, the entry was not prohibited by the second section of the act of 1830, or the circular of 1837. To extend the preëmptive right of the complainant over the entire quarter, would cover improvements of another individual, made about the same time as those on which his preëmption is founded. This would disregard the express provision of the law, which gives to each settler, where there are two upon the same quarter section, eighty acres.

As the right set up by the complainant arises under an act of Congress, and the decision of the Supreme Court of Arkansas was against that right, this court has jurisdiction of the case.

We have not considered any right equitable or legal, as arising under the New Madrid locations, laid upon the land in dispute. Such right, if any existed, is not presented in the pleading, in such a form as to require its consideration and decision. It therefore remains wholly unaffected by the decree.

The facts in the case are exceedingly voluminous and complicated; but we have considered them, and the legal and equitable bearing they have upon the title of the parties. Upon this view, we are brought to the conclusion that the entries on which the defendants' patents were issued, were void, so far as they interfere with the claim of the complainant, for the reasons stated, and that, consequently, the patents are also void. The decree of the Supreme Court of Arkansas is therefore reversed; and the cause is remanded to that court, with instructions to enter a decree in pursuance of this opinion. And in order to give more definitely our views, we state, that, on a full consideration of the pleadings and proof in the case, we consider that the two entries of eighty acres each, made in the name of Samuel Plummer and Mary Louisa Jenbeau, on the south-east quarter of section number three, in township one north, and in range twelve, west of the fifth principal meridian, south of the Arkansas River, are void so far as they interfere with the preëmptive right of Matthew Cunningham to one half of the said quarter; and that Roswell Beebe, and the heirs of Chester Ashley, deceased, defendants, shall execute a deed of quitclaim to the said Cunningham, on his paying or tendering to them the minimum price of the public land, with interest from the sixth of June, 1838, the time the above entries were made, to one half of the above quarter section, by east and west, or north and south lines, so as to include his improvement on the quarter section, or, if such a division cannot be made, that they convey to him, as aforesaid, a joint interest of one half in the quarter section.

And the court order that the decree shall in no respect affect any right which may or does exist, under the New Madrid locations, in the defendants or other persons, if any there be.

Order.

This cause came on to be heard on the transcript of the record from the Supreme Court of the State of Arkansas, and was argued by counsel. On consideration whereof, it is now here ordered, adjudged, and decreed, by this court, that the decree of the said Supreme Court in this cause be, and the same is hereby, reversed, with costs, and that this cause be, and the same is hereby, remanded to the said Supreme Court, for further proceedings to be had therein in conformity to the opinion of this court.

MARY LUCINDA BOSLEY, HENRY BOSLEY, MARY JANE DAVIS, SALLY ANN DAVIS, JAMES BOSLEY AND MELDRID BOSLEY, (INFANTS,) BY THEIR GUARDIAN AND NEXT FRIEND JOHN BOSLEY, AND JOHN BOSLEY SON OF THE SAID JOHN, v. MARGARET E. WYATT, EXECUTRIX OF ELIZABETH N. BOSLEY, DECEASED.

James Bosley, in his will, after sundry specific devises and bequests, devised and bequeathed all his lands and other real estate in Baltimore, Cecil, and Alleghany counties, in Maryland, and also in Florida, and his house and lot in Santa Croix, and all the real estate he might have elsewhere, to his wife Elizabeth, her heirs and assigns, in trust to sell the same and divide the net proceeds thereof, with all the residue of his estate, equally between herself and the children of his brother.

After making his will, he sold all of the lands, particularly mentioned in the residuary clause of the will above stated, except some lands lying in Baltimore county. At the time of making the codicil hereafter-mentioned, he held some of the proceeds of these sales in bonds and other securities, and with the residue had purchased other property.

He afterwards made a codicil, by which he devised his summer residence, in Baltimore county, to his wife, and also the securities he held for the lands sold in Cecil county, and directed all the property he had acquired after the date of his will to be sold, and the proceeds to be equally divided between his wife and her sister Margaret. Then followed a residuary clause in the following words:

"Lastly, my pew in St. Paul's Church and all my other property, real or personal, and all money in bank belonging to me at the time of my decease, I give, devise and bequeathe unto my said wife Elizabeth and her heirs forever; and I ratify and confirm my said last will in every thing except where the same is hereby revoked and altered as aforesaid."

The residuary clause in this codicil is inconsistent with that in the will, and consequently revokes it. But the devise of the property, specifically mentioned in the will, is not revoked by the clause in the codicil.

After the execution of the codicil, the testator agreed to lease some land for the term of ninety-nine years, renewable forever, a ground rent being reserved upon the same. The lessee was to pay cash for a part, and the residue of the purchase-money was to remain on interest, as ground rent, which the lessee could extinguish at any time by the payment of the principal sum.

This property was a part of that which was specifically mentioned in the will, and not revoked by the clause in the codicil.

But the conduct of the testator, in making this agreement, so altered the condition of the property that it amounted to a revocation of the devise, and manifests an intention on his part, when taken in connection with other circumstances of the case, to give it to his wife under the residuary clause in the codicil.

THIS was an appeal from the Circuit Court of the United States for the District of Maryland.

The bill was filed by the plaintiffs in error, who were the children of Dr. John Bosley, mentioned in the will of James Bosley.

That part of the will which gave occasion to the controversy is stated in the opinion, as are also the material facts in the case.

The Circuit Court decided that the residuary devise in the will was revoked by the residuary clause in the codicil; that the devise of the property, specifically mentioned in the will, was not revoked by the clause in the codicil, and ordered an account to be taken of such part as remained subject to the trust, one half of the proceeds whereof to be paid over to the complainants; and that the testator's agreement, made after the date of the will and the codicil, to lease a part of that real estate for a term of ninety-nine years, the principal sum payable at the option of the lessee, operated to revoke the devise as to that part.

From this decree, the complainants appealed to this court.

It was argued by M. Mayer, for the appellants, and Mr. Campbell and Mr. Johnson, for the appellees.

Mr. Mayer, for the appellants, made the following points.

1. The final clause of the codicil institutes no new residuary devisee and legatee; and the words supposed to effect that, are not the appropriate, nor any constructive phrase, for a residuary disposition in a will; and those words (which are, " all other my property, real or personal,") must be construed either — 1st, to comprise all property " other" than the pew, and so to purport to annul all devises and bequests of will and codicil,

except those in favor of Mrs. Bosley; which result must condemn the paragraph as incongruous and absurd; or, 2dly, to point to only property *ejusden generis* with the pew, and with the real property just in a preceding clause given to Mrs. Bosley and Miss Noel, and being the acquisitions subsequent to the date of the will; or, 3dly, must be rejected altogether as incapable of any consistent or reasonable application; or, as militating against the general intent of the testator, of dedicating his estate (with but small exceptions) to the children of John Bosley, and to Mrs. Bosley. 3 P. Wms. 112; 3 Atk. 61; 3 My. & Cr. 661; 1 Eq. Ca. Abr. 301; pl. 14; 1 Bro. C. C. 127, 39; 1 Russ. 146; 2 Atk. 113; 1 Jarman, 395, '9, 417; Greenl. Cruise [Devises] 133 and note to ch. 8, §39; 6 Watts, 192; 3 Peters, 117, 118; 11 Gill & J. 206; 2 Paige, 22; 8 Mass. 3; 11 Ed. 528; 22 Maine, 257, 413; 4 B. & Cres. 620; 2 Wms. Ex'rs, 799, 790; 6 Peters, 83, 84; 5 Ves. 247; 10 Wheat. 239; 13 Peters, 173; 5 Ves. Jr. 247; 21 E. C. L. 352; 1 Jarman, 594, 595, 596.

2. The paragraph adverted to, is no residuary disposition; because, a specific bequest follows it to Mrs. Bosley, which would be utterly needless and idle, if it were preceded by the supposed all-comprehending residuary appropriation. 13 Ves. Jr. 39; 1 Russ. 149; 3 Atk. 61; 1 Jarman, 595, 598, 599, 600.

3. There is, by those words, no revocation of the residuary devise and bequest of the will, because, the codicil, in erms following those words, confirms the will, except where the same is (by the codicil) "revoked and altered." The testator introduces several express revocations into his codicil; and to only those revocations must he be understood to refer — and to modifications, by name of "alterations," of his will — for any interferences with the will, as meant to be revoked, or affecte" by the codicil. If the words in question touch at all the residuary disposition of the will, they must affect it only as a revocation; and, leaving out of view mere modifications, or "alterations," the inquiry is, what revocation the testator meant should trench upon the broad confirmation his codicil gives to the will, thus declared as of continuing force? The will speaks anew from the date of the codicil, even without any confirmatory reference to it in the codicil, and the two acts are thus intimately allied; and any revocation of any part of the will, imputed to the codicil, must be by words as precise and unequivocal, and positive, as are the terms of the dispositions supposed to be revoked.

The testator has given his own limitation to the effect of his "alterings" of his will, or of any estate disposed of by it, by declaring, in the codicil, that where Mrs. Bosley, (under the clause next to the last,) shall "alter" any estate, it shall nevertheless take the course prescribed in the will, and that "alteration" is not, in his view, and by the law of his will, the same as revocation; and he thus precludes the idea that he had in view any revocations but those he had expressly declared in the codicil. ·3 Mason, 486; 10 B. & Cres. 895, (21 E. C. L. 192); 3 Pick. 216; 5 Johns.·C. R. 534; 1 Wms. Ex'rs, 114, 116; 21 Eng. C. L. R. 352; 4 Kent, 531; 8 Cowen, 58; 1 Jarman, 189, 395; 2 How. Rep: 580.

4. The will and codicil being thus blended and coöperative, the codicil avails as a republication of the will, except where such an inference at law is, by the express terms or necessary construction of the codicil, excluded. The will, in this relation · to the codicil, is to be treated as if inserted in the codicil. If so, if even there be those contradictory residuary dispositions, the residuary estate must, as modern adjudications now deal with such contrariant clauses, be shared by the parties named or embraced in both clauses. This construction would virtually restore the residuary· clause of the will, as the only rule; because, as under the construction just asserted, Mrs. Bosley and the children, the subjects of the two clauses, share equally, by the will, in the residuary estate. 14 Pick. Rep. 521; 6 Johns. C. R. 375; 3 My. & Cr. 376; 1 Jarman, 202, 397, 412; 2 Atk. 374; 2 My. & Keen, 165; Yelv. 209; ·Cro. Eliz. 9; Grcenl. Cruise, (Dev.) 149, (marg.); 10 B. & Cres. 895, (21 E. C.·L. 192.)

5. The agreement of the testator to lease a part of his land in Baltimorc county, had not the effect to revoke the devise of that part of the land in favor of the complainants, and only modified the devise so as to give the rent and reversion on the lease, in place of the land. This construction applies also to the lot and house by the will devised to "Old Sarah," and, subsequently to the codicil, agreed to be leased to William Hollins, as stated in the defendant's schedule. The privilege, accorded by the agreement of lease, to extinguish the rent and so acquire the reversion, does not render the transaction a sale, and give to the contracting lessee the equitable fee of the land. If the agreements for leasing revoked the devises of these pieces of property, then the testator died intestate as to them; the agreements dating after the codicil. Greenl. Cruise, 105. 109, (note to 106); 2 Ves. Jr. 428; 1 Jarman, 167, 171, 172; 4 Kent, 530; 7 T. R. 399; S. C. 1 B. & Pull. 576; Cro. Car. 23; Cro. Jac. 49; 1 Vern. 97; 3 Bro. Parl. Ca. 12; 2 Chipman, 74; 4 Greenl. 341; 3 Ves. Jr. 685; 1 Maryland Ch. Decis. 36; Cro Eliz. 9.

The counsel for the appellee made the following points.

1. That the residuary clause in the codicil revokes the residuary clause in the will. 4 Black. 381; 4 Kent, 535, (note); 3 Greenl. Cruise, 139; Rowley v. Eyton, 2 Mer. 128; Rogers v. Pettis, 1 Addams, (Prerog.) 30.

2. That the decree of the court below was right; because, if no part of the specific property devised by the last clause in the will, which contains also the residuary devise, was not revoked by the last clause in the codicil, a large part of that specific property was subsequently disposed of, by the testator, and other parts of it otherwise specifically devised by the codicil.

3. Because that portion of such property so specifically devised by said last clause in the will, his lands in Baltimore county, was revoked by the testator's agreement of lease, afterwards executed by Mrs. Bosley, by her lease to Armstrong, on the 18th of January, 1845, for the term of ninety-nine years, renewable forever. 7 Bac. Ab. tit. Wills and Testaments, G. 344; 4 Kent, Com. 528 to 530, and cases there cited, 6 ed.; Colegrave v. Manley, 6 Madd. 84; Ward v. Moore, 4 Madd. 368; 5 Pick. 112; 7 Johns. Ch. Rep. 261.

Mr. Chief Justice TANEY delivered the opinion of the court.

The dispute in this case arises out of the will and codicil of James Bosley, late of the city of Baltimore. The will was executed in 1828, and the codicil in 1839. He died in December, 1843.

In his will, after sundry specific devises and bequests, he devised and bequeathed all his lands and other real estate, in Baltimore, Cecil, and Alleghany counties, in Maryland, and also in Florida, and his house and lot in Santa Croix, and all the real estate he might have elsewhere, to his wife Elizabeth N. Bosley, her heirs and assigns, in trust to sell the same to the best advantage, and directed the net proceeds, together with all the residue of his estate, real, personal, and mixed, not therein before devised, to be equally divided — one half to his wife, and the other to the children of his brother, Dr. John Bosley. After making his will, and previous to the codicil, he sold all of the lands particularly mentioned in the residuary clause of the will above stated, except some lands lying in Baltimore county, and except also his Florida land and part of that in Alleghany county, of which it seems he had been unable to obtain possession. And at the time of making the codicil, he held some of the proceeds of these sales in bonds and other securities, and with the residue had purchased other property.

By the codicil he devised his summer residence, situated in

Baltimore county, to his wife, and also the securities he held for the lands sold in Cecil county,—and directed all the property he had acquired after the date of his will to be sold and the proceeds to be equally divided between his wife and her sister, Margaret E. Noel. Then follows a residuary clause in the following words:

"Lastly, my pew in St. Paul's Church, and all my other property, real or personal, and all money in bank belonging to me at the time of my decease, I give, devise and bequeathe unto my said wife Elizabeth N. Bosley, and her heirs forever; and I ratify and confirm my said last will in every thing except where the same is hereby revoked and altered as aforesaid."

Upon this will and codicil, the appellants, who are the children of Dr. John Bosley, claim the one half of this personal property left by the testator at his death, and also one half of the lands not specifically devised, upon the ground that the residuary clause in the will is not revoked by that in the codicil.

This claim is altogether untenable. The residuary clause in the codicil is inconsistent with that in the will, and consequently revokes it.

There is another claim, however, which presents a question of more difficulty.

It appears that at the time of making his will the testator held, in fee-simple, fifty acres of land in Baltimore county; and that in 1842, after the execution of the codicil, he entered into a contract with a certain Horatio G. Armstrong, whereby he covenanted that in consideration of the payment of two thousand dollars, at the times specified in the agreement, and the annual ground rent of two hundred and ten dollars, payable semiannually, he would lease the said land to Armstrong, his executors, administrators, and assigns, for ninety-nine years, renewable forever, with the right to the said Armstrong to extinguish the ground rent, upon the payment of three thousand five hundred dollars at any time, to the said James Bosley, his heirs and assigns. The testator died before the cash payments were made; and the money was afterwards received by his, widow, and the lease executed by her according to the terms of the covenant.

As this was a part of the land in Baltimore county, and was therefore specifically devised in the residuary clause of the will, it was not revoked by the general devise of the residue of his real and personal property in the codicil. The question therefore is, whether the contract with Armstrong was an implied revocation of the devise in the will.

The adjudged cases upon implied revocations are collected together in 4 Kent's Com. 528, and the rule he deduces from them is this, "that the same interest which the testator had when he made his will should continue to be the same interest; and remain unaltered to his death, and that the least alteration in that interest is a revocation." A valid agreement or covenant to convey, which equity will specifically enforce, will operate in equity as a revocation of a previous devise of the land. Walton v. Walton, 7 Johns. Ch. Rep. 258.

In the case before us, the interest which the testator had in this land at the time of making his will, was converted into money by his contract with Armstrong. It was a sale and an agreement to convey his whole interest in the land. It is therefore unlike the case of a lease for years, or of ninety-nine years renewable forever, in which the lessor retains the reversion — and does not bind himself to convey it on any terms to the lessee.

The form of the contract adopted in this instance, between the testator and Armstrong, is in familiar use in the sale of lots in the city of Baltimore and the adjacent country. It has nearly if not altogether superseded the old forms of contract where the vendor conveyed the lands and took a mortgage to secure the payment of the purchase-money — or gave his bond for the conveyance and retained the legal title in himself until the purchase-money was paid. And it has taken the place of these forms of contract, because it is far more convenient, both to the seller and the purchaser. For it enables the vendee to postpone the payment of a large portion of the purchase-money until he finds it entirely convenient to pay it; and at the same time it is more advantageous to the vendor, as it gives him a better security for the punctual payment of the interest; and while an extended credit is given to the vendee, it is to the vendor a sale for cash. For if his ground rent is well secured, he can at any time sell it in the market, for the balance of the purchase-money left in the hands of the vendee. It will be observed that the rent reserved is precisely the interest on the amount of the purchase-money remaining unpaid. And when it must be admitted that a sale in which a bond of conveyance is given, and the title retained by the vendor, to secure the payment of the purchase-money, is in equity a revocation, there would seem to be no good reason for holding otherwise in the case before us, where the vendor is equally bound to convey when the whole purchase-money is paid. A distinction between the cases would rest on a difference in form rather than of substance and principle. It would moreover make the revocation depend upon the will of a stranger, and not upon that of the testator. For if Armstrong had paid to him in his lifetime, the whole amount of the purchase-money, as he had a right to do under the contract, it is very clear that the devise would then have been revoked. And if the purchaser's omission to pay prevents the contract from being a revocation, the validity of the devise is made to depend, not upon the will or the act of a testator, but that of a stranger, over which the testator has no control. We think a distinction leading to that result cannot be maintained, and that the devise in question was revoked by the contract with Armstrong.

The counsel for the appellants, however, contends, that if the will is revoked, and the land converted into money, yet there was a legal reversionary interest remaining in him; and that the rent reserved, being incident to the reversion and pertaining to the realty, cannot pass under a bequest of money or personal estate.

But it must be remembered that the residuary clause in the codicil gives to his wife all his real as well as personal property, not otherwise disposed of; and therefore is broad enough to embrace the interest in question, although, in contemplation of law, it belongs to the realty.

We do not mean to say, that every residuary clause in a codicil will pass land specifically devised in a will, where, by some act of the testator, the devise is impliedly revoked after the codicil was executed. There are adjudged cases upon certain wills where it has been held otherwise. But whether the property passes to the devisee or descends to the heir, as in a case of intestacy, must depend upon the intention of the testator, to be gathered from the will and codicil. It is always necessarily a question of intention. No two wills, probably, were ever written in precisely the same language throughout; nor any two testators die under the same circumstances in\relation to their estate, family, and friends. And it would be very unsafe as well as unjust to expound the will of one man, by the construction which a court of justice had given to that of another, merely because similar words were used in paticular parts of it.

Undoubtedly there are fixed rules of law in relation to the construction of certain words and phrases in a will, which have been established by a long course of judicial decisions; and which have become landmarks of property, and cannot therefore be disturbed. But in most of the cases in which they have been applied, it is to be feared that they have not accomplished, but defeated, the testator's intentions.

They owe their origin to the principles of the feudal system, which always favored the heir at law, because it was its policy to perpetuate large estates in the same family. And, acting upon this principle, the English courts of justice have, in some instances, placed the narrowest possible construction on the words of a will. And a testator sometimes being held to die intestate as to portions of his property, and left it to descend to his heir, when a fair and reasonable interpretation, according to the ordinary acceptation of the words used, plainly showed that the whole estate was intended to be devised to another.

It has not been the disposition of courts of justice, in modern times, to extend the application of these rigid technical rules; but rather to carry out the intention of the testator, when no fixed rule of legal interpretation stands in the way. And this is, and ought to be, more especially the case in this country. For wills here are most frequently drawn by persons unacquainted with legal phraseology, and ignorant of the meaning which the law attaches to the words they use. The property devised is, perhaps, in the greater number of cases, the fruits of the testator's own industry. And the policy and institutions of the country are adverse to the feudal policy of favoring the heir at the expense of the devisee; and of construing, for that purpose, the words of the will in their most restricted sense, although that construction obviously defeats the intention of the testator.

But the question, arising upon this will and codicil, does not depend upon any word or phrase to which the law has affixed a certain and definite meaning. The words used are legally sufficient to pass the property to his widow, and the only question is, was that his intention, as we gather it from the will and codicil, considered together? We think it was.

Eleven years elapsed between the date of the will and that of the codicil. The situation of the testator's property had undergone considerable changes during that time; and his mind also had materially changed as to the manner of disposing of it. The lands mentioned in the residuary clause of his will, had, with a very small exception, been sold. And the property he purchased with the proceeds of these sales or otherwise acquired after the date of the will, was devised by the codicil to his wife and her sister, and not, as before, divided between his wife and his brother's children; and the whole of his personal estate is given exclusively to his wife, instead of the one half only bequeathed in the will. The land, which has given rise to this controversy, was also sold by the testator in his lifetime, and two thousand dollars of the purchase-money had become personalty, and as such, unquestionably passed to the wife, by the residuary clause in the codicil. The testator's remaining interest in this property, was also money, and not land; but by reason of the form in which he contracted to sell it, this portion of the money belonged to the realty. It is impossible to suppose, after looking at these bequests to his wife, that he meant to die intestate of this money, and to divide this small portion of his estate in two parts, giving her the two thousand dollars, but withholding from her the residue, and leaving it to be claimed by whoever might chance to be his heir at law at the time of his death. On the contrary, it is manifest, from the whole context of the will and codicil, that he did not mean to die intestate of any portion of his property; and that what did not pass to others by a specific devise or bequest, should go to his wife. The codicil is evidently drawn by unskilful hands, and therefore, according to settled principles of law, must receive a fair and liberal interpretation to accomplish the intent. And as that intent is apparent in favor of the widow, it ought not to be defeated by a narrow and technical construction of particular words.

It was suggested, in the argument, that the appellants might be entitled to a remainder in fee, in the two lots on which, it would seem from the will and the codicil, that two old servants of the testator were living. But this point, very properly, was not pressed. For the lots mentioned in that clause of the will, in which a remainder in fee is given to the appellants after the death of Mrs. Bosley, are lots on which there were improvements, and which yielded an income. The lots in question were not of that description. They yielded no income, and consequently are not embraced in that devise.

Upon the whole, therefore, we think the decree of the Circuit Court was right, and must be affirmed.

Order.

This cause came on to be heard on the transcript of the record from the Circuit Court of the United States for the District of Maryland, and was argued by counsel. On consideration whereof, it is now here ordered, adjudged, and decreed, by this court, that the decree of the said Circuit Court in this cause be, and the same is hereby, affirmed with costs.

Dissenting, Mr. Justice GRIER.

JOHN F. ENNIS, ADMINISTRATOR DE BONIS NON OF JOSEPH ZOL-KOWSKI AND OTHERS, v. J. H. B. SMITH, ADMINISTRATOR OF GEORGE BOMFORD, LEWIS JOHNSON, ADMINISTRATOR DE BONIS NON OF THADDEUS KOSCIUSKO, JAMES CARRICO, SAMUEL STOTT, GEORGE C. BOMFORD, JACOB GIDEON, ULYSSES WARD, AND JONATHAN B. H. SMITH.

Origin of the fund in controversy.

Mr. Jefferson's letter concerning it.

General Kosciusko made four wills. One in the United States, in 1798; another in Paris, in 1806; the third and fourth were made at Soleure, in Switzerland, whilst he was sojourning there in 1816 and 1817.

The first and second wills were revoked by the third, and he died intestate as to his estate in the United States.

But the first will, before it was known that he had made the others, was probated by Mr. Jefferson, in Virginia, and when Mr. Jefferson learned that the General had made other wills, he transferred the fund to the Orphans' Court of the District of Columbia. The Orphans' Court managed the fund for some time, and then Benjamin L. Lear was appointed the administrator of Kosciusko, with the will annexed. He died, leaving a will, and George Bomford one of his executors. Bomford qualified as such, and afterwards became the administrator of Kosciusko de bonis non. He took into his possession, as executor, the estate of Lear, and also the funds of Kosciusko, which had been administered by Lear, and first made his return to the Orphans' Court of the administered funds of Kosciusko, as executor of Lear. Afterwards they were returned by him to the Orphans' Court, as administrator de bonis non of Kosciusko. The Orphans' Court deeming that his sureties as administrator de bonis non of Kosciusko, were insufficient, or that they were not liable for any waste of them, on account of the funds having been received by him as executor of Lear, and not as administrator de bonis non, called upon him for other sureties, under the act of Congress of the 20th February, 1846. He complied with the call, and gave as sureties, Stott, Carrico, and George C. Bomford, and Gideon, Ward, and Smith.

The original bonds of Bomford were given to the Orphans' Court, under the law of Maryland, which prevailed without alteration in that part of the District of Columbia which had been ceded by Maryland, until Congress passed the act of the 20th February, 1846. The defendant Stott, Carrico, and George C. Bomford, and Smith, Ward, and Gideon, became the sureties of Bomford, as administrator de bonis non of Kosciusko, under the act of 20th February, 1846.

In the State of Maryland, if an executor or administrator changes any part of an estate from what it was into something else, it is said to be administered. If an administrator de bonis non, possesses himself of such changed estate, of whatever kind it may be, and charges himself with it as assets, his sureties to his original bond, as administrator de bonis non, are not liable for his waste of them. They are only liable for such assets of the deceased as remain in specie, unadministered by his predecessor, in the administration. Such is the law of Maryland, applicable to the sureties of Bomford, in the bond given when he was appointed administrator de bonis non of Kosciusko.

But when other sureties are called for by the Orphans' Court, under the third section of the act of February 20, 1846, and are given, they do not bear the same relation to the administrator that his original sureties did, and they will be bound for the waste of their principal to the amount of the estate, or funds which he has charged himself by his return to the Orphans' Court, as administrator de bonis non, when it called for additional sureties, and for such as the administrator may afterwards receive.

The bonds taken by the Orphans' Court in this case, were properly taken under the act of the 20th February, 1846.

General Kosciusko's Olographic will of 1816, contains a revoking clause of all other wills previously made by him, and not having disposed of his American funds in that will, nor in the will of 1817, he died intestate as to such funds. The second article in the will of 1817, "Je lègue tous mes effets, ma voiture, et mon cheval y comprise à Madame et à Monsieur Zavier Zeltner, les homme ce dessus,"—record, 105—is not a residuary bequest to them of the rest of his estate, not specifically disposed of in the wills of 1816 and 1817.

General Kosciusko was sojourning in Switzerland when he died, but was domiciled in France, and had been for fifteen years.

His declarations are to be received as proof that his domicil was in France. Such declarations have always been received, in questions of domicil, in the courts of France, in those of England, and in the courts of the United States.

The presumption of law is, that the domicil of origin is retained, until residence elsewhere has been shown by him who alleges a change of it. But residence elsewhere repels the presumption, and casts upon him who denies it to be a domicil of choice, the burden of disproving it. The place of residence must be taken to be a domicil of choice, unless it is proved that it was not meant to be a principal and permanent residence. Contingent events, political or otherwise, are not admissible proofs to show, where one removes from his domicil of origin, for a residence elsewhere, that the latter was not meant to be a principal and permanent residence. But if one is exiled by authority from his domicil of origin, it is never presumed that he has abandoned all hope of returning back. The abandonment, however, may be shown by proof. General Kosciusko was not exiled by authority. He left Poland voluntarily, to obtain a civil status in France, which he conscientiously thought he could not enjoy in Poland, whilst it continued under a foreign dominion.

Personal property, wherever it may be, is to be disturbed in case of intestacy, according to the law of the domicil of the intestate. This rule may be said to be a part of the *jus gentium*.

What that law is when a foreign law applies, must be shown by proof of it, and in the case of written law, it will be sufficient to offer, as evidence, the official publication of the law, certified satisfactorily to be such. Unwritten foreign laws, must be proved by experts. There is no general rule for authenticating foreign laws in the courts of other countries, except this, that no proof shall be received, "which presupposes better testimony behind, and attainable by the party." They may be verified by an oath, or by an exemplification of a copy under the great seal of the State or nation whose law it may be, or by a copy proved to be a true copy, by a witness who has examined and compared it with the original, or by the certificate of an officer authorised to give the law, which certificate must be duly proved. Such modes of proof are not exclusive of others, especially of codes and accepted histories of the law of a country. See also the cases of Church *v.* Hubbart, in 2 Cranch, 181, and Talbot *v.* Seeman, in 1 Cranch, 7. In this case, the Code Civil of France, with this indorsement, "Les Garde des Sceaux de France a la Cœur Supreme Des Etats Unis," was offered as evidence to prove that the law of France was for the distribution of the funds in controversy. This court ruled that such indorsement was a sufficient authentication, to make the code evidence in this case, and in any other case in which it may be offered. By that code, the complainants named in this suit as the collateral relations of General Kosciusko, are entitled to receive the funds in controversy, in such proportions as are stated in the mandate of this court to the court below.

The documentary proofs in this cause, from the Orphans' Court, of the genealogy of the Kosciusko family, and of the collateral relationship of the persons entitled to a decree, and also of the wills of Kosciusko, are properly in evidence in this suit.

The record from Grodno is judicial; not a judgment *inter partes*, but a foreign judgment *in rem*, which is evidence of the facts adjudicated against all the world.

Mr. Justice *Catron* did not sit in this cause.

THIS was an appeal from the Circuit Court of the United States for the District of Columbia, holden in and for the county of Washington, sitting as a Court of Equity.

The whole case is set forth in the opinion of the court.

The appellants were those who filed the bill in the Circuit Court, which was dismissed by that court.

It was argued by *Mr. Tochman* and *Mr. Johnson*, for the appellants, and by *Mr. Redin, Mr. Marbury*, and *Mr. Coxe*, for the appellees.

The points raised by the counsel for the appellants, were the following:

I. Was Kosciusko's domicil, at the time of his death, in France, as the appellants charge, or was it in Poland, as the appellees maintain?

It could not be in Poland, since Kosciusko left it, because of its subjugation by the foreign powers, in 1794. Vattel's Law of Nations, Book I. chap. 16, § 195.

It was in France, by his own choice, since 1806 until 4th of June, 1816. (Wills of 1806 and 1816, and conclusions resulting from the admission of the appellees.) Story's Confl. of Laws, § 44–46, § 8–47, § 14.

It continued to be in France until his death, upon the principle of law laid down in 1 Starkie on Evid. (Philad. ed. of 1842, p. 53, "Presumption as to Continuance.") 1 American Leading Cases, by Hare & Wallace, p. 710, § 3, and the authorities therein referred to; Story's Confl. of Laws, § 47, § 16

II. Has the will of 1816 been proved? Have the letters of administration *de bonis non* to Lewis Johnson been issued with the wills of 1798, 1806, and 1816, as alleged in the bill? Does the will of 1816 revoke the wills of 1798 and 1806? Is the residue of Kosciusko's property liable for the legacies stated in the wills of 1816 and 1817?

The original will of 1816 was proved, recorded, and is lodged for safe keeping in France, and its authenticated exemplification with the French probate was proved and recorded in the Orphans' Court for the District of Columbia, pursuant to the rules laid down in Toller on Evid. p. 71. Van Rensselear *v.* Morris, 1 Paige's Rep. 13; Story's Confl. of Laws, notes to § 514 b, on p. 432 of the 2d ed.; Statute of Maryland of 1785, chap. 46, § 2; De Sobre *v.* De Laistre, 2 Har. & Johns. 191.

The letters of administration *de bonis non* to Lewis Johnson were issued with the will and other two, as charged in the bill, proved by the decretal of the Orphans' Court, and the deposition of the record of the wills.

The court below had, and this court has now, the power of deciding what effect each of these three wills of Kosciusko should have upon the final disposition of the property sought to be recovered. 1 Jarman on Wills, 4, 22, 23, &c.

For this purpose the law of the domicil of Kosciusko at the time of his death must be resorted to. Jarman on Wills, 3, 4; Story's Confl. of Laws, § 465, 467, 468, 479 f, 479 m.

The will of 1798 cannot take effect, because of the uncertainty of its dispositions and objects of the bounty; the will of 1806 is null and void, not being executed according to either of the forms prescribed by the laws of France for making wills; but, good or bad, they have been both revoked by the will of 1816.

The will of 1816, containing the revoking clause of former wills, is a good and valid olographic will, proved by the depositions on p. 15 and 16 of the record. Arts. 970, 999, 1001, of the Civil Code of Napoleon.

Parol evidence, referred to in the answers, has not been produced; but, if it were produced, it could not be received, to impeach the will of 1816, nor to prove its revocation. Civil Code of Napoleon, Arts. 1035, 1036; 12 Wheaton's Rep. 175; Toller on Exec. 76; 1 Madd. Ch. Pr. 81, 552, 555; 2 Starkie on Evid. Part I. Phil. ed. of 1842, 756, and Part II. p. 1284, note a; 1 Greenleaf on Evid. § 273, 290.

The word "effets," used in the 2d clause of the will of 1817, being restrained by the words "ma voiture et mon cheval y comprise," passes only property of "ejusdem generis," and nothing else. 1 Jarman on Wills, 692 f; 13 Ves. 36, 45.

Independent of this, the French word "effets" signifies only such property as is about the person. Dictionaire Francais et Anglais, par les Professeur Fleming et Tibbins; Dictionaire de l'Academie Francaise.

Admitted, that for the legacies specified in the will of 1816, the property sought to be recovered, and every other property of Kosciusko, would be liable — but all these legacies had been paid.

The legacies made by the will of 1817 being legacies of specific funds, which were invested in Switzerland and in England, and of such specific property which was left in the house where Kosciusko died, in Switzerland, none of them can charge any other property; but whatever may be the law in this respect, the proof is that these legacies have also been paid.

The accidental omission, in the proceedings, of Mr. and Mrs. Zavier Zeltner, legatees under the will of 1817, is immaterial: first, because they take only such property in kind as comes within the definition of the word "effets," restrained by the words "ma voiture et mon cheval y comprise," and should claim it from those persons in Switzerland in whose possession these "effets" were left; secondly, because, by the law of France, upon the death of the testator or intestate, the property vests in the lawful heirs, who stand *in loco* of legal representatives of the deceased at common law. Civil Code of Napoleon, Art. 724; Story's Confl. of Laws, § 507, 508, 516.

It follows, from the above rule, that when the lawful heirs of Kosciusko recover the property which is not wanted here by local administrator, all claimants residing in Europe, whether they are legatees or creditors, will have a right to establish there their claims. It would be immaterial, then, were all the claimants residing in Europe omitted in these proceedings, as no decree *pro confesso* taken here will bar their claims there. Civil Code of Napoleon, Arts. 724, 870, 873, 1011, 1025, 1026.

Admitting, for the sake of argument, the existence of such European claims, this is no defence; the appellees in such a case should bring money into court — show good reasons of their apprehension for safety, and pray that the appellants may interplead their right with other claimants. 2 Story's Com. on Eq. § 805, 809, &c.; Mitf. Eq. Plead. by Jeremy, p. 48, 49.

III. Have the appellants proved that Kosciusko died unmarried and without issue, and that they are his next of kin, entitled to the residue of undisposed of property? " In civil cases, slight evidences of right or title are sufficient — as against a stranger who possesses no color of title." 1 Starkie on Evid. Phil. ed. of 1842, p. 544. In case of Folger's Lessee *v.* Simpson, (1 Yeates's Rep. 17,) *ex parte* affidavit, made in England, was held to be sufficient evidence of pedigree against strangers. Kingston *v.* Lesley, 10 Sergeant & Rawle's Rep. 383. The appellees are all strangers, having no color of title to the estate of Kosciusko. The appellants, to establish their title thereto, produce a decree of the nobility of the Government of Grodno, and a decree of the Court of Kobryn, in the province of Lithuania, formerly Poland, now a part of the Empire of Russia, which were proved as to their authenticity, and as to the competency of the tribunals which passed them; first, in the Orphans' Court for the District of Columbia, in the course of legal proceedings against Bomford, deceased administrator, and subsequently, by depositions taken under the commission in the case.

The originals of these foreign decrees, written in the Russian language, are on file in the court below. Their translations will be found on p. 73, Exhibit A, and on p. 80, Exhibit B. These translations are judicial — they were made under oath, taken in open court. The originals, written in the Russian language, are not in the record, from reasons stated in the answer of the clerk of the court below.

The authenticity of these documents has been established by the testimony that the seal of the Assembly of the Nobility on the decree of pedigree, (marked A, on p. 73,) and the seal of the Court of Kobryn in the decree (marked B, on p. 80,) are genuine seals, which alone is sufficient, under the principles laid down in 6 Wendell's Rep. 484; 1 Paine's Rep. 614; Norris's Peake's Evid. 58, conjointly with 60, 108, and 109; 3 East's Rep. 222; Act of Maryland, of 1785, ch. 46, § 6.

Though the foregoing authorities do not require that the signatures be proved, to establish the authenticity of a decree or judgment — the appellants proved two of the signatures on the decree of pedigree, marked A, on p. 80, by the deposition — which, upon the principle laid down in Gresley's Eq. Evid. p. 120, and the authorities therein referred to, would be sufficient, were it deemed necessary to prove the signatures.

The seals and signatures not proved, (which are appended to the certificates, purporting to attest the signatures and seals of the Assembly of the Nobility of Grodno, and of the Court of Kobryn,) are useless appendages, the law not admitting such certificates as evidence. 13 Peters's R. 209; 2 Cranch's R. 187.

The competency of the jurisdiction of the Assembly of the Nobility of Grodno, and of the Court of Kobryn, in matters decided upon by the exhibited decrees of pedigree, &c., is proved by the depositions of witnesses skilled in law, which depositions prove also that the decree of the Assembly of the Nobility, marked A, on p. 73, falls within the scope of such as are called *in rem*, and bind everybody.

Depositions taken in the Orphans' Court are evidence in this case, upon the principle laid down in 1 Starkie on Evid. Phil. ed. of 1842, p. 315 — the more so when they were brought before the court below, through the medium of a commission taken in the case.

Independent of this witness, Judge Kalussowski was reëxamined under the commission, and another witness, Tysowski was examined under it.

The decrees, marked A and B, are as conclusive evidence to prove pedigree in this country, as they are in the country from which they come, upon principles laid down in 1 Starkie on Evid. Phil. ed. of 1842, p. 253, " Judgments *in rem.*" Id. p. 30, " Reputation, in what cases evidence." 2 Starkie on Evid. id. ed. part 1, p. 842; 1 Id. 275; Norris's Peake's Evid. 101, 104–6; 1 Starkie on Evid. id. ed. 285–6, 295–6; 1 Greenleaf on Evid. §§ 525, 543; Story's Confl. of Laws, § 593.

The objection that the decree of pedigree, marked A, was obtained upon *ex parte* proceedings, &c., cannot be sustained, when it is proved that it was obtained upon such proceedings as the law of the country from which it comes prescribes, (depositions on pp. 85, 69, 70, of the record.) 4 Peters's R. 472, 475; Story's

Confl. of Laws, §§ 605, 608; Peake's Evid. 101, 104-106; 1 Greenleaf on Evid. § 547.

The city of Grodno is the capital, and the seat of the government of the Province of Lithuania, which is called Government of Grodno — just as is called the government of the United States, "Government of Washington." Encyc. Brit. vol. 10, p. 799; Cycl. of Soc. for Diff. of Useful Knowledge, vol. 11, p. 455. Hence comes the incongruity of the testimony, in calling the official seal of the nobility of Grodno " the Government of Grodno's official seal," "a Government seal of Lithuania." But that both these expressions mean to speak of the seal of the nobility of Grodno, proves the fact that both witnesses had before them the document with the seal described in its body, on p. 80 of the record, as the seal of the nobility of Grodno.

Nor can the testimony of these witnesses be impeached by giving it a different construction than the nature of the case admits of, the appellees having neglected to cross-examine them, (Starkie on Evid. Phil. ed. of 1842, pp. 197, 212, 214, 316, 317, 577,) though their counsel were present at the taking of depositions, and cross-examined one witness on other matters.

Independent of the above, witness Kalussowki explained himself as to his testimony by deposition.

The Assemblies of Nobility, when called upon to decide on pedigree, issue as many original copies of decrees as there are interested parties.

In this case, four original copies of such decree were issued, and delivered to the appellants. The original copy, of which the translation is marked A, on p. 73 of the record, is one of these four copies. None of these copies is " better evidence." Each of them is evidence of the same decree for all purposes.

·Reference is made that a certain Pole, Klimkiewicz, filed a bill claiming the estate, as next of kin of Kosciusko. This individual attempted to impose in the premises — when, upon the death of the former counsel of the appellants, they had no one here to take care of their claim. This suit abated by the death of Klimkiewicz and of administrator Bomford, and its papers formed no part of the record in the court below.

The residue of Kosciusko's estate goes to the appellants, as his next of kin, upon the principle laid down in 1 Jarman on Wills, 3, 4, &c.; Civil Code of Napoleon, art. 750.

IV. Are the defendants liable to account, as is charged in the bill, on pp. 6, 8, of the record ?

The decree dismissing the bill against Jonathan B. H. Smith, as administrator of the estate of Bomford, is not questioned — Bomford having died insolvent, (pp. 48, 109, of the record.)

As to the same Jonathan B. H. Smith, trustee of the property which Bomford delivered to him as counter security, with the deed of trust, on p. 23 of the record, he is bound to account for it to the appellants, upon the principle laid down in 1 Story's Com. on Eq. § 502; Eq. Abridg. 93, K. 5; Comm. Dig. Chancery, 4, D. 6; Wright v. Morley, 11 Ves. 22. He is bound also to account, upon the same principle, for the sum of $4,156.92, for rents, &c., which he admitted to hold in his hands — in the answer on p. 49 of the record — and for such after rents as accrued since the filing of that answer.

Lewis Johnson, administrator *de bonis non* of Kosciusko's estate, in his original answer, (p. 29 of the record,) admitted, that at the time of the filing of it he had under his control stock of the Bank of Washington of the nominal value of $5,580.00 — of which the market price was then 60 per 100 — and $200 in cash. In his amended answer, (on p. 62 of the record,) he informed the court that said bank refused to pay him further dividends, under "pretence" that this stock does not belong to Kosciusko's estate; and on p. 63 of it, he admitted that he had in hands $268.28 in cash. In view of these admissions, the decree of the court below, dismissing the bill against him as administrator *de bonis non*, is erroneous; he ought to account for the cash and the certificate of the stock which he holds.

As to the liability of the sureties of Bomford:

This is the only point upon which the court below delivered a written opinion. It is not in the record, the Judges not having filed it in the case, but it will be found in a separate pamphlet, published by the appellees.

Grounds upon which the court below dismissed the bill against the sureties, are as follows:

First, because the original assets of Kosciusko having been converted into money, by Lear, the first administrator, this money and the evidences of the new investments could not (in the opinion of the court below) pass lawfully to Bomford as the administrator *de bonis non* of the estate of Kosciusko, but he ought to have administered them as Lear's executor, (pp. 9, 12, 13, of the opinion); secondly, because Bomford, administrator *de bonis non*, "converted and used" the funds of Kosciusko's estate before the date of the bonds, (id. 14); thirdly, because the act of Congress of 1846, (chap. 8,) and the bonds obtained under it, are prospective, and not retrospective, (id. 16-21); fourthly, because what is retained by the first administrator cannot go to the administrator *de bonis non*, (id. 21-24); fifthly, variances of the bonds referred to in the bill, and exhibited as evidence, were alleged, (id. 7,) but the court expressed no opinion as to it.

The counsel for the appellees made the following points, many of which were divided into subdivisions. *Mr. Coxe* argued points 1, 2, 4, and 5. *Mr. Redin*, points 7 and 8, and part of 3. *Mr. Marbury* the remaining subdivision of 3, and point 6.

The appellees, the sureties of Bomford, contend:

I. That the Circuit Court had no jurisdiction of the cause. Act of 21st Feb. 1801, § 5; 3d March, 1801, § 3; Judicial Act of 1789; Strawbridge v. Curtis, 3 Cranch, 267.

II. That the claim must be made through the administrator of Kosciusko's domicil.

The administration in the District of Columbia, if the domicil was, as the complainants allege, in France, was merely ancillary, and, after paying debts, &c., the residue of the estate ought to be remitted to France, to the executors under the wills of 1816 and 1817; and complainants, all being or representing foreign parties, must proceed against such foreign executors, and cannot sue the ancillary administrator here; and the bill makes no case in which a foreign distributee can maintain an action here. Story's Confl. Laws, § 513, and cases cited in the notes.

III. That if the appellants have proved themselves to be the true representatives of Kosciusko, and can claim directly, the defendants, as sureties of Bomford, as administrator *de bonis non* of Kosciusko, are not liable to them,—

1. Because the whole of the original assets were converted into money by Lear in his life, except Bank of Columbia stock; and because the money and new securities on hand at his death passed to Bomford, as executor of Lear, for distribution, and Bomford's sureties, in that capacity, if any, are answerable; that Bomford had no legal right or authority, as administrator *de bonis non*, to receive such money and securities; and the defendants, as sureties for him in that character, are liable only for what he could lawfully and rightfully receive in virtue of his office as such administrator; that their bond does not cover what is claimed.

2. Admitting Bomford came rightfully, as administrator *de bonis non*, into possession of the money and securities left by Lear, the sureties are not liable to the full extent of the complainant's claim; because Bomford wasted and converted to his own use, prior to the date of the bonds, as shown by complainant's proof, $30,625.47, part of said assets, for which the sureties are not liable, their bonds being prospective and not retrospective.

3. The third ground upon which the sureties are not liable to complainants is, that there is a fatal variance between the bonds as charged in the bill, and the bonds as exhibited by complainants to prove the charge; and further, that said bonds are void.

IV. That there is no proof in this cause that the appellants are the next of kin of Kosciusko.

V. If the complainants are the next of kin, and if there be liability on the part of the sureties, there was no intestacy by Kosciusko as to these funds; but if the will of 1798 be revoked, or its trusts cannot be carried out, then the will of 1817 disposes of the whole fund to Mr. and Mrs. Zavier Zeltner, and intercepts the claim of the next of kin.

As to the trust of the will of 1798, vide 2 Story Eq. §§ 1169, 1172, 1176; Brocket's case, 9 How.; Girard's, 2 How.; Bap. Ass'n, 4 Wheaton.

Kosciusko did not intend to die intestate as to any of his property; this is shown by his frequent wills, and by the introductory clause in the will of 1817.

The words of the will of 1817, in the introductory clause are, "*mes biens;*" in the clause of gift (the second) " *tous mes effets, ma voiture, et mon cheval y comprise.*"

Standing alone, the words are broad enough to pass his whole estate. " *Mes biens,*" meaning " estate," " what a man is worth," and " *tous mes effets.*" " all or the whole of my effects or property."

The words " *tous mes effets* " would pass the whole residue; and the introduction of the words, " my carriage and horse included," was not for the purpose of restricting or qualifying the former terms, but resulted from the testator's anxiety that those articles should pass under the general terms.

The expression is " included; " and the rule of *ejusdem generis* is inapplicable. The clause in this will of 1817 comes within the qualifying cases upon that rule, of Fleming *v.* Burrows, 1 Russ. C. C. 277; Kendal *v.* Kendal, 4 Russ. C. C. 360, (2 Wm's Ex'ors, 1019); Arnold *v.* Arnold, 2 Mylne & Keen, 365, (2 Wm's Ex'ors, 1019); Parker *v.* Marchant, 1 Younge & Collier C. C. 290; Rop. on. Leg. 210, 211.

Mr. and Mrs. Zavier Zeltner are not made parties in this bill.

VI. If there was intestacy, then it is not proved where the domicil of Kosciusko was at the time of his death; nor is the law or rule of representation or succession shown; these must be stated in the bill, and proved as stated.

The bill states that Kosciusko was a native of Poland, and died at Soleure, in Switzerland, intestate, and possessed of a large personal estate in the United States.

It is alleged that France was the domicil of the intestate at the time of his death, and that by the law of France, then in force, the succession to the whole of the said estate was cast upon the descendants of his sisters, representing the parents living at the time.

The defendants contend —

1. That there is no evidence to prove the domicil, as alleged. Mere residence, is not in itself proof of a change of domicil; it must be *animo manendi.* Story's Confl. of Laws, § 89; 1 Cur. E. R. 856; 2 Id. 897; 7 Clark & Fin. 876.

2. That the law of the assumed domicil is not set forth in the bill.

3. That there is no evidence in the case, to prove the law of France providing for the succession of an intestate's personal estate.

To prove this law, as alleged, the complainants offered in evidence a printed volume of the Code Napoleon. To the admissibility of which, for such purpose, the defendants objected; and they rely on 1 Greenleaf, §§ 487, 488; 3 Wend. Rep. 173; 5 Id. 375, 384, and 389.

The defendants also contend, that if the printed volume of the code be received as admissible, the law as contained in the Code does not entitle the complainants to the succession of said estate, as claimed by them. They refer to the Code, book 1, § 11; book 3, § 726.

VII. That proper parties are not made.

1. Lear's sureties, as administrator of Kosciusko, ought to have been made parties.

2. So ought Bomford's sureties, as executor of Lear.

3. So ought Bomford's original sureties, as administrator *de bonis non* of Kosciusko.

4. And so ought Mr. and Mrs. Zavier Zeltner, the residuary legatees in the will of 1817.

There is no averment in the bill, of the insolvency of any of the omitted sureties to excuse the omission.

The averment goes no further than that the original sureties of Bomford, as administrator *de bonis non*, are dead, and the bond is open to the plea of limitations. Story's Eq. Pl. § 169, and note 5; Madox v. Jackson, 3 Atk. 406; Cockburn v. Thompson, 16 Ves. 321, overruling Stanley v. Cook, Moseley's Rep. 383, &c.

VIII. That the remedy against the sureties was at law on the bond, and not in equity.

The sureties severally filed demurrers, general and special, to the complainants' bill; in support of which, they contend that the complainants have a free and unobstructed remedy at law against them on their bonds, and have, therefore, no right to bring them before the court as parties in this cause.

In the case of Richardson v. Jones, (3 Gill & J. 163,) it was held that a court of chancery had no jurisdiction (on petition by a trustee acting under a decree of the Chancellor to sell land,) to order the purchaser and his sureties, who had given a bond for the purchase-money, to bring the same into court, to be paid to the trustee. The court say, the contract on this bond is a purely legal one, and can be enforced by an action at law and trial before a jury.

In the case of Boteler & Belt v. Brookes, (7 Gill & J.) 143, on petition to the Chancellor to compel the sureties in a trustee's bond (he being dead and insolvent,) to bring the proceeds of a sale made by the trustee, into court, the court held that the obligation of the sureties on their bond was purely legal, and could be enforced in a court of law only.

In Brooke v: Boteler et al. (12 Gill & J. 307,) it was held that a bill in chancery might be maintained against sureties in a bond, when there could be no remedy at law. In the particular case, the trustee being dead, insolvent, and there being no administration on his estate, there could be no order by the court for the payment of the complainants' claim. At page 317, the court say, " No person could maintain a suit at law in such case, until payment was awarded by order of the court under whose decree the land was sold, and demanded of the trustee."

The cases in 4 Munford's Rep. 289; 2 Edw. Ch. Rep. 67; 9 Porter's Rep. 697; were determined on the ground that a preliminary judgment, and execution against the administrator, was necessary to establish a *devastavit*, before suit could be maintained against sureties in an administration bond; and the court say that a complainant would be without remedy, if not allowed to sue in chancery.

It was said this would not be allowed in an ordinary case, where the administrator was alive, and within the reach of the common-law courts, and a judgment could be obtained against him. Bolton v. Powell, 8 Eng. L. and E. Rep. 165.

But by the act of Assembly of Maryland, 1798, c. 101, sub. c. 8, § 15, and sub. c. 11, § 1, distribution is to be made when the debts are paid. A distributee may sue at law on the administration bond, against the sureties, after the lapse of thirteen months, without having first obtained judgment and issued execution against the administrator. 7 Gill & J. 475.

More than thirteen months had elapsed between the filing of the new bonds and the filing of the bill.. A right of action at law had accrued on the bonds before the filing of the bill.

Again; the complainants do not in their bill aver that there was a surplus in the hands of Bomford, as administrator *de bonis non*, after the payment of debts, to which they, as distributees of the estate of Kosciusko, under the French law, are entitled. Which omission, the defendants say, is bad on demurrer Stevens v. Frost, 2 Younge & Coll. 297.

Mr. Justice WAYNE delivered the opinion of the court.

The purpose of this suit is to recover for the descendants of the sisters of General Kosciusko, the funds which he owned in the United States at the time of his death.

Several points are suggested by the pleadings.

We will consider such of them as we think necessary, after having stated the origin of the fund in controversy, and the management of it, from the time that Kosciusko placed it under the care of Mr. Jefferson until the death of Colonel Bomford, the administrator *de bonis non*, in eighteen hundred and forty-eight.

General Kosciusko came to the United States early in our revolutionary war, to join our army. He did so at first as a volunteer. In October, 1776, he received from Congress the commission of Colonel of Engineers. He served with great distinction until the close of the war, and then retired from the army, after our independence had been acknowledged, with the rank of Brigadier-General. He stood prominently with those great men of our own country, with whom he had given seven years of his life to secure its freedom and nationality. He returned to Poland, poorer than when he came to us, and was, in fact, our creditor for a part of his military pay.

His subsequent career in Europe is a part of its history. All that we can say of it in connection with this case, is, that he returned to the United States after he was released from the prisons of Catherine, by her son and successor, the Emperor Paul. Whilst he was absent from the United States, a military certificate for twelve thousand two hundred and eighty dollars and fifty-four cents, had been issued, as due to him for services during the war. Not having been, for several years, in a situation to claim or to receive it, until his return to the United States, in 1798, Congress passed an act in 1799, (6 Stat. at Large, 32,) directing the Secretary of the Treasury to pay to him the amount of the certificate, with interest from the first day of January, one thousand seven hundred and ninety-three, to the thirty-first of December, one thousand seven hundred and ninety-seven. It was not a gratuity, but a simple act of justice, graduated then by the inability of our country to do more. It yet remains for us to give some national testimonial of his virtues, and of his services in the war of our independence. Seven years of peril and suffering, of wise forecast in counsels of war, and of dauntless bravery in the field, may claim from our people grateful recollections, and the expression of them in the best way that they can be commemorated by art. The cadets at West Point, unaided by the Government, have reared to his memory a monument there, and it is the only memorial of him upon the face of our land.

That military certificate, with a part of the interest upon it, was the basis of the fund now in controversy.

It was paid to Kosciusko, was invested in American stocks in his own name, and placed under the care and direction of Mr. Jefferson.

In a letter from Mr. Jefferson, in answer to one from H. E. M. De Politica, the Russian Minister at Washington, of the 27th of May, 1819, written by the latter, at the instance of the Viceroy of Poland, to make inquiries about the fund, Mr. Jefferson says: "A little before the departure of the General from America, in 1798, he wrote a will, all with his own hand, in which he directed that the property he should possess here, at the time of his death, should be laid out in the purchase of young negroes, who were to be educated and emancipated — of this will he named me executor, and deposited it in my hands. The interest of his money was to be regularly remitted to him in Europe. My situation in the interior of the country, rendered it impossible for me to act personally in the remittances of his funds, and Mr. John Barnes, of Georgetown, was engaged, under a power of attorney, to do that on commission; which duty he regularly and faithfully performed, until we heard of the death of the General. We had, in the mean time, by seasonably withdrawing a part of his funds from the bank in which he had deposited them, and lending them to the government during the late war, (with England,) augmented them to seventeen thousand one hundred and fifty-nine dollars sixty-three cents, to wit: $12,499.63, in the funds of the United States, and $4,600 in the Bank of Columbia, at Georgetown. I delayed for some time the regular probate of the will, expecting to hear from Europe, whether he had left any will there, which might affect his property here. I thought that prudence and safety required this, although the last letter he wrote me before his death, dated September 15th, 1817, assured me of the contrary, in these words: ' Nous avançons tous en age, c'est pour cela, mon cher et respectable ami, que je vous prie de vouloir bien (et comme vous avez tout le pouvoir,) arranger qu' apres la mort de notre digne ami, Mr. Barnes, quelqu'un d'aussi probe que lui prenne sa place, pour que je reçoive les interêsts ponctuellement de mon fonds; duquel, après ma mort, vous savez, la destination invariable, quant à présent faites pour le mieux comme vous pensez.'

" *Translation.*

" We all grow old, and for that reason, my dear and respectable friend, I ask you, as you have full power to do, to arrange it in such a manner that, after the death of our worthy friend, Mr. Barnes, some one, as honest as himself, may take his place, so that I may receive the interest of my money punctually ; of which money, after my death, you know the fixed destination. As for the present, do what you think best.'

"After his death, a claim was presented to me, on behalf of Kosciusko Armstrong, son of General Armstrong, of three thousand seven hundred and four dollars, given in Kosciusko's lifetime, payable out of this fund ; and, subsequently, came a claim to the whole, from Mr. Zeltner, under a will made there. I proceeded, on the advice of the Attorney-General of the United States, to prove the will, in the State Court of the District in which I reside, but declined the executorship.   When the General named me his executor, I was young enough to undertake the duty, although, from its nature, it was likely to be of long continuance ; but, the lapse of twenty years, or more, had rendered it imprudent for me to engage in what I could not live to carry into effect.   Finding, now, by your letter of May 27th, that a relation of the General's also claims the property ; that it is likely to become litigious, and age and incompetence to business admonishing me to withdraw myself from entanglements of that kind, I have determined to deliver the will, and the whole subject, over to such court of the United States as the Attorney-General of the United States shall advise, (probably it will be that of the District of Columbia,) to place the case in his hands, and to petition that court to relieve me from it, and to appoint an administrator, with the will annexed. Such an administrator will probably call upon the different claimants to interplead, and let the court decide what shall be done with the property.   This I shall do, sir, with as little delay as the necessary consultations will admit; and, when the administrator is appointed, I shall deliver to him the original certificates which are in my possession.   The accumulating interest and dividends remain, untouched, in the Treasury of the United States, and Bank of Columbia."

The facts of this letter are referred to and admitted, in the answer of the defendants, but we preferred to give them in the language of the writer.

Mr. Jefferson carried out his intentions, and letters of administration were granted to the late Benjamin F. Lear.   He received, in different kinds of stock, and in dividends, which had accrued since the death of Kosciusko, $25,931.43½; $4,100.62½ of which, were applied by him for the payment of United States six per cents, which had been purchased on account of the estate, by the direction of the Orphans' Court, when it had the control of the fund.   It is not necessary, for the purposes of this suit, to inquire into the correctness of Mr. Lear's accounts of his administration.   There is nothing on the record making them doubtful. He died in 1832, and it appears, from the books and papers from which the final account of his administration was made, that the funds in his hands had been increased to $31,-785.27. Colonel Bomford, his successor, charged himself with that sum.

The accounts of both, however, must be looked into, for another purpose. And that is, to determine, from the changes made by Lear in the funds, and in his mode of managing them, in what official relation to Lear Bomford received them, and why it is, though he did so as the executor of Lear, that the defendants in this suit, by becoming his bondsmen, under the act of the 20th February, 1846, have made themselves liable for the *devastavit* of their principal. And here we will consider that point of the case.

It appears, from the accounts of Lear, that he thought he was authorized, as administrator, to change the funds of the estate into other funds, and to lend them upon private securities, without the permission of the Orphans' Court. Most, if not all of them, in whatever way invested by him, were in his own name, at the time of his death. Bomford took them, as his executor, and settled an account with the Orphans' Court, in which he charged himself, as executor of Lear, with all the stocks, bonds, mortgages, and other securities for the payment of money, and the money of the estate, which Lear had, as administrator, at the time of his death. In fact, the funds, excepting the stock of the Bank of Columbia, were converted into money, in Lear's hands, and Bomford took them, as his executor, with the obligation, as such, to account for the same to whomsoever might be entitled to Kosciusko's estate. This being so, the question arises, whether or not his sureties, as executor of Lear, were not liable for any waste of the estate by him, instead of his sureties, as the administrator of Kosciusko, upon the ground that the latter were only liable, by their bonds, for so much as he received as administrator, and not for what he had possessed himself of, as the executor of Lear.

Bomford, it must be remembered, was the executor of Lear, and became, also, by appointment of the Orphans' Court, the administrator *de bonis non cum testamento* of Kosciusko, under the laws of Maryland, as they were of force in that part of the District of Columbia which had been a part of Maryland when Congress took jurisdiction over the same. His bonds, in both relations to the two estates of Lear and Kosciusko, were given under that law; and the obligations of himself and his sureties are determined by what has been the judicial interpretation and administration of it in Maryland, uncontrolled by any decisions of other courts elsewhere.

We understand, by the laws of Maryland, as they stood when Congress assumed jurisdiction over the District of Columbia, that the property of a deceased person was considered to be administered, whenever it was sold, or converted into money, by the administrator or executor, or in any respect changed from the condition in which the deceased left it. It did not go to the administrator *de bonis non*, unless, on the death of the executor or administrator, it remained in specie, or was the same then that it was when it came to his hands. When the assets have been changed, it is said, in Maryland, that the property has been administered. In that sense, all the funds received by Lear, and changed by him into other securities, were administered by him. If this suit, then, had been brought against the first sureties of Bomford, in his original bond as administrator *de bonis non* of Kosciusko, they would not have been answerable. For any waste of the estate of Kosciusko, the remedy would have been against him and his sureties, as executor of Lear, and if the assets had been wasted by Lear, Lear's sureties would have been answerable. Nor would the circumstance that Bomford charged himself with these assets, as administrator *de bonis non*, make any difference. His sureties could be made liable only for the assets which legally came to his hands; that is, for what remained in specie, unadministered. Nor could he make them liable for more, by charging himself, in his account as administrator, with any property which had been changed by his predecessor, or administered, as it is said to be, in Maryland, when such a change is made, by an administrator or executor.

Such being the law as to the responsibility of Lear and his sureties, and of Bomford and his original sureties, it was urged in the court below, as we see from the decision of the learned Judge who gave that court's opinion, and here also in argument by the counsel of the defendants, that it applied equally to Bomford's second and third sets of sureties, who became so under the act of Congress of the 20th February, 1846. 9 Stat. at Large, 4. So the court below decided, but we think it did so erroneously. The error consists in this, that the bonds of these defendants were treated as if they were the same as the original bonds given by the first sureties of Bomford under the Maryland law, and that the relations of Bomford to the estate of Kosciusko were precisely such as they were when he came into the possession of the Kosciusko funds, as the executor of Lear. The argument was this: that as Bomford had, from the character of the assets at the death of Lear, a valid right to them, as Lear's executor, and was bound by law to administer them as Lear was, that he would not have any legal right in them as administrator *de bonis non*, to bind these defendants as his sureties for any of his defaults; particularly as it appears from his accounts, including the last of them, that he charges himself with a balance of $43,504.40, in his ninth account; the items of which related to transactions which had taken place before the date of either of the bonds of the defendants.

Now, upon such a state of facts, it must be admitted that Bomford himself was bound for the amount stated by him to be due, in an account of assets of the estate of Kosciusko, and that his original sureties were not under the Maryland law, for those assets which had been administered by Lear.

For what purpose then, it may be asked, did the Orphans' Court call upon Bomford, after he had rendered his eighth account, to give other sureties, under the penalty, if he did not do so, that he would be displaced as administrator, and that another administrator would be appointed in his stead, unless it was to secure that amount for which he had become personally liable, though it had been originally received by him as executor, but for which there were no sureties in fact, when the defendants became so? They became his sureties under the 3d section of the act of 1846. 9 Stat. at Large, 4. That section provides, that, whenever the Orphans' Court shall be satisfied that the security which has been taken, or which may hereafter be taken from an executor or administrator, is insufficient, by reason of the removal or insolvency of any of the sureties, or because the penalty of the bond is too small, or from any cause whatever, that the court may call upon the administrator or executor to give additional security, and if there shall be a failure to comply with such order, the court is empowered to appoint another administrator in the stead of the first, and to require, from him removed, to hand over to his successor the unadministered assets, and to enforce compliance with such an order by fine and attachment or any other legal process. The act, and the proceedings of the Orphans' Court under it, towards the administrator, Colonel Bomford, cover exactly such a case as this. The object of the law, and the purpose of the court, was to get from the administrator additional and adequate security, for the funds which he had stated in his sworn account to be still unadministered in his hands, without any regard to the fact which could not then have been known to the court, whether they had been misused or not by him; but which, from his rendered account, it might properly have been inferred had not been. The act permits the court, in the cases mentioned in the 3d section, not only to take security for assets which might in future come to the hands of the administrator, but for such as he had already received and returned to the court as in his hands, or of which he ought to have made a return, and which may not have been properly administered.   If that be not the proper interpretation of the act, it would be nugatory and idle.   Instead of the power of the court being enlarged by it, it would be just as powerless to act in the cases mentioned in the 3d section, as it had been under the law of Maryland.   The bonds of the defendants were manifestly given with reference to the accounts which had been filed in the Orphans' Court by Colonel Bomford.   They must have so understood it; for in one of them the action of the Orphans' Court, under the law of 1846, is recited, and the record shows that the sureties in the other took from their principal a counter security, to indemnify them on account of his failure to discharge all of his duties as administrator.   The bonds of the defendants are distinguishable from the original bonds which the administrator gave, the latter having been given before any inventory was returned, or account stated in the court, and when no particular sum was due from the administrator; and the bonds of these defendants were given for a sum certain, returned to the court by the administrator, due by him in that character.

All of us concur in thinking that the bonds of the defendants were properly taken under the act of 1846.   That the Orphans' Court called for them to secure the amount with which the administrator then stood charged, and such as he might afterwards get.   They were accepted and approved by the court for that purpose, and the sureties gave them with a full knowledge of the state of the account which the administrator had filed.   All of us think, also, that they are answerable for his waste. unless something else in the case can relieve them.

The first objection is, that Kosciusko did not die intestate as to his personal property in the United States, and that the same passed, by the second article of the will of 1817, to M. and Madame Zavier Zeltner, of Soleure, in Switzerland.

2. That there is no proof in the case that Kosciusko was domiciled at his death in France, and if he was, that the complainants have failed to prove what the law of France was at that date, for the distribution of the personal estate of one who dies domiciled there.

3. It is also said, that it is not proved that those persons named in the bill as being entitled to the fund sued for, have such a relationship to Kosciusko as entitled them to receive it.

We will consider these objections in their order.

Kosciusko made four wills.   One of them in the United States, in 1798, which, after his death, Mr. Jefferson proved in the Court of Albemarle, in Virginia.   His second will was made in Paris, in 1806, in which he charged the fund mentioned in the first will with a legacy to Kosciusko Armstrong.   His third and fourth wills were made at Soleure, in Switzerland; the third on the 4th of June, 1816, and the fourth on the 10th October, 1817. It is not denied that he made the first, second, and fourth wills, but the defendants attack the third on account, as they suppose, that the probate of it had been taken in the Orphans' Court in Washington, without due proof of its execution; and they rely upon the fourth will to show that it contains a residuary article in favor of Monsieur and Madame Zeltner, after the payment of specific legacies.

We think that all of the wills have been proved according to the rules of evidence, and that the authenticated exemplification of that of 1816, from the registry of it in France, recorded in the Orphans' Court for the District of Columbia, is all that can be required. With these wills in view, we have the means to decide the effect of them on the property in controversy.

The olographic will of 1816, contains a revoking clause. It is in these terms: " Je revoque tous les testaments et codiciles que j'ai pu faire avant le présent auquel seul je m'arrête comme contenant mes dernières volantes." Translated in the record: " I revoke all the wills and codicils which I may have made previous to the present, to which alone I confine myself, as containing my last wishes."

The right to revoke a will exists now in every nation, though the exercise of it is differently regulated. It may be done by an express revocation, or by certain acts, which of themselves infer, or from which the law infers, a revocation. "Ambulatoria est voluntas defuncti usque ad vitæ supremum excitum." Nor can one bind himself in a testament not to make another. "Nemo potest in testamento suo cavere, ne legis in suo testamento locum habeant; quia nec tempore, aut conditione finiri obligatio hæridis legatorum nomine potest." Dig. Lib. 34, tit. 4 l. 4; Dig. Lib. 30, tit. 1, l. 55. In England, the manner of revocation is prescribed by the 6th and 22d sections of the Statute of Frauds. In Spain and in Holland, a will may be revoked by an act confined to the revocation of that testament, without making any other disposition; or by making another testament which expressly revokes the former, if either manner as it may be used, is executed with the forms and solemnities which the law required to give validity to the first will. By the customs of Paris and Normandy, revocations could be made by a simple declaration before two notaries, or before one notary and two witnesses, without its being done in any prescribed form. And by the same customs, a declaration in the handwriting of a testator, and signed by himself, revoked his testament, and the effect of it was to make him intestate. Law 25, tit. 1, p. 6; Voet. lib. 28; tit. 3, n. 1; Matth. de Success; disp. 8, n. 18. But we learn from Touiller and from the Code Civil, that these customs were abolished, and that in France, wills may be revoked in whole or in part, by a subsequent will, or by an act before notaries, containing a declaration of such intention. Touillier liv. 3, tit. 2; Don. et Test. ch. 5, n. 619; Pothier des Don. Test. ch. 6, § 2, § 1; Art. Code Civil, 969, 1035 – 36 – 38.

The will of 1816 was made at Soleure, while Kosciusko was sojourning there, after he had left Vienna, in 1815, whither he had gone from Paris, at the instance of the Emperor Alexander, that he might be advised with concerning the affairs of Poland. It is an olographic will, wholly written in the handwriting of the testator, according to the 970th article of the Code Civil. It gives specific legacies to persons residing in France, charged upon funds owned by the testator in France, and his executor was a notary at Morcu, in the department of Seine and Marne, which is the opening of the will, the testator says, in the department of his residence, at Berville.

Within the month of Kosciusko's death, the will was taken to Paris, and recorded there, pursuant to law. The executor having received authority from the proper tribunal to act as such, paid, according to the will, the legacies given by it. See arts. Code Civil, 999, 1000. The wills, then, of 1798 and of 1806, were revoked by the will of 1816, and as the testator did not make in it any disposition of his American funds, he died intestate as to them, unless the second article in the will of 1817, has the effect of a residuary bequest to the persons named in it.

It is, " I bequeathe all of my effects, (*effets,*) my carriage and my horse included, to Madame and to Mr. Zavier Zeltner, above named." It will be seen, by the first clause in the will, that they are the father and mother of Emilie Zeltner, to whom he bequeathed about fifty thousand francs of France, charged upon funds in England, in the hands of Thompson, Bonard & Co.

We shall be aided, in the construction of the second article of the will of 1817, by keeping in mind what were the relations between himself and the Zeltner family, as they are disclosed by his wills of 1816 and 1817. He makes them, in both wills, his legatees, except a legacy to General Baszkoyski; two small legacies to his executors; two thousand francs to the poor, and one thousand for his own burial. His chosen friends were without fortune. He says so in that memorable letter which he wrote to the Emperor Alexander, after the allies had entered Paris, in 1814; from which it may be seen, when his country was nearest his heart, that his friend was there too. Fletcher's Poland: Harp. Fam. Lib. 301; Ozinski, 4, p. 175. To the two daughters of that friend, Andrew Lewis Zeltner, with whom he had lived for fifteen years, he gives all of his funds in

France, amounting to ninety-five thousand francs, excepting a legacy to his executor. To the daughter of Zavier Zeltner, with whom he was staying when the wills of 1816 and 1817 were made, and where he died, he bequeathes fifty thousand francs; and it is to him and to his wife, that he says, I bequeathe all my effects, my carriage and horse included. From its place in the will of 1817, and from the connection of the words " all my effects, with my carriage and horse included," it would be a very strained construction, to make the words, all of my effects, comprehend his personal estate in the United States, it being neither alluded to in any way in this will, nor in that of 1816. Except in so far as it might, under the will of 1816, have been applied to the payments of the legacies given in that will, upon the failure of the funds upon which they were first charged. Effects, in French, or the word *effets*, has the same meaning in common parlance and in law, that it has in English. Its meaning properly in either, when used indefinitely in wills, but in connection with something particular and certain, is limited by its association to other things of a like kind. It is from the subject-matter of its use, that intention of something else is to be implied; and that of course may be larger or less. In some instances in wills, the word has carried the whole personal estate. When in connection with words of themselves of larger meaning, or of fixed legal import, as there were in the case of Bosley v. Bosley, decided at this term of the court, such a clause in a will is residuary. 5 Madd. Ch. Rep. 72; 6 Madd. Ch. Rep. 119; Cowper, 299; 15 Vesey, 507.

Such being the rule, it is our opinion, that the second article in the will of 1817, is not residuary, and that it has no relation to the funds in controversy.

It follows, then, that as the wills of 1798 and of 1806. were revoked by the will of 1816, and as no disposition was made in it, or in the will of 1817, of the funds in controversy, that General Kosciusko died intestate as to them, and that they may be distributed to his relations who may be entitled to inherit from him, according to the law of his domicil at the time of his death.

We now proceed to the question of domicil.

In the will of 1806, he describes himself as " an officer of the United States of America, in their revolutionary war against Britain, and a native of Lithuania, in Poland, at present residing in Paris." In the will of 1816, made at Soleure, his language is: " I, the undersigned Thaddeus Kosciusko, residing at Berville, in the township Genevraye, of the department of Seine and Marne, (being now) or at present at Soleure, in Switzerland." In the will of 1817, nothing is said of his residence. The record shows that he went from the United States to France in 1798, that he was there in 1806, when he said he resided at Paris. There is no proof that he was not continuously in France until 1815, when he went to Vienna. We know, too, historically, that he left it in June of that year for Soleure, when he found out that it had been determined in the Congress of Vienna to erect the Duchy of Warsaw into a kingdom, without including in it his native province of Lithuania.

We do not, however permit the historical facts just alluded to, or any other of a like kind, to have any weight in forming our conclusion concerning his domicil at the time of his death. The facts in the record are sufficient for that purpose.

In the first place, his declarations that his residence was in France, in the way they were made in his wills, with an interval of ten years between them, would, upon the authority of adjudged cases, be sufficient to establish, *primâ facie*, his domicil in France. Such declarations have always been received in evidence, when made previous to the event which gave rise to the suit. They have been received in the courts of France, in the courts of England, and in those of our own country. In two questions of domicil in France, such declarations in a power of attorney, and in other instruments, were received as evidence. Denisart, tit. Domicil, § 1. In the English courts there are many cases in which like declarations have been offered and received. 5 Term Rep. 512, and the observations of Mr. Evans, axon et un 2 Poth. Obl. App. No. 16, § 11. Rawson v. Haigh, 2 Bing. 99; 9 Moore, 217; S. C. W. & M. 353. Lord Tenterden, 1 Bing. N. C.; 5 C. & P. 575; 1 Taylor, 376. In the United States, the case of Gorham v. Canton, (5 Greenleaf, 266,) is to the same effect; and in Massachusetts, in the cases of Thorndike v. Boston, (1 Metcalf,) and Kilburn v. Bennett, (3 Metcalf, 199,) it was ruled that in a case where the question of domicil was raised, the declarations and letters of a party whose domicil was disputed, were admissible in evidence, especially if made previous to the event which gave rise to the suit. We find, also, in 8 Pickering, 476, that the will of a grandfather in 1774, in which he was described as being of O. and another will, in which he is described as resident in O., were admissible evidence to prove that the grandfather had obtained a settlement at O.

Kosciusko's domicil of origin was Lithuania, in Poland. The presumption of law is that it was retained, unless the change is proved, and the burden of proving it is upon him who alleges the changes. Somerville v. Somerville, 5 Vesey, 787; Voet, Pand. tit. 1, 5, N. 99.

But what amount of proof is necessary to change a domicil of origin into a *primâ facie* domicil of choice? It is residence elsewhere, or where a person lives out of the domicil of origin. That repels the presumption of its continuance, and casts upon him who denies the domicil of choice, the burden of disproving it. Where a person lives, is taken *primâ facie* to be his domicil, until other facts establish the contrary. Story's Com. 44, 6 Rule; Bruce *v.* Bruce, 2 Bos. & Pul. 228, Note 239; 3 Ves. 198, 291; Hagg. Consist. 374, 437. It is difficult to lay down any rule under which every instance of residence could be brought, which may make a domicil of choice. But there must be to constitute it actual residence in the place, with the intention that it is to be a principal and permanent residence. That intention may be inferred from the circumstances or condition in which a person may be as to the domicil of his origin, or from the seat of his fortune, his family and pursuits of life. Pothier, Introd. Gen. aux Cout. p. 4; D'Argentié, Cout. Art. 449; Touillier, lib. 1, tit. 3, n. 371; 1 Burge, Com. Confl. Laws, 42, 43. A removal which does not contemplate an absence from the former domicil for an indefinite and uncertain time is not a change of it. But when there is a removal, unless it can be shown or inferred from circumstances that it was for some particular purpose, expected to be only of a temporary nature, or in the exercise of some particular profession, office, or calling, it does change the domicil. The result is, that the place of residence is *primâ facie* the domicil, unless there be some motive for that residence not inconsistent with a clearly established intention to retain a permanent residence in another place. The facts in the case, place the residence of Kosciusko in France, under the principle just stated.

It is averred in the bill that France was his residence. The defendants deny it, admitting, however, that, from the time he left the United States, he was a sojourner in France and Switzerland until he died. But they aver that he did not remove to France at any time of his life with the intention to make it his permanent residence. And they further charge that he never did abandon the hope that circumstances would favor his return to Poland, when its political condition would permit him to resume his rights and duties as a citizen of it. Such an averment implies that he had voluntarily left Poland for France, without having been forced to do so, and that his return depended upon political contingencies, which might never happen, and which we know did not occur. It places upon the defendants the burden of proving the intention, the complainants having shown, and the defendants having admitted, that he had *primâ facie* a domicil in France. They have not done so. There is nothing in the record disproving the averment of his domicil in France, and we must, from his own declarations and other proofs in the record, receive it as a fact that he was domiciled there at the time of his death.

The error of the argument and of the averment against Kosciusko's domicil in France is this: that they considered him a forced exile from Poland, and that he had only made France his asylum during banishment.

In such a case, it is true, a person cannot be presumed to have abandoned all hope of return to his country, whatever length of time may have passed since he was driven from it. But Kosciusko is not placed in that predicament by any proof in the case. Nor could such proof have been made; for it is well known, when he was liberated by the Emperor Paul, that it was done without restraint or inhibition of any kind. He was offered high military command and presents of princely amount, which he declined to accept. He came to the United States, and afterwards went voluntarily to France, where he lived for fifteen years. He could have returned to Poland at any time, if he had chosen to do so. Not having done so, the conclusion ought to be that he abandoned his residence there for a residence in France, which cannot be affected, as to its permanency, by any event which might have happened to induce him to change it again to the domicil of his origin. This is coincident with the fact that he had been made a French citizen by a decree of the National Assembly of France, in August, 1792. Knowing that such a naturalization would not have the effect of investing him with the privileges of a native-born citizen, if he did not become domiciled in France, unless his residence there was expressly dispensed with in the letters of naturalization, he went to France to get a civil status which he could not conscientiously enjoy in Poland whilst it continued to be under a foreign dominion. Pothier, Tr. des Personnes, &c. P. 1, tit. 2, § 3; Denesart, tit. Aubaine.

These general principles of jurisprudence in respect to domicil, by which Kosciusko's has been determined, are such as the courts of France would have ruled in this case.

Kosciusko's intestacy as to the funds in controversy, and his domicil having been determined, we will now state the law as to the right of succession in such cases.

For several hundred years upon the continent, and in England, from reported cases, for a hundred years, the rule has been, that personal property, in cases of intestacy, is to be distributed by the law of the domicil of the intestate at the time of his death. It has been universal for so long a time that it may now be said to be a part of the *jus gentium*. Lord Thurlow speaks of it as such in the House of Lords, in the case of Bruce v. Bruce. Erskine, in his Institutes of the Law of Scotland, (B. 3, tit. 9, § 4, 644,) says, this rule is founded on the laws of nations. He says, "When a Scotsman dies abroad *sine animo remanendi*, the legal succession of his movable estate in Scotland must descend to his next of kin according to the law of Scotland; and where a foreigner dies in this country *sine animo remanendi*, the movables which he brought with him hither ought to be regulated, not by the law of the country in which they locally were, but that of the proprietors *patria*, or domicil whence he came, and whither he intends again to return. This rule is founded in the law of nations, and the reason of it is the same in both cases, that since all succession *ab intestatio* is grounded upon the presumed will of the deceased, his estate ought to descend to him whom the law of his own country calls to the succession, as the person whom it presumes to be most favored by the deceased."

The law of Scotland had been different in this particular, but it was brought into harmony with the law of the rest of Europe by the decision of the House of Lords, in Bruce *v.* Bruce, 6 Brown's Par. Cases, 550, 566; 2 Bos. & Pul. 226, 230, 231; Lord Stair's Institutes, B. 3, tit. 8, § 5; Hogg & Lashley, House of Lords, June 25th, 1788; Robertson on Personal Success. 131; Omman *v.* Bingham, House of Lords, March 18, 1776; Colville & Landor *v.* Brown & Brown, Dict. Success. Ap. p. 1, 4; W. & S. 28.

The earliest case reported in the English books, is that of Pipon *v.* Pipon, Am. 6, 27. Lord Hardwicke recognized in it the rule that the personal estate, in cases of intestacy, followed the person, and becomes distributable according to the law or custom of the place where the intestate lived. Among other reasons given by him is, that a contrary rule would be extremely mischievous, and would affect our commerce. No foreigner could deal in our funds but at the peril of his effects going according to our laws, and not those of his own country. He reaffirmed the same in a few years afterwards, in Thorne *v.* Watkins, 2 Ves. 35. Lord Kenyon did the same when he was Master of the Rolls in 1787, in Killpatrick *v.* Killpatrick, which will be found cited in Robertson on Personal Succession, 116. In 1790, the House of Lords acted upon the rule, in Bruce *v.* Bruce, and two years afterwards, in Hogg *v.* Lashley. Many cases followed in the English courts, and the only question since has been, what was the domicil of the intestate at the time of his death? In the United States the rule has been fully recognized. 14 Martin, Lou. 99; 3 Paige, 182; 2 Gill & Johns. 193, 224, 228.

The rule prevails, also, in the ascertainment of the person who is entitled to take as heir or distributee. It decides whether primogeniture gives a right of preference, or an exclusive right

36*

to take the succession; whether a person is legitimate or not to take the succession; whether the person shall take *per stirpes* or *per capita*, and the nature and extent of the right of representation. Story's Conflict of Laws.

But it is objected, before the rule can be applied in this suit against the defendants, that the complainants must prove what the law of France is for the distribution of the fund. It is said that has not been done.

For this purpose, the Code Civil of France was offered in evidence, but it was objected to.

It is true, that the existence of a foreign law, written or unwritten, cannot be judicially noticed, unless it be proved as a fact, by appropriate evidence.

The written foreign law may be proved, by a copy of the law properly authenticated. The unwritten must be by the parol testimony of experts. As to the manner of authenticating the law, there is no general rule, except this : that no proof shall be received, " which presupposes better testimony behind, and attainable by the party." They may be verified by an oath, or by an exemplification of a copy, under the great seal of a State, or, by a copy, proved to be a true copy by a witness who has examined and compared it with the original, or by a certificate of an officer, properly authorized, by law, to give the copy; which certificate must be duly proved. But such modes of proof as have been mentioned, are not to be considered exclusive of others, especially of codes of laws and accepted histories of the law of a country. In Picton's case, Lord Ellenborough said : " The best writers furnish us with their statements of the law, and that would certainly be good evidence upon the same principle as that which renders histories admissible. There is a case, continued Lord Ellenborough, in which the History of the Turkish Empire, by Cantemir, was received by the House of Lords, after some discussion. I will, therefore, receive any book that purports to be a history of the common law of Spain. B. N. P. 248, 249; 30 How. St. Tr. 492; 2 Phil. Ev. 123; 1 Salk. 281: Morris v. Harmer, 7 Pet. 554; 3 Cary, 178; 11 Clark & Fin.; Russel's Peerage Cases; 3 Wend. 173, Lord Tenterden, in Lacon v. Heggins, (Stark. Rep. 178,) admitted a copy of the Code Civil of France, produced by the French Consul, who stated that it was an authentic copy of the law of France, upon which he acted in his office, and that it was printed at the office for printing the laws of France, and would be acted upon in the French courts. In the Russel Peerage case, Lord Campbell said : " The most authentic form of getting at foreign law, is to have the book which lays down the law. Thus, we have had the Code Napoleon in our courts. It is better than to examine a witness, whose memory may be defective, and who may have a bias influencing his mind upon the law." The Supreme Court of New York has held, that an unofficial copy of the Commercial Code of France, could not be proved by the French Consul residing at New York, though he stated it to be conformable to the official publications; and that it was an exact copy of the laws furnished by the French government to its Consul at New York. Had it been an official copy, and sworn to be such, by the Consul, it would have been received in evidence, as the Irish Statutes were, in Jones v. Maffet, (5 Serg. & Rawle, 523,) where they were sworn to by an Irish barrister, and that he received them from the King's printer, in Ireland. In Church v. Hubbart, (2 Cranch,) this court said, that the edicts of Portugal, offered in evidence, would have been admissible, if the copies of them had been sworn to be true copies, by the American Consul at Lisbon, instead of his having given his consular certificate, that they were true copies, because it was not one of the functions of a Consul to authenticate foreign laws in that way.

The court say, " The paper offered to the court is certified to be a copy compared with the original. It is impossible to suppose that this copy might not have been authenticated by the oath of the Consul, as well as by his certificate." It will be seen, that what the court required, was a verification of the original, upon oath, and that then the edicts would have been admissible in evidence. They were municipal edicts, too, it should be remembered, and not one of those marine ordinances of a foreign nation, on a subject of common concern to all nations, which may, according to the manner of its promulgation, be read as law, without other proof. Talbot v. Seeman, 1 Cranch, 1.

The rule of this court has always been, since those cases were decided, " that the laws of a foreign country, designed only for the direction of its own affairs, are not to be noticed by other countries, unless proved as facts; and, that the sanction of an oath is required for their establishment, unless they can be verified by some other such high authority, that the law respected not less than the oath of an individual."

The question in this case, is, has the Code Civil, which was offered in evidence, a verification equivalent to the oath of an individual?

Opinions and cases may be found in conflict with the cases cited, but, from a perusal of many of them, we find that they have been formed and decided without a careful discrimination between what should be the proof of foreign written and unwritten law; and when written laws, either singly or in statute books, or in codes, have been offered in evidence, without a sufficient authentication that they were official publications, by the government which had legislated them; or when written laws have been offered, properly proved to be official, but which were equivocal in their terms, and in the judicial administration of which there have been, or may be, various interpretations, making it necessary to call in experts, as in cases of an unwritten law, to state how the law offered in evidence is administered in the courts of the country of which it is said to be the law. In England, until recently, it was not doubted that a foreign written law was admissible in evidence, when properly authenticated. But, in the Sussex Peerage case, 1844, (in 11 Clark & Finnelly, 115,) several of the Judges gave their opinions upon the subject. Lord Brougham, in that case, differed from Lord Campbell, and said that the Code Napoleon ought not to be received in an English court, and that before it could be received from the book, that an expert, acquainted with the text and the interpretation of it, must be called. And so it was ruled, afterwards, by Erle, Justice, in 1846, in Cocks *v.* Purdy, (2 C. & K. 269,) in which fragments of a code were offered as evidence. But his Lordship's opinion, and the case of Clark *v.* Purdy, must be taken, subject to the facts upon which the point arose. In the first, it was, whether Doctor Wiseman, who had been called as a witness, could refer, whilst giving his evidence of the law of Rome on the subject of marriage, to a book, whilst it was lying by him. In the other case, fragments of laws were offered. This point had been settled by Lord Stowell, in Dalrymple *v.* Dalrymple, 2 Hagg. 54. Lord Brougham again expressed the same opinion, in his sketch of Lord Stowell, in the second series of the Statesmen of the Time of George III., 76. But Lord Langdale, who also sat with the other Judges, in the Sussex Peerage case, gave the rule, with its qualifications, in the case of the Earl of Nelson *v.* Lord Bridport, 8 Beav. 527 After stating the rule, coincidently with the opinion of Lord Brougham, he says: " Such I conceive to be the general rule, but the case to which it is applicable admits of great variety. Though a knowledge of foreign laws is not to be imputed to the Judge, you may impute to him such a knowledge of the general art of reasoning, as will enable him, with the assistance of the bar, to discover where fallacies are probably concealed, and in what cases he ought to require testimony more or less strict. If the utmost strictness was required, in every case, justice might often stand still; and I am not disposed to say that there may not be cases, in which the Judge may not, without impropriety, take upon himself to construe the words of a foreign law, and determine their application to the case in question; especially, if there should be a variance or want of clearness in the testimony."

Notwithstanding the differences in the cases cited, we think that the true rule in respect to the admissibility of foreign law in evidence, may be gathered from them. In our view it is this, that a foreign written law may be received, when it is found in a statute book, with proof that the book has been officially published by the government which made the law. Such is the foundation of Lord Tenterden's ruling, in Lacen v. Higgens, 3 Starkie's Rep. 178. The case in 5 Sergeant & Rawle, 523, has the same basis. Though there are other reasons for the admission of the laws of the States into the courts of the United States as evidence, when they are officially published, yet they are only received when the genuineness of the publication is apparent. This court has so ruled in Hind v. Vattier, 5 Peters, 398, and in Owings v. Hull, 9 Peters, 607-625. It is true that we are called upon, as Judges, to administer the laws of the States in the courts of the United States, and that the States of the Union are not politically foreign to each other, but there is no connection between them in legislation, and we only take notice of their laws judicially, when they are found in the official statute books of the State.

With these views, it remains for us to show that the Code Civil, offered in evidence in this case by the complainants, to prove their right to the succession of the intestate estate of General Kosciusko, is authenticated in such a way that it may be received by the court for the purpose for which it was offered. It was sent to the Supreme Court, in the course of our national exchanges of laws with France. It is one of the volumes of the Bulletin des Lois à Paris L' imprimerie royalé, with this indorsement, "Les Garde des Sceaux de France à la Court Supreme Des Etats Unis." Congress has acknowledged it by the act, and the appropriation which was given to the Supreme Court to reciprocate the donation. We transmitted to the Minister of Justice official copies of all the laws, resolutions, and treaties of the United States, and a complete series of the decisions of this court. We do not doubt, whenever the question shall occur in the courts of France, that the volumes which were sent by us will be considered sufficiently authenticated to be used as evidence. The gift and the reciprocation of it, are the fruits of the liberal age in which we live. We hope for a continuance of such exchanges between France and the United States, and for a like intercourse with all nations. Business men, jurists, and statesmen, will readily appreciate its advantages. It will save much time and expense when questions occur in the courts of different nations, involving the rights of foreigners, if the written laws of every nation were verified in all of them, by certified official publications to the governments of each. In the now rapid transit of persons and property, out of the sovereignties to which they belong, into the different parts of the world, such a verification would often speed and save the rights of emigrants, sojourners, and merchants.

We think that the Code Civil, certified to the court as it is, is sufficiently authenticated to make it evidence in this suit, and that it would be so in any other case in which it may be offered.

We proceed to state the law from it, applicable to the case.

It has been determined that the domicil of General Kosciusko was in France at the time of his death, that he died intestate as to his funds in the United States, and that they were to be distributed according to the law of his domicil.

It has been proved that he survived his parents, died without issue, and that these complainants are the lineal descendants of two of his sisters, one of whom died before her brother, and the other afterwards.

The fact of their relationship, notwithstanding the objection which was made to the proof of it, is sufficient. The proofs are decrees of the Court of Nobility, of the Government of Grodno, and, another of the Court of Kobryn, in the Russian province of Lithuania. The originals are in the Orphans' Court, and were filed in it, in the regular course of judicial proceeding, Both of them are authenticated copies of judicial proceedings in the courts from which they are brought. The competency of the jurisdiction of those courts, in the matters decided in the decrees, is proved by witnesses skilled in the law of the governments of Lithuania. Lithuania we know to be now a Russian province, governed by its own laws, except as they may be modified by the Emperor's edicts. It is divided into three governments, Wilna, Grodno, and Minsk, with a Governor-General over them. The decree of the Assembly of the Department of Grodno, is an exemplified copy of that made on the 7th May, 1843, in the case of the heirs of Kosciusko, and contains the genealogical chart of the descendants of the sisters of Kosciusko.

It is not a judgment *inter partes*, but a foreign judgment *in rem*, and is evidence of the facts adjudicated against all the world. The decree from the court of Kobryn is also proved to be a judicial record. From both we learn that the persons named in the bill of the complainants, are the collateral kinsmen of General Kosciusko. By the laws of France, they may take his estate by succession.

We shall reverse the decision of the court below, and direct the funds in controversy to be divided among them, according to the 750th article of the Code, which is, that in ease of the previous decease of the father and mother of a person dead without issue, his brother and sister, or their descendants, are called to the succession, to the exclusion of ancestors and other collaterals.

All of the objections which were made against the rendition of a decree in favor of the complainants, having been considered and overruled, it only remains for us to announce the sum for which the decree shall be given, and the proportions to be paid by the defendants, as the sureties of Bomford, under the act of. 1846.

It has been heretofore stated that these bonds were given under that act, to secure the amount then returned to the Orphans' Court by the administrator, and such assets as he might afterwards receive in that character. In his ninth account, he charges himself with a balance from the eighth account of $41,914.47, and after giving the estate credit for the sums subsequently received, and claiming credits, he admits that there was due to the estate on the 7th of June, 1847, $43,504.40, including the stock of the Bank of Washington, which was after his death transferred to Lewis Johnson, who became the administrator of Kosciusko, with the will annexed.

We shall enter a decree against the defendants for the sum of $37,924.40, with interest from the 7th June, 1847, until the same shall be paid.

The said decree is to be binding upon the sureties, Carrico, Stott, and George C. Bomford, and upon the sureties Gideon, Ward, and Smith, jointly and severally in the proportion which their respective bonds bear to the sum decreed, and the costs which have accrued in this suit. But in the event that the sureties in either bond do not pay the sum decreed against them, or any part thereof, then the sureties in the other bond shall be answerable for and pay the same to the extent of their respective bonds.

We shall also order a decree to be entered against the defendant, Lewis Johnson, not subjecting him to any costs from his having been made a defendant in this suit, directing him to turn over to the complainants the stock of the Bank of Washington, to which he is entitled as the administrator *de bonis non* of Kosciusko, and the dividends which have accrued thereon, allowing to him out of the same, the costs incurred as administrator, commissions, and such reasonable counsel fees as may have been paid by him for services in matters pertaining to this case, in the Orphans' Court, and to this suit, after his account shall be filed, and be credited to him in the Orphans' Court.

Order.

This cause came on to be heard on the transcript of the record from the Circuit Court of the United States for the District of Columbia, holden in and for the County of Washington, and was argued by counsel. On consideration whereof, it is now here ordered, adjudged, and decreed, by this court, that the decree of said Circuit Court dismissing the complainants' bill in this cause, be, and the same is hereby, reversed and annulled. And this court proceeding to render such decree as the said Circuit Court ought to have rendered, doth order, adjudge and decree, as follows :

First. That the legal domicil of Thaddeus Kosciusko, the party under whom the complainants below claim, was, at the period of his death, in 1817, in France.

Second. That as to the property and fund in controversy, he, the said Kosciusko, died intestate, his will of the 4th of June, 1816, in the proceedings mentioned, having revoked his prior will of 5th of May, 1798, and 28th of June, 1806, and without disposing of said fund, and the same not having been disposed of by the will of 10th October, 1817.

Third. That the said property and fund is to be distributed according to the law of France, the place of his domicil at the time of his death.

Fourth. That by the said law of said domicil, at said period, the said property belongs in equal moieties to the collateral kindred who were the lineal descendants of the two sisters in the case mentioned, of said Kosciusko, and complainants in the bill mentioned, that is to say, one moiety thereof to Hippolitus Estho and Roman Estho, grandsons of his sister Ann, and to Louisa Narbut, her granddaughter, a widow, and in the proportions between them of one half of said moiety to said Hippolitus Estho, and the other half of said moiety to said Roman Estho and Louisa Narbut, in equal shares, — and the other moiety thereof to Vlandislaus Wankowieg, to Hippolitus Wankowieg, Adam Bychowiec, and to Michael Szyrma, also complainants, and in the proportions between them, as follows, that is to say, to Vlandislaus Wankowieg and Hippolitus Wankowieg, each of them one half of five sevenths, and of one third to each of another seventh, and to Michael Szyrma, one third of a seventh, and to Adam Bychowiec, one seventh.

Fifth. That the defendants' sureties in the bond of the 7th May, 1846, for $20,000, in the proceedings mentioned, taken under the authority of the act of Congress of the 20th of February, 1846, that is to say, James Carrico, Samuel Stott, and George C. Bomford, and the other defendants' sureties in the other bond therein mentioned, also taken under said act of Congress, and dated 4th of January, 1847, for $40,000, that is to say, Jacob Gideon, Ulysses Ward, and Jonathan B. H. Smith, are each, and to the extent hereinafter decreed, responsible to the complainants for the amount also hereinafter decreed.

Sixth. It is further adjudged and decreed, that there is due, and that the same be paid, by said defendants, to the complainants above named, in the proportions herein stated, the sum of $37,924 $\frac{48}{100}$ with interest on said sum, at the rate of six per centum, from the 7th day of June, 1847, till paid; that is to say, that the said defendants, James Carrico, Samuel Stott, and George C. Bomford, are jointly and severally bound to pay to said complainants, of said $37,924 $\frac{48}{100}$, the sum of $12,641.46$\frac{2}{3}$, with interest thereon. as aforesaid, from the 7th of June, 1847, till paid, and one third of the costs of this suit, in both courts, and they are hereby ordered and decreed to pay the same. And that the said defendants, Jacob Gideon, Ulysses Ward, and Jonathan B. H. Smith, are jointly and severally bound to pay to said complainants, the balance of said sum of $37,924 $\frac{48}{100}$, being the sum of $25,282.93$\frac{2}{3}$, with interest from the 7th of June, 1847, till paid, and two thirds of the said costs; and they are hereby ordered and decreed to pay the same.

Seventh. And it is further ordered, adjudged, and decreed, that, in the event the said sureties in the first bond, to wit: James Carrico, Samuel Stott, and George C. Bomford, do not pay the said $12,641.46$\frac{2}{3}$, with interest, and one third of the costs, so decreed to be, paid by them, as aforesaid, and every part thereof, that then the said Jacob Gideon, Ulysses Ward, and Jonathan B. H. Smith, the sureties in the second bond, as aforesaid, are bound to pay the same, and every part thereof, to the extent of the penalties of their said bond. And that, in the event that the said Jacob Gideon, Ulysses Ward, and Jonathan B. H. Smith, the sureties in the second bond, do not pay the said $25,282.93$\frac{2}{3}$, with interest and two thirds of the costs, so decreed to be paid by them, as aforesaid, and every part thereof, that then the said James Carrico, Samuel Stott, and George C. Bomford, the sureties in the first bond, as aforesaid, are bound to pay the same, to the extent of the penalty of their said bond.

And it is further ordered, adjudged, and decreed, that the defendant, Lewis Johnson, administrator *de bonis non* of Thaddeus Kosciusko, transfer and deliver over to said named complainants the stock of the Bank of Washington, belonging to him, as such administrator, amounting at its par value, to the sum of $5,580, together with all the dividends which have accrued on the same, less the costs of his administration, and reasonable counsel fees, and such commissions, as administrator, as the Orphans' Court may legally allow.

And it is further ordered, adjudged, and decreed, that the said sums of money and stock, so decreed to be paid and transferred by the above-named defendants, be paid and transferred to the above-named complainants, Hippolitus Estho, Roman Estho, Louisa Narbut, Vlandislaus Wankowiez, Hippolitus Wankowiez, Adam Bychowiec, and Michael Szyrma, in the proportions stated and adjudged in the preceding fourth clause of this decree.

Eighth. It is further ordered, adjudged, and decreed, that the decrees *pro confesso* against Roman Estho, Louisa Narbut, born Estho, Thadea Emilie Wilchelmine Zeltner, Maria Charlotte Julia Marguerette Zeltner, Bonnisant Pere, General Baszkoyski, Emilie Zeltner, Mr. and Mrs. Edward Zeltner, Zavier Amieth, Dr. Sheërer, Miss Ursula Zeltner, and Kosciusko Armstrong, by the said Circuit Court be, and the same is hereby, affirmed.

And lastly. It is ordered, adjudged, and decreed, that this cause be, and the same is hereby, remanded to the said Circuit Court, with directions to that court to carry the aforesaid decree of this court into effect.

WILLIAM H. WINDER, PLAINTIFF IN ERROR, *v.* ANDREW D. CALDWELL.

Where a *scire facias* was issued to enforce a lien upon a house under the lien law of the District of Columbia, there was no necessity to file a declaration.

Where the contract between the owner and the builder, (who was also the carpenter,) stipulated for a forfeiture per diem in case the carpenter should delay the work, the court below ought to have allowed evidence of such delay to be given to the jury by the defendant, under a notice of set-off, and also evidence that the work and materials found and provided upon and for the building, were defective in quality and character, and far inferior in value to what the contract and specification called for.

A master builder, undertaker, or contractor, who undertakes by contract with the owner to erect a building, or some part or portion thereof, on certain terms, does not come within the letter or spirit of the act of Congress passed March 2, 1833, (4 Stat. at Large 659,) entitled an Act to secure to mechanics and others, payment for labor done and materials furnished in the erection of buildings in the District of Columbia.

THIS case was brought up, by writ of error, from the Circuit Court of the United States for the District of Columbia, holden in and for the county of Washington.

It was an action of *scire facias*, brought by Caldwell against Winder, upon a claim filed under the act of Congress passed

March 2, 1833, entitled "An Act to secure to mechanics and others, payment for labor done and materials furnished in the erection of buildings in the District of Columbia." 4 Stat. at Large, 659.

Caldwell, in March, 1849, filed his claim in the clerk's office, consisting of the gross sum of $10,500, claimed·as due under a special agreement, and the further sum of $4,086 for extra work — the items of the extra work being particularly mentioned in the claim.

Upon this claim the writ of *scire facias* issued March 20, 1849. No declaration was filed. The defendant appeared and pleaded *non assumpsit*, upon which issue was·joined.

Upon the trial, the jury found a verdict for the plaintiff in the sum of $4,746, with interest from 9th March, 1849.

Upon the trial, the plaintiff took three bills of exceptions, and the defendant, ten. The substance of them all is stated in the opinion of the court.

It .was argued by *Mr. Davidge*, for the plaintiff in error, and *Mr. Bradley* and *Mr. Lawrence*, for the defendant in error.

The counsel for the plaintiff in error made the following points.

I. That, under the act of 1833, the mechanics and material-men who do the work and provide the materials for the building, are entitled to the lien, and not he who merely contracts with them to do and provide such work and materials.

1. Because the law *totidem verbis*·confines the lien to those "employed in furnishing materials for, or in the erecting or constructing" the building.

2. Because the only debts secured by the law are those contracted for work done and materials furnished for the building.

3. Because the 2d clause of the·1st section of the act plainly shows that a mere contractor is not within its provisions.

4. Because the· contractor not being within the letter, is still less within the spirit of the law, the object of which was to allow those whose property, whether work or materials, had been advanced upon the credit of the building, to follow that property after it had become part of the building. In the present case, the work and materials advanced, or a large portion of them, were not the property of· the contractor.

5. Because if the contractor be held within the law, the building would be subjected· to double liens and double recoveries. And, more than this, a sub-contractor, not advancing either work or materials, might, with equal justice, claim the lien, and the property would then be subjected to .triple liens for the same benefit.

6. Because the mechanics and material-men are, by the law, expressly authorized to institute proceedings against the contractor, the basis of which is, that they have found and provided the work and materials for the building.

7. Because the law contemplates but one lien for the same work or materials, and if there be two or more, the satisfaction which the owner is entitled to, under the last clause of the 1st section could not be entered. Act of 1833, (4 Statutes at Large, p. 659); Penn. Lien Laws of 1803, (Pamphlet L. 591); of 1806, (4 Smith's L. 300); and of 1836, (Pamphlet L. 695); Jones v. Shawhan, 4 W. & S. 257, 264; Hoatz v. Patterson, 5 W. & S. 537, 539; Haley v. Prosser, 8 W. & S. 133, 134; Whitman v. Walker, 9 W. & S. 183, 187; Bolton v. Johns, 5 Barr's Penn. Rep. 145, 150.

But, further, the act of 1833 cannot be regarded as giving a lien to the contractor in this case, unless it, an affirmative statute, without a repealing clause or negative words, be held to repeal a former law passed in *pari materia*, and between which and the act of 1833 there is no necessary repugnancy. The act of Maryland, passed December 19, 1791, provided as follows:

" X. And for the encouragement of master-builders to undertake the building and finishing houses within the said city, by securing to them a just and effectual remedy for their advances and earnings, be it enacted, that for all sums due and owing, on written contracts, for the building any house in the said city, or the brickwork, or carpenters' or joiners' work thereon, the undertaker or workmen employed by the person for whose use the house shall be built, shall have a lien on the house and the ground on which the same is erected, as well as for the materials found by him; provided the said written contract shall have been acknowledged before one of the commissioners, a justice of the peace, or an alderman of the corporation of Georgetown, and recorded in the office of the clerk for recording deeds herein created, within six calendar months from the time of acknowledgment as aforesaid; and if, within two years after the last of the work is done, he proceeds in equity, he shall have remedy as upon a mortgage, or if he proceeds at law within the same time, he may have execution against the house and land, in whose hands soever the same may be; but this remedy shall be considered as additional only, nor shall, as to the land, take place of any legal encumbrance made prior to the commencement of such claim." 2 Kilty's Laws of Md. act 1791, ch. 45, §.10.

This law gives a lien to the contractor or to the workmen employed by the owner, but it requires, 1. That there shall be a contract in writing; 2. That such contract shall be acknowledged; and 3. Recorded within six months after acknowledgment.

In the present case there was a written contract, but it was neither acknowledged nor recorded; and, besides, the remedy adopted is wholly different from that given by the act of 1791.

Is that law repealed by the act of 1833? It is not in any portion; or, if at all, not so far as concerns the right of the contractor.

It is not repealed, in whole or in part, expressly or by direct terms. Is it by necessary implication?

There must be, to repeal by implication, a positive repugnancy between the provisions of the new law and those of the old; and even then the old law is repealed only *pro tanto*, to the extent of the repugnancy. Wood v. The United States, 16 Pet. 342, 362; Daviess et al. v. Fairbairn et al. 3 How. 636, 646; Beals v. Hale, 4 How. 37, 53; Chesapeake & O. C. Co. v. Baltimore & O. R. R. Co. 4 Gill & J. 1, 152, 153; Dwarris on St. 673, 674, 675.

A later statute, which is general, does not abrogate a former, which is particular. 6 Rep. b. 19; Dwarris on St. 674.

Statutes in *pari materia*, are to be taken together and compared in the construction of them. The United States v. Freeman, 3 How. 556; Dwarris on St. 699.

Statutes are to be construed with reference to the existing law. Four things are to be considered; what was the law before the act; the mischief not provided against; the remedy provided; and the reason of that remedy. Heydon's case, 3 Co. 7.

The mischief which required the passage of the act of 1833, was twofold: 1. The law gave no lien to mechanics contracting with the undertaker or contractor. 2. It gave no lien whatever to the material-man, unless he was at the same time undertaker, or a workman contracting directly with the owner.

The whole object of the law of 1833, was to supply the omissions of the act of 1791. It was designed to be auxiliary merely, and not to repeal the provisions of the existing law.

Certainly no reason can be assigned why the salutary provision of the act of 1791, requiring a contractor to enter into a written contract, and have the same acknowledged and recorded, was intended to be annulled.

The act of 1701 is not obsolete, but has been recognized as in full force. Homans v. Coombe, 3 Cranch, C. C. Rep. 366 — decided in 1828.

II. The court below erred in refusing to instruct the jury that the plaintiff was not entitled to recover for the work and materials done and provided under the special agreement.

1. Because the act of 1833 is inapplicable to cases where work

and materials are furnished under a special agreement. Jones v. Shawhan, 4 W. & S. 257, 262; Hoatz v. Patterson, 5 Id. 537, 538; Haley v. Prosser, 8 Id. 133, 134; Witman v. Walker, 9 Id. 183, 187; Barton v. Johns, 5 Barr's Penn. R. 145, 150; Act of 1791, ch. 45, § 10; United States v. Barney, 2 Hall's Law J 128; Ex parte Lewis, 2 Gallis. 483; Hostler's case, Yelv. 66; Bac. Abr. Trover, E.; 2 Rol. Abr. 92, Justification, pl. 2; Chapman v. Allen, Cro. Car. 271; Bul. N. P. 45; Brennan v. Currint, Sayre, 224; S. C. cited 3 Selw. N. P. 1163; Stone v. Lingwood, 1 Str. 651; Collins v. Ongley, cited Selw. N. P. ubi sup.; Stevenson v. Blakelock, 1 Maule & Selw. 535; and see, also, Boyce v. Anderson, 2 Pet. 155.

2. Because the special agreement in this case was inconsistent with the retention of a lien. Peyroux et al. v. Howard, 7 Pet. 324, 344; Chase v. Westermore, 5 Maule & Selw. 180; Scarfe v. Morgan, 4 Mee. & W. 270; Stoddard Woolen Man. v. Huntley, 8 N. H. 441; Hutchins et al. v. Olcutt, 4 Verm. 549; Bailey v. Adams, 14 Wend. 201; Welch v. Mandeville, 5 Wheat. 277.

III. The court erred in refusing to submit to the jury the question whether the work and materials, or what part thereof, were supplied upon the credit of the building. Hills v. Elliott, 16 S. & R. 56; Hinchman v. Graham, 2 S. & R. 170.

IV. A declaration should have been filed. Foster on Scire Facias, 72 Law. Lib. p. 350.

V. The judgment rendered was general and in personam. The proceeding was in rem, and the last clause of the act of 1833, expressly prohibits the rendition of a judgment in the scire facias, against any other property than the building against which the lien existed.

VI. The court erred in refusing to instruct the jury that the plaintiff was not entitled to recover for the portion of work and materials performed, and furnished under the special agreement, more than three months before the claim was filed.

VII. The claim, so far as it related to the special agreement, was not filed in conformity with the requirements of the law, and the court erred in refusing to instruct the jury to that effect. See the claim, R. 9; McDonald v. Lindall, 3 Rawle, 492.

VIII. The court erred in excluding from the jury, evidence of defects in the work and materials furnished, under the special agreement. Withers v. Greon, 9 Howard, 213; Van Buren v. Digges, 11 How. 461. Notice of set-off had been given. R. 5.

IX. The court erred in refusing evidence of delay, the demurrage money mentioned in the agreement, being liquidated damages, and not a penalty. Fletcher v. Dyche, 2 T. R. 32; Huband v. Grattan, 1 Alc. & Napier, 389; Crisdee v. Bolton, 3 C. & P.

240; Leighton *v.* Wales, 3 M.' & W. 545; 2 Poth. Obl. by Evans, 81, &c; Noble *v.* Bates, 7 Cow. 307; 2 Greenleaf on Ev. §§ 257, 258, 259, and cases cited; Van Buren *v.* Digges, 11 How. 461; Tayloe *v.* Sandiford, 7 Wheat. 17.

The points on behalf of the defendant in error, were—

First. That this act is not repugnant to the act of 1791, but is remedial, cumulative, and auxiliary. That it was designed to give a lien to every person who, whether under a parol contract, oral or written, or a contract under seal, should thereafter furnish materials for or do work upon any dwelling or other building in the city of Washington during its erection, for the owner or for the contractor.

That if the building was constructed by contract, no person who did work or furnished materials to such contractor, could have the lien, unless within thirty days after being so employed, he should give notice in writing to the owner, that he was so employed to work or furnish materials, and that he claimed the benefit of that act.

These points are presented in the 3d, 6th, 7th, 8th, 9th, and 10th exceptions.

1. The first sentence of the act of 1833, is in the most general and comprehensive terms. 7 B: & C. 643.

2. The second sentence expressly contemplates the case of a contract, and provides a remedy for those employed by the contractor.

There is no such provision in any one of the laws of Pennsylvania referred to by plaintiff, and under which the decisions of the courts of that State were made.

3. The act of 1791 expressly recognizes and provides for two sets of liens, the one by the contractor, the other by the workmen. So does the act of 1833.

4. The act of 1791 contemplated a statutory mortgage; provided for contracts of a certain description, viz. those in writing acknowledged before a justice, and recorded in the clerk's office within six months, and gave a remedy in equity.

This act is not repugnant to that. It extends the remedy and provides a new one, (not for those who have made their contracts and recorded them under the law of 1791,) but to all persons who have done work or furnished materials for the building, without pursuing the remedy given by that law. It provides a different remedy. It gives an absolute lien in all cases for two years, to be enforced upon a claim filed by *scire facias* or personal action; or if no claim is filed, then by personal action.

The act of 1791 provides a lien to commence from the date

of the contract, if recorded within six months. The act of 1833 gives a lien from the commencement of the work.

There is no repugnancy between them. The two provisions may well stand together, the latter as cumulative to the former. 3 How. 645–6.

They are both affirmative statutes, and such parts of the prior statute as may be incorporated into the subsequent one as consistent with it, must be considered in force. Id. 644–5.

They are in *pari materia*; they must be taken together as if they were one law. Id. 564.

A thing which is within the intention of the makers of the statute, is as much within the statute as if it were within the letter. Id. 565.

Here the intention cannot admit of dispute. It was to protect all who furnished skill, time, labor, or materials, to the erection of the building, without regard to the manner of their employment. They might make their contract under the act of 1791, and obtain a remedy in equity under that act; or they might proceed under the law of 1833, and seek their remedy at law only. Both laws require a recording as notice. The law of 1833 has received this construction from its passage, and hundreds of mortgages now existing, rest upon it.

Unless it repeals the act of 1791 by necessary implication, it may be merely affirmative, or cumulative, or auxiliary. 16 Pet. 362–3.

The more natural, if not necessary inference is, that the legislature intended the new law to be auxiliary to and in aid of the purposes of the old law, even when some of the cases provided for may be equally within the reach of each. Id. 363.

In construing an act, (and equally so in acts in *pari materia*, 3 How. 564, 2 T. R. 504,) if there are expressions not so large in one part as those used in another, but upon a view of the whole act they can collect from the more large and extensive expression of the legislature, their intention, it is the duty of the Judges to give effect to the larger expressions. Per Lord Tenterden, 7 B. & C. 643.

A second law on the same subject does not repeal a former one without a repealing clause, or negative words, unless so clearly repugnant as to imply a negative. But if they be not so contrary or so repugnant that the last act expresses or implies a negative of the first, then they may continue to stand together. And if such be the case here, a mortgage of city property, recorded in conformity with either law, would be valid. Many cases of this kind, very analogous, are cited in Foster's case, 11 Coke, 63 64; 4 How. 53.

We contend that both acts are in force, and the parties may

proceed under either. But if the act of 1833 repeals the act of 1791, we contend further that its provisions clearly embrace written contracts for construction.

Second. If the contractor or person who had done work or furnished materials for the owner, files his claim in the clerk's office, as provided by the act of 1833, within three months after the last work is done by him, under the same written contract, or under an implied contract, during the progress of the work, that claim will relate back to the commencement of the building and cover the work and materials mentioned in it and used in the erection of the building. 4th and 5th exceptions.

1. The language of the act is explicit. "Every . . . . . building hereafter constructed and erected, &c., shall be subject to the payment of the debts contracted for, or by reason of any work or materials found and provided by any person or persons, &c., employed in furnishing the materials for, or in the erecting and constructing such house or other building, before any other lien which originated *subsequent to the commencement* of such other house or building, &c.: Provided, That no such debt, &c., shall remain a lien on such house or other building, longer than two years from the commencement of the building thereof, unless, &c., a claim be filed within three months after performing the work or furnishing the materials."

It could not have been designed by the legislature to deprive a lumber-merchant of his lien, if there was an understanding between himself and the owner that he should furnish the lumber for the building from time to time, as it should be required, and it should occur, in the course of the erection of the building, that more than three months should elapse between filing one order and the giving of a new one.

2. If the work is done by contract, and there is an express or tacit understanding between the parties that alterations may be required by the owner and executed by the contractor during the progress of the work, it would be in direct violation of the spirit of the law, and the obvious intent of the legislature to deprive the contractor of his lien, unless he from time to time, and every three months recorded his claim.

3. The language of the act is, within three months after *performing the work* or *furnishing* the materials. This means, by the force of the terms, after performing the last work or furnishing the last materials used in the progress of the building; not that he shall record his claims *toties quoties* three months shall elapse. This would be requiring the party to accumulate costs, the thing the legislature designed to avoid, and to do a vain thing, which the law never requires.

4. Much more will this construction apply to a contract, as in

this case, for work and materials for a building which contemplated eighteen months in its construction.

As to the pleadings.

1. No declaration is required on the appearance of the defendant to a *scire facias* under this act. In Blake *v.* Dodemead *et ux.* (2 Str. 775,) it is said there is no such thing as a declaration on a *scire facias*, the plea is to the writ, and *narratio* and *breve* in this case are the same.

Vaughn *v.* Floyd, 1 Sid. 406. The *scire facias* disclosed the facts on which it was founded, and required an answer from the defendant; it was said to be in the nature of a declaration.

Bank of Scotland *v.* Fenwick, 1 Exch. 796, (per Rolfe.) The declaration, in fact, sets out the writ, and is in the same form as the writ.

Nunn *v.* Claxton, 3 Exch. 715. Although called a declaration, it is "merely a mode of entering the writ on the record."

See, also, Herd *v.* Brustowe, Cro. Eliz. 177; Tidd's Prac. 8th ed. 1140.

2. The nature of the relief intended, the object of the legislature to give a mortgage, and the writ being provided as notice of the action, the court may well, as the Circuit Court has heretofore, consider it as setting forth the facts on which it is founded, a narrative in the nature of a declaration, make it part of the record, and require the defendant to plead to it. The statute itself, in the second section, would seem to contemplate the same thing.

Second, as to the form of the judgment.

The writ is not to show cause why execution should not issue against the property mentioned in it, but to show cause why the court ought not to render judgment for the sum demanded upon the record aforesaid.

This is the conclusion of the declaration.

The judgment is responsive. It must be the same after the pleading "as in personal actions for the recovery of debts."

The judgment, then, is right. But the record being in the same court, the statute regulates the form and extent of the execution which may issue on that judgment.

Mr. Justice GRIER delivered the opinion of the court.

Caldwell, who was plaintiff below, entered into a contract with Winder, " to furnish all the materials and do all the carpenter work required to a certain house to be erected in the city of Washington," for the sum of ten thousand dollars. After the house was finished, the contractor filed a lien against the building, claiming this sum, together with sundry charges for extra work. A *scire facias* was issued to enforce this claim, and a trial had, in the course of which, numerous bills of exception were sealed by the court at the defendant's instance, which form the subjects for our consideration in this case.

1. The want of a declaration, though not the subject of exception below, has been urged here as an error. But we think this objection is without foundation.

A *scire facias* is a judicial writ used to enforce the execution of some matter of record on which it is usually founded; but though a judicial writ, or writ of execution, it is so far an original that the defendant may plead to it. As it discloses the facts on which it is founded, and requires an answer from the defendant, it is in the nature of a declaration, and the plea is properly to the writ. In the present case the bill of particulars of the plaintiff's claim is filed of record under the statute which gives this remedy, and it is recited in the writ and thereby made part of it, so that any further pleading on his part, to set forth the nature of his demand, would be wholly superfluous.

2. In the written contract between the parties, given in evidence on the trial, it is stipulated that "the work is to be promptly executed, so that no delay shall be occasioned to the builder by having to wait for the carpenter's work;" and also, "that in any and every case in which the carpenter shall occasion delay to the building the sum of twenty-five dollars per day shall be deducted for each and every day so delayed, from the amount to be paid by this contract."

The defendant, under a notice of set-off, offered to prove "that in consequence of the plaintiff's not being ready to put up his work according to said contract, delay was occasioned by him in the construction of the building of not less than three weeks;" and also, "that the work and materials found and provided upon and for the said building, were defective in quality and character, and far inferior in value to what said contract and specification called for."

The refusal of the court to permit such evidence to go to the jury, is the subject of the first two bills of exception.

The statute which authorizes this proceeding, gives the defendant liberty "to plead and make such defence as in personal actions for the recovery of debts." Had the plaintiff below brought his action of assumpsit on the contract, the right to make this defence cannot now be doubted. For, although it is true, as a general rule, that unliquidated damages cannot be the subject of set-off, yet it is well settled that a total or partial failure of consideration, acts of nonfeasance or misfeasance, immediately connected with the cause of action, or any equitable defence arising out of the same transaction, may be given in evidence in mitigation of damages, or recouped; not strictly by way of defalcation or set-off, but for the purpose of defeating the plaintiff's action in whole or in part, and to avoid circuity of action. Without noticing the numerous cases on this subject, it is sufficient to say that the cases of Withers *v.* Green, (9 How. 214,) and Van Buren *v.* Digges, (11 How. 461,) decided in this court, are conclusive of the question. The court below, therefore, erred in the rejection of the testimony offered.

3. The remaining bills of exception, involve, in fact, but one prominent and important question, and the decision of it will dispose of this case.

The right to file a "mechanic's lien," as it is usually denominated, is claimed by the plaintiff, under the act of Congress of March 2d, 1833, entitled, "An act to secure to mechanics and others, payment for labor done and materials furnished, in the erection of buildings in the District of Columbia." The first section of this act, defines the persons who shall be entitled to this peculiar security and remedy, as follows :

"All and every dwelling-house, or other building, hereafter constructed and erected within the city of Washington, in the town of Alexandria, or in Georgetown, in the District of Columbia, shall be subject to the payment of the debts contracted for, or by reason of any work done, or materials found and provided by any brickmaker, bricklayer, stonecutter, mason, lime-merchant, carpenter, painter and glazier, ironmonger, blacksmith, plasterer and lumber-merchant, or any other person or persons employed in furnishing materials for, or in erecting and constructing such house or other building, before any other lien which originated subsequent to the commencement of such house, or other building. But if such dwelling-house or other building, or any portion thereof, shall have been constructed under contract, or contracts, entered into by the owner thereof, or his or her agent, with any person or persons, no person who may have done work for such contractor or contractors, or furnished materials to him, or on his order or authority, shall have or possess any lien on said house or other building, for work done, or materials so furnished, unless the person or persons employed by such contractor to do work on, or furnish materials for, such building, shall, within thirty days after being so employed, give notice in writing to the owner or owners of such building, or to his or to their agent, that he or they are so employed to work or to furnish materials, and that they claim the benefit of the lien granted by this act."

Does a master-builder, undertaker, or contractor, who undertakes, by contract with the owner, to erect a building, or some part or portion thereof, on certain terms, come within the letter or spirit of this act, or within any of the classes enumerated, as entitled to this special remedy.? Such persons have an opportunity, and are capable of obtaining their own securities. They do not labor as mechanics, but superintend work done by others. They are not tradesmen in lumber, or other materials for building, but employ others to furnish materials. If such contractor should by accident be a carpenter, or an owner or vendor of lumber, yet he deals not with the owner in this capacity, but as an undertaker, who has covenanted for his own securities.

The title to this act shows its policy and intention. It is to secure, to "mechanics and others, payment for labor done and materials found;" and the persons enumerated in the first section are, plainly, those mechanics and tradesmen whose personal labor or property have been incorporated into the building, and not the agents, supervisors, undertakers, or contractors, who employed them. The act contemplates two conditions, under which such labor and materials may have been furnished: First, on the order of the owner, who may act without the intervention of any middleman, and thus become indebted directly to his mechanics and tradesmen. Or, secondly, when they have been furnished on the order of a contractor or undertaker. In such cases, the mechanic, or material-man, if he intends to look to the credit of the building, and not to that of the contractor with whom he deals, must give notice to the owner of the building, within thirty days, of his intention to claim this security. The contractor, though mentioned in the act, is not enumerated among those entitled to its benefit. The aim and policy of this act is also obvious. Experience has shown that mechanics and tradesmen, who furnish labor and materials for the construction of buildings, are often defrauded by insolvent owners and dishonest contractors. Many build houses on speculation, and after the labor of the mechanic and the materials are incorporated into them, the owner becomes insolvent, and sells the buildings, or encumbers them with liens; and thus, one portion of his creditors are paid at the expense of the labor and property of others. Or, the solvent owner, who builds by the agency of a contractor or middleman, pays his price and receives his building, without troubling himself to inquire what has been the fate of those whose labor or means have constructed it. These evils required a remedy, and such a one as is given by this act. Its object is, not to secure contractors, who can take care of themselves, but those who may suffer loss by confiding in them. It is not the merit of the contractor, that gave rise to the system, but the protection of those who might be wronged by him, if the owner were not compelled thus to take care of their interests before he pays away the price stipulated. But the contractor is neither within the letter nor the spirit of the act.

A question has been made in the argument, whether the act of Maryland, of 19th of December, 1791, formerly in force in this district, is supplied or repealed, by the act of Congress now under consideration. But as the proceedings in this case are not within or under the act of Maryland, the question is not before us for decision. The plaintiff claims his right to support this proceeding, under the act of Congress alone, and if that fails him, his only resource is to his action on his contract. That he has mistaken his remedy, the court entertain no doubt.

If precedent were needed to justify this construction of the act of Congress, it may be found in the reports of the Supreme Court of Pennsylvania, where similar legislation has always received the same construction. See Jones *v.* Shawhan, 4 Watts & Serg. 257; Hoatz *v.* Patterson, 5 W. & S. 537, &c.

4. It is unnecessary to notice particularly the exception to the form of the judgment. It is certainly not in the form required by the act; and although the act may be construed to prescribe the effect rather than the form of the judgment, there is no reason why the form should differ from the effect; or that, in words, it should give the plaintiff any thing more than the law gives him, viz. execution of the property described in the *scire facias.*

The judgment of the Circuit Court is, therefore, reversed, and *venire de novo* awarded.

Order.

This cause came on to be heard on the transcript of the record from the Circuit Court of the United States for the District of Columbia, holden in and for the county of Washington, and was argued by counsel. On consideration whereof, it is now here ordered and adjudged, by this court, that the judgment of the said Circuit Court in this cause, be, and the same is hereby, reversed, with costs, and that this cause be, and the same is hereby, remanded to the said Circuit Court, with directions to award a *venire facias de novo.*

THE SALMON FALLS MANUFACTURING COMPANY, PLAINTIFF IN ERROR, *v.* WILLIAM W. GODDARD.

The statute of frauds in Massachusetts, is substantially the same as that of 29 Car. 2, and declares that no contract for the sale of goods, &c., shall be valid, &c "unless some note or memorandum in writing of the bargain, be made, and signed by the party to be charged thereby, or by some person thereunto by him lawfully authorized."

The following memorandum, viz.: "Sept. 19, W. W. Goddard, 12 mos. 300 bales S. F. drills, 7¼; 190 cases blue do. 8⅜. Credit to commence when ship sails; not after December 1st, delivered free of charge for trackage. The blues, if color satisfactory to purchasers. R. M. M. W. W. G."—is sufficient to take the case out of the statute.

If the terms are technical or equivocal on the face of the instrument, or made so by reference to extraneous circumstances, parol evidence of the usage and practice in the trade, is admissible to explain the meaning.

It was competent also to refer to the bill of parcels delivered for the purpose of explanation. It was made out and delivered by the seller, in the course of the fulfilment of the contract, acquiesced in by the buyer, and the goods ordered to be delivered after it was received.

THIS case was brought up, by writ of error, from the Circuit Court of the United States for the District of Massachusetts.

The facts are set forth in the opinion of the court, and also the rulings of the Circuit Court. The bill of exceptions extended over thirty pages of the printed record.

It was argued by *Mr. Goodrich*, for the plaintiff in error, and by *Mr. Johnson* and *Mr. Davis*, with whom was *Mr. Choate*, for the defendant in error.

The points made by the counsel for the plaintiff in error, were the following:

I. The evidence before the jury was competent and sufficient to authorize them to find that the bill of parcels had been adopted, recognized, and acted upon by the defendant, as the contract between himself and the plaintiffs.

II. The bill of parcels constitutes a contract known as a bargain and sale, by force of which the title to the property passed, without delivery, without payment of the price. It purports on its face a sale *in presenti.*

III. The paper signed by the defendant, dated 19th September, (Record, p. 11,) is a sufficient compliance with the statute of frauds, and the first position taken, and the first instruction asked in the court below, should have been sustained.

Addison on Contracts, 80. "It is not necessary that all the particulars of the contract should appear upon the face of the written memorandum. Any note, acknowledging the fact of the sale, mentioning the name of the vendor and the thing sold, and signed by the purchaser or his agent, will take the case out of the statute."

Penniman *v.* Hartshorn, 13 Mass. 87; Egerton *v.* Matthews, 6 East, 307, as to the description of the goods being sufficiently certain.

Even if it should be considered essential that the particular bales and cases should be selected, this was done, and thereupou the writing attached. See Record, p. 13, letters. The first letter set apart No. 8180 to 8679. The 100 cases blue drills were set apart at the counting room of Mason & Lawrence, on 11th October.

The second letter called for No. 8480 to 8679 — 200 bales, thus leaving set apart, 300 bales from No. 8180 to 8479.

In considering this position and instruction, the plaintiffs relied upon their usage, to require notes upon all sales made upon credit, which was known to Goddard.

This usage was competent, as constituting a part of the contract, as one of the incidents of the credit which was given.

Hutton *v.* Warren, 1 Mees. & Wels. 466; Grant *v.* Maddox, 15 Id. 737; Syers *v.* Jonas, 2 Wels. Hurls. & Gor. 111. In an action for the price of tobacco sold, evidence is admissible to show that by the established usage of the tobacco trade, all sales are by sample, although not so expressed in the bought and sold notes. Tibbets *v.* Sumner, 19 Pick. 166.

The contract is certain as to the parties, as to the number of bales, the price per yard, so that the amount of the purchase may be computed.

It is well established that a signature, by initials, is good; but the fact, whose initials they are, must be settled by the jury, upon proof. So, also, it is submitted, that it is the province of the jury to determine the character in which the parties signed. It was for them to say whether Goddard, by signing his initials and writing underneath the provision as to credit, and that the contract as to the blues might be abandoned, if color not satisfactory to the purchaser, is or is not sufficient, and was designed by the defendant to designate himself as the purchaser. That he did so design, is apparent, also, from the fact that his name is written at the top of the paper, prior to that of any other person.

In determining this question, it is competent for the jury to look at the situation of the parties and of the property, in aid and in explanation of the paper, for the purpose of attaching or locating the paper.

Whether a party signed as a witness, or as a party, is often determined from the location of his signature upon the paper.

Higgins *v.* Senior, 8 Mees. & Wels. 844. It may be shown that a party, whose name does not appear upon the paper, is bound as a contracting party, where an agent signs his own name instead of that of the principal.

Why not show, upon the same principle, or infer from the paper, the character and purpose in and for which a party signs?

The provision in this paper, that the goods are to be delivered free of truckage, does not prevent the passing of the property, without and before delivery—and without payment.

Phillimore v. Barry, 1 Camp. 513. "If goods are sold to be paid for in thirty days, and if not carried away at the end of that time, warehouse rent to be paid—the property of the goods vests absolutely in the purchaser, and they remain at his risk from the moment of the sale."

King v. Meredith, 2 Camp. 639. "The fact that the carrier is to be paid by the vendor, will not defeat the vesting of the property."

Wackerbath v. Masson, 3 Camp. 270. "Where, in a contract for the sale of sugar, there is the following term, 'free on board a foreign ship,' the seller is not bound to deliver it into the hands of the purchaser, but only to put it on board a foreign ship, which it is the duty of the purchaser to name."

IV. The following instructions, asked for by the plaintiff below, and refused, ought to have been given by the court to the jury.

Instruction third, asked by the plaintiffs. That if the jury are satisfied that Mason & Lawrence were the general agents and factors of the plaintiffs; that the memorandum of September 19, 1850, was executed by the parties whose initials are affixed, and was delivered by defendant to them; and that the invoice or bill of parcels, dated 30th of September, 1850, was delivered by Mason & Lawrence to defendant, in furtherance of said contract, as containing a particular specification and enumeration of the bales and cases mentioned in the memorandum, or contract of September 19th, and was received and retained by him as a true invoice, or bill of parcels, they are to be taken as parts of one contract, and together constitute a memorandum or contract in writing, binding upon both parties, and not void within the statute of frauds.

Eighth instruction asked. If the jury are satisfied that the two papers exhibited by the plaintiffs, severally dated September 19, and September 30, 1850, relate to the same transactions and things, and manifestly relate to the same contract and transaction, they are to be construed together, and so taken, constitute a sufficient written note or memorandum of the contract, within the statute of frauds.

Whether the two papers, the one dated the 19th, the other the 30th of September, constituted the contract of the parties as finally settled, is a question of fact, exclusively for the determination of the jury—the construction of the papers is partly a matter of fact, and partly matter of law.

Addison on Contracts, 80, 81. "The contract may be authenticated and established through the medium of letters and separate writings, provided they refer to each other, and to the same persons and things, and manifestly relate to the same contract and transaction."

Jackson v. Lowe, 1 Bing. 9. This case recognizes the position that two papers may be regarded from the same context and subject-matter of the papers, as referring to the same contract. It also recognizes the cases cited as to bills of parcels. See also Smith's Mer. Law, 407.

Dobell v. Hutchinson, 5 Neville & Man. 251. "And where, upon such contract, (a paper signed only by the purchaser,) it does not appear upon the face of it, or by reference, of whom the property is purchased, letters, written by persons in the character of vendors, may be connected with the contract, for the purpose of supplying this defect."

V. The evidence before the jury was competent and sufficient to authorize the jury to find a delivery and acceptance, to and by the defendant.

VI. The defendant is estopped to set up the statute, or to say that no delivery and acceptance has been made.

The points made by the counsel for the defendant in error, were the following.

I. The memorandum in this case is insufficient to satisfy the requirements of the statute of frauds.

" No contract for the sale of any goods, wares, or merchandise, for the price of fifty dollars or more, shall be good and valid, unless the purchaser shall accept and receive part of the goods so sold, or shall give something in earnest to bind the bargain, or in part payment, or unless some note or memorandum in writing of the bargain be made and signed by the party to be charged thereby, or by some person thereunto by him fully authorized." Rev. Stat. of Mass. ch. 74, § 3. p. 473.

1. The memorandum of September 19, is insufficient, since it cannot be understood without reference to parol evidence.

a. It does not clearly set out or evidence that a sale has been made, or whether a contract for a future sale has been made, or only proposals offered, leading to a sale not yet agreed on.

b. It does not ascertain who is vendor and who is vendee. Addison on Contracts, 80; Bailey v. Ogden, 3 Johns. R. 399; Smith's Mer. Law, 451.

c. The price is uncertain. Addison, 80; Smith's Mer. Law, 451, and the cases in his note; 5 B. & C. 583; 2 B. & C. 627; 1 N. R. 252; Laythrop v. Bryant, 2 Bing. N. C.; 10 Bing. 217, 227, 383, 482.

d. The time of commencement of credit s uncertain; what ship, and what December, are uncertain.

e. The name of the plaintiff is not on the contract; nor the name nor initials,of any person then his agent. R. M. M. are not the initials of any person then an agent of the plaintiff. Mason and Lawrence were the agents, and, to avail the plaintiff, he must produce a written contract, containing his name or their names. Higgins v. Senior, 8 Mees. & Wels. 844; Shaw et al. v. Phinney, 13 Met. 456.

To the various insufficiencies aforesaid, and to the general principles on which the statute of frauds is construed: Ide v. Stanton, 15 Vt. 685; Adams v. McMillan, 7 Porter, 73; Champion v. Plummer, 4 B. & P. 252; Elmore v. Kingscote, 5 B. & C. 583; Hoadley v. McLaine, 10 Bing. 482; Acebal v. Levy, 10 Bing. 170; Cooper v. Smith, 11 East, 103; Kain v. Old, 2 B. & C. 205; Parkhurst v. Van Cortlandt, 1 J. C. R. 280; Abeel v. Ratcliffe, 13 Johns. 297; Goss v. Nugent, 5 B. & Ad. 58; Stowell v. Robinson, 3 Bing. N. S. 928; Harvey v. Grabham, 5 Ad. & Ellis, 61; Ford v. Yates, 2 Man. & Granger, 549; 2 Kent's Com. 511, 6th ed.; Story on Sales, § 269, p. 212; 1 N. H. 157; 3 Greenleaf, 340; 4 Scott's N. R. 504; 23 Wendell, 270, 275; 5 Phil. Evidence, (Cowen's last ed.) 84; 16 Wendell, 28, 32.

2. The bill made out by Rien, dated September 30, cannot be connected with the memorandum of September 19, to form a note within the statute.

a. Neither contains any reference to the other.

b. The only one signed by defendant and on which only he can be charged, (that of September 19,) does not anticipate, provide for, or in any manner adopt, the paper of September 30, written long afterwards; and it cannot be deemed to be amended, completed, or altered by such subsequent unanticipated paper.

Addison on Cont. 80, 81, and cases there cited; 5 Phil. Ev. (Cowen's last ed.) 84; Boydell v. Drummond, 11 East, 142; 1 St. on Ev. 603; 1 Greenl. on Ev. § 268; Chitty on Cont. 314–16; Sandiland v. Marsh, 2 B. & A. 680; Coles v. Trecothick, 9 Ves. 250; Tawney v. Crowther, 2 Bro. Ch. Cases, 320, n. a; Story on Sales, § 272, p. 216.

3. The bill of sale of September 30th is in itself insufficient as a memorandum, as not signed by the defendant, or by any one authorized by him to sign it for him.

A. Neither Mason nor Rien had any express authority from the defendant to sign for him, and their position gave them no implied authority to do so.

Commission merchants stand upon a different footing from brokers and auctioneers; being agents for one party only, they can only bind their principals. 13 Met. 456; Sewall v. Fitch, 8 Cow. 215; Dixon v. Bromfield, 2 Chit. Rep. 205;

Wright v. Dunnell, 2 Camp. 203; Fairbrother v. Simmons, 5 B. & A. 333; 1 R. & M. 325, Raynard v. Linthorn; Smith's Merc. Law, 455, and cases cited; 1 Bl. 599; 1 Esp. 105; 7 E. 569.

B. There was no subsequent ratification by the defendant of the act of Rien.

a. The language of the defendant is perfectly consistent with the idea that he had a right to insist upon having the goods, as the bill sufficiently bound the plaintiff, and is therefore no necessary ratification.

b. The silence of defendant was no ratification. Rien was an officious intermeddler in the business, (if he had assumed to act as agent for defendant,) so far as defendant is concerned; and it is holden by some, though denied by others, that in such case, even after notice from such person of his act, silence is no ratification. 1 Livermore, Agency, 50; Story on Agency, 251; and note.

But defendant had no notice from Rien that he had assumed to act for him, and so silence would not amount to ratification, even under the worst view of the law for the defendant. McLean v. Dunn, 1 M. & P. 761; and all cases hold that, to a ratification of an unauthorized agency, knowledge that there has been an assumption of agency for the very party ratifying is indispensable.

c. There was no express ratification of Rien's act by defendant.

The view which the court took at the *nisi* hearing of the case of Batters v. Sellers, 5 H. & J. 117, seems impregnable. See, too, 5 Phil. Ev. (Cowen's last ed. 358,) Hawkins v. Chace, 19 Pick. 502; Graham v. Musson, 5 Bing. N. C. 603.

3. Even if the memorandum of the bargain of September 19 was sufficient within the statute, yet unless there was a subsequent delivery to, and acceptance of, goods by the defendant, the property, under the special circumstances, did not pass, and remained the plaintiff's at the time of the fire.

a. The memorandum leaves it doubtful, whether a sale *in presenti*, or a contract, or proposals towards a contract, for a future sale, were intended. The probable, if not necessary inference, from the face of the paper, is, that no present sale is made.

1. No specific goods are designated.

2. An election to reject or deny any contract as to part, at the mere pleasure of the purchaser, is reserved.

3. Credit is not to commence until a future uncertain event.

4. Delivery is thereafter to be made.

a. The goods in fact were not at the time selected, or set apart; and of course no property therein could or did pass; this aids also the inference from the face of the paper, that no present sale was intended.

c. When plaintiff subsequently selected them, the property would not pass, certainly under such a contract, until defendant accepted them, and thus adopted the particular designation; and this he never did. In Rhode *v.* Thwaites, (6 B. & C. 388,) there was such actual acceptance by the buyer.

e. The plaintiff was permitted to prove that he had a right t. a note before delivery; and he would have a lien for this; which affords some ground of additional argument to show that the property did not pass.

II. There was no delivery by the plaintiff, nor acceptance by the defendant, sufficient to take the case out of the operation of the statute requiring a demand.

Mr. Justice NELSON delivered the opinion of the court.

This is a writ of error to the Circuit Court of the United States for the District of Massachusetts.

The suit was brought by the plaintiffs in the court below, to recover the price of three hundred bales of brown, and of one hundred cases of blue drills, which they had previously sold to the defendant.

The contract for the purchase was made with the house of Mason & Lawrence, agents of the plaintiffs, in Boston, on the 19th September, 1850, and a memorandum of the same signed by the parties. A bill of parcels was made out under date of 30th September, stating the purchase of the goods by the defendant, carrying out prices, and footing up the amount at $18,565.03; also the terms of payment—note at twelve months, payable to the treasurer of the plaintiffs. This was forwarded to the defendant on the 11th October, and in pursuance of an order from him, the three hundred bales were sent from their establishment at Salmon Falls by the railroad, and arrived at the depot in Boston on the 30th October, of which notice was given to the defendant on the same day, and a delivery tendered. He requested that the goods should not be sent to his warehouse, or place of delivery, for the reason, as subsequently stated by his clerk, there was no room for storage. The agents of the plaintiffs the next day renewed the tender of delivery by letter, adding that the goods remained at the depot at his risk, and subject to storage, to which no answer was returned. On the night of the 4th November, the railroad depot was consumed by fire, and with it the three hundred bales of the goods in question. The price was to be paid by a note at twelve months, which the defendant refused to give, upon which refusal this action was brought.

The court below, at the trial, held that the written memorandum made at the time of entering into the contract between the agents of the plaintiffs and the defendant, was not sufficient to take the case out of the statute of frauds, and as there was no acceptance of the goods, the plaintiffs could not recover.

As we differ with the learned Judge who tried the cause, as to the sufficiency of the written memorandum, the question upon the statute is the only one that it will be material to notice. The memorandum is as follows:

" Sept. 19;— W. W. Goddard, 12 mos.
300 bales S. F. drills, . . . $7\frac{5}{8}$
100 cases blue do. . . . $8\frac{3}{4}$
" Credit to commence when ship sails:
not after Dec. 1st—delivered free of
charge for truckage.
" The blues, if color satisfactory to purchasers. R. M. M.
w. w. G."

The statute of Massachusetts on this subject is substantially the same as that of 29 Car. II. ch. 3, § 17, and declares that no contract for the sale of goods, &c., shall be valid, &c., " unless some note or memorandum in writing of the bargain be made, and signed by the party to be charged thereby, or by some person thereunto by him lawfully authorized."

The word " bargain," in the statute, means the terms upon which the respective parties contract; and in the sale of goods, the terms of the bargain must be specified in the note or memorandum, and stated with reasonable certainty, so that they can be understood from the writing itself, without having recourse to parol proof; for, unless the essential terms of the sale can be ascertained from the writing itself, or by a reference contained in it to something else, the memorandum is not a compliance with the statute.

This brief note of the contract, however, like all other mercantile contracts, is subject to explanation by reference to the usage and custom of the trade, with a view to get at the true meaning of the parties, as each is presumed to have contracted in reference to them. And although specific and express provisions will control the usage, and exclude any such explanation, yet, if the terms are technical, or equivocal on the face of the instrument, or made so by reference to extraneous circumstances, parol evidence of the usage and practice in the trade, is admissible to explain the meaning. 2 Kent C. 556, and n. 3; Id. 260, and n.; Long on Sales, 197, ed. 1839, 1 Gale & Davis. 52.

Extraneous evidence is also admissible to show that a person whose name is affixed to the contract, acted only as an agent, thereby enabling the principal either to sue or be sued in his own name; and this, though it purported on its face to have been made by the agent himself, and the principal not named. Higgins *v.* Senior, 8 M. & Wels. 834; Trueman *v.* Loder, 11 Ad. & Ell. 589. Lord Denman observed, in the latter case, "that parol evidence is always necessary to show that the party sued is the party making the contract, and bound by it; whether he does so in his own name, or in that of another, or in a feigned name, and whether the contract be signed by his own hand (or that of an agent) are inquiries not different in their nature from the question, Who is the person who has just ordered goods in a shop? If he is sued for the price, and his identity made out, the contract is not varied by appearing to have been made by him in a name not his own."

So the signature of one of the parties is a sufficient signing to charge the firm. Soames *v.* Spencer, 1 D. & R. 32; Long on Sales, 58.

It has also been held, in the case of a sold note which expressed "eighteen pockets of hops, at 100s.," that parol evidence was admissible to show that the 100s. meant the price per cwt. Spicer *v.* Cooper, 1 Gale & D. 52; 5 Jurist, 1036.

The memorandum in that case was as follows: "Sold to Waite Spicer, of S. Walden, 18 pos. Kent hops, as under July 23, 1840; 10 pos. Barlow East Kent, 1839 ; 8 pos. Springall Goodhurst Kent, 1839, 100s. Delivered, JOHN COOPER."

Evidence was admitted on the trial to prove that the 100s. was understood in the trade to refer to the price per cwt., and the ruling approved by the King's Bench. Lord Denman put a case to the counsel in the argument to illustrate his view, that bears upon the case before us. Suppose, he said, the contract had been for ten butts of beer, at one shilling, the ordinary price of a gallon—and intimated that the meaning could hardly be mistaken.

Now, within the principles above stated, we are of opinion that the memorandum in question was a sufficient compliance with the statute. It was competent to show, by parol proof, that Mason signed for the firm of Mason & Lawrence, and that the house was acting as agents for the plai..tiffs, a company engaged in manufacturing the goods which were the subject of the sale; and also to show, that the figures 7¼ and 8¾, set opposite the three hundred bales and one hundred cases of goods, meant seven and a quarter cents, and eight and three quarter cents per yard.

The memorandum, therefore, contains the names of the sellers, and of the buyer—the commodity and the price—also, the time of credit, and conditions of the delivery; and, in the absence of any specified time or place of delivery, the law will supply the omission, namely, a reasonable time after the goods are called for, and usual place of business of the purchaser, or his customary place for the delivery of goods of this description.

In respect to the giving of the note, which was to run during the period of the credit, it appears to be the uniform custom of the house of Mason & Lawrence, to take notes for goods sold of this description. The defendant was one of their customers, and knew this usage; and it is a presumption of law, therefore, that the purchase was made with reference to it, there being no stipulation to the contrary in the contract of the parties.

We are also of opinion, even admitting that there might be some obscurity in the terms of the memorandum, and intrinsic difficulty in a proper understanding of them, that it would be competent, under the circumstances of the case, to refer to the bill of parcels delivered, for the purpose of explanation. We do not say that it would be a note in writing, of itself sufficient to bind the defendant within the statute; though it might be to bind the plaintiff.

It was a bill of sale made out by the seller, and contained his understanding of the terms and meaning of the contract; and having been received by the buyer, and acquiesced in, (for the order to have the goods forwarded was given after it was received,) the natural inference would seem to be, that the interpretation given was according to the understanding of both parties. It is not necessary to say that this would be the conclusion, if the bill differed materially from the written contract; that might present a different question; but we think it is so connected with, and naturally resulting from, the transaction, that it may be properly referred to for the purpose of explaining any ambiguity or abbreviations, so common in these brief notes of mercantile contracts.

A printed bill of parcels, delivered by the seller, may be a sufficient memorandum within the statute to bind him, especially, if subsequently recognized by a letter to the buyer. 2 B. & P. 238 D.; 3 Esp. 180. And generally the contract may be collected from several distinct papers taken together, as forming parts of an entire transaction, if they are connected by express reference from the one to the others. 3 Ad. & Ell. 355; 9 B. & Cr. 561; 2 Id. 945; 3 Taunt. 169; 6 Cow. 445; 2 M. & Wels. 660; Long on Sales, 55, and cases.

In the case before us, the bill of parcels is not only connected with the contract of sale, which has been signed by both parties, but was made out and delivered in the course of the fulfilment of it; has been acquiesced in by the buyer, and the goods ordered to be delivered after it was received. It is not a memorandum sufficient to bind him, because his name is not affixed to it by his authority; but if he had subsequently recognized it by letter to the sellers, it might have been sufficient. 2 B. & P. 238; 2 M. & Wels. 653; 3 Taunt. 169.

But although we admit, if it was necessary for the plaintiffs to rely upon the bill as the note or memorandum within the statute, they must have failed, we think it competent, within the principle of the cases on the subject, from its connection with, and relation to, the contract, to refer to it as explanatory of any obscurity or indefiniteness of its terms, for the purpose of removing the ambiguity.

Take, for example, as an instance, the objection that the price is uncertain, the figures $7\frac{1}{4}$ and $8\frac{3}{4}$, opposite the 300 bales and 100 cases of drills, given without any mark to denote what is intended by them.

The bill of parcels carries out these figures as so many cents per yard, and the aggregate amount footed up; and after it is received by the defendant, and with a knowledge of this explanation, he orders the goods to be forwarded.

We cannot doubt but that the bill, under such circumstances, affords competent evidence of the meaning to be given to this part of the written memorandum. And so, in respect to any other indefinite or abbreviated item to be found in this brief note of a mercantile contract.

For these reasons, we are of opinion, that the judgment of the court below, must be reversed, and the proceedings remitted, with directions to award a *venire de novo*.

Mr. Justice CATRON, Mr. Justice DANIEL, and Mr. Justice CURTIS, dissented.

DANIEL, Justice, dissenting.

Upon the point made in this case, on the Statute of Frauds, I entirely concur in the exposition of the law just announced by the court. With respect, however, to the proceedings ordered by this court to be taken in this case in the Circuit Court, I am constrained to dissent from the decision of my brethren. My opinion is, that under the 2d section of the 3d article of the Constitution, the courts of the United States could not take cognizance of the controversy between these parties; and that therefore the proper direction to the Circuit Court would have been to dismiss this suit for want of jurisdiction. My reasons, for the conclusion here expressed, having been given in detail in the case of Rundle et al. v. The Delaware and Raritan Canal Company, during the present term, it is unnecessary to repeat them on this occasion.

Mr. Justice CURTIS.

I have the misfortune to differ from the majority of my breth-ren, in this case, and, as the question is one which enters into the daily business of merchants, and at the same time involves the construction of a statute of the Commonwealth of Massa-chusetts, I think it proper to state, briefly, the grounds on which I rest my opinion.

The first question is, whether the writing of the 19th of Sep-tember is a sufficient memorandum within the 3d section of the 74th chapter of the Revised Statutes of Massachusetts. The writing is in these words and figures.

"Sept. 19.   W. W. Goddard, 12 mos.

$\quad$ 300 bales S. F. drills $\quad$. $\quad$. $\quad$ $7\frac{1}{4}$,

$\quad$ 100 cases blue $\quad$ " $\quad$. $\quad$. $\quad$ $8\frac{1}{4}$.

Cr. to commence when ship sails; not after Dec'r 1st; de-livered free of charge for truckage. $\qquad$ R. M. M.

$\hfill$ W. W. G.

The blues, if color is satisfactory to purchaser."

Does this writing show, upon its face, and without resorting to extraneous evidence, that W. W. Goddard was the purchaser of these goods? I think not. Certainly it does not so state in terms, nor can I perceive how the fact can be collected from the paper, by any certain intendment. If it be assumed that a sale was made, and that Goddard was a party to the transaction, what is there, on the face of the paper, to show whether God-dard sold or bought? Extraneous evidence that he was the seller, would be just as consistent with this writing, as extrane-ous evidence that he was the purchaser. Suppose the fact had been, that Mason was the purchaser, and that the writing might be explained by evidence of that fact; it would then be read that Goddard sold to Mason, on twelve months' credit; and this evidence would be consistent with every thing which the paper contains, because the paper is wholly silent as to the fact whether he was the seller or the purchaser. In Bailey et al. v. Ogden, (3 Johns. Rep. 398,) an action for not accepting sugars, the memorandum was:

"14 December.

$\quad$ J. Ogden & Co.—Bailey & Bogart.

$\qquad$ Brown, $12\frac{1}{4}$, $\quad$ } $\quad$ 60 and 90 days.

$\qquad$ White, $16\frac{1}{4}$. $\quad$ }

$\quad$ Debenture part pay."

Mr. Justice Kent, who delivered the opinion of the court, enu-merating the objections to the memorandum, says, no person can ascertain, from this memorandum, which of the parties was seller, and which buyer; and I think it would be difficult to show that the memorandum now in question is any more intelligible, in reference to this fact.

Indeed, I do not understand it is supposed, that, in the absence of all extraneous evidence, it could be determined by the court, as matter of law, upon an inspection of the paper alone, that Goddard was the purchaser of these goods. The real inquiry is, whether extraneous evidence of this fact is admissible.

Now, it is true, the statute requires only some note, or memorandum, in writing, of the bargain; but I consider it settled, that this writing must show who is vendor, and who is purchaser. In Champion v. Plumer, (1 B. & P. New Rep. 252,) the memorandum contained the name of the vendor, a description of the goods, and their price, and was signed by the vendee; yet it was held that the vendee could not maintain an action thereon, because it did not appear, from the writing, that he was vendee, though it was clearly proved by parol.

In Sherburn et al. v. Shaw, (1 N. H. Rep. 157,) the plaintiffs caused certain real estate to be sold at auction, and the defendant, being the highest bidder, signed a memorandum, agreeing to take the property; this memorandum was written on a paper, headed, "Articles of sale of the estate of Jonathan Warner, deceased," containing the terms of the sale; and this paper was also signed by the auctioneer. Yet the court, through Mr. Justice Woodbury, who delivered the opinion, held that, as the paper failed to show that the plaintiffs were the vendors, it was radically defective. Here, also, there was no doubt that the plaintiffs were the vendors, but extraneous evidence to supply this fact was considered inadmissible.

It seems to me that the fact that the defendant was the purchaser, is, to say the least, as necessary to be stated in the writing as any other fact, and that to allow it to be proved by parol, is to violate the intent of the statute, and encounter the very mischiefs which it was enacted to prevent. Chancellor Kent, (2 Com. 511,) says, "the contract must, however, be stated with reasonable certainty, so that it can be understood from the writing itself, without having recourse to parol proof." And this position rests upon a current of authorities, both in England and America, which it is presumed are not intended to be disturbed. But how can the contract be understood from the writing itself, when that fails to state which party is vendor and which purchaser?

I am aware that a latent ambiguity in a contract may be removed by extraneous evidence, according to the rules of the common law; and that such evidence is also admissible to show what, in point of fact, was the subject-matter called for by the terms of a contract. Bradlee v. Steam P. Co. 16 Pet. 98. So when an act has been done by a person, and it is doubtful whether he acted in a private or official capacity, it is allowable to prove by parol that he was an agent and acted as such. But these cases fall far short of proving that when a statute requires a contract to be in writing, you may prove by parol the fact that the defendant was purchaser, the writing being silent as to that fact; or that a writing, which does not state who is vendor and who purchaser, does contain in itself the essentials of a contract of sale.

It is one thing to construe what is written; it is a very different thing to supply a substantive fact not stated in the writing. It is one thing to determine the meaning and effect of a complete and valid written contract, and it is another thing to take a writing, which on its face imports no contract, and make it import one by parol evidence. It is one thing to show that a party, who appears by a writing to have made a contract, made it as an agent, and quite a different thing to prove by parol that he made a purchase when the writing is silent as to that fact. The duty and power of the court is a duty and power to give a construction to what is written, and not in any case to permit it to be added to by parol. Least of all when a statute has required the essential requisites of a contract of sale to be in writing, is it admissible, in my judgment, to allow the fact, that the defendant made a purchase, to be proved by parol. If this fact, which lies at the basis of the action and to which every other is but incidental, can be proved by evidence out of the writing signed by the defendant, the statute seems to me to be disregarded.

It has been argued that the bill of parcels, sent to Goddard by Mason and Lawrence, and received by him, may be resorted to for the purpose of showing he was the purchaser. But it is certainly the law of Massachusetts, where this contract was made, and the case tried, as I believe it is of most other States, and of England, that unless the memorandum which is signed contains a reference to some other paper, no paper, not signed by the party to be charged, can be connected with the memorandum, or used to supply any defect therein. This was held in Morton et al. *v.* Dean, (13 Met. R. 385,) a case to which I shall have occasion more fully to refer hereafter. And in conformity therewith, Chancellor Kent lays down the rule in 2 Com. 511, and refers to many authorities in support of it. I am not aware that any court has held otherwise.

That this bill of parcels was of itself a sufficient memorandum under the statute, or that it was a paper signed by the defendant, or by any person by him thereunto lawfully authorized, I do not understand to be held by the majority of the court.

Now the memorandum ot the 19th September, is either sufficient or insufficient, under the statute. If the former, there is no occasion to resort to the bill of parcels to show who was vendor, and who purchaser; because, if the latter, it cannot, consistently with the statute, be made good by another paper not signed, and connected with it only by parol. To charge a party upon an insufficient memorandum, added to by another independent paper, not signed, would be to charge him when there was no sufficient memorandum signed by him, and therefore in direct conflict with the statute. It does not seem to me to be an answer, to say that the bill of parcels was made out pursuant to the memorandum. If the signed memorandum itself does not contain the essentials of a contract of sale, and makes no reference to any other paper, in no legal sense is any other paper pursuant to it—nor can any other paper be connected with it, save by parol evidence, which the statute forbids. In point of fact, it would be difficult to imagine any two independent papers more nearly connected, than a memorandum made and signed by an auctioneer, and the written conditions read by him at the sale. Yet it is settled, that the latter cannot be referred to, unless expressly called for by the very terms of the signed memorandum. Upon what principle does a bill of parcel stand upon any better ground?

The distinction, heretofore, has been between papers called for by the memorandum by express reference, and those not called for; this decision, for the first time, I believe, disregards that distinction, and allows an unsigned paper, not referred to, to be used in evidence to charge the purchaser.

In my judgment, this memorandum was defective in not showing who was vendor, and who purchaser, and oral evidence to supply this defect was not admissible.

But if this difficulty could be overcome, or if it had appeared on the face of the paper, that Goddard was the purchaser, still, in my judgment, there is no sufficient memorandum. I take it to be clearly settled, that if the court cannot ascertain from the paper itself, or from some other paper therein referred to, the essential terms of the sale, the writing does not take the case out of the statute. This has been so often decided, that it is sufficient to refer to 2 Kent's Com. 511, where many of the cases are collected.

The rule stated by the Chancellor, as a just deduction from the authorities, is, " Unless the essential terms of the sale can be ascertained from the writing itself, or by a reference contained in it to something else, the writing is not a compliance with the statute; and if the agreement be thus defective, it cannot be supplied by parol proof, for that would at once introduce all the

.39 *

mischiefs which the statute of frauds and perjuries was intended to prevent."

The statute, then, requires the essential terms of the sale to be in writing; the credit to be allowed to the purchaser is one of the terms of the sale.

And if the memorandum shows that a credit was to be given, but does not fix its termination, it is fatally defective, for the court cannot ascertain, from the paper, when a right of action accrues to the vendee, and the contract shown by the paper is not capable of being described in a declaration. The rights of the parties, in an essential particular, are left undetermined by the paper. This paper shows there was to be a credit of six months, and contains this clause —"Cr. to commence when ship sails: not after Dec'r 1st." According to this paper, when is this credit to commence? The answer is, when ship sails, if before December 1st. What ship? The paper is silent.

This is an action against Goddard for not delivering his note on twelve months' credit, and it is an indispensable inquiry, on what day, according to the contract, the note should bear date. The plaintiffs must aver, in their declaration, what note Goddard was bound to deliver, and the memorandum must enable the court to say that the description of the notes in the declaration is correct. They attempt this by averring, in the declaration, that the contract was for a note payable in twelve months from the sailing of a ship called the Crusader, and that this ship sailed on the sixth day of November. But the writing does not refer to the Crusader; and if oral evidence were admissible to prove that the parties referred to the Crusader, this essential term of their contract is derived from parol proof, contrary to the requirement of the statute. It was upon this ground the case of Morton et al. v. Dean, and many other similar cases, have been decided. In that case, there was a memorandum signed by the auctioneer, as the agent of both parties, containing their names, as vendor and vendee, the price to be paid, and a sufficient description of the property. But it appeared that there were written or printed conditions read at the sale, but not referred to in the memorandum, containing the terms of credit, &c., and therefore that the memorandum did not fix all the essential parts of the bargain, and it was held insufficient.

But, further; even if oral evidence were admissible to show that the parties had in view some particular vessel, and so to explain or render certain the memorandum, no such evidence was offered, and no request to leave that question of fact to the jury, was made. Mason, who made the contract with Goddard, was a witness, but he does not pretend the parties had any particular vessel in view, still less that they agreed on the

Crusader as the vessel, the sailing of which was to be the commencement of the credit. I cannot perceive, therefore, how either of the counts in this declaration is supported by the evidence, or how a different verdict could have lawfully been rendered.

The count for goods sold and delivered, was clearly not maintained, because, when the action was brought, the credit had not expired, even if it began on the 19th of September. One of the special counts avers, that the notes were to be due twelve months from the 80th of September; but this is inconsistent with the written memorandum, and there is no evidence to support it. The other special counts all declare for a note due twelve months after the sailing of the Crusader, but, as already stated, there is no evidence whatever to support this allegation, and a verdict of the jury, affirming such a contract, must have been set aside.

It may be added, also, that no one of the prayers for instructions, contained in the bill of exceptions, makes the fact that the parties had reference to the Crusader, any element of the contract, but that each of them asks for an instruction upon the assumption that this necessary term of the contract had not been in any way supplied.

I consider the language of Chief Justice Marshall, in Grant *v.* Naylor, (4 Cranch, 234,) applicable to this case. That great Judge says: "Already have so many cases been taken out of the statute of frauds, which seem to be within its letter, that it may well be doubted whether the exceptions do not let in many of the mischiefs against which the rule was intended to guard. The best Judges in England have been of opinion that this relaxing construction of the statute ought not to be extended further than it has already been carried, and this court entirely concurs in that opinion."

I am authorized to state that Mr. Justice CATRON concurs in this opinion.

Order.

This cause came on to be heard on the transcript of the record from the Circuit Court of the United States for the District of Massachusetts, and was argued by counsel. On consideration whereof, it is now here ordered and adjudged by this court, that the judgment of the said Circuit Court in this cause be, and the same is hereby, reversed, with costs, and that this cause be, and the same is hereby, remanded to the said Circuit Court, with directions to award a *venire facias de novo.*

WILLIAM D. NUTT, EXECUTOR OF ALEXANDER HUNTER, DE-
CEASED, PLAINTIFF IN ERROR, v. PHILIP H. MINOR.

Where the marshal of the District of Columbia engaged the services of a clerk for
a stipulated sum per annum, and the service continued without any new agreement,
and the jury were instructed that they might imply a new agreement to pay the
clerk at a different rate, this instruction was erroneous. There was nothing in the
evidence from which the jury could imply such new agreement.

THIS case was brought up, by writ of error, from the Circuit
Court of the United States for the District of Columbia, holden
in and for the county of Washington.
The facts are stated in the opinion of the court.

It was argued by *Mr. Bradley* and *Mr. Davis*, for the plaintiff in error, and by *Mr. Lawrence*, with whom was *Mr. Carlisle*,
for the defendant in error.

Mr. Justice CATRON delivered the opinion of the court.
Alexander Hunter was appointed marshal of the District of
Columbia in 1834, and continued to fill that office by reappoint-
ments, until June, 1848, at which time he died. Shortly after
he entered on the duties of his office, in 1834, he appointed
Daniel Minor his deputy for the county of Alexandria, where a
separate court was held and jurisdiction exercised; and for that
county Daniel Minor was practically marshal.
Philip H. Minor, the plaintiff below, was the brother of Daniel
Minor, who, being desirous to obtain the office of clerk to the
marshal for Philip H., applied to Hunter for this purpose, and
advised him to employ Philip H. as his clerk, and Hunter agreed
to do so; Daniel and Philip came up from Alexandria to Washington, and, in the marshal's room, a conversation took place between Philip H. Minor, Hunter the marshal, and Daniel Minor
the deputy. Hunter proposed to give, as salary for the service,
two hundred dollars per annum, and that Daniel Minor as deputy for Alexandria county, should give one hundred dollars,
making the salary three hundred dollars. Daniel Minor insisted
that the salary should be larger; Hunter replied, that he was
just in office and did not know what the profits would be, nor
what the value of the duties to be discharged by the clerk would
be; and that he did not feel justified in giving a larger salary.
Daniel Minor then offered, that if Hunter would pay two hundred and fifty dollars, he would pay one hundred and fifty
towards the salary, which was agreed to by Hunter and Daniel
Minor on the one part, and by Philip H. Minor on the other.
Daniel Minor, who was the principal witness, testified to the

foregoing facts for the plaintiff below, on the trial; and further deposed, that he took his brother Philip aside and conversed with him out of the hearing of Hunter, and advised him to take the offer for a year, small as it was; and accordingly Philip H. assented; that nothing was said about a continuance of the agreement after the first year.

Daniel Minor further deposed, that he told his brother Philip, in the foregoing conversation, "that the substance of the matter was an agreement confined to one year, and that the compensation would be afterwards made adequate to the services, and the value of the office; and that this was urged upon Philip as an inducement to agree to the engagement for the year; but that Hunter did not authorize the witness Daniel Minor, to promise Philip H. that he would be engaged after the first year at a higher compensation."

Daniel Minor also deposed, that he suggested to Hunter during the first year's service, that the salary of Philip H. should be increased, but Hunter declined doing so. The agreement was precise: Hunter was to pay 250 dollars, and Daniel Minor 150 dollars as clerk hire, per annum; nor was the contract limited to one year, so far as Hunter entered into it; it was general, at the rate stipulated, for any length of time that Hunter might remain in office, or that Philip H. Minor might see proper to serve, and Hunter and Daniel Minor see proper to retain him as clerk. It is most obvious that the court and jury held Hunter bound by what Daniel Minor promised in the absence of Hunter, and without his knowledge, and contrary to his consent. There is an entire absence of proof, that Hunter ever assented, by word or act, to raise the salary of Philip H. Minor as clerk; nor does it appear that the latter at any time applied to Hunter in person, and insisted, or even suggested that his salary should be increased, until February, 1847, when the letter offered in evidence was written; on the contrary, he received the salary of 400 dollars, as at first stipulated, for fourteen years, regularly crediting himself with it on the marshal's books, each year.

If we reject Daniel Minor's evidence as incompetent to bind Hunter, so far as he used persuasions in Hunter's absence to induce Philip H. Minor to hope, and probably believe, that Hunter would raise his salary, then the case, as proved by the plaintiff below, rests alone on the special agreement made in 1834; and we think it must be stripped of all these conversations between Daniel Minor and his brother, to which Hunter never assented.

Nutt was sued as Hunter's executor, for work and labor, care and diligence, done and performed by Minor in and about the business of Hunter in his lifetime, and at his special instance and request. And also for sundry matters and things properly

chargeable in an account therewith filed; and on these allegations of a *quantum meruit*, Hunter's estate was charged for 400
dollars per annum, in addition to the 400 dollars annually paid on
the special agreement, running through the whole time of Minor's
service; and a verdict was had, and a judgment rendered for five
thousand and fifty-five dollars and seventy-three cents, against
the estate, which was held responsible, regardless of the fact
that Daniel Minor was bound to pay one hundred and fifty dollars of the four hundred, from April, 1834, to June, 1847, when
Alexandria county was retroceded to Virginia by Congress.

On this state of facts, the court was asked to instruct the jury,
(among other things) that "if from the whole evidence aforesaid, the jury shall find that in April, 1834, the plaintiff entered
into the employment of the deceased to serve him as clerk at a
salary of 400 dollars for a single year, and thereafter continued
to serve the said Hunter as clerk aforesaid, during the whole
time mentioned in said account and declaration, and that no
new agreement was made between the said plaintiff and said
Hunter, for a compensation different from that which was as
aforesaid first agreed upon between them; and if they shall further find that said Hunter in his lifetime fully paid said plaintiff
for his said services, at the rate aforesaid, then the plaintiff is
not entitled to recover in this action; which instruction the court
refused to give as prayed, but did modify the same by inserting
the words "express or implied" between the words "agreement" and "was made."

By thus modifying the instruction, the court told the jury, in
substance, that they might find on the allegation of a *quantum
meruit*, for work and labor done, and for services performed, and
hold that an agreement to pay on Hunter's part, might be "implied," because of the performance of the services; and, that a
verdict might be found equal to the value of such services, according to the proof, deducting therefrom the amount already
paid on the special agreement; and that such agreement did
not preclude the plaintiff below from recovering additional
compensation, to any amount that the jury should think he was
entitled to. That the instruction as given did reject the special
agreement, and leave the jury free to imply a new promise arising on the *quantum meruit*, for labor and services, is manifest;
and therefore we are of opinion, that the instruction as propounded, ought to have been given without an addition of the
words "express or implied," as inserted by the Circuit Court

The letter, offered in evidence, was a plain attempt on the part
of the plaintiff to make evidence for himself. It could only be
offered for the purpose of showing that Hunter was thereby
notified of Minor's unwillingness to act as clerk after the notice,

unless his compensation was increased, and that he would quit unless there was an increase; or as evidence to be taken in connection with other subsequent proof, showing that Hunter assented to the propositions contained in the letter. But as Hunter not only refused to sanction the demand set up, but indignantly resisted, and resented it, the letter could be of no value to establish a new promise; nor can it be of any value as notice that additional compensation would be claimed for services rendered thereafter, because the plaintiff, with full knowledge of Hunter's determined rejection of the claim, continued to perform his duties as clerk, and to receive his salary of 400 dollars as usual, and thereby submitted to Hunter's assumption that the salary was governed by the special agreement made in 1834. We are of opinion that this letter should have been objected to as evidence, and the party offering it compelled by the court to state for what purpose it was offered; so that it might have been inspected and passed on by the court, without being read to the jury. As, however, this course was not pursued at the trial by the defendant's counsel, and a general objection made to reading the letter for any purpose, we do not think the court erred in admitting the evidence in the first instance, although it ought certainly to have been rejected and taken from the jury, after the evidence was closed, had a motion been made to this effect, because it was unsustained by other evidence that Hunter assented to the claim made by the letter. But as no motion was made to withdraw this piece of evidence, the court properly left it with the jury.

We order that the judgment of the Circuit Court be reversed, and that the cause be remanded for another trial.

Order.

This cause came on to be heard on the transcript of the record from the Circuit Court of the United States for the District of Columbia, holden in and for the county of Washington, and was argued by counsel. On consideration whereof, it is now here ordered and adjudged, by this court, that the judgment of the said Circuit Court in this cause be, and the same is hereby, reversed, with costs, and that this cause be, and the same is hereby, remanded to the said Circuit Court, with directions to award a *venire facias de novo*.

THE PHILADELPHIA AND READING RAILROAD COMPANY, PLAINTIFF IN ERROR, v. ELIAS H. DERBY.

Where a suit was brought against a railroad company, by a person who was injured by a collision, it was correct in the court to instruct the jury, that, if the plaintiff was lawfully on the road, at the time.of the collision, and the collision and consequent injury to him were caused by the gross negligence of one of the servants of the defendants, then and there employed on the road, he was entitled to recover, notwithstanding the circumstances, that the plaintiff was a stockholder in the company, riding by invitation of the President, paying no fare, and not in the usual passenger cars.

And also, that the fact that the engineer having the control of the colliding locomotive, was forbidden to run on that track at the time, and had acted in disobedience. of such orders, was no defence to the action.

A master is liable for the tortious acts of his servant, when done in the course of his employment, although they may be done in disobedience of the master's orders.

·THIS case was brought up, by writ of error, from the Circuit Court of the United States for the Eastern District of Pennsylvania.

It was an action on the case brought by Derby, for an injury suffered upon the railroad of the plaintiff in error.

The declaration, in ten counts, was, in substance, that on the 15th day of June, 1848, the defendants, being the owners of the railroad, and of a certain car engine called the Ariel, received the plaintiff into the said car, to be safely carried therein, upon, and over the said railroad, whereby it ·became the duty of the defendants to use proper care and diligence that the plaintiff should be safely and securely carried, yet, that the defendants, not regarding their duty in that behalf, conducted themselves so negligently by their servants, that, by reason of such negligence, while the car engine Ariel was upon the road, and the plaintiff therein, he was precipitated therefrom upon the ground, and greatly injured. Defendants pleaded not guilty.

On the 22d of April, 1851, the cause came on to be tried, and the evidence was, in substance, as follows :

In the month of June, 1848, the plaintiff, being a stockholder in the said railroad company, came to the city of Philadelphia, for the purpose of inquiring into its affairs, on his own account and as the representative of other stockholders. On the.15th of June, 1848, the plaintiff accompanied John Tucker, Esq., the President of the said company, over the railroad, for the purpose of viewing it and the works of the company.

They proceeded in the ordinary passenger train of the company, from the city of Philadelphia, (the plaintiff paying no fare for his passage,) as far as the city of Reading.

On arriving at Reading, the plaintiff inspected the machine-shops of the defendants, there situate, and remained for that purpose about half an hour after the departure of the passenger train towards Pottsville, which latter place is about the distance of ninety-two miles from Philadelphia.

By order of Mr. Tucker, a small locomotive car engine, called the Ariel was prepared for the purpose of carrying the plaintiff and Mr. Tucker further up the road. This engine was not constructed, or used, for the business of the said defendants, but was kept for the use of the President and other officers of the company, their friends and guests.

On this engine, the plaintiff and Mr. Tucker, accompanied by the engineer and fireman, and a paymaster of defendants, proceeded, following the passenger train, until they reached Port Clinton, a station on the line of the railroad.

After leaving Port Clinton, when about three miles distant from it, going round a curve, the passengers on the Ariel saw another engine called the Lycoming, of which S. P. Jones was the conductor, approaching on the same track. The engineer of the Ariel immediately reversed his engine, and put down the break. Mr. Tucker, the plaintiff, and the fireman, jumped from the Ariel, to avoid the impending collision. After they had jumped, the engineer also left the Ariel, having done all he could do to stop it. The plaintiff, in attempting to jump, fell, and received the injury of which he complains.

The engineer of the Lycoming, when he saw the approach of the Ariel, reversed his engine and put down the break. He did not leave the Lycoming till after the collision. At the time of the collision, the Lycoming was backing. The engines were but slightly injured by it.

On the night of the 14th or the morning of the 15th of June, a bridge, on the line of the railroad above Port Clinton, was burnt. In consequence of this, one of the tracks of the railroad was blocked up by empty cars returning to the mines, and stopped by the destruction of the bridge. For this reason a single track only could be used for the business of the road between Port Clinton and the burnt bridge.

Lewis Kirk, an officer of the said company, (master machinist and foreman,) went on in the passenger cars from Reading, towards Pottsville, informing the plaintiff and Mr. Tucker, that he would give the proper orders to have the track kept clear for the Ariel. On arriving at Port Clinton he did give an order to Edward Burns, despatcher at Port Clinton, (an officer of said company, charged with the duty of controlling the starting of engines,) that no car should be allowed to go over the road until he the said Kirk returned.

This order was communicated in express terms by Burns to Jones, the conductor of the Lycoming. Jones replied that he would go, and would take the responsibility, and, contrary to his orders, did go up the road towards the burnt bridge, and on his return met the Ariel, and the collision ensued, as above stated. Jones had the reputation of being a careful and competent person, no previous disobedience of orders by him had ever occurred, and he was discharged by the defendants immediately after the accident, and because of it.

On the trial the plaintiff below requested the court to charge the jury,—

I. That if the plaintiff was lawfully upon the railroad of the defendants at the time of the collision, by the license of the defendants, and was then and there injured by the negligence or disobedience of orders of the company's servants, then and there employed on the said railroad, the defendants are liable for the injury done to the plaintiff by such collision.

II. That if the defendants, by their servants, undertook to convey the plaintiff along the Reading Railroad, in the car Ariel, and while so conveying, him, through the gross negligence of the servants of the company then and there employed on the said railroad, the collision occurred, by which the plaintiff was injured, that the defendants are liable for the injury done to the plaintiff by such collision, although no compensation was to be paid to the company for such conveyance of the plaintiff.

III. That if the collision, by which the plaintiff was injured, was occasioned by the locomotive Lycoming, then driven negligently or in disobedience of orders upon the said road by J. P. Jones, one of the company's servants, then having control or command of the said locomotive, that the defendants are liable for the injury to the plaintiffs, caused by such collision.

And the counsel for the defendants below requested the court to charge the jury,—

1. That the damages, if any are recoverable, are to be confined to the direct and immediate consequences of the injury sustained.

2. That if the jury believe the plaintiff had paid no fare, and was passing upon the railroad of the defendant as an invited guest, in order to entitle him to recover damages he must prove gross negligence, which is the omission of that care which even the most thoughtless take of their own concerns.

3. That the defendants would be liable in damages to a passenger who had paid passage-money upon their contract to deliver him safely, for slight negligence, but to an invited guest, who paid no fare or passage-money, they will not be responsible unless the jury believe that there was not even slight diligence on the part of the agents of the defendants.

4. That the employer is not responsible for the wilful act of his servant.

5. That if the jury believe that the conductor of the engine Lycoming wilfully, and against the express orders of the officer of the company communicated to h'im, by running his engine upon the track above Port Clinton, caused the collision, the defendants are not responsible for any injury or loss resulting from such wilful disobedience.

6. That if the jury believe that every reasonable and proper precaution was taken to have the track of the railroad clear for the passage of the Ariel, and collision ensued solely by reason of the wilful disobedience of the conductor of the Lycoming, and of the express orders duly given by an agent of the company, the plaintiff cannot recover.

7. That if the jury believe that the conductor of the Lycoming, and all the officers of the company in any wise connected with the collision, were carefully and prudently selected, and that the collision ensued and the injury resulted to the plaintiff, an invited guest, by the wilful disobedience of one of them to an order duly communicated, then the plaintiff cannot recover.

The learned Judge charged the jury as requested, on all the points offered by the plaintiff.

And the learned Judge charged on the first and second points offered by the defendants, as requested, and also on the third point of the defendants, with the explanation, that though all the other agents of the defendants acted with diligence, yet if one of the agents used no diligence at all, then the defendants could not be said to have shown slight diligence.

As to the fourth point, the learned Judge charged as requested by the defendants, with this explanation, that though the master is not liable for the wilful act of his servant, not done in the course of his employment as servant, yet if the servant disobeys an order relating to his business, and injury results from that disobedience, the master is liable, for it is his duty to select servants who will obey. The disobedience in this case is the *ipsa negligentia,* for it is not pretended by the defendants that the Lycoming was intentionally driven against the Ariel.

On the fifth, sixth, and seventh points of the defendants, the learned Judge refused to charge as requested.

The learned Judge further said, that it is admitted that the plaintiff was injured through the act of Jones, the conductor of the Lycoming, that the plaintiff was lawfully on the road by the license of the defendants; then, in this view of the case, whether he paid fare or not, or was the guest of the defendants, made no difference as to the law of the case.

The jury found a verdict for the plaintiff, and assessed the damages at three thousand dollars.

A writ of error brought the case up to this court.

It was argued by *Mr. Campbell* and *Mr. Fisher*, for the plaintiff in error, and *Mr. Binney* and *Mr. Wharton*, for the defendant in error.

The points made by the counsel for the plaintiff in error, were the following:

I. The plaintiff stood in such relation to the defendants at the time of the accident, that he cannot by law recover.

II. The plaintiff suffered no damage from any act with which the defendants are by law chargeable.

These propositions cover the whole case; yet it may be proper to direct the attention of the court to two others, which, although included in the latter, are made more specific by referring to the points and charge of the court.

III. That the learned Judge erred while affirming the third and fourth points of the defendants, in the explanation by which that instruction was accompanied. The points and explanations referred to, were,

3. That the defendants would be liable in damages to a passenger who had paid passage-money, upon their contract to deliver him safely, for slight negligence; but to an invited guest, who paid no fare, or passage-money, they will not be responsible, unless the jury believe that there was not even slight diligence on the part of the agents of the defendants.

4. That the employer is not responsible for the wilful act of his servant or agent.

The learned Judge charged as requested on the third point, with the explanation, that though all the other agents of the defendants acted with diligence, yet, if one of the agents used no diligence at all, then the defendants could not be said to have shown slight diligence.

The learned Judge also charged as requested on the fourth point with this explanation, that though the master is not liable for the wilful act of his servant, not done in the course of his employment as servant, yet, if the servant disobeys an order relating to his business, and injury results from that disobedience, the master is liable; for it is his duty to select servants who will obey. The disobedience in this case is the *ipsa negligentia*, for it is not pretended by the defendants that the Lycoming was intentionally driven against the Ariel.

IV. The learned Judge erred in refusing to charge as requested by the 5th, 6th, and 7th points of the defendants.

5. That if the jury believe that the conductor of the engine Lycoming wilfully, and against the express orders of the officer of the company, communicated to him, by running his engine upon the track above Port Clinton, caused the collision, the de-

Philadelphia and Reading Railroad Company *v,* Derby.

fendants are not responsible for any injury or loss resulting from such wilful disobedience.

6. That if the jury believe every reasonable and proper precaution was taken to have the track of the railroad clear for the passage of the Ariel, and the collision ensued solely by reason of the wilful disobedience of the conductor of the Lycoming, and of the express orders duly given by an agent of the company, the plaintiff cannot recover.

7. That if the jury believe that the conductor of the Lycoming, and all the officers of the company, in any wise connected with the collision, were carefully and prudently selected, and that the collision ensued, and the injury resulted to the plaintiff, an invited guest, by the wilful disobedience of one of them to an order duly communicated, then the plaintiff cannot recover.

I. The plaintiff stood in such relation to the defendants at the time of the accident, that he cannot by law recover.

The plaintiff was a stockholder of the defendants; he was on the road as an invited guest, and paid no fare; was not carried in the way of their business, nor in a car used for such purpose. He voluntarily left the passenger train at Reading, and took his seat in the Ariel, with full knowledge of the service to which it was devoted, and the character of the engine itself. He was himself the president of a railroad company.

Being no passenger, and not carried by the company, even gratuitously, in the way of their business, he was in the car and was carried as a stockholder and a guest.

What were his legal rights, and what the obligations of the defendants?

. It was contended:

1. That no cause of action can arise to any person by reason of the occurrence of an unintentional injury while he is receiving or partaking of any of those acts of kindness which spring from mere social relations. No contract exists, and no such duty as can give a cause of action, is by law cast upon either party in such relation. Such was the position of the plaintiff.

Upon principles somewhat analogous to the one now presented it has been ruled, "Si un hoste invite un al supper, et le nuit esteant farr spent et luy invite a stayer la tout le nuit, fit soit apres robbe uncore le hoste ne serra charge pur ceo, car cest guest ne fuit ascur traveller. 1 Rolle's Abr. 3.

"And if a man set his horse at an inn, though he lodge at another place, that makes him a guest, for the innkeeper gains by the horse, and therefore that makes the owner a guest, though he be absent. Contra, if goods left there by a man, because the innkeeper hath no advantage by them." York *v.* Grenaugh, 2 Ld. R. 868.

40 *

" So where one leaves his horse at an inn, to stand there by agreement at livery, although neither himself nor any of his servants lodge there, he is reputed a guest for that purpose, and the innkeeper hath a valuable consideration, and if that horse be stolen, he hath an action upon the common custom of the realm. But, as in the case at bar, where he leaves goods to keep, whereof the defendant is not to have any benefit, and goes from thence for two or three days, although he saith he will return, yet he is at liberty, and is not a guest during that time, nor is the innkeeper chargeable as a common hostler for the goods stolen during that time, unless he make a special promise for the safe keeping of them, and the action ought to be grounded upon it." Greeley v. Clark, Cr. Jac. 188.

" For if a man be lodged with another who is not an innholder on request, if he be robbed in his house by the servants of him who lodged him, or any other, he shall not answer for it." Cayle's case, 4 Rep. 32.

"And therefore, if a neighbor who is no traveller, as a friend, at the request of the innholder, lodges there, and his goods be stolen, &c., he shall not have an action." Cayle's case, Id. 33.

The principles on which rights and obligations, arising from particular relations, are founded, are stated by Shaw, C. J. in Farwell v. Boston & Worcester Railroad Co. 4 Metcalf, 58.

And it may be proper to refer to that class of cases based upon the principle, that unless the parties met upon the terms of contract, none can be inferred, or, in the words of Mr. Justice Williams, in Davies v. Davies, (38 Engl. C. L. R. 46,) that the evidence must show " that the parties came there on the terms that they were to pay and be paid, but if that was not so, there can be no *ex poste facto* charge made on either side."

And to the same effect are the actions brought upon claims for services rendered, when the relations of the parties do not justify the inference of contract, · Strine v. Parsons, 5 Watts & S. 357. The case of a woman who lived with the decedent (whose estate was sued) as his wife. Walker's Estate, 3 Rawle, 343. An action by a son for services rendered after he arrived at full age. And also Candor's Appeal, 5 Watts & S. 216; Hacks v. Stewart, 8 Barr, 213.

2. The plaintiff, being a stockholder as well as guest, and availing himself of an opportunity to inspect, for his own interest as for that of others, the line of the road, their shops, &c., he cannot, by reason also of this relation, recover.

He was in the car, as already stated, as a stockholder, and not carried by the company in the way of their business, but for his own benefit, and for the interest of other stockholders whom he represented, and for whom he was acting as agent. No contract was entered into with him, and he occupied, in this regard, no other relation than any other officer or agent of the company or coproprietor of the road.

One agent injured by another agent, cannot recover from their common principal. Farwell v. Boston & Worcester Railroad Co. 4 Metcalf R. 49; Brown v. Maxwell, 6 Hill, 592; Murray v. South Carolina Railroad Co. 1 McMullan, 385; Coon v. Railroad Co. 6 Barbour, 231; Priestly v. Fowler, 3 Mees. & Welsb. 1.

If the defendant in error owned half the stock of the road, or being so the owner, the company was unincorporated, (its charter cannot affect this relation,) or if the charter had created an individual liability in the shareholders, what duty did the law impose upon the other proprietors towards him, while he was on the road by their license, without compensation, to inspect its condition for his own benefit? It is submitted he went there like any other tenant in common, or joint proprietor, without right to claim against his coproprietors for the negligence of any of their common servants.

II. The plaintiff suffered no damage from any act with which the defendants are by law chargeable.

The gist of the action is, the neglect by the servant of the defendants of some duty imposed upon them by law, for which negligence they are sought to be held responsible.

1. It is first to be observed, that this liability of the defendants, if any, is not affected by their corporate character, and if under like circumstances an individual would not be liable, a corporation will not.

" A corporation will be liable for an injury done by its servants, if under like circumstances an individual would be responsible." The First Baptist Church v. Schenectady & Tr. R. R. Co. 5 Barb. Sup. Ct. Rep. N. Y. 79. " Indeed the same rule should be applied to a corporation as should be applied to an individual who carries on a business solely through the medium of agents and servants." Pratt, J., Coon v. The Utica R. R. Co. 6 Barb. S. C. R. 231; Philadelphia R. R. Co. v. Wilt, 4 Wharton, R. 146.

" The power and duty of an engine driver must be the same, simply as such, whether he be employed by a corporation or a joint stock company, or an ordinary partnership, or an individual. The driver appointed by a corporation, or company, or partnership, carrying on the business of carriers of passengers or goods, must, as such, have the same duties and powers." Per Parke, B. 3 Welsby, H. & G. 277; Con. v. R. R. Co.

2. That an individual would not, under the facts in this case, have been liable, is, it is submitted, clear, from the following

authorities, and the principles upon which the decisions are based:

"A master is chargeable with the acts of his servant, but when he acts in the execution of the authority given him by his master, and then the act of the servant is the act of the master." Per Holt, C. J., Middleton v. Fowler, 1 Salk. 282.

"In civil matters, to render one man amenable for another's misconduct, it must ever be established that the latter, in committing the injury, was all the while acting under the authority, and with the assent, express or implied, of the former." Hammond's Nisi Prius, 80.

"Hence it is, that the principal is never liable for the unauthorized, the wilful, or the malicious act or trespass of the agent." Per Story, J., Princip. and Agt. § 456.

In McManus v. Crickett, Lord Kenyon cites these cases, as illustrating the rule:

"If my servant, contrary to my will, chase my beasts into the soil of another, I shall not be punished."

"If I command my servant to distrain, and he ride on the distress, he shall be punished, not I." 1 East, 106.

"In order to render a master liable for a trespass committed by the servant, it is necessary to show that the acts were done while the servant was acting under the authority of the master. . . . To render him liable, it must be shown that the commission of the trespasses was in the execution of his order, or with his assent or approbation." Per Waite, J., Church v. Mansfield, 20 Conn. 287.

In Armstrong v. Cooley, (5 Gill's Rep. 512,) it was said, by Treat, C. J., "Even when the act is lawful, the principal is responsible for the manner of its performance, if done in the course of his employment, and not in wilful violation of his instructions." Thus declaring that, in the latter case, he would not be liable.

"It should here be observed, that the ground of the principal's liability cannot be that he has selected an agent who is more or less unworthy, and placed him in a situation which enables him to become the instrument of mischief to his neighbor, because that would hold him responsible; not alone for the acts done by the other, in his capacity *quatenus* agent, but even for a wilful default." Ham. N. P. 81.

This principle is exemplified in the case next cited, which, with the following, it is submitted, rule the cause now before the court.

Joel v. Morrison, 25 Eng. C. L. Rep. 512. In this case, the plaintiff was knocked down by the defendant's horse and cart, then driven by one of his servants accompanied by another.

The defendant proved that his horse and cart were only in the habit of being driven out of the city, and did not go into the city (where the act happened) at all. Thesiger, counsel for the plaintiff, suggested that the defendant's servants might have gone out of their way, for their own purposes, or might have taken the cart at a time when it was not wanted for the purpose of business, and have gone to pay a visit to some friend. He was observing that, under these circumstances, the defendant was liable for the acts of his servants—but, per Parke, B., " He is not liable, if, as you suggest, these young men took the cart without leave."

Wilson v. Peverley, (2 N. Hamp. Rep. 548,) was an action on the case against the master. It appeared that, by the defendant's orders, a fire was set on his land, and the charge of it given to a hired laborer. That the defendant left home, directing the laborer, after setting the fire, to employ himself in harrowing other land in the neighborhood. That the laborer, after his master's absence, and before he commenced harrowing, carried brands from that fire into the ploughing field, to consume some piles of wood and brush there collected, and on his way dropped some coals, from which another fire arose, and did all the injury complained of. That carrying fire from one field to another was dangerous, and was not in conformity to any express authority of his master; that the laborer was accustomed to work under the particular directions of his master, and could conveniently have harrowed, without first burning the piles of wood, though to burn them first is the usual course of good husbandry. A verdict was taken for the plaintiff, subject to the opinion of the court. Judgment was afterwards given for the defendant, and the Judge (Woodbury) said: "The next ground on which a master is liable for wrongs of his servant, is, that the wrongs are performed by the servant in the negligent and unskilful execution of business specially intrusted to the servant, but the principle does not reach wrongs caused by carelessness in the performance of an act, not directed by the master, as a piece of business of some third person, or of the servant himself, or of the master, but which the master did not, either expressly or impliedly, direct him to perform. . . . Thus, a piece of labor might be very properly performed at one time, and not at another; as, in this case, the setting of a fire in the neighborhood of much combustible matter. And if the master, when the fire would be highly dangerous in such a place, forbore to direct it to be kindled, and employed his servant in other business, it would be unreasonable to make him liable, if the servant, before attending to that business, went in his own discretion, and kindled the fire to the damage of third persons.

The master *quoad hoc*, is not acting in person, or through the servant, neither *per se*, nor *per aliud*, and the doctrine of *respondeat superior*, does not apply to such an act, it being the sole act of the servant."

It appears by the evidence, as applied to these rules:

1. Jones was not acting in execution of the authority given him by his master, the company, which is deemed essential by Lord Holt.

2. In committing the injury, he was not all the while, or at any time, acting under the authority, or with the assent of the company, things, says Hammond, ever to be established to make the principal liable.

3. His act was contrary to the will and express direction of the company, which, under the cases approved by Lord Kenyon, in McManus *v.* Crickett, would discharge the master from liability.

4. The company directed him to do one thing, and not to do another; yet, he did the latter, and did not do the former; therefore, according to the rule approved by Lord Kenyon, he, and not the company, is liable to the plaintiff.

5. His whole conduct was unauthorized by the defendants, who are, therefore, not liable, under the authority of Story and Waite, Js

6. His acts were "in wilful violation of his instructions," and, therefore, as stated in the opinion of Treat, C. J., the defendants are not liable.

7. He took and run the car "without leave," in which case, says Parke, B., the principal is " not liable."

8. Nor are the defendants liable because Jones was in the performance of a piece of business of the defendants, because they did not, either expressly or impliedly, direct him to perform it; and if, as Judge Woodbury said, it would be unreasonable to make the principal liable for an act done by the servant, without authority, but only on his own discretion, with what reason can the principal be made responsible for the wilful violation of his orders?

It is hence submitted, that the defendants are not by law chargeable with the damages resulting from the wilful and disobedient act of one of their servants, and that the second point is maintained.

(The argument upon the remaining points, is necessarily omitted.)

The points made by the counsel for the defendant in error, were the same ruled by the court below, and were stated as follows:

The three points made by the defendant in error, and affirmed by his honor, Judge Grier, who tried the cause, are found on the record. ·They are as follows :

I. That if the plaintiff was lawfully upon the railroad of the defendants, at the time of the collision, by the license of the defendants, and was then and there injured by the negligence or disobedience of orders of the company's servants, then and there employed upon the said railroad, the defendants ·are liable for the injury done to the plaintiff by such collision.

Two principles sustain this point.

I. That every person (or corporation) whose negligence or carelessness causes damage to another person, is *primâ facie* responsible to such person therefor.

II. That a corporation is liable to third persons for the damage done by its servants through negligence or disobedience of orders, in the course of their employment.

I. To the first principle, as an axiom of the law, it is not deemed necessary to cite authorities.

II. In support of the second, the authorities which follow are cited, the principles being first given as stated by eminent text-writers.

In Story on Agency, p. 465, ch. 17, § 452, the rule is laid down as follows :

" It is a general doctrine of law, that, although the principal is not ordinarily liable, (though he sometimes is,) in a criminal suit, for the acts or misdeeds of his agent, unless, indeed, he has authorized or coöperated in those acts or misdeeds ; yet, he is held liable to third persons in a civil suit for the frauds, deceits, concealments, misrepresentations, torts, negligences, and other malfeasances or misfeasances and omissions of duty of his agent in the course of his employment, although the principal did not authorize, or justify, or participate in, or, indeed, know of such misconduct, or even if he forbade them, or disapproved of them.   In all such cases, the rule applies, *Respondeat superior;* and it is founded upon public policy and convenience; for in no other way could there be any safety to third persons in their dealings, either directly with the principals, or indirectly with him through the instrumentality of agents.   In every such case, the principal holds out his agent as competent, and fit to be trusted; and thereby, in effect, he warrants his fidelity and good conduct in all matters of the agency."   And in note 2, the learned author, in commenting upon a passage in 1 Blackstone's Comm. 432, adds, " for the master is liable for the wrong and negligence of his servant, just as much when it has been done contrary to his orders and against his intent, as he is, when he has coöperated in, or known the wrong."

"A master is ordinarily liable to answer in a civil suit for the tortious or wrongful acts of his servant, if those acts are done in the course of his employment in his master's service; the maxims applicable to such cases, being, *Respondeat superior*, and *Qui facit per alium, facit per se.* This rule, with some few exceptions, is of universal application, whether the act of the servant be one of omission or commission, whether negligent, fraudulent, or deceitful, or even if it be an act of positive malfeasance or misconduct; if it be done in the course of his employment his master is responsible for it, *civiliter*, to third persons. And it makes no difference that the master did not authorize, or even know of the servant's act or neglect; for even if he disapproved of or forbade it, he is equally liable, if the act be done in the course of the servant's employment. Smith on Master and Servant, p. 152; Law Lib. Jan. 1852, p. 130.

"If a servant is acting in the execution of his master's orders, and by his negligence causes injury to a third party, the master will be responsible, although the servant's act was not necessary for the proper performance of his duty to his master, or was even contrary to his master's orders." Smith on Master and Servant, p. 157; Law Lib. Jan. 1852, p. 134.

The following authorities establish conclusively the principles above stated. Sleath *v.* Wilson, 9 Carrington & Payne, 607, (38 E. C. L. 249.)

If a servant, without his master's knowledge, take his master's carriage out of the coach-house, and with it commit an injury, the master is not liable; because he has not in such case intrusted the servant with the carriage. But whenever the master has intrusted the servant with the control of the carriage, it is no answer that the servant acted improperly in the management of it; but the master, in such case, will be liable, because he has put it in the servant's power to mismanage the carriage, by intrusting him with it. Therefore, where a servant, having set his master down in Stamford street, was directed by him to put up in Castle street, Leicester Square; but instead of so doing, went to deliver a parcel of his own, in the Old Street Road, and in returning along it, drove against an old woman, and injured her; it was held, that the master was responsible for his servant's act.

Mr. Justice Erskine states the law in the clearest manner. "Whenever the master has intrusted the servant with the control of the carriage, it is no answer that the servant acted improperly in the management of it. If it were, it might be contended that if a master directs his servant to drive slowly, and the servant disobeys his orders and drives fast, and through his negligence occasions an injury, the master will not be liable.

But that is not the law : the master, in such a case, will be liable, and the ground is, that he has put it in the servant's power to mismanage the carriage, by intrusting him with it."

The case of Joel v. Morrison, (6 Carrington & Payne, 501, 25 E. C. L. 511,) is to the same point,—but the servant in that case was acting against his master's implied commands, and not his express.   The master was held liable.   In Brown v. Copley, (7 Mann. & Granger, 566, 49 E. C. L. 566.) Sergeant Talfourd, *arguendo*, puts the case, previously put by way of illustration by Mr. Justice Erskine, in Sleath v. Wilson,— "As, if a coachman were driving his master, and were ordered not to drive so fast, but he nevertheless continued to do so, the master would be responsible for the injury."   To which Mr. Justice Cresswell assents, saying,—"In that case, the coachman would still be driving for his master, though driving badly."

It is not pretended, in the present case, that Jones disobeyed the order given him, to attend to any private business of his own ; he was still "driving" (his locomotive) "for his master," "though driving badly."

Nor did the damage ensue from the breach of the express order not to run up the railroad until the Ariel had passed. Jones ran his locomotive up the road without harming any one. It was on his return down the road that he encountered the Ariel.

And in Croft v. Alison, (4 Barn. & Ald. 590, 6 E. C. L. 528,) in an action for the negligent driving of the defendant's coachman, whereby the plaintiff's carriage was upset, it appeared that the accident arose from the defendant's coachman striking the plaintiff's horses with his whip, in consequence of which they moved forward, and the carriage was overturned. At the time when the horses were struck, the two carriages were entangled.   The defendant was held liable for the damage caused by his servant's act, although wanton, as it was done in pursuance of his employment.   And *per curiam*, "The distinction is this; if a servant driving a carriage, in order to effect some purpose of his own, wantonly strikes the horses of another person, and produce the accident, the master will not be liable. But if, in order to perform his master's orders, he strikes, but injudiciously, and in order to extricate himself from a difficulty, that will be negligent and careless conduct, for which the master will be liable, being an act done in pursuance of the servant's employment."

The third point of the defendant in error, and sustained by his Honor who tried the cause. is as follows :

III. That if the collision by which the plaintiff was injured was occasioned by the locomotive Lycoming, then driven negligently, or in disobedience of orders, upon the said road, by J. P. Jones, one of the company's servants, then having control or command of the said locomotive, that the defendants are liable for the injury to the plaintiff, caused by such collision.

This point merely applies the general principles of the first point to the facts proved, and is virtually comprehended in it. It therefore needs no further notice.

The second point of the defendant in error, sustained by his Honor who tried the cause, is as follows:

II. That if the defendants, by their servants, undertook to convey the plaintiff along the Reading Railroad, in the car Ariel, and while so conveying him, through the gross negligence of the servants of the company, then and there employed upon the said railroad, the collision occurred by which the plaintiff was injured, that the defendants are liable for the injury done to the plaintiff by such collision, although no compensation was to be paid to the company for such conveyance of the plaintiff.

The principle of this point is identical with that of the second point presented by the plaintiffs in error themselves, and which was duly affirmed by his Honor in his charge, and the principle is in entire harmony with the third point of the plaintiffs in error, which was also duly affirmed by his Honor.

As both parties, therefore, seem to have agreed in their views on these points as presented as above to his Honor for adoption, and which were duly adopted by him, it can hardly be necessary to refer to the authorities on which the doctrine is based.

The leading case in point is that of Coggs v. Barnard, (Lord Raymond, 909,) the celebrated case under the law of bailments. The principle of that case is that, " If a man undertakes to carry goods safely and securely, he is responsible for any damage they may sustain in the carriage through his neglect, though he was not a common-carrier, and was to have nothing for the carriage."

This case has been commented upon with great ability, and at much length in 1 Smith's Leading Cases, p. 82, and the American authorities upon the point are collected by Messrs. Hare and Wallace, p. 227.

Mr. Smith states the general principle in these words, viz. " The confidence induced by undertaking any service for another, is a sufficient legal consideration to create a duty in the performance of it."

Among the numerous American cases affirming this principle, is Thorne v. Deas, (4 Johns. 84,) in which Chief Justice Kent says, "If a party who makes this engagement," (the gratuitous performance of business for another,) "enters upon the execution of the business, and does it amiss, through the want of due care, by which damage ensues to the other party, an action will lie for this misfeasance."

A principle to which the defendant in error's second point also refers, is the liability of an unpaid agent for gross negligence only.

In the later cases, the English courts have found considerable difficulty in distinguishing with precision between negligence and gross negligence. In Wilson v. Brett, (11 Mees. & Wels. 113,) Baron Rolfe observes, "that he could see no difference between negligence and gross negligence; that it was the same thing, with the addition of a vituperative epithet."

And see Hare and Wallace's American note, p. 242, with the American cases there cited, and which are collected and commented on at much length, and the true principle stated, that any negligent conduct, which causes injury or loss, is actionable.

The defendant in error might perhaps have been entitled to ask the benefit of a rule less rigid in its bearing upon himself; but as the conduct of the railroad company in discharging Jones, the conductor, showed their own estimate of the grossness of the negligence in question, the defendant in error was content to ask the ruling of the point in its milder form, and the finding of the jury established the grossness of the negligence. The question of what is gross negligence being for the jury, see Storer v. Gowen, 6 Shepley, 174; Whitney v. Lee, 8 Metcalf, 91; Angell on Carriers, p. 12.

Mr. Justice GRIER delivered the opinion of the court.

This action was brought by Derby, the plaintiff below, to recover damages for an injury suffered on the railroad of the plaintiffs in error. The peculiar facts of the case, involving the questions of law presented for our consideration, are these:

The plaintiff below was himself the president of another railroad company, and a stockholder in this. He was on the road of defendants by invitation of the president of the company, not in the usual passenger cars, but in a small locomotive car used for the convenience of the officers of the company, and paid no fare for his transportation. The injury to his person was caused by coming into collision with a locomotive and tender, in the charge of an agent or servant of the company, which was on the same track, and moving in an opposite direction. Another agent of the company, in the exercise of proper care and caution, had given orders to keep this track clear. The driver of the colliding engine acted in disobedience and disregard of those orders, and thus caused the collision.

The instructions given by the court below, at the instance of plaintiff, as well as those requested by the defendant, and refused by the court, taken together, involve but two distinct points, which have been the subject of exception here, and are in substance as follows:

1. The court instructed the jury, that if the plaintiff was lawfully on the road at the time of the collision, and the collision and consequent injury to him were caused by the gross negligence of one of the servants of the defendants, then and there employed on the road, he is entitled to recover, notwithstanding the circumstances given in evidence, and relied upon by defendant's counsel as forming a defence to the action, to wit: that the plaintiff was a stockholder in the company, riding by invitation of the president—paying no fare, and not in the usual passenger cars, &c.

2. That the fact that the engineer having the control of the colliding locomotive, was forbidden to run on that track at the time, and had acted in disobedience of such orders, was not a defence to the action.

1st. In support of the objections to the first instruction, it is alleged, " that no cause of action can arise to any person by reason of the occurrence of an unintentional injury, while he is receiving or partaking of any of those acts of kindness which spring from mere social relations; and that as there was no contract between the parties, express or implied, the law would raise no duty as between them, for the neglect of which an action can be sustained."

In support of these positions, the cases between innkeeper and guest have been cited, such as 1 Rolle's Abr. 3, where it is said, " If a host invite one to supper, and the night being far spent, he invites him to stay all night, and the guest be robbed, yet the host shall not be chargeable, because the guest was not a traveller;" and Cayle's case, (4 Rep. 52,) to the same effect, showing that the peculiar liability of an innkeeper arises from the consideration paid for his entertainment of travellers, and does not exist in the case of gratuitous lodging of friends or guests. The case of Farwell v. The Boston and Worcester Railroad Company, (4 Metcalf, 47,) has also been cited, showing that the master is not liable for any injury received by one of his servants, in consequence of the carelessness of another, while both are engaged in the same service.

But we are of opinion, that these cases have no application to the present. The liability of the defendants below, for the negligent and injurious act of their servant, is not necessarily founded on any contract or privity between the parties, nor affected by any relation, social or otherwise, which they bore to each other. It is true, a traveller, by stage coach, or other public conveyance, who is injured by the negligence of the driver, has an action against the owner, founded on his contract to carry him safely. But the maxim of "*respondeat superior*," which, by legal imputation, makes the master liable for the acts of his servant, is wholly irrespective of any contract, express or implied, or any other relation between the injured party and the master. If one be lawfully on the street or highway, and another's servant carelessly drives a stage or carriage against him, and injures his property or person, it is no answer to an action against the master for such injury, either, that the plaintiff was riding for pleasure, or that he was a stockholder in the road, or that he had not paid his toll, or that he was the guest of the defendant, or riding in a carriage borrowed from him, or that the defendant was the friend, benefactor, or brother of the plaintiff. These arguments, arising from the social or domestic relations of life may, in some cases, successfully appeal to the feelings of the plaintiff, but will usually have little effect where the defendant is a corporation, which is itself incapable of such relations or the reciprocation of such feelings.

In this view of the case, if the plaintiff was lawfully on the road at the time of the collision, the court were right in instructing the jury that none of the antecedent circumstances, or accidents of his situation, could affect his right to recover.

It is a fact peculiar to this case, that the defendants, who are liable for the act of their servant coming down the road, are also the carriers who were conveying the plaintiff up the road, and that their servants immediately engaged in transporting the plaintiff were not guilty of any negligence, or in fault for the collision. But we would not have it inferred, from what has been said, that the circumstances alleged in the first point would affect the case, if the negligence which caused the injury had been committed by the agents of the company who were in the immediate care of the engine and car in which the plaintiff rode, and he was compelled to rely on these counts of his declaration, founded on the duty of the defendant to carry him safely. This duty does not result alone from the consideration paid for the service. It is imposed by the law, even where the service is gratuitous. "The confidence induced by undertaking any service for another, is a sufficient legal consideration to create a duty in the performance of it." See Coggs v. Bernard, and cases cited in 1 Smith's Leading Cases, 95. It is true, a distinction has been taken, in some cases, between simple negligence, and great or gross negligence; and it is said, that one who

41*

acts gratuitously is liable only for the latter. But this case does not call upon us to define the difference, (if it be capable of definition,) as the verdict has found this to be a case of gross negligence.

When carriers undertake to convey persons by the powerful but dangerous agency of steam, public policy and safety require that they be held to the greatest possible care and diligence. And whether the consideration for such transportation be pecuniary or otherwise, the personal safety of the passengers should not be left to the sport of chance or the negligence of careless agents. Any negligence, in such cases, may well deserve the epithet of "gross."

In this view of the case, also, we think there was no error in the first instruction.

2. The second instruction involves the question of the liability of the master where the servant is in the course of his employment, but, in the matter complained of, has acted contrary to the express command of his master.

The rule of "*respondeat superior*," or that the master shall be civilly liable for the tortious acts of his servant, is of universal application, whether the act be one of omission or commission, whether negligent, fraudulent, or deceitful. If it be done in the course of his employment, the master is liable; and it makes no difference that the master did not authorize, or even know of the servant's act or neglect, or even if he disapproved or forbade it, he is equally liable, if the act be done in the course of his servant's employment. See Story on Agency, § 452; Smith on Master and Servant, 152.

There may be found, in some of the numerous cases reported on this subject, dicta which, when severed from the context, might seem to countenance the doctrine that the master is not liable if the act of his servant was in disobedience of his orders. But a more careful examination will show that they depended on the question, whether the servant, at the time he did the act complained of, was acting in the course of his employment, or in other words, whether he was or was not at the time in the relation of servant to the defendant.

The case of Sleath *v.* Wilson, (9 Car. & Payne, 607,) states the law in such cases distinctly and correctly.

In that case a servant, having his master's carriage and horses in his possession and control, was directed to take them to a certain place; but instead of doing so he went in another direction to deliver a parcel of his own, and, returning, drove against an old woman and injured her. Here the master was held liable for the act of the servant, though at the time he committed the offence, he was acting in disregard of his master's orders; because the master had intrusted the carriage to his control and care, and in driving it he was acting in the course of his employment. Mr. Justice Erskine remarks, in this case: "It is quite clear that if a servant, without his master's knowledge, takes his master's carriage out of the coach-house, and with it commits an injury, the master is not answerable, and on this ground, that the master has not intrusted the servant with the carriage; but whenever the master has intrusted the servant with the control of the carriage, it is no answer, that the servant acted improperly in the management of it. If it were, it might be contended that if a master directs his servant to drive slowly, and the servant disobeys his orders, and drives fast, and through his negligence occasions an injury, the master will not be liable. But that is not the law; the master, in such a case, will be liable, and the ground is, that he has put it in the servant's power to mismanage the carriage, by intrusting him with it."

Although, among the numerous cases on this subject, some may be found (such as the case of Lamb v. Palk, 9 C. & P. 629) in which the court have made some distinctions which are rather subtile and astute, as to when the servant may be said to be acting in the employ of his master; yet we find no case which asserts the doctrine that a master is not liable for the acts of a servant in his employment, when the particular act causing the injury was done in disregard of the general orders or special command of the master. Such a qualification of the maxim of *respondeat superior*, would, in a measure, nullify it. A large proportion of the accidents on railroads are caused by the negligence of the servants or agents of the company. Nothing but the most stringent enforcement of discipline, and the most exact and perfect obedience to every rule and order emanating from a superior, can insure safety to life and property. The intrusting such a powerful and dangerous engine as a locomotive, to one who will not submit to control, and render implicit obedience to orders, is itself an act of negligence, the "*causa causans*" of the mischief; while the proximate cause, or the *ipsa negligentia* which produces it, may truly be said, in most cases, to be the disobedience of orders by the servant so intrusted. If such disobedience could be set up by a railroad company as a defence, when charged with negligence, the remedy of the injured party would in most cases be illusive, discipline would be relaxed, and the danger to the life and limb of the traveller greatly enhanced. Any relaxation of the stringent policy and principles of the law affecting such cases, would be highly detrimental to the public safety.

The judgment of the Circuit Court is therefore affirmed.

Mr. Justice DANIEL dissents from the decision of this court in this car ·, upon the ground that the said railroad company being a corporation, created by the State of Pennsylvania, is not capable of pleading or being impleaded, under the 2d section of the 3d article of the constitution, in any of the courts of the United States; and that therefore the Circuit Court could not take cognizance of the controversy between that corporation and the plaintiff in that court.

Order.

This cause came on to be heard, on the transcript of the record, from the Circuit Court of the United States for the Eastern District of Pennsylvania, and was argued by counsel. On consideration whereof, it is now here ordered, and adjudged, by this court, that the judgment of the said circuit court, in this cause be, and the same is hereby, affirmed, with costs and interest until the same is paid at the same rate per annum that similar judgments bear in the courts of the State of Pennsylvania.

HENRY WEBSTER, PLAINTIFF IN ERROR, v. PETER COOPER.

A will, executed in 1777, which devised certain lands in Maine, to trustees and their heirs to the use of Richard (the son of the testator) for life, remainder, for his life in case of forfeiture, to the trustees to preserve contingent remainders; remainder to the sons of Richard, if any, as tenants in common in tail, with cross remainders; remainder to Richard's daughter Elizabeth, for life; remainder to trustees to preserve contingent remainders during her life; remainder to the sons of Elizabeth in tail, — did not vest the legal estate in fee simple in the trustees. The life estate of Richard, and the contingent remainders limited thereon, were legal estates.

No duties were imposed on the trustees which could prevent the legal estate in these lands from vesting in the *cestuis que use*; and although such duties might have been required of them relating to other lands in the devise, yet this circumstance would not control the construction of the devise as to these lands.

The devise to Elizabeth for life, remainder to her sons as tenants in common, share and share alike, and to the heirs of their bodies, did not give an estate tail to Elizabeth, under the rule in Shelly's case. But upon her death, her son (the party to the suit) took as a purchaser, an estate tail in one moiety of the land, as a tenant in common with his brother.

One of the conditions of the devise was, that this party, as soon as he should come into possession of the lands, should take the name of the testator. But as he had not yet come into possession, and it was a condition subsequent, of which only the person to whom the lands were devised over, could take advantage, a non-compliance with it was no defence, in an action brought to recover possession of the land.

The son, taking an estate tail at the death of Elizabeth, in 1845, could maintain a writ of entry, and until that time had no right of possession. Consequently, the adverse possession of the occupant only began then.

In 1848, the Legislature of Maine passed an act declaring that no real or mixed action should be commenced or maintained against any person in possession of lands, where such person had been in actual possession for more than forty years, claiming to hold the same in his own right, and which possession should have been adverse, open. peaceable, notorious, and exclusive. This act was passed two years after the suit was commenced.

The effect of this act was to make the seisin of the occupant during the lifetime of Elizabeth, adverse against her son, when he had no right of possession.

This act, which thus purported to take away property from one man and vest it in another, was contrary to the constitution of the State of Maine, as expounded by the highest courts of law in that State. And as this court looks to the decisions of the courts of a State to explain its statutes, there is no reason why it should not also look to them to expound its constitution.

THIS case was brought up, by writ of error, from the Circuit Court of the United States for the District of Maine.

The facts are set forth in the opinion of the court.

Upon the trial in the Circuit Court, the demandant's (Webster's) counsel, prayed the court to instruct the jury as follows:

1. That the act of the Legislature of Maine, of the year 1848, ch. 87, is not applicable to any case in which the title of the demandant had accrued before the passage of said act.

2. That said act is not applicable to the present action, the same having been commenced before the passage of said act.

3. That said act is void, because it is in violation of the constitution of the State of Maine, (Art. 1, § 21,) and because it is retrospective in its operation upon vested rights of the demandant.

4. That said act is void, because it is in violation of the Constitution of the United States, as being a law impairing the obligation of contracts.

5. That by the true and legal construction of the will of Florentius Vassall, said Elizabeth Vassall took only an estate for life in the demanded premises.

6. That by the true and legal construction of the will of Florentius Vassall, the demandant took a remainder in tail male, as tenant in common with said Henry Edward Fox, in the demanded premises expectant on the life estate of said Elizabeth Vassall.

7. That the demandant is not barred from recovering one undivided half of the demanded premises by the statutes of limitation of the States of Maine or Massachusetts, or any of them.

8. That if the demandant shows a right to recover one undivided half of the demanded premises, he may recover the same under the writ in this case, although he therein demands the whole of said demanded premises.

9. That it is not necessary, for the purpose of enabling the demandant to recover in this action, that he should have taken the name of Vassall.　　　F. DEXTER and E. H. DAVEIS,
Counsel for Henry Webster.

But the honorable Judges, who presided at the said trial, declined to give to the jury any of the said instructions so prayed for by the demandant's counsel; but, on the contrary thereof, did instruct the jury, that by the true and lawful construction of the said will of Florentius Vassall, no legal estate in the demanded premises, or any part thereof, was ever vested in the demandant, but that, if the legal estate in the demanded premises was, and by force and effect of the said will, vested in any person or persons, it was thereby vested and continued to be in the trustees named in said will, viz., Lord Viscount Falmouth, Lord Viscount Barrington, and Charles Spooner, Esq., the survivors and survivor of them, and the heirs of such survivor; and that, therefore, the demandant could not maintain the present action to recover the same, and that it was, therefore, unnecessary to instruct the jury upon the other points mentioned in the demandant's prayer for instructions; whereas the said counsel for the demandant respectfully insist that the said Judges ought not so to have instructed the jury, but ought to have instructed them upon the matters and in the manner prayed for by the said counsel as aforesaid; and they did, therefore, except in law to the said instruction and said refusal of the said Judges; and, inasmuch as the several matters aforesaid do not appear by the record of said verdict, the said counsel have made and tendered to the said Judges this, their bill of exceptions, and pray that the same may be allowed.

All which being considered, and found conformable to the truth of the case, the presiding Judge has allowed this bill of exceptions, and hath thereto put his seal, this 28th day of April, in the year one thousand eight hundred and fifty-one.

[SEAL.]   LEVI WOODBURY,
Ass. Jus. Sup. Court.

The case was argued in this court by *Mr. Daveis*, with whom was *Mr. Dexter*, for the plaintiff in error, and by *Mr. Allen*, for the defendant in error.

The counsel for the plaintiff in error, made the following points:

1. A devise to A, and his heirs, to the use of, or in trust for B, vests the legal estate immediately in B. 2 Jarm. on Wills, 196, 198, 199; Hill on Trustees, Part 2, ch. 1, p. 229; 1 Greenl. Cruise, 346–7, note; Webster *v.* Gilman, 1 Story's R. 499, 515.

2. Where duties are imposed on the trustees which make it necessary that they should take the legal estate, the extent and duration of that estate are limited to exactly that quantity of interest which the purposes of the trust require. 2 Jarm. 213;

Hill on Trustees, Part 2, ch. 2; 1 Greenl. Cruise, 348, note; Doe *v.* Ironmonger, 3 East, 533; Robinson *v.* Grey, 9 East, 1; Curtis *v.* Price, 12 Ves. 89; Doe *v.* Hicks, 7 T. R. 433; Doe *v.* Barthorp, 5 Taunt. 382, 385; Doe *v.* Simpson, 5 East, 163; 1 Hill. Real Prop. ch. 22, § 21, and §§ 27 to 31.

3. There are no duties imposed on the trustees by the will in this case, in relation to the demanded premises, nor is there any other expression of the intention of the testator to give them the legal estate.

4. The only duties imposed are, by the terms of the will, expressly confined to other lands, viz., to the Friendship and Greenwich plantations. And the purposes of those duties have been fully performed and discharged. Whether the trustees took a legal estate in those plantations at any time, may depend on the local law in Jamaica. Under our laws they would take but a chattel interest, as they were only to apply the rents and profits. Hill on Trustees, 240, 241, and cases cited to the second point.

5. The successive remainders limited to the use of the same trustees, to preserve contingent remainders in case of forfeiture, show that it was not the intention of the testator that the legal estate should vest in them originally. Curtis *v.* Price, 12 Ves. 100; Doe *v.* Hicks, 7 T. R. 433, 437; Fearne, Cont. Rem. 177, 178; Hill on Trustees, 240–1.

6. The act of Maine, 1848, ch. 87, is void as impairing the obligation of contracts. Fletcher *v.* Peck, 6 Cranch, 87, 137; 3 Story on Const. § 1385.

7. It is void, as it takes away vested rights. Wilkinson *v.* Leland, 2 Pet. S. C. R. 657, 658, Story, J.; Society, &c. *v.* Wheeler, 2 Gall. 105, 141; Ham *v.* McClaws, 1 Bay, 93; Bowman *v.* Middleton, 1 Bay, 252; Dash *v.* Van Kleek, 7 Johns. 502, Kent, Ch. J.; Call *v.* Hagger, 8 Mass. 423; 1 Kent, 455.

Taking away all remedy, is taking away the right. Bronson *v.* Kinzie, 1 How. 317, 318; Bruce *v.* Schuyler, 4 Gilman, R. 221, 277; Story on Const. § 1379; Sturges *v.* Crowninshield, 4 Wheat. 207; Gilmer *v.* Shooter, 2 Mod. R. 310.

8. It is void as against the constitution of Maine. Proprietors, &c. *v.* Laborce, 2 Greenl. 275, 294; Oriental Bank *v.* Freeze, 18 Me. R. 109, 112; Austin *v.* Stevens, 11 Shepley, 520; Constitution of Maine, Art. 1, §§ 1, 19, 21.

9. The will in this case gave a life estate only in the demanded premises to Elizabeth Vassall, with remainder to her sons as tenants in common. Willis *v.* Hiscox, 4 Myl. & Cr. 197; Right *v.* Creber, 5 Barn. & Cres. 860; Doe *v.* Laming, 2 Burrow, 1100; Backhouse *v.* Wells, 1 Eq. Abr. 184; White *v.* Collins, 1 Com. 289; Sisson *v.* Seabury, 1 Sumn. 235; Dingley *v.* Dingley, 5 Mass. 535; Webster *v.* Gilman, 1 Story, 499, 514; 2 Jarm. 235, 315; Fearne, Cont. Rem. 150.

10. "Sons" and "children" are words of purchase, and not of limitation. 2 Jarm. 343, 344, 352 to 356; 1 Rolle's Abridg. 837, pl. 13; Buffar v. Bradford, 2 Atk. 220; Lowe v. Davis, 2 Ld. Raym. 1561; Goodtitle v. Herring, 1 East, 264; Walker v. Snow, Palm. 359; Archer's case, 1 Coke, 66; Lisle v. Gray, 2 Lev. 223; Dingley v. Dingley, 5 Mass. R. 535; 1 Fearne, Cont. R. 150, 151, &c.; 2 Jarm. 301, 302, &c.; Doe v. Simpson, 5 Scott, 770; Doe v. Webber, 1 B. & Ald. 713; Sisson v. Seabury, 1 Sumn. 235.

The word "sons" has been held to control the words "heirs of the body," to make them words of purchase. Lowe v. Davies, 2 Ld. Raym. 1561; Lisle v. Gray, 2 Lev. 223; Goodtitle v. Herring, 1 East, 264; cited 2 Jarm. 301, 302; and also "issue male;" Mandeville v. Lackey, 3 Ridgw. P. C. 352.

The word "son" in the singular, can create an estate tail only when used as *nomen collectivum*, and where it is the manifest intention of the testator to give such an estate. Mellish v. Mellish, 2 B. & C. 520; cited 2 Jarm. 320.

11. The devise to the sons of Elizabeth Vassal as tenants in common, shows that it was not the testator's intention to give her an estate tail. These words control even the words "issue of the body," so that they take as purchasers. Doe v. Burnsall, 6 D. & E. 30; Burnsall v. Davy, 1 Bos. & P. 215; Doe v. Collins. 4 D. & E. 294.

12. The plaintiff's right of entry accrued at the death of Elizabeth, in 1845, and is not barred by adverse possession. Wells v. Prince, 9 Mass. 508; Wallingford v. Hearl, 15 Mass. 471; Angell on Lim. 42; 2 Sugd. Vend. 216, 323, 324.

13. The condition of taking the name of Vassal, is subsequent, and no one but the devisee over can take advantage of it. Gulliver v. Ashby, 4 Burrows, 1929; Taylor v. Mason, 9 Wheat 325, 349; Finlay v. King's Lessee, 3 Pet. 347, 374; 1 Jarm. 805.

14. The plaintiff can recover a moiety in this action. 6 Dane's Abr. 61; Dewey v. Brown, 2 Pick. 387; Somes v. Skinner, 3 Id. 52; Holyoke v. Haskins, 9 Id. 259; Rev. Stat. Maine, p. 610, §§ 12, 13.

Mr. Allen, for the defendant in error, made the following points:

1. That there is no error in the District Court in declining to give the instructions requested by said plaintiffs in error, as contained in the assignment of errors, from No. 1 to No. 9, both inclusive. Because, if there is no error in the tenth assignment, but the instruction therein given, was correct, plaintiff in error was not prejudiced by the withholding the instructions in the

preceding nine requests. Greenleaf v. Birth, 5 Pet. R. 132; Binney v. Chas. & Ohio Canal Co. 8 Pet. R. 214; U. S. Bank v. Planters Bank, Gill & Johns. R. 439; Watts & Serg. 391.

2. But if. the instructions in first four assignments of errors had been material and injurious to plaintiff in error, they were correct and not erroneous; that the act of the Legislature of Maine of the year 1848, ch. 87, is valid and not liable to any legal objection, and is not in violation of the constitution of Maine, Art. 1, § 21, or of the Constitution of the United States. Phalen v. Virginia, 8 How. U. S. 168. " Such acts (Lim.) giving peace and quiet, may be said to effect or complete divesture or transfer of rights, yet as reasons have led to their validity, cannot be questioned." Id. S. P. 585, Mills v. St. Clair County. " Such laws do not impair the obligation of contracts within the sense of the Const. U. S." Townsend v. Jemison, 9 How. U. S. 407, 419, 420; and cases cited 10 How. U. S. 395, 401, 402, Bal. & Susquehanñah R. R. v. Nesbit.

" No real or mixed action for the recovery of any lands in this State, shall be commenced or maintained against any person in possession of such lands, where such person or those under whom he claims, have been in actual possession for more than forty years, and claiming to hold the same in his, her, or their own right, and which possession shall have been adverse, open, peaceable, notorious, and exclusive. To take effect in one day after approval." Act of Maine, Aug. 11, 1848.

3. The said act may apply to actions then pending. Thayer v. Seavey, 11 Maine Rep. 284; Bacon v. Callender, 6 Mass. Rep. 309; 2 Gall. Rep. 315, 319. Stat. Lim. Rhode Island, no objection that it went into immediate operation. Story, J.

4. There was no error in the Circuit Court in refusing to give the instructions in the 5th and 6th assignment. They were properly declined; and cannot be assigned for error if the instruction in the 10th assignment was properly given.

5. There is no error in withholding the instructions requested in the 7th and 8th assignment. They were rightly withheld; and plaintiff was not injured thereby. The same may be said of the 9th instruction, contained in 9th assignment of errors.

6. No error in the Circuit Court in giving the instruction in the 10th assignment of errors.

1st, The fee-simple and whole legal estate in the premises was by the will of F. Vassal devised to Lord Falmouth and others and their heirs, as trustees; this action cannot be maintained, not being in their names or that of their heirs. Sanders, Uses & Trusts, 190–1, 197, 202, 3–4. 2 Jar. on Wills, 198–9, 202; Leicester v. Biggs, 2 Taunt. Rep. 109; Biscoe v. Perkins, 1 Ves. & Bea. 485; White v. Parker, 1 Scott, 542; Harton v.

Harton, 7 D. & E. 652; Gregory v. Henderson, 4 Taunt. 772; Cursham v. Newland, 2 Moo. & Scott, 113; Tompkins v. Willon, 2 Barn. & Ald. 84; Brewster v. Striker, 2 Comstock's Rep. 19, and note, 581–2.

2d. The purposes for which the legal estate was originally devised to the trustees, still continue to exist, viz., to preserve the remainders; viz., to "same trustees" for George Barrington in tail and his issue male and his issue female. In same manner to Richard Barrington and issue — same manner to William Barrington and issue; then to testator's granddaughter, Louisa Barrington and her fourth son and 'daughters, then to Rose Hening May and her issue; the words "same trustees" prior to each devise in remainder. On failure of all these to the use of the ministers and wardens of Westmoreland. 2 Jar. on Wills, 200, 202, 203–228. It was the intention of the testator that the legal estate should remain in the trustees until all the remainders should be executed. It is so expressed in the will.

3d. It is agreed that the persons named in said will, or devises in remainder, after the failure of issue of Elizabeth Vassal, or their lineal descendants, are now living.

4th. Trustees must hold the legal estate, as long as any of the remainders are outstanding; repetition of devise to same trustees to preserve six now unexecuted remainders, Jar. 222.

5th. Necessary that the trustees should hold the legal estate for other purposes, viz., out of the rents and profits &c., they were to purchase negroes, cattle and stock, and other utensils.

They were to appoint agents, attorneys, and managers. 2 Barn. & Ald. 84; Id. 554; 2 Jar. 223–5; 6 Barn. & Cress. 420; Morton v. Barrett, 22 Maine Rep. 257. Testator recommends that trustees should appoint his son Richard manager, at their discretion. They are to approve marriage jointures — assumes that money will pass through their hands — they may deduct and retain; discretion as to time of paying £10,000 — gives L. Falmouth 100 guineas for a ring; the other £50 cash for same purpose. Record, 29.

6th. The imbecility of testator's son Richard and the infancy of his granddaughter Elizabeth is a sufficient reason why he should devise the legal estate to trustees; still less, could he anticipate, with any certainty, the existence of unborn sons of his granddaughter. All the estates were over 3000 miles distant. Not named in the will in what State in New England his lands were situate. Trustees most competent to look them up. The cestui que trusts most incompetent.

7th. Another object of testator in giving the legal estate to trustees, would be to prevent cestui que trusts from docking the entailment and defeating subsequent remainders by common recovery, without the legal estate, they could make no legal tenant to the precipe.

8th. It is competent for defendant to urge and maintain this objection. And to show the legal title in others, and thereby disprove plaintiff's seisin. Cutler v. Lincoln, 3 Cush. Rep. 128.

Tenant may give in evidence, title of a third person, without claiming under said third person for the purpose of disproving plaintiff's seisin in a writ of entry. Jack. on Real Actions, 157; Stearns on Real Actions, 365, 380–9; Hall v. Stevens, 9 Met. Rep. 418.

9th. In this case, defendant has no need of invoking that principle; for plaintiff himself introduces the will, by which it is seen that the legal title is in other persons than the plaintiff.

10th. The acquiescence of Lady Holland, the mother of plaintiff, in the open, exclusive, and adverse possession of defendant, and those under whom he claims from the time of her divorce from her first husband, till her decease, (a period of about fifty years) tends to prove that neither she nor her second husband ever claimed the legal estate to be in her.

No error in four first assignments. See brief, 2d point.

1. If the court should decide that there is error in the tenth assignment, and that the legal estate is not in the trustees, it is then contended that there is no error in withholding the instructions from the 5th and 9th requests; for if the legal estate was in the *cestui que trusts*, Elizabeth, mother of plaintiff, took an estate tail, and not for life only, and she is barred by the Statute of Limitations of Massachusetts and Maine, and so is the plaintiff. Shelly's case, 1 Coke, R. 93; 2 Jar. 241 to 249; Doug. 321, 324; Soule v. Soule, 5 Mass. R. 61; 19 Ves. 175; Malcom v. Malcom, 3 Cush. 472.

2. Plaintiff takes, by limitation under the will, an estate tail. Co. R. lib. 6, fol. 17, Wyld's case; Robinson v. Robinson, 1 Burr. R. 38; 2 Jar. 271, 272, 287; Chandler v. Smith, 7 D. & E. 532; Pearson v. Vickers, 5 East, R. 548; Jesson v. Wright, 2 Bligh, R. 258; Coulson v. Coulson, 2 Strange, R. 1125; Brook v. Astley, 3 Burr. R. 1570; 4 Barn. & Cress. 610; 1 Barn. & Ald. R. 944; Parkman v. Bowdoin, 1 Sumn. R. 359; Fearne on Remain. 118, 124; 4 Kent's Com. 214 to 232.

3. Sons, at time of will unborn, words of limitation. Wharton v. Graham, 2 W. Black. R. 1083; 1 Vent. 231, cited by Hale, C. J., in King v. Snelling; Byfield's case, 1 East, R. 229; Doe dem Cook v. Cooper, 2 Barn. & Cress. 524; 2 Barn. & Adol. R. 87; 4 Id. 43; 5 Id. 421; 2 Jar. 394 to 470; 4 Barn. & Cress. 610; 1 Moore, 682, pl. 939; Sondy's case, 9 Co. R. 127; Inman v. Barnes, 2 Gall. 315; 15 Ves. R. 546.

Rule in Shelly's case in force in Massachusetts till March 8th,

1792, 14 years after probate of this will. Davis *v.* Hayden, 9 Mass. 514 ; 4 Pick. 206 ; 15 Pick. 104 ; 7 Met. R. 172 ; Id. 425 ; Jones *v.* Morgan, 1 Brown, C. C. 206, Lord Thurlow. Plaintiff sues as tenant in tail. Shoemaker *v.* Sheely, 2 Den. 485.

Mr. Justice CURTIS delivered the opinion of the court.

Henry Webster, an alien, and subject of Great Britain, brought his writ of entry in the Circuit Court of the United States for the District of Maine, to recover possession of a parcel of land described in the count. He claims title under a will of Florentius Vassall. At the trial, the parties agreed on the following facts :

" It is agreed, by the parties, that the following statement of facts is true, namely, that the demanded premises belonged to the proprietors of the Kennebec Purchase, and were by them duly granted and assigned to Florentius Vassall, one of the proprietors in fee, in the year 1756, being included in the grant recorded in the records of the proprietary.

" That Florentius Vassall made his will September 20th, 1777, and died at London, 1778, seised of the lands in question, they then being unoccupied wild lands. The will was afterwards duly proved in the Prerogative Court of Canterbury, September 14, 1778, a copy of which will, with its exemplifications, has been duly filed and recorded in the Probate Office for the county of Kennebec ; which will was offered in evidence, as copied, and makes a part of this case. (C.)

" Richard Vassall, named in the will, died about 1795, leaving only one child, Elizabeth Vassall, who married Sir Godfrey Webster, deceased, about the first day of January, 1793, by whom she had issue, two sons, namely, Sir Godfrey Vassall Webster, who died in the lifetime of said Elizabeth, without issue, and Henry Webster, the demandant. ' Said Elizabeth, afterwards, namely, in January, 1796, was legally divorced from her husband, the said Sir Godfrey Webster, and on the first day of July, 1797, she was legally joined in marriage with Richard Henry Fox, afterwards Lord Holland, by whom she had issue, one son, Henry Edward Fox, who is now living. All charges upon the land devised have been satisfied, and they are not now subject to any life estate, estate for years, or outstanding terms, under the will. Said Lord Holland died on the ——— 1841 ; said Lady Holland died in the fall of the year 1845. The persons named in said will as devisees in remainder, after the failure of the issue of said Elizabeth, or their lineal descendants, are now living in England, as is the said Henry Edward Fox, son of said Elizabeth. That said Florentius Vassall, was, at the time of said grant, a resident in Boston, State of Massachusetts; that he, on or before the year 1775, left his said residence, went to England, and never returned; and that neither he, nor any of the devisees named in said will, have ever resided within the limits of the United States since that time. The premises demanded, being the matter in dispute, are of greater value than two thousand dollars.

" The tenant, and those from whom he legally derives title to said demanded premises, have been in the quiet, undisturbed, open, notorious, and exclusive possession and occupation of said premises for and during the term of fifty years next preceding the commencement of this action, he and they claiming to hold the same adversely to any claim of said demandant, or any other person, as his and their own property in fee-simple."

These facts, together with the will of Florentius Vassall, made the case. By this will the testator devised three plantations in Jamaica, and all his lands in New England, (which included the demanded premises,) to Lord Falmouth, Lord Barrington, and Mr. Charles Spooner, and their heirs, to the uses, upon the trusts, and for the intents and purposes, and with and subject to the powers and provisos therein expressed. The will then proceeds to declare, in respect to all the lands in New England, as follows: To the use of my son, Richard Vassall, for and during his life, and from and after the determination of that estate by forfeiture, or otherwise, during his life, to the use of the three trustees during the life of Richard Vassall, in trust to preserve the contingent uses and estates thereinafter mentioned, and for that purpose to make entries and bring actions as occasion shall require, but nevertheless to permit Richard Vassall to take the rents of the premises to his own use during his life. The testator then declares the remainder, after the death of Richard, to be to the use of the son and sons of Richard, to be equally divided between them, share and share alike, as tenants in common, and not as joint tenants, and to the several and respective heirs male of the bodies of such sons, with cross remainders among them; and in default of such issue male of Richard, subject to a term of years, which it is agreed is not outstanding, to the use of Elizabeth Vassall, the daughter of Richard, for her life, with remainder as before stated to the trustees for the life of Elizabeth to preserve contingent remainders, in case of forfeiture of her life estate; and then follows the provision under which the demandant claims title, which is therefore given in the words of the will. "And from and immediately after the decease of the said Elizabeth Vassall, to the one or all and every the son and sons of the said Elizabeth Vassall, to be begotten to be divided between or amongst such sons, if more than one, share and share alike, and they to take

42 *

as tenants in common, and not as joint tenants, and the several and respective heirs male of the body and bodies of all and every such son and sons issuing." Then follow remainders to the other daughters of Richard, as tenants in common in tail general, with cross remainders; remainder to the daughters of Elizabeth Vassall, as tenants in common in tail general, with cross remainders, — with successive remainders to George and Richard, and William Barrington, testator's grandsons, for life; remainder to their sons, as tenants in common in tail male; remainder to testator's granddaughter, Louisa Barrington, for life, and her sons in common in tail male; remainder to her daughters, as tenants in common in tail general; remainder to testator's daughter, Elizabeth Barrington, for life; remainder to her other sons "in tail male successively;" remainder to her future daughters, as tenants in common in tail; remainder to testator's nephew May, for life; remainder to his sons in common in tail male; remainder to his daughters in common in tail; remainder to the minister and wardens of Westmoreland, &c.

These are the most material provisions of the will of these lands, and are sufficient to show its general structure, in reference to the questions which have been made concerning its legal effect.

The first of these question is, whether, by force of the will, the demandant took any, and if any, what legal estate in these lands on the decease of his mother, Elizabeth Vassall.

It is insisted, by the tenant's counsel, that the trustees took the legal estate in fee simple, and that the estates limited to Richard Vassall for life, and to the others, by way of remainder, were only equitable estates, and consequently the demandant cannot maintain this action.

But whether we look to the evident intent of the testator, or to the settled technical meaning of the language he has employed, we think it clearly appears that the life estate of Richard Vassall and the contingent remainders limited thereon were legal estates, and that the trustees did not hold the fee-simple under this will. The instrument was drawn in England, evidently by a skilful draughtsman, and is in strict conformity with well-known precedents. It employs technical language with accuracy, and all the various provisions of the will, though numerous and complicated, compared with the usually simple testamentary dispositions of property in this country, are capable of being clearly understood and fully executed. The substance of the devises of these lands, may be stated to be: to the trustees and their heirs to the use of Richard for life, remainder, for his life in case of forfeiture, to the trustees to preserve contingent remainders; remainder to the sons of Richard, if any, as tenants in common in tail, with cross remainders; remainder to Richard's daughter Elizabeth for life; remainder to trustees to preserve contingent remainders during her life; remainder to the sons of Elizabeth in tail, the demandant being the elder of her two sons.

A devise to the trustees and their heirs to the uses mentioned, carries the legal estate to the *cestuis que use*, unless the will has imposed on the trustees some duty, the performance of which requires the legal estate to be vested in them. And in that case they would take an estate exactly commensurate with the exigencies of their trust. Morrant v. Gough, 7 B. & C. 206; Kenrick v. Lord Beauclerck, 3 B. & P. 178; 10 Bythewood on Con. 214; Jarm. on Wills, 198–9; Nielson v. Lagow, 12 How. 110, 111; 1 Greenl. Cruise, 346–7, note.

The testator has not imposed on the trustees any duties, connected with these lands, which in any way interfere with the existence of legal estates in the different beneficiaries named in the will. On the contrary, the sole duties to be performed by them, in reference to these lands, are to take the life estates, in case of forfeiture, and hold them, so that the future remaindermen may not be deprived of the legal estates limited to them by way of contingent remainders, which require the preservation of the particular estates to support them.

Whether the trustees took and held any legal estate in either of the plantations in Jamaica, it is not necessary to determine. It was argued that they did, because they have some duties to perform concerning two of them, and that the testator employs the same language in devising these two plantations to the trustees, as he does in devising the lands in New England. But it by no means follows that the same words devising to trustees two parcels of land, must necessarily vest the legal estates in both parcels in the trustees, because they take a legal estate in one of those parcels. They may take a legal estate in one, because subsequent parts of the will require them to do acts in reference to it, which can be done only by the holder of the legal estate, and then the law assigns to them such an estate as the due execution of their trust demands; while at the same time, by force of the statute of uses, or of wills, the other land, as to which no duties are required of the trustees, goes to the *cestuis que use.*

So far as this will operates on the lands in New England, there is nothing to prevent the usual and settled operation of a devise to uses, which is, to vest the legal estate in the *cestuis que use;* and it is placed beyond all doubt that it was not intended the trustees should hold the fee, because there are express limitations of life estates to them to preserve contingent remainders, which would be wholly inoperative if they took the fee, and is sufficient of itself to control any doubtful intent, according to Doe *v.* Hicks, 7 T. R. 433; Curtis *v.* Price, 12 Ves. 100.

Our conclusion is that the legal estates in the New England lands, were to go to the beneficiaries named in the will.

It is further urged by the tenant's counsel, that the legal effect of the devise to Elizabeth Vassall for life, remainder to her sons, as tenants in common, share and share alike, and to the heirs of their bodies, gave an estate tail to Elizabeth Vassall, under the rule in Shelly's case, which was in force in Massachusetts, within whose limits these lands lay at the time this will took effect. There is no doubt this rule made part of the law of Massachusetts until the 8th of March, 1792, when it was abolished by statute, so far as it respects wills. Bowers *v.* Porter, 4 Pick. 198; Steel *v.* Cook, 1 Met. 282. But in our opinion, the rule in Shelly's case is not applicable to this devise. That rule is, that when the ancestor, by any gift or conveyance, takes an estate of freehold, and in the same gift or conveyance an estate is limited, either immediately or mediately, to his heirs in fee or in tail, that the words heirs, &c., are words of limitation, and not of purchase.

Here the life estate is limited to Elizabeth Vassall, and the remainder to her sons as tenants in common, share and share alike, and the heirs of their bodies. The fee tail is not limited to the heirs in tail of the first taker. The heir in tail was this demandant; and the remainder is not limited to him, but to him and his brother, as tenants in common. It is not a question, therefore, whether the same persons shall take by descent or purchase, which alone is the matter determined by the rule in Shelly's case; for the two sons could not take an estate tail from their mother as tenants in common. They must take as purchasers, or not take at all; and there is no rule of law which forbids such a devise, nor can the rule in Shelly's case be applied to it. On the contrary, it is well settled that a limitation by way of remainder to the sons of the first taker, as tenants in common, manifests the intent of the testator that the ancestor should not take an estate in fee or in tail, and that the sons may and do take as purchasers. Doe *v.* Burnsall, 6 T. R. 30; Burnsall *v.* Davy, 1 B. & P. 215; Gilman *v.* Elvy, 4 East, 313, Doe *v.* Collins, 4 T. R. 294; 4 Greenl. Cruise, 389.

Our opinion is, that upon the decease of his mother, this demandant took, as a purchaser, an estate tail in one moiety of these lands, as a tenant in common with his brother.

It was objected that the devise to him was upon the condition that as soon as he should come into the actual possession of the lands devised, he should take and use the surname of Vassall; but it is enough to say that he does not appear to have yet come into such actual possession, and that if this condition subsequent were broken, only the person to whom the lands are devised over can by an entra take advantage of it.   Taylor v. Mason, 9 Wheat. 325; Finley v. King, 3 Pet. 347.

Under the Revised Statutes of Maine, c. 145, § 13, the demandant may recover according to his title, provided he has a right of entry; and this raises the only remaining question, whether he has such a right, or whether it is barred by an act of the Legislature of Maine, passed on the eleventh day of August, 1848, which is as follows:

An act, in addition to the one hundred and forty-seventh chapter of the Revised Statutes.

Sec. 1. No real or mixed action for the recovery ot any lands in this State shall be commenced or maintained against any person in possession of such lands, where such person, or those under whom he claims, have been in actual possession for more than forty years, and claiming to hold the same in his or their own right, and which possession shall have been adverse, open, peaceable, notorious, and exclusive.

Sec. 2. This act shall take effect at the end of one day, from and after its approval by the governor.

This action was commenced on the fourteenth of April, 1846, and, consequently, had been pending upwards of two years, when the above act was passed. The inquiry is, what is its effect upon this action, and the title of the demandant? That it was intended to be retrospective, and to bar a recovery in actions then pending, upon proof of such seisin by the tenant as the act describes, is plainly indicated. Under the constitution of the State of Maine, can it so operate? To determine this question, it is necessary to take into view the legal rights of the demandant and tenant, when this act was passed, and the change in those rights attempted by the act.

The demandant, on the deeease of his mother, in 1845, became constructively seised of an estate tail, and had a right of entry into these lands. The actual seisin of the tenant and those under whom he claims, though adverse to all persons having estates in possession under the will of Florentius Vassall, for a period of time sufficient to bar their right of entry, did not become adverse as against the demandant, until he acquired an estate in possession, by the decease of his mother; and, consequently, when he brought this action, he was lawfully entitled to one moiety of the land, as tenant in tail, having an estate of inheritance which he could convey by deed, and upon which, being disseised, he could maintain a writ of entry. In other words, the land was his property, and, as such, he had a right to re-cover and hold it. Rev. Stat. c. 147, § 3.

The effect of the act is, to make the seisin of the tenant, and of those under whom he claims, adverse as against the demand-ant, during the time he had no right of possession, and thus to deprive him of his right of entry, and destroy his estate in the land. The actual operation of this law upon the demandant's title, would have been expressed in words, if it had been said in the statute that, whereas, up to that time an actual wrongful seisin had been by law adverse only against those having estates in possession, and so, those coming in by way of remainder, were well entitled to the land, however long that actual wrong-ful seisin might have been continued; yet, thereafter, those who have come in by way of remainder, shall not be deemed entitled to the land, because such actual seisin shall be taken to be ad-verse as against them, and they shall not be allowed to main-tain an action for the recovery of the land to which they had lawful title when the action was brought. It is only by giving this construction to the law, that it can be made to operate at all, on the demandant's title. It requires a possession for forty years, "adverse, open, peaceable, notorious, and exclusive." Adverse to whom? Exclusive of whom? If adverse to, and exclusive of, the demandant, who came into the title by way of remainder, less than three years before the act was passed, then, according to the law of the State existing down to the passage of the act, no actual wrongful seisin could be adverse to him until he had an estate in the land entitling him to its possession. But we cannot suppose this law meant to enact merely, that forty years' exclusive and actual seisin should bar an action by one having title to the possession during the whole of that period, because, by the Revised Statutes, (c. 147, § 1,) twenty years was sufficient; and, therefore, we are forced to conclude, that the intention of the legislature was, to make an actual seisin, for forty years, sufficient to destroy a title which had be-come vested, by way of remainder, before the act was passed, and which was a valid title by the then existing law.

Under the constitution of the State of Maine, as expounded by the highest court of that State, is it in the power of the legislature to pass a retrospective law, thus operating to destroy an estate in lands?

We think this case not distinguishable from the case of the Proprietors of the Kennebec Purchase *v.* Laboree et al. 2 Greenl. Rep. 275. That was a writ of entry to recover a tract of land. The principal question was, whether an act of the legislature concerning disseisin, was valid in its retrospective operation. Prior to the passage of this act an entry under a deed, duly registered, which described a tract of land by metes and bounds, and actual possession of a part of that tract, operated, by the law of Maine, as a disseisin of the true owner of the whole tract described in the deed. But an entry, without such a deed, gave seisin, as against the owner, only of so much of the land as was actually occupied; and this occupation was required to be equivalent to what is figuratively described in the common law as *pedis possessio;* that is, open, notorious, and exclusive, such as at once to give notice to all, of the nature and extent of the possession and claim, and show the exercise of the exclusive dominion over the land, and the appropriation of it to the use and benefit of the possessor. This being the state of the law when the action was brought, a law was passed, one section of which was in these words:

" Be it further enacted; that, in any writ or action which has been, or may hereafter be brought, for the recovery of any lands, &c., it shall not be necessary for limiting the demandant and barring his right of recovery, that the premises defended shall have been surrounded by fences, or rendered inaccessible by other obstructions; but it shall be sufficient if the possession, occupancy, and improvement thereof, by the defendant, or those under whom he claims, shall have been open, notorious, and exclusive, comporting with the ordinary managements of similar estates in the possession and occupancy of those who have title thereunto, or satisfactorily indicative of such exercise of ownership as is usual in the improvement of a farm by its owner; and no part of the premises demanded and defended shall be excluded from the operation of the aforesaid limitation, because, such part may be woodland or without cultivation."

The Supreme Court of Maine held, that so far as this act attempted to change the law of disseisin in respect to titles existing when it was passed, the act was inoperative and void, because in conflict with the constitution of that State. The opinion of the court, delivered by Mellen, Chief Justice, contains an elaborate and searching analysis of the subject, and it is evident, that learned court considered it with all the care demanded by a question of so much delicacy and importance, and brought to its adjudication sound principles of constitutional jurisprudence The principles of this decision have been recognized in subsequent cases, (Oriental Bank v. Freeze, 18 Maine Rep. 109; Austin v. Stevens, 24 Maine Rep. 520; Preston v. Drew, 5 Law Reporter, 189,) and we are not aware that it has ever been questioned, or denied to be a just exposition of the constitutional law of that State. The result of the decision is, that the constitution of the State has secured to every citizen the right of " acquiring, possessing, and enjoying property;"

and that, by the true intent and meaning of this section, property cannot, by a mere act of the legislature, be taken from. one man and vested in another directly; nor can it, by the retrospective operation of law, be indirectly transferred from one to another, or be subjected to the government of principles in a court of justice, which must necessarily produce that effect.

According to this decision, the act now in question is inoperative, as respects this action, and the demandant's title, on which it is founded. For, unless by a retrospective operation it subjects his title to the government of a new law of disseisin, which, in effect, transfers his property to the tenant, it can have no operation; and whether such an effect can be produced by an act of the Legislature of Maine, under the constitution of that State, was the precise question adjudicated by the Supreme Court in the case referred to, which adjudication we understand to contain an established principle in the fundamental law of that State.

The thirty-fourth' section of the Judiciary Act, (1 Statute at Large, 92,) as well as the rule of general jurisprudence, as to the operation of the *lex loci* upon titles to land, requires us to determine this case according to the law of the State of Maine. In ascertaining what that law is, this court looks to the decisions of the highest court of that State; and where the question turns upon the construction to be given to the constitution of the State, and we find a construction made by the highest State Court very soon after the constitution was formed, acquiesced in by the people of the State for nearly thirty years, and repeatedly confirmed by subsequent judicial decisions of that court, we cannot hesitate to adopt it, and apply it to this case, to which, in our judgment, it is justly applicable. Such has been the uniform course of this court. McKeen v. Delancy's Lessee, 5 Cr. 22; Polk's Lessee v. Wendall, 9 Cr. 87; Gardner v. Collins, 2 Pet. 58; Shelly v. Guy, 11 Wheat. 351; Green v. Neal, 6 Pet. 291, are some of the cases in which this course has been followed, and its reasons explained. The question has usually been concerning the construction of a statute of a State. But we think there is no sound distinction between the construction of a law enacted by the legislature of a State, and the construction of the organic law, ordained by the people themselves. The exposition of both belongs to the judicial department of the government of the State, and its decision is final, and binding upon all other departments of that government, and upon the people themselves, until they see fit to change their constitution; and this court receives such a settled construction as part of the fundamental law of the State.

In conformity with these principles, we are constrained to.

hold the law now in question to be inoperative upon the demandant's title, and consequently, that he is not barred by it from maintaining this action.

The judgment of the Circuit Court must be reversed, and a *venire de novo* awarded.

Order.

This cause came on to be heard on the transcript of the record from the Circuit Court of the United States for the District of Maine, and was argued by counsel. On consideration whereof, it is now here ordered and adjudged, by this court, that the judgment of the said Circuit Court in this cause, be, and the same is hereby, reversed, with costs, and that this cause be, and the same is hereby, remanded to the said Circuit Court, with directions to award a *venire facias de novo*.

ABRAM SHEPPARD AND JOHN DUNCAN, PLAINTIFFS IN ERROR, *v.* PEYTON S. GRAVES.

It is a bad mode of pleading, to unite pleas in abatement and pleas to the merits. And if after pleas in abatement, a defence be interposed, going to the merits of the controversy, the grounds alleged in abatement become thereby immaterial and are waived.

When a plea is filed to the jurisdiction of the court, upon the ground that the plaintiff is a resident of the same State with the defendant, it is incumbent on the defendant to prove the allegation.

It is of no consequence whether the date of a promissory note be at the beginning or end of it.

THIS case was brought up, by writ of error, from the District Court of the United States for the District of Texas.

The facts are all set forth in the opinion of the court.

It was argued by *Mr. V. E. Howard* and *Mr. Ballinger*, in a printed argument, for the plaintiffs in error, and *Mr. Davidge* and *Mr. O. F. Johnson*, for the defendant in error.

The points made by the counsel for the plaintiffs in error, were the following:

1. The court erred in admitting the notes in evidence, because there was a variance between the notes offered and those described in the petitions.

The petitions alleged, that the notes were "executed and delivered at Matagorda," but did not allege that they bore date at Matagorda, as was found to be the fact on their being produced.

It was the plaintiff's duty to give a perfect description of his notes, so as to prevent the possibility of the defendants being ever sued upon them again, and if so, that this record should be a bar.

The place at which the notes bore date on their face, was essential to their description. When the objection was made, the plaintiff could have amended, and given an accurate description; but refusing to do this, it was error in the court to admit the notes.

· Thus, the words "value received," are material in a description of the note; and if omitted, the variance will be fatal. 1 Chitty's Pleadings, 339, note 1, ed. 1833; Saxon v. Johnson, 10 Johns. R. 418.

2. The court erred in refusing to instruct the jury, " that, upon the issue as to the citizenship of plaintiff, the burden of proof was on the plaintiff to show such citizenship as entitled him to sue ;" and in giving the instruction, " that the plaint ff was to be considered a citizen of Louisiana, as alleged in his petition, unless it was pleaded and proved that he was a citizen of Texas."

There was a proper plea to the jurisdiction of the court, presenting the issue as to the citizenship of plaintiff.

It was not necessary that the plea should be verified by affidavit. Hartley's Digest, art. 690, § 31, Practice, act 1846.

Besides, there was no demurrer or exception taken to the plea for want of an affidavit; and if one had been necessary, it was waived by the plaintiff taking issue on the fact.

The rule which at first prevailed in the courts of the United States, required the plaintiff, on the general issue, to prove citizenship as alleged. Catlett & Keith v. Pacific Insurance Company, Paine's C. C. R. 594.

It was afterwards decided, however, that a plea in abatement was necessary to raise the question of citizenship. D'Wolf v. Rabaud et al. 1 Peters, 476. See 498.

The courts of the United States are courts of limited jurisdiction; and although a plea to the merits admits the jurisdiction, yet when jurisdiction is denied by a proper plea, it must be shown by the plaintiff. See 1 Cowen & Hill's Notes to Phillips's Ev. p. 487, note 376, and authorities referred to ; Maples v. Wightman, 4 Conn. R. 376 ; Wooster v. Parsons, Kirby's R. 27.

The counsel for the defendant in error contended, that there was no variance between the note alleged in the petition of defendant in error, (R. 1 and 2,) and that offered in evidence.

1. The petition alleged the place where the note bore date, in the usual form, even under the English practice, and with greater

certainty than is required by the law of Texas. But, had there been no such allegation, the omission would have been immaterial. 1 Saund. Pl. and Ev. 260.

2. That there was no error in the refusal of the court below to grant the first prayer of the·plaintiffs in error, which plainly tended to mislead the jury, is manifest, and, indeeu, is conceded by the brief filed by their counsel.

3. The court was right in refusing to instruct the jury, "that upon the issue as to the citizenship of plaintiff, the burden of proof was on the plaintiff to show such citizenship as entitles him to sue;" and in giving the instruction, "that the plaintiff was to be considered a citizen of Louisiana, as alleged in his petition, unless it was pleaded and proved that he was a citizen of Texas."

Exception to the capacity of the plaintiff below to sue in the District Court, could only be taken by plea in abatement. Conard v. The Atlantic Ins. Co. 1 Pet. 386, 450; D'Wolf v. Rabaud et al. Id. 476, 498; Evans v. Gee, 11 Pet. 80, 83; Sims v. Hundley, 6 How. 1, 5; Smith v. Kernochen, 7 How. 198, 216.

Such being the case, and as the obligation of proving any fact lies upon the party who substantially asserts the affirmative of the issue, the burden of proof was necessarily upon the defendants below.

The plea is strictly affirmative in its character, alleging, in terms and substance, that the plaintiff was not entitled to sue in the District Court, because he "is, and was at the commencement of this suit, a citizen of the State of Texas." Being introductive of new matter, and concluding, as it very properly does, with a verification, the defendants below, who pleaded it, held the affirmative, inseparably connected with which was the *onus probandi.* 1 Saund. Pl. and Ev. 8, 13, 16, 22; Union Bank of Maryland v. Ridgeley, 1 Harris & Gill, 415–419; Smith v. Dovers, 2 Doug. 428; Jackson on Pleading in Real Actions, 62, 65; Fowler v. Coster, 1 Moo. & Malk. 241; S. C. 3 C. & P. 463; Colstone v. Hiscolls, 6 C. & P. 666.

Indeed, the definition of a plea in abatement, (in the nature of which is a plea to the jurisdiction, or to the person of the plaintiff,) is, that by it the defendant "shows cause why he should not be impleaded, or if impleaded, not in the manner and form he now is." Bac. Abr., Abatement.

Whenever the plea is to the jurisdiction, it must state another jurisdiction. Id.

4. The plea in abatement was a nullity, not having been filed in time. Act of May 13, 1846, §§ 23, 24, 26, 27; Laws of Texas, 1846, pp. 369, 370.

Process was regularly served on one of the defendants below,

May 31, 1850; on the other, October 12, 1850. The court met on the first Monday of December, 1850. The plea was not filed until January 6, 1851.

Mr. Justice DANIEL delivered the opinion of the court.

The defendant in error, in conformity with a mode of practice in the State of Texas, instituted an action at law against the plaintiffs in error upon their promissory note. That note was in the words following:

" On the first day of January, 1850, we jointly and severally promise to pay to Peyton S. Graves, or order, at the counting house of R. & D. G. Mills, in Brazoria County, the sum of $1,845.94, for value received, with eight per cent. interest thereon, from the first day of January, till paid.

ABM. SHEPPARD.
JOHN DUNCAN.

" Matagorda, Sept'r 23d, 1844."

The petition sets forth, that Peyton S. Graves, a citizen and inhabitant of Louisiana, represents, that Abram Sheppard and John Duncan, both citizens and residents of the county of Matagorda, in the State of Texas, are jointly and severally indebted to the petitioner in the sum of $1,845.94, with interest thereon, at eight per cent. per annum, from the first day of January, 1844, until paid—for that heretofore, to wit, at Matagorda, in the State of Texas, on the 23d day of September, 1844, the said Sheppard, who signs his name Abm. Sheppard, and the said Duncan, executed and delivered to the petitioner, their joint and several promissory note, dated September 23d, 1844, and signed Abm. Sheppard and John Duncan, by which, &c.

Upon the summons issued against each of the defendants, the marshal returns, that he had executed the summons on the 12th of October, 1850, serving each of them with a certified copy of the petition and summons, and with regard to Duncan, the return farther states that the original summons, was also exhibited to him. The plaintiffs in error appeared to the action, and attempted to interpose several defences in the nature of pleas in abatement. They first allege jointly, that the court could not take cognizance of the cause, because the plaintiff below, was not, at the commencement of the suit, a citizen of Louisiana, but of the State of Texas.

The defendant Sheppard, then pleads separately, that the marshal's return upon the summons was not legal, and should be quashed, because it does not state, that the marshal had delivered to the defendant in person, a copy of the citation, and of the petition accompanying it; and that the return was not made and signed by the deputy purporting to make and sign the same.

The defendant Duncan also pleads separately in abatement, that the citation calls upon him to answer the complaint against him and Abraham Sheppard, whereas the true name of said Sheppard is Abram, and not Abraham; and he also insists upon the insufficiency of the return to the summons, because, as he alleges, that return does not state that the marshal delivered to him in person, a copy of the citation, or of the petition accompanying it.

In addition to these pleas in abatement, the defendants below interposed a defence upon the merits in the nature of the general issue, by which they deny all and singular the matters stated in the petition, and say that they are not indebted to the plaintiff as he has alleged, and in this defence they conclude to the country, whilst in the introduction thereto, they declare that they do not waive their several pleas in abatement, but fully rely upon the same. After this series of heterogeneous defences, the plaintiff moved the court to strike out the plea to the jurisdiction and all the other pleas in abatement tendered by the defendants, assigning, as the grounds of this motion, that those pleas were not filed within the time required by law.

Upon the trial of the cause, the court seems to have considered the case as standing before it upon all the defences attempted, but ruled out the several pleas in abatement, though whether for the insufficiency of those pleas in point of law, for the want of proof to sustain them, or for their irregularity in the order of pleading, does not certainly appear from this record. The jury upon the issue joined upon the merits, rendered a verdict for the plaintiff for the sum of $2,788.89, for which judgment was given with costs.

The incongruities in practice, which mark the progress of this case in the court below, are much to be regretted, as having a tendency to confound the proceedings in courts of justice; proceedings calculated to define and distinguish the rights of parties litigant, and to conduct the courts to a correct adjudication upon those rights; proceedings indeed founded upon, and as it were sanctified by, an experience of their usefulness, and even of their necessity. Thus it has ever been received as a canon of pleading, that matters which appertain solely to the jurisdiction of a court, or to the disabilities of the suitor, should never be blended with questions which enter essentially into the subject-matter of the controversy; and that all defences involving inquiries into that subject-matter imply, nay admit, the competency of the parties to institute such inquiries, and the authority of the court to adjudicate upon them. Hence it is, that

43 *

pleas to the jurisdiction or in abatement, are deemed inconsistent with those which appertain to the merits of a cause; they are tried upon different views as to the relations of the parties, and result in different conclusions. A striking illustration of the mischiefs flowing from the departure from the rule just stated, is seen in the practice attempted in the case before us. If it could be imagined that the plea to the jurisdiction and the plea to the merits, could be regularly committed to the jury at the same time, the verdict might involve the following absurdities. Should the finding be for the plaintiff, the judgment would, as to the defendant, be upon one issue, that of *respondeas ouster*, and upon the other, that he pay the debt, as to the justice of which he was commanded to answer over. Should the finding be for the defendant, the judgment upon one issue must be that the debt was not due, and upon the other, that the court called upon so to pronounce, had no authority over the case. So that in either aspect there must, under this proceeding, be made and determined one issue, which is incongruous with and immaterial to the other. A practice, thus fraught with confusion and perplexity, and one endangering the rights of suitors, it is exceedingly desirable should be reformed, and we are aware of no standard of reformation and improvement more safe or more convenient than that which is supplied by the time-tested rules of the common law. And by one of those rules, believed to be without an exception, it is ordained, that objections to the jurisdiction of the court, or to the competency of the parties, are matters pleadable in abatement only, and that if after such matters relied on, a defence be interposed in bar and going to the merits of the controversy, the grounds alleged in abatement become thereby immaterial, and are waived.

With respect to the exception taken to the ruling of the District Court, as to the obligation of the defendant to prove his averment of the plaintiff's residence in the State of Texas, and not of Louisiana, as set forth in the petition, were the decision of this question deemed requisite here, we should say that the true doctrine applicable to the question is this: that although in the courts of the United States it is necessary to set forth the grounds of their cognizance as courts of limited jurisdiction, yet wherever jurisdiction shall be averred in the pleadings, in conformity with the laws creating those courts, it must be taken *prima facie* as existing, and that it is incumbent on him who would impeach that jurisdiction for causes *dehors* the pleading, to allege and prove such causes; that the necessity for the allegation and the burden of sustaining it by proof, both rest upon the party taking the exception. Such, we think, would be the proper rule resulting from the intrinsic character of the exception, and such we consider the doctrine enunciated in the cases of Conrad *v.* The Atlantic Insurance Company, in 1 Pet. 386, and D'Wolf *v.* Rabaud et al. Id. 476.

This doctrine we are unwilling to disturb. The cases just referred to, as well as those of Sims *v.* Hundley, in 6 Howard, and Smith *v.* Kernochen, (7 Id. 198,) expressly affirm the common-law principle of pleading, herein before mentioned, that the question of the residence or of the right of the parties to sue, as incident to residence, cannot be inquired into under the general issue.

The plea of a misnomer of the defendant Sheppard, by the insertion of two superfluous letters in his christian name, and the still more captious and unmeaning distinction attempted between serving the defendants with a certified copy of the petition and summons in this suit, and a delivery of that petition and summons to the defendants in person, is disposed of by the same rule which displaces, as irrelevant and immaterial, the exception taken to the jurisdiction.

The question of variance between the note and the description of it in the petition, it is not easy to comprehend, unless indeed it is intended by the defendants to insist, that a note should have its date inserted at its beginning only, and cannot be dated at the termination of it; for the note at the bottom bears upon it the date as well as the place of its execution, viz. Matagorda, September 23, 1844, and the description and the petition accord with both these facts. It is true, the petition contains a recital that Matagorda is within the State of Texas, but by no extreme of cavil can this recital be converted into a misdescription of the note. Upon the whole case, we think the judgment of the District Court was correct, and we accordingly order it to be affirmed.

Order.

This cause came on to be heard on the transcript of the record from the District Court of the United States for the District of Texas, and was argued by counsel. On consideration whereof, it is now here ordered and adjudged by this court, that the judgment of the said District Court in this cause be, and the same is hereby, affirmed, with costs and interest, until the same is paid, at the same rate per annum that similar judgments bear in the courts of the State of Texas.

ABRAM SHEPPARD AND JOHN DUNCAN, PLAINTIFFS IN ERROR, *v.* PEYTON S. GRAVES.

In this case, as in the preceding, it is decided, that where the plaintiff averred enough to show the jurisdiction of the court and the defendant pleaded in abatement that the plaintiff was disabled from bringing the suit, on account of residence, it was incumbent upon the defendant to sustain the allegation by proof.

Until that was done, it was not necessary for the plaintiff to offer any evidence upon the subject.

THIS case was brought up by writ of error, from the District Court of the United States for the District of Texas.

The parties were the same as those in the preceding case, and the point upon which the decision of the court turned was the same as one of those decided in the preceding case.

It was argued, in conjunction with the other, by the same counsel.

Mr. Justice DANIEL delivered the opinion of the court.

This is a suit between the parties to the case No. 65, and is in all its features essentially the same with the former case with one exception, which will be pointed out.

In this suit, as in No. 65, the defendants below demurred to the petition, pleaded in abatement to the regularity of the service of process, to the disability of the plaintiff on the score of residence, and then interposed a defence in the nature of the general issue, but tendered no proofs in support of their defences, either in abatement or in bar. The plaintiff, to sustain the jurisdiction of the court upon the question of residence, and to meet the pleas in abatement, offered to read the deposition of two witnesses Rugely and Blair, residents of the city of New Orleans, in the State of Louisiana, taken *de bene esse* before a Commissioner in the city of New Orleans, under the act of Congress of 1789. The reading of these depositions was objected to by the defendants, because the Commissioner did not certify that the witnesses resided at a greater distance than one hundred. miles from the place of trial, but stated only that they were residents of the city of New Orleans, within the Eastern District of the State of Louisiana, and beyond the jurisdiction of the District Court of Texas. The court permitted the introduction of oral evidence to prove that the city of New Orleans was at a greater distance than one hundred miles from Galveston, the place of trial; and ruling also that the court itself knew judicially the mail routes and distances thereof, and that New Orleans, the place of taking said depositions, was more than one hundred miles from Galveston, the place of trial, permitted the depositions to be read in evidence.

Whether the District Court erred in allowing an omission in the certificate of the Commissioner to be supplied by oral evidence, or could regularly act upon knowledge assumed to be within its judicial cognizance, we do not consider it necessary to examine, in order to dispose of the case before us. It must be recollected that the defendants below, attempted no proof whatsoever in support of any of their pleas. The plaintiff having averred enough to show the jurisdiction of the court, and nothing having been adduced to impeach it, that jurisdiction remained as stated, and the plaintiff could lose nothing by adducing either imperfect evidence, or no evidence at all, in support of that which clearly existed, and which he, under the circumstances, could not be called on to sustain. Even then had the case in the District Court stood upon an issue regularly formed upon the pleas in abatement, the evidence of the depositions was wholly unnecessary — the ruling of the court upon that evidence was immaterial, and should not impair the strength of the plaintiff's case, which was perfect without it. But the exception to the ruling of the court on this point, must be unavailable upon another view, as given in our consideration of the preceding case. By interposing the plea of the general issue after their several pleas in abatement, the defendants have effectually waived those pleas, and surrendered the positions covered by them. The judgment of the Circuit Court must in this case also be affirmed.

Order.

This cause came on to be heard on the transcript of the record from the District Court of the United States for the District of Texas and was argued by counsel. On consideration whereof, it is now here ordered and adjudged by this court that the judgment of the said District Court in this cause be, and the same is hereby, affirmed, with costs, and interest until the same is paid, at the same rate per annum that similar judgments bear in the courts of the State of Texas.

SAMUEL MARSH, WILLIAM E. LEE, AND EDWARD C. DELAVAN, PLAINTIFFS IN ERROR, v. EDWARD BROOKS, AND VIRGINIA C. HIS WIFE, CHARLES P. BILLON, AND FRANCIS E. HIS WIFE, WALTER G. REDDICK, AND DABNEY C. REDDICK.

This court decided, in 8 Howard, 223, that the recitals in a patent for land, referring to titles of anterior date, were not of themselves sufficient to establish the titles thus recited.

The titles themselves being now produced, it is decided, that a permit, given by the Lieutenant-Governor of Upper Louisiana, in 1799, to a person to form an establish-ment on the Mississippi, followed by actual possession and improvement, entitled the occupant to 640 acres, including his improvements, although the Indian title was not then extinguished.

It was not the practice of the Spanish government to make treaties with the Indian tribes, defining their boundaries; but to prevent settlements upon their lands without special permits. Such permits, however, were usual.

The construction of the treaty between the United States and the Sac and Fox Indians, must be that the latter assented to an occupancy which was as notorious as their own.

The act of Congress, approved April 29, 1816, (3 Stat. at Large, 328,) confirming certain claims to land, confirmed this one, although the Recorder of Land Titles, in his report, made in 1815, had added these words, "if Indian title extinguished." These words were surplusage.

THIS case was brought up, by writ of error, from the District Court of the United States for the Southern District of Iowa.

It was before this court at January term, 1850, and is reported in 8 Howard, 223.

The children and heirs of Thomas F. Reddick, (the defendants in error,) were the plaintiffs in the court below, having brought their action by writ of right, according to the practice of the courts in Iowa, to recover 640 acres of land upon the right bank of the Mississippi River.

The acts of Congress and the patent to Reddick are set forth in 8 Howard, to which the reader is referred. But the plaintiffs having offered additional evidence, it may be proper to bring the whole into one view. In the former trial the plaintiffs relied on the recitals in the patent to Reddick to prove the title of Tesson: but this court having decided that those recitals were insufficient, the evidence produced upon the trial of the present suit in the District Court was the following:

Plaintiffs' Evidence.

1. The plaintiffs proved, that Louis Honoré Tesson settled on the land in controversy, in 1798, and on the 30th of March, 1799, obtained from the Spanish government, a written permit to settle thereon, which is recited at length in the record.

2. That Tesson had possession, and inhabited, cultivated, and had houses and orchards and fields on said lands, in 1798, 1799, 1800, and until 1805; and that all his right, under the permit and settlement, passed, by mesne conveyances, to said Thomas F Reddick.

3. That said Reddick duly presented and proved before the Recorder of Land Titles at St. Louis, his claim, and claim of title from Tesson to said land; and that said Recorder, by his report, dated November 1st, 1815, reported on said claim his opinion, as follows: "Granted 640 acres, if Indian rights extinguished."

4. The act of Congress, approved April 29th, 1816, (3 U. S. Stat. at Large, p. 328, ch. 155,) "for the confirmation of certain claims to land in the Western District of the State of Louisiana, and in the Territory of Missouri."

5. That on the 17th of May, 1838, a patent certificate, (No. 1157,) was delivered, by the Recorder of Land Titles at St. Louis, to Edward Brooks, (one of the original plaintiffs,) for the land referred to in the report of November 1st, 1815.

6. A patent of the United States, issued to Thomas F. Reddick, described as assignee of Joseph Robidoux, assignee of Louis Honoré Tesson, for the lands in controversy, dated the 7th February, 1839.

7. They also proved, that they, the plaintiffs, were the heirs and legal representatives of said Reddick; and that the defendants were in possession of the land in controversy, at the commencement of the suit, and rested their case.

Defendants' Evidence.

The defendants then gave in evidence:

1. The treaty between the United States and the Sac and Fox Indians, (7 U. S. Stat. at Large, 229,) made at Washington on the 4th of August, 1824, by the first article whereof, these Indians ceded to the United States all their right and title to the lands claimed by them between the Mississippi and the Missouri rivers, and a northerly line, running from the Missouri, at the entrance of the Kansas River, north 100 miles, to the northwest corner of the State of Missouri, and thence east to the Mississippi; but with the understanding " that the small tract of land lying between the rivers Des Moines and Mississippi, and the section of the above line between the Mississippi and the Des Moines, is intended for the use of the half-breeds belonging to the Sac and Fox nations; they holding it, however, by the same title, and in the same manner, that other Indian titles are held."

2. The act of Congress, approved June 30th, 1834, (4 U. S. Stat. at Large, ch. 167, p. 740,) " to relinquish the reversionary interest of the United States in a certain Indian reservation lying between the rivers Mississippi and Des Moines."

3. That the land in controversy is included within the interior boundary lines of the Sac and Fox half-breed reservation, referred to in the treaty of 1824, and act of Congress of 1834.

4. The act of Congress of July 1st, 1836, (6 U. S. Stat. at Large, p. 661,) by which the United States relinquished to the heirs of said Thomas F. Reddick, their right in the lands embraced in said patent—but reserving any older or better claim not emanating from the United States, and providing, that in case said lands should be included in any reservation theretofore

made under treaty with any Indian tribe, Reddick should be authorized to make another location on unappropriated lands.

5. That the 640 acres of land referred to in said act of Congress, of July 1st, 1836, lie within the exterior boundary lines of said Sac and Fox half-breed reservation, made by the treaty of August 4th, 1834.

6. That the land in controversy is worth more than $2000.

The defendants then rested their case.

The plaintiffs then prayed the court to instruct the jury—

1. That under the treaty with Fra ce, of the 30th April, 1803, and the several acts of Congress passed in pursuance thereof, for settlement of titles in the Territory of Missouri, Tesson and Reddick, as his assignee, had a valid subsisting interest in he land in controversy, at the date of the report made by the Recorder, which was not divested by the reservation in the treaty with the Sac and Fox Indians, or the act of Congress of the 30th June, 1834.

2. That the claim of Tesson, and of Reddick, as his assignee, as reported, was substantially confirmed by the act of Congress, approved April 27th, 1816.

3. That the patent, taken in connection with other evidence, conveyed to the plaintiffs a fee-simple title to the land in controversy, and overrides the title set up by defendants.

These instructions were given by the Court.

The defendants then prayed the court to instruct the jury –

1. That under the report of the Recorder of Land Titles, given in evidence by the plaintiffs, they are not entitled to recover the land, unless their title thereto has been confirmed by an act of Congress. This instruction was given by the court.

2. That the true construction of the act of Congress of the 29th of April, 1816, given in evidence by the plaintiffs, does not confirm their title to the lands sued for, if the Indian title to the same was not at that time extinguished.

3. That the treaty of August 4th, 1824, with the Sac and Fox Indians, is a recognition by the United States, at the date of said treaty, of the Indian right to the lands in controversy; the same being within the Sac and Fox half-breed reservation.

4. That the Indian title to the land in controversy was not extinguished prior to the 4th of August, 1824.

5. That the plaintiffs have shown no right to recover the land in controversy in this suit.

The first of these instructions, prayed for by the defendants, was given by the court; but the second, third, fourth, and fifth instructions, as prayed, were refused to be given.

The defendants, by their counsel, excepted to the rulings and decisions of the court in giving the instructions prayed for by the plaintiffs, and in refusing to give the second, third, fourth, and fifth instructions, prayed for by the defendants.

The jury, under these instructions, found a verdict for the plaintiffs, and a bill of exceptions brought these several rulings before this court for review.

It was argued by *Mr. Butler*, for the plaintiffs in error, and *Mr. Geyer*, for the defendants in error.

Mr. Butler, for the plaintiffs in error, made several points. The one upon which the decision of the court chiefly turned, was the following:

II. The District Court erred, in giving to the jury the several instructions prayed for by the counsel for the plaintiffs below.

1. The instruction, "that under the treaty with France of the 30th of April, 1803, and the acts of Congress, Tesson, and Reddick as his assignee, had a valid subsisting interest in the land in controversy, at the date of the report made by the Recorder, which was not divested by the reservation in the treaty with the Sac and Fox Indians, or the act of Congress of the 30th of June, 1834," was erroneous.

(After analyzing the treaty, and the several acts of Congress from that time to 1815, *Mr. Butler* came to the following conclusion:)

Neither under the, treaty, nor under any one of the above-cited acts, or all of them combined, had Reddick, as the assignee of Tesson, a valid subsisting interest in the land in controversy, at the date of the Recorder's report, November 1, 1815.

- 1. Under the treaty, every species of title to lands in Louisiana, emanating from the French or Spanish governments — whether perfect and complete, or inchoate and incomplete — was recognized and protected as "property;" but mere permits to make settlements on such lands, even when lawfully granted by such authorities, conferred no right of property within the meaning of the treaty. Les Bois v. Bramell, 4 How. 463; Soulard & Smith v. United States, 4 Pet. 511; Smith v. United States, 10 Id. 326; Wherry v. United States, 10 Id. 328; Chouteau v. Eckhart, 2 How. 344; Menard's heirs v. Massey, 8 Id. 293, 308, 806; Bissell v. Penrose, 8 Id. 317; Landes v. Brant, 10 Id. 348; Glenn v. United States, 13 Id. 250; Heirs of Vilemont v. United States, 13 Id. 261.

2. The equitable claim of settlers under such permits, upon the justice or bounty of the government, to complete their titles, devolved, after the treaty of cession, on Congress, who, by the several statutes above cited, have acted upon and regulated the subject. Cases above cited.

3. No specific quantity, and no definite location, are men·
tioned in the written permit to Tesson; he is merely permitted
to establish himself, for the purpose of trade·with the Indians,
at the head of the rapid of the River Des Moines. No survey
could have been made, nor was any made or contemplated,
under this permit; nor did any interest, in any particular tract,
pass by it to Tesson. United States v. Forbes, 15 Peters, 173;
Same v. Buyck, Id. 215; Same v. O'Hara, Id. 275; Same v.
Delespine, Id. 319; Same v. Miranda, Id. 153; Same v. King,
3 How. 773; Same v. Lawton, 5 Id. 10; Same v. Villalobos,
10 Id. 541; Same v. Boisdore, 11 Id. 62; Same v. Lecompte,
Id. 115; Same v. Vilemont, 13 Id. 261; Bissell v. Penrose,
8 Id. 317.

4. Tesson, after making his establishment, was to apply to
the Governor-General, to obtain a grant of a convenient space
for the use of his establishment; and, until the obtaining of
such grant, Tesson neither had, nor could equitably claim, any
interest whatever in any specific tract or lot.

5. This permit to Tesson was, therefore, a mere license to·
reside and trade in the Indian country; it was wholly insuffi-
·cient to extinguish the Indian title in any particular tract, or to
sever any particular tract from the public domain; and, unless
confirmed by Congress, and duly located by their authority,
Tesson had, and could have no standing, under said permit, in
a court of justice. Cases above cited.

See, as to the Indian title, and the proceedings necessary to
extinguish it, the following cases: — United States v. Arredon-
do, 6 Pet. 691, 741; Mitchell v. United States, 9 Id. 711; S. C.
15 Id. 52, 83, 88; United States v. Fernandez, 10 Id. 303; Marsh
v. Brooks, 8 How. 223; Gaines v. Nicholson, 9 Id. 356; United
States v. D'Auterive, 10 Id. 624.

6. Whatever power, under the acts of Congress passed prior
to the date of the Receiver's report, that affair might have to
grant or confirm to Tesson's assignee, as a donation, the land
claimed by him, neither of said acts had, by itself, confirmed his
claim.

The first branch of the instruction now under review — that
Tesson and his assignee, on the 1st of November, 1815, had a
subsisting interest in the land in controversy — was, therefore,
erroneous.

Mr. Geyer, for the defendants in error, divided his points as
follows:

That a complete title to the land in controversy was vested
in Thomas F. Reddick, on the 29th of April, 1816, whether the
"Indian rights" had, or had not, then been extinguished; and

the title so vested has not been divested or impaired, by any subsequent treaty or act of Congress.

A confirmation of a title by act of Congress, not only renders it a legal title, but furnishes higher evidence of that fact than a patent, inasmuch as it is a direct grant of the fee by the government itself, whereas a patent is only an act of its ministerial officer. Grignon's Lessee v. Astor, 2 How. 319, S. P.; Simms's Lessee v. Irvine, 3 Dal. 405; Strother v. Lucas, 12 Pet. 410.

The grant to the half-breeds by the act of 30th of June, 1834, does not affect the grant to Reddick, by the act of 29th of April, 1816. It is a principle applicable to every grant, that it cannot affect preëxisting titles. Polk's Lessee v. Wendall, 5 Wheat. 293; 9 Cr. 87; Patterson v. Loinn, 11 Wheat. 380; Stoddard et al. v. Chambers, 2 How. 284.

II. The confirmation by the act of 29th April, 1816, vested in Reddick the title, subject only to the Indian right of occupancy, if not then extinguished. All grants by the government are subject to such rights, whether expressly reserved or not, but as soon as they are extinguished by cession or otherwise, the grantee of the government acquires full dominion over the property. Fletcher v. Peck, 6 Cranch, 87, 137, 143; Mitchell v. United States, 9 Pet. 711; United States v. Hernandez, 10 Pet. 304.

III. The report of the Recorder of Land Titles is an approval of the claim of Reddick, and a recommendation that six hundred and forty acres of land be granted to him, " if Indian rights extinguished." Referring it to Congress to determine the whole question. Congress must therefore be understood to have decided that the Indian rights were extinguished, or to have made the grant subject to such rights, and in either case the title of the defendants in error is complete; all such rights having been extinguished before the commencement of the suit.

IV. Although the grantee of the government takes, subject to the Indian right of occupancy, the existence of such right is not presumed, nor is the grantee bound to prove its extinguishment in an action against a mere intruder, especially where, as in this case, the grant is by an act of Congress.

V. If the Indian right of occupancy could be set up as a bar to a recovery under a grant by act of Congress, which is denied, it was incumbent on the defendants below to prove the existence of such right at the time of the commencement of the suit. No such proof was made; on the contrary, so far as the evidence discloses the existence of any claim by any Indian tribe, that claim appears to have been extinguished in 1824, so that at that time, if not before, Reddick acquired the absolute dominion and right of possession.

VI. The permit granted by the Spanish Government to Louis Honoré Tesson, to settle upon, occupy, and cultivate the land in controversy, as his property, excluded all Indian rights. The grants of the Spanish government were not subject to Indian rights, but operated as extinguishments of such rights on the lands granted. At the date of the treaty by which Louisiana was acquired, the title of Tesson, though incomplete, was property protected by the treaty; that title, with all its incidents, was recognized by the laws of the United States, and confirmed by the act of 29th April, 1816; so that according to the record, no Indian right of occupancy existed since 1798.

VII. If the existence of an Indian right had been recognized by the treaty of 4th August, 1824, as asserted in the third refused instruction, such recognition would not have affected the title of Reddick, granted in 1816. But that treaty recognizes no such right; it is merely a relinquishment of a claim by the Sacs and Foxes, a quitclaim by the Indians, and not a recognition of their title by the United States.

The Sacs and Foxes, by a treaty of 3d November, 1804, (Stat. at Large, vol. 7, p. 84,) ceded to the United States all their claim to the lands east of a line drawn from a point on the Missouri River, opposite the mouth of Gasconade, to a point on the River Jeffreon, thirty miles above its mouth, thence down that river to the Mississippi River, and up the same to the mouth of Wisconsin River, &c.

The Great and Little Osages, by a treaty of 10th November, 1808, ceded to the United States all lands "northwardly of the Missouri River." A survey of the boundary was provided for in the seventh article, and was made in 1816; the north boundary being coincident with the north boundary of the now State of Missouri.

The Osages, as well as the Sacs and Foxes, had set up claims to lands north of the Missouri, and both relinquished to the United States. But in 1824, the Sacs and Foxes still pretended to have a claim within the bounds of the State of Missouri, which is relinquished by the treaty of 1824.

It cannot be assumed that the title to the country, embracing the land in controversy, was in the Sacs and Foxes at any time; nor can the party claiming under a grant of the Spanish Government, confirmed by act of Congress, be required to prove that it was not, or that their treaty of 1804 included the land granted. The party who undertakes to maintain a possession against such a title, by showing an outstanding title or right of occupancy, takes upon himself the burden of proving it.

Mr. Justice CATRON delivered the opinion of the court.

This case was before us in 1850, and is reported in 8 Howard. We then held that as the patent to Reddick's heirs of 1839 was younger than the treaty of 1824, and the confirming act of 1836, by which the title of the United States was *primâ facie* vested in the Sac and Fox half-breeds, the patent could not prevail. Nor could its recitals be relied on to give it legal effect from an earlier date than it had on its face.

The judgment was then reversed, and the cause remanded for another trial, and an intimation given, that probably additional evidence might be adduced on a subsequent trial, which would establish an earlier and better title in the plaintiffs, than that of the half-breeds. That trial has taken place, and the case is now before us, with the evidence to which the recitals in the patent of Reddick's heirs, to some extent, refer. This evidence consists of a permit given by the Lieutenant-Governor of Upper Louisiana to Louis Honoré Tesson, to establish himself at the head of the rapids of the River Des Moines, (being a great rapid in the River Mississippi,) and having formed his establishment, he was assured that then it would be the duty of the Governor-General of Louisiana, residing at New Orleans, to procure for said Honoré, a concession of sufficient space to render the establishment available and useful to the trade of the country in peltries, and so that said Honoré might exercise an oversight of the Indians, and keep them in the fidelity which they owed to His Catholic Majesty; the object being to increase the trade with the Indians on that border; and in which said Honoré was permitted to be a participant, and to trade with the Indians in that part of His Majesty's dominions; nor were any rival traders to be allowed to deal with the Indians, except such as had a passport for that purpose, signed by the Lieutenant-Governor. This stipulation was made in March, 1799. Honoré was then in possession of the land in dispute, and had improvements on it; and he improved it further under the permit of 1799, and continued there until 1805. He had houses, orchards, and fields.

Thos. F. Reddick's claim was regularly derived by assignments from Honoré. Reddick's heirs, claimed a league square, on the assumption that the permit to settle and inhabit, entitled Honoré to this quantity. But the Recorder at St. Louis, acting as Commissioner, rejected the claim for a league square; and properly, as we think; there being only a promise of title in future, but no concession of land, in the Lieutenant-Governor's permission to Honoré to establish himself, and occupy the premises, and trade with the Indians. As, however, Honoré held actual possession, and had improved the land in an expensive

44*

and substantial manner, he was beyond question entitled to six hundred and forty acres, including his improvements, under our acts of Congress securing this quantity to actual settlers, had the land laid within that part of Louisiana to which the Indian title was extinguished, at the time when the occupancy existed. Being uncertain whether Honoré was entitled, by reason of his inhabitation and cultivation within territory to which the Indian title was not extinguished, the Recorder, in his tabular statement, granted the six hundred and forty acres, "if Indian rights extinguished." And this expression has embarrassed the title for more than thirty years. There were many claims in the Recorder's report and tabular statement, in which this one is found; and by the act of April 29, 1816, all of them were confirmed without exception, and without any notice having been taken of the Recorder's remark, referring to an existing Indian title to the land. That the Sacs and Foxes did claim the country generally, where this land lies, is not controverted; nor was their claim ceded to the United States till 1824. And this raises the question whether, according to Spanish usage, whilst that power governed Louisiana, an existing Indian claim to territory precluded inhabitation and cultivation under a permit to inhabit and cultivate a particular place designated in the permit, and which was in the Indian country. Spain had no treaties with any of the Indian tribes in Louisiana, fixing limits to their claims, so far as we are informed. The Indians were kept quiet, and at peace with Spanish subjects, by kind treatment and due precautions, which did not allow obtrusion on lands claimed by them, without written permits from the Governor; but that such permits were usual, cannot be doubted. The county of St. Charles lies in the fork of the Mississippi and Missouri rivers; it was settled, and the village of St. Charles established there, twenty years and more before we acquired Louisiana; and yet, by the treaty of November 3d, 1804, this section of country was ceded to the United States, by the Sac and Fox tribes, extending from the Missouri River, opposite to the mouth of the Gasconade, to the Janfilione, or "North 2 rivers," as now known; which empties into the Mississippi, in the county of Marion, in the State of Missouri. This country was as solemnly ceded, as was the country north of that cession, by the treaty of 1824; and which treaty is here set up in opposition to Reddick's title. The treaty of 1804 was duly ratified by the Senate of the United States, and apparently sanctioned, retrospectively, the Sac and Fox claim to the old county of St. Charles, in like manner that the treaty of 1824 recognized an existing Indian claim to the half-breed tract, where the land in dispute lies.

And again in 1808, the Osages ceded to the United States all the lands east of a line running from Fort Clark on the Missouri River, situate a few miles below the mouth of the Kansas; thence, due south to the River Arkansas, and down the same to the Mississippi; up the same to Sullivan's line; then west to the north-west corner, being a point one hundred miles due north of the mouth of the Kansas River; and with this line south to the north bank of the Missouri opposite the mouth of the Kansas. Sullivan's line was run in 1816, in execution of the Osage treaty of 1808, and is the northern boundary of the half-breed tract, and the line referred to in the treaty of 1824 with the Sacs and Foxes, and which the Osage treaty of 1808, included.

This treaty had every sanction that a ratification by our Senate could give it, and is a recognition of an ·Indian title in the Osages to nearly all the territory now embraced in the State of Missouri, and the greater part of Arkansas; and of an Osage right to the land claimed by Reddick up to November, 1808; and yet the county and town of St. Louis, the seat of government in Upper Louisiana during the existence of the Spanish colonial government there, the post of New Madrid, the county, town, and post of St. Charles,—were all within the cession made by the Osages; and within which cession, lay a great mass of Spanish orders of survey and grants, in regard to which this country has been legislating and adjudicating for nearly fifty years, without any one ever supposing that such concessions were affected by these loose Indian pretensions set up to the country at a time when the concessions were made; pretensions that the Spanish government notoriously disregarded, further than a cautious policy required. If permits to inhabit and cultivate were given in so many other instances, regardless of Indian claims, no reason exists why Honoré Tesson, could not lawfully improve the land in dispute under his permit; and in view of this notorious state of facts, the treaty of 1804 with the Sacs and Foxes, by an additional article, declared that nothing in that treaty contained should affect the claim of any individual (or individuals, if more than one) who had obtained grants of land from the Spanish government beyond the boundary lines of the country then ceded to the United States, on lands claimed by the Sacs and Foxes, but not ceded by that treaty; provided, that such grants had at any time been made known to the said Indian tribes, and recognized by them.· That the large, valuable, and notorious improvements were made by Honoré, at a place where the Sacs and Foxes themselves resided at the time, is a historical fact. He resided there as notoriously as they did. His claim to this property was transferred to Reddick, and was occupied for twenty-five years under Tesson and Reddick, and his heirs before the treaty of 1824 was made. It was held and improved by authority of the Spanish government, and claimed as individual property, to which the Indian right of possession did not extend; of this the Indians never complained, nor do they now complain; no half-breed owner and Indian descendant is defending this suit; it is defended by trespassers, showing no color of claim under the half-breeds, or any one else; shelter is sought under the assumption that Honoré's permit and inhabitation were neither known or recognized by the Sacs and Foxes, and that therefore, the additional article of the treaty of 1804, cannot protect the title of Reddick. We concur with the opinion of Mr. Attorney-General Grundy, in his report of 1839 on Reddick's title, to the Secretary of the Treasury, (Opinions of Attorney-Gen., 1230,) that it must be presumed that the Indians both had knowledge and assented to Honoré's claim; and we are furthermore of opinion, that the Indian tribes, and the half-breeds, who claim under them, must be held to knowledge, and to consent, that Honoré took and held, rightful possessions, from the fact of his open and notorious actual occupancy, and holding for himself, in their midst. This is the settled rule in other cases, and no reason is seen why it should not apply in this case. The reasons are quite as strong, and the rule quite as necessary in its application here, as it was in the case of Landes v. Brant, (10 How. 375,) where we enforced the rule. We are therefore of opinion that the supposed Indian right of occupancy did not affect the confirmation by Congress in this case, and that the remark of the recorder, " If Indian rights extinguished," was surplusage, and which remark Congress properly disregarded.

That the confirmation of 1816 carried the title with it, if the confirmation was valid, has so often been decided by this court, that it is not open to discussion; nor is it disputed here on behalf of the defendants below. The confirming act of 1816, however, ordered that a patent should issue according to a survey afterwards to be made, in all cases confirmed by the act. This has been done. The patent recites the necessary facts to connect the confirmation with the patent, and gives date to it by relation, as a legal title, from the 29th of April, 1816, according to the boundaries set forth in the patent; and as this ruling covers all the instructions that were given in the court below, and all such as were refused, we order that the judgment be affirmed.

Order.

This cause came on to be heard on the transcript of the

record from the District Court of the United States for the Southern District of Iowa and was argued by counsel. On consideration whereof, it is now here ordered and adjudged by this court that the judgment of the said District Court in this cause be, and the same is hereby, affirmed with costs.

JOHN JACKSON, PLAINTIFF IN ERROR, v. SAMUEL HALE, GEORGE C. MANY, AND JOHN V. AYER.

Where a warehouseman gave a receipt for wheat which he did not receive, and afterwards the quantity which he actually had was divided amongst the respective depositors, an action of replevin, brought by the assignee of the fictitious receipt, could not be maintained when, under it, one of these portions was seized.

Evidence offered to show that the wheat in question was assigned to the defendant, was objected to by the plaintiff in the replevin; but such objection was properly overruled. The plaintiff had shown no title in himself.

So also, evidence was admissible to show that the receiver of the fictitious certificate had never deposited any wheat in the warehouse.

The defendants in this case were the assignees of the original warehouseman, and were not responsible, unless it could be shown that wheat was deposited, which had come into their possession.

THIS case was brought up by writ of error from the District Court of the United States for the District of Wisconsin.

The facts are stated in the opinion of the court.

It was argued by *Mr. Lawrence*, for the plaintiff in error, and by *Mr. Lee*, and *Mr. Seward*, for the defendants in error.

Mr. Lawrence, for the plaintiff in error, made the following points.

First. The Judge of the District Court erred in ruling upon the admission of testimony, that a depositary, when there is a joint interest in the deposit, may change the joint interest of depositors into an interest in severalty, by mere setting apart, without delivery made.

Second. The court erred in holding, that a depositor, having a joint interest in one description of property, his depositary could confer a title upon him, to the extent of such joint interest, from deposits of a different description; or that if his deposits were in part winter wheat, &c., his depositary might set apart to him the spring wheat of other depositors, and such act of the depositary would give title.

Third. Testimony was improperly admitted, that " the property rose in value after it was taken in replevin," and "that the agent of the plaintiff was told that the wheat belonged to parties," in whom defendants had pleaded property—as also the evidence to contradict the receipt.

Fourth. The Judge of the District Court should not have decided to refuse a new trial, if defendants would consent to remit a part of the recovery for detention, when a recovery had been secured by testimony taken under objection.

Mr Chief Justice TANEY delivered the opinion of the court.

It appears, in this case, that C. H. Hutchinson was a warehouseman at the city of Ranasho, (formerly Southport,) in Wisconsin, and in that character had received on deposit large quantities of wheat from different persons, which, by common consent, was mingled in general mass.

On the 22d of February, 1850, Hale, Many, and Ayer, the defendants, succeeded Hutchinson in the business and possession of this warehouse; and at the time the possession was transferred, the portions of wheat to which the several depositors were respectively entitled, were separated and put into different bins; and the old receipts given by Hutchinson, surrendered.

In this division, 7000 bushels, which had been deposited at different times by Adams & Son, were placed in a separate bin for them; and they, as well as Hutchinson and Hale, Many and Ayer, were present when the division was made.

Previous to this, however, and while Hutchinson was still carrying on business at the warehouse, he gave the following receipt to Hubbard, Faulkner & Co.

Received into store, Southport, January 19, 1850, for account of Messrs. Hubbard, Faulkner & Co., four thousand bushels of spring wheat, deliverable on board vessel free of charge, on return of this receipt, and not insured against fire.

4000 bushels of wheat.   C. L. HUTCHINSON.

Hubbard, Faulkner & Co. never deposited any wheat at the warehouse, but paid Hutchinson $2,640 as the price of the quantity mentioned in the receipt; and afterwards sold it to John Jackson, the plaintiff in error, for $1,050, and indorsed and delivered to him the receipt.

The plaintiff, claiming to be entitled to this quantity of wheat under this assignment, sued out a writ of replevin against the defendants, and the marshal, under the direction of the agents of the plaintiff, replevied and delivered to him 4000 bushels of wheat, part of the 7000 bushels, placed in a bin for Adams & Son, as herein before mentioned.

The defendants appeared and pleaded sundry pleas, and among others, property in Adams & Son. And at the trial, the jury found for the defendants, and that the wheat taken, was the property of Adams & Son; and its value, $2,640; and assessed damages for the detention, at the sum of four hundred dollars.

Upon a motion made by the plaintiff, for a new trial, the court it seems, were of opinion that a new trial should be granted, unless the defendant remitted all the damages assessed as aforesaid, beyond the interest on the value of the wheat from the day it was taken under the replevin, to the day of trial. And under this opinion of the court, the defendants remitted all of the damages, except one hundred and one dollars, and the judgment was thereupon accordingly entered.

Upon this judgment the present writ of error is brought.

The facts above stated, are set out in an exception taken by the plaintiff. The statement shows, that Hubbard, Faulkner & Co., in whose favor the warehouse receipt was given by Hutchinson, never deposited any wheat in this warehouse, but paid for this receipt in money. And the plaintiff offers no evidence but the receipt itself to show that Hutchinson had any wheat of his own in this warehouse at the time it was given, or at any other time; and in the division which took place when the possession was transferred to the defendants, none was set apart as belonging to Hutchinson.

Upon such a state of facts, it is difficult to see how any question of law could have arisen, open to dispute. The plaintiff indeed objected to the evidence offered to prove that the wheat replevied was, in the division of the general mass, set apart in a bin as the property of Adams & Co. But if there was any thing in the objection, (and clearly there was not,) it would not avail the plaintiff unless he could show that it belonged to him. For he could not maintain the replevin unless he proved that the wheat was his property. And if he had no wheat there, it was perfectly immaterial whether it was lawfully divided, or remained in general mass. And if the want of a legal division among the owners, prevented it from being specifically the property of Adams & Co., it would equally prevent it from being the separate property of the plaintiff, even if he was entitled to the quantity he claimed in the general mass.

So, too, he excepts to evidence offered to prove that Hubbard Faulkner & Co. had never deposited any wheat in the warehouse. The evidence was undoubtedly admissible. For whether they had done so or not, was the fact in dispute. Besides, the plaintiff himself had already proved the fact by his own witness, Faulkner, who stated that Hubbard, Faulkner & Co. paid money to Hutchinson for the wheat. They did not, therefore, deposit it themselves. And as regards the damages remitted, certainly the plaintiff is not injured by having the judgment rendered against him for a smaller sum instead of a larger. If either party had a right to complain of the opinion of the court under which the *remittitur* was entered, it was the defendants, and not the plaintiff. For, if a party uses the process of the law wilfully and oppressively, his conduct may be considered by the jury in estimating the damages sustained by the injured party. And proof of the conduct of the agents of the plaintiff in this respect, and also of the damage sustained by the defendants by the loss of a favorable market, were properly submitted to the consideration of the jury.

The receipt of Hutchinson, upon which the plaintiff relied, did not prove, or tend to prove, that the wheat taken on the replevin was the wheat therein mentioned — or that any wheat belonging to Hutchinson, or to Hubbard, Faulkner & Co., ever came to the hands of the defendants. It showed that Hutchinson held so much wheat for Hubbard, Faulkner & Co. But the defendants are not answerable for his contracts, or his warehouse receipts, unless it is shown that the property came into their possession. And there is not the slightest evidence to show that any wheat, belonging either to Hutchinson or to Hubbard, Faulkner & Co., was ever in the warehouse after it was transferred to the defendants.

The judgment of the District Court is affirmed, with costs.

Order.

This cause came on to be heard on the transcript of the record from the District Court of the United States for the District of Wisconsin, and was argued by counsel. On consideration whereof, it is now here ordered, and adjudged by this court, that the judgment of the said District Court, in this cause be, and the same is hereby, affirmed, with costs, and interest until the same is paid, at the same rate per annum that similar judgments bear in the courts of the State of Wisconsin.

JAMES STEPHENS, APPELLANT, v. ISAAC H. CADY.

Where the copy-right of a map was taken out under the act of Congress, and the copperplate engraving seized and sold under an execution, the purchaser did not acquire the right to strike off and sell copies of the map.

The court below decided that an injunction to prevent such striking off and selling, could not issue, without a return of the purchase-money. This decision was erroneous.

A copy-right is a "property in notion, and has no corporeal tangible substance," and is not the subject of seizure and sale by execution. It can be reached by a creditor's bill in chancery, but in such case, the court would probably have to decree a transfer in the mode pointed out in the act of Congress.

THIS was an appeal from the Circuit Court of the United States for the District of Rhode Island, sitting as a Court of Equity.

The facts are stated in the opinion of the court.

It was submitted on printed argument by the appellant, in proper person. No counsel appeared for the appellee.

Mr. Justice NELSON delivered the opinion of the court.

This is an appeal from the Circuit Court of the United States for the District of Rhode Island.

The bill was filed by the appellant in the court below, to restrain the defendant from printing and publishing a map of the State of Rhode Island and Providence Plantations, in violation of the complainant's copy-right.

The facts are briefly these: The complainant, on the 23d of April, 1831, took out the copy-right of a map, the title of which is as follows: "A Topographical Map of the State of Rhode Island and Providence Plantations, surveyed trigonometrically and in detail, by James Stephens, topographer and civil engineer, Newport, R. I., 1831, the right whereof he claims as author, in conformity with the act of Congress, entitled an act to amend the several acts respecting copy-rights," and since then has been engaged in printing, publishing, and vending the said maps, by virtue of the copy-right thus obtained. In March, 1846, a judgment was recovered against him, in the Common Pleas of Bristol county, Massachusetts, for $194.23, upon which an execution was issued, and the copperplate engraving of the map in question seized, and sold, and bid off by the defendant for the sum of $245, he being the highest bidder. Having thus become entitled to the property in the engraving, he claimed the right to print and publish the maps, and in pursuance of this supposed right, he has been engaged in printing, publishing and vending the same.

On the hearing upon the bill, answer, and proofs, the court below differed in opinion, as to the effect of the sale of the copperplate engraving of the map; but agreed that no injunction could issue without a repayment of the purchase-money, which was refused by the complainant; whereupon the court dismissed the bill with costs.

The single question in the case is, whether or not the property acquired by the defendant in the copperplate, at the sheriff's sale, carried with it, as an incident, the right to print and publish the map engraved upon its face.

Upon this question the court below divided in opinion, but finally agreed in dismissing the bill.

The appellee has not followed the case into this court, and we have not, therefore, been favored with the grounds and reasons relied on for sustaining the decree; nor have we been furnished with the reasons of the court for the same. The ground upon which the decision was ultimately placed, namely, the refusal of the complainant to refund the purchase-money, is certainly not satisfactory; for if the copy-right of the map, or any right to print or publish the same, passed with the purchase of the plate, as incidental, as there is nothing in the facts of the case to invalidate the sale, the title became complete in the purchaser, and could not be rightfully interfered with. But if otherwise, then there was no ground for imposing the repayment of the purchase-money, as a condition to the relief prayed for; the injunction should have been awarded, and the defendant directed to account.

But from the consideration we have given to the case, we are satisfied that the property acquired by the sale in the engraved plate, and the copy-right of the map secured to the author under the act of Congress, are altogether different and independent of each other, and have no necessary connection. The copy-right is an exclusive right to the multiplication of the copies, for the benefit of the author or his assigns, disconnected from the plate, or any other physical existence. It is an incorporeal right to print and publish the map, or, as said by Lord Mansfield in Millar v. Taylor (4 Burr. 2396,) " a property in notion, and has no corporeal tangible substance."

The engraved plate and the press are the mechanical instruments, or means by which the copies are multiplied, as the types and press are the instruments by which the copies of a book are produced. And to say that the right to print and publish the copies, adheres to and passes with the means by which they are produced, would be saying, in effect, that the exclusive right to make any given work of art necessarily belonged to the person who happened to become the owner of the tools with which it was made; and that if the defendant in this case had purchased the stereotyped plates of a book, instead of the engraved plate, he would have been entitled to the copy-right of the work, or at least, to the right to print, publish, and vend it; and yet, we suppose that the statement of any such pretension is so extravagant as to require no argument to refute it. Even the transfer of the manuscript of a book will not, at common law, carry with it a right to print and publish the work, without the express consent of the author, as the property in the manuscript, and the right to multiply the copies, are two separate and distinct interests. 4 Burr. 2330, 2396; 2 Eden, R. 329; 2 Atkyns, R. 342; 2 Story, R. 100.

Lord Mansfield observed, in Millar v. Taylor, that "no disposition, no transfer of paper upon which the composition is written, marked, or impressed, (though it gives the power to print and publish,) can be construed a conveyance of the copy, (by which he means copy-right, as appears from a previous part of his opinion,) without the author's express consent 'to print and publish,' much less against his will."

Now, it seems to us, that the transfer of the manuscript of a book by the author would, of itself, furnish a much stronger argument for the inference of a conveyance of the right to multiply copies, than exists in the case of a transfer of the plate in question, or of the stereotype plates, as the ideas and sentiments, or in other words, the composition and substance of the work, is thereby transferred. But the property in the copy-right is regarded as a different and distinct right, wholly detached from the manuscript, or any other physical existence, and will not pass with the manuscript unless included by express words in the transfer.

The copperplate engraving, like any other tangible personal property, is the subject of seizure and sale, on execution, and the title passes to the purchaser, the same as if made at a private sale. But the incorporeal right, secured by the statute to the author, to multiply copies of the map, by the use of the plate, being intangible, and resting altogether in grant, is not the subject of seizure or sale by means of this process — certainly not at common law. No doubt the property may be reached by a creditor's bill, and be applied to the payment of the debts of the author, the same as stock of the debtor is reached and applied, the court compelling a transfer and sale of the stock for the benefit of the creditors. 20 J. R. 554; 5 J. Ch. 280; S. C. 4 Id. 687; 1 Paige, 637. But in case of such remedy, we suppose, it would be necessary for the court to compel a transfer to the purchaser, in conformity with the requirements of the copy-right act, in order to invest him with a complete title to the property. The first section of that act provides, that the author of any map, chart, &c., his executors, administrators, or legal assigns, shall have the sole right of printing, publishing, and vending the same, during the period for which the copy-right has been secured. And the seventh section forbids any person from printing, publishing, or selling the map or chart, under heavy penalties, without the consent of the proprietor of the copy-right, first obtained in writing, signed in the presence of two credible witnesses. Act of Congress, Feb. 3, 1831.

An assignment, therefore, that would vest the assignee with the property of the copy-right, according to the act of Congress, must be in writing, and signed in the presence of two witnesses, and it may, I think, well be doubted whether a transfer even by a sale, under a decree of a court of chancery, would pass the title so as to protect the purchaser, unless by a conveyance, in conformity with this requirement. 6 B. & Cr. 169; 1 Car. & P. 558; R. & M. 187; D. & K. 215.

It is unnecessary, however, to express an opinion upon the point. It is sufficient, for the purposes of this case, to say, that the right in question is wholly independent of, and disconnected from, the engraved plate; and, that there is no foundation for the defence set up, that it passed as appurtenant to the sale and transfer of the property, in the engraved plate, from which the copies of the map were struck off.

For these reasons, we are of opinion that the decree below, must be reversed with costs, and the proceedings remitted, with directions that a decree be entered for the complainant, in conformity with this opinion.

Order.

This cause came on to be heard on the transcript of the record from the Circuit Court of the United States for the District of Rhode Island, and was argued by counsel. On consideration whereof, it is now here ordered, adjudged, and decreed by this court, that the decree of the said Circuit Court in this cause be, and the same is hereby, reversed, with costs, and that this cause be, and the same is hereby, remanded to the said Circuit Court, with directions to enter a decree therein, in conformity to the opinion of this court.

L. I. STAINBACK ET AL., CLAIMANTS OF THE SHIP WASHINGTON, HER TACKLE, &C., APPELLANTS, v. WILLIAM A. RAE, IN HIS OWN RIGHT, AND AS ADMINISTRATOR OF JOSEPH PORTER WHEELER, DECEASED, AND EDMUND CROSBY, MASTER, OWNERS OF THE SHIP MARY FRANCES, AND FREDERICK TUDOR, OWNERS OF THE CARGO OF SAID SHIP, APPELLEES.

Where a collision takes place between two vessels at sea, which is the result of inevitable accident, without the negligence or fault of either party, each vessel must bear its own loss.

Mr. Justice Curtis did not sit in this cause, having been of counsel in the court below.

THIS was an appeal from the Circuit Court of the United States for the District of Massachusetts, in admiralty.

The facts are stated in the opinion of the court.

It was argued by *Mr. Badger* and *Mr. Lawrence*, for the appellants, and by *Mr. Goodrich*, for the appellees.

The points made by the counsel for the appellants, were the following :

First. That the watch on board the Washington, was usual, proper, and safe ; and that consequently, no negligence is imputable to her.

Second. That in the state of the weather, and the position of the two vessels in respect to each other, it was impossible that the Washington could have discovered the Mary Frances at a greater distance than a quarter of a mile, and highly improbable that she could have discovered her at more than half that distance ; and that under such circumstances, considering the admitted rate at which the two vessels were approaching each other, it was impossible for the Washington, by any manœuvre whatever, to have avoided the collision.

Third. That if the Mary Frances, as stated by some of her witnesses, discovered the Washington ten minutes, and as stated by others, five minutes, before the collision, the two vessels must have been at a distance of two miles, or at least one, from each other, and it was in her power, by changing her course, to have avoided the collision ; and if, as stated by the same witnesses, she perceived that the Washington had not discovered her, it was her duty to have done so, and consequently the collision is attributable to the fault, not of the Washington, but of the Mary Frances.

And hence, that the collision was either a mere misfortune, without fault in either party, or without fault on the part of the Washington, and, in either view, the decree must be reversed.

Mr. Goodrich, for the appellees, contended,

1. That on the night of the collision, the weather was fair and starlight overhead, with a hazy horizon, and that the night was not unusually dark.

2. The ships being each closehauled on the wind, neither was materially to windward of the other, and each crew was equally favorably situated to see the other ship, and to hear hailing from the other ship.

And if either ship was to windward of the other, and for this reason less favorably situated in those respects, it was the Mary Frances.

3. That the crew of the Mary Frances had a good look-out

45 *

before, and at the time of the collision, and used all due care to prevent it; and that they actually saw and hailed the Washington in time to prevent the collision; and that the crew of the Washington did no act to avoid the collision, and the collision was attributable to the absence of a good look-out on board the latter ship.

4. The appellees maintain, that the rule of the sea is, that where two vessels, closehauled on the wind, approach each other, and must meet unless the course of one is changed, the vessel having her starboard tacks on board, must keep her course, and the one having her larboard tacks on board, must bear up and give way. The Alexander Wise, 2 Wm. Robinson, Adm. R. 65, 68; The Virgil, Id. 201; The Mary Stewart, Id. 244; The Chester, 3 Haggard, Adm. R. 316; The Ligo, 2 Id. 356, 360; Clapp v. Young, 6 Law Reporter, 111–13; 1 Conkling's Admiralty Practice, 303–6; The Europa, 14 Jurist, 627, (2 Law and Eq. R. 562–4); The Genesee v. Fitzhugh, 12 Howard, 443; Walsh v. Rogers, 13 Id. 283; Pritchard's Admiralty Digest, art. 12, p. 156; 1 Bell's Com. 583.

5. That the appellees having made out a *primá facie* case of want of skill and care on the part of the crew of the Washington, the burden of proof is on the appellants to show that due care and skill was used. Authorities previously cited. The George, 9 Jurist, 282, 4; Notes of Cases, 161; Pritchard's Admiralty Digest, art. 114, 116, and 117, p. 137, tit. Damage.

6. That appellees are entitled in law to recover compensation for freight and cargo, as well as for the ship of appellants. See 3 Kent's Com. 6 ed. 232, § 8; Story on Bailments, ch. 6, §§ 599, 602, 608, and case of Dundee, note to § 609; 1 Bell's Com. 580.

12. The Washington was in fault, because her officers and crew did not maintain that constant care and vigilance which her position required.

A. The Washington, having her larboard tacks on board, was bound to give way.

B. No officer, and only two men on deck, attending to the navigation of the ship—one, McCoy, was at the wheel, the other, Simmons. a boy, was on the look-out.

C. A large ship, with noisy passengers, nearing the land, under full sail, in a hazy night, should have had at least two men on the look-out.

D. No sufficient look-out before the call to the pumps.

E. The Washington might have avoided the collision.

Mr. Justice NELSON delivered the opinion of the court.

This is an appeal from the Circuit Court of the United States for the District of Massachusetts, in admiralty.

The libel charges, that the ship Mary Frances, laden with ice, was on a voyage from Boston to New Orleans, and that on the 11th December, 1847, at about half-past three o'clock in the morning, while on her starboard tack, in the prosecution of the voyage, she was struck by the ship Washington, nearly midships on her larboard side, breaking in her bulwarks and stanchions, and starting her planks and timbers, so that in a few hours she filled with water, and the master and hands were obliged to abandon her, and she went to the bottom.

The respondents, in their answer, state, that the ship Washington, at the time mentioned in the libel, was upon the high seas between George's Shoals and the south shore of Nantucket Island, at a distance of about sixty miles from land; that the wind was blowing a moderate breeze from the south-south-west, and the Washington, with all her reefs out, with courses free, and main-topgallant sails, jib, and flying-jib, and fore and main-topmast-stay-sails set, was sailing full and by, upon her larboard tack, and steering due west by the compass, and as near the wind as possible; that she had a competent watch on deck, keeping a good look-out, the weather being dark and hazy towards the horizon, especially to the leeward of the ship, but the stars visible above. That while she was thus pursuing her course, at about half-past three o'clock in the morning, the Mary Frances was seen about four points on the lee bow of the Washington, and was then in the act of running up, and did immediately run up into the wind athwart the hawse of the Washington; and, that instantly, on the discovery of the Mary Frances, and of the course she was pursuing, the helm of the Washington was put hard up, and every endeavor made by the hands on deck to put her before the wind, and to avoid a collision.

The facts, as proved on the part of the libellants, are substantially as follows:

That about half-past three o'clock, on the morning of the 11th December, 1847, the hands on board the Mary Frances, while she was standing to the eastward, on her starboard tack, the wind from the south-south-west, closehauled, descried the Washington something less than a quarter of a mile distant, about a point and a half forward of the Mary Frances's larboard beam, some of the hands say, on the larboard bow two or three points. The Washington was standing to the westward when first seen, and orders were immediately given to put the helm hard down, and, at the same time, the hands cried out to those on board the Washington, to keep off. The collision took place, as estimated, from five to seven minutes after the Washington was first discovered. The Mary Frances was struck midships, on the larboard side, her bulwarks stove in, and her planks below the white streak on the opposite side were broken, and all her forerigging carried away. The ship was abandoned with thirteen feet of water in her hold, being a wreck, and wholly unmanageable. The Washington was not at first seen plainly, as the weather was hazy. The second mate of the Mary Frances, who had charge of the watch, and one of the first to descry the Washington, says the weather was hazy and thick, the sky was overcast, no moon or stars visible. The Mary Frances was about 320 tons burden; the Washington about 500 tons

The evidence, on behalf of the respondents, is substantially as follows:

The Washington was bound from Liverpool to Virginia by the way of New York, and had on board a cargo of salt, and some 170 steerage passengers. She was on her larboard tack, closehauled, the wind about south-south-west. The man at the wheel states, that an order was given from the deck, "put the helm hard up, there is a ship into us;" that the order was obeyed instantly, but the collision immediately followed. Simmons, one of the hands, states, that he was on the weather side of the Washington's windlass on the look-out; that the weather was dark, cloudy, and hazy; that he descried the Mary Frances about a minute and a half or two minutes before the collision; that she was on the lee bow of the Washington, between three and four points; that at first he could not determine her course on account of the thick weather. When he first saw her he sang out to the man at the wheel to put helm hard up. The witness heard a noise or hail about half a minute before he descried the Mary Frances, but could not determine whence it came; supposed it might be from some of the passengers, as they were in the habit of making a noise.

This witness is substantially corroborated by several others on board the Washington. Part of the watch were at the pumps at the time the collision took place.

The testimony on both sides agree, that each vessel was going at the rate of five and a half knots the hour.

The court below decreed in favor of the libellants.

Upon a careful perusal of the evidence in behalf of the libellants and the respondents, it is apparent that there is much less discrepancy and contradiction among the witnesses called by the respective parties, as to the material facts, than are usually found in these collision cases.

All agree as to the state of the weather — thick, hazy and dark; as to the direction of the wind — from the south-south-west; the course of the vessels — the Mary Frances on the starboard tack, standing south-east, and the Washington on the larboard, standing nearly due west; the rate of speed—fiye and a half knots the hour. And even as it respects the distance the vessels were from each other when first descried, there is very little, if any difference.

According to the witnesses on board the Mary Frances, the Washington was less than a quarter of a mile distant, when she was first seen. The distance of the former vessel, when first seen by the hands on board the Washington, is not stated directly; but Simmons, the look-out, testifies, she was seen from one and a half to two minutes before the collision, which, regarding the combined speed of the two vessels, must have been at about the same distance. The probability is, that the two vessels were much nearer each other than a quarter of a mile, when first seen. The chief mate of the Mary Frances, who was asleep in his berth at the time, but immediately afterwards on deck, fixes the distance the vessel could be seen in that state of the weather at about two hundred yards; and this corresponds with the opinion expressed by the master of the Washington, where he says the Mary Frances might have been seen at a distance of about four times her length. The answer of the experts is that the distance a vessel could be seen in such weather would be uncertain. The course the two vessels were steering was calculated to increase the difficulty, and embarrass the look-out in descrying the vessel ahead, for, as they were approaching each other by the wind, they presented to the eye the edges of the sails, and not the breadth of them, as in other positions.

There is some apparent discrepancy between the witnesses of the two vessels in respect to their relative position at the time they were first seen. The hands on board the Mary Frances state, when they first descried the Washington, she was two or three points on their larboard bow, one of them states, she was a point and a half forward of their larboard beam.

The hands on board the Washington state that the Mary Frances was on their lee bow when first seen, which would place the Washington to the windward. This may be reconciled probably by what is stated by the experts, who agree, that two vessels, approaching each other as these were, the hands on each would necessarily see the approaching vessel over the lee bow, and which may have led those on board the Washington to suppose this vessel was on the weather side.

The manœuvre of each, on discovering the other, it is agreed, was proper; and, indeed, the only one that could have afforded any chance of preventing the collision. The Mary Frances was thrown into the wind by putting her helm h rd down, and the Washington bore away before the wind by putting her helm hard up. The orders were not only proper and skilful, but were promptly given and instantly executed; and unless fault can be imputed to the latter vessel in not descrying the Mary Frances sooner, so as to have afforded time for these manœuvres to have avoided the disaster, we do not see how she can be properly chargeable with the consequences; and as to that, the difficulty, if not impossibility of discovering a vessel ahead at a greater distance than the Mary Frances was seen by the hands on the Washington, the relative position of the two vessels while approaching each other by the wind, presenting only the edges of the sails instead of their breadth, and in thick and hazy weather, such as existed in this case, in connection with the combined speed of the vessels at the time, seem to furnish evidence sufficient to repel any such imputation. The two vessels must have come together probably in less than two minutes after they were first seen. The look-out appears to have been competent and sufficient, and such is, as we understand it, the opinion of the experts examined, and who were selected by both the parties.

Indeed, the fact that the Mary Frances must have been seen about the same time by the hands of the Washington that she was seen by those on board of the Mary Frances, and which we think is fairly borne out by the evidence, of itself, should be regarded as conclusive against the charge of fault in this respect.

We are of opinion, therefore, that the collision was the result of an inevitable accident, arising out of one of the perils of navigation, and, in judgment of law, is not attributable to the fault of either party. And in such cases the settled rule in admiralty in England is, that each vessel must bear its own loss, which rule has been heretofore recognized by this court, but has not been before directly applied. 2 Dodson's Adm. R. 83; Woodrop Sims, 1 How. Rep. 28; Id. 89; 3 Kent's Com. 231; Abbot on Shipping, Pt. 3, ch. 1, and Pt. 4, ch. 10, § 10; 2 Brown's Civ. & Adm. Law, 204-7; 5 How. Rep. 503, and cases.

The rule is not uniform upon the continent, as several of the maritime states in such cases apportion the loss upon the two vessels. Abbot, 224, 230; 2 Brown's Civ. & Ad. Law, 204-6; 3 Kent's Com. 230, 231, 232.

But we think it more just and equitable, and more consistent with sound principles, that where the loss happens from a collision which is the result of inevitable accident, without the negligence or fault of either party, each should bear his own.

There seems no good reason for charging one of the vessels with a share of a loss resulting from a common calamity beyond that happening to herself, when she is without fault, and therefore in no just sense responsible for it.

Our opinion is, that the decree of the court below must be reversed, with costs, and the proceedings remitted, with directions to enter a decree dismissing the libel with costs.

Order.

This cause came on to be heard on the transcript of the record from the Circuit Court of the United States for the District of Massachusetts, and was argued by counsel. On consideration whereof, it is now here ordered, adjudged, and decreed, by this court, that the decree of the said Circuit Court in this cause be, and the same is hereby, reversed, with costs, and that this cause be, and the same is hereby, remanded to the said Circuit Court with directions to dismiss the libel with costs.

ELISHA BLOOMER, APPELLANT, *v.* JOHN W. McQUEWAN, ALLEN R. McQUEWAN, AND SAMUEL DOUGLAS, PARTNERS, UNDER THE NAME OF McQUEWANS & DOUGLAS.

The patent for Woodworth's planing machine was extended from 1842 to 1849, by the Board of Commissioners.

Under that extension, this court decided, in Wilson *v.* Rousseau, (4 How. 688,) that an assignee had a right to continue the use of the machine which he then had.

In 1845, Congress, by a special act, extended the time still further from 1849 to 1856. Under that extension, an assignee has still the same right.

By the cases of Evans *v.* Eaton, (3 Wheaton, 548,) and Wilson *v.* Rousseau, (4 How. 688,) these two propositions are settled, viz.:

1. That a special act of Congress in favor of a patentee, extending the time beyond that originally limited, must be considered as ingrafted on the general law.
2. That, under the general law in force when this special act of Congress was passed, a party who had purchased the right to use a planing machine during the period to which the patent was first limited, was entitled to continue to use it during the extension authorized by that law, unless there is something in the law itself to forbid it.

But there is nothing in the act of Congress, passed in 1845, forbidding such use; and, therefore, the assignee has the right.

Mr. Justice Curtis, having been of counsel, did not sit on the trial of this cause, and *Mr. Justice Wayne* was absent.

THIS was an appeal from the Circuit Court of the United States for the Western District of Pennsylvania, sitting as a Court of Equity.

It was a bill filed by Bloomer, who claimed under Wilson, the assignee of Woodworth's planing machine. The whole of

Wilson's title is set forth in the report of the case of Wilson v. Rousseau, 4 Howard, 646, as is also the act of Congress passed on the 26th February, 1845, (4 How. 662,) extending the patent for seven years from the 27th of December, 1849.

McQuewan claimed, through two *mesne* assignments from Woodworth and Strong, by virtue of a license granted on the 8th of November, 1833.

The bill and answer covered a great deal of ground, which need not be noticed in this report.

Amongst other averments was this, that the license conveyed no right to use the machine during the extension for seven years from 1849, under the act of Congress passed in 1845; and the decision of the court being in favor of the defendants below upon this point, it is unnecessary to state all the points and arguments upon other matters.

The court below were divided in opinion, and the bill was of course dismissed. Bloomer appealed to this court.

It was argued by *Mr. Keller* and *Mr. St. George T. Campbell*, for the appellant, and *Mr. Dunlop*, for the appellees.

The fourth point made by the counsel for the appellant was as follows:

IV. Whether the licensee of a right to use the patented machine for the original term of the patent, is entitled to continue the use of the same during the extension by Congress.

The facts in this regard appearing by the record, are

1. That Collins and Smith, who were assignees for the first term of the district in question, granted to Barnet the right for the city of Pittsburg and Allegany county, "to construct and use during the residue of the said terms of fourteen years," the patented machine, and by the same assignment covenanted "not themselves to construct and use," nor to give license to any other person than Barnet "during the terms aforesaid," and Barnet covenanted not to construct more than fifty machines "during the terms aforesaid."

. (The word "terms" is used in the plural, as it will be perceived by the assignment that the grantors were the owners also of the Emmons patent, and that the limitation of his right applied to the duration of both.)

2. Barnet assigns all his "right, title, interest, and claim of the within patent for Woodworth's planing machine to G. Warner and John W. McQuewan, their heirs and assigns," except seven rights previously given.

3. It seems to have been granted, below, that Warner had assigned his license to McQuewan, and McQuewan to the two

co-defendants, and that the machine was made during the first term of the patent; hence arises the question, have the appellees the right to continue its use during the congressional extension?

For the appellants it is submitted:

1. That this question, and the principles upon which it must be decided, have been already passed upon by this court.

In Wilson v. Rousseau, (4 Howard,) the question was of the right of the licensee to continue the use of the machine during the extension by the commissioner. The court were divided in opinion. In that delivered as their judgment, the right of the licensee to the continued use was put exclusively upon the terms of the 18th section, which were, "The benefit of such renewal shall extend to assignees and grantees of the right to use the thing patented, to the extent of their respective interests therein." Without that provision it is conceded by the learned judge, in delivering the opinion of the court, "that all the rights of assignees or grantees, whether in a share of the patent or to a specified portion of the territory held under it, terminate at the end of the fourteen years, and become reinvested in the patentee by the new grant."

"From that date he is again possessed of 'the full and exclusive right and liberty of making, using, and vending to others the invention,' whatever it may be, not only portions of the monopoly held by assignees and grantees, as subjects of trade and commerce, but the patented articles or machines throughout the country, purchased for practical use in the business affairs of life, are embraced within the operation of the extension. This latter class of assignees and grantees are reached by the new grant of the exclusive right to use the things patented. Purchasers of the machines, and who were in the use of them at the time, are disabled from further use immediately, as that right became vested exclusively in the patentee. Making and vending the invention are prohibited by the corresponding terms of his grant."

And the learned Judge, in expressing the opinion of the court, further declared that the provision in the 18th section, above referred to, was "intended to restore or save to them," (those in use of the thing patented at the time of the renewal,) "that right which, without the clause, would have been vested again exclusively in the patentee."

And the learned Judges who dissented from the opinion of the court did so upon the ground that even this clause of the 18th section did not confer upon the licensees the right claimed in their behalf.

Thus it is clear that the extension of a patent by lawful

authority revests in the patentee every right originally possessed by him, and that unless the law, by virtue of which it is
extended, contains a provision in favor of licensees or assignees,
their right to use ends with the term of their license. (This, of
course, does not apply to cases where the patentee has covenanted to grant any subsequently acquired extensions — none
such is pretended in this case.)

Applying, then, these principles to the act extending this
patent, (February 26, 1845,) it will be seen that it contains no
such provision as is to be found in the 18th section of the act
of 1836; and that, therefore, in accordance with the opinion of
all the judges, the entire right was reinvested in the patentee.

The general power to renew and extend a patent is conferred
by the 18th section of the act of 1836, which, after providing for
the proof of the prerequisites, declares that "it shall be the duty
of the Commissioner to renew and extend the patent, by making
a certificate thereon of such extension for the term of seven
years from and after the expiration of the first term."

The act in question provides that the patent "be, and the
same is hereby extended for the term of seven years from and
after the 27th of December, 1849, and the Commissioner of
Patents is hereby directed to make a certificate of such extension in the name of the administrator of William Woodworth,
and append an authenticated copy thereof to the original letters-
patent," &c.; the words being substantially the same as these,
judicially construed, and the intention being still further marked,
as well by the omission of any provision for the licensees, as by
the express insertion of the name of the party in whose favor
the extension was made, and to whose benefit it was intended
to enure.

The principles upon which the judgment in Wilson *v.* Rousseau, is founded, are, it is submitted, if possible, more conclusively applicable to the case of such an extension by Congress
than to one made by the Commissioner.

Such, too, has been the application made of them by many
of the learned Judges in their circuits. By Mr. Justice Nelson,
July 22, 1850, in Gibson *v.* Gifford, in a written opinion delivered
by him; by the late Mr. Justice Woodbury, July, 1850, in Mason
v. Tallman, also in a written opinion; and by Mr. Justice Mc
Lean, October 22, 1850, in Bloomer *v.* Stately.

The opinion of Mr. Justice Woodbury refers to similar decisions made by the late Justice McKinley, by Judge Ware, and
Judge Sprague.

It may be proper, with reference to the argument founded
upon the supposed intention of Congress, (not declared in the
words of the act as already shown,) to permit a continued use

during the congressional extension of machines licensed under the original term, to annex a list of the patents, extended by special acts, and thus to refer to the provisions in each, expressly declaring, where such was intended, the existence of such right, and providing for its mode of exercise or enjoyment.

The absence of such provision in the act of 1845, must, it is submitted, conclusively negative any idea of such intention, even if the judicially decided effect of such an act did not render a reference to such a source for interpretation, unnecessary.

I. January 21, 1808, to Oliver Evans, 6 Stat. at Large, 70. (With special provision for parties then using invention.) Under this act the cases of Evans v. Jordan, 9 Cranch, 199, and Evans v. Eaton, 3 Wheat. 454, were decided.

II. March 3, 1809, to Amos and William Whittemore, 6 Stat. at Large, 80, (without provision for licensees.)

III. February 7, 1815, Oliver Evans (steam engine,) 6 Stat. at Large, 147, (with proviso that no greater sum should be charged for constructing and using, than was during prior term, and subject to existing patent laws.)

IV. March 3, 1821, Samuel Parker, 6 Stat. at Large, 262, (subject to provision of then existing patent laws.)

V. March 2, 1831, John Adamson, 6 Stat. at Large, 458, (without proviso or reference to existing laws.)

VI. March 3, 1831, Samuel Browning. 6 Stat. at Large, 467, (without proviso and reference to existing laws.)

VII. May 19, 1832, Jethro Wood, 6 Stat. at Large, 486, (proviso in favor of licensees that the price shall not be advanced.)

VIII. June 30, 1834, Thomas Blanchard, Stat. at Large, 589, (with special proviso in favor of licensees.) (It may not be improper to refer to the opinion of B. F. Butler, Attorney-General, May 25, 1837, that under this act the United States had no right to use, except on the conditions of the original grant.)

IX. March 3, 1835, Robert Eastman, 6 Stat. at Large, 613, (without proviso or reference to existing laws.)

X. July 2, 1836, James Barron, 6 Stat. at Large, 678, (extending two patents without proviso in reference to existing laws, and the other with provisos in reference to licensees.)

XI. February 6, 1839, Thomas Blanchard, 6 Stat. at Large, 748, (with proviso in favor of licensees.)

XII. March 3, 1845, William Gale, 6 Stat. at Large, 895, (authorizing renewal of patent under eighteenth section of act of 1836, although it had expired, and subject to the restrictions of that act.)

XIII. March 3, 1843, Samuel K. Jennings, 6 Stat. at Large, 899, (directing Commissioner to renew patent, subject to provisions of existing laws.)

XIV. February 26, 1845, William Woodworth, 6 Stat. at Large, 936, (extending patent. Commissioner to certify to the extension in the name of the administrator — no proviso in favor of licensees, or reference to existing laws.)

XV. February 15, 1847, Thomas Blanchard, 9 Stat. at Large, 683, (with proviso in favor of licensees, on terms to be agreed or adjusted by the Circuit Court, &c.)

The point that, by an accidental error in the bill, the word " fourteen " was inserted, instead of " twenty-eight," is not deemed a proper subject of objection in this court. No such ground appears to have been taken below; the patent itself forms part of the record, and an amendment would have been, it is submitted, instantly allowed by the court below, had the objection been there made. That the patent on its face was for twenty-eight years, forms one of the objections of the appellees to its validity, and the error complained of is set right by answer of the defendants themselves.

It is not deemed necessary by the appellants to present any authorities to meet the point argued by the appellees, that an act of Congress, extending a patent for seven years, is unconstitutional and void.

It is therefore submitted that the decree should be reversed, and that the appellant is entitled to a perpetual injunction and an account.

The counsel for the appellees made several points, amongst which was the following:

1. That defendants are protected as assignees.

The bill (pages 14 to 20) asserts, and the answer admits, that the respondents claim to use the machine they are alleged to have infringed, as assignees, from 1833, the year of their purchase, under assignments from the original patentee. Being then assignees under the original patent, can they claim to continue unmolested in the use of the machine they purchased and paid for, and have erected and used for seventeen years?

Was it the design of the act of 1845, to bring disasters upon the respondents, to deprive them of the rights they had acquired in good faith, to depreciate their property, to render useless their establishments, in which they had invested large sums of money, to destroy their business, and disable them from the performance of their contracts? Such flagrant outrages are not to be imputed to a statute, unless the terms of it imperatively demand it.

The language of the act calls for no such harsh, unreasonable, and impolitic construction. It is a simple extension of the patent of 1828, and nothing more. Could any design in Congress to spread such disasters, be predicated of the simple meaning of this statute?

Chief Justice Gibson, of Pennsylvania, has laid down a rule which must commend itself to the judgment of every one,—that in the construction of statutes, the Judges, when one of those cases of hardship occurs, which continually arise, should do what their consciences irresistibly persuade them the legislature would have done, if the occurrence had been foreseen. Pennock v. Hart, 8 S. & R. 369.

And can any one doubt that if the idea of the propriety of protecting the purchasers of rights, and the uses of the thing patented, had been suggested, but they would immediately have inserted such a clause?

This act of 1845 is a private act, made for the special benefit of a particular individual, and should not have such construction as will be detrimental to others. Chief Justice Parsons, in the case of Coolidge v. Williams, has laid down the rule to be that private statutes, made for the accommodation of particular citizens or corporations, ought not to be construed to affect the rights or privileges of others, unless such construction results from express words, or from necessary implication. 4 Mass. 145.

There are no express words in this statute, which demands the construction contended for by the plaintiff.

We may appeal, too, to the language of Mr. Justice Washington, in the case of Evans v. Jordan, that arguments founded upon hardship, would be entitled to great weight, if the language of the act was not so peremptory as to forbid a construction at variance with the clear meaning of the legislature 9 Cranch, 199.

There are no words in this act to justify such savage construction as urged by the plaintiff. It declares a simple extension of the patent, and manifestly intends an extension similar to that which may be conferred by the Patent-Office, under which the rights of persons, using the invented machine under license, are protected in the enjoyment of it.

The same learned Chief Justice of Massachusetts, has also declared in the case of Wales v. Stetson, that in the consideration of the provisions of any statute, they ought to receive such a reasonable construction if the words and subject-matter will admit of it, as that the existing rights of the public or individuals be not injured. 2 Mass. 146.

If the legislature meant a simple extension of the patent for seven years, is it not a reasonable construction to suppose that it meant an extension, as ordinarily understood; as an extension of the nature of the extensions of the Patent-Office, and with the restrictions and privileges of such extensions? Is it not reasonable to conclude that they had in their mind the general act of 1836, and the clause which gave to purchasers and users of the thing patented, the right to continue that use? Is it not a reasonable construction that they meant that this special act should be construed in reference to the general law of the land? The language of the act is, that the patent of 1828 "be extended for seven years." Now what benefit would that extension be, even to complainant, without an incorporation with the general law? How could he be assignee of the right? how could he enjoy the use of the patent? how could he pretend to recover damages, without an appeal for aid to the act of 1836? The plaintiff is obliged to invoke the aid of the general law, to maintain this very action. The very plaintiff in this cause is an assignee, and undertakes to maintain this action in his own name, by calling into requisition the act of 1836.

The rule of law undoubtedly is, that laws on the same subject are to be construed together; that laws on the same subject are to be construed *pari passu*, and with reference to parallel legislation. This is clearly the rule as to general laws, which in relation to the same subject, are to be construed as one act. They are to be construed, too, in reference to parallel legislation. Penn *v.* Hamilton, 2 Watts. 60; 17 S. & R. 81; 7 Id. 404.

The right of appeal, given by the Pennsylvania act relating to divorces *a vinculo matrimonii*, was extended by implication, to the act of 1817, respecting divorces *a mensa et thoro*. Roberts *v.* Roberts, 9 S. & R. 191.

So the right to appeal from justices' judgments, in cases of contracts, was held to extend to trespass, to which the powers of magistrates had been extended, without expressly giving the right of appeal. 4 S. & R. 73.

And this wise and safe rule of construction has been held to apply to statutes which have been repealed, or may not have been noticed by the statutes to be construed. Rex *v.* Loxdale, 1 Burr. 447.

And Lord Mansfield, in that case, said, " that where there are different statutes *in pari materia*, though made at different times, or even expired, and not referring to each other, they shall be taken and construed together, as one system." In the expressive language of Tilghman, Ch. J., of Pennsylvania, in one of the cases cited, they were so blended together as to form one statute.

And from the cases cited from Burrow, this blending of statutes, this analogy of legislation, is not confined to public statutes, but that public laws may receive aid in their construction from private laws, and *vice versa;* for his Lordship says, in the case cited, page 448, that the act of Parliament, of 1740, relating to St. Martins, and the overseers of that parish, (which was, I apprehend, clearly a private act,) which extended the number of overseers of the poor to be appointed by two justices, under the general act of 43 Elizabeth, to the number of nine, " shows " (says the Chief Justice) " the construction put by the legislature themselves, upon the 43 Elizabeth, on this head, and excepts this very large parish of St. Martins. out of it.

I need not burden your honors with any name of books on this, so obvious a rule of construction. This case, in Burrow, was carefully considered; it had been argued several times before Ch. J. Ryder, and afterwards before Lord Mansfield, by great counsel, and if any case is entitled to respect of courts, it is a case so considered, and so decided.

· But we have cases nearer home, and more german to this very matter of private acts, in relation to these very patent-rights.

In the case of Evans v. Eaton, (3 Wheat. 454,) it was declared, that an act of Congress, authorizing the Secretary of State to issue a patent to Oliver Evans, for his improvements in the manufacture of flour, " was ingrafted on the general act for the promotion of useful arts, and that the patent was issued under both acts," the public and the private one.

So in the case of Evans v. Jordan, 9 Cranch, 199, which was an action to recover damages under the same private act, Washington, J., said, in declaring the opinion of the court, that " it should be recollected, that the right of the plaintiff to recover damages for using his improvement, after the issuing of his patent, arises, not under this law, but the general law of 1793."

If the plaintiff is obliged to invoke the aid of the act of 1836, he must take the whole of it. It is a well-established rule of law, that he who claims the benefit of his title, must admit its disadvantages. *Qui sentit commodum sentire debet et onus.*

Mr. Chief Justice TANEY delivered the opinion of the court.

The bill in this case was filed by the appellants, on the 6th of July, 1850, in the Circuit Court of the United States, for the Western District of Pennsylvania, to obtain an injunction restraining the appellees from the use of two of Woodworth's planing machines in the city of Pittsburg. The term for which Woodworth's patent was originally granted, expired in 1842, but it was extended seven years by the board established by the 18th section of the act of 1836. And afterwards, by the act of Congress of February 26, 1845, this patent was extended for seven years more, commencing on the 27th of December, 1849, at which time the previous extension would have terminated.

It appears, from the pleadings and evidence in the case, that, shortly after the passage of the act of Congress of 1845, William Woodworth, the administrator of the patentee, in whose name the certificate of extension was directed to be issued, assigned all his right to James G. Wilson, from whom the appellant purchased the exclusive right to construct and use this machine, and to vend to others the right to construct and use it, in a large district of country described in the grant. Pittsburg, in which the machines in question are used, is included within these limits. And the right which the appellant purchased was regularly transferred to him by Wilson, by an instrument of writing duly recorded in the Patent-Office.

In the year 1833, during the term for which the patent was originally granted, the defendants purchased the right to construct and use a certain number of these machines within the limits of the city of Pittsburg and Alleghany county; and the right to do so was regularly transferred to them by different assignments, deriving their title from the original patentee. The two machines mentioned in the bill were constructed and used by the respondents soon after the purchase was made, and the appellees continued to use them up to the time when this bill was filed. And the question is, whether their right to use them terminated with the first extension, or still continues under the extension granted by the act of 1845.

The Circuit Court decided that the right of the appellees still continued, and upon that ground dismissed the appellant's bill. And the case is now before us upon an appeal from that decree.

In determining this question we must take into consideration not only the special act under which the appellant now claims a monopoly, but also the general laws of Congress in relation to patents for useful improvements, and the special acts which have from time to time been passed in favor of the particular patentees. They are statutes in *pari materia;* and all relate to the same subject, and must be construed together. It was so held in the case of Evans v. Eaton, (3 Wheat. 518,) where the court said that the special act of Congress in favor of Oliver Evans, granting him a new patent for fourteen years, for his improvements in manufacturing flour and meal, was ingrafted on the general act for the promotion of useful arts, and the patent issued in pursuance of both. The rule applies with more force in the present case; for this is not the grant of a new patent, but an enlargement of the time for which a patent previously extended under the act of 1836, should continue in force.

Indeed, this rule of construction is necessary to give effect to the special act under which the appellant claims the monopoly. For this law does not define the rights or privileges which the patent shall confer, nor prescribe the remedy to which he shall be entitled if his rights are infringed. It merely extends the duration of the patent, and nothing more. And we are necessarily referred, therefore, to the general law upon the subject to ascertain the rights to which the patent entitled him, and also the remedy which the law affords him if these rights are invaded.

Now, the act of 1836, in express terms, gives the benefit of the extension authorized by that law to the assignees and grantees of the right to use the thing patented to the extent of their respective interests therein. And under this provision it was decided, in the case of Wilson v. Rousseau, (4 Howard, 688,) that the party who had purchased and was using this planing machine during the original term for which the patent was granted, had a right to continue the use during the extension. And the distinction is there taken between the grant of the right to make and vend the machine, and the grant of the right to use it.

The distinction is a plain one. The franchise which the patent grants, consists altogether in the right to exclude every one from making, using, or vending the thing patented, without the permission of the patentee. This is all that he obtains by the patent. And when he sells the exclusive privilege of making or vending it for use in a particular place, the purchaser buys a portion of the franchise which the patent confers. He obtains a share in the monopoly, and that monopoly is derived from, and exercised under, the protection of the United States. And the interest he acquires, necessarily terminates at the time limited for its continuance by the law which created it. The patentee cannot sell it for a longer time. And the purchaser buys with reference to that period; the time for which exclusive privilege is to endure being one of the chief elements of its value. He therefore has no just claim to share in a further monopoly subsequently acquired by the patentee. He does not purchase or pay for it.

But the purchaser of the implement or machine for the purpose of using it in the ordinary pursuits of life, stands on different ground. In using it, he exercises no rights created by the act of Congress, nor does he derive title to it by virtue of the franchise or exclusive privilege granted to the patentee. The inventor might lawfully sell it to him, whether he had a patent or not, if no other patentee stood in his way. And when the machine passes to the hands of the purchaser, it is no longer within the limits of the monopoly. It passes outside of it, and is no longer under the protection of the act of Congress. And if his right to the implement or machine is infringed, he must seek redress in the courts of the State, according to the laws of the State, and not in the courts of the United States, nor under the law of Congress granting the patent. The implement or machine becomes his private, individual property, not protected by the laws of the United States, but by the laws of the State in which it is situated. Contracts in relation to it are regulated by the laws of the State, and are subject to State jurisdiction. It was so decided in this court, in the case of Wilson v. Sanford and others, 10 Howard, 99. Like other individual property, it is then subject to State taxation; and from the great number of patented articles now in use, they no doubt, in some of the States, form no inconsiderable portion of its taxable property.

Moreover, the value of the implement or machine in the hands of the purchaser for use, does not in any degree depend on the time for which the exclusive privilege is granted to the patentee; nor upon the exclusion of others from its use. For example, in the various patented articles used in agriculture, in milling, in manufactures of different kinds, in steam-engines, or for household or other purposes, the value to the purchaser is not enhanced by the continuance of the monopoly. It is of no importance to him whether it endures for a year or twenty-eight years. He does not look to the duration of the exclusive privilege, but to the usefulness of the thing he buys, and the advantages he will derive from its use. He buys the article for the purpose of using it as long as it is fit for use and found to be profitable. And in the case before us the respondents derive no advantage from the extension of the patent, because the patentee may place around them as many planing machines as he pleases, so as to reduce the profits of those which they own to their just value in an open and fair competition.

It is doubtless upon these principles that the act of 1836 draws the distinction between the assignee of a share in the monopoly, and the purchase of one or more machines, to be used in the ordinary pursuits of business. And that distinction is clearly pointed out and maintained in the case of Wilson v. Rousseau, before referred to.

Upon the authority, therefore, of the cases of Evans v. Eaton, and Wilson v. Rousseau, these two propositions may be regarded as settled by judicial decision: 1. That a special act of Congress in favor of a patentee, extending the time beyond that originally limited, must be considered as ingrafted on the general law; and 2. That under the general law, in force when this special act of Congress was passed, a party who had purchased the right to use a planing machine during the period to which the patent was first limited, was entitled to continue to use it during the extension authorized by that law.

Applying these rules to the case before us, the respondents

must be entitled to continue the use of their planing machines during the time for which the patent is extended by the special act of Congress, unless there is something in the language of the law requiring a different construction.

But there is nothing in the law to justify the distinction claimed in this respect on behalf of the patentee. Its language is plain and unambiguous. It does not even grant a new patent, as in the case of Oliver Evans. It merely extends the time of the monopoly to which the patentee was entitled under the general law of 1836. It gives no new rights or privileges, to be superadded to those he then enjoyed, except as to the time they should endure. The patent, such as it then was, is continued for seven years longer than the period before limited. And this is the whole and only provision contained in this special act. In order, therefore, to determine the rights of the patentee during the extended term, we are necessarily referred to the general law, and compelled to inquire what they were before this special act operated upon them, and continued them. Indeed, the court has been obliged to recur to the act of 1836, in every stage of this suit, to guide it in deciding upon the rights of the parties, and the mode of proceeding in which they are to be tried. It is necessarily referred to in order to determine whether the patent under which the complainant claims, was issued by lawful authority, and in the form prescribed by law; it was necessary to refer to it in the Circuit Court in order to determine whether the patentee was entitled to the patent, as the original inventor, that fact being disputed in the Circuit Court; also, for the notices to which he was entitled in the trial of that question; and for the forum in which he was authorized to sue for an infringement of his rights. And the rights of the appellant to bring the case before the court for adjudication is derived altogether from the provisions of the general law. For there is no evidence in the record to show that the machines are worth two thousand dollars, and no appeal therefore would lie from the decision of the Circuit Court, but for the special provision in relation to patent cases in the act of 1836. And while it is admitted that this special act is so ingrafted on the general law, as to entitle the patentee to all the rights and privileges which that law has provided, for the benefit and protection of inventors, it can hardly be maintained that the one in favor of the purchaser of a machine is by construction to be excepted from it, when there are no words in the special act to indicate that such was the intention of Congress.

This construction is confirmed by the various special acts which have been passed from time to time, in favor of particular inventors, granting them new patents after the first had expired or extending the time for which they were originally granted. Many of these acts have been referred to in the argument, some of which contain express provisions, protecting the rights of the purchaser under the first term, and others contain no provision on the subject, and merely grant a new patent, or, as in the case before the court, extend the duration of the old one. And in several instances special laws in favor of different inventors have been passed within a short time of each other, in one of which the rights of the previous purchaser are expressly reserved, and in the other there is no provision on the subject. And the act of March 3, 1845, authorizing the patent of William Gale, for an improvement in the manufacture of silver spoons and forks to be extended, was passed only a few days after the act in favor of Woodworth, and Gale's patent is subjected in express terms to the conditions and restrictions in the act of 1836, and consequently protects previous purchasers from a new demand.

It has been contended, on behalf of the appellant, that the insertion of these restrictions in one special law, and the omission of them in another, shows that, in the latter, Congress did not intend to exempt the purchaser from the necessity of obtaining a new license from the patentee. And that Congress might well suppose that one inventor had stronger claims upon the public than another, and might, on that account, give him larger privileges on the renewal.

But this argument only looks to one side of the question, that is, to the interest and claims of the inventor. There is another, and numerous class of persons, who have purchased patented articles, and paid for them the full price which the patentee demanded, and we are bound to suppose that their interests and their rights would not be overlooked or disregarded by Congress. And still less, that any distinction would be drawn between those who purchased one description of patented machines and those who purchased another. For example, the act granting a new patent to Blanchard, in 1834, for cutting or turning irregular forms, saves the rights of those who had bought under the original patent. And we ought not to presume, without plain words to require it, that while Congress acknowledged the justice of such claims in the case of Blanchard, they intended to disregard them in the case of Woodworth. Nor can it be said that the policy of Congress has changed in this respect after 1834, when Blanchard's patent was renewed. For, as we have already said, the same protection is given to purchasers in the special law, authorizing the renewal of Gale's patent, which was passed a few days after the law of which we are speaking.

The fair inference from all of these special laws is this, that

Congress has constantly recognized the rights of those who purchase for use a patented implement or machine; that in these various special laws the patentee and purchasers of different inventions were intended to be placed on the same ground; and that the relative rights of both parties under the extension, by special act of Congress, were intended to be the same as they were when the extension was granted under the general law of 1836. It would seem that in some cases the attention of the legislature was more particularly called to the subject, and the rights of the purchaser recognized and cautiously guarded. And when the provision is omitted, the just presumption is, that Congress legislated on the principle decided by this court in Evans v. Eaton, and regarded the special law as ingrafted on the general one, and subject to all of its restrictions and provisions, except only as to the time the patent should endure. Time is the only thing upon which they legislate. And any other construction would make the legislation of Congress, on these various special laws, inconsistent with itself, and impute to it the intention of dealing out a different measure of justice to purchasers of different kinds of implements and machines; protecting some of them, and disregarding the equal and just claims of others.

And if such could be the interpretation of this law, the power of Congress to pass it would be open to serious objections. For it can hardly be maintained that Congress could lawfully deprive a citizen of the use of his property after he had purchased the absolute and unlimited right from the inventor, and when that property was no longer held under the protection and control of the General Government, but under the protection of the State, and on that account subject to State taxation.

The 5th amendment to the Constitution of the United States declares, that no person shall be deprived of life, liberty, or property, without due process of law.

The right to construct and use these planing machines, had been purchased and paid for without any limitation as to the time for which they were to be used. They were the property of the respondents. Their only value consists in their use. And a special act of Congress, passed afterwards, depriving the appellees of the right to use them, certainly could not be regarded as due process of law.

Congress undoubtedly have power to promote the progress of science and useful arts, by securing for limited times, to authors and inventors, the exclusive right to their respective writings and discoveries.

But it does not follow that Congress may, from time to time, as often as they think proper, authorize an inventor to recall rights which he had granted to others; or reinvest in him rights of property which he had before conveyed for a valuable and fair consideration.

But we forbear to pursue this inquiry, because we are of opinion that this special act of Congress does not, and was not intended to interfere with rights of property before acquired; but that it leaves them as they stood during the extension under the general law. And in this view of the subject, the appellant was not entitled to the injunction he sought to obtain, and the Circuit Court were right in dismissing the bill.

As the decision on this point disposes of the case, it is unnecessary to examine the other grounds of defence taken by the appellees.

The decree of the Circuit Court must be affirmed.

Mr. Justice McLEAN and Mr. Justice NELSON dissented.

Mr. Justice McLEAN.

Woodworth's patent bears date the 27th of December, 1828, and runs for fourteen years. On the 29th of July, 1830, the patentees conveyed to Isaac Collins and Barzillai C. Smith the right to construct, use, and vend to others, the planing machine invented within several States, including Pennsylvania, except the city of Philadelphia. On the 19th of May, 1832, Collins and Smith transferred to James Barnet the right to construct and use, during the residue of the aforesaid term of fourteen years, fifty planing machines, within Pittsburg and Alleghany county, for which he agreed to pay four thousand dollars. Barnet agreed not to construct or run more than fifty machines during the term aforesaid, and Collins and Smith bound themselves not to license during the term, nor to construct or use themselves during the term, or allow others to do so, in the limits of Pittsburg and Alleghany county.

On the 27th of December, 1842, the patent expired, but it was renewed and extended for seven years, under the act of 1836. This extension expired in 1849; but Congress, on the 26th of February, 1845, passed an act which provided that "the said letters-patent be, and the same is hereby, extended for the term of seven years, from and after the twenty-seventh day of December, 1849."

The patentee, by deed dated the 14th of March, 1845, and also by a further deed dated the 9th of July, 1845, conveyed to James E. Wilson all his interest as administrator in the letters patent under the extension by the act of Congress. And Wilson, on the 4th of June, 1847, for the consideration of twenty-five thousand dollars, gave to Bloomer, the plaintiff, a license to construct and use, and vend to others to construct and use, during the two extensions, "all that part of Pennsylvania lying west of the Alleghany Mountains, excepting Alleghany county, for the first extension, which expires on the 27th day of December, 1849, and the States of Virginia, Maryland, Kentucky, and Missouri, excepting certain parts of each State."

The defendants continued to run their machines during the residue of the fourteen years, for which the patent was granted, and during the first extension; and the complainant filed his bill to enjoin the defendants from running their machines under the second extension, by the act of Congress.

The contract of the defendants was entered into the 19th of May, 1831, and under it Barnet had a right "to construct and use during the residue of the aforesaid term of fourteen years, fifty planing machines," &c. The patent expired on the 27th of December, in 1842. The contract of defendants was made the 19th of May, 1832, leaving about nine years and six months for the patent to run, and this was the time limited by the contract, and for which the consideration of four thousand dollars was paid. This was not left to construction from the life of the patent, but the contract expressly declared the right was purchased "for the residue of the aforesaid term of fourteen years."

This term was enjoyed by the defendants, and under the decision of this court, in the case of Wilson v. Rousseau et al. (4 Howard, 646,) the seven years' extension under the act of 1836, was also enjoyed by the defendants. This construction of the act of 1836, in my judgment, was not authorized, and was not within the intention of the law, as was expressed at the time. That extension having expired, another extension is claimed under the act of Congress. This claim is set up to an injunction bill, filed by the complainant, who is the assignee of the patent for a part of Pennsylvania and other States. And by the decision of four of my brethren, just delivered, the defendants are to enjoy this extension, making fourteen years beyond their control. This would seem to imply, that, under the act of 1836, and under the act of 1845, the assignees were the favored objects of Congress. But this is not the case. The patentee who made the invention, and through whose ingenuity, labor, and expense, a great benefit has been conferred on the public, in justice, is entitled to remuneration, and that only was the ground of extension, whether under the law of 1836, or the special act of 1845.

This, as well as the former decision, was influenced by the consideration that the owners of the machines are, in equity, entitled to run them so long as the exclusive right of the patent shall be continued. It is said that the machines are property, and that no act of Congress should deprive the owners of the use of their property. But in this view, the property of the patentee seems not to be taken into the account. He is the meritorious claimant for protection. The assignee for a specific time, rests upon his contract. He has conferred no benefit on society. His investment was made with an exclusive reference to his own advantage. He has no more claims upon the public sympathy than he who rents a mill, a farm, or engages in a business, open to all who expect a profit by it.

But the hardship is supposed to exist, in the fact that, to use the right, a planing machine must be constructed at an expense of some four or five hundred dollars, and this will be lost to the occupier, if by an extension he shall not be permitted to run his machine. The answer is, when he entered into the contract he knew, or is presumed to have known, that the patent might be extended under the law of 1836 or by special act, and if he desired an interest under the renewed patent, he should have provided for it in his contract. Having failed to do this, it would seem to be unjust that, under a contract to run the machine less than ten years, he should be entitled to run it sixteen years. The consideration paid was limited to the term specified in the contract. But, it is answered, that the assignee expected to run his machine after the termination of the contract on which the exclusive right would end and become vested in the public.

Let us examine this plea, and it will be found that a great fallacy prevails on this subject. A right that is common, is no more valuable to one person than another, as all may use it. The injury, then, consists, so far as the licensee is concerned, in the reduction of the value of his machine, by the extension of the exclusive right in the patentee, to the exclusion of the assignee. It is true this deprives him of the monopoly which his contract secured to him. But he has enjoyed this to the extent of his contract, and for which he has paid the stipulated consideration. Now his only equitable plea to run his machine during the renewed patent, arises alone from the supposed difference in the value of his machine, under the renewal, without a license, and where the right becomes vested in the public.

If there had been no renewal, the licensee might run his machine, and any other person might run one. It is a fact known to every observing individual, when a new business is set up, as a planing machine, supposed to be very profitable generally, a competition is excited, which reduces the profit below a reasonable compensation for the labor and expense of the business. If the monopoly continued, as enjoyed under the contract, the consideration paid for the monopoly would be added to the profits, which would make them large. But when the monopoly ceases, the profits, if not destroyed, are reduced by competition, at least as low, if not below the ordinary profit of capital employed in other investments.

If the business of the county or city required the number of planing machines in operation, the licensee could sell his machine at a reasonable reduction for the time it had run. The machines of the defendant had run, probably, from twelve to fifteen years. A considerable reduction would be expected by the purchaser, as a machine could not be expected to last more than twenty years. But suppose it can be used thirty, then one half of the value must be deducted for the wear of the machine fifteen years, which would reduce it to some two hundred and fifty or three hundred dollars.

But suppose the exclusive right should be continued in the patentee, by an extension of it seven years. Then, if the machines were not more numerous than the public required, they would be wanted by their owners, or by others disposed to engage in the business. And I hazard nothing in saying, that, after deducting the compensation from the profits, paid for the exclusive right, they would be larger than could be hoped for, where the right was common. . Under such circumstances, I can entertain no doubt, that a machine would sell for more money, under the extension of the patent, than where the right goes to the public.

The idea that to refuse the use of a machine under the extension of a patent, is an unjust interference with property, I think, is unfounded. There is no interference with the property in the machine. The owner may sell it to any one who has a license to use it. It is not the property in the machine that is complained of, but because the right to run it longer than the contract provided for, is not given. The licensee has used the franchise, as long as he purchased and paid for it; and can he in justice claim more than his contract. The extension of the right to use, while the extended patent continues, does a wrong to the patentee, by taking his property, without compensation, and giving it to the licensee. The franchise is property, and it can no more be transferred to another, without compensation or contract, than any other property. It would seem that this description of property is not governed by contract. That a contract to use the franchise ten years, does not mean what is expressed, but may mean a right for twenty years, or any other term to which the patent may be extended.

Every man who has sense enough to make a contract, takes into his estimate the contingency of a loss, to some extent, in going out of the business. He fixes his own time for the contract, and if he wishes to provide for the contingency arising from the renewal of a patent, he can embrace it in his contract for a stipulated compensation.

It may be true, that, unless the contrary appear, when the patentee sells a planing machine, a right to use it may be applied. But the right to construct and the right to use, are distinct. Some purchase of the patentee the right to construct the machine, others to use it. This planing machine cannot be compared to a plough, or any other article which may be considered the product of the patent. The machine is the instrument through which the plank is planed. The plank is the product, and may be sold in the market as other property. But the planing machine cannot be used, without a license. The law protects the franchise, by prohibiting the use of the machine without a license. When Barnet purchased the franchise for the fifty machines, he did not buy the machines for a term as long as the machines could run, but for nine years and six months. The contract, neither expressly nor impliedly, extended beyond that term.

In this view, I think that I am not mistaken, and if I am not, the license is not injured a dollar by the termination of his right to run his machine, as fixed in his contract. But, on whom is the injury inflicted by extending the contract of the licensee with the patentee, and that without compensation? In the present case, the patentee has been injured, by the use of the fifty machines, at least four thousand dollars, the amount agreed to be paid for the right to run them less than ten years. And must not the property of the patentee be taken into the account, as well as the imagined rights of the licensee?

The patentee is justly considered a public benefactor. He has conferred a great benefit upon the world; and he is entitled, under our laws, to at least a compensation for his expense, ingenuity, and labor.

That the patentee is the only one whose interests are regarded, as the ground of extending the patent in the act of 1836, is clear. Now, suppose the patentee has assigned the whole of the patent, without receiving such a compensation as the law authorizes; there can be no doubt he is entitled, on that ground, to a renewal of the patent; and yet, under the decision now given, his assignees would receive all the benefits of the renewal. Should not this fact cause doubts whether the rule of construction of the statute can be a sound one, which defeats its avowed object? If this be the consequence of the assignment of the entire interest by the patentee, any partial assignment must produce the same result, though to a more limited extent. A principle which will not bear this test is not sound.

The act of 1845, extending this patent, annexed no conditions. The exclusive right was extended to the administrator of Woodworth for seven years, from the 27th of December, 1849. But the decision now given, in effect declares this exclusive right is not given. Indeed the object of Congress must be defeated if the machines, in operation at the time of the passage of the act, are to be continued without compensation. It is presumed there are few places where planing machines were not constructed before 1849, the time the renewal took effect, if the public required them. On this supposition, the extension of the patent can be of little or no benefit to the heirs of the patentee. Congress could have granted the act only upon the ground to remunerate the heirs of the inventor.

There seems to be a great mistake as to the profits of this patent. It was a valuable patent, but, as in all other cases, its value excited the rapacity of men who seek to enrich themselves by taking the property of others. The records of the courts show, that piracies were committed on this patent in every part of the country; and that to sustain it, much expenditure and labor have been required. It is stated that the sum of near two hundred thousand dollars has been thus expended to establish this patent. Congress have extended many patents; in some instances conditions have been imposed, in others, the franchise has been extended unconditionally. Now, where the patent is extended by act of Congress, without conditions, I am unable to perceive how the court can impose conditions. Such an act would be legislation, and not construction.

By the act of the 15th February, 1847, the patent of Thomas Blanchard, for cutting irregular forms out of wood, brass, or iron, was extended for fourteen years, from the 20th of January, 1848: " Provided that such extension shall enure to the use and benefit of the said Thomas Blanchard, his executors and administrators and to no other persons whomsoever, except that a *bona fide* assignee of the invention, by virtue of an assignment from the patentee heretofore made, shall have the benefit of this act, upon just, reasonable, and equitable terms, according to his interest therein. And if the said Thomas Blanchard, his executors or administrators, cannot agree with such assignee, the terms shall be ascertained and determined by the Circuit Court of the United States for the district in which such assignee resides, to be decreed upon a bill to be filed by such assignee for that purpose. And provided further, that no assignee shall have the benefit of this act unless he shall, within ninety days from its passage, agree with the said Thomas Blanchard as to the consideration upon which he is to have it, or file his bill," &c.

Every one must perceive the justice and propriety of this act; under the decision now given, the assignee of Blanchard would have had the benefit of the extension without paying for it. This act, extending Blanchard's patent, was passed two years after the decision of this court in Wilson v. Rousseau, which, under the act of 1836, gave the benefit of the extension to the assignee. This must have been known to Congress, and yet they deemed a special provision in behalf of the assignee necessary. This act, and several others of a similar character, cannot fail to convince every one that Congress did not suppose that the courts have power to annex a condition to a legislative grant.

In the case of Evans v. Jordan and Morehead, (9 Cranch, 199,) this court held, that the act of January, 1808, for the relief of Oliver Evans, does not authorize those who erected their machinery between the expiration of their old patents and the issuing of the new one, to use it after the issuing of the latter.

The above act extended the patent fourteen years, " provided that no person who may have heretofore paid the said Oliver Evans for license to use the said improvements, shall be obliged to renew said license or be subject to damages for not renewing the same; and provided also, that no person who shall have used the said improvements, or have erected the same for use, before the issuing of the said patent, shall be liable to damages therefor."

This was a much stronger case for equitable considerations than the one before us. Evans's patent had expired. His improvements were free to the public, and they were adopted by the defendants before he made application to Congress for a renewal of his patent. I will cite the reasoning of the Supreme Court on that case. " The language," they say, " of this last proviso is so precise, and so entirely free from all ambiguity, that it is difficult for any course of reasoning to shed light upon its meaning. It protects against any claim for damages which Evans might make, those who have used his improvements, or who may have erected them for use, prior to the issuing of his patent under this law. The protection is limited to acts done prior to another act thereafter to be performed, to wit, the issuing of the patent. To extend it, by construction, to acts which might be done subsequent to the issuing of the patent, would be to make, not to interpret, the law." " The injustice of denying to the defendants the use of machinery which they had erected after the expiration of Evans's first patent, and prior to the passage of this law, has been strongly urged as a reason why the words of this proviso should be so construed as to have a prospective operation. But it should be recollected that the right of the plaintiff to recover damages for using his improvement after the issuing of his patent, under this law although it had been erected prior thereto, arises not under this law, but under the general law of the 21st of February, 1793. The provisos in this law profess to protect, against the operation of the general law, three classes of persons — those who had paid Evans for a license prior to the passage of the law ;. those who may have used his improvements ; and those who may have erected them for use before the issuing of the patent."

And the court say, " The legislature might have procceded still further, by providing a shield for persons standing in the situation of these defendants. It is believed that the reasonableness of such a: provision could have been questioned by no one. But the legislature have not thought proper to extend the protection of these provisos beyond the issuing of the patent under that law ; and this court would transgress the limits of the judicial power by an attempt to supply, by construction, this supposed, omission of the legislature. The argument founded upon the hardship of this and similar cases, would be entitled to great weight if the words of this proviso were obscure and open to construction. But considerations of this nature can never sanction a construction at variance with the manifest meaning of the legislature, expressed in plain and an unambiguous language."

The above views do not conflict with the opinion of the court in Evans v. Eaton, 3 Wheat. 454. In that case the court say, " Some doubts have been entertained respecting the jurisdiction of the courts of the United States, as both the plaintiff and defendants are citizens of the same State. The fifth section of the act to promote the progress of useful arts, which gives to every patentee a right to sue in a Circuit Court of the United States, in case his rights be violated, is repealed by the third section of the act of 1800, which gives the action in the Circuit Court of the United States where a patent is granted, 'pursuant' to that act, or to the act for the promotion of useful arts. This patent, it has been said, is granted, not in pursuance of either of those acts, but in pursuance of the act 'for the relief of Oliver Evans.' but this court is of opinion, that the act for the relief of Oliver Evans, is ingrafted on the general act for the promotion of useful arts, and that the patent is issued in pursuance of both. The jurisdiction of the court is therefore sustained "

There can be no question that the special law extending the grant, as to its validity, is subject to the general patent law. The right was intended to be exclusive, if it be established that Evans was the original inventor of the improvements claimed, and such improvements were stated with the necessary precision.

And also that it came under the class of cases on which suit could be brought in the courts of the United States, without regard to the citizenship of the parties. But it could not have been intended to apply to any contract subsequent to the patent, and it could only be held to embrace those general provisions of the patent law which relate to the validity of the patent. Under the act of Congress, a specification was necessarily filed, and it seems to be the practice to issue a patent under the act. This, it appears to me, is unnecessary, as the grant in the act is sufficient. But the schedule is necessary to show the nature and extent of the claim, and these must be sustained on those principles which apply to patents generally.

To give any other construction to the above remarks of the court, would be in direct contradiction to the language used, and the principle decided, in the case above cited from Cranch. In fact, the remark that the relief of Evans was ingrafted on the general law, was made in reference to the jurisdiction of the court, and cannot be extended beyond that and other questions, in relation to the validity of the patent.

This argument of the court, in Evans v. Jordan, applies with all its force and authority to the case before us; and I need only say it was the language of Marshall, of Story, of Washington, and of the other Judges of the court, except Judge Todd, who appears to have been absent. I can add nothing to the weight of the argument; but I will proceed to name the Judges of this court who have given opinions opposed to the decision of this case by four of my brethren.

Mr. Justice Wayne being sick, did not sit in the case. In Wilson v. Rousseau, he held that, under the act of 1836, the licensee had no right to run his machine under the extended patent.

Mr. Justice Curtis having, as counsel, given an opinion opposed to the right of the defendants, did not sit in the case. Mr. Justice Thompson and Mr. Justice Story had both given opinions against the right of the assignee, unless under a special assignment. This was the opinion of Mr. Justice Woodbury, as expressed in 'the case of Wilson v. Rousseau. Mr. Justice McKinley gave an opinion against the right of the assignee under the act of 1845, extending Woodworth's patent. The same decision has been frequently given, by the Justices of this bench, in the second and seventh circuits.

Sustained by the authority of seven Justices of this court, and by an argument of the Supreme Court, above cited, which, I think, is unanswerable, I shall deem it to be my duty to bring the same question now decided, when it shall arise in my circuit, for the consideration and decision of a full bench.

Order.

This cause came on to be heard on the transcript of the record from the Circuit Court of the United States for the Western District of Pennsylvania, and was argued by counsel. On consideration whereof, it is now here ordered, adjudged, and decreed by this court, that the decree of the said Circuit Court in this cause be, and the same is hereby, affirmed, with costs.

LESSEE OF IRWIN H. DOOLITTLE AND OTHERS, PLAINTIFFS, *v.* LEVI BRYAN AND OTHERS, DEFENDANTS.

A sale of land by a marshal on a *venditioni exponas*, after he is removed from office, and a new marshal appointed and qualified, is not void.

Such sale being returned to the court and confirmed by it, on motion, and a deed ordered to be made to the purchaser at the sale, by the new marshal, such sale being made, is valid.

THIS case came up from the Circuit Court of the United States for the District of Ohio, on a certificate of division in opinion between the Judges thereof.

The following was the entire record in the case:

THE UNITED STATES OF AMERICA,
District of Ohio, ss.

At a Circuit Court of the United States, for the District of Ohio, began and held at the city of Columbus, in said district, on the third Tuesday in the month of October, in the year of our Lord one thousand eight hundred and fifty-one, and of the independence of the United States of America the 76th, before the Honorable John McLean and the Honorable Humphrey H. Leavitt, Judges of said court; among other proceedings had, were the following, to wit:

The lessee of IRWIN B. DOOLITTLE et al. }
v. } In ejectment.
LEVI BRYAN et al. }

In this case, the lessors of the plaintiff, being citizens of Illinois, brought their action of ejectment to recover possession of one thousand acres of land in the State of Ohio; the declaration being duly served on the tenants in possession, they appeared and entered into the consent rule, and filed the general issue. On the trial, two points arose, on which the opinions of the Judges were opposed, to wit:

1. Whether a sale of land by a marshal, on a *venditioni exponas*, after he is removed from office, and a new marshal appointed and qualified, is void?

2. Whether such sale, being returned to the court, and confirmed by it on motion, and a deed ordered to be made to the purchaser, at the sale, by the new marshal, such sale being made, is valid?

And the counsel for the lessors of the plaintiff, moved the court to certify the above points, for decision, to the Supreme Court, under the statute.

The practice to confirm the marshal's sale, is under the fifteenth section of the State statute "regulating judgments and executions," and is as follows:

" That if the court to which any writ of execution shall be returned by the officer, for the satisfaction of which any lands or tenements may have been sold, shall, after having carefully examined the proceedings of such officer, be satisfied that the sale has, in all respects, been made in conformity to the provisions of this act, they shall direct their clerk to make an entry thereof on the journal, that the court are satisfied with the legality of such sale, and an order that the said officer make to the purchaser a deed for such lands and tenements."

October 27, 1851.

From the arguments of counsel, the following appeared to be the dates of the several transactions.

On the 19th of February, 1829, a *venditioni exponas* came to the hands of William Dougherty, then the marshal of Ohio. The writ was returnable to the July term, 1829.

On the 20th of April, 1829, Dougherty was removed from office.

On the 11th of May, 1829, John Patterson was qualified as marshal.

On the 10th of July, 1829, Dougherty sold the land in question.

At the July term, 1829, the writ of *venditioni exponas* was returned, by which it appeared that the land was sold to Levi Bryan, one of the defendants. The sale was confirmed by the court, and Patterson, the then marshal, ordered to convey the land to Bryan, the purchaser.

The counsel upon both sides agreed that the plaintiffs in ejectment could not recover unless this was a void sale.

It was argued by *Mr. Stanberry*, for the plaintiffs, and *Mr. Corwin*, for the defendant.

Mr. Justice GRIER delivered the opinion of the court.

On the trial of this case in the Circuit Court, two points arose, in which the Judges were divided in opinion, and which have been accordingly certified to this court.

1. Whether a sale of land by a marshal, on a *venditioni exponas*, after he is removed from office, and a new marshal is appointed, is void?

2. Whether such sale, being returned to the court and confirmed by it, on motion, and a deed ordered to be made to the purchaser at the sale, by the new marshal, such sale being made, is valid?

If the first of these questions be answered in the negative, the second will be answered affirmatively, as an undisputed consequence.

Whether a sale, made by a marshal after he is removed from office, on a writ of *venditioni exponas*, is void, will depend on the construction of the third section of the act of May 7, 1800, ch. 45, and whether it is a repeal of the provisions on this subject, contained in the twenty-eighth section of the Judiciary Act of 1789, chap. 20.

So much of the latter act as is material to our inquiry, is as follows: "Every marshal or his deputy, when removed from office, or when the term for which the marshal is appointed shall expire, shall have power, notwithstanding, to execute all such precepts as may be in their hands respectively at the time of such removal or expiration of office," &c.

The third section of the act of 1800 enacts: "That whenever a marshal shall sell any lands, tenements, or hereditaments, by virtue of process from a court of the United States, and shall die or be removed from office, or the term of his commission expire, before a deed shall be executed for the same by him to the purchaser; in every such case the purchaser or plaintiff, at whose suit the sale was made, may apply to the court from which the process issued, and set forth the case, assigning the reason why the title was not perfected by the marshal who sold the same; and thereupon the court may order the marshal, for the time being, to perfect the title, and execute a deed to the purchaser, he paying the purchase-money and costs remaining unpaid. And where a marshal shall take in execution any lands, &c., and shall die or be removed from office, or the term of his commission expire before a sale or other final disposition made of the same, in every case the like process shall issue to the succeeding marshal, and the same proceedings shall be had, as if such former marshal had not died or been removed, or the term of his commission had not expired. And the provisions in this section contained, shall be and they are hereby extended to all the cases respectively which may have happened before the passing of this act."

There is no express repeal of the act of 1789 to be found in this act of 1800. Nor does it contain any negative terms which are necessarily contrary to the previous affirmative act. A latter act is never construed to repeal a prior act unless there be a contrariety or repugnancy in them, or at least some notice taken of the former act so as to indicate an intention to repeal it. The law does not favor a repeal by implication unless the repugnance be quite plain. hence it has been decided that, although two acts of parliament be seemingly repugnant, yet if there be no clause of *non obstante* in the latter they shall, if possible, have such construction that the latter may not be a repeal of the former by implication; Dwarris on Stat. 674, and cases cited.

The purview of the clause of the act of 1789, now in question, is to define the powers of a marshal having process in his hands at the time he is removed or his office expires; it authorizes him to execute process previously directed to him. The act of 1800 is evidently intended to confer rights on the parties to have the same acts performed by the new marshal. It gives cumulative rights and powers, for the benefit of suitors.

That such is its purview and policy, is evident from its language — "the purchaser or the plaintiff," it is said, "may apply, and the court may order the new marshal for the time being;" and although "may" is changed into "shall," in the latter clause of the section, it is not necessarily inconsistent with, nor repugnant to the power conferred on the marshal to execute precepts in his hands, by the act of 1787. The latter act does not set aside or make void process or precepts in the hands of the outgoing marshal, or require him to hand them over to the new officer. It authorizes "like process" to issue to him; and the word "shall" is used because it is the most proper in conferring a power on the officer, and is not incompatible with the choice given to the plaintiff in the first clause of the section. The laws of the several States affecting liens on land, and the process by which they may be sold for the satisfaction of judgments, differ very widely. In some, by attachment a lien is created at the institution of the suit. In others, the judgment becomes a lien at the time of its rendition; while in others, the execution and levy first give a lien. In some, lands are sold on a *fi. fa.*, while in others it can be sold only on a *vinditioni exponas*. Under the act of 1789, a doubt might have been entertained, whether land attached should be sold by the officer who had originally attached it, and whether, if process issued to a new officer, it might not be a relinquishment of the lien of the original attachment, as by fiction of law the land, like personal property attached, might be considered in the custody of the officer who attached it. Again, an officer, going out of office, may have an execution in his hands which has created a lien; if the act were construed so as imperatively to require a new or "like process" to issue to the new officer, the lien, and with it the debt, might be lost. In other cases, on the contrary, a marshal may be, and often is, removed from office, because money, which once gets into his hands, cannot be got out again, and a plaintiff may much prefer to relinquish his execution and take a new one. Doubts, also, may have arisen whether a *venditioni exponas* could legally issue to the new marshal, where the former one had levied on the land and had it condemned. All these difficulties are obviated by the act of 1800, not by repealing the general powers given by the act of 1789, but by conferring certain powers on the new officer, where it is found expedient or necessary that he should exercise them.

. It is an argument entitled to great weight in the construction of these statutes, — that different constructions have been given them in different States, and the practice under them has been more or less conformed to the State practice, without, perhaps, a proper regard to these acts. In some, the act of 1800 has been overlooked altogether. A sharp or stringent construction, which should now declare the latter to be a repeal of the powers conferred by the former, might have the effect of unsettling titles to land to an extent the court may not be able to anticipate. In the present case, it is said, the land was sold in 1829. The purchaser paid his money and obtained his deed upon the faith of a judgment of the court that the sale was regular, and has held the land under this title ever since. Hundreds of similar cases may probably be found, where the same objections to the sale exist. Under such circumstances a court should be even astute in avoiding a construction which may be productive of much litigation and insecurity of titles.

We therefore answer the first question proposed, in the negative; which involves, as a necessary consequence, an affirmative answer to the second, so far as it affects the case before us. But we do not mean to say that the confirmation of a void sale by the court, would make it valid.

Order.

This cause came on to be heard, on the transcript of the record, from the Circuit Court of the United States for the District of Ohio, and on the points or questions on which the Judges of the said Circuit Court were opposed in opinion and which were certified to this court for its opinion, agreeably to the act of Congress in such case made and provided, and was argued by counsel. On consideration whereof, it is the opinion of this court,—

1. " That a sale of land by a marshal, on a *venditioni exponas*, after he is removed from office, and a new marshal appointed and qualified," is not void.

2. That " such sale being returned to the court, and confirmed by it on motion, and a deed ordered to be made to the purchaser, at the sale, by the new marshal, such sale being made, is valid."

Whereupon it is now here ordered and adjudged, by this court, that it be so certified to the said Circuit Court.

SAMUEL VEAZIE AND LEVI YOUNG, PLAINTIFFS IN ERROR, *v.* WYMAN B. S. MOOR.

The River Penobscot is entirely within the State of Maine, from its source to its mouth. For the last eight miles of its course it is not navigable, but crossed by four dams erected for manufacturing purposes. Higher up the stream there was an imperfect navigation.

A law of the State, granting the exclusive navigation of the upper river to a company who were to improve it, is not in conflict with the 8th section of the 1st article of the Constitution of the United States, and a license to carry on the coasting trade did not entitle a vessel to navigate the upper waters of the river.

THIS case was brought up from the Supreme Judicial Court of the State of Maine, by a writ of error issued under the 25th section of the Judiciary Act.

The facts in the case are stated in the opinion of the court.

It was argued by *Mr. Paine*, for the plaintiffs in error, and by *Mr. Kelley* and *Mr. Moor*, for the defendant in error:

The following propositions were contended for, in an elaborate brief, filed by the counsel for the plaintiffs in error:

1. That the constitutional power of Congress in question, embraces the right to adopt any means reasonably necessary, in their opinion, to the successful prosecution of commerce among the States and with foreign nations.

2. That Congress has adopted, as such means, the whole commercial marine of the country, every part of which, as a unit, is under their entire control and regulation, without regard to the waters on which the navigation is carried on.

3. That to constitute a part of this commercial marine, no other qualifications are necessary than those prescribed by Con

gress in the several acts regulating the registry and enrolment of vessels, and such registry or enrolment is evidence of a compliance with the prescribed conditions.

4. That any vessel so enrolled, being licensed, has an unrestricted right to navigate all the navigable waters of the United States. wherever they may be found serviceable to its use.

5. That the power of Congress to regulate commerce is as extensive on land as water, and is irrespective of both;—that these compose no part of commerce or navigation, but are subject to be adopted as ways or thoroughfares of it, whenever they may be required by the wants of either;—and that in legislating upon the subject, Congress has not discriminated between one class or body of navigable waters and another, but has made all such waters free for the uses of navigation, wherever any portion of the commercial marine of the country may exist.

6. That under the statute of 1831, March 2, § 3, the plaintiffs' boat is expressly included as provided for by said act, and is thus embraced within the power of Congress, even if not included in the general provisions of the acts regulating the " coasting trade."

7. That the right of Congress to regulate " commerce with the Indian tribes," extends to and embraces the Penobscot tribe of Indians, and the Legislature of Maine has no right to restrict the people to, or deprive them of, any particular mode of intercourse or trade with them.

8. That any act of a State Legislature contravening such right of navigation, as does the act set forth in defendants' bill of complaint, is absolutely null and void.

The points made by the counsel for the defendant in error, were thus stated:

The only question here is, whether the grant to Moor is in conflict with that provision of the Constitution which gives Congress the right to regulate commerce.

A party alleging that a State law is unconstitutional, takes on himself the burden of establishing these three propositions:

First. That the matter or subject in controversy is within the legislative jurisdiction of Congress.

Second. That Congress has *de facto* legislated on the subject, and embraced it within regulations established by its legislation; and

Third. That the party impeaching the law, has himself acquired rights in the subject-matter which is in controversy, and that these rights have been invaded by the legislation of the State.

47*

Applying these rules to this case, plaintiffs are bound to show,
First. That the navigation of the Penobscot River, above Old-town Falls, is within the jurisdiction of Congress.

Second. That Congress has embraced this navigation in its legislation, and provided regulations for it; and

Third. That they have acquired rights in that navigation under the legislation of Congress, which rights have been impaired by the law of the State.

Plaintiffs must establish all three of these propositions. It is not enough for them to establish any two of them. If they fail in any one of them, they have no ground to stand upon.

1st. As to the first of these propositions. The grant being confined to waters wholly internal, plaintiffs can carry on no navigation by means of those waters, with any foreign nation, nor with any other State. We think this is almost too plain for argument. Moor v. Veazie, 32 Maine Rep. 843; Wilson v. Blackbird Co. 2 Pet. 250; 3 Kent's Com. 458; Livingston v. Van Ingen, 9 Johns. Rep. 506; Gibbons v. Ogden, 17 Id. 488; Id. 9 Wheat. 1; New Bedford Bridge case, 1 Wood. & Minot, 404; Kellogg v. Union Company, 12 Conn. 7; Passenger case, 7 How. 283; Brown v. Maryland, 12 Wheat. 419; New York v. Miln, 11 Pet. 102; 3 Cowen, 713.

Again. This grant is not in conflict with the power of Congress to regulate commerce with the Indian tribes.

1. Because commerce, in this connection, does not include navigation. 32 Maine, 343.

2. Because the constitution manifestly refers only to independent tribes with which the general government may come in conflict; not to those small remnants of tribes scattered over the country, which are under State jurisdiction and guardianship. 32 Maine, 343.

2d. We hold that plaintiffs entirely fail to establish the second proposition, to wit: That the navigation of these waters is embraced within the actual legislation of Congress. None of the acts cited were ever intended to apply to waters wholly within the limits of a State, and which could not be reached by vessels from foreign ports, or from other States.

Again. We contend that if Congress has, or should pass any acts interfering with commerce purely internal, they would be unauthorized and void. Passenger case, 7 How. 283; Genesee Chief, 12 Id. 443.

3d. As to the third proposition, the case fails to show that plaintiffs have acquired any rights in the navigation of the waters of the upper Penobscot, under any regulation of Congress, or in any other way or manner.

Assuredly there can be no pretence that plaintiffs were engaged in any commerce on those waters with any foreign nation, o with any other State. Nor is there any fact or evidence in the case tending to show that they were engaged in commerce with the Penobscot tribe. It does not appear that they traded or had any intercourse with that tribe, nor that they wished or intended to have any such intercourse. The Penobscots are not represented here. They do not complain of the grant. There is no fact going to show that this grant has any bearing or effect on any commerce to which they are parties. If they have any ports of entry or clearance, for aught the case finds, such ports may be as hermetically sealed as those of Japan.

If plaintiffs fail to show that they have acquired rights which have been taken away, they cannot complain, even if the act was most palpably against the constitution. Wheeling Bridge case, 13 Howard, 518; East Hartford v. Hartford Bridge Company, 17 Conn. Rep.

Mr. Justice DANIEL delivered the opinion of the court.

The questions raised upon this record, however subdivided or varied they may have been in form or number, are essentially and properly restricted to the power and the duty of this court, to inquire into the constitutional obligation of the law of the State of Maine, upon which the decision of the Supreme Court of that State was founded; for if that law and the privileges conferred thereby, be coincident with the eighth section of article 1st of the constitution, they can be assailable here upon no just exception.

It is insisted, however, that the statute of the State of Maine is in derogation of the power vested in Congress by the article and section above mentioned, " to regulate commerce with foreign nations, and among the several States, and with the Indian tribes." We will examine the character of this objection with reference to the facts disclosed by the record, and with reference also to the provisions of the statute in question, as they have been designed to operate on those facts; and as these last are all agreed by the parties, there can be no need of a comparison of the testimony to ascertain their verity.

The River Penobscot is situated entirely within the State of Maine; having its rise far in the interior of the State, it is not subject to the tides above the city of Bangor, near its mouth. Between the city of Bangor and Old Town, a distance of eight miles, the Penobscot passes over a fall, is crossed by four dams erected for manufacturing purposes, and for the above space is not, at this time, and never has been, navigable; but there is a railroad from Bangor to the steamboat landing at Old Town. On the 30th day of July, 1846, the Legislature of Maine, by law. enacted, that "William Moor and Daniel Moor, Jr., their associates.and ·assigns, were authorized to' improve the navigation of the Penobscot River above Old Town, and for that purpose, were authorized to deepen the channel of the river, to cut down and remove any gravel or ledge, bars, rocks, or other obstructions in the bed thereof; to erect in the bed, on the shore or bank of said river, suitable dams and locks, with booms, piers abutments, breakwaters, and other erections to protect the same; to build upon the shore or bank of said river, any canal or canals to connect the navigable parts of said river, or (in case it shall be deemed the preferable mode of improvement,) any railroads for the like purpose.

After providing the modes of acquiring lands or gravel on the shores or in the bed of the river, and for compensating the owners of property used in the prosecution of the contemplated improvement, the act proceeds to limit the time for the completion of the undertaking, within particular *termini* therein. named, to the period of seven years from its date; and farther requires that, within the period thus limited, the grantees shall build and run a steamboat between those· *termini*, and shall, within the same time, make a' canal and lock around the falls of the river, or a railroad to connect the route above with that below the falls.

Then follows section fourth of the statute, containing the provision objected to. It is in these words: " If said .William Moor and Daniel Moor, Jr., their associates and assigns, shall perform the conditions of this grant as contained in the preceding section, the sole right of navigating said river by boats propelled by steam from said Old Town so far up as they·shall render the same navigable, is hereby granted to them for the term of twenty years· from and after the completion of the improvement, as provided in the third section.of this act." The defendant in error, who is assignee of the original grantees from the legislature, having made certain improvements in the river by the removal of rocks, and by deepening the channel in other places, so as to enable boats to run therein, with two and a half feet less of water than was requisite for navigation previously to these improvements, and all within the limit prescribed to him by law, built, and on the 27th of May, 1847, placed upon the said river, the steamboat Governor Neptune, and ran her from Old Town over the Piscataquis Falls, to a place called Nickaton. In the spring of the year 1847, the defendant in error placed on the river the steamboat Mattanawcook, and ran her to Lincoln, till obstructions were removed by him at a place called the Mohawk Rips, above the Piscataquis Falls; and has also built and is now running upon the river, another steamboat called the Sam Houston, in addition to the Governor Neptune and the Mattanawcook.

The plaintiff in error, Samuel Veazie, built the steamboat Governor Dana, and, in conjunction with the other plaintiffs, Levi and Warren R. Young, ran her upon the Penobscot River between Old Town and the Piscataquis Falls, from the 10th day of May, 1849, until they were arrested by an injunction granted at the suit of the defendant in error. The steamboat Governor Dana was enrolled and licensed for the coasting trade, at the custom-house at Bangor. The Penobscot tribe of Indians own all the islands in the Penobscot River above Old Town Falls, some of which they occupy; and this tribe always have been, and now are, under the jurisdiction and guardianship of the State of Maine.

Upon this state of facts agreed, the Supreme Judicial Court of Maine, after argument and advisement, at its June term, 1850, decreed, that the plaintiffs in error be perpetually enjoined to desist and refrain from running and employing the steamboat Governor Dana, propelled by steam, for transporting passengers or merchandise on said river, or any part thereof above Old Town, and also from building, using, and employing, any other boat propelled by steam on that part of the said river for that purpose, without the consent of the said Wyman B. S. Moor, obtained according to law, until the said Moor's exclusive right shall expire. The court farther decreed to the defendant in error, the sum of one thousand and fifty-two dollars and forty-five cents, for damages and expenses incurred by him, by reason of the interference with his rights on the part of the plaintiffs in error.

Upon a comparison of this decree, and of the statute upon which it is founded, with the provision of the Constitution already referred to, we are unable to perceive by what rule of interpretation either the statute or the decree can be brought within either of the categories comprised in that provision.

These categories are, 1st. Commerce with foreign nations. 2dly. Commerce amongst the several States. 3dly. Commerce with the Indian tribes. Taking the term commerce in its broadest acceptation, supposing it to embrace not merely traffic, but the means and vehicles by which it is prosecuted, can it properly be made to include objects and purposes such as those contemplated by the law under review? Commerce with foreign nations, must signify commerce which in some sense is necessarily connected with these nations, transactions which either immediately, or at some stage of their progress, must be extra-territorial. The phrase can never be applied to transactions wholly internal, between citizens of the same community, or to a polity and laws whose ends and purposes and operations are

restricted to the territory and soil and jurisdiction of such community. Nor can it be properly concluded, that, because the
products of domestic enterprise in agriculture or manufactures,
or in the arts, may ultimately become the subjects of foreign
commerce; that the control of the means or the encouragements
by which enterprise is fostered and protected, is legitimately
within the import of the phrase *foreign commerce*, or fairly implied in any investiture of the power to regulate such commerce.
A pretension as far reaching as this, would extend to contracts
between citizen and citizen of the same State, would control the
pursuits of the planter, the grazier, the manufacturer, the mechanic, the immense operations of the collieries and mines and
furnaces of the country; for there is not one of these avoca-
tions, the results of which may not become the subjects of
foreign commerce, and be borne either by turnpikes, canals, or
railroads, from point to point within the several States, towards
an ultimate destination, like the one above mentioned.   Such a
pretension would effectually prevent or paralyze every effort at
internal improvement by the several States; for it cannot be
supposed, that the States would exhaust their capital and their
credit in the construction of turnpikes, canals, and railroads,
the remuneration derivable from which, and all control over
which, might be immediately wrested from them, because such
public works would be facilities for a commerce which, whilst
availing itself of those facilities, was unquestionably internal,
although intermediately or ultimately it might become foreign.

The rule here given with respect to the regulation of foreign
commerce, equally excludes from the regulation of commerce
between the States and the Indian tribes the control over turnpikes, canals, or railroads, or the clearing and deepening of
watercourses exclusively within the States, or the management
of the transportation upon and by means of such improvements.
In truth, the power vested in Congress by article 1st, section
8th of the Constitution, was not designed to operate upon matters like those embraced in the statute of the State of Maine,
and which are essentially local in their nature and extent. The
design and object of that power, as evinced in the history of
the Constitution, was to establish a perfect equality amongst
the several States as to commercial rights, and to prevent unjust
and invidious distinctions, which local jealousies or local and
partial interests might be disposed to introduce and maintain.
These were the views pressed upon the public attention by the
advocates for the adoption of the Constitution, and in accordance therewith have been the expositions of this instrument
propounded by this court, in decisions quoted by counsel on
either side of this cause, though differently applied by them.

Boyden v. Burke.

Vide The Federalist, Nos. 7 and 11, and the cases of Gibbons *v.* Ogden, 9 Wheat. 1; New York *v.* Milne, 11 Peters, 102; Brown *v.* The State of Maryland, 12 Wheat. 419; and the License cases in 5 Howard, 504.

The fact of procuring from the collector of the port of Bangor a license to prosecute the coasting trade for the boat placed upon the Penobscot by the plaintiff in error, (the Governor Dana,) does not affect, in the slightest degree, the rights or condition of the parties. These remain precisely as they would have stood had no such license been obtained. A license to prosecute the coasting trade, is a warrant to traverse the waters washing or bounding the coasts of the United States. Such a license conveys no privilege to use, free of tolls, or of any condition whatsoever, the canals constructed by a State, or the watercourses partaking of the character of canals exclusively within the interior of a State, and made practicable for navigation by the funds of the State, or by privileges she may have conferred for the accomplishment of the same end. The attempt to use a coasting license for a purpose like this, is, in the first place, a departure from the obvious meaning of the document itself, and an abuse wholly beyond the object and the power of the government in granting it.

Upon the whole, we are of the opinion that the decision of the Supreme Judicial Court of the State of Maine is in accordance with the Constitution of the United States, and ought to be, and is hereby, affirmed.

Order.

This cause came on to be heard on the transcript of the record from the Supreme Judicial Court of the State of Maine, and was argued by counsel. On consideration whereof, it is now here ordered and adjudged by this court, that the judgment of the said Supreme Judicial Court in this cause be, and the same is hereby, affirmed with costs.

URIAH A. BOYDEN, PLAINTIFF IN ERROR, *v.* EDMUND BURKE.

Where an action was brought against the Commissioner of Patents for refusing to give copies of papers in his office, and no special damage was set out in the declaration, evidence of the professional pursuits of the applicant was not admissible.

Where the application was made through a third person, letters of both parties to this third person were admissible in evidence, as part of the *res gestæ*.

Patents are public records, and it is the duty of the Commissioner to give authenticated copies to any person, on payment of the legal fees.

But the party entitled to such services must request their performance in a proper manner, and not accompany his demand with insult or abuse.

Hence, the Commissioner could not be held responsible for refusing to comply with a demand couched in such language.

But when a second application was made, in a proper manner, the Commissioner ought to have complied with it.

THIS case was brought up by writ of error from the Circuit Court of the United States for the District of Columbia, holden in and for the county of Washington.

Boyden was a citizen of Massachusetts, and Burke was Commissioner of Patents at the time when the transactions took place which were the subject of the suit.

The ground of the action was, that Burke wilfully, maliciously, and corruptly, and with intent to injure Boyden, had refused to give copies of certain patents.

The bills of exceptions referred to certain letters, which will be mentioned chronologically.

On the 14th December, 1847, Boyden wrote a long letter to Burke, too long to be inserted. The following extract from it will be sufficient:

"If, in your letter of August 10, 1847, you mean by the 'office' yourself, or the author of the letters which I have received from you, you prescribe two conditions in said letter which are inconsistent, viz., that my letters to you, or to the author of those letters subscribed by you, should be both respectful and proper. It is improper to treat a person respectfully while it is known that he is unworthy of respect; therefore, it is impossible to comply with your prescriptions. The claim of unworthy office-holders to have people, as they say, respect the offices they hold, while it is known that the incumbents are unworthy of respect, is absurd. Do you mean, when you urge people to respect 'the office,' to have them respect you merely because you hold the office, while it is known that you are unworthy of respect? This is a free country!" &c. &c.

On the same day Mr. Boyden wrote to Mr. Greenough, in Washington, as follows:

BOSTON, MASS., December 14, 1847.

SIR, — Your letter of the 23d ult. was duly received. I wrote to Mr. Burke to-day, criticizing his conduct, and informing him that I wish him to deliver to you a certified copy of each of the following patents, including drawings, specifications, and claims, or of all of them which are recorded in the Patent-Office: George W. Henderson and John E. Cayford's patent, dated April 14, 1830, Charles Kenzie's patent, dated July 1, 1836, and J K. Millard's patent, dated May 9, 1846.

You will oblige by tendering the fees for those copies if he declines furnishing them; and if you obtain them, I wish you to send them by mail to me at Boston.   Respectfully,
(Signed)   URIAH A. BOYDEN.
        Test: JOHN A. SMITH, *Clk.*

Mr. Greenough, accordingly, called upon Mr. Burke, who declined to cause the copies to be prepared for him, as the agent of Mr. Boyden, and addressed to Mr. Greenough an explanatory letter, from which the following is an extract:

" Of these reasons, for declining to cause the copies to be made for him, which you requested, you were duly apprised. And you were also informed, as Mr. Boyden himself has been informed, that, until he comes to the conclusion to treat this office with the civility which the customs and rules of official intercourse require, this office will have no intercourse with him, directly or through the agency of others.   When he concludes to conduct his intercourse with this office with decency and propriety, his business will be attended to."

On the 20th of January, 1848, Mr. Burke made the following memorandum, which he handed to Mr. Laskey, who had called for the same papers:

PATENT-OFFICE, January 20, 1848.

Mr. R. H. Laskey, as the agent of Uriah A. Boyden, calls for the following copies of patents, including drawings, specifications, and claims, or of all of them, which are recorded in the Patent-Office, viz., George W. Henderson and John E. Cayford's patent, dated April 14, 1830; Charles Kenzie's patent, dated July 1, 1846; and J. K. Millard's patent, dated May 9, 1846; for which he offers to pay the usual fees required by law for copies.

I hereby refuse to give him the copies called for for Mr. Boyden, or to transact any other business for Mr. Boyden with Mr. Laskey.   I do not refuse copies of any patents or other papers which Mr. Laskey requires for himself or for any other person, except Mr. Boyden.   I refuse to do any business for Mr. Boyden, whether he applies for the same personally or by agent, until he comes to the conclusion to observe, in his communications with this office, or its official head, the proprieties usually observed in official intercourse.   When he comes to the conclusion to address this office, or its head in respectful language, any business which he may have with it will be done as it is done for other persons, whether he applies in person or by agent.

EDMUND BURKE.

Mr. Boyden soon afterwards brought his action against Burke, as above stated.

On the trial of the cause, the plaintiff's counsel took four bills of exceptions; the first three of which related to evidence, and the fourth an exception to a general instruction, that the plaintiff was not entitled to recover.

They were as follows:

First Exception.

On the trial of the issue in this cause, the plantiff, to maintain the issue on his part joined, offered to give evidence tending to show that he is a citizen of the United States, residing in Boston, in the State of Massachusetts; that he is a civil engineer and machinist, and as such was, in the month of January, 1848, engaged in making improvements in "Turbines" and "water-wheels;" that this fact was known to the defend ant; that the defendant was at the same time Commissioner of Patents; that the plaintiff, in order to see what machinery having in view the same purpose, had been theretofore patented, as well to guard himself against any suit by such previous patentees, for any alleged infringement of their said patents, as also to avoid any infringement thereof, and to save himself time, labor, and expense, required copies of certain patents then of record in the Patent-Office, and which had been theretofore issued to the persons mentioned in the memorandum of January 20th; that, on the 20th day of January, 1848, the said plaintiff applied to the said defendant, as Commissioner of Patents, as aforesaid, for copies of the said patents, and tendered himself ready, and "offered to pay the usual fees required by law for copies," and the defendant thereupon, as Commissioner, as aforesaid, answered the said application in writing, as follows.

To all which evidence, so as aforesaid offered by the plaintiff, and to every part thereof, except the said memorandum last above mentioned, the defendant by his counsel objects, as inadmissible upon the issue joined, and the court refused to permit the said evidence, so objected to, to be given; and thereupon, the plaintiff, by his counsel, excepts thereto.

Second Exception.

The plaintiff then read in evidence, without objection, the memorandum made by the defendant, dated 20th January, 1848, and then gave evidence tending to show that, on or about the 22d day of December, 1847, J. J. Greenough, by authority of the plaintiff, called at the Patent-Office to obtain for him copies of three several patents, which had theretofore been issued by said office for "Turbines" or "water-wheels;" that he was referred by the clerk, to whom he applied, to the defendant, and informed defendant, that he had been requested by the plaintiff to obtain for him copies of those patents, and defendant refused, saying he would not have any thing to do with Mr. Boyden, directly or indirectly, or words to that effect; and, upon his cross-examination, witness stated, that he asked Mr. Burke to give him in writing his reasons for so refusing, which he then and there promised to do; and some days after the witness received a letter from the defendant containing those reasons, which letter he had transmitted to the plaintiff; and then, upon cross-examination, the counsel for the defendant called upon the plaintiff to produce said letter, and the plaintiff, admitting he had said letter then in court, refuses to produce the same, on the ground that the said letter, if produced, would not be evidence; but the court, overruling the objection of the defendant, ordered the same to be produced, and thereupon the said letter was produced by the plaintiff; and the defendant, by his counsel, offers to read the same in evidence, and the plaintiff, by his counsel, objects thereto, but the court permits the same to be read in evidence, and it is read accordingly, as follows; and the plaintiff, by his counsel, excepts thereto, &c. &c.

Third Exception.

And here the plaintiff rested; and thereupon the defendant offered to read, in evidence, a letter addressed to him by the plaintiff, dated 14th December, 1847, and also a letter from plaintiff to J. J. Greenough, which it is admitted is the same letter referred to in the testimony of said Greenough, as containing the authority under which he applied for the copies of patents, as testified by him in his examination by the plaintiff, which letter bears date the 14th December, 1847, to the admissibility of which said letters, or either of them, as evidence in this cause, the plaintiff, by his counsel, objects, and the court overrules the said objection, and permits both of said letters to be read in evidence; and the handwriting of the plaintiff thereto being admitted, the same are read accordingly, and the plaintiff, by his counsel, excepts thereto, &c. &c.

Fourth Exception.

And thereupon, and upon the whole evidence aforesaid, the defendant prayed the court to instruct the jury that upon the evidence aforesaid, if the same is believed by the jury, the plaintiff is not entitled to recover in this action; which instruction the court gave, and the plaintiff, by his counsel, excepts thereto, &c. &c.

Upon these exceptions, the case came up to this court, and was argued by *Mr. Bradley*, for the plaintiff in error, and *Mr. Coxe*, for the defendant in error.

Mr. Bradley contended that the Circuit Court erred in each one of the above rulings.

First. The defendant was, by law, bound to give the copies asked for, if they could be made consistently with the public interest.

1. The Patent Office is for certain purposes an office of public record, in like manner as the office in which the titles to real property are recorded :

From the very name; tne object; the nature of the contract between the government and the patentee; the effect of the granting the patent as to the right granted; and the notice implied; the manner in which the title is secured, and by which a right under it is, to be transferred; the necessity to prevent litigation; to prevent conflicts; to avoid the expenditure of time and money.

2. For like reasons, if no provision were made by law for copies, still the keepers of those records should be bound to give them.

3. The original statute, and each successive one, made provision for such copies. Act 10th April, 1790, 1 Stat. at Large, 109, § 1, 2, 3; Act 21st February, 1793, Id. 318, § 1, 4, 11; Act 4th July, 1836, 5 Stat. at Large, 118, § 4, 5, 11; Act 3d March, 1837, Id. 191, § 1, 2, 12; Act 3d March, 1839, Id. 353, § 2, 8; Act 29th August, 1842, Id. 542, § 2, 6.

The law, in terms, provides copies in cases in which they are to be used as evidence, and makes them evidence. It does not stop here, but directs copies of the records, drawing, and other papers deposited in the office, to be given to any person making application for them, on their paying certain fees therefor.

It requires a record of the claim, specification, drawings, the patent therefor, and the assignment thereof. It imposes heavy penalties upon an infringement of the patent, and makes these records notice of the particulars of the right granted.

Its design, in authorizing copies to every person applying for them, is obvious; that is, protection against the danger of incurring these penalties. The reason for requiring copies in such cases, is obviously the same as that which requires them to be given in cases of contest. Prevention is often better than redress.

Second. The duty was purely ministerial, involving no discretion; and it will be further contended —

1. The general proposition, that, for a refusal by a public officer to do a mere ministerial act, to the injury of another's right, an action will lie.

2. The injury is to be compensated in damages, and if the officer has acted in good faith, the measure of damages is the

actual injury sustained; if he has acted wilfully, maliciously, corruptly, or by color of his office, with intent to injure, the party injured will be entitled to recover such damages as the jury may see fit to give.

As to the first branch of this second point, Tracy & Ballestier v. Swartwout, 10 Pet. 80; 9 How. 259.

As to the second branch, Huckle v. Money, 2 Wils. 205; Beardmore v. Carrington, Id. 244; Dinsman v. Wilkes, 12 How. 401 – 406; Day v. Woodworth, 13 How. 371.

Third. Evidence is admissible, in this last case, to show that the officer knew the nature of the injury he was inflicting, and therefore it was competent for the plaintiff to give in evidence the facts stated in plaintiff's bill of exceptions, not as indicating a measure of damages, but to give the jury some knowledge of the nature, character, and degree of the injury, as a guide in forming an estimate of the extent to which they might rightfully go in inflicting punitive as well as compensatory damages. Marest v. Harvey, 5 Taunt. 442; Woert v. Jenkins, 14 Johns. 352; Whipple v. Walpole, 10 N. H. Rep. 130; Wallace, Jr. R. 164; and cases under second point.

Fourth. The letter written by the defendant to Mr. Greenough, set out in the 2d bill of exceptions, was not evidence for any purpose.

1. Mr. Greenough had no authority to require it.

2. It was but an amplification of his first refusal, and not explanatory of it.

3. It was the party's own letter, offered in evidence by himself, not originally called for by plaintiff, and not in any manner admitted or acquiesced in by him. Farlie v. Denton, 3 C. & P. 103; 14 E. C. L. R. 227, 228; Healey v. Thatcher, 8 C. & P. 338; 34 E. C. L. R. 442; Whifford v. Buckmeyer & Adams, 1 Gill, 127, 140; Van Buren v. Digges, 11 How. 461, 477; Towle v. Stevenson, 1 Johns. Ca. 112; Champlin v. Tilley, 3 Day, 306; Antoine v. Coit, 2 Hall, N. Y. 40, 46, 47.

Fifth. The letter to the defendant, set out in the 3d bill of exceptions, was not evidence for the defendant for any purpose. The letter from the plaintiff to Mr. Greenough was admissible to show his authority from the plaintiff, and shows conclusively that he had no authority to ask for or to receive defendant's written statement, set out in the 2d exception.

But the letter written by plaintiff to defendant, on the 14th December, 1847, was not evidence in mitigation of his refusal on the 22d December, 1847, or on the 2d January, 1848; and it could have been admissible for no other purpose.

That letter would have reached here on the 18th December,

Boyden *v.* Burke.

1847, at furthest, by due course of mail, and the defendant had abundant time to get cool before the 22d of that month.

The refusals were both given deliberately, wilfully, with the intent to punish, that is, to injure the plaintiff, and the malice is so much the greater.

Mr. Coxe, for the defendant in error, made the following points:

1. That the Circuit Court ruled according to law on all the points raised in the bills of exception.

2. That the action is founded upon a misconception of the 4th section of the act of Congress of July 4th, 1836.

3. That if the plaintiff's case is embraced by that section, the evidence in the record furnishes a complete justification of the acts of defendant.

4. That the declaration sets forth no legal cause of action.

Mr. Justice GRIER delivered the opinion of the court.

The bills of exception, taken by the plaintiff to the rejection and admission of testimony on the trial, have not been supported.

The declaration charges, that the defendant, Burke, was Commissioner of Patents, and as such was bound to grant to applicants therefor, copies of patents, &c., on payment of fees. That the plaintiff tendered the customary fees and demanded copies of certain patents, which defendant refused to give him, to the damage of plaintiff, $10,000, &c.

As no special damage is alleged, the court very properly, refuse to receive evidence tending to prove it.

A demand for certain copies was made through the agency of Mr. Greenough, but accompanied with a letter from plaintiff to defendant, requesting him to deliver the copies to Mr. Greenough. This letter, with the answer of defendant thereto, was properly received as part of the *res gestæ,* or as a conversation between the parties, reduced to writing.

A bill of exceptions was also taken to the charge of the court, who instructed the jury, "that, upon the evidence before them, the plaintiff was not entitled to recover."

As the plaintiff had shown a demand of the copies, with tender of fees, and a refusal of defendant, he had made out his case as laid in his declaration, and was entitled to a verdict for nominal damages, unless by law he was not entitled to demand such copies, or defendant had shown a sufficient excuse for refusing them. Patents are public records. All persons are bound to take notice of their contents, and consequently should have a right to obtain copies of them. The patent law of 1836, § 4, enacts that "any person making application therefor may have certified copies," &c. These records being in the care and custody of the Commissioner of Patents, it is his duty to give authenticated copies to any person who shall demand the same, as soon as he conveniently can, on payment of the legal fees. Where there is a right on the one side, and a corresponding duty imposed on the other, a refusal to perform such duty, on the reasonable request of the party entitled to demand it, will subject the officer to an action. But the party entitled to such services must request it in a proper manner. He has no right to accompany his demand with personal insult, or vulgar abuse of the officer. Those to whom the people have committed high trusts, are entitled at least to common courtesy, and are not bound to submit to the insolence or ill temper of those who disregard the decencies of social intercourse. A demand, accompanied with rudeness and insult, is not a legal demand. The letter, accompanying the plaintiff's demand in this case, was taunting, insulting, and libellous, indicating a want of taste and temper. And if the case had rested here, we could have found no fault with the instruction of the court. But the plaintiff showed another demand, some two weeks after the first, by his agent, which was made in a proper manner, and unaccompanied with any insulting missive. The defendant was not justified in refusing this demand on account of the former misconduct of the plaintiff, or to enforce an apology by withholding his rights. Ill manners or bad temper do not work a forfeiture of men's civil rights. While the want of an apology for his previous rudeness and insult might well justify the defendant in refusing all social intercourse with the plaintiff, yet it could not release him from the obligations imposed upon him by his official station, or entitle him to disregard the rights guaranteed to the plaintiff by the laws of the land.

The court below erred, therefore, in not instructing the jury that if they believed the testimony, the plaintiff was entitled to a verdict for nominal damages.

The judgment is reversed, and a *venire de novo* awarded.

Order.

This cause came on to be heard on the transcript of the record from the Circuit Court of the United States for the District of Columbia, holden in and for the county of Washington, and was argued by counsel. On consideration whereof, it is now here ordered and adjudged by this court that the judgment of the said Circuit Court, in this cause be, and the same is hereby, reversed with costs; and that this cause be, and the same is hereby, remanded to the said Circuit Court with directions to award a *venire facias de novo*.

WILLIAM F. WALKER AND SAMUEL M. PUCKETT, APPELLANTS, v. GEORGE S. ROBBINS, LLOYD W. WELLS, ABIJAH FISHER, AND ROBERT H. McCURDY.

A bill in chancery will not lie for the purpose of perpetually enjoining a judgment, upon the ground that there was a false return in serving process upon one of the defendants. Redress must be sought in the court which gave the judgment, or in an action against the marshal.

Moreover, the defendant in this case, by his actions, waived all benefit which he might have derived from the false return; and no defence was made on the trial at law, impeaching the correctness of the cause of action sued on, and in such a case, resort cannot be had to equity to supply the omission.

THIS was an appeal from the Circuit Court of the United States for the Southern District of Mississippi, sitting as a Court of Equity.

The facts in the case are set forth in the opinion of the court.

It was argued by *Mr. Freeman*, for the appellants, and *Mr. Crittenden*, (Attorney-General,) for the appellees.

Mr. Justice CATRON delivered the opinion of the court.

William F. Walker, Samuel M. Puckett, and John Lang, filed their bill against Robbins and others, praying a perpetual injunction against a judgment at law recovered in the Circuit Court of the Mississippi District, alleging, among other grounds of relief, that William F. Walker, one of the complainants, was not served with notice to appear and defend the suit at law.

The deputy marshal returned the original writ, " Executed on William F. Walker, 6th of April, 1840, personally." More than ten years afterwards the deposition of the deputy (Cook) was taken in Texas, when he testified that his return was false; that he did not notify Walker, but indorsed the writ executed, intending to execute it after the indorsement was made, and therefore he let it stand, although he never did notify Walker.

Assuming the fact to be that Walker was not served with process, and that the marshal's return is false, can the bill, in this event, be maintained? The respondents did no act that can connect them with the false return; it was the sole act of the marshal, through his deputy, for which he was responsible to the complainant, Walker, for any damages that were sustained by him in consequence of the false return. This is free from controversy; still the marshal's responsibility does not settle the question made by the bill, which is, in general terms, whether a court of equity has jurisdiction to regulate proceedings, and to afford relief at law, where there has been abuse, in the various details arising on execution of process, original, mesne, and final. If a court of chancery can be called on to correct one abuse, so it may be to correct another; and in effect, to vacate judgments, where the tribunal rendering the same would refuse relief, either on motion, or on a proceeding by *audita querela*, where this mode of redress is in use.

In cases of false returns affecting the defendant, where the plaintiff at law is not in fault, redress can only be had in the court of law where the record was made, and if relief cannot be had there, the party injured must seek his remedy against the marshal.

We are of the opinion, however, that the return was not false; but if it was, that Walker waived the want of notice by pleading to the action. The suit was against Walker, Puckett and Lang. The latter employed David Shelton as his attorney to defend the suit. Lang told Shelton to put in pleas for all the defendants who had been served with process. Upon examination, Shelton found that process had been served on Walker, Lang, and Puckett, and he put in a joint plea for them. Afterwards, Shelton, the attorney, met both Walker and Lang in Jackson, where the court sat, and spoke to them in each other's presence, about the defence of the case; and a conversation was held with them, in which they promised Mr. Shelton that another attor. ·, William Seiger, should be associated with him in defending the suit. The questions likely to arise in the case were stated by Lang and Walker, and they were especially anxious to know from Shelton whether Mr. Shields, the principal to the note sued on, would be competent as a witness on their behalf. The cause was tried at a subsequent term, on the issue made by the plea put in by Shelton, and a verdict and judgment rendered.

No defence was nade on the trial at law, impeaching the consideration of the note sued on, either on the ground that Green had not delivered the bank-notes, as stipulated by him; nor on the ground that usury entered into the transaction because the notes were at a discount of from forty to fifty per cent. Neither was any proof introduced on the hearing of this chancery suit in the Circuit Court, tending to show that Green failed to deliver the bank-notes, although the respondents put the fact in issue; and as the face of the note imported a consideration, no further evidence to sustain it was required from the respondents.

They admit that the bank-notes were at the rate of discount stated in the bill, but insisted they were of equal value to Shields as if they had been at par; and this the bill admits would have been the case, had Shields received them according to his agreement with Green; and there being no proof to the contrary, we must assume that they were duly received. But whether they were duly delivered or not, is immaterial. The defendants in the suit at law had an opportunity to make their defence there, and having failed to make it, cannot be heard in a Court of Equity. By way of authority, we need only repeat, as the settled rule, what was adjudged in the case of Creath v. Sims, (5 Howard, 204,) that whenever a competent defence shall have existed at law, the party who may have neglected to use it, will never be permitted to supply the omission and set it up by bill in chancery.

This court has never departed from the foregoing rule, nor allowed the circuit courts to depart from it in cases brought here. Nor can we do so without violating the sixteenth section of the Judiciary Act of 1789, in its true sense. Apparent aberrations may be found, but they are only apparent.

We order that the decree below be affirmed.

Order.

This cause came on to be heard on the transcript of the record from the Circuit Court of the United States for the Southern District of Mississippi, and was argued by counsel. On consideration whereof, it is now here ordered, adjudged, and decreed by this court, that the decree of the said Circuit Court in this cause be, and the same is hereby, affirmed, with costs.

HENRY D. HUFF, JOHN BULLEN, AND SAMUEL HALE, PLAINTIFFS IN ERROR, v. CHAMPION J. HUTCHINSON, WHO SUES FOR THE USE OF WILLIAM W. HURLBUT, JOSEPH A. SWEETZER, PHILIP VAN VALKENBURGH, AND GEORGE S. PHILLIPS.

Where the marshal of the District of Wisconsin attached property at the suit of creditors in New York, and then gave it up upon the execution of a bond to himself, for the use of those creditors, it was within the jurisdiction of the District Court of the United States for Wisconsin, to entertain a suit by the marshal, suing upon the bond for the New York creditors, against the claimants in Wisconsin, although both parties resided in the same State.

The name of the marshal was merely formal; the real plaintiffs were averred to be citizens of New York.

It was not a good exception upon the ground of variation between the evidence and declaration, that the latter stated the bond to have been given to Hutchinson as marshal of the District of Wisconsin, and the former said the State of Wisconsin. They mean the same thing.

Judgment having been rendered for the plaintiffs in the attachment, by a court having jurisdiction over the subject, it was too late to object to those proceedings in a suit upon the bond, in which they were collaterally introduced.

The bond given to the marshal was in conformity with the statute.

The objections, that the declaration on the bond did not show the jurisdiction of the court in the attachment suit; that the verdict was entered for the amount due instead of the penalty of the bond, and that the recovery was for a sum greater than was claimed by the *ad damnum* in the declaration, were not sufficient for a new trial.

THIS case was brought up, by writ of error, from the District Court of the United States for the District of Wisconsin.

The facts are stated in the opinion of the court.

It was argued by *Mr. Chatfield*, for the plaintiffs in error, and by *Mr. Lee* and *Mr. Seward*, for the defendants in error.

Mr. Justice McLEAN delivered the opinion of the court.

This case is brought before us by a writ of error from the District Court for the District of Wisconsin.

The action was commenced on a bond given by the plaintiffs in error to Champion J. Hutchinson, United States Marshal, for the State of Wisconsin, and his successor in office, in the penal sum of five thousand six hundred dollars, for the payment of any judgment within sixty days after its rendition, in a suit which William Hurlbut and others had commenced in the District Court, against Huff, by attachment, and in which a judgment was rendered for the plaintiffs, for two thousand eight hundred and eighty-four dollars and forty-eight cents, and costs.

. To the declaration the defendants pleaded in abatement, that at the commencement of the suit, Huff, Bullen, and Hale, were citizens of the State of Wisconsin, and that the said Champion J. Hutchinson was also a citizen of the same State.

To this plea a demurrer was filed; and the District Court sustained the demurrer.

The declaration stated that Hutchinson, late marshal, sues for the use of William W. Hurlbut, Joseph A. Sweetzer, Philip Van Valkenburgh, and George S. Phillips, citizens of the State of New York, plaintiffs. The bond was given to the marshal in pursuance of the statute of Wisconsin, regulating proceedings against debtors by attachment, and the name of Hutchinson was merely formal, as he had no interest in the suit. The real plaintiffs were those named in the declaration, for whose use the suit was brought, and who are averred to be citizens of New York.

The District Court did not err in sustaining the demurrer. In McNutt *v.* Bland & Humphreys, (2 How. 10,) this court held, in such a case, the Circuit Court had jurisdiction.

After the demurrer was sustained, the defendants filed a plea of *nil debet.*

On the trial, a bill of exceptions was taken to the rulings of the court, which will now be considered.

The first exception was to the introduction of the bond as evidence, because it varied from the declaration. The alleged variance consisted in this: The declaration states the bond to have been given to Hutchinson, as marshal of the District of Wisconsin, and in the bond he is described as the marshal for the State of Wisconsin. As the State of Wisconsin is the same in fact and in law, as the District of Wisconsin, there was no variance.

Objection was made to the introduction of the writ of attachment in evidence, on the same ground of variance as above stated to the bond. There was no necessity of introducing this evidence, as the condition of the bond referred to the judgment to be obtained, but the court did not err in admitting it.

Other objections were made to the affidavit on which the attachment was issued, to the return of the writ, &c. These objections were unsustainable. The court had jurisdiction of the writ by attachment, and the judgment obtained in that case was collateral to a suit on the bond. ` Objections, therefore, could not be made to the proceedings in attachment, however erroneous they might be.

In the case of Voorhees et al. v. The Bank of the United States, (10 Pet. 449,) this court say, " So long as this judgment remains in force, it is in itself evidence of the right of the plaintiff to the thing adjudged, and gives him a right to process to execute the judgment. The errors of the court, however apparent, can be examined only by an appellate power." That was a procedure by attachment, and there were many errors on the face of the record, which would have required an appellate court to reverse the judgment; but they could not be considered when the record of the judgment was introduced collaterally.

It was objected that the bond did not pursue the statute. 1. That it should have been in double the amount of the goods attached. 2. That the bond described in the declaration is in the penalty of $5,600, to pay whatever judgment should be obtained. The 13th section of the statute, which regulates the giving of the bond, provides that "it may be in a penalty of double the amount specified in the affidavit, annexed to the writ, as due to the plaintiff, conditioned for the payment of any judgment which may be recovered by the plaintiff in the suit commenced by such attachment, within sixty days after such judgment shall be rendered." The bond is within the statute.

The bond being given in the name of Hutchinson, as marshal, and his successor in office, the suit is well brought in the name of Hutchinson, though he has been succeeded in office by another. The name of the obligee being used as matter of form, the action may be brought in the name of the late marshal or his successor.

Several grounds were taken in arrest of judgment.

1. Because the declaration on the bond, does not show that the District Court had jurisdiction in the attachment suit. Such showing was unnecessary, as that court had general jurisdiction of such cases.

2. Because the verdict is informal, in being entered for the amount due, when it should have been for the penalty of the bond. This is a mere informality, and no ground for arresting the judgment.

3. Because the recovery is for a sum greater than is claimed by the *ad damnum* in the declaration. The action was debt, and the damages laid were only required to cover the interest.

There was no error in the District Court in overruling the motion in arrest of judgment.

The judgment of the District Court is affirmed.

Order.

This cause came on to be heard on the transcript of the record from the District Court of the United States for the District of Wisconsin, and was argued by counsel. On consideration whereof, it is now here ordered and adjudged, by this court, that the judgment of the said District Court in this cause be, and the same is hereby, affirmed, with costs, and interest until the same is paid, at the same rate per annum that similar judgments bear in the courts of the State of Wisconsin.

JOHN G. GOESELE AND OTHERS, APPELLANTS, *v.* JOSEPH M. BIMELER AND OTHERS.

A society called Separatists, emigrated from Germany to the United States. They were very poor, and one of them, in 1817, purchased land in Ohio, for which he gave his bond, and took the title to himself. Afterwards, they adopted two constitutions, one in 1819, and one in 1824, which they signed, and in 1832 obtained an act of incorporation. The articles of association, or constitutions of 1819 and 1824, contained a renunciation of individual property.

The heirs of one of the members who signed these conditions, and died in 1827, cannot maintain a bill of partition.

From 1817 to 1819, the contract between the members and the person who purchased the property, vested in parol, and was destitute of a consideration. No legal rights were vested in the members.

The ancestor of these heirs renounced all right of individual property, when he signed the articles, and did so upon the consideration that the society would support him in sickness and in health; and this was deemed by him an adequate compensation for his labor and property, contributed to the common stock.

The principles of the association were, that land and other property were to be acquired by the members, but they were not to be vested with the fee of the land. Hence, at the death of one of them, no right of property descended to his heirs.

There is no legal objection to such a partnership; nor can it be considered a forfeiture of individual rights for the community to succeed to his share, because it was a matter of voluntary contract.

Nor do the articles of association constitute a perpetuity. The society exists at the will of its members, a majority of whom may at any time order a sale of the property, and break up the association.

The evidence shows that they are a moral, religious, and industrious people.

THIS was an appeal from the Circuit Court of the United States for the District of Ohio, sitting as a Court of Equity.

The bill was filed by John G. Goesele and six other persons, as heirs at law of Johannes Goesele, deceased, against Bimeler and twenty-four other persons, members of the Society of Separatists.

The facts of the case are stated in the opinion of the court.

The Circuit Court dismissed the bill, and the complainants appealed to this court.

It was argued by *Mr. Quinn*, for the appellants, and by *Mr. Stanberry* and *Mr. Ewing*, for the appellees.

Mr. Quinn, for the appellants, stated the facts in the case, the articles of association made in 1819 and 1824, and then made the following points:

1st. That the purchase being made for the use of all the members of the company, the purchase-money paid with the issues and profits of their joint labor or joint means, and the title taken by Bimeler, either with or without a fraudulent intention, makes him a trustee of the legal estate, holding to the use of the members of the company, each of whom own an undivided portion of the whole trust or equitable estate.

2d. That this trust, or equitable estate, is an estate of inheritance, alienable and descendible like any other fee. 8 Ohio R. 398; 9 Ohio R. 145. And that of such an estate Johannes Goesele died seised in 1827.

Here we think the argument properly ends, and that the complainants are entitled to an account and partition. But to the case made upon the articles, we say —

1st. That if the articles of 1819 constituted a partnership, (which we think they did not,) it became dissolved by Johannes Goesele's death, or by the first change in its constituent parts.

2d. That the articles of 1824 are void for no less than four different reasons.

1. Because there is no grantee or assignee to take the property from the natural persons. Sloan v. McConahy, 4 Ohio R. 169. The society being unincorporated. 4 Wheat. 1.

2. Because the trusts are vague and uncertain. 3 Kent's Com. 303; Bacon's Ab., Uses and Trusts, 256; Tomlins's L. Dict., Trusts; Story's Eq. § 979 to § 1070; 12 Ohio R. 287; 5 Mass. 504; Swan's Ohio Stat. 319; 2 Spencer's Eq. 106; 7 Eng. Com. Law R. 267.

3. Because they create a perpetuity. Story's Eq. § 974, n.; 10 Ohio R. 4; 2 Spencer's Eq. 93, et seq. 106; 4 Ohio R. 515; Lord Deerhurst v. Duke of St. Albans, 5 Mad. 235; 4 Kent's Com. 267, 271; 1 Cox, 324; 1 Bing. 104.

4. Because they are the work of imposition, and a scheme of Bimeler to defraud his *cestui que trusts*.

In addition to these two exceptions taken to the articles of 1824, two others are made, which are alike common to both, and which, in their natural order, lie in advance of those just taken. They are—

1st. That no articles were executed, some of the members having failed to sign; among whom is the defendant Bimeler, who now claims protection under them.

2d. That the so-called Separatists' society, at Zoar, is not an association or community, but is an institution of a master and his slaves, or what the Roman jurists characterized as *societas leonina*. Story on Part. § 18.

Bimeler, upon the face of his pleadings, presents five points of defence.

1. That by the articles, there is a surrender of property, and that in consequence no property descended to Goesele's heirs.

2. That the institution is to be taken as a general partnership, with the principles of succession ingrafted upon it, and its property is to be taken as personalty.

3. That in virtue of the act of incorporation, passed in 1832, the entire property passed to the corporation.

4. That Johannes Goesele's labor was not worth more than his support.

5. That the property has been improved with regard to a common ownership, and cannot now be divided.

The *first* of these points, we say, admits the first objection made to the articles of 1824, viz., the want of an assignee. For, while it claims a surrender, it does not show to whom that surrender was made.

Upon the *second* point, we think the articles do not constitute a partnership; yet, if they do, we think it is a waiver of the whole defence; for, if the members were partners, they owned the property. But a partnership, with the principle of succession ingrafted upon it, would be a corporation, which individuals have not the power of making. In the consideration of these points, the following cases are cited: Miles v. Fisher, 10

Ohio Rep. 1; Story on Part. § 273, § 18; 15 Johns. Rep. 159; 11
Mass. Rep. 469; Swan's Ohio Statutes.

The *third* point, namely, that Goesele's property passed to a
corporation, five years after his death, is not the law.   8 Pick.
Rep. 455.

Upon the *fourth* point, we say that, whether Goesele's labor
was worth more or less than his support, is a matter after which
the court will not inquire; but, finding him a member of the
company, and a joint owner of the estate, will presume his
share equal to that of the other members. If, however, it makes
the inquiry, it will find that he contributed about twice or three
times his proportionate share.

The *fifth* and last point presented on the face of the pleadings, namely, that the property has been improved with regard
to a common ownership, and is incapable of division, we cannot but regard as trifling.   And yet we find that depositions,
covering no less than thirty pages of printed record, have been
taken to prove this point, together with one other of similar
importance, namely, that the members are well clothed, well
fed, and are contented.

One other point was raised by the defendant, Bimeler, at the
hearing below, and will probably be raised again.   It is, that
" the society is a charity," or rather that the property is a donation to charitable use.   This, we say, it is not, and cite Ambler,
652; Story's Eq. § 1156, 4th ed., § 1182, 1183; Rabb *v.* Read,
5 Rawle's Rep. 154; Chase's Ohio Statutes, 1066; Swan's Ohio
Statutes, 782; 4 Wheat. 1.

We are advised that it will be insisted that the society is
what is called a universal partnership.   If it is, it will not help
the defence; for such partnerships differ from ordinary partnerships only in the extent of the investment; that is, the members
invest their all, all their labor, property, and skill; but in every
other particular, including the causes of dissolution, they are
governed by the same rules that govern ordinary partnerships.
Were they, however, such as is claimed by the defence, they
would be corporations.

Again, we are advised that it will be claimed that the articles
are a contract for survivorship.   To this we answer, that nothing
can be farther from both the letter and spirit of the instruments.
Instead of its being provided that one shall survive to the estate of another, it is expressly provided, that no one shall survive to, or even have any thing; and in this particular the first
decedent and the last survivor are placed in precisely the same
situation.   Nothing could be more foreign from the intention,
than that the last survivor and his heirs should take the whole
property, to the exclusion of the heirs of all the other members.

That Goesele once owned the property, is admitted; and Bimeler claims to be nothing but a trustee. In this situation, when called upon by the *cestui que trust* to convey the legal title, he endeavors to defend himself by saying, that *cestui que trust* assigned his interest to a third person. This kind of defence cannot be sustained. For as he is a mere stakeholder, by his own showing, he must file his bill of interpleader, and bring that third party before the court to litigate the right.

He claims protection, too, under instruments which he never signed, but which he got others to sign, by representing that he would also be a subscriber.

Great complaint is made from the other side, that we are endeavoring to infringe upon their liberties by prohibiting them from living in community. This is not so. Mr. Bimeler and his adherents may live in any way they please, provided they live on their own property; but we are unwilling to give them our property to enable them to live in any way whatever. They say, too, that the appointment of a receiver or a partition will break up the society. If it does, it ought to be broken up; for it is an evidence that the members do not wish to live as they do.

The articles of 1833 purport to be a revision of those of 1819 and 1824, and also to be an acceptance of an act of incorporation passed in 1833; but they form a society entirely different from the one created by the act, for which reason, we think, the grant of corporate power has been rejected. A grant of corporate power must be received as it came from the hands of the legislature, or it is not received at all. Kirk v. Newill, 1 T. R. 71.

Their by-laws, too, which are required by the statute to be consistent with the laws of the United States and the State of Ohio, are opposed to public policy.

They require the alienating rights which are unalienable, and close the doors of the courts of justice against the citizen. Constitution of Ohio, §§ 1, 16, Bill of Rights; 1 Blackf. 122; 19 Wend. 77. Deprive the husband of his curtesy and the widow of her dower. 4 Kent, 131; 3 Id. 30, e; 2 Spencer's Eq. 104; 1 Eden, 415. Their trusts are also vague and uncertain. They are also executory, and, to divest the member of his property, are without consideration.

Under these articles, as well as under those of 1824, if they are sustained, Bimeler will eventually take the whole property in absolute ownership. He still holds the legal title. The members, according to his defence under the articles of 1824, hold an use while they remain members; consequently, when they cease to be members, either by death or otherwise, the use estate becomes extinct, and his legal title takes the absolute property. The same is the case under the articles of 1833, supposing the company to be incorporated; for by that arrangement the corporation holds the use estate in trust for the use of the members. When the members die, then the corporation dies, and, as a consequence, there is nobody to look after the trust; therefore, whether the company is or is not incorporated, Bimeler's legal title will eventually take the whole estate.

Such an advantage, to be acquired by an agent over his principals, a preacher or pastor over his people, and a trustee over his *cestui que trusts*, cannot be sustained by any enlightened system of jurisprudence.

Mr. Stanberry's brief was as follows:

I propose, in the first place, to consider the character and legal condition of this association, as it stood upon the mere agreements of 1819 and 1824, before it became clothed with a corporate capacity.

It is said it was simply a partnership, liable to the incidents of that condition, and subject to the operation of all the ordinary causes of dissolution. That, in point of fact, it was dissolved by the first death which happened amongst its members, and was capable of dissolution and partition of its real estate, at any time, at the instance of any member.

If it were a pure partnership, these results would have followed. But I claim this association is not of that character.

The original agreement provides for a perfect community of property, real and personal, and for a succession or survivorship among members on the Tontine principle. It guards, with great care, against the dissolution of the body. Its property consisted, at the beginning, of a common stock of money and chattels, contributed in unequal proportions by the members, with which, and the labor of the members, real estate and personalty, to a very large amount, were in process of time accumulated. The legal title to the real estate has always been vested in Joseph M. Bimeler, one of the members. The business of the society has been various. Agriculture, manufactures, and merchandise, have been carried on simultaneously. From 1817 to 1833, a period of seventeen years, during which it was unincorporated, various changes took place in the body of the society, by deaths, withdrawals, expulsions, and admissions of members.

With this general outline, we can enter upon the inquiry which is opened by the objections on the other side.

And first, we say, this was not a mere partnership, nor the members tenants in common. The agreement for community of property, the mutual surrender of all individual property into the common stock, and the express stipulations against any reclamation in the case of withdrawal, and for the preservation of the common property, for the exclusive use and perpetual enjoyment of the members, in succession, are inconsistent with the incidents of mere partnership or tenancy in common.

There can be no question as to the intent of these stipulations. The only doubt is as to their legal practicability.

The actual practicability of such a society is demonstrated in this instance. For the sixteen years in which it existed without a charter it fulfilled all the purposes of its formation, and secured the comfort and well-being of its members, beyond the common lot.

But, it is said, there are legal difficulties which the agreement of the parties cannot surmount. Let us consider them.

1. It is said, upon the death of a member, the society was dissolved *ex necessitate*. This consequence, though generally true as to partnerships, does not follow where the agreement provides against it. It is not an inevitable consequence. The doctrine of dissolution upon the death of a partner, only obtains where the deceased partner has a continuing interest in the property or profits of the association. It is not just that the surviving partners should be obliged to carry on the business, without his coöperation, for the benefit of his estate. Story on Partnership, 453.

I have said this society was not an ordinary partnership. It very closely resembles that sort of partnership in the civil law, which is called universal. " Universal partnerships (*des societies universelles*) are contracts by which the parties agree to make a common stock of all property they respectively possess — they may extend it to all property, real or personal, or restrict it to the personal only. They may, as in other partnerships, agree that the property itself shall be common stock, or that the fruits only shall be such; but property which may accrue to one of the parties, after entering into the partnership, by donation, succession, or legacy, does not become common stock, and any stipulation to that effect, previous to the obtaining of the property aforesaid, is void." "An universal partnership of profits includes all the gains that may be made, from whatever source, whether from property or industry, with the restriction contained in the last article, and subject to all legal stipulations between the parties." Civil Code of Louisiana, art. 2800, 2801.

These universal partnerships have been adopted into the common law. Mr. Justice Story thus defines them : " By universal partnerships, we are to understand these, that where the parties agree to bring into the firm all their property, real, personal, and mixed, and to employ all their skill, labor, services, and diligence, in trade or business, for the common and mutual benefit, so that there is an entire communion of interest between them. Such contracts are within the scope of the common law, but they are of very rare existence." Story on Part. 104.

Such a form of association being within the scope of the common law, can it be doubted that, by the mutual consent and agreement of the members, the effect of a dissolution by death may be provided against?

In England, and in the United States, large associations and joint stock companies exist, under agreements which protect the members, *inter sese,* from the ordinary incidents of partnership, such as dissolution by death, bankruptcies, assignments, &c. Collyer on Part. 614; Livingston v. Lynch, 4 Johns. Ch. Rep. 573.

This association is a general partnership, with the principle of survivorship ingrafted upon it. In this particular it takes the character of a Tontine, which is a society with the benefit of survivorship, the longest liver taking the common property in absolute ownership. Encyclopædia Brit. vol. 37, art. Tontine; Encyclopædia Amer. vol. 12, art. Tontine.

I can see no objection to this provision as to ownership. Certainly as to personalty there can be no difficulty; but it is said, in so far as the real property of the company is concerned, there can be no joint tenancy, no right of survivorship, in Ohio; and that upon a death of a member, his interest in the real estate passes to his heirs at law, and that at any time the right to partition might be asserted.

As to that, it is to be considered, in the first place, that this is a partnership, and that the real estate is, by the articles of association, expressly made a part of the common stock. This, in equity, stamps it with the character of personalty. Summer v. Hampson, 8 Ohio Rep. 328.

Fortunately for the society, the title to its real estate has always been well vested in one individual. No question can be raised in this case as to the condition of that legal title, and as to the equitable title or use, that was in the members before the act of incorporation, and since then it is in the corporate body.

I do not doubt, however, that as a general principle, equitable estates follow the same rules as to descent, &c., with legal estates. What I mean to say in reference to the legal, as distinguished from the equitable, title. is, that there is a necessity. it should vest somewhere, and conform to general rules as to transfer, descent, &c.

Being relieved, in this case, from any difficulty as to the condition of the fee in the real estate of this society, all we have

:o look to, is merely the equitable interest or use which enured :o the members, who stood in the relation of *cestuis que trust* :o Bimeler, the holder of the legal title. As I have before said, this interest in partnership property is viewed in this court simply as personalty.

But if that were not so, if it were strictly an interest in real estate, and to be made conformable to the rules which govern real property, I deny that the principle of survivorship may not be grafted upon it.

Our court has said, in an early case, (Sergeant *v.* Steinberber, 2 Ohio Rep. 126,) that the estate by joint tenancy does not exist in Ohio. That case only required of the court to decide that it does not exist here by mere operation of law. But that the principle of survivorship may not be provided for and exist by limitation, in Ohio, has never been decided. On the contrary, we have reported cases which recognize it. Miles *v.* Fisher, (10 Ohio, 1,) is a case of that character. The court say in that case, " Laying out of view the doctrine of survivorship, resulting from joint tenancy, an incident of the estate depending on the law and not on the act of the party, we find the testator, by express words, limiting the estate to three trustees and the survivor. The estate well passes by these vords to the survivor for life, the remainder in fee is not disposed of."

There is, then, no objection to survivorship by express limitation or agreement. This being so, there has been no descent to any heirs of the deceased members of the society, and there is no present right of partition in any of the living members.

It is also said that even as to the personal property, it is difficult to fix its ownership distinct from the individual right of each member making the contribution, and that the idea of accumulation for an unincorporated body is a fallacy.

This difficulty is altogether fanciful. The members of this partnership are in no way uncertain, for no one is a member whose name is not subscribed to the articles of association: It is a large partnership. The accumulation is for the partners, not for an ideal company or mere abstraction. The property loses its individuality as to ownership the instant the owner becomes a member. It stands like the property of any other partnership. The partners are joint owners. No formal transfer or delivery is necessary; the possession by one partner is the possession of all.

Objection is also made to this association, that the principle of community and succession of property among the members, involves a *perpetuit* There is nothing like a perpetuity in it. The society has the perfect right of disposal over all its property, real as well as personal, and this power of disposal is wholly inconsistent with the idea of perpetuity, which only exists where property is so limited that no living agency can unfetter it.

It is further urged that this society is contrary to the genius of our free institutions — that its constitution enforces perpetual service and adherence to a particular faith, and that it is aristocratic in its tendency.

If there were any thing in such objections, the constitution answers them all. So far from being at all aristocratic, this society is a pure democracy. All the officers are chosen by ballot, every member, male and female, having an equal voice; and the body of the society reserves to itself the power of removing officers, and changing the form of government at pleasure. All distinctions of rank or wealth are abolished, and a perfect equality provided for. No single dogma in religion or politics is announced, no unusual restraint on marriage, nor subserviency to any doctrine out of the common way, exist; and so far from any enforcement of perpetual service being provided for, the right is reserved for every member to retire from the society at pleasure, with the single condition that no claim is to be set up for services or property contributed. The powers which the society confides to its officers are temporary, and so distributed as to prevent any one member or officer from engrossing too much power.

Besides this liberal frame of government, the constitution, by very full enactments, provides for the education of the children, the comfort and support of all the members, and the peaceable settlement of all controversies by domestic tribunals. It is impossible to hold that such a constitution is contrary to public policy, or in any sense illegal. To say that such a society cannot exist under our form of government is a libel on our free institutions.

Here are a number of persons, who, in the exercise of their mature judgment, and following their own peculiar views, have thought it best, more than thirty years ago, to associate as one family, in a communion of property. From that time to the present, through an entire generation, their experiment has been successful. They have lived in peace, plenty, and happiness, beyond the common lot. The legislature has given them a charter to perpetuate their social existence; and now it is urged that, in this land of liberty, the right does not exist to live in this way; a very bright idea, truly! If a despot proclaimed such an edict, forbidding men to pursue their own mode of life, in their own inoffensive way, we could understand it; but it is quite new as a democratic idea.

(*Mr. Stanberry* then cited and examined the cases of Waite *v.* Merrill et al. 4 Greenleaf, 102 ; Schriber *v.* Rapp, 5 Watts, 351 ; Gass and Bonta *v.* Wilhite et al. 2 Dana, 170. He then contended that this society was protected by the doctrine of charities, and by its act of incorporation.)

Mr. Ewing's brief was as follows.

1st. The executor or administrator of Goesele is not a party to this suit; therefore no question as to personal property can arise.

I now state the proposition as applying to property purely personal, but will, in the course of my argument, show that it controls also the real estate owned by this association, to which the law attributes the qualities and consequences of personalty.

2d. This suit, therefore, involves nothing but title to real estate, and the question is, did Goesele die seised of an inheritable estate in the lands and tenements named in the bill.

We have the object and terms of the original purchase from no other source than the answer of Bimeler. He says he purchased it for the Separatist society, took a deed in his own name, and gave his own bonds for the payment of the purchase-money. P. 6.

And it was purchased with the understanding at the time that it should be paid for with the means and labor of those of the Separatists who would settle upon it, and that each should have thereof in proportion to the amount that he or she should contribute to paying therefor. P. 14.

It is obvious, at once, that here was yet no partnership. And there was yet no contract between Bimeler and either or all of the other parties which equity could enforce.

No one was yet bound to Bimeler, that he should go upon the land or pay for any part of it; as a correlative proposition, Bimeler was not bound to hold the land, or any part of it, in trust for any of them. Both parties must be bound or neither. Goesele, however, went on to the land, and built a small log-house on a town lot in Zoar, previous to 1819. Some conflict in the evidence about the building. He went into a house.

He was still under no contract to pay for any of the land. He still had no right to any definite part or amount, on making payment, unless it may have been the town lot on which his house was built.

He had yet paid nothing, applied nothing; had no contract which equity could regard.

If, the hour before the execution of the articles of April 5th, 1819, Goesele had claimed a definite portion of the land, and offered to pay for it in proportion to the cost of the whole, a court of equity could not have denied it to him.

If Bimeler had declared that he would thenceforth hold the land to his own use, and that his associates should have none of it, equity could not have relieved them by decreeing to them parts of the land. The law, however, would have given them a *quantum meruit* for the labor which they had performed.

Or, if I be mistaken in this, and he had any interest in the land which equity could recognize, it was held by such loose and uncertain tenure, that he could abandon it by any word or deed showing a purpose not to retain or rely upon it. Goesele, therefore, was entitled to nothing, except what the articles of brotherhood and association gave him.

The genuineness of the articles is doubted, and we are called upon for proof that Goesele signed them. We are content that the court should regard them as not in evidence, and especially that Goesele never signed them. If that be so, we think it very clear that he never had any right whatever, except to a compensation in money for his services, if he rendered any, of value beyond his maintenance, nursing, and burial. But this is a question which none but his administrator is competent to litigate.

But he had rights under those articles of association, and as his counsel is probably not seriously disposed to repudiate them, I will inquire what the rights were which were conferred by them.

Waiving, for the present, the question whether this was or was not a charitable association, and, as such, protected by the law of charities, I will examine it as a mere attempt to dispose of property and give it direction.

I will suppose Bimeler to have signed the articles, as he intended to be bound by them, and would have signed them had the land been paid for and his notes taken up, and he did sign soon after this was done.

Then if the articles were good to transfer real estate in equity, they were good to transfer personalty, and equally good to limit and direct the real estate transferred.

What title to the real estate do these articles vest in Goesele? It is to be borne in mind, that down to this time Bimeler had the legal estate, and Goesele had no interest in it which a court of equity could regard.

The articles give to Goesele a right to live upon, and enjoy a fair proportion of the land, during his life; to raise and have his children educated and maintained upon it; to take part, with others, under rules agreed upon between themselves, in its management and control. These rights, however, were conferred subject to conditions and forfeiture.

But the conditions were complied with, namely, that he should surrender whatsoever property he had, to the association, and live and labor with them during his life. He did not incur a forfeiture; he had then purchased this right, and he enjoyed it; he lived, died, and was buried in the lands with his brethren in the faith.

Can there be a doubt that all the parties were competent to make this contract? But if there be a doubt, can a question now arise as to their competency, since both parties kept it, and executed it faithfully to the end?

No complaint on either side, of wrong or violation, until the contract, as far as Goesele was concerned, was completely executed and ended.

But if this contract could not be legally entered into by Goesele with the other members, no valid contract whatever was entered into by him or for him.

Bimeler agreed to surrender this land to the association, to be held in this manner, and on these conditions. He never did agree, and never would have agreed, to surrender it to these one hundred and fifty men and women as a partnership, subject to the consequences of partnerships, dissolution by the death or withdrawal of a member, and consequent partition, at least three times a year, of land and personalty.

If equity cannot sustain the contract which the parties did make for themselves, it will not make a contract for them which they never did make, and never intended to make, and which would defeat all their objects.

But it will carry out the contract according to their intent, as far forth as the principles of law will permit. This will readily and without a single difficulty, that I can discover, dispose of Goesele's interest, and consequently of this case.

Goesele might, without the violation of any rule of law, give his labor and property, if he had any, in consideration of the provision for life herein made for him.

Bimeler might, in like manner, bind his land in equity to make good such provision.

3d. But I do not, for myself, perceive any serious difficulty in transmitting the property, with the personalty and the equitable title to the realty, in the manner adopted by these articles.

Cannot a man transfer the equitable title to his real estate to ten men, designated as those who live on it and have signed the article of transfer with him, to be used and enjoyed by them as long as they shall abide by the terms of the article, and giving a right to the persons, to whom he so transfers, to vest the same right in others, in succession, who shall enter into the same article in future, and comply with its conditions, the majority having, as in this case, the power to sell and dispose of the property, but required to apply the proceeds to the same object?

This is not a perpetuity in the common-law sense of the term; it does not tie up real estate, for it may be disposed of at any time. Such a limitation of the real estate, or its proceeds, would be good, by the laws of Ohio, for the lives in being; and each tenant for life, by his own signature, if the full estate at any time vested in him or them, could equally well transmit it to another life, and so in succession, a majority being at all times able to terminate the succession at pleasure.

4th. But if I be wrong in this, and difficulty arise as to the final disposition of the property, when the end cometh, which is not yet, that difficulty is removed by the law of charitable uses, considered in Mr. Stanberry's brief.

5th. And if this be not a charity, and as such protected by equity, and if the contract made by the parties for themselves be invalid for the purposes intended, it is still good as a partnership with succession, by the express agreement of the parties, an agreement, so far, unobjectionable. All the property owned in common, real as well as personal, is necessary to carry on the partnership; it is, therefore, all personalty in equity. And the partners, or a majority of them, can readopt their rules or change them at pleasure, and transmit their property by succession as heretofore, or divide between the partners.

6th. But if it were indeed a partnership, we have not the necessary parties in court. The property is all personalty, and neither executor nor administrator of Goesele is in court.

Mr. Justice McLEAN delivered the opinion of the court.

This case comes before the court on an appeal from the Circuit Court of the District of Ohio.

In their bill the complainants represent that they are the heirs at law of Johannes Goesele, who died at Zoar, in the county of Tuscarawas, Ohio, in the year 1827; that the said Johannes, in his lifetime, associated himself with the defendants, Bimeler and others, and formed a society of Separatists, and in the year 1817 they purchased of one Godfrey Haga, of Philadelphia, a tract of land situated in said county, containing 5,500 acres; that afterwards other purchases were made, which, when added to the first purchase, amounting to 10,000 acres, with a large number of town lots, and other property procured about the same time; that these purchases were made on behalf of Goesele, deceased, and his associates, and for their use, and the purchase-money was paid by their joint labor and money; that Bimeler acted fraudulently as their agent, in taking the deed and title papers to himself and his heirs forever.

They further represent that many of his associates sold their interest to their ancestor, on leaving the society. And the defendants allege, that, as heirs of their ancestor, they are entitled to one hundredth portion of the estate now held by Bimeler; and that they have requested the defendants to make partition of the estate, which has been refused; that Bimeler, although often requested, has refused to convey to the complainants any part of the estate; and they pray that he may be compelled to give a full and true description of the property held by him as stated; and that on a final hearing he may be decreed to make partition of the said property, and to make a good deed in fee-simple to the complainants, for so much of the said property as may be found to belong to them.

In the year 1817, the members of the above association emigrated from Germany to the United States. They came from the Kingdom of Wertemberg, where they had been known for years as a religious society called Separatists. They were much persecuted on account of their religion. Goesele, the ancestor of the complainants, with another member, had been imprisoned for nine years; and the safety of Bimeler depended on his frequent changes of residence, and living in the utmost privacy. In that country they sought to establish themselves by purchasing land, but they found that the laws would not allow them this privilege. Disheartened by persecution and injustice, they came to this country in pursuit of civil and religious liberty. When they arrived at Philadelphia, they were in a destitute condition. They were supported while in that city, and enabled to travel to the place where they now live, by the charities of the Friend Quakers of Philadelphia and of the city of London. These contributions amounted to eighteen dollars to each person. A large majority of the society consisted of women and children.

While at Philadelphia, Bimeler, the head and principal man of the association, purchased, in his own name, from Godfrey Haga, the five thousand five hundred acres of land, as stated in the bill. A credit of thirteen years was given, three years without interest. A deed to Bimeler and his heirs was executed for the land, the 7th of May, 1818; a mortgage to secure the consideration of $15,000 was executed. On their arrival at the place of their destination, they found it an unbroken forest; their means were exhausted, and they had no other dependence than the labor of their hands. They were no strangers to a rigid economy, and they were industrious from principle.

At the time of their settlement at Zoar, they did not contemplate a community of property. On the 15th of April, 1819, articles of association were drawn up and signed by the members of the society, consisting of fifty-three males and one hundred and four females. In the preamble they say, "that the members of the society have, in a spirit of Christian love, agreed to unite in a communion of property, according to the rules and regulations specified." The members renounce all individual ownership of property, present or future, real or personal, and transfer the same to three directors, elected by themselves annually; that they shall conduct the business of the society, take possession of all its property, and account to the society for all their transactions. Members who leave the society are to receive no compensation for their labor or property contributed, unless an allowance be made them by a majority of the society.

These articles continued in force until the 18th of March, 1824, when amendatory articles were drawn up and signed by the members at that time, consisting of sixty males and one hundred females. In these articles an entire union of property is declared, and a renunciation of individual ownership. Males of the age of twenty-one, and females of the age of eighteen, become members by signing the articles. New members are received in this way. The directors elected by the society conduct the affairs of the association, and provide for the boarding, lodging, and clothing of the members. The directors are to apply themselves for the common benefit of the society, provide for the children, determine disputes among the members, with a right of appeal to the board of arbitration. Other provisions were made for the expulsion of members, and the general good order and welfare of the society.

In the year 1832, the society was incorporated by a law of the State, which gave to them the ordinary powers of a corporation. On the 14th of May, 1833, a constitution was adopted under the act, which was signed by fifty-one males and one hundred and three females. The constitution embodies substantially the regulations contained in the preceding articles, and some others conformably with the corporate powers conferred.

This is the outline of the association formed at Zoar. It appears a different plan was at first adopted. Each family was to select from the general tract as many acres as it could pay for, and improve it, living on its own industry, and from the same source paying for the land. But this plan was found impracticable, and in less than two years it was abandoned, and the first articles of association were adopted.

The ancestor of the complainant, as stated, died in 1827, a member of the society. His name was signed to the articles of 1819 and 1824. There was no evidence in the case conducing to prove any contract, except that which arises from the articles referred to. On the first payment made for the land, it appeared that Goesele paid a small sum that remained unexpended of the eighteen dollars he received at Philadelphia.

The answer denies the allegations of the bill charging fraud, and every allegation to charge the defendants, except the purchase of the land and the articles referred to.

It appears, by great industry, economy, good management, and energy, the settlement at Zoar has prospered more than any part of the surrounding country. It surpasses, probably, all other neighborhoods in the State in the neatness and productiveness of its agriculture, in the mechanic arts, and in manufacturing by machinery. The value of the property is now estimated by complainant's counsel to be more than a million of dollars. This is a most extraordinary advance by the labor of that community, about two thirds of which consists of females.

In view of the facts stated, it is not perceived how the case made in the bill can be sustained. A partition is prayed for; but there is no evidence on which such a right can be founded. The plan, as stated, first agreed upon at Zoar, for individual proprietorship and labor, was abandoned in less than two years. It was a parol contract, no consideration being paid. No right was acquired by the ancestor of the complainant on this ground. He then signed the first articles, which, like the amended articles, renounced individual ownership of property, and an agreement was made to labor for the community, in common with others, for their comfortable maintenance. All individual right of property became merged in the general right of the association. He had no individual right, and could transmit none to his heirs. It is strange that the complainants should ask a partition through their ancestor, when, by the terms of his contract, he could have no divisible interest. They who now enjoy the property, enjoy it under his express contract.

But if there were a right of partition by the complainants, there is no such statement in the bill as would authorize the court to decree it. For the time that Goesele lived, what was the value of his labor in comparison with the labor of the others? Twenty-five years have elapsed since his death. The property has increased in value seven hundred per cent.; and of this property partition is prayed. But there is not a shadow of evidence to sustain the right. The proofs and the statements in the bill are as remote and inconsistent as can well be conceived.

The fraud charged on Bimeler, in the purchase of the land, if true, could not help the case made in the bill. But the charge has no foundation. Bimeler purchased the land in his own

51 *

name, and became responsible for the payment of the consideration. And he retained the title until the purchase-money was paid, and an act of incorporation was obtained, when he signed the articles, and placed the property under the control of the society, he having no greater interest in it than any other individual. But, before this, he openly declared that he held the land in trust for the society. As an honest man, he could not change, if in his power, the relation he bore to the vendor, until the consideration was paid. In this matter, the conduct of Bimeler is not only not fraudulent, but it was above reproach. It was wise and most judicious to secure the best interests of the association.

The articles of 1819 and 1824 are objected to as not constituting a contract which a court of equity would enforce. And it is said that chancery will not enforce a forfeiture. As a general rule, chancery may not enforce a forfeiture; but will it relieve an individual from his contract, entered into fairly, and for a valuable consideration? What is there in either of these articles that is contrary to good morals, or that is opposed to the policy of the laws? An association of individuals is formed under a religious influence, who are in a destitute condition, having little to rely on for their support but their industry; and they agree to labor in common for the good of the society, and a comfortable maintenance for each individual; and whatever shall be acquired beyond this shall go to the common stock. This contract provides for every member of the community, in sickness and in health, and under whatsoever misfortune may occur. And this is equal to the independence and comforts ordinarily enjoyed.

The ancestor of the complainants entered into the contract fairly and with a full understanding of its conditions. The consideration of his comfortable maintenance, under all circumstances, was deemed by him an adequate compensation for his labor and property contributed to the common stock. But it is not shown that Goesele or any other member contributed to the general fund, with the exception of a small sum by Goesele, which, probably, could not have exceeded five dollars. The members of the association were poor, and were unable to contribute any thing but labor. In this way the land purchased by Bimeler was paid for.

The complainants speak of the interest of their ancestor in the real and personal estate, owned by the association, and their counsel contend that the articles did not divest him of either, but both descended to his heirs at law at his death.

This argument does not seem to comprehend the principles of the association. Land and other property were to be acquired by the members, but they were not to be vested with the fee of the land. While they remained in the society, under its general regulations, the products of their labor on the land and otherwise were applied, so far as necessary, to their support. Beyond this, they were to have no interest in the land or in the personal property. Many of the members were aged females, others, from sickness or disease, were unable to labor, but every one, whether able to labor or not, was provided for by the labor of the community. This was a benevolent scheme, and from its character might be properly denominated a charity. But from the nature of the association and the object to be attained, it is clear the individual members could have no rights to the property, except its use, under the restrictions imposed by the articles. The whole policy of the association was founded on a principle which excluded individual ownership. Such an ownership would defeat the great object in view, by necessarily giving to the association a temporary character. If the interests of its members could be transferred, or pass by descent, the maintenance of the community would be impossible. In the natural course of things the ownership of the property in a few years, by transfer and descent, would pass out of the community into the hands of strangers, and thereby defeat the object in view.

By disclaiming all individual ownership of the property acquired by their labor, for the benefits secured by the articles, the members give durability to the fund accumulated, and to the benevolent purposes to which it is applied. No legal objection is perceived to such a partnership. If members separate themselves from the society their interest in the property ceases, and new members that may be admitted, under the articles, enjoy the advantages common to all.

The counsel for the complainants imagine the original members possessed property, real and personal, before they entered into the association, which is contrary to the facts of the case, and then contend that, having executed no conveyance of the property, on the death of the member it descended to his heirs at law.

It is always desirable that legal principles should be applied to the facts of the case. When the members first formed the association they were destitute of property. The purchase of the land by Bimeler had been made, but not paid for; and the members had no means of payment but by the labor of their hands. This they agreed to give, in consideration of being supported in sickness and in health, disclaiming, at the same time, any individual claim of ownership to any property which should be acquired by the community. This statement of facts obviates many of the objections urged by complainants' counsel. If the members of the association had no interest in the land when they signed the articles, no conveyance of it by them was necessary. They stipulated a compensation for their future labor in the support to be given them, and disclaimed the own-ership of all property acquired.

It is said, where a member is excommunicated or leaves the society he forfeits his rights, and that chancery will not enforce a forfeiture. What is the extent of this forfeiture? It is the right to a support from the society. And this is certainly rea-sonable. Can a member expect to be supported by the society, when he refuses to perform his part of the contract which en-titles him to a support? He claims pay for his labor. He has been paid for this, in pursuance of his own contract. In sick-ness and in health he has been clothed and fed, and a home provided for him. But he claims payment for property which he surrendered to the association at the time he became a member of it, by signing the articles. The ownership of this property he relinquished to his associates as a part of the con-tract; and for the considerations named, all the demands for such property in the language of the articles signed, "the individual abolished and abrogated for himself and his heirs."

Can property thus conveyed be deemed forfeited, if not recoverable? A forfeiture is against the will of the owner. Where property is conveyed under a fair contract and for a valuable consideration, is not the term forfeited misapplied, if such conveyance be held valid? Chancery is not asked to enforce a forfeiture in this case. No property is shown to have been transferred to the association by the ancestor of the com-plainants. But if property had been given by the ancestor, would a court of chancery direct such property to be surren-dered or paid for against the express contract of the owner? The surrender or giving up of the property was a part of the consideration on which the association stipulated to support him. It cannot be separated from that agreement. And it is clear, where the fault of not carrying out the contract is not attributable to the association, but to the member, he cannot have the aid of a court of chancery.

Do the articles constitute a perpetuity? We all think that they do not. They provide for the continuance of the associa-tion an indefinite period of time, in the exercise of the discre-tion of its members. But there is no obligation to this extent. The majority of the members may require a sale of the property and break up the association. In fact the majority governs, by the election of officers. Members may be expelled from the society and new ones admitted, under established rules. Whilst the society has the means of perpetuating its existence, it may be said to depend for its continuance, on the will of a majority of its members.

As the law now stands in England, a conveyance by executory devises, to be good, cannot extend beyond a life or lives in being, and twenty-one years and the fraction of another year, to reach the case of a posthumous child. Atkinson v. Hutchinson, 3 P. Wms. 258; Long v. Blackall, 7 Term, R. 100.

There are many depositions in the case, taken in behalf of the complainants, by persons who have been expelled from the society, or, having left it, show a strong hostility to Bimeler. They represent his conduct as tyrannical and oppressive to the members of the association, and as controlling its actions absolutely. And several instances are given to impeach his moral character and his integrity. Two of the witnesses say that he drives a splendid carriage and horses.

In regard to the carriage, it is proved to be a very ordinary one, worth about three hundred dollars, one of his horses worth about twenty dollars and the other thirty or forty. By respectable persons out of the society, Bimeler's character is sustained for integrity and morality, and several instances are given where, even in small matters, he deferred to the decision of the trustees against his own inclination. And many facts are proved wholly inconsistent with the charge of oppression.

That Bimeler is a man of great energy and of high capacity for business, cannot be doubted. The present prosperity of Zoar is evidence of this. There are few men to be found any where, who, under similar circumstances, would have been equally successful. The people of his charge are proved to be moral and religious. It is said that, although the society has lived at Zoar for more than thirty years, no criminal prosecution has been instituted against any one of its members. The most respectable men who live near the village say, that the industry and enterprise of the people of Zoar have advanced property in the vicinity ten per cent.

Bimeler has a difficult part to act. As the head and leader of the society, his conduct is narrowly watched, and often misconstrued. Narrow minds, in such an association, will be influenced by petty jealousies and unjust surmises. To insure success these must be overcome or disregarded. The most exemplary conduct and conscientious discharge of duty may not protect an individual from censure. On a full view of the evidence we are convinced that, by a part of the witnesses, great injustice is done to the character of Bimeler. On a deliberate consideration of all the facts in the case, we think there is no ground to authorize the relief prayed for by the complainants. The decree of the Circuit Court is therefore affirmed.

Order.

This cause came on to be heard on the transcript of the record from the Circuit Court of the United States for the District of Ohio, and was argued by counsel. On consideration whereof it is now here ordered, adjudged, and decreed by this court, that the decree of the said Circuit Court in this cause be, and the same is hereby, affirmed with costs.

JOHN DEACON, APPELLANT, v. CHARLES OLIVER AND ROBERT M. GIBBES, EXECUTORS OF ROBERT OLIVER, DECEASED.

Under the attachment laws of Maryland, a share in the Baltimore Mexican Company, which had fitted out an expedition under General Mina, was not, in 1827, the subject of an attachment under a judgment, whether such share was held by the garnishee under a power of attorney to collect the proceeds, or under an equitable assignment to secure a debt.

The answers of the garnishee to interrogatories filed, were literally correct. He had not in his hands any "funds, evidences of debt, stocks, certificates of stock," belonging to the debtor, nor "any acknowledgment by the Mexican government," on which an attachment could be laid.

THIS was an appeal from the Circuit Court of the United States for the District of Maryland, sitting as a court of equity.

The bill was filed by John Deacon, the surviving partner of Baring, Brother & Company, of London, under the following circumstances:

In 1821, Baring, Brother & Company obtained a judgment, in the Circuit Court of the United States for the District of Maryland, against one Lyde Goodwin for $60,000, upon a bill of exchange, to be released on payment of $41,006.58, with interest and costs. Goodwin was at this time the owner of one ninth share in the Mexican Company, the history of which is given in the report of the case of Gill v. Oliver's Executors, 11 How. 529. This judgment was kept alive until the issuing of the attachment hereafter spoken of, in 1826.

On the 19th of July, 1823, the government of Mexico passed a decree, declaring that General Mina, amongst other persons, was a benefactor of his country; and on the 28th of June, 1824, another decree, acknowledging the debts contracted by the Generals declared to have been benefactors.

On the 11th of January, 1825, Lyde Goodwin addressed a

letter to Mr. Oliver, which is too long to be inserted, but which was of the following tenor. He states the claim to have been acknowledged by Mexico; that the amount of his original proportion of the claim, exclusive of interest, was twenty thousand dollars; that his object in proposing to assign his interest therein was, 1st, to secure to Oliver the sum he already owed him; and 2d, to obtain barely the means of support for the present, and that the additional sum he would acquire, should not exceed $2,000.

Between this date and June, 1825, Oliver paid to Goodwin $2,000, and received an assignment of the share from Brown, the trustee in insolvency of Goodwin.

On the 22d of March, 1825, the company appointed Oliver their attorney to prosecute the claim, and informed him that Goodwin was entitled to a commission of five per cent. in addition to his one ninth share.

On the 28th of October, 1826, an attachment under the act of Maryland, of 1715, was issued upon the judgment against Goodwin, and laid in the hands of Oliver, as garnishee. At the same time, the following interrogatories were filed, which the garnishee was required to answer.

Interrogatory 1. Had you, at the time of laying the attachment in the above cause, in your hands, or at any other time, and when, any funds, evidences of debt, stocks, certificates of stock, belonging to Lyde Goodwin, or any acknowledgment of debt due by the government of Mexico to the said Lyde Goodwin?

2. Did not the said Lyde Goodwin transfer to you some certificate of stock, or evidence of debt due by the said Mexican government to Goodwin, or some document of that character, and when did such transfer take place?

3. Had you not a claim against said Goodwin, secured by a transfer or pledge of some certificate of stock, or document of a public character, showing that Goodwin was entitled to receive some funds from the Mexican government? If so, what was the amount of your claim so secured, and what was the security; was, or was not, the balance or remaining credit, under your control at the time of laying the attachment? State particularly how your claim was secured.

4. Do you know any other matter or thing that may be of advantage to the plaintiffs, in the above cause? If so, state it as fully as if you were particularly interrogated thereto.

In December, 1827, Oliver filed the following answers:

1. To the first interrogatory he answers: That he had not, at the time of laying the attachment in the above cause in his hands, nor at any other time, any funds, evidences of debt,

stocks, or certificates of stocks, belonging to Lyde Goodwin, or any acknowledgment of debt due by the government of Mexico, but that he had a power of attorney signed by said Lyde Goodwin, in conjunction with several other persons, claimants of a debt alleged to be owing by the Mexican government, and authorizing him to claim and receive the same for the benefit of said Goodwin's assignees and others.

2. To the second interrogatory he answers: That the said Goodwin did not transfer to him any certificates of stock or evidences of debt due by the Mexican government, or documents of that character, unless the before-mentioned power of attorney may be called one.

3. To the third interrogatory he answers: That he had, and still has, a large claim against said Goodwin for money lent him from time to time; that he is not secured for this debt, and never has been secured, by a transfer or pledge of some certificate of stock, or document of a public character, showing that Goodwin was entitled to receive some funds from the Mexican government, unless the aforesaid power of attorney be deemed such, but which he does not admit it to be.

4. To the fourth interrogatory he answers: That he knows nothing.

On the 10th of January, 1829, the counsel for the Barings caused the following entry to be made upon the docket, relative to the attachment: "Discontinued without costs."

On the 30th of May, 1829, Oliver obtained from Goodwin the following paper:

"Being indebted to Robert Oliver, of Baltimore, upwards of nine thousand dollars, I hereby assign, transfer, and make over to the said Robert Oliver, in payment of my debt to him, the following objects, which were assigned to him many years ago, to secure the payment of the said debt due by me, to wit, all my undivided ninth part, and right, title, and interest of every kind whatsoever, in the claim on the government of Mexico for supplies furnished, and advances made, to the late General Mina, or the proceeds thereof, and which claims are under the control of the said Robert Oliver and his agent, John Mason, Jr., now in Mexico; also a claim on a certain Louis Merwin, who died some years ago in Havana. The object and intention of this assignment, is to make a full and complete transfer to the said Robert Oliver of all my right, title, and interest, as aforesaid, for which said Robert Oliver has agreed to balance my account on his books, and to consider the same as satisfactorily settled; and I hereby authori⸱ and order all my agents, or those holding any powers of atto⸱ ey or instructions from me relative to the aforesaid property, to account with the said Robert Oliver for the same, or the proceeds thereof.

"L. GOODWIN.

" Baltimore, May 30, 1829.

" Witness — JOHN THOMAS.

" I confirm the above agreement. ROBERT OLIVER."

This claim was prosecuted under the treaty between the United States and Mexico, with the following result:

On the 11th of April, 1850, there were paid to Oliver's executors (he having died in 1834) the following sums, being net proceeds:

On account of Goodwin's commissions	22,143.12
" " " his share	35,110.47
	$57,253.59

In November, 1850, Deacon filed his bill against the executors, alleging that the answers of Oliver were untrue and evasive, by means of which deception the attachment had been discontinued; that at the time when it was laid, Oliver had under his control the evidences of debt due by the Mexican government; that so far from having a mere power of attorney from Goodwin to collect the debt, he had a transfer of the claim for the purpose of security, which, being irrevocable, was, by the laws of Maryland, the subject of an attachment, &c.

The executors of Oliver answered, and upon a hearing of the cause, the Circuit Court dismissed the bill, when the complainant appealed to this court.

It was argued by *Mr. Davis* and *Mr. Howard*, for the appellant, and *Mr. Campbell* and *Mr. Johnson*, for the appellees.

As the decision rested mainly upon one point of the case, namely, that, at the time of laying the attachment, Oliver had no interest which was attachable, many of the arguments of counsel upon other points, are omitted.

The following extract from the brief of Mr. Davis contains his view of the leading points of the case.

1. That a debt due by a foreign or domestic government is assignable, passing, by insolvency, to executors or administrators, and liable for debts of claimant, and liable to all the incidents of other debts, excepting that it cannot be enforced by suit. Comegys *v.* Vasse, 1 Pet. 193, 215, 217; Sheppard *v.* Taylor, 5 Pet. 675; Plater *v.* Scott, 6 Gill & Johns. 116; Gorgier *v.* Mieville, 3 Barn. & Cress. 45; 10 E. C. L. R. 16.

2. That the Court of Appeals of Maryland have decided,

that, by the local law, the share of Lyde Goodwin, now in controversy, and his commissions, did not pass to his insolvent trustee in 1817, because then under the ban of the public policy of the country; but that after the decrees of 19th July, 1823, and 28th June, 1824, of Mexico, it became a fair and valid debt, due by the Mexican government, and as such was assignable, and did pass by the assignment of Goodwin of 1825, and 30th May, 1829.

3. That the Supreme Court have pronounced ·the above to have been the decision of the Court of Appeals; and that being on a question of local municipal law, not involving any law of the United States, such decision could not be reviewed by them. Gill *v.* Oliver's Ex's, 11 How. 529; Williams *v.* Oliver's Ex's, 12 Id. 111, 125.

4. That the award of the Mexican commission and the decree of the Court of Appeals, are conclusive upon Robert Oliver's representatives and in our favor, of the nature and origin of the fund, of the validity and assignability of the funds, and its liability to all legal incidents of a valid legal claim, from 1824 down to this time. Comegys *v.* Vasse, 1 Pet. 212; Sheppard *v.* Taylor, 5 Id. 708, 709, 713; Frevall *v.* Bache, 14 Id. 97; De Vallingan *v.* Duffy, Id. 290, 291; Barry *v.* Patterson, 6 Har. & Johns. 203, 204.

II. That the assignment of 1825 was a mortgage on the fund to secure the prior debt of Goodwin to Oliver, and the $2,000 then advanced; subject to which Goodwin remained owner of the fund, and Oliver was accountable to him.

1. This appears from Goodwin's letter to Oliver, 11th January, 1825; his receipt, 15th February, 1825; Brown's assignment, 21st March, 1825; and Goodwin's receipt, 24th March, 1825; and the assignment of 30th May, 1829.

The letter did not propose a sale; there was no estimate of the value of the claim; Goodwin considered it likely to be received in a year, and looked on it as worth $20,000, or more.

His objects he said were— 1st. To secure a debt he then owed, but if it were a sale for $2,000, it secured nothing; 2d. To obtain the bare means of support for the present. He then plainly looked to the remainder of the fund as his support for the future.

The additional sum I shall want shall not exceed $2,000," is the language of a borrower, and implies a previous loan now to be added to. The receipts are, on account of his share, or interest.

The assignment, signed by Brown, mentions no value given. It was a mere precaution to preclude a possible claim. The assignment of 1829, May 30, finally, is express and decisive as to the former assignment, being for security merely, and itself purports to assign and relinquish the remaining right of Goodwin. It recites a debt of $9,000; but the answer shows only $8,500, including the $2,000. So it continued to be a debt, and so was not a payment on a sale. If it were a sale, then "the words to secure you the sum I already owe you," must be construed to make that sum a part of the consideration of the sale; and it also would cease to be a debt. If it were a sale, then the assignment of 30th May, 1829, would not only recite a falsehood, but be an absurdity. It cannot be half sale and half mortgage; a sale for $2,000 and a mortgage for $6,000.

The assignment of 1825 was therefore a mortgage, agreed by the act of the parties to be worth $8,000, and considered by Goodwin worth more than $20,000, and likely to be paid in cash in a year.

2. That such an assignment is in law a mortgage, or security merely, the following cases prove: 1 Story Eq. Jur. § 1018; 1 Cruise (by Greenleaf) tit. 15, ch. 1; Conway v. Alexander, 7 Cranch, 218, 241; Hughes v. Edwards, 9 Wheat. 489; Morris v. Nixon, 1 How. 118, 122, 123, 124, 126, 127, 130, 131; Dougherty v. McCalgan, 6 Gill & Johns. 275, 280, 281.

3. That on mortgage, or pledge, or transfer, by way of security, the mortgagor is treated as the substantial owner, subject to the lien of the creditor. His right to redeem is an incident inseparable. It may be assigned or pass to his representatives, or to his insolvent trustee, or in bankruptcy, or a judgment creditor may claim to stand in his place and to redeem.

This principle applies to securities of chattels as well as of lands, and to choses in action as well as to either. Morris v. Nixon, 1 How. 123, 124, 126, 129; 5 Johns. R. 345; 2 Story Eq. Jur. §§ 1023, 1052; Dougherty v. McCalgan, 6 G. & J. 281, 282; Hudson v. Warner & Vance, 2 Har. & G. 415; Hartley v. Russel, 2 Sim. & Stu. 244; Milne v. Walton, 2 Younge & Col. 354, 362.

III. That, therefore, Lyde Goodwin retained such a property and interest in the claim on Mexico, after its assignment to Oliver, as was liable in some way to be subjected to the payment of his debts by judgment. Being an equitable interest in a chose in action, it could not be subjected to the common-law execution of *fieri facias*.

It could then be reached by one of two processes only; either, 1st, by attachment in the nature of an execution; 2d, by bill in equity to subject the surplus.

The appellant insists that it could be subjected by either of those modes, and that the laying the attachment was a fit preliminary; and that the fraud is the same in either view.

1. By execution of attachment.

a. The act of 1715, § 7, gives any judgment creditor of any person right, in lieu of any other execution, to sue out an attachment against the goods, chattels, and credits, of the defendant, in his own hands, or in the hands of any other person.

The policy of our law is to subject every species of property to execution. Somerville *v.* Brown, 5 Gill, 422.

It is an execution. Baldwin *v.* Wright, 3 Gill, 246.

The attachment was intended to cover every species of property not liable to be taken by *fi. fa.*, and for which, before plaintiff had been driven into equity to get hold of; and that it would not lie where a *fi. fa.*, lay. For example —

Fi. fa. lay only for chattels held by *legal title.* 10 G. & J. 226, 261; Harding *v.* Stevenson, 6 H. & J. 267. Attachment covers that by *equitable title.*

Legal estates in land, by the act of 1732, are sold on *fi. fa.* Equitable estates, as equities of redemption, by attachment, but not to *fi. fa.* Ford *v.* Philpot, 5 Har. & J. 312; 5 Johns. R. 336.

Goods consigned to merchants who had lien on them were not liable to *fi. fa.*, but were to attachment. 6 Har. & Johns. 267, 268; Nathan *v.* Giles, 5 Taunt. 558.

The lien of a judgment could not be sold on *fi. fa.*, but the judgment could be attached, and court could execute it. Wells *v.* Ghiselin, 1 Har. & McH. 91.

Surplus money in sheriff's hands could not be taken on *fi. fa.* but might by attachment. 1 Har. & Johns. 546; 5 Har. & Johns. 312.

Attachment lies for a credit or a chose in action, or for stocks, because they are not liable to *fi. fa.* Evans, Pr. 364.

But chattels in defendant's possession were not liable to attachment, because they could be taken by *fi. fa.* 3 Har. & McH. 594, 615, 616, 617.

Thus the policy of the attachment law was to give a residuary execution, covering every case not before covered. The words goods and chattels, and lands, covering interests in lands, and goods and chattels, which could not be taken by *fi. fa.* and credits, being used to designate every thing in the nature of a chose in action.

b. The claim on the Mexican government, assigned by Goodwin, was a credit of Goodwin in the hands of Oliver, and so liable to attachment in his hands.

The statute does not confine the attachment to credits in the hands of the debtor, but extends it to the credits of the defendant in the hands of the plaintiff, or any other person.

The most common case is the attaching the credit in the

hands of the debtor, or person owing the money to the defendant.

But the act does not define the subject-matter on which the attachment may be laid by any reference to the person in whose hands it may happen to be. The credit is the thing attached; it may be attached in the hands of the plaintiff, or any other person.

May, then, a credit be in the hands of any person but the debtor, who himself directly owes the money to the defendant?

A credit is a right to demand money from some one. It is equivalent to the legal phrase, a chose in action — a thing to be sued for.

Now, a right in A to recover money from B for the use of C, is matter of every day occurrence.

If D have judgment against C, may he not lay an attachment in the hands of A, who holds a credit or chose in action against B for the benefit of C, especially if B be out of the State?

2. The modern law recognizes the assignability of choses in action, operating an actual transfer *proprio vigore* of the title of the chose in action, or credit, from the assignor to the assignee, vesting the latter with all the rights of the former, the possession of the evidences, and the right to enforce the claim, as effectually as a bargain and a sale of lands. 2 Story, Eq. Jur. § 1057; Comegys v. Vasse, 1 Peters, 213, 215, 217; Spring v. S. C. Ins. Co. 8 Wheat. 268; Bohlen v. Cleveland, 5 Mason, 174; Harrison v. Sterry, 5 Cranch, 289, 300, 302; Evans et al. v. Merriken, 8 G. & J. 39, 46–49; Ex parte South, 3 Swanst. 372, 373; Conrad v. Atlantic Ins. Co. 1 Peters, 386, 441; Black v. Zacharie, 3 How. 483, 512.

As between successive assignments, the title vests according to the dates, a former being liable, however, to be postponed to a later one by failure to notify the person liable to the assignor in proper time. Anderson v. Tompkins, 1 Brock. 456; Hudson v. Warner and Vance, 2 H. & G. 415, 418, 427, 432; Houston v. Nowland, 7 G. & J. 480, 493; Loveridge v. Cooper, 3 Russ. 1; Cooper v. Tynmore, 3 Russ. 60; 3 How. 483, 512.

3. By the assignment of 1825, therefore, the chose in action or credit belonging to Goodwin, and due by Mexico, was vested in and held by Oliver for the benefit of Goodwin, after paying his debt. He held the evidences, the sole legal right to prosecute and control it, to collect and receipt for it.

To refuse to apply the attachment to such a case, is to withdraw from its reach half the cases it was provided to remedy, forcing the judgment creditor back into a suit in equity; e. g. all cases where a credit or chose in action of a judgment debtor is in the hands of any one, except the person ultimately liable to pay the money.

A consignee has sold goods and taken notes of the purchaser, not yet due, to the consignor. The goods could have been attached — may not their proceeds, in the shape of notes, in the hands of the consignee, on a judgment against the consignor?

Chattels and choses in action are assigned in trust, the debtors living out of reach of process, to sell and pay to A B. The chattels may be attached in the hands of the trustee — may not the bonds and notes be attached, so as to bind the proceeds when collected?

United States stock is held by a trustee for A B. It is an obligation to pay money; may the stock — the right to receive the money, not merely the quarterly instalment, be attached; and, if so, in whose hands but the trustee's?

So stocks of all non-resident corporations will escape execution, unless they be attachable in any hands holding the certificates for the person entitled to receive the proceeds.

The stock, like the debt, is a credit, the money payable ultimately by one person; but the right to receive it, the title to it, being in the hands of a third party for the owner, with the evidences on which alone it is payable. It is case of a credit in the hands of such party, and may be attached there.

The very point has been decided twice in Massachusetts. N. E. M. Ins. Co. v. Chandler, 16 Mass. 274, 279; 6 Mass. 339, 342.

The Massachusetts law uses the words, "goods, effects, and credits," equivalent to "goods, chattels, and credits." Attachment laid on goods and notes for collection in the garnishee's hands. Erskine v. Staley, 12 Leigh, 406.

Or put the case of a legacy specific, of a note, or chose in action, where executor is here, and person liable on the chose in action beyond process.

c. The attachment was rightly laid in Oliver's hands, for it must be laid in the hands of the possessor of the thing attached. Van Brunt v. Pike & Ward, 4 Gill, 270, 276.

And possession of the evidences, together with the assignment, vests the possession of the chose in action in transferee. Dearle v. Hall, 3 Russ. 1; Farmers' Bank of Delaware v. Beaston, 7 G. & J. 428, 429; Gardner v. Lochlan, 4 Myl. & Craig, 129, 133; Black v. Zacharie, 3 How. 483, 512.

That Oliver is legally chargeable with the possession of the evidences of debt, since they were under his control, and should have so stated it. Morrice v. Livaby, 2 Bevan, 500; Attorney-General v. Bailiff of E. R., 2 Myln. & K. 35; 2 Danl. Ch. Pr. 259, 260; Woods v. Morsell, 105, 107.

d. That the money had not been actually received, was no obstacle to a judgment of condemnation, with a stay of execution till it should be collected; for the court has power to modify its judgments and process to suit the exigency of each case; e. g. where property is subject to a lien, to have it ascertained was to get at the surplus. Davidson's Lessee *v.* Beatty, 3 H. & McH. 594; Pratt *v.* Law, 9 Cranch, 456, 496; Serg. on Attach. 91, 94; 2 Rawl. 227.

And where laid in the hands of a debtor, on a debt not yet due, no plea of *nulla bona* is allowed; but condemnation is given, and execution stayed till debt due. Somerville *v.* Brown, 5 Gill, 399; Serg. on Attach. 101, 102, 109.

Or where papers detained abroad. 4 Dall. 253; 2 Binney, 453; Serg. on Attach. 145.

So the court could have condemned Goodwin's interest, and either have sold it or evited its collection.

e. That the attachment, by way of execution, applies to all judgments, without regard to the residence of the defendant. 1 D. L. M. 22, 23; Act 1715, ch. 40.

1. The operative words of the section giving the remedy are of the widest possible scope.

2. The use of the word "absent" before defendant, occurs only in the last clause of the section requiring notice of the garnishee.

3. They only create a doubtful implication, which is not sufficient to limit the universality of the enacting words.

4. This section expressly dispenses with the prerequisites prescribed in the 1st and 2d sections, providing for the protection of absent defendants.

5. The 5th section of the act implies, that an attachment may be levied on the goods of a resident. (Printed out of place, 1 D. L. M. 763.)

6. The oldest forms of attachment, by way of executions, apply to residents. 2 Harris's Entries, 611; 2 Evans's Harris, 377.

7. The defendant must have been in the State before judgment could have been recovered; yet 2d section prescribes no way to show the removal.

8. The law of 1831, ch. 321, is declaratory, and not binding; the United States courts ought not to be allowed to raise an implication, so as to do by construction what it could not do by enactment.

9. It contravenes the whole purpose and policy of the attachment, by way of execution.

f. If, therefore, the court think the assignment of 1825, or any assignment before October, 1826, covered the commissions on the Mervin claim, they are covered by the above reasoning.

But if not, yet Oliver, holding possession of the evidences, the right to receive the proceeds, and being the party directed to pay Goodwin, he held Goodwin's claim to the commissions as agent, sufficiently to make him a fit garnishee, as having that credit in his hands.

Though the court doubt as to the commissions and Mervin debt, that will not affect the mortgage of the share in the company.

This fund could have been reached by bill in equity.

(*a.*) A bill in equity is competent to compel the application of the equitable property, the choses in action and equities of redemption of a judgment debtor which cannot be reached by *fi. fa.* to the satisfaction of the judgment. Scott *v.* Scholly, 8 East, 467, 508, 509; Clayton *v.* Anthony, 6 Rand. 285; Dold *v.* Geiger, 2 Grat. 112; Halley *v.* Williams, 1 Leigh, 140; Hadden *v.* Spader, 20 Johns. Rep. 554, 563, 564, 568; 2 Johns. C. C.; McDermott *v.* Strong, 4 Johns. C. R. 687, 690, 692; Bayard *v.* Hoffman, 4 Johns. C. R. 450; Spader *v.* Davis, 5 Johns. C. R. 280; Hallett *v.* Thompson, 5 Page, 583; Griffith *v.* Fred. County Bank, 6 Gill & Johns. 424; Harris & Chauncey *v.* Alcock, 10 Gill & Johns. 251, 252; McDonald *v.* Bank U. S. 2 Pet. 107.

(*b.*) An execution is usually required as precedent to suit in equity.

The attachment was such an execution. Even if no condemnation could have been had under it; yet neither can an equitable interest in chattels or land be sold under a *fi. fa.* at common law. But the *fi. fa.* is held to bind them, and a bill lies in equity to sell them.

So here, the attachment was the most appropriate form of execution to bind an interest, in the nature of a credit or chose in action, as preliminary to a bill in equity, to have it applied to the satisfaction of the judgment.

(*c.*) To this preceeding the facts of the assignment, by way of mortgage to, and the possession of the evidences by Oliver, were as essential as to the sustaining of the attachment.

The untrue denials in the answers of Oliver equally misled the plaintiff to the abandonment of his remedy.

The fraud gives the plaintiff an equal equity now to call on the court to do him justice by subjecting the fund to his judgment, after paying Oliver his debt and expenses.

The points raised by the counsel for the appellees were as follows:

The theory of the bill is, that the appellant had, by the attachment on the judgment of himself and co-plaintiffs, entitled himself to condemnation of Goodwin's funds, alleged to be in

Deacon v. Oliver et al.

Oliver's hands as garnishee, and that Oliver, by his false and fraudulent answers, having deprived him of his legal right to such condemnation, equity will compel Oliver's estate to pay the money which, but for his unconscientious conduct, would have been recovered at law.

A right to condemnation, then, as against Oliver, and the loss of that right through his fraud and falsehood, are essential, on the appellant's own showing, to his success.

Neither of these elements are found in the case, as it appears on pleadings or proofs.

1st. The attachment was issued against law, and would, at the trial, (which never came on, because the plaintiffs in the attachment discontinued it,) have been quashed, and is therefore to be regarded as void. Act of Maryland, 1715, chap. 40, § 6; Waters & Caton, 1 Harris & McHenry, 407; Harden & Moores, 7 Harris & Johnson, 4.

2d. The attachment was irregular and void for another reason; that the act of 1715, (above referred to,) and adopted by the 100th rule of the Circuit Court of Maryland, authorized no such writ in the case of a resident defendant. Act of 1831, chap. 321.

3d. But conceding the attachment to have been regular, it could only take the "lands, tenements, goods, chattels, or credits," of Goodwin, in Oliver's hands, (see Writ, 19, 20,) and there being none of these things in his hands, there was nothing to attach, and of course nothing to condemn. Houston & Nowland, 7 Gill & Johnson, 480; Meeker and Wilson, 1 Gallison, 419; Act of Maryland, 1810, chap. 160; Ford & Philpot, 5 Harris & Johnson, 312; Campbell & Morris, 3 Harris & McHenry, 535; 9 Cranch, 477.

4th. If there was any thing in Oliver's hand at the time of the attachment, it was only Goodwin's claim on the government of Mexico, for assistance rendered to Mina, in his attempt to revolutionize Mexico when a province of Spain, in violation of our neutrality acts; and such a claim has been decided by the Maryland courts, in the case of Goodwin's trustee against these appellees, to be of such a character that the law of Maryland will not recognize its existence, and of course no condemnation could be had of it.

5th. The discontinuance of the attachment was the voluntary act of the appellant; and as he was not bound by Oliver's answers to the interrogatories in attachment, but might have tested their truth by bringing the attachment to trial, his failure to proceed at law gives him no right to come into equity.

6th. Oliver's answers were true. Goodwin's share in the Mexican Company was assigned to Oliver absolutely in 1825, and no interest therein remained in Goodwin at the time of the attachment. Goodwin's interest in his commissions and his claim on Mervin were not assigned to Oliver till May, 1829, nearly two years after the answers, and at the time of the attachment Oliver had no interest whatever in either of these claims.

Mr. Justice GRIER delivered the opinion of the court.

Without attempting to give a history of the facts of this case, as exhibited in the pleadings and proofs, or noticing all the objections of the equity of the bill, we think there are two of its charges or allegations, on which its whole equity rests, and which the complainant has failed to substantiate.

1. That there were in the hands of Robert Oliver at the time the attachment was laid, any chattels, rights, or credits of Lyde Goodwin, "which were bound by said attachment."

2. That Robert Oliver was guilty of falsehood or fraudulent concealment of facts, in his answers to the interrogatories proposed to him as garnishee in the attachment.

In 1816, and previous to his insolvency, Lyde Goodwin had become a shareholder in the Baltimore Mexican Company, to the extent of one ninth part. This company had furnished means to General Mina to fit out a warlike expedition against Mexico, then a dependency of Spain. The expedition of Mina had failed, and he had perished with it. This transaction of the company was illegal, and punishable as a misdemeanor, with fine and imprisonment. The contract was therefore void in law, and could not be the foundation of any debt, nor could the stock thus created be treated in law as a thing of value; and from the uncertainty of its future prospects, its value in the market was little better. It was merely possible that Mexico, if successful in her struggle for independence, might, at some future day, assume the payment of the debts contracted by Mina, and if, as it was possible, or perhaps probable, that at some day still further in the future the payment may be obtained. Goodwin's title in this possibility or expectancy, or whatever it might be called, was supposed to have passed to Brown, his assignee, under the insolvent act. Afterwards, in 1824, Mexico having achieved her independence, passed a decree promising to acknowledge "the debts that may be proven to have been contracted for the service of the nation by the Generals declared *bene meritos de la patria*," of whom Mina was one. This renewed the hopes of the company, that possibly something might be recovered hereafter on this pledge of the Mexican government; and Robert Oliver was appointed the attorney on the part of the company to prosecute their claim. Lyde Goodwin being in actual want of the means of subsistence, persuaded Robert Oliver to advance him the sum of two thousand dollars, and take a transfer from Brown, his insolvent trustee of this claim, as security.

In this situation of affairs, the attachment of Baring, Brothers & Co. was served on Robert Oliver, as garnishee of Lyde Goodwin, in 1827. Now it is admitted that Oliver was a creditor of Lyde Goodwin, and not a debtor. His power of attorney put him in possession of nothing which could be attached as the property of Goodwin. The insolvent assignment was supposed to have vested Goodwin's interest in this expectancy, in Brown. If it did not do so, as has since been decided, Oliver had no title to Goodwin's claim. And if it did, and if Oliver held it merely as a security for the sum advanced by him, the equitable assignment taken as such security, was his own ; it was but an instrument to obtain satisfaction for his debt; it conferred nothing but a right in equity. Whether it was valid or invalid, absolute or defeasible, it did not constitute him a debtor of Lyde Goodwin, or put him in possession of any of his credits or effects, so as to subject him to an attachment as Goodwin's garnishee. It was not till after the death of Robert Oliver, and more than ten years after the attachment of complainant was discontinued, that the United States made the Convention of April, 1839, with Mexico, under which Commissioners were appointed, before whom this claim of the Baltimore Company was proved, and acknowledged by Mexico as a just debt. Then for the first time, this uncertain claim or equity, assumed the form of a credit, and an existence as a legal chose in action. But in that character it never existed in the hands of Robert Oliver. If, at the time the attachment was served on him, the claim of Lyde Goodwin had existed as a debt due him by a citizen of Maryland, and Oliver held an equitable transfer either absolute or defeasible, it is abundantly evident that the proper person to be made garnishee in an attachment, would have been the debtor, not the equitable claimant of the debt. He has but an equity or a bare right, but whatever it is, it is his own, and his claim is in hostility both to the plaintiff and defendant in the attachment.

The whole foundation of the complainant's equity in this bill rests on the averment, that the interest of Lyde Goodwin, whatever it was, in this Mexican claim, " was bound by the attachment laid in the hands of Robert Oliver, as garnishee." The Merwin claim not having been assigned till after the attachment was withdrawn, need not be noticed. The decision of this point against the averment of the bill, would dispose of the case.

But as we think the charges made in the bill against Robert

Oliver, of false and fraudulent concealment, have not been sustained, it is due to the memory of one who always sustained a high reputation as a merchant and man of honor, to notice this point.

It must be remembered that the purpose of the interrogatories was to ascertain whether Oliver had in his hands any credits or effects of Lyde Goodwin, subject to attachment; and also that Brown, the insolvent assignee of Goodwin, was supposed to have had the title to Goodwin's interest vested in him. The legitimate inquiry was, therefore, not whether Brown had abused his trust, by selling or mortgaging the trust property for the benefit of Goodwin; or whether Oliver's claim under the assignee was valid or not. This inquiry was wholly irrelevant in the investigation, under the attachment proceeding. Nor was Oliver bound, in that investigation, to make any disclosure of the strength or weakness of his own title, which was hostile to that of the plaintiff. The discovery sought, was not of Oliver's equities, but of Goodwin's assets. Oliver's answers to the interrogatories were drawn, no doubt, by learned counsel, fully aware of the nature of the proceedings, and the rights of the parties under them. The answers were strictly true to the letter. The garnishee had not in his hands, "any funds, evidences of debt, stocks, certificates of stock, belonging to Lyde Goodwin, nor any acknowledgment by the Mexican government to said Lyde Goodwin," on which the attachment could be laid. What claims or securities he himself had as a creditor of Goodwin, the plaintiff in that proceeding had no right to inquire, nor was Oliver bound to answer. If he had nothing which the plaintiff could attach, it was no fraud on plaintiff to keep his own counsel, and make no disclosure as to the nature of his own securities.

The decree of the Circuit Court is therefore affirmed.

Order.

This cause came on to be heard on the transcript of the record from the Circuit Court of the United States for the District of Maryland, and was argued by counsel. On consideration whereof, it is now here ordered, adjudged, and decreed, by this court, that the decree of the said Circuit Court in this cause be, and the same is hereby, affirmed, with costs.

INDEX.

PRINCIPAL MATTERS.

CHANCERY (*Continued*).

condition to levy an execution, if the fraudulent obstacle should be removed. *Ibid.*

10. It is proper to make a prior encumbrancer, who holds the legal title, a party to the bill, in order that the whole title may be sold under the decree; for the purpose of such a decree, the prior encumbrancer is a necessary party; but the court may order a sale subject to the encumbrance, without having the prior encumbrancer before it, and in fit cases it will do so. *Ibid.*

11. If the prior encumbrancer is out of the jurisdiction, or cannot be joined without defeating it, it is a fit cause to dispense with his presence, and order a sale subject to his encumbrance, which will not be affected by the decree. *Ibid.*

12. Where real estate is in the custody of a receiver, appointed by a court of chancery, a sale of the property under an execution issued by virtue of a judgment at law, is illegal and void. *Wiswall v. Sampson,* 52.

13. The proper modes of proceeding pointed out, to be pursued by any person who claims title to the property, either by mortgage, or judgment, or otherwise. *Ibid.*

14. Where there was a judgment at law against a defendant in Mississippi, and he sought relief in equity, upon the ground that the consideration of the contract was the introduction of slaves into the State, and consequently illegal; a court of equity will not grant relief, because the complainant was *in pari delicto* with the other party. *Sample v. Barnes,* 70.

15. Moreover, such a defence would have been good at law, and the averments, that deception was practised to prevent the complainant from making the defence, are not sustained by the evidence in the case. And, further, after the judgment, the complainant gave a forthcoming bond, thus recognizing the validity of the judgment. *Ibid.*

16. Where an antenuptial contract was alleged to have been made, and the affidavits of the parties claiming under it alleged that they never possessed or saw it; that they had made diligent inquiry for it, but were unable to learn its present existence or place of existence; that inquiry had been made of the guardian of one of the children, who said that he had never been in possession of it, and did not know where it was; that inquiry had been made at the recording offices in vain, and that the affiants believed it to be lost; secondary proof of its contents ought to have been admitted. *De Lane v. Moore,* 253.

17. Whether recorded or not, it was binding upon the parties. If recorded within the time prescribed by statute, or if reacknowledged and recorded afterwards, notice would thereby have been given to all persons of its effect. *Ibid.*

18. If it was regularly recorded in one State, and the property upon which it acted was removed to another State, the protection of the contract would follow the property into the State into which it was removed. *Ibid.*

19. But where no suit was brought until eight or nine years after the death of the husband, and then the one which was brought was dismissed for want of prosecution; another suit against the executors who had divided the property, comes too late. *Ibid.*

20. A cour. has a right to set aside its own judgment or decree, dismissing a bill in chancery, at the same term in which the judgment or decree was rendered, on discovering its own error in the la r, or that the consent of the complainants to such dismissal was obtained by fraud. *Doss v. Tyack,* 298.

21. A verdict on an issue to try whether a sale was fraudulent, finding the same to be fraudulent, will not be set aside on a certificate or affidavit of some of the jurors, afterwards made, as to what they meant. *Ibid.*

22. A Chancellor does not need a verdict to inform his conscience, when the answer denies fraud in the abstract, whilst it admits all the facts and circumstances necessary to constitute it, in the concrete. *Ibid.*

23. Releases given by the complainants, in the present case, decided to cover the matters in controversy, and, therefore, to put an end to all claim by them; inasmuch as there is no proof that they were obtained by fraud or circumvention. *Perkins v. Fourniquet,* 313.

24. Where a title to land in the State of Coahuila and Texas was obtained in 1833, by a mother for, and in the name of her daughter, and, in 1836, the father of the daughter conveyed it away by a deed executed in Louisiana, this deed was properly set aside by the District Court of Texas. *Hoyt v. Hammekin,* 346.

25. It was not executed either according to the laws of Louisiana, or those of Coahuila and Texas. *Ibid.*

CHANCERY (*Continued.*)

26. Two statutes of Mississippi, one passed in 1843, and the other in 1846, provide that where the charter of a bank shall be declared forfeited, a trustee shall be appointed to take possession of its effects, and commissioners appointed to audit accounts against it. *Peale* v. *Phipps*, 368.

27. Where these steps had been taken, and the commissioners had refused to allow a certain account, the Circuit Court of the United States had no right to entertain a bill filed by the creditors to compel the trustee to pay the rejected account. There was a want of jurisdiction. *Ibid.*

28. The cases upon this point, examined. *Ibid.*

29. A claim by the trustee, in re-convention, was not a waiver of the exception to the jurisdiction. *Ibid.*

30. A will, executed in 1777, which devised certain lands in Maine, to trustees and their heirs to the use of Richard (the son of the testator) for life, remainder, for his life in case of forfeiture, to the trustees to preserve contingent remainders; remainder to the sons of Richard, if any, as tenants in common in tail, with cross remainders; remainder to Richard's daughter Elizabeth, for life; remainder to trustees to preserve contingent remainders during her life; remainder to the sons of Elizabeth in tail, — did not vest the legal estate in fee simple in the trustees. The life estate of Richard, and the contingent remainders limited thereon, were legal estates. *Webster* v. *Cooper*, 489.

31. No duties were imposed on the trustees which could prevent the legal estate in these lands from vesting in the *cestuis que use;* and although such duties might have been required of them relating to other lands in the devise, yet this circumstance would not control the construction of the devise as to those lands. *Ibid.*

32. The devise to Elizabeth for life, remainder to her sons as tenants in common, share and share alike, and to the heirs of their bodies, did not give an estate tail to Elizabeth, under the rule in Shelly's case. But upon her death, her son (the party to the suit) took as a purchaser, an estate tail in one moiety of the land, as a tenant in common with his brother. *Ibid.*

33. One of the conditions of the devise was, that this party, as soon as he should come into possession of the lands, should take the name of the testator. But as he had not yet come into possession, and it was a condition subsequent, of which only the person to whom the lands were devised over, could take advantage, a non-compliance with it was no defence, in an action brought to recover possession of the land. *Ibid.*

34. The son, taking an estate tail at the death of Elizabeth, in 1845, could maintain a writ of entry, and until that time had no right of possession. Consequently, the adverse possession of the occupant only began then. *Ibid.*

35. A bill in chancery will not lie for the purpose of perpetually enjoining a judgment, upon the ground that there was a false return in serving process upon one of the defendants. Redress must be sought in the court which gave the judgment, or in an action against the marshal. *Walker* v. *Robbins*, 584.

36. Moreover, the defendant in this case, by his actions, waived all benefit which he might have derived from the false return; and no defence was made on the trial at law, impeaching the correctness of the cause of action sued on, and in such a case, resort cannot be had to equity to supply the omission. *Ibid.*

37. A society called Separatists, emigrated from Germany to the United States. They were very poor, and one of them, in 1817, purchased land in Ohio, for which he gave his bond, and took the title to himself. Afterwards, they adopted two constitutions, one in 1819, and one in 1824, which they signed, and in 1832 obtained an act of incorporation. The articles of association, or constitutions of 1819 and 1824, contained a renunciation of individual property. *Goesele* v. *Bimeler*, 590.

38. The heirs of one of the members who signed these conditions, and died in 1827, cannot maintain a bill of partition. *Ibid.*

39. From 1817 to 1819, the contract between the members and the person who purchased the property, vested in parol, and was destitute of a consideration. No legal rights were vested in the members. *Ibid.*

40. The ancestor of these heirs renounced all right of individual property, when he signed the articles, and did so upon the consideration that the society would support him in sickness and in health; and this was deemed by him an adequate compensation for his labor and property, contributed to the common stock. *Ibid.*

CHANCERY (*Continued.*)

41. The principles of the association were, that land and other property were to be acquired by the members, but they were not to be vested with the fee of the land. Hence, at the death of one of them, no right of property descended to his heirs. *Ibid.*

42. There is no legal objection to such a partnership; nor can it be considered a forfeiture of individual rights for the community to succeed to his share, because it was a matter of voluntary contract. *Ibid.*

43. Nor do the articles of association constitute a perpetuity. The society exists at the will of its members, a majority of whom may at any time order a sale of the property, and break up the association. *Ibid.*

44. The evidence shows that they are a moral, religious, and industrious people. *Ibid.*

45. Under the attachment laws of Maryland, a share in the Baltimore Mexican Company, which had fitted out an expedition under General Mina, was not, in 1827, the subject of an attachment under a judgment, whether such share was held by the garnishee under a power of attorney to collect the proceeds, or under an equitable assignment to secure a debt. *Deacon v. Oliver*, 610.

46. The answers of the garnishee to interrogatories filed, were literally correct. He had not in his hands any "funds, evidences of debt, stocks, certificates of stock," belonging to the debtor, nor "any acknowledgment by the Mexican government," on which an attachment could be laid. *Ibid.*

COLLISION BY LAND AND WATER.

1. Where a suit was brought against a railroad company, by a person who was injured by a collision, it was correct in the court to instruct the jury, that if the plaintiff was lawfully on the road, at the time of the collision. and the collision and consequent injury to him were caused by the gross negligence of one of the servants of the defendants, then and there employed on th. road, he was entitled to recover, notwithstanding the circumstances, that the plaintiff was a stockholder in the company, riding by invitation of the President, paying no fare, and not in the usual passenger cars. *P. & R. R. R. Co. v. Derby*, 468.

2. And also, that the fact that the engineer having the control of the colliding locomotive, was forbidden to run on that track at the time, and had acted in disobedience of such orders, was no defence to the action. *Ibid.*

3. Where a collision takes place between two vessels at sea, which is the result of inevitable accident, without the negligence or fault of either party, each vessel must bear its own loss. *Steinback v. Rae*, 532.

COMMERCIAL LAW.

1. Under a policy insuring against the usual perils of the sea, including barratry, the underwriters are not liable to repay to the insured, damages paid by him to the owners of another vessel and cargo, suffered in a collision occasioned by the negligence of the master or mariners of the vessel insured. *Gen. M. Ins. v. Sherwood*, 352.

2. A policy cannot be so construed as to insure against all losses directly referable to the negligence of the master and mariners. But if the loss is caused by a peril of the sea, the underwriter is responsible, although the master did not use due care to avoid the peril. *Ibid.*

3. It is of no consequence whether the date of a promissory note be at the beginning or end of it. *Sheppard v. Graves*, 505.

4. Where a warehouseman gave a receipt for wheat which he did not receive, and afterwards the quantity which he actually had was divided amongst the respective depositors. an action of replevin, brought by the assignee of the fictitious receipt, could not be maintained when, under it, one of these portions was seized. *Jackson v. Hale*, 525.

5. Evidence offered to show that the wheat in question was assigned to the defendant, was objected to by the plaintiff in the replevin; but such objection was properly overruled. The plaintiff had shown no title in himself. *Ibid.*

6. So, also, evidence was admissible to show that the receiver of the fictitious certificate had never deposited any wheat in the warehouse. *Ibid.*

7. The defendants in this case were the assignees of the original warehouseman, and were not responsible, unless it could be shown that wheat was deposited, which had come into their possession. *Ibid.*

CONSTITUTIONAL LAW.

1. A State, under its general and admitted power to define and punish offences against its own peace and policy, may repel from its borders an unacceptable population, whether paupers, criminals, fugitives, or liberated slaves; and, consequently, may punish her citizens and others who thwart this policy, by harboring, secreting, or in any way assisting such fugitives. *Moore v. People of Illinois*, 13.

2. It is no objection to such legislation, that the offender may be liable to, punishment under the act of Congress for the same acts, when injurious to the owner of the fugitive slave. *Ibid.*

3. The case of Prigg *v.* The Commonwealth of Pennsylvania, (16 Peters, 539,) presented the following questions, which were decided by the court:
   1. That, under and by virtue of the Constitution of the United States, the owner of a slave is clothed with entire authority in every State in the Union, to seize and recapture his slave, wherever he can do it without illegal violence or a breach of the peace.
   2. That the government of the United States is clothed with appropriate authority and functions to enforce the delivery, on claim of the owner, and has properly exercised it in the act of Congress of 12th February, 1793.
   3. That any State law or regulation, which interrupts, impedes, limits, embarrasses, delays, or postpones, the right of the owner to the immediate possession of the slave, and the immediate command of his service, is void. *Ibid.*

4. This court has not decided that State legislation. in aid of the claimant, and which does not directly or indirectly delay, impede, or frustrate the master in the exercise of his right under the Constitution, or in pursuit of his remedy given by the act of Congress, is void. *Ibid.*

5. It belongs exclusively to the political department of the government to recognize or to refuse to recognize a new government in a foreign country, claiming to have displaced the old and established a new one. *Kennett v. Chambers*, 38.

6. Until the political department of the government acknowledged the independence of Texas, the Judiciary were bound to consider the old order of things as having continued. *Ibid.*

7. While the government of the United States acknowledged its treaty of limits and of amity and friendship with Mexico as still subsisting and obligatory, no citizen of the United States could lawfully furnish supplies to Texas to enable it to carry on a war with Mexico. *Ibid.*

8. A contract made in Cincinnati, after Texas declared itself independent, but before its independence was acknowledged by the United States, whereby the complainants agreed to furnish, and did furnish money to a General in the Texan army, to enable him to raise and equip troops to be employed against Mexico, was illegal and void, and cannot be enforced in a court of the United States. *Ibid.*

9. The circumstance, that the Texan officer agreed, in consideration of these advances of money, to convey to them certain lands in Texas, of which he covenanted that he was then the owner, will not make the contract valid, when it appears upon the face of it, and by the averments in the bill, that the object and intention of the complainants, in advancing the money, was to assist Texas in its military operations. *Ibid.*

10. A contract made in the United States, at that time, for the purchase of land in Texas, would have been valid even if the money was afterwards used to support hostilities with Mexico. But in this case it was not an ordinary purchase; but the object of the complainants, as avowed in the contract and the bill, was to aid Texas in its war with Mexico. *Ibid.*

11. The contract being absolutely void by the laws of the United States at the time it was made, the circumstance that it was valid in Texas, and that Texas has since become a member of the Union, does not entitle the. complainants to enforce it in the courts of the United States. *Ibid.*

12. No contract can be enforced in the courts of the United States, no matter where made or where to be executed, if it is in violation of the laws of the United States, or is in contravention of the public policy of the government, or in conflict with subsisting treaties. *Ibid.*

13. By the law of Pennsylvania, the River Delaware is a public navigable river, held

53 *

CONSTITUTIONAL LAW (*Continued.*)

by its joint sovereigns in trust for the public. *Rundle* v. *Delaware & Raritan Canal Co.* 80.

14. Riparian owners, in that State, have no title to the river, or any right to divert its waters, unless by license from the States. *Ibid.*

15. Such license is revocable, and in subjection to the superior right of the State, to divert the water for public improvements, either by the State directly, or by a corporation created for that purpose. *Ibid.*

16. The proviso to the provincial acts of Pennsylvania and New Jersey, of 1771, does not operate as a grant of the usufruct of the waters of the river to Adam Hoops and his assigns, but only as a license, or toleration of his dam. *Ibid.*

17. As, by the laws of his own State, the plaintiff could have no remedy against a corporation authorized to take the whole waters of the river for the purpose of canals, or improving the navigation, so, neither can he sustain a suit against a corporation created by New Jersey for the same purpose, who have taken part of the waters. *Ibid.*

18. The plaintiffs, being but tenants at sufferance in the usufruct of the water to the two States who own the river as tenants in common, are not in a condition to question the relative rights of either to use its waters without the consent of the other. *Ibid.*

19. This case is not intended to decide whether a first license, for private emolument, can support an action against a later licensee of either sovereign or both, who, for private purposes, diverts the water to the injury of the first. *Ibid.*

20. The case of League *v.* De Young & Brown, (11 How. 185,) considered and again established, 79.

21. Under the tenth article of the treaty of 1842, between the United States and Great Britain, a warrant was issued by a commissioner, at the instance of the British Consul, for the apprehension of a person who, it was alleged, had committed an assault, with intent to murder, in Ireland. *In re Kaine*, 103.

22. The person being arrested, the Commissioner ordered him to be commited, for the purpose of abiding the order of the President of the United States. *Ibid.*

23. A *habeas corpus* was then issued by the Circuit Court of the United States, the District Judge presiding, when, after a hearing, the writ was dismissed, and the prisoner remanded to custody. *Ibid.*

24. A petition was then presented to the Circuit Judge, at his chambers, addressed to the Justices of the Supreme Court, and praying for a writ of *habeas corpus*, which was referred by the Circuit Judge, after a hearing, to the Justices of the Supreme Court, in bank, at the commencement of the next term thereof. *Ibid.*

25. At the meeting of the court, a motion was made, with the papers and proceedings presented to the Circuit Judge annexed to the petition, for writs of *habeas corpus* and *certiorari* to bring up the defendant and the record from the Circuit Court, for the purpose of having the decision of that court examined. *Ibid.*

26. The motion was refused; the writs prayed for denied, and the petition dismissed. *Ibid.*

27. Where the Supreme Court of a State certified that there was "drawn in question the validity of statutes of the State of Ohio," &c., without naming the statutes, this was not enough to give jurisdiction to this court, under the 25th section of the Judiciary Act. *Lamb* v. *Walker*, 149.

28. Nor, in this case, would the court have had jurisdiction if the statutes had been named, because, —

29. In 1816, the Legislature of Ohio passed an "act to prohibit the issuing and circulation of unauthorized bank paper," and, in 1839, an act amendatory thereof; and the question was, whether or not a canal company, incorporated in 1837, was subject to these acts. In deciding that it was, the Supreme Court of Ohio only gave a construction to an act of Ohio, which neither of itself, nor by its application, involved in any way a repugnancy to the Constitution of the United States, by impairing the obligation of a contract. *Ibid.*

30. The case of the Commercial Bank of Cincinnati *v.* Buckingham's Executors, (5 How. 317,) examined and sustained. *Ibid.*

31. The State of Texas was admitted into the Union on the 29th of December, 1845, and from that day the laws of the United States were extended over it. *Calkin* v. *Cocke*, 227.

CONTRACTS (*Continued.*)

5. The circumstance that the Texan officer agreed, in consideration of these advances of money, to convey to them certain lands in Texas, of which he covenanted that he was then the owner, will not make the contract valid when it appears upon the face of it, and by the averments in the bill, that the object and intention of the complainants in advancing the money was to assist Texas in its military operations. *Ibid.*

6. A contract made in the United States at that time for the purchase of land in Texas, would have been valid even if the money was afterwards used to support hostilities with Mexico. But in this case it was not an ordinary purchase; but the object of the complainants, as avowed in the contract and the bill, was to aid Texas in its war with Mexico. *Ibid.*

7: The contract being absolutely void by the laws of the United States at the time it was made, the circumstance that it was valid in Texas, and that Texas has since become a member of the Union, does not entitle the complainants to enforce it in the courts of the United States. *Ibid.*

8. No contract can be enforced in the courts of the United States, no matter where made or where to be executed; if it is in violation of the laws of the United States, or is in contravention of the public policy of the government or in conflict with subsisting treaties. *Ibid.*

9. Where there was a judgment at law against a defendant in Mississippi, and he sought relief in equity. upon the ground that the consideration of the contract was the introduction of slaves into the State, and consequently illegal; a court of equity will not grant relief, because the complainant was *in pari delicto* with the other party. *Sample* v. *Barnes*, 70.

10. Moreover, such a defence would have been good at law, and the averments, that deception was practised to prevent the complainant from making the defence, are not sustained by the evidence in the case. And, further, after the judgment, the complainant gave a forthcoming bond, thus recognizing the validity of the judgment. *Ibid.*

11. In 1834, Burden obtained a patent for a new and useful improvement in the machinery for manufacturing wrought nails and spikes, which he assigned to the Troy Iron and Nail Factory, and also covenanted that he would convey to that company any improvement which he might thereafter make. *Troy Iron and Nail Factory* v. *Corning*, 193.

12 In 1840, he made such an improvement, for making hook and brad-headed spikes, with a bending lever, which he assigned to the Troy Iron and Nail Factory, in 1848. *Ibid.*

13. Before this last assignment, however, viz., in 1845, Burden made an agreement with Corning, Horner, and Winslow, in which, among other things, it was agreed, that both parties might thereafter manufacture and vend spikes of such kind and character as they saw fit, notwithstanding their conflicting claims. *Ibid.*

14. Owing to the peculiar attitude of the parties to each other at the time of making this agreement, and the language used in it, it cannot be construed into permission to Corning, Horner, and Winslow, to use the improved machinery patented by Burden in 1840; and the right to use it, having passed to the Troy Iron and Nail Factory, a perpetual injunction upon Corning, Horner, and Winslow will be decreed. *Ibid.*

15. Where the marshal of the District of Columbia engaged the services of a clerk for a stipulated sum per annum, and the service continued without any new agreement, and the jury were instructed that they might imply a new agreement to pay the clerk at a different rate, this instruction was erroneous. There was nothing in the evidence from which the jury could imply such new agreement. *Nutt* v. *Minor*, 464.

COPY-RIGHT.

1. Where the copy-right of a map was taken out under the act of Congress, and the copperplate engraving seized and sold under an execution, the purchaser did not acquire the right to strike off and sell copies of the map. *Stephens* v. *Cady*, 528.

2. The court below decided that an injunction to prevent such striking off and selling, could not issue, without a return of the purchase-money. This decision was erroneous. *Ibid.*

3. A copy-right is a " property in notion, and has no corporeal tangible substance,"

COPY-RIGHT (*Continued*).

and is not the subject of seizure and sale by execution. It can be reached by a creditor's bill in chancery, but in such case, the court would probably have to decree a transfer in the mode pointed out in the act of Congress. *Ibid.*

DEED.

In the State of Ohio, it is not a sufficient description of taxable lands to say, "Cooper, James, 5 acres, section 24, T. 4, F. R. 1." A deed made in consequence of a sale for taxes under such a description, is void. The courts of Ohio have so decided, and this court adopts their decision. *Raymond* v. *Longworth*, 76.

DELAWARE RIVER.

See PENNSYLVANIA.

DEVISES.

See WILLS.

DISTRICT OF COLUMBIA.

1. For some of the principles which govern sureties in bonds before the Orphans' Court, see *Ennis* v. *Smith.*
2. A master builder, undertaker, or contractor, who undertakes by contract with the owner to erect a building, or some part or portion thereof, on certain terms, does not come within the letter or spirit of the act of Congress passed March 2, 1833, (4 Stat. at Large, 659,) entitled an act to secure to mechanics and others, payment for labor done and materials furnished in the erection of buildings in the District of Columbia. *Winder* v. *Caldwell*, 434.

DOMICIL.

1. General Kosciusko was sojourning in Switzerland when he died, but was domiciled in France, and had been for fifteen years. *Ennis* v. *Smith*, 401.
2. His declarations are to be received as proof that his domicil was in France. Such declarations have always been received, in questions of domicil, in the courts of France, in those of England, and in the courts of the United States. *Ibid.*
3. The presumption of law is, that the domicil of origin is retained, until residence elsewhere has been shown by him who alleges a change of it. But residence elsewhere repels the presumption, and casts upon him who denies it to be a domicil of choice, the burden of disproving it. The place of residence must be taken to be a domicil of choice, unless it is proved that it was not meant to be a principal and permanent residence. Contingent events, political or otherwise, are not admissible proofs to show, where one removes from his domicil of origin for a residence elsewhere, that the latter was not meant to be a principal and permanent residence. But if one is exiled by authority from his domicil of origin, it is never presumed that he has abandoned all hope of returning back. The abandonment, however, may be shown by proof. General Kosciusko was not exiled by authority. He left Poland voluntarily, to obtain a civil status in France, which he conscientiously thought he could not enjoy in Poland, whilst it continued under a foreign dominion. *Ibid.*

DUTIES — CUSTOM-HOUSE.

1. The State of Texas was admitted into the Union on the 29th of December, 1845, (9 Stat. at Large, 108,) and from that day the laws of the United States were extended over it. *Calkin & Co.* v. *Cocke*, 227.
2. Consequently, on the 30th of January, 1846, the revenue laws of Texas were not in force there, and goods seized for a non-compliance with those laws, were illegally seized. *Ibid.*

EJECTMENT.

1. In the State of Ohio, it is not a sufficient description of taxable lands to say, "Cooper, James, 5 acres, section 24, T. 4, F. R. 1." A deed made in consequence of a sale for taxes under such a description is void. The courts of Ohio have so decided, and this court adopts their decision. *Raymond* v. *Longworth*, 76.
2. This court decided, in 8 Howard, 223, that the recitals in a patent for land, referring to titles of anterior date, were not of themselves sufficient to establish the titles thus recited. *Ibid.*
3. The titles themselves being now produced, it is decided, that a permit given by the Lieutenant-Governor of Upper Louisiana, in 1799, to a person to form an

EVIDENCE (*Continued.*)

according to the law of the domicil of the intestate. This rule may be said to be a part of the *jus gentium. Ennis* v. *Smith*, 401.

13. What that law is when a foreign law applies, must be shown by proof of it, and in the case of written law, it will be sufficient to offer, as evidence, the official publication of the law, certified satisfactorily to be such. Unwritten foreign laws must be proved by experts. There is no general rule for authenticating foreign laws in the courts of other countries, except this, that no proof shall be received, " which presupposes better testimony behind, and attainable by the party." They may be verified by an oath, or by an exemplification of a copy under the great seal of the State or nation whose law it may be, or by a copy, proved to be a true copy by a witness who has examined and compared it with the original, or by the certificate of an officer authorized to give the law, which certificate must be duly proved. Such modes of proof are not exclusive of others, especially of codes and accepted histories of the law of a country. See also the cases of Church *v.* Hubbart, in 2 Cranch, 181, and Talbot *v.* Seeman, in 1 Cranch, 7. In this case, the Code Civil of France, with this indorsement, "Les Garde des Sceaux de France a la Cour Supreme des Etats Unis," was offered as evidence to prove that the law of France was for the distribution of the funds in controversy. This court ruled that such indorsement was a sufficient authentication to make the code evidence in this case, and in any other case in which it may be offered. By that code, the complainants named in this suit as the collateral relations of General Kosciusko, are entitled to receive the funds in controversy, in such proportions as are stated in the mandate of this court to the court below. *Ibid.*

14. The documentary proofs in this cause, from the Orphans' Court, of the genealogy of the Kosciusko family, and of the collateral relationship of the persons entitled to a decree, and also of the wills of Kosciusko, are properly in evidence in this suit. *Ibid.*

15. The record from Grodno is judicial; not a judgment *inter partes,* but a foreign judgment *in rem,* which is evidence of the facts adjudicated against all the world. *Ibid.*

16. Where the contract between the owner and the builder, (who was also the carpenter,) stipulated for a forfeiture per diem in case the carpenter should delay the work, the court below ought to have allowed evidence of such delay to be given to the jury by the defendant, under a notice of set-off, and also evidence that the work and materials found and provided upon and for the building, were defective in quality and character, and far inferior in value to what the contract and specification called for. *Winder* v. *Caldwell,* 434.

17. Where the marshal of the District of Columbia engaged the services of a clerk for a stipulated sum per annum, and the service continued without any new agreement, and the jury were instructed that they might imply a new agreement to pay the clerk at a different rate, this instruction was erroneous. There was nothing in the evidence from which the jury could imply such new agreement. *Nutt* v. *Minor,* 464.

18. The statute of frauds in Massachusetts, is substantially the same as that of 29 Car. 2. and declares that no contract for the sale of goods &c., shall be valid, &c., "unless some note or memorandum in writing of the bargain be made, and signed by the party to be charged thereby. or by some person thereu by him lawfully authorized." *Salmon Falls Co.* v. *Goddard,* 447..

19. The following memorandum, viz.: "Sept. 19, W. W. Goddard, 12 mos. 300 bales S. F. drills, 7¼; 190 cases blue do. 8¾. Credit to commence when ship sails; not after December 1st, delivered free of charge for truckage. The blues, if color satisfactory to purchasers. R. M. M. W. W. G."—is sufficient to take the case out of the statute. *Ibid.*

20. If the terms are technical or equivocal on the face of the instrument, or made so by reference to extraneous circumstances, parol evidence of the usage and practice in the trade, is admissible to explain the meaning. *Ibid.*

21. It was competent, also, to refer to the bill of parcels delivered for the purpose of explanation. It was made out and delivered by the seller, in the course of the fulfilment of the contract, acquiesced in by the buyer, and the goods ordered to be delivered after it was received. *Ibid.*

22. Where a warehouseman gave a receipt for wheat which he did not receive, and afterwards the quantity which he actually had was divided amongst the respective depositors, an action of replevin, brought by the assignee of the fictitious

JURISDICTION (*Continued.*)

of *habeas corpus* and *certiorari* to bring up the defendant and the record from the Circuit Court, for the purpose of having the decision of that court examined. *Ibid.*

11. The motion was refused; the writs prayed for denied, and the petition dismissed. *Ibid.*

12. Where the Supreme Court of a State certified that there was "drawn in question the validity of statutes of the State of Ohio," &c., without naming the statutes, this was not enough to give jurisdiction to this court, under the 25th section of the Judiciary Act. *Lawler* v. *Walker*, 149.

13. Nor, in this case, would the court have had jurisdiction if the statutes had been named, because, —

14. In 1816, the Legislature of Ohio passed an "act to prohibit the issuing and circulation of unauthorized bank paper," and, in 1839, an act amendatory thereof; and the question was, whether or not a canal company, incorporated in 1837, was subject to these acts. In deciding that it was, the Supreme Court of Ohio only gave a construction to an act of Ohio, which neither of itself, nor by its application, involved in any way a repugnancy to the Constitution of the United States, by impairing the obligation of a contract. *Ibid.*

15. The case of the Commercial Bank of Cincinnati *v.* Buckingham's Executors, (5 How. 317,) examined and sustained. *Ibid.*

16. Two statutes of Mississippi, one passed in 1843, and the other in 1846, provide that where the charter of a bank shall be declared forfeited, a trustee shall be appointed to take possession of its effects, and commissioners appointed to audit accounts against it. *Peale* v. *Phipps*, 368.

17. Where these steps had been taken, and the commissioners had refused to allow a certain account, the Circuit Court of the United States had no right to entertain a bill filed by the creditors to compel the trustee to pay the rejected account. There was a want of jurisdiction. *Ibid.*

18. The cases upon this point, examined. *Ibid.*

19. A claim by the trustee, in re-convention, was not a waiver of the exception to the jurisdiction. *Ibid.*

20. When a plea is filed to the jurisdiction of the court, upon the ground that the plaintiff is a resident of the same State with the defendant, it is incumbent on the defendant to prove the allegation. *Sheppard* v. *Graves*, 505.

21. Where the marshal of the District of Wisconsin attached property at the suit of creditors in New York, and then gave it up upon the execution of a bond to himself, for the use of those creditors, it was within the jurisdiction of the District Court of the United States for Wisconsin, to entertain a suit by the marshal, suing upon the bond for the New York creditors, against the claimants in Wisconsin, although both parties resided in the same State. *Huff* v. *Hutchinson*, 587.

22. The name of the marshal was merely formal; the real plaintiffs were averred to be citizens of New York. *Ibid.*

23. It was not a good exception upon the ground of variation between the evidence and declaration, that the latter stated the bond to have been given to Hutchinson as marshal of the District of Wisconsin, and the former said the State of Wisconsin. They mean the same thing. *Ibid.*

24. Judgment having been rendered for the plaintiffs in the attachment, by a court having jurisdiction over the subject, it was too late to object to those proceedings in a suit upon the bond, in which they were collaterally introduced. *Ibid.*

25. The bond given to the marshal was in conformity with the statute. *Ibid.*

26. The objections, that the declaration on the bond did not show the jurisdiction of the court in the attachment suit; that the verdict was entered for the amount due instead of the penalty of the bond, and that the recovery was for a sum greater than was claimed by the *ad damnum* in the declaration, were not sufficient for a new trial. *Ibid.*

JURY.

1. Upon a trial in New York, a juror became ill, and was discharged before any evidence was given, and before the plaintiffs' counsel had concluded his opening address. The court ordered another juror to be sworn, and proceeded with the trial. The defendant cannot object to this. It is the practice in New York, and the Circuit Court had a right to follow it. *Silsby* v. *Foote*, 218.

2. One of the specifications of the patent being for a combination of certain parts of mechanism necessary to produce the desired result, it was proper for the

LANDS, PUBLIC (*Continued.*)

13. The titles themselves being now produced, it is decided, that a permit given by the Lieutenant-Governor of Upper Louisiana, in 1799, to a person to form an establishment on the Mississippi, followed by actual possession and improvement, entitled the occupant to 640 acres, including his improvements, although the Indian title was not then extinguished. *Marsh v. Brooks*, 514.

14. It was not the practice of the Spanish government to make treaties with the Indian tribes, defining their boundaries; but to prevent settlements upon their lands without special permits: such permits, however, were usual. *Ibid.*

15. The construction of the treaty between the United States and the Sac and Fox Indians, must be that the latter assented to an occupancy which was as notorious as their own. *Ibid.*

16. The act of Congress, approved April 29, 1816, (3 Stat. at Large, 328,) confirming certain claims to land, confirmed this one, although the Recorder of Land Titles, in his report, made in 1815, had added these words, "if Indian title extinguished." These words were surplusage. *Ibid.*

LIEN.

1. Where a *scire facias* was issued to enforce a lien upon a house under the lien law of the District of Columbia, there was no necessity to file a declaration. *Winder v. Caldwell*, 434.

2. Where the contract between the owner and the builder, (who was also the carpenter,) stipulated for a forfeiture per diem in case the carpenter should delay the work, the court below ought to have allowed evidence of such delay to be given to the jury by the defendant, under a notice of set-off, and also evidence that the work and materials found and provided upon and for the building, were defective in quality and character, and far inferior in value to what the contract and specifications called for. *Ibid.*

3. A master builder, undertaker, or contractor, who undertakes by contract with the owner to erect a building, or some part or portion thereof, on certain terms, does not come within the letter or spirit of the act of Congress passed March 2, 1833, (4 Stat. at Large, 659,) entitled an act to secure to mechanics and others, payment for labor done and materials furnished in the erection of buildings in the District of Columbia. *Ibid.*

MAINE, STATE OF

See CONSTITUTIONAL LAW.

MANDAMUS.

1. A rule will be refused for the judges of the Circuit Court of the District of Columbia, to show cause why a *mandamus* should not issue, unless a case is presented which *primâ facie* requires the interposition of this court. *Ex parte Taylor*, 3.

2. Such a case is not presented where the Circuit Court decided that, under an act of Congress, an affidavit was sufficient to hold a party to special bail. That court had the power, by the act, to exercise its judicial discretion. *Ibid.*

3. This act of Congress regulated the subject, and not the statute of Maryland, passed in 1715. *Ibid.*

4. Where there was a blank in the record of the Circuit Court, in the taxation of the costs recovered by the plaintiff, and the judgment being affirmed by this court, a mandate with the same blank went down to the Circuit Court; and a motion was there made to open the original judgment for the purpose of taxing the costs, which motion was refused by the court, such refusal cannot be reached by a *mandamus* from this court. *Ex parte Many*, 24.

5. The refusal of the court was not a ministerial act, but an exercise of judicial discretion. This court could issue a *mandamus* for the Circuit Court to proceed to judgment, but such a writ would not be appropriate to the present case. *Ibid.*

MASTER AND SERVANT.

A master is liable for the tortious acts of his servant, when done in the course of his employment, although they may be done in disobedience of the master's order. *P. & R. R. R. Co. v. Derby*, 468

NONSUIT.

The courts of the United States have not the power to order a nonsuit against the wishes of the plaintiff. *Silsby v. Foote*, 219.

PATENTS.

1. In a patent for improvements upon the machinery used for making pipes and tubes from lead or tin when in a set or solid state, by forcing it, under great pressure, from out of a receiver, through apertures, dies, and cores, the claim of the patentees was thus stated: " What we claim as our invention, and desire to secure by letters-patent, is the combination of the following parts, above described, to wit, the core and bridge, or guide-piece, the chamber, and the die, when used to form pipes of metal, under heat and pressure, in the manner set forth, or in any other manner substantially the same." *Le Roy* v. *Tntham*, 156.

2. The Circuit Court charged the jury, "that the originality did not consist in the novelty of the machinery, but in bringing a newly-discovered principle into practical application, by which an useful article of manufacture is produced, and wrought pipe made as distinguished from cast pipe." *Ibid.*

3. This instruction was erroneous. *Ibid.*

4. Under the claim of the patent, the combination of the machinery must be novel. The newly-discovered principle, to wit, that lead could be forced by extreme pressure, when in a set or solid state, to cohere and form a pipe, was not in the patent, and the question whether it was or was not the subject of a patent, was not in the case. *Ibid.*

5. In 1834, Burden obtained a patent for a new and useful improvement in the machinery for manufacturing wrought nails and spikes, which he assigned to the Troy Iron and Nail Factory, and also covenanted that he would convey to that company any improvement which he might thereafter make. *Troy Iron and Nail Factory* v. *Corning*, 193.

6. In 1840, he made such an improvement, for making hook and brad-headed spikes, with a bending lever, which he assigned to the Troy Iron and Nail Factory, in 1848. *Ibid.*

7. Before this last assignment, however, viz., in 1845, Burden made an agreement with Corning, Horner, and Winslow, in which, amongst other things, it was agreed, that both parties might thereafter manufacture and vend spikes of such kind and character as they saw fit, notwithstanding their conflicting claims. *Ibid.*

8. Owing to the peculiar attitude of the parties to each other at the time of making this agreement, and the language used in it, it cannot be construed into a permission to Corning, Horner, and Winslow, to use the improved machinery patented by Burden in 1840; and the right to use it, having passed to the Troy Iron and Nail Factory, a perpetual injunction upon Corning, Horner, and Winslow will be decreed. *Ibid.*

9. Under a notice given by the defendant, that the invention claimed by the plaintiff was described in Ure's Dictionary of Arts, Manufactures, and Mines, and had been used by Andrew Ure, of London, it was not competent to give in evidence a very large book. The place in the book should have been specified. *Silsby* v. *Foote*, 219.

10. Nor, under the notice, was the book competent evidence that Andrew Ure, of London, had a prior knowledge of the thing patented. The notice does not state the place where the same was used. *Ibid.*

11. One of the specifications of the patent being for a combination of certain parts of mechanism necessary to produce the desired result, it was proper for the court to instruct the jury that the defendants had not infringed the patent, unless they had used all the parts embraced in the plaintiffs' combination; and the jury were to find what those parts were, and whether the defendants had used them. *Ibid.*

12. When a claim does not point out and designate the particular elements which compose a combination, but only declares, as it properly may, that the combination is made up of so much of the described machinery as effects a particular result, it is a question of fact which of the described parts are essential to produce that result, and to this extent, not the construction of the claim, strictly speaking, but the application of the claim, should be left to the jury. *Ibid.*

13. The patent for Woodworth's planing-machine was extended from 1842 to 1843, by the Board of Commissioners. *Bloomer* v. *McQuewan*, 539.

14. Under that extension, this court decided, in Wilson v. Rousseau, (4 How. 688,) that an assignee had a right to continue the use of the machine which he then had. *Ibid.*

PATENTS (*Continued.*)

15. In 1845, Congress, by a special act, extended the time still further from 1849 to 1856. *Ibid.*
16. Under that extension, an assignee has still the same right. *Ibid.*
17. By the cases of Evans *v.* Eaton, (3 Wheat. 548,) and Wilson *v.* Rousseau, (4 How. 688,) these two propositions are settled, viz.:
    1. That a special act of Congress in favor of a patentee, extending the time beyond that originally limited, must be considered as ingrafted on the general law.
    2. That, under the general law, in force when this special act of Congress was passed, a party who had purchased the right to use a planing-machine during the period to which the patent was first limited, was entitled to continue to use it during the extension authorized by that law, unless there is something in the law itself to forbid it. *Ibid.*
18. But there is nothing in the act of Congress, passed in 1845, forbidding such use; and, therefore, the assignee has the right. *Ibid.*
19. Where an action was brought against the Commissioner of Patents for refusing to give copies of papers in his office, and no special damage was set out in the declaration, evidence of the professional pursuits of the applicant was not admissible. *Boyden* v. *Burke,* 576.
20. Where the application was made through a third person, letters of both parties to this third person were admissible in evidence, as part of the *res gesta.* *Ibid.*
21. Patents are public records, and it is the duty of the Commissioner to give authenticated copies to any person, on payment of the legal fees. *Ibid.*
22. But the party entitled to such services must request their performance in a proper manner, and not accompany his demand with insult and abuse. *Ibid.*
23. Hence, the Commissioner could not be held responsible for refusing to comply with a demand couched in such language. *Ibid.*
24. But when a second application was made in a proper manner, the Commissioner ought to have complied with it. *Ibid.*

PAYMENT.
See EVIDENCE.

PENNSYLVANIA.
1. By the law of Pennsylvania the River Delaware is a public navigable river, held by its joint sovereigns in trust for the public. *Rundle* v. *Delaware & Raritan Canal Co.,* 80.
2. Riparian owners, in that State, have no title to the river, or any right to divert its waters, unless by license from the States. *Ibid.*
3. Such license is revocable, and in subjection to the superior right of the State, to divert the water for public improvements, either by the State directly, or by a corporation created for that purpose. *Ibid.*
4. The proviso to the provincial acts of Pennsylvania and New Jersey, of 1771, does not operate as a grant of the usufruct of the waters of the river to Adam Hoops and his assigns, but only as a license or toleration of his dam. *Ibid.*
5. As by the laws of his own State, the plaintiff could have no remedy against a corporation authorized to take the whole waters of the river for the purpose of canals, or improving the navigation; so, neither can he sustain a suit against a corporation created by New Jersey for the same purpose, who have taken part of the waters. *Ibid.*
6. The plaintiffs being but tenants at sufferance in the usufruct of the water to the two States who own the river as tenants in common, are not in a condition to question the relative rights of either to use its waters without consent of the other. *Ibid.*
7. This case is not intended to decide whether a first license, for private emolument, can support an action against a later licensee of either sovereign, or both, who, for private purposes, diverts the water to the injury of the first. *Ibid.*

PLEAS AND PLEADINGS.
1. Where the declaration, in an action of assumpsit, contained the following counts: —1. On a promissory note; 2. *Indebitatus assumpsit* for the hire of slaves; 3. An account stated; 4. *Quantum valebut* for the services of slaves; 5. Work and labor, goods sold and delivered, and money lent and advanced; 6. Money had and received; 7. An account stated; 8. A special agreement for the hire of slaves. And the defendant pleaded,—1. The general issue; 2. Statute of limitations; 3. Payment. And the jury found a verdict for "the defendant

PRACTICE.

1. An appeal will not lie to this court from a refusal of the court below to open a prior decree, and grant a rehearing. The decision of this point rests entirely in the sound discretion of the court below. *Wylie v. Coxe*, 1.

2. The case of Brockett *v.* Brockett, (2 How. 240,) explained. *Ibid.*

3. Two appeals having been taken, one from the original decree, and the other from the refusal to open it, the latter must be dismissed, and the case stand for hearing upon the first appeal. *Ibid.*

4. A motion for a mandate upon the court below, to carry the decree into execution, overruled. *Ibid.*

5. A rule will be refused for the judges of the Circuit Court of the District of Columbia, to show cause why a *mandamus* should not issue, unless a case is presented which *primâ facie* requires the interposition of this court. *Ex parte Taylor*, 3.

6. Such a case is not presented where the Circuit Court decided that, under an act of Congress, an affidavit was sufficient to hold a party to special bail. That court had the power, by the act, to exercise its judicial discretion. *Ibid.*

7. This act of Congress regulated the subject, and not the statute of Maryland, passed in 1715. *Ibid.*

8. Where a motion was made, under the 12th section of the Judiciary Act, to remove a cause from a State Court to the Circuit Court of the United States, notwithstanding which the State Court retained cognizance of the case, and it was ultimately brought to this court under the 25th section of the Judiciary Act, a motion to dismiss it for want of jurisdiction cannot be sustained. The question will remain to be decided upon the full hearing of the case. *Kanouse v. Martin*, 23.

9. Where there was a blank in the record of the Circuit Court, in the taxation of the costs recovered by the plaintiff, and the judgment being affirmed by this court, a mandate with the same blank went down to the Circuit Court; and a motion was there made to open the original judgment for the purpose of taxing the costs, which motion was refused by the court, such refusal cannot be reached by a *mandamus* from this court. *Ex parte Many*, 24.

10. The refusal of the court was not a ministerial act, but an exercise of judicial discretion. This court could issue a *mandamus* for the Circuit Court to proceed to judgment, but such a writ would not be appropriate to the present case. *Ibid.*

11. A reargument of a case decided by this court will not be granted, unless a member of the court, who concurred in the judgment, desires it; and when that is the case, it will be ordered without waiting for the application of counsel. *Brown v. Aspden*, 25.

12. And this is so, whether the decree of the court below was affirmed by an equally divided court or a majority; or whether the case is one at common law or chancery. *Ibid.*

13. The rules of the English Court of Chancery have not been adopted by this court. Those which are applicable to a court of original jurisdiction, are not appropriate to an appellate court. *Ibid.*

14. Upon a trial in New York, a juror became ill, and was discharged before any evidence was given, and before the plaintiffs' counsel had concluded his opening address. The court ordered another juror to be sworn, and proceeded with the trial. The defendant cannot object to this. It is the practice in New York, and the Circuit Court had a right to follow it. *Silsby v. Foote*, 218.

15. The court having erroneously refused to allow the plaintiff to offer a paper in evidence, as a disclaimer of part of a patent, afterwards refused to allow the defendants to offer the same paper in evidence for the purpose of prejudicing the plaintiffs' rights. This last refusal was correct. The reason given was erroneous; but this is not a sufficient cause for reversing the judgment. *Ibid.*

16. The courts of the United States have not the power to order a nonsuit against the wishes of the plaintiff. *Ibid.*

17. Where the declaration, in an action of assumpsit, contained the following counts:—1. On a promissory note; 2. *Indebitatus assumpsit* for the hire of slaves; 3. An account stated; 4. *Quantum valebat* for the services of slaves; 5. Work and labor, goods sold and delivered, and money lent and advanced; 6. Money had and received; 7. An account stated; 8. A special agreement for the hire of slaves: And the defendant pleaded,—1. The general issue; 2. Statute of limitations; 3. Payment;—and the jury found a verdict for "the defendant upon the issue joined as to the within note of four hundred and fifty-

PRACTICE (*Continued.*)

six dollars, and the within account" — this verdict, although informal, was sufficient to authorize to enter a general judgment for the defendant. *Downey* v. *Hicks*, 240.

18. An objection cannot be made in this court to a release under which a witness was sworn, unless the objection was made in the court below, and an exception taken. *Ibid.*

19. The sixty-second rule of this court, (13 Howard,) is as follows: "In cases where a writ of error is prosecuted to the Supreme Court, and the judgment of the inferior court is affirmed, the interest shall be calculated and levied from the date of the judgment below, until the same is paid, at the same rate that similar judgments bear interest, in the courts of the State where such judgment is rendered. The same rule shall be applied to decrees for the payment of money, in cases in Chancery, unless otherwise ordered by this court. This rule to take effect on the first day of December term, 1852. *Perkins* v. *Fourniquet*, 328.

20. Before this rule, interest was to be calculated at six per cent., from the date of the judgment in the Circuit Court to the day of affirmance here; and the confirmation of the report of the clerk, in the case of Mitchell v. Harmony, (13 Howard, 149,) was under the rules then existing. *Ibid.*

21. So, also, where a case from Mississippi was affirmed, at December term, 1851, the mandate from this court should have been construed to allow interest at six per cent. from the date of the decree in the court below, to the date of the affirmance in this court. Therefore, it was erroneous either to allow six per cent. until paid, or to allow the current rate of interest in Mississippi, in addition to the six per cent. allowed by this court. *Ibid.*

22. The several rules upon this subject examined and explained. *Ibid.*

23. A statute of Mississippi directs that where the defendant cannot be found, a writ of *capias ad respondendum* shall be served, by leaving a copy thereof with the wife of the defendant, or some free white person above the age of sixteen years, then and there being one of the family of the defendant, and found at his usual place of abode, or leaving a copy thereof at some public place, at the dwelling-house or other known place of residence of such defendant, he being from home, and no such free white person being found there willing to receive the same. *Harris* v. *Hardeman*, 334.

24. The Circuit Court of the United States adopted a rule that the *capias* should be served personally, or, if the defendant be not found. by leaving a copy thereof at his or her residence, or usual place of abode, at least twenty days before the return day thereof. *Ibid.*

25. The marshal made the following return to a writ of *capias*: "Executed on the defendant Hardeman, by leaving a true copy at his residence." *Ibid.*

26. This service was neither in conformity with the statute nor the rule. *Ibid.*

27. Therefore, when the court gave judgment, by default, against Hardeman, and an execution was issued, upon which a forthcoming bond was given, and another execution issued, and at a subsequent day the court quashed the proceedings, and set aside the judgment by default, this order was correct. *Ibid.*

28. When the judgment by default was given, the court was not in a condition to exercise jurisdiction over the defendant, because there was no regular service of process, actual or constructive. *Ibid.*

29. The cases upon this point, examined. *Ibid.*

30. Moreover, when the proceedings were quashed, they were still *in fieri*, and not terminated; and any irregularity could be corrected, on motion. *Ibid.*

31. A sale of land by a marshal, on a *venditioni exponas*, after he is removed from office, and a new marshal appointed and qualified, is not void. *Doolittle* v. *Bryan*, 563.

32. Such a sale being returned to the court, and confirmed by it on motion, and a deed ordered to be made to the purchaser at the sale, by the new marshal, such sale, being made, is valid. *Ibid.*

RAILROADS.

1. Where a suit was brought against a railroad company, by a person who was injured by a collision, it was correct in the court to instruct the jury, that if the plaintiff was lawfully on the road, at the time of the collision, and the collision and consequent injury to him were caused by the gross negligence of one of the servants of the defendants, then and there employed on the road, he was entitled to recover, notwithstanding the circumstances that the plaintiff was a stockholder in the company, riding by invitation of the President, paying no fare, and not in the usual passenger cars. *P. & R. R. R. Co.* v. *Derby* 468.

WILLS (*Continued.*)

law of Maryland, which prevailed without alteration in that part of the District of Columbia which had been ceded by Maryland, until Congress passed the act of the 20th February, 1846. The defendants, Stott, Carrico, and George C. Bomford, and Smith, Ward, and Gideon, became the sureties of Bomford, as administrator *de bonis non* of Kosciusko, under the act of 20th February, 1846. *Ibid.*

12. In the State of Maryland, if an executor or administrator changes any part of an estate from what it was into something else, it is said to be administered If an administrator *de bonis non* possesses himself of such changed estate, of whatever kind it may be, and charges himself with it as assets, his sureties to his original bond, as administrator *de bonis non*, are not liable for his waste of them. They are only liable for such assets of the deceased as remain in specie, unadministered by his predecessor in the administration. Such is the law of Maryland, applicable to the sureties of Bomford, in the bond given when he was appointed administrator *de bonis non* of Kosciusko. *Ibid.*

13. But when other sureties are called for by the Orphans' Court, under the third section of the act of February 20, 1846, and are given, they do not bear the same relation to the administrator that his original sureties did, and they will be bound for the waste of their principal to the amount of the estate or funds, which he has charged himself by his return to the Orphans' Court, as administrator *de bonis non*, when it called for additional sureties, and for such as the administrator may afterwards receive. *Ibid.*

14. The bonds taken by the Orphans' Court in this case were properly taken, under the act of the 20th February, 1846. *Ibid.*

15. General Kosciusko's Olographic will, of 1816, contains a revoking clause of all other wills previously made by him, and not having disposed of his American funds in that will, nor in the will of 1817, he died intestate as to such funds. The second article in the will of 1817, "Je lègue tous mes effets, ma voiture, et mon cheval y comprise à Madame et à Monsieur Xavier Zeltner, les homme ce dessus," record 105, is not a residuary bequest to them of the rest of the estate, not specifically disposed of, in the wills of 1816 and 1817. *Ibid.*

16. General Kosciusko was sojourning in Switzerland when he died, but was domiciled in France, and had been for fifteen years. *Ibid.*

17. His declarations are to be received as proof that his domicil was in France. Such declarations have always been received, in questions of domicil, in the courts of France, in those of England, and in the courts of the United States. *Ibid.*

18. The presumption of law is, that the domicil of origin is retained, until residence elsewhere has been shown by him who alleges a change of it. But residence elsewhere repels the presumption, and casts upon him who denies it to be a domicil of choice, the burden of disproving it. The place of residence must be taken to be a domicil of choice, unless it is proved that it was not meant to be a principal and permanent residence. Contingent events, political or otherwise, are not admissible proofs to show, where one removes from his domicil of origin for a residence elsewhere, that the latter was not meant to be a principal and permanent residence. But if one is exiled by authority from his domicil of origin, it is never presumed that he has abandoned all hope of returning back. The abandonment, however, may be shown by proof. General Kosciusko was not exiled by authority. He left Poland voluntarily, to obtain a civil status in France, which he conscientiously thought he could not enjoy in Poland, whilst it continued under a foreign dominion. *Ibid.*

19. Personal property, wherever it may be, is to be disturbed in case of intestacy, according to the law of the domicil of the intestate. This rule may be said to be a part of the *jus gentium*. *Ibid.*

20. What that law is when a foreign law applies, must be shown by proof of it, and in the case of written law, it will be sufficient to offer, as evidence, the official publication of the law, certified satisfactorily to be such. Unwritten foreign laws must be proved by experts. There is no general rule for authenticating foreign laws in the courts of other countries, except this, that no proof shall be received, "which presupposes better testimony behind, and attainable by the party." They may be verified by an oath, or by an exemplification of a copy under the great seal of the State or nation whose law it may be, or by a copy, proved to be a true copy by a witness who has examined and compared it with the original, or by the certificate of an officer authorized to give the law, which certificate must be duly proved. Such modes of proof are not ext